THE RIFT

The Exile Experience
of South Africans

THE RIFT

The Exile Experience
of South Africans

Hilda Bernstein

Jonathan Cape
London

First published 1994

1 3 5 7 9 10 8 6 4 2

© Hilda Bernstein 1994

Hilda Bernstein has asserted her right under the Copyright, Designs and Patents Act, 1988
to be identified as the author of this work

First published in the United Kingdom in 1994 by
Jonathan Cape
Random House, 20 Vauxhall Bridge Road, London SW1V 2SA

Random House Australia (Pty) Limited
20 Alfred Street, Milsons Point, Sydney,
New South Wales 2061, Australia

Random House New Zealand Limited
18 Poland Road, Glenfield,
Auckland 10, New Zealand

Random House South Africa (Pty) Limited
PO Box 337, Bergvlei, South Africa

Random House UK Limited Reg. No. 954009

A CIP catalogue record for this book is available from the British Library

ISBN 0–224–03546–0

Designed by Rowan Seymour
Printed in Great Britain by
Mackays of Chatham PLC,
Chatham, Kent

For my children, involuntary exiles;
and to the memory of all those who died in exile.

'Exile is strangely compelling to think about but terrible to experience. It is the unhealable rift forced between a human being and a native place, between the self and its true home; its essential sadness can never be surmounted.'

Edward Said

Contents

Without Whom . . .

It was only possible to make this book with the assistance of many people.

The Arbetarrorelsens Internationello Centrum in Stockholm gave me an initial grant, the spur I needed to begin. I was then bribed into signing a contract with Candida Lacey, my editor, who arranged an advance generous enough to enable me to undertake the journeys that were necessary. Her enthusiasm for the book supported me during three years' work. She has worked meticulously with me to construct and edit this book.

The arduous task of transforming the spoken word – the tapes – into print-outs was performed by Beryl Baker, without whose uncomplaining co-operation I should not have been able to proceed.

Rusty Bernstein did major work in assisting to select and edit the interviews. In effect, through his editing and many critical suggestions, he co-partnered the book. He is a problem-solver, without whom I could not have come to terms with the word processor.

The research undertaken by Robyn Slovo was invaluable and has become part of the book.

The generous hospitality of friends, without whom I would have had to stay in hotels while travelling, enabled me to come out on a tight budget; the bonus was the pleasure of their company. I was hosted by Eve and Tony Hall and Pat and Hugh Lewin in Zimbabwe; Pamela dos Santos in Mozambique; Lia Gorter in Holland; Edith Anderson and Indres Naidoo in Berlin; Nomsa Gertz-Mketo in Hamburg; Vibeke Bidstrup in Copenhagen; Fritz and Mala Dullay in Århus, Denmark; Madi Gray in Sweden; Hamid and Zaby Bhyat in Toronto; Lily Mah-sen and Keith Rimstad in Ottowa; Mary and Ben Clarke in Los Angeles; Dunja Sagov in New York.

In addition I received valuable assistance in choosing and contacting exiles from Barbara Masekela, Billy Modise, Vernon September, Tim Maseko, Zena and Mervyn Susser, Cedric Mayson, and many others. In Toronto Fatima Bhyat was my organiser, chauffeur, guide and friend. Esther Levitan undertook two interviews for me in Norway.

Introduction

Concerning the label 'Emigrant'.

Exile is predicated on the existence of, love for, and bond with, one's native place; what is true of all exile is not that home and love of home are lost, but that loss is inherent in the very existence of both.

Edward Said

To be rooted is perhaps the most important and least recognised need of the human soul.

Simone Weil

I started to write this book at a time when many South Africans had left their homes as long as thirty years ago, and there was still no hope of return. And old friends were dying – friends who had left, as we had, a long time ago. Dying, and leaving no record of their lives except in frail memories of those who had been close to them. What about all those years in exile? I had never asked them about themselves, what made them leave home, what happened, how they felt . . .

I wanted simply to record something of the lives of our people, to let them speak a few words before it was all lost. For a period that spanned three decades, from the late 1950s to 1990, so many of us – 30,000? 60,000? nobody knew exactly – were excluded from South Africa's contemporary history, yet still irrevocably tied to it. We were exiles not because of war or famine or religious persecution, but because of apartheid. And this defines the nature of this book: the exile experience is its motif, but the politics of apartheid is its essential core.

Exiles are those who leave with the intention of returning. They have not chosen to emigrate. They do not regard themselves as refugees, although they were so classified by organisations such as the UNHCR and others.

Sometimes refugees become exiles. And some exiles, losing the intention of returning and abandoning political involvement, become émigrés. But even these often remain involved with the passion of apartheid politics, however peripherally.

This does not mean that all my exiles were political activists. Some chose to leave only to better their education which was restricted by Bantu Education and the limitations of the ethnic colleges. Their intention was to return; it was their opposition abroad to apartheid that turned them into exiles. Some left because their parents took them into exile; the children did not choose exile. Some women left to be with a husband or boyfriend who had been driven into exile; some young white males left to escape conscription into an army fighting in the townships and in Angola. Some were sent out by the organisations to which they belonged, either on specific missions, or because their own situation had become too dangerous to themselves or their colleagues. Many were driven out by the various 'bans' they were placed under – a teacher would be banned from entering any school or educational establishment, an industrial worker from any factory, a journalist or writer from publishing or writing anything whatsoever, as I myself had been.

But whatever fuelled their departure, the majority left under circumstances of intolerable stress. Many were students who had been participating in school boycotts and protests and so found themselves permanently on the run, debarred from ever returning to school again, driven to living underground; many of these were ultimately driven out of South Africa by the persecution of their families and the threats to their siblings, who were sometimes taken as hostages. And some had already suffered imprisonment, detention, often torture; and when released, lived aware of their own impotence against constant threats to their liberty and safety, imperilled by a strait-jacket of bans and prohibitions.

The reasons for leaving South Africa often determined the exiles' future direction; and, more important, influenced their psychological adjustment to their new life. Those who went primarily to seek an education denied to them in South Africa generally fulfilled their expectations, and often went further than they had anticipated; although that could still not eliminate the pain, the loneliness and alienation of a life in exile. Those who were sent out or who left at the advice of their organisations continued their fight for justice, to bring an end to apartheid, for no material reward. Their time in exile was simply a projection into a different dimension of the continuing struggle in which they were involved.

But many political activists, dispersed across continents, were to suffer an even sharper sense of loss. In South Africa they had enjoyed a status, a purpose, and a strongly-knit comradeship, bound together by mutual danger that demanded mutual trust. In exile they often found themselves parted not only from their families, but also from their comrades with whom they had met secretly and in danger, and lived through endless hours of meetings, arguing, debating, hammering out decisions. The bonds that had held them together had been essential for their survival.

In exile the purpose that had fired their lives was fractured. They ceased to belong to the coherent community they left behind, and did not find – or did not wish to seek – a way to belong to the new world in which they found themselves. For them, exile is alienation.

Exile exacts its price not only from those who leave, but also from those who are left: parents and siblings; and wives and children left by husbands who fled across the border, often without a word of farewell and leaving behind no money for material needs. The women went to work and brought up families alone and in loneliness, shouldering the total burden of responsibility and care, often through silent years without any communication from the one who had left. Survivors with a total hole in their lives that could never be filled.

Many who left concealed their intention to depart from those closest to them – parents, wives (mostly; few women left husbands), brothers and sisters – both for self-protection and to protect those left behind from reprisals and allegations of complicity. Then their lives were haunted by the unresolved departure – not having said goodbye. For years there could be no communication by letter or by phone with any member of the family. In the pervasive atmosphere of terror in South Africa, families could be implicated by intercepted letters and phone calls. Parents did not know where their daughters or sons had gone, whether they were alive, whether they had been detained or murdered by police or soldiers, or even if they were dead or where their remains were buried. Without the rites of farewell the one who had departed was already within the realm of the dead.

Abrupt and secret departure added a sense of guilt to the exiles' pain of unresolved separation from the closest members of the family. Some mothers left babies, believing they would be reunited within a short time – only to meet them again when they were strangely grown, as did Tembeka Ngeleza, who gave her daughter to her mother; or Eleanor Kasrils, who did not recognise her daughter and ran to greet the wrong person many years later; and Eleanor Khanyile who left a baby son she would not see again until he was an adult. The years of loss and suffering of the mothers are only one part of the picture; the other is the alienation, the resentment and feelings of rejection suffered by the children who were left behind.

Terror, persecution, struggle and resistance brought out waves of exiles, to the huge deprivation of South Africa as a whole. Over a span of more than thirty years many of the most politically conscious, the most able and gifted people in all fields and of all races, left their own country. Lost, therefore, the doctors, the teachers, the organisers, the diplomats, the politicians, the leaders who had so much to contribute to South Africa, but were denied that right by apartheid. Lost too the careers of many fine writers, painters and musicians, because life in exile – as Ngugi has written – means removal from the material basis of the artist's inspiration. South Africa has been deprived of so much in the creative field that could have enriched the society.

The deprivations inflicted by apartheid extended to all the countries of southern Africa, holding their own development hostage to blackmail by physical incursions, by arms and by terror. Mozambique is today impoverished, devastated by the long war organised and financed by South Africa, because its very existence was regarded as a threat to apartheid. The Frontline States – Botswana, Lesotho, Swaziland – into which the exiles flooded and found some protection – were yet unable to protect themselves from becoming victims of the very system which produced the exiles.

Military incursions into these countries killed not only South Africans, but also native peoples. And the Death Squads, kidnapping and assassinating both within South Africa and outside, reached out into Lesotho, Botswana, Zambia, Zimbabwe, Mozambique and as far away as France and Britain. Some of the survivors of those horrors are here in this book: Ma-Mia who lost her husband, her daughter and her son; Grace Cele, who relates a story both terrible and bizarre; Bunie Sexwale, who lay on the earth with her daughters, watching her home bombed and burnt to ashes; and many others, including Joyce Diphale who was the target of an assassination attack, and Captain Dirk Coetzee, head of the Death Squad that went to kill her.

All exiles are torn away from their past and projected into everything that is unfamiliar, but the South Africans carried a huge part of their history with them into exile. I was struck by the potency of the South African question and the emotive intensity that events in their homeland held for the exiles; and how that was passed on to their children. Even those who have spent more of their lives outside South Africa than in, and even those who became émigrés making their new country a permanent home, speak of how they still turn first to the 'foreign news' in their daily paper, seeking, before all else, any item from South Africa.

That deep involvement in all things South African transferred itself into anti-apartheid political activity in the country of exile. The environment of exile politics has usually turned out to be sterile and demoralising, the parties and groups, frustrated and ineffectual, split and dissolve in internecine warfare. Unusually the South African exiles did not succumb to this corrosion. They not only survived with a remarkable degree of unity but built organisations that fundamentally influenced international affairs. In a large part it was their efforts that brought this comparatively small country, with a population of less than 40 million at the very edge of the huge African continent, geographically removed from centres of the developed world, to a front position in world affairs. The internal political struggle in South Africa has been long and ongoing, its external – that is exile – component perhaps paralleled only by that of the Palestinians.

The loneliness of exile and the loss of family reinforced the unity of the one coherent homeland group they found outside – the ANC. Within that political community, exiles in clusters in such places as Lusaka, London and Mazimbu found a new family. It is because the internal struggle was blacked out by the censorship and punitive laws of the South African regime during vital years that the political activities of the exile community have taken on such importance. From inside, silence. But outside, a relentless campaign to make the world understand the meaning of apartheid. A handful of students meeting in a basement room in London set in motion a worldwide campaign that became an essential factor in bringing apartheid down. A few ANC leaders, sent into exile in 1960 in anticipation of the organisation being outlawed, developed the force inside and outside the country which has sealed the fate of apartheid. Exile provided the climate not only for survival, but also for resurgence and triumph.

Out of the fragmentation and incoherence of exile, they built strong and coherent structures with such success that the political system that had driven them out became known and reviled throughout the world. Today, when condemnation of apartheid stretches across the spectrum of democratic nations, and is now acknowledged as being 'wrong' and a 'mistake' even by the very architects of the system itself, it is difficult to recall how those early exiles were ignored, their voices faint and unpublished, their cause not considered news-worthy.

Most exiles leave their own country in retreat, after suffering a major defeat: a military coup, war, revolution; the Spanish after Franco overthrew the Republican government in civil war; the Chileans when Allende was murdered and the Colonels took over. Such exiles take the trauma and pessimism of defeat with them. And though many organise to recover lost terrain, the scars of defeat rarely fade. They tend to live in their own past, an essentially sterile scattering, growing smaller and more isolated as the years pass.

The South African exile experience is uniquely different. Exile was neither the aftermath of a lost war nor of a defeated coup or revolution. Although there had been a disastrous shattering of their political leadership in the 1960s, no one concerned with the politics of resistance interpreted that as final defeat. Those political activists who went into exile saw themselves as part of a continuing and rising struggle at home. The link between 'home' and 'exile' politics ebbed and flowed with the fortunes of the struggle at home – a struggle temporarily forced into retreat from time to time, but never extinguished, constantly reborn. The link was steadily renewed by successive waves of exiles, coming out at different times over a period of more than thirty years.

Each wave brought out its own type of people. Those who left in the late fifties and early sixties were mainly adult, often middle-aged, and highly political, with a history of engaging in public political struggle.

Those of the seventies, and specifically of the huge exile wave after 1976, were overwhelmingly young, largely male; and though fired with political passion, they were often without real ideology or political programmes. They were of a generation who had been cut off from access to information about their own country, their own history, and from political theory and the history of struggle. The 'elders' who might have passed on this knowledge were either themselves in exile, or on Robben Island or Pretoria Central prison. Or perhaps keeping discreetly quiet. 'Mandela' was a remote name, used by some parents as a warning of what happens to those who follow the path of resistance to law and authority. The 1976 Soweto rebels came out with no history in their heads. They believed themselves to be the first revolutionaries, the first to confront the apartheid state; and their anger was often without political objective. They learned the history of their country only when they had left it – the long story of struggle, oppression and resistance.

But those who went into exile in the eighties came from the reborn internal resistance to the terror, a wave of determined people, black and white, hardened by life-threatening activity in popular armed and unarmed resistance, experienced in work both above and underground.

It was this constant stream over more than three decades that contributed to the uniqueness of the South African exile experience. Ours was not a static, fossilised community of ageing individuals living on the memories of a glorious past, but part of a continuity of resistance, constantly in touch with home through the injection of new life from those most recently out.

Even so, as the flow of exiles increased remorselessly, individual lives unravelled – in one sense more completely for South Africans than for many other exiles. The exodus into exile which follows famine, war or religious or national persecution is usually an exodus of whole families, often of whole communities. But the South Africans left their country, in the main, as individuals, fleeing by themselves or in small ad hoc groups of strangers, leaving behind all familial ties. They came into an alien world alone. They had ceased to belong. They became strangers, even when received without hostility, they remained outsiders.

For some this 'strangeness' has been a virtue to be emphasised and exploited. 'Clutching difference like a weapon to be used with stiffened will, the exile jealously insists on his or her right to refuse to belong,' writes Edward Said. And Breyten Breytenbach writes in *Long March*: 'You end up speaking all languages with an accent, even the distant one of your youth, the one kept for love and anger. You have acquired the knack of fitting in pretty well with any society – you do a good impersonation of the cosmopolitan – but in fact you probably never really penetrate beneath the surface concerns of those around you. You are engaged with an elsewhere that cannot be reached. Isn't that the defining characteristic of an exile?'

Although the driving force of South African politics of change has been a progressive nationalist passion, we are living in an age where multi-ethnic nations are in a state of disintegration, contending for the right to split into separate states. But South African nationalism is going in precisely the opposite direction. This is another feature which sets our experience of exile apart. Our driving motive and national passion has been towards the binding together of different ethnic groups, towards unity, not separateness. That spirit of unity in diversity has spilled out into the homogenous, non-factional nature of our exile politics.

This has not been a seamless, painless achievement, however much it is welcomed in theory and accepted in practice. Black South Africans have the advantage of feeling that they are part of a consonant community. (Tribalism, despite the efforts of apartheid to foster it, despite the Bantustans, played a very minor role in black politics until the establishment of Inkatha.) They can relate easily to compatriots in exile. White exiles, already alienated from their own communities, often from their own families, may yet need to prove their credentials for acceptance in the movement: read Simon Dunkley's painful attempt to cross the line between white and black at Crossroads; and Barry Gilder's joy at his acceptance in the camps of Umkhonto we Sizwe. Black Consciousness, which raised the pride and self-awareness of a generation of young urban blacks, had the effect of pushing white opponents of apartheid into a kind of isolation, making them feel unacceptable and useless. Several whites went into exile during this period precisely because for them there was no political home at home. They found it in exile.

An extraordinary feature of the exiles' politics is the absence of a spirit of revenge. The young people who erupted from the township schools in 1976 went out fired by anger, seeking revenge, their intention to get a gun and to shoot those who had been shooting them. Once outside they became subject to a very positive political education. They were given books to read – books prohibited in South Africa. They were told the history of their own immediate past. The continuity of their lives had been fractured under apartheid, the history of their parents' lives obliterated. If memory is the continuity principle for people, then history is the continuity principle for nations. By erasing essential areas of history the development of a nation is halted, distorted. Memory and history must merge and reinforce each other so that humans can recognise and understand their lives. 'The Movement' – that vaguely defined but concretely existing body – gave back to these young people their own history, and with it an understanding of the nature of society. The anger remains, but the racial direction of it has changed. They speak of radical change, but not of revenge. For all its failings and omissions, this is the gift bestowed by the ANC on the future of South Africa.

For apartheid's exiles have the grand vision of an extraordinary mix of a racially, tribally variegated society living in harmony in the future.

Narrow nationalist exclusiveness has been largely subsumed in the drive for nationhood. From their so disparate social, economic, class and race backgrounds the exiles achieve a singular bonding. For all the hardships, the deprivations, the alienation and loneliness of exile, they feel themselves still part of something grand, positive, unifying and heroic. 'We are fighting for a democratic, unitary, non-racial, non-sexist South Africa,' they say. They believe that to the depth of their being.

Exile, as so many of those I interviewed told me, was difficult – 'very very difficult.' It was necessary to adjust to living in cold and hostile environments, usually with little, often no income. For black South Africans, Europe sharpened the sense of dislocation: Alpheus Mangezi, on his first day as a social worker in Glasgow, finds a car with a uniformed chauffeur waiting for him; the chauffeur is white, calls him 'Sir' and opens the door for him – perhaps only a South African can appreciate how really bizarre is this experience. Oliver Tambo confronts his first public meeting in exile, a sea of all-white faces; Irene Beck stands with her children at the back of the bus in Århus, Denmark, because she did not know that a 'Coloured' woman was allowed to sit next to white passengers.

Race and class mitigate or exacerbate the pains and difficulties of exile. And adjustment to those difficulties were also mediated by the actual place of settlement: the continent, the country, the town.

In Europe exiles were assessed visually, skin colour being the defining factor. White South Africans could merge into the structures of Western society, outwardly integrated regardless of their inner alienation. In Britain their accent was often an advantage, not a liability – their class could not be predicated from the way they speak – that immediate giveaway for native Brits. So they could be colonials, 'one of us'. But blacks are from elsewhere.

Black South Africans found adjustment easier in the Frontline States. Climate, ambience, often language crossed the frontiers drawn arbitrarily by imperial invaders, which cut tribes apart without separating language, culture and custom. There the exiles felt close to home, could even look across the rivers to the blue horizons of their own country.

But living in the Frontline States was hazardous; none felt safe from South African military incursions and the Death Squads, whether or not they were involved in the underground. Here, by contrast, whites were disadvantaged, often arriving without political credentials since the nature of political resistance during the late seventies and eighties had precluded a public face. So who are you? A genuine refugee from apartheid? A plant? A spy? White exiles moved in black Africa dogged by suspicion.

Yet even in Africa, especially further north, colour could not protect against the culture shock. Africa proved as alien to many blacks as Europe did to whites. The exiles were urban people. They came from large towns, industrially developed centres, even though they had lived among the unmade streets, shacks and matchbox houses in Alexandra Township and Soweto. They arrived in 'liberated' towns like Dar es Salaam and suffered culture-shock, comparing the dusty, pot-holed, tin-roofed, decrepit capital of Tanzania not with Crossroads or Khyalit-sha – the concealed 'Third World' sector of South Africa – but with 'their' cities of Johannesburg, Port Elizabeth, Cape Town. And they were shocked by free Africa.

People tend to believe that their culture is the measure of all culture. In the developed West there is a widespread belief that African culture and customs are 'backward'. There is a lack of understanding, often a total misinterpretation of social customs, even of body language. So black South Africans who went to live in Western countries were often intoler-ably patronised. Katleho Moloi relates that, after she had made a speech at a meeting in London, Ontario, a Canadian woman said to her: 'Good speech! And good grammar too!' Katleho speaks six languages. Billy Modise speaks of what he called 'positive racism' in Sweden – it didn't deny him opportunities but treated him like an outgrown adolescent. Others recall just as sharply being treated with the kindness and patience that is usually reserved only for children, or the handicapped.

But of course, they were handicapped; all exiles are, by the abrupt rupture of their lives, the terror and dislocation that went before, the uncertainty about the shape of the life into which they have been forced. This they are unable to share with foreigners. And who are the foreigners? Them or us? No points of contact. No shared background, no shared experience. And especially no shared experience of living constantly under terror. Most exiles, black and white, looked normal, spoke normally. Yet they would take years and years to adjust to the 'normal' world, not to wake and listen with tension when a car stops outside at night, not to be constantly vigilant, suspicious of all strangers; to loosen the disciplines and secretiveness that had once been so essential for survival.

So many of those who had left with no visible luggage bore with them all the mental baggage of their past, of growing up under apartheid. The scars of that skewered society marked them like tattoos – deprivation, humiliation, anger.

Underlying the exile experience was the inability to describe the reality of living under apartheid; the past on which it rests; the alienation of colonialism which concealed history and distorted culture; the terrible impress of inferiority, which made Black Consciousness such a potent and powerful magic for the restoration of self. So the double loss of self-esteem, inside their country and outside, sometimes gives rise to belligerence and over-compensation.

You husband your weaknesses. These are the souvenirs of your native land . . . You demand to be treated respectfully; your edges become sharper and your paranoia more acute. In fact, your evaluation of dignity becomes a taut string. You are invited to New York for a conference? Insist upon being put up in the best hotel!

Breyten Breytenbach

The effort to compensate for what has been lost brought the exiles together in protective groups wherever there were enough of them. Despite the enormous time-consuming, money-consuming sprawl of London and Lusaka, there was comfort, reassurance, strength to be drawn from ceremonial celebrations of dates, from a nostalgia that excluded the strangers among whom they lived, from a renewal of commitment – almost an assertion of superiority, that their lives held something different and momentous, in which their friends in the host country could never truly share. The raised clenched fist, the familiar slogans, the singing of Nkosi Sikelele at every South African gathering – these were the rituals that drew all together in a net. We belong! It is you – our sympathisers, our hosts – who are the outsiders. Thus exile itself becomes a political statement, a defiance, a justification.

There are exiles who recognise what they have gained; which does not invalidate the reality of their loss, but adds another dimension to the exile experience. They recognise that through knowledge of an enlarged world, they have been enriched by immersion in language, culture and ways of life that could not have been possible within the confines of their own country.

Seeing the entire world as a foreign land makes possible originality of vision. Most people are principally aware of one culture, one setting, one home; exiles are aware of at least two, and this plurality of vision gives rise to an awareness of simultaneous dimensions, an awareness that – to borrow a phrase from music – is contrapuntal. For an exile, habits of life, expression or activity in the new environment inevitably occur against the memory of these things in another environment. Thus both the new and the old environments are vivid, actual, occurring together contrapuntally.

Edward Said

There are many gaps in this book, stories that were not or perhaps could not be told. Too many men speak of their own strength, of how they gained maturity in the face of loss and loneliness, but will not speak of what happened to a father, a brother, a comrade; and unless persistently questioned, will often not even mention a wife and children left behind. So the men persist in the assertion of their own strength, while the women persist in their protection of those men who are close to them. Their silences or denials conceal those who could not make it through 'the long march', those who broke, who fled, who dissolved in an alcoholic fog, who became lost in a maze of mental disorder.

Alcoholism, breakdown and mental collapse were the visible manifestations of the traumas, the sufferings, the disorientation of exile. The stories of these people were inaccessible to me, the victims dead, their friends and relatives silent in their protectiveness.

Very soon the memories slide into the past, become blurred, distorted, especially now when for so many the long exile has come to an end. I wanted to pick up some of the threads of their exile experience. Was their drive for political coherence all that they have in common? South Africa is so deeply split by economic and social conditions and status; so wholly segregated by the barriers of race. And the exiles reflect this, ranging across the spectra of origins, race, colour, religions, social and cultural, economic and educational backgrounds.

They are the products of Bantu education and pre-Bantu education, adults and children. They are women and men from commerce and industry; they are artists, journalists, athletes, labourers, lawyers, doctors, priests, peasants, professors, and many are political activists. They speak a variety of languages, have a variety of origins. They are Anglicans, Methodists, Jews, Catholics, Muslims, atheists. They are those who left to avoid military service, and those who left with the single intention of getting a gun and returning in a new ANC army. They are those who found the guns and the military training they sought, and sometimes used both; and those who instead found themselves studying philosophy at a European university. They are a variety of committed nationalists and patriots, and those who wanted to put the whole of South Africa behind them – only to discover how deeply they were South African after they had left there.

The exiles' stories that are most profoundly moving are those told by women. Often this is because women were prepared to speak of their emotions, and did not fear the loss of status by exposing pain and weaknesses. While the men would present a recital of movements from place to place, few of them would speak of hardship or of pain, for that would reflect on their organisation as well as their own strength. Few would speak of fear, or nervousness or cowardice. They clung as much as possible to their perception of a man's status in South Africa, which is a very chauvinist society.

The women, on the other hand, were forced by the fact of exile to discard the roles assigned to them by custom or tradition. In totally new lives in strange countries, they re-made themselves, became independent and strong, usually while bearing alone the burden of raising a young family. 'The elephant does not feel the weight of his trunk,' said one woman when I asked was this not difficult. There is really no parallel experience of this by the men. These women, like the ones left behind at home by the male exiles, are truly the 'guardians of continuity' without whom the fissures in society would have widened into impassable chasms.

Voices that are rarely heard are those of the children. They often express deep anger and resentment towards their activist parents, while at the same time revealing their love and admiration for them – a dichotomy that remains unresolved. 'I knew he was on the side of good,' said Christopher Kasrils, 'but I didn't really understand why he was putting his politics before us.' Gloria Nkadimeng thought 'my Dad didn't like me much. He's much more in love with his cause than with us, his children.' Robyn Slovo spoke of her mother, 'I just wanted her to say she was frightened, and that she missed me.' Pren Naicker felt he never knew his father.

People do not tell all their secrets. We all keep areas of our lives that we do not wish to expose to anyone. Often memories are too painful, deliberately eradicated or covered over with a hard skin. Exiles, like old soldiers recounting the experiences of war, recall only what is tolerable. And yet from these selected, selective threads, there emerge patterns and pictures that illuminate the experience of exile, not only in the specific, but also in the universal. Patterns of the nature of South African society in all its crudity, its sophistication, its paradoxes; of the nature of the struggle against that society, and how it changed and developed over the years; of the primary importance of international solidarity and the spread worldwide of the knowledge of and opposition to apartheid; of the position of women inside and outside the home, casting light on the struggles of women everywhere; of the meaning of culture and of the ways we absorb new cultures without discarding the old; of the pervasive presence of racialism, even in the countries which opened their arms to the exiles from racialism. Patterns of prejudice, of loyalty, of weakness and of strength; of the role, positive and negative, of the extended family; of love and of hate, of courage and betrayal; and most of all, of the unsuspected human resources summoned up by hardship and adversity – strengths that never would have emerged in less strenuous circumstances and that for so many ensured the survival of self.

I began interviewing exiles in 1989, which was before President De Klerk's volte face of 2 February, 1990, when he unbanned a large number of illegal organisations including the African National Congress, the Pan African Congress and the Communist Party. From that date the status of exiles changed, for the possibility of return was opened up for tens of thousands. Before 2 February, 'going home' was a dream deferred over the years, all the more sweet because of its remoteness. Return was insubstantial, while the longing for it remained clear and unconditional.

But the opportunity of return revealed the irreparable nature of exile. It exposed lesions that will never heal. For once the legal obstacles to fulfilling that dream were removed, then ambivalence blurred the clarity of the perception.

The reality of return was easier for those who had left in the 1980s, easier for the thousands of young people in the ANC's army living in camps in different parts of Africa. They had been uprooted, but not transplanted. For those living at the ANC school and farms in Tanzania, and those working in the ANC apparatus in Zambia, the problems of return were more logistic than emotional. They had remained South African communities, unassimilated into their host countries.

Yet even for these there are formidable practical and psychological problems. For they return to a country cemented into the rigid mould of apartheid, to communities still as deeply riven, little changed by the removal of laws from the statute books; a society in which social and economic conditions, customs, habits, ideas and perceptions are those imposed by apartheid and still strongly entrenched. They may now share the same bus queues, but the black townships to which they return at night – Soweto, Langa, Lenasia, Mitchell's Plain – are worlds apart from the lush white suburbs of Parktown, Rivonia or Rondebosch.

Exiles begin life all over again each time they step into a new country. They who have been strangers, never feeling wholly part of their host country however much acceptance and hospitality they have been given, knowing they are outsiders in someone else's country, now face the prospect of becoming outsiders in their own. They know in their hearts that they can never return completely, for it is not possible to cast out those changes deep within that come through immersion in a different world. So they focus their concerns on the practical problems – will they find jobs at their age? Will they find a place to live? And where – in the slums of the townships, or the walled, razor-wired, barricaded white suburbs? But underlying is the real anxiety, the recognition that none can return to the familiar.

They have been irrevocably changed; but the country they left has also changed. Many exiles have moved forward educationally, while siblings and friends left at home moved backwards in a disintegrating educational system. But then politically the exiles have been left behind. 'You feel as though this stream has cast you aside,' says Lauretta Ngcobo. 'Even when you have tried to drift on, you feel as though you are at the edge.' All through the years South African exiles sang songs, the songs they brought with them from home. But at home they are singing different songs now.

Some exiles left home fifteen, twenty, twenty-five, even thirty years ago. A new generation has grown up in exile – those who left a country they were too young to recall now, and those who were born and have lived their whole lives 'outside'. They go to British or German, Zambian or Canadian schools. They mingle with children of their host country, they assimilate different cultures, learn to speak different languages, and do not know or forget their own. Perhaps they are always aware that they do not quite fit in, but they strive. And they adjust. Then they grow up, get jobs, marry, and have their own children. They know about South Africa – but at second hand; and their spouses and children only at third hand. Nandi Vileika's father is Swedish. Nomsa Gertz, once married to a fellow South African, is now married to a German, with children by both marriages. Pren Naicker's Russian wife is afraid of going to South Africa.

Despite the tremendous centrifugal force of South Africa and its struggles, wherever they stayed the exiles began to put down roots. Paul Tabori writes: 'Those of my exile friends who would listen I tried to advise by stressing the simple truth that it was very difficult to lead a suitcase life – that after a while they had to unpack, literally and symbolically.' Those who did unpack their suitcases and managed to build a family life in exile are faced with competing pulls which threaten to shatter that family. 'The returning person inhabits a different reality . . . The one thing certain is that he will feel a new kind of homesickness, a new kind of grief.'* Those who stay must part with those who will return. And those who return will leave families and friends who have grown into communities around them. The wound of that second separation can be as sharp and painful as the first.

'Home' is still the name they give to the country they left behind, but home is now elsewhere, not simply in location but also through custom and habit, possessions, neighbours, jobs; and through the culture they have absorbed from their host countries. So there is the paradox of exile. Abdul Minty and Dumisani Kumalo have each spent the major portion of their lives – up to thirty years – working full-time in the Anti-Apartheid organisations, sacrificing their educational and career opportunities, to concentrate only on this: to end apartheid. And now they stand face to face with the reality that they do not wish to live in South Africa again.

Exile was a desertion, however imperative, and nothing can wholly restore that unravelled relationship. But it changed the pictures on the retina of our minds, so that now we have double vision. We have had to find a way of reconciling the way we had seen things from 'home', and the way they look to us now from the changed place. Thus it locates us and our objectives beyond parochial boundaries.

'The immediate physical environment is no longer a problem,' states Billy Modise, 'it is my home wherever I am . . . that is what I think exile has meant to me. My world has become the whole world, and everywhere I am a citizen.'

'The planet has become a small city, so home should be everywhere,' says Hotep, an exile in America. We are no less citizens of our own country because we now understand that we are citizens of the world.

---

* L. and R. Grinberg, *Migration and Exile*, Yale University Press.

Selecting the Exiles

I expect South Africans who read this book may be critical of the choice both of those included and those left out.

A large number of the exiles in this book are politically committed; many full-time activists. I did not intend any limitation on political orientation, and there are people from different organisations, and from none. But because of my own past activities and associations as a member of the ANC I was more readily accepted by those whose own political leanings were similar to mine. I did seek out others, sometimes encountering suspicion and reservations. It was not easy.

A few exiles who I approached did not want to be interviewed; but not many. Most spoke openly and often at great length. Quite obviously many of the exiles could have been included in any one of two or three different categories. So the choice of section was often an arbitrary one, governed by the extent to which the potency of the story as a whole centred around a particular subject.

Where do the exiles' stories begin? Crossing the border is only one of a long series of events which are crucial to that culminating act. Why go into exile? Some background material had to be included. The past is essential for understanding the present. It is for this reason that some of the exiles' stories are more about pre-exile than post. The past is the apartheid phenomenon, and that becomes the pivot around which life in exile revolves. The children of exiles know this all too well; the shadow of apartheid is a constant presence in their lives.

In the end the exile experience is inextricably woven into the experience of apartheid, with all its remorseless brutalities, its cruel absurdities, its degradations. The extent to which individual exiles were able to confront and adjust to life in exile has been conditioned by the conflicts of life under apartheid.

The names of people interviewed are real names. There may be some confusion of names, because many people working full-time in the ANC or serving in the ranks of Umkhonto were given new names for reasons of security. Sometimes these new names have become so well-used that they have been adhered to by the holders in place of their lesser-known birth names.

The place and date of each interview is given at the beginning of each interview.

Some South African Words,
Usages and Idioms

BAKKIE: A small delivery van or pick-up truck.

BY THEN: Does not imply any movement of time or events. It is used interchangeably with 'at that time', as in: 'I was very young by then,' or: 'I was very shy by then.'

CLAP or KLAP: Derived from the Afrikaans 'klap' – a blow, a hit, a strike. As in 'They clapped me,' meaning 'They struck me.'

DAGGA: Marijuana.

DONGA: A gully or gulch, often the result of erosion.

ELDERLY or ELDERLIES: Does not necessarily refer to actual age, but to the people of an earlier generation. As: 'The elderlies came back from Robben Island.'

HAU!: An expression of astonishment.

HIPPOS and CASPIRS: Different types of armoured personnel carriers, used by the South African army and by the police in their suppression actions in the black townships.

JA: All South Africans use 'Ja' – literally 'yes' in Afrikaans. It is a long drawn-out yaaaah, used regardless of whether the speaker is using English or Afrikaans or one of the African languages, very often as a confirmation: 'I did go there. Ja.' Or reflectively: 'It was hard, ja.'

LATE: Is a euphemism, meaning 'dead'. As used in customary English obituaries: 'The late Mr X,' here used as in 'I heard my father was late.'

MK: Shorthand for Umkhonto we Sizwe – the Spear of the Nation – the military wing of the African National Congress.

NE?: Meaning 'Not so?'

NO: Used frequently not to imply a negative, but almost as an introduction to a statement, such as English speakers use 'Well . . . ' As, for instance: 'What have you been doing?' 'No. I just went for a walk.'

OR and TG: The ANC's two most important officials in exile during the period from 1960 to 1990; Oliver Tambo, the President General, and Tom Nkobi, the Treasurer General.

PAP: The staple South African food; a dry porridge made from maize meal – known locally as 'mealie-meal' or 'mielie meal'.

PONDOKKIE: Shack.

SCHOOL and SCHOOLING: A compendium word to cover virtually all education – lower, higher and what in the West is known as 'post-school'. Used generally by adults to refer equally to University, College or vocational Institutional training.

SKIPPING and FOOTING: 'To skip' is slang for crossing the border illegally in flight; 'footing' is walking, generally long distances.

STANDHOLDER: Owner of an urban plot of land (very unusual among Africans).

THE COUNTRY or INSIDE: Exile talk for South Africa. Depending on its context, 'Inside' may also mean 'In prison'.

Mazimbu Words

CHARLOTTES: The nurseries for babies at Mazimbu, named after ANC pioneer Charlotte Maxake.

MPANDO: Literally 'choosing' – generic term for the periodic distribution of clothing or other goods to Mazimbu residents and students.

FRYING: Slang term – origin unknown – for the private selling of clothes or other items from Mpando – even stolen items.

Frontline States and Forward Areas

FRONTLINE STATES: When Mozambique and Angola became independent in 1974 after the collapse of Portuguese colonialism, they joined with Tanzania, Zambia and Botswana in a Frontline States alliance to coordinate resistance to South Africa and Southern Rhodesia. After its independence in 1980 Zimbabwe joined the Frontline alliance and the grouping was instrumental in forming the Southern African Development Coordination Conference (SADCC) together with Lesotho, Malawi and Swaziland, in an effort to reduce economic dependence on South Africa and to promote regional co-operation. All the Frontline States, with the exception of Tanzania – presumably protected by its distance from direct incursions – were subject to direct armed incursions, military attacks, sabotage and Death Squad operations by South Africa.

Later the term Frontline States came to refer to all the SADCC countries, including Tanzania.

FORWARD AREAS: A term used in ANC and anti-apartheid circles to denote those areas outside South Africa which have been used as a springboard for military or political infiltration into South Africa – particularly Botswana, Lesotho, Swaziland, and to a lesser extent, Southern Zimbabwe and Mozambique.

States in the Forward Areas sometimes had ambivalent attitudes towards the South African freedom fighters in their areas. They accepted the exiles – refugee centres were established by UNHCR in Botswana and Swaziland. But military and quasi-military activities on their soil exposed them to reprisals from South Africa: They therefore tried to restrain such activities as far as possible – or to give South Africa the impression that they were doing so. Botswana and Swaziland, for instance, prohibited exiles from possessing firearms and prosecuted those found with them. Swaziland police constantly arrested politically active exiles – allegedly on South African prompting – jailed them for short periods, and often deported them; but not back to South Africa.

CRAIG WILLIAMSON: a Captain (later Major) in the South African Security Police, who worked for ten years as an infiltrator into organisations close to the ANC. Started his undercover work in NUSAS, the National Union of South African Students, and used that to get promotion to the post of assistant director to the IUEF – the International University Exchange Fund – based in Geneva. This organisation, set up to help Latin American and South African student exiles, allowed Williamson to gather confidential information not only on this organisation but also on the ANC, PAC and SACP.

The IUEF closed down early in 1981 after Williamson was unmasked, leaving debts of R134,000. Williamson returned to South Africa and took charge of the Death Squad responsible for assassinating white activists, both inside and outside the country. Ruth First, Jenny and Katryn Schoon and David Webster died at his direction, and Albie Sachs was badly injured.

INTELLIGENCE ORGANISATIONS: Names have changed from time to time, and precise contemporary names are not always used by people interviewed. The SPECIAL BRANCH intelligence agency was set up during the second World War as a division of the police force – also known as the Security Police. Its successor was the BUREAU OF STATE SECURITY, set up by Prime Minister P.W. Botha as an almost personal apparatus within the military – convenient acronym: BOSS. BOSS was finally dissolved, more in spirit than in substance, and its functions were taken over by the South African Defence Force's CIVIL CO-OPERATION BUREAU – CCB CCB – a thuggish and criminal 'counter-insurgency' unit operating virtually outside the law.

Acronyms

AAM	Anti-Apartheid Movement
ANC	African National Congress
BC	Black Consciousness (or Black Consciousness Movement)
BOSS	Bureau of State Security (see above)
BPC	Black Peoples Convention
CCB	Civil Co-operation Bureau (see above)
COD	Congress of Democrats
COSAS	Congress of South African Students
COSAWR	Committee of South African War Resisters
CUSO	Canadian University Service Overseas
FAPLA	People's Armed Forces for the Liberation of Angola
FRELIMO	Mozambique Liberation Front
IDAF	International Defence and Aid Fund
IUEF	International University Exchange Fund
NUSAS	National Union of South African Students
OAU	Organisation for African Unity
SACTU	South African Congress of Trade Unions
SADCC	Southern African Development Co-ordination Conference
SADF	South African Defence Force
SAIC	South African Indian Congress
SAP	South African Police
SASO	South African Students Organisation
SB	Special Branch – or any variant
SECHABA	Magazine issued by the ANC
SIDA	Swedish Institute for Development Agencies
SOMAFCO	The Solomon Mahlangu Freedom College
SWANU	South West African National Union
TANU	Tanzanian African National Union
UDF	United Democratic Front
UNHCR	United Nations High Commission for Refugees
UNIP	United National Independence Party (of Zambia)
UNISA	University of South Africa – correspondence courses only
WUS	World University Service

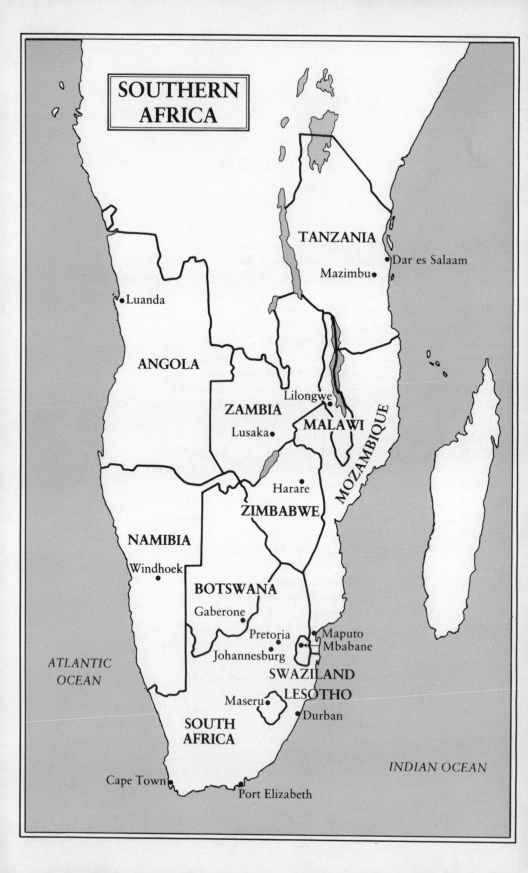

SOUTHERN AFRICA

TANZANIA

• Dar es Salaam

Mazimbu •

• Luanda

ANGOLA

ZAMBIA

Lilongwe •

MALAWI

Lusaka •

MOZAMBIQUE

Harare •

ZIMBABWE

NAMIBIA

Windhoek •

BOTSWANA

Gaberone •

Pretoria •

Maputo
Mbabane

Johannesburg •

SWAZILAND

ATLANTIC
OCEAN

Maseru •

LESOTHO

• Durban

SOUTH
AFRICA

INDIAN OCEAN

Cape Town •

Port Elizabeth

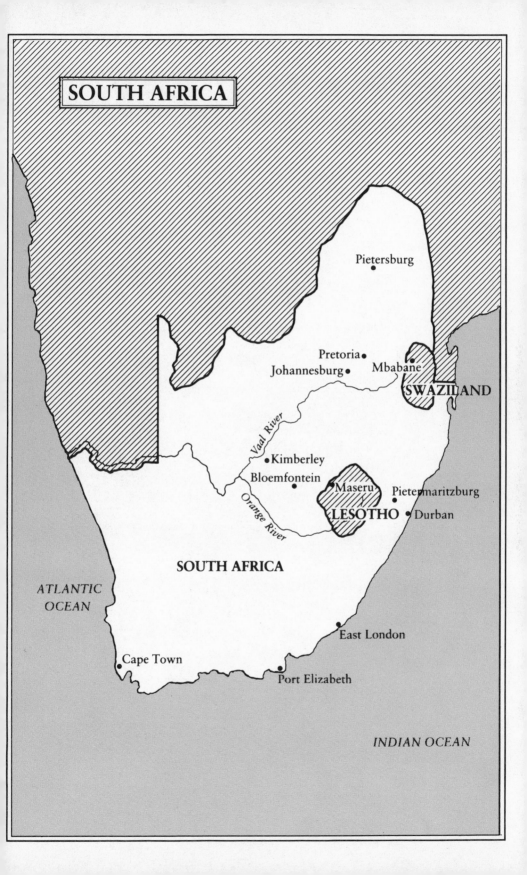

PART ONE

Crossing the Frontier

Trail-Blazers: the 1960s

There are two episodes in contemporary South African history that are like lines drawn across the political landscape, or ravines; as though the earth's plates moved, opening up fissures that could never be bridged between the irrevocable past and the developing future.

These two events are known by the place and the year: Sharpeville, 1960. Soweto, 1976.

They changed the history of our country, the lives of our people, and the perceptions of the rest of the world. And they sent, first hundreds, then thousands, then tens of thousands into exile.

On a warm sunny day, 21 March 1960, towards the end of summer, a crowd of perhaps two thousand people gathered outside the police station at Sharpeville, a black township near Vereeniging, fifty miles from Johannesburg. They were there in a protest against the pass laws organised by the Pan-Africanist Congress, a movement that had broken away from the ANC. Shortly after one o'clock, without any warning, the police began firing into the crowd. Sixty-nine people were killed – mostly shot in the back as they were running away. A hundred and eighty were injured. In the late afternoon a short, sharp, high-veld rainstorm washed the blood from the streets of Sharpeville.

'For nearly fifty years', writes Allister Sparks, 'black South Africans had pursued their struggle against oppression and exploitation with consummate patience. Politely, deferentially, they had petitioned the white government for a better deal and had been ignored . . . Sharpeville was the turning point when black Nationalist politics was outlawed, when it went underground and switched from strategies of non-violence to those of a guerilla struggle . . . When, with the black opposition silenced, what little public debate there had been between black and white ceased and the possibility of a political solution to the race conflict was replaced by the certainty of confrontation.'

OLIVER TAMBO
London 1990

The Sharpeville massacre precipitated the departure from South Africa of Oliver Tambo, who had already been selected by the ANC to be their representative overseas.

At one time Tambo had hoped to become an Anglican priest; but he trained as a lawyer and for some time ran a practice in Johannesburg together with Nelson Mandela. At the time he left he was deputy-president of the ANC. After Chief Luthuli's death he became president.

By chance he had arrived in Cape Town the day before Sharpeville, and was with Ronald Segal when he heard the news. Ronald offered to drive him across the border to Bechuanaland.

This was the beginning of three decades of exile. For Ronald Segal and Frene Ginwala it was entirely unplanned. Both found themselves caught up in the drama, where they took on functions that were imposed by chance of circumstance; and then because of the role they had played in the escape of Oliver Tambo and the Indian leader, Yusuf Dadoo, were themselves unable to return.

Oliver Tambo began a thirty-year odyssey in which he travelled the world, at first with little status and often no acceptance; gradually to become recognised as the spokesperson for those who had no votes, no human rights within South Africa – the black majority – and their principal organisation, the African National Congress.

'In 1964, when Nelson Mandela and other leaders were sentenced to life imprisonment,' he relates, 'the number of volunteers leaving South Africa to join us was constantly growing. Fortunately there were places where they could be trained. In African countries there was Ethiopia, Tanzania, Egypt, Nigeria, Morocco and Algeria. And there was China and the USSR, as well as the GDR. After the 1976 uprising there was a big explosion of young people leaving South Africa. Many of them wanted to join Umkhonto we Sizwe. The problem then was not the question of training, but how to return them to South Africa when they were trained. Remember at this stage South Africa was surrounded by countries that were not yet independent, or that were sympathetic to the apartheid regime – the Rhodesias and Angola and Mozambique, still under Portuguese rule. And many of these exiles were very young. That was when Nyerere, then President of Tanzania, offered us land for a school.'

Under Oliver Tambo the ANC's external mission established itself first in London, then in Dar es Salaam, later to Morogoro (near the ANC school); and finally to Lusaka in Zambia. Understanding of the meaning of apartheid in the outside world grew slowly, assisted by resistance inside the country and anti-apartheid organisations outside.

'Gradually white South Africa was forced to yield. It took a long time, and in latter years the situation became intolerable – such harsh repression, torture, cruelties, so many people dying and even more prepared to die. Gradually white South Africa began to realise that there was no end to this. They had to change. The oppressed can't change – it's not possible. They have to force the oppressor to change. It was the action of people inside who refused to be silenced, who rose again and again, together with boycotts and sanctions applied from outside that began the process of change. At the time when de Klerk made his announcement about his change in policy we were waiting to deliver representatives to a number of countries, including Jamaica, Caracas, Portugal, Spain – in fact, the ANC had official representatives in more countries in the world than the apartheid regime.

'I never had a home really. I could not say that I would ever be home on a certain day or leave on another. After I left South Africa my wife had to leave the country by herself with the children, work, bring them up, do everything on her own. And later when I was transferred to Africa it was even worse. My family remained in London, and I was able to visit them only when passing through on some other assignment.

'But my heart was given to the struggle and nothing else would come first. I felt that people depended on me, and I gave my life to it. I didn't think I was playing an important role. I simply had a duty to perform, and went on performing it as long as possible. I responded to a challenge when it came. There was one thing that I was convinced about – that apartheid was doomed to end, that whatever time it took it was doomed to die, and all of us would one day make our country together. Given that as a challenge that I accepted, then all else was subject to it.'

For thirty years of exile he took the reality of apartheid all over the world. More than any other this quiet, gentle and friendly man held the disparate forces and individuals in the ANC together in a remarkable unity of activity and purpose.

In 1989 he suffered a stroke which limited his work, although he made a good recovery. With the release of his old friend and partner, Nelson Mandela, the demands on him relaxed.

Oliver Tambo and Nelson Mandela formed the ANC Youth League at Fort Hare University when they were students there in the early 1940s. Both were expelled from the university for their political activities.

In the changed climate of October 1991, Tambo returned in triumph to the university to be installed as Chancellor – the first appointment made by the university after the dead hand of Bantu Education had been lifted. It was, he said, a happy and emotional occasion that linked the distant past to the bright future we are all striving to build.

Oliver Tambo died in Johannesburg on 24 April 1993.

RONALD SEGAL
London 1990

'I think for many exiles it's going to be a very tough recognition to reach – that that is the only function that they will really have. Because they are too old. Or have been away too long.'

> He has written fourteen books, starting with *Tokoloshe*, a political fantasy; and including an autobiography *Into Exile*; *A Dictionary of African Politics*; *African Profiles*; and books on India, America, a biography of Trotsky, a world atlas; and *The Race War*, the first attempt to tell world history from the black point of view.
>
> After graduating he took a second degree at Trinity College, Cambridge, and won a fellowship to the University of Virginia, USA. But he resigned his fellowship and returned to South Africa after reading about the packing of the Senate to remove coloured voters from the common voters' roll.
>
> With money left to him by his father, he started a magazine, *Africa South*.

I became involved in Congress campaigns, and started agitating for an economic boycott. I launched the boycott of Nationalist goods at a meeting on campus at the University of Cape Town – a huge meeting.

I got a series of threatening phone calls that clearly emanated from the Special Branch. They said, 'You have fourteen days to live. We are watching wherever you go.' And then they would phone and say: Thirteen days to live. Twelve days. Eleven days.

For a young spoilt white, born to the purple of commerce, this was not a comfortable experience. But it's my hatred of bullies that probably got me into politics in the first place. And by the fourth or fifth day I was flaming mad. I mean, I went from panic, through alarm, to absolute fury!

One night I was having dinner at my mother's house and we suddenly heard a most extraordinary bang. We rushed outside, and there was the large Chrysler Imperial which I had inherited from my father, in a sheet of flame. We called the police. And when the head of the squad came in the house, he looked at me, and I looked at him. And he knew that I knew that he knew that the police were behind this. Two hours later when I went back to my flat, there were further threatening messages written on the windows.

> His office was raided. Then his passport was confiscated, and he was issued with banning orders prohibiting him from all gatherings for five years.

Then came Sharpeville. The major centre of PAC support was the Cape Peninsula, where the ANC was weakest, and the PAC found a political vacuum to fill. All of a sudden, in the wake of the Sharpeville Massacre, the PAC was tumultuously evident.

In Cape Town there was a great march. I was a Capetonian – and those thousand miles between Cape Town and Johannesburg are a lot of miles between cultures, political systems and establishments. I hardly knew Oliver Tambo, but I was so distressed by the PAC dominance of what looked in Cape Town like a popular black insurrection, that I phoned him. I said, 'Something must be done. You can't abandon, almost by default, the leadership.' He said, 'You'll be hearing from us.' He was obviously – not surprisingly – keen to get me off the phone!

The following day I got a phone call. Would I come to the office of the Garment Workers. I went along and there was Oliver. We were both banned, both prohibited from communicating with each other. And there we sat talking. He told me about the ANC plans for a national stay-at-home.

As we were talking, the door opened, a head came through, and a voice said: You'd better go! The Special Branch are next door examining the files. We tiptoed down the stairs, the two of us, went into Plein Street. And as we hit the pavement, the newspaper boys were shouting: CONGRESS BANNED! CONGRESS OUTLAWED!

Oliver said: There is a standing order of the National Executive that, should this happen, I should go abroad to start an organisation for what will follow. And I said, thinking and not thinking: I'll take you!

I borrowed my mother's chauffeur's coat. Oliver would sit next to me dressed as a chauffeur since no one in the platteland questions the existence of a black servant sitting next to a white master. I got money from my family in case it was needed, and we set off for Johannesburg, a twenty-five hour journey. The following evening we set off for what was then Bechuanaland – I think it was a four hour drive. We had no problems. We got into Bechuanaland. Oliver reported to the District Commissioner, and I drove back to Johannesburg.

I woke in the morning to find a State of Emergency had been declared. I think I decided that I would go back across the border to think things out, since it had proved to be so easy. Should I take *Africa South* out?

Oliver was in the House of Chiefs, a little way outside of Lobatsi. I went straight to see him, and he was sitting in the sun with a bead necklace and a cross at the end of it. It had never occurred to me that he was a devout Anglican.

Back at my hotel, I heard a radio announcement by the then Minister of Foreign Affairs that two most dangerous agitators, Oliver Tambo and Ronald Segal, had escaped. We then became the centre of international attention. Journalists started descending on Bechuanaland. But for a number of days I was absolutely alone in this appalling place, in this hotel. They now knew who I was. And the farmers used to come in to look at me, and then come up and threaten me.

It wasn't the fear I'd had when they threatened to kill me in Cape Town. Once you'd had that, you know, I really wasn't frightened. But I was lonely. I was terribly, terribly lonely. I didn't know where I was going, what I would do with the rest of my life. And I refused to move in with Oliver because, if I left that hotel, it was as much as raising some sort of white flag. One evening I came into the bedroom; and there was a parcel on the bed. And I thought, 'Well, this is . . . this is it. It must be a bomb.' No message, nothing. Just a brown paper parcel. And I thought, 'If it's not today, it will be tomorrow.' So I opened the parcel. And what was inside was a packet of matzos. It was Passover, which of course I had completely forgotten! And a message that somebody passing through Bechuanaland had been asked by my mother to bring it.

I'm not a crier. But that was one of the very, very few times in my post-childhood life that I just burst into tears. I was overwhelmed. I felt such a wild longing for my home again, and it was a long, long time . . . I loathed Lobatsi. I felt if I didn't leave at once I would spend the rest of my life in that sullen town, besieged by the sun and the hot dust, the only relief a short walk down the street to the railway-line and back.

I decided I must phone my brother – he was an industrialist in Southern Rhodesia at the time – and Frene Ginwala who was the agent for *Africa South* in Dar es Salaam, in order to get papers of some sort. The question was: if we drove out through Southern Rhodesia – then part of the Central African Federation – would the Federal Government try to hand us back to the South Africans?

Eventually I took it on myself – and in retrospect it was a very rash thing to do – to say to Oliver, 'Look, I think we should go, drive across the border and see what happens.' We were half a mile from the border when a cloud of dust came towards us, and a car screeched to a stop. It was my brother, coming from Southern Rhodesia. It was an extraordinary coincidence. He had come with a message that we would certainly be arrested, and almost certainly returned over the border, so we went back to Francistown on the northern border. A day or two later I got a call from Frene to say that she had got hold of Indian Government papers for us, and had arranged for a plane.

The only workable, practical airfield was run by the Witwatersrand Native Labour recruiting organisation. And they had refused permission for a plane to land to collect us, so it needed to be a plane that could land on the veld. Three, four, five days later, we drove down to Palapye in the centre of Bechuanaland, the plane arrived at five o'clock in the morning, we took off. We landed in Blantyre – the plane could only do six hundred mile leaps, and until the last moment we didn't know whether we would be allowed to leave Blantyre. But we did. And we were taken to Dar es

Salaam, and Julius Nyerere was there with his arms outstretched, flung them around me – and that was the beginning of my exile.

I published *Africa South in Exile* from London until I got a letter from the South Africa Reserve Bank telling me that my funds had been frozen. They then operated a most illegal, and unique form of discrimination against me. They refused to recognise that I had emigrated, and therefore refused me any emigration allowance funds of any sort. They refused to accept the alternative, that I was technically therefore still in South Africa, and so entitled to write cheques on my account. So they effectively neutralised my funds. I was forced on to my own resources.

Tony Godwin, who was the chief editor of Penguin Books, suggested that I start an African series of books. I said: That's a marvellous idea. And I founded the Penguin African Library, which I edited, I think until about 1985. It was almost a quarter of a century, and has pioneered African studies in all sorts of ways, certainly in popularising new perceptions in Africa.

Do I want now to return to South Africa? That's a very difficult question after thirty years. Yes. For what? For how long? On what basis?

My wife leads a very productive life, running a community art studio. My children are twenty-four, twenty-six, twenty-eight, and all have lives of their own. I would go if there was something creative for me to do. I don't mean something important, I don't mean something prestigious, because really at the age of fifty-seven I've done what I can or will do what I can through my books. If it was felt that I could be useful, really useful, I would go. And I would commute with London. But what I do not wish is to be a part of a bureaucracy, almost as though I'm part of the luggage of return.

And I think for many exiles it is going to be a very tough recognition to reach – that they are too old. Or have been away for too long.

FRENE GINWALA
London 1990

'People don't take you seriously as a woman, they don't take you seriously politically. They see you as a technician.'

She has a law degree and a doctorate in history. In the first years of Tanzanian independence she edited the newspaper of the new ruling party. She could have gone far in the academic world. Instead she has used all her skills working full-time for the liberation movement, without the reward of money or honours.

At the time of this interview, she was head of the Political Committee of the office of the President of the ANC.

I left to help get Oliver Tambo out of the country. It was 1960, 22 March. I was back in South Africa from studying overseas, I had to do courses in South Africa to finish my legal training.

There was some general talk about ANC representatives coming out of the country. I don't know if I understood all the implications of setting up an ANC foreign mission – which I was told was what Tambo was coming out for.

Britain had just made a statement that Tanganyika was going to be developed as a self-governing colony, with African interests paramount. We had good friends in Tanganyika who were now also becoming powerful. It might be possible for us to use it as a staging-post. I was asked, would I sound people out as to what was possible; and would I help. I agreed.

I was doing an interview for the BBC with Monty Naicker on the evening of 21 March, when the phone rang. It was Walter Sisulu who said something about my going to see my parents who were in Mozambique. I talked to Monty and I told him that I'd had these discussions with Sisulu, and I didn't really know what I was supposed to do. And he said, 'Go and see your parents!'

So the next morning I went to Mozambique, that's how I left South Africa.

I knew I had to do something about the plan to set up ANC foreign missions. But I didn't really know what. While I was in Lourenco Marques, I heard on the radio that Tambo was in Bechuanaland. Now there was an incredible coincidence! I had been working for *Africa South*, and it was Ronald Segal – the founder of *Africa South* – who drove Tambo to Bechuanaland. Tambo was stuck there. So I just now felt obligated; I had to do something.

I made my way to Salisbury (now Harare) and made the transportation arrangements for Oliver, Ronald, and Yusuf Dadoo, who had joined them; and arrangements for them to be allowed to land in Tanganyika. By then there was a State of Emergency in South Africa. There'd been the attack on Verwoerd, ja; there'd been the hue and cry after us; and world publicity that I was in Dar es Salaam and had helped people to get out. So I stayed in Tanganyika.

An office had been set up for a South African United Front – the SAIC, the ANC, PAC, SWANU and SWAPO. I wasn't part of that office, and I was able to act independently to channel our people in and out of South Africa. Mandela came out; Mlangeni, Mhlaba, Wilton Mkwayi – all those leadership people. But also a lot of young comrades who were coming in and out.

I set up a newspaper there called *Spearhead*, a monthly journal. It was before Tanganyika's independence although four TANU ministers were in the government at that time. Independence didn't come until December 1961. So then I worked there as a journalist – until I got deported. There was – to put it mildly – a mix-up as far as the Tanzanians were concerned. I was declared a prohibited immigrant, yet I left on a Tanzania travel document. I had had a bad accident with my leg, so when I was declared a PI I came to the UK to go into hospital. The PI order was lifted, but I didn't go back immediately.

I spent more than a year getting my leg right – bone grafts and so on. Then I started work producing radio programmes and writing scripts for something called the Transcription Centre, which was non-profit making. And we used to make programmes for Africa particularly, primarily on culture.

I wanted to write about South Africa. A lot of the way our history was being interpreted was wrong, and I had it in my head that I needed a doctorate if I was going to write history that anyone would pay attention to. But I found that, with a law degree, I couldn't get to do a postgraduate degree in history. So it just remained a prospect.

Oxford University used to run a course for training potential diplomats from the newly liberated countries; and I used to be invited to talk at seminars and courses. So on one occasion I said to George Bennett, who was organising them, 'I find it very strange that I can't come and study, but I can come and teach.' He said, 'Well, do you want to come and study?' I'd never thought of going to Oxford then. So he arranged for me to be admitted.

I got to Oxford in 1967 or 1968 and I'd begun work when I got a letter from Nyerere, saying he wanted to see me; he had something he wanted me to do; would I come and see him? So I arranged to go to Tanzania to see him during the December holidays. When I got there, he said that they were nationalising the local newspapers. We'd often talked in the past about newspapers; and he wanted me to edit the national paper.

I remember saying that I didn't think I was constitutionally able to edit a government newspaper. And he joked, and said that that was precisely why he wanted someone like me. Anyway, he agreed that he would give us a Charter which would establish that the paper would be independent, though it would be government owned. I said I couldn't really accept without consulting the President of the ANC.

So I went to Lusaka and spoke to President Tambo. And he said no, I should go. It's important! And so I didn't finish my doctorate. In February I went to Tanzania to edit the official newspaper.

Now had you wanted an identikit picture of who should be the editor of a Tanganyikan newspaper, you will come up with: an Asian woman connected to a liberation movement, known as a radical, who had formerly been deported from the country! [Laughs]

I survived it for just over eighteen months, when I was dismissed because we had written an editorial attacking General Mamare, who had executed members of the Communist Party in the Sudan. What I was not aware of was that Mamare was about to pay a state visit to Tanzania.

But I'm not sure of the exact reasons behind it. I thought we'd done a lot, much more than anyone had expected. We exposed stories of the forced marriages in Zanzibar – young women were being forcibly married by leaders of the Revolutionary Council. There was a whole range of issues that we took up. Nyerere never interfered. Obviously if I had problems, I would go and talk to him. I was conscious of the fact that he was technically editor of *The Standard*, and that I was a presidential appointment. So I took great care not to embarrass him. But he never said, 'Don't do this' or 'Do that'.

There were two things which I felt very good about. First, that we made it a paper of discussion. We carried endless discussions on policy, and we opened them to everybody. The other thing is that we made it into a training paper.

Many of the staff and others thought we were hostile to the government. This whole notion of a campaigning, discussing paper was something very alien. Also, being a woman in charge of them – inevitably some of it was because I was a woman, but it was never expressed as such.

But after the article attacking General Mamare, I was dismissed. I came back to Oxford and I finished my doctorate, and got myself a place in chambers, with a view to practising here.

In the meantime there was the coup in Portugal, and changes in Mozambique. So I decided to go back to Mozambique to see my parents, which I did, and then came back to Britain.

By then things had changed quite dramatically. Mozambique was going to be independent, and the decision was taken that I should work full-time for the ANC. It was decided I should work on the establishment of a DIP – Department of Information and Publicity. So for a year I worked setting up the machinery we needed, and since then I've been working for the ANC. So I really never went back to law.

Working as a woman in the ANC is difficult on two counts. As a woman people don't take you seriously politically. They see you as a technician. It doesn't happen now, but before, if a committee was ever set up, they'd look around and they'd say that so-and-so, a man, would be the chair, and you, as the woman, would be the secretary to take the notes. In fact, for many years I used to make an absolute point of refusing to take the notes.

Always combined with being a woman has been the matter of being an Indian, not an African. I've been on delegations where people have come to me assuming I'm the secretary to the delegation, and things of that kind. Mmm. I think it's getting better. There's a bigger recognition. But it's still, at a personal level, very problematic. It takes a lot out of you. One doesn't like what it does to you as a person. It makes you aggressive, it makes you prickly when it's not necessary. That, I think, in a sense is a price you pay. But sometimes you don't like yourself.

How do you feel about having abandoned a professional career to give all your expertise and energies to the ANC?

That's also a profession! [Laughs] I left a very good job to work full-time for the movement. I was earning I think twice as much at the time I went to Oxford as I'm earning today! And that was twenty years ago!

I can't see myself not being in the ANC. To be very honest, had I been able to see myself not being in the ANC, I'd have left years ago, because of the frustrations. I've been tempted many times. But when it comes down to it, I cannot imagine myself being outside.

So, I see myself going back with the ANC – although after thirty years I know it will be going back to a foreign country. I want to work much more on women. I've been doing a lot more work on it – research, agitating within the movement, pushing, putting forward proposals, ideas. And I'd like to work in that field if it's possible. When I go back, I will work with the ANC.

If there's a constituent assembly, I think I'll probably try and run for it. It's something I want to do, because it would give meaning, take further what one's been doing. Also I think it's very very important. If we don't push the women's issue now, and if women don't get in and do things at every level, we're going to be left behind. So it's more important than ever now. I can't see myself doing anything else.

Ja, there were times when I tried to go back to law. I could have, after leaving Tanzania. I was doing very well in radio before I went there. I was probably the only woman editing a national newspaper on the continent of Africa at that time. So I could have moved on from there into those areas, had I wanted that kind of professional recognition. Sometimes, even now, it does give me a small sort of pleasure, a boost for my confidence when – for instance, immediately after the unbanning of the ANC – I was offered jobs at home. It did mean that as a journalist I had some kind of professional recognition, even though I wasn't working as a journalist in that period. Or when I get invited in my own right to deliver a lecture here or open a conference there, or something like that.

Because in the ANC, when you're battling on, at times you feel you don't get recognition. It's not that you want personal aggrandisement. But you do want to feel that what you are doing is actually having an impact. It has value. And you do often feel devalued in the movement, I think. Particularly women.

THOMAS TITUS NKOBI
Lusaka 1990

'There's not a time, not a year, not a week, where I could say I just rest. Nothing! No!'

He is the ANC's TG – Treasurer General – a burly, cheerful man, with a booming voice, now sixty-seven years old.

My father was a taxi-owner and also a standholder in Alexandra Township, outside Johannesburg.

The conditions in Alexandra Township were really appalling. You find a family of six sharing one room – bedroom, kitchen, living-room – with children sleeping in the same room with the parents, and so on. Because of lack of sleeping accommodation then you'll get boys who are about sixteen who don't like to live in that condition, who will go out and go look for places to stay and sleep. And as soon as the boy does that, he starts to come into contact with the gangs. I escaped this moving around with gangs – because my father was a very strict person.

I used to collect rents for my father. And sometimes you come into a place where the people are staying, you look at the lady of that house – perhaps the husband is away at work – and you say, 'Well mummy. I've come to collect rent.' And she says, 'My child, I've no money.' I was sent by my father to go and collect this money. I had a duty to perform. And at the same time, you look at this person, you see there's a lot of starvation there and no other alternative. You were torn into whether to go on asking for the rent money or you just leave it. But I couldn't say to my father, 'No. I'm not going to collect this money.' It is then the time when I decided no, the best way of doing this is really to participate in politics.

At that time, I had known leading people from the ANC – J. B. Marks, Dan Tloome, Walter Sisulu, Mandela, Tambo – when they used to address meetings in Alexandra Township. I don't think I used to miss a meeting. I was still schooling, ja. Very energetic, lot of energy, also a sportsman, and I used to run the mile. During those days, I think in the Transvaal I was the best person in the mile.

The Unity Movement held annual conferences in Bloemfontein at the same time that the ANC had conferences there.

We used to go to Bloemfontein. As students, we used to leave the Unity Movement Conference and go and listen to the debates in the ANC Conference. They were quite different. They were more theoretical at the Unity Movement Conference. At the ANC Conference they were discussing real things which worry the people. They were discussing bread; they were discussing starvation; they were discussing lack of land; they were discussing exorbitant rents; they were discussing Pass Laws. It appealed to us that, no, there is something here as compared with the Unity Movement. I think we did that for almost three years, in and out. And then finally I decided: no, I think our home is here in the ANC.

Then I started. I was at that time – in spite of the fact that there were these school hours – becoming more active also in the branches of the ANC, discussing and so on and so forth. I think the climax, the real thing came in 1957 when there was the second Alexandra bus boycott. When we started, I was the chairman of that. It's where I saw that if you are a leader, then you have the responsibility and discipline of a leader.

The same year I was made the National Organising Secretary of the ANC. I started moving all over South Africa. I think I'm the real most travelled native in South Africa, [Laughs] in town, in the rural areas and so on. I continued from 1957 till 1960, when the Movement was banned. 1960. But I was still the National Organiser.

Oh, there was a lot of harassment! Jeepers! One outstanding harassment, which I don't think I'll ever forget, was when I was sent to Bloemfontein to go and organise for a national strike. When I left Johannesburg I was given illegal leaflets which were calling upon the people to strike.

He was arrested in Bloemfontein.

Then they took me to the police station. The whole day they didn't do anything. At half past seven they put on the manacles . . . the handcuffs. I never in my life experienced such pains. They make tight! You know, even if you are still, you are not moving, they penetrate. You move, they penetrate. From half past seven until two o'clock in the morning.

I had a suit, a nice suit. I was supposed to look like a gentleman, not to be suspected as a subversive. I look quite respectable. At one o'clock a.m. I didn't have my jacket; I didn't have my shirt; I didn't have my trousers. The only thing which remained on me was a tie and my underwear. They had beaten me – I don't know what they did with them. They beat me up and they make me sit on my haunches. And I was sitting there; I was just thinking what to do.

Then I decided to say to them, 'Yes. I'm going to speak.' They say, 'Kom jong!' I went. I just dipped my head down and I say to him, 'I don't think you are doing justice to the government of this country. You want to force me to tell the government of South Africa lies – that I know where is Mandela when I don't know it. That will not give you credit.' That kind of liberated me from these things. Honestly. Immediately afterwards they took me upstairs, right upstairs. They are mocking at me. 'Meneer Nkobi. You see the galaxy of the lights of Bloemfontein? Every native is fast asleep, contented, no problem. You are from Johannesburg to come and cause trouble here.' And he took his revolver out. He says, 'I can shoot you, drop you down; then I can say the native was running away from custody. Nothing will happen. Duma Nokwe will bark for two weeks, Sisulu will bark for two weeks, and it will be the end. Your children will not be having a father. You'll be gone as a dog.'

Then I said to him – I could see this is the end – then I said, 'Who I am? I'm nothing compared to great men whom you have killed. You kill me, I'm nothing. But there are greater man you have killed, but the struggle goes on.' They had hit me here, [demonstrating the chest] just in this part here. I thought really I was falling. And I just fell where I was standing.

They pour water on me, I woke up. I could see, well I'm still alive. Then they took me down; they took me into a car. I was really certain that they are now going to eliminate me in the bush. They drove and drove until we reached a police station somewhere in the Orange Free State. The Chief of the Special Branch says, 'Oh, are they still handcuffing you, man?' He ordered them to unlock it. I started shaking like a fowl which you have cut its head. I wanted to stand but I couldn't. And they were laughing.

You know, there was only one person I thought of in this world – my son. He was a young fellow. He was just, you know, born. I said, 'Well, now I will not see that boy.'

They put me there for twenty-nine days ex communicado. No word from anybody. Nothing. But one day a white policeman in uniform came to me and said, 'What have you done? Why are these people so interested in you?' I said, 'I don't know. They haven't told me.' He says, 'Are you not Mandela?' I says, 'No; I'm not Mandela.' But he says, 'Now look! They say that nobody should speak to you. I'm a policeman, but you know I don't like what they are doing. Can you give me an address of one of your people so that I can inform them that you are here?' I said, 'Please! Don't come and talk to me in this thing. Go away.' He left.

At eleven o'clock he came back. He says, 'Please! I mean,' he says, 'they will just sentence you.' And so, even if it is a trap, I gave him the name of Reverend Tangle. Eleven o'clock. At five o'clock I was demanded to appear in court, dead or alive. I don't want to carry on with this story, but this person by the name of Coetzee, the first name is Bart, he's a uniformed policeman. He says, 'Please! One day when you are free, please remember me.' I said, 'Well, I will. I will.'

It really sort of gave me a kind of . . . a psychological insight, ja, that these people know now that at least one day we'll be free! The marks which were left by the handcuffs remained with me for years. For years. For years.

In 1961 I was put under house arrest for five years. Then one day Govan Mbeki came and met with us, and said, 'My friend, you must leave the country, work outside.' And indeed I was picked up, raced to the border, and I found myself in Lobatsi. No, I never told my family I was going – not an inch. It's painful, absolutely! What can you do? I didn't also want them to know where I was. But those who sent me out did inform my wife that I have left. Ja.

I flew to Tanzania. And – well, I did so many work within the Movement. There's not a time, not a year, not a day, not a week where I could say I just rest. Nothing! No.

Now I'm still travelling, like I used to do in South Africa. But it is different. The difference is that at home I was talking to my people to come into the Movement, to mobilise them. But now here I'm like a beggar. I'm going from one place to another, asking for funds to assist us in our liberation. That is what I do wherever I go.

The problems of exile are enormous. Socially, psychologically, financially. You sometimes think about home, but that is not a very big major problem. The problem is, how do we maintain the cohesion of the movement outside? Because there's a tremendous kind of psychological impact on our people. You get people who really need some psychiatric . . . they break up. Some of them come here to me, as the person who's in charge of real day-to-day needs. When they come here it's – I have no shoes. I have no clothes, I have no place to sleep. My child is sick. I need . . . All these kinds of things. No work. No work, ja. It's one of the most difficult departments of this Treasury. It is really the nerve centre. But you are not dealing with real politics about constitutional guidelines, discussions about the Freedom Charter, what it means.

I was here in 1964. There was a house, and the first people who came from Tanzania after their military training were on their way home. They remained in that house for six solid months without going out, waiting to be moved on. Only at night they would go out and exercise in the yard. It was a core, really a core which you can't find today. People who were committed. Who knew what they were doing. Prepared to sacrifice.

They included even our President. I stayed with him at a place called Gwaganazinga Makedi. He was sleeping, our President – sleeping on the floor together with his men there. Sleeping on the floor. Not a word. Not a complaint.

Then came this exodus of young people who had no political experience or understanding. Some of them left home not because they were political. For some of them it was the question of adventure. Others committed some crimes of some kind. But they were not politically grounded with the policy of the ANC. They were interested in training in the art of war; they were not interested to go to school.

One of our policies which we were trying to teach was that education is essential. There's this new phrase: 'Liberation first! Education afterwards.' We said: That is wrong. Education is the root, because without education you can never be a good soldier. A soldier, we were telling them, a soldier is not the one who just shoot and kill. A soldier is the one who is mentally alert. There are a lot of things today in the army which needs well-educated people. We are dealing with machines which need sciences, which need mathematics – not just shoot.

The exile life has got problems that you'd never expect. Never, never! And we didn't have the capacity, in fact, to contain them. There are new problems. One problem which I'm having in my mind, as a person who is responsible for day-to-day needs of these people, is that we are creating people who will be completely useless for that revolution. They do nothing. They eat and do nothing. Because they are sure of their pap, their clothes, therefore they are not interested to develop themselves.

Another of the problems which is facing the Movement is the question of pregnancy of small children. It's one of the greatest problems this movement is facing. A young man should be thinking about girls not as something to satisfy his own emotion, but must look at her as a sister, as a comrade in arms. As a comrade in arms. That is the kind of spirit which we must create among ourselves.

RUTH MOMPATI
Lusaka 1990

'The hardest thing – I missed the childhood of my children.'

> She looks like the schoolteacher she once was, with an air of gentle authority. She is on the National Executive of the ANC and was their Chief Representative in the United Kingdom for three years.

I have six aunts. The first one had about twelve children herself, and the others had six, five, four. I have a whole army of first cousins. Where we lived, a little village called Ganyesa in the district of Vryburg, the nearest school was six miles away. And my father left Ganyesa to go and work in town because he wanted us to go to school. It always surprised me that he moved for that.

My father never went to school himself; he taught himself to read and write in the mines. But as we grew older we got to learn that my father felt that we will be more free if we are educated – we will live better lives. Then when we got to Vryburg town, we went to school there – three girls – my brothers died; one was eighteen when he died, the other one was sixteen; one died from TB, the other from dysentry, yes. And there was nothing that could be done. The third brother died as a baby. I came after him. There were three girls left.

At that time, you either became a nurse or a teacher, or you went for domestic science, which really meant being a glorified domestic servant.

And so my mother decided that we should become teachers. When I qualified I went to teach in a small village called Tlhakgameng. It was a very nice village with a spring running, almost dividing the village into two. It was very beautiful and had a rich soil. They grew wheat – you know, in that type of climate, you can have two crops a year. They grew vegetables – all kinds of vegetables, beautiful. And they had fruit trees. The first fruit was in November which was apricots, and the last fruit was in April, quinces. In between, you had all sorts of fruits – grapes, apples, figs, plums, peaches, and then berries, gooseberries, strawberries – all sorts of berries. The people made a living on this. It was one of the villages that was chosen under apartheid as not suitable for black people to live in. It has been removed now.

My father died when I was fourteen, my mother had to work. My father, he believed in cattle and goats – not in money in the bank. When he realised that he was going to die, he said to my mother, 'Don't remove the girls from school. I know people are going to discourage you and tell you that they are going to get married. Let them go to school until they finish, and they will look after you.' And that's exactly what my mother did.

I loved teaching because I love children. So I think if I had to live my life all over again, I would still choose teaching. Perhaps I would look for higher qualifications, but I think I would teach.

I went to teach and I joined the Teachers Union. We women were paid less than men, and as soon as you got married, your post became temporary, because you were supposed to go and sit and look after your husband and have children. So we used to discuss most of this – and, of course, also better teaching conditions. Then when we began to look at the Bantu Education Act itself, a number of teachers felt that they couldn't teach under Bantu education.

But then I got married in 1952 and I moved to Johannesburg, where I immediately joined the ANC. Towards the end of 1953 I got a job with Oliver Tambo and Nelson Mandela in their lawyers' office, yes. I was interested always in women's questions. The position of women always seemed a challenge to me.

That challenge was being met by women through the formation of the Federation of South African Women, in April 1954. Ruth took part in the inaugural meeting. She was in the thick of the Federation's nationwide campaigns; and in the forefront of the historic march organised by the Federation, when 20,000 women went to the seat of government in Pretoria to protest against the extension of Pass Laws to women. Through her own leading role in that resurgence, Ruth was selected to go abroad for a year.

That year became half a lifetime.

In 1962 – the ANC was underground by then – I was sent out for political training. After my training I was to return. I had been divorced in 1959, and I had custody of the children. I left my two sons with my mother; also my sister helped. I told them I was going to school. I said, 'No, I'm just going to school, I want to further my studies. I'm coming back after a year.'

At the end of the year, in July, I was preparing to come back when I came across a newspaper which said people at Rivonia had been arrested. I was shattered, because if so many of the leaders had been arrested then it meant it was going to be difficult to get home. But I still continued with my preparations.

And then I saw in the newspapers that Bartholomew Hlapane was giving evidence for the prosecution at a political trial. That shattered me even more. I didn't believe it. He was my contact and we had worked together during the State of Emergency, right through.

But I just didn't believe it until I came back to Africa. I went to Tanzania. And then many more were arrested, people I had worked with. But I still wanted to go back, because I'd left a baby of two and a half years, and a child of six years. And I just couldn't think of not going home. When they said, 'No. You'll be arrested,' I said, 'So what? I'll go. I'll be released after some time.' They said, 'You have got a very big sentence coming. Hlapane's singing. You will go in for a long time. It's a waste – we need people outside now, in the external mission. I said, 'No, you need people. But you don't need me. I need my children; my children need me at home.'

It was very difficult but it was decided I should stay in exile. And in the first years, contact was very difficult. I didn't have contact with the children. The organisation suggested that I should try to get the children out. I thought it would be easy. But it took a very long time – ten years. Ten years! Ten years of real agony. Sometimes I would be so sick, just because of the children. I remember when once I spent the whole time preparing a little sort of . . . I would prepare albums, you know, buy little books and put in pictures – because you don't know what to write to children – with birds and animals. And then send it to them on their birthdays; and things like that, because what else could I send them, living in exile and dependant on solidarity for everything?

In Tanzania we had already a mission. And some twenty-one South African nurses who had come out to teach in Tanzania, so we formed very strong women's organisations. Then I got involved with international work in West Africa, Sudan, Ghana, Mali, Nigeria, yes. I met women representatives from Guinea-Bissau and Angola. We built a relationship with the women's organisation of Mozambique.

More people began to arrive, people from the leadership like J. B. Marks, Duma Nokwe, Moses Kotane. Oliver Tambo moved from London to work from Africa. And then the MK people started arriving – people who came for training, young people. You know, you saw these young girls coming in, and you say to them, 'But you can't be going for military training. Have you come for school?' They said, 'No. We've come for training.'

I came to Zambia in 1966, thinking that I would be able to make contact with my children, but I couldn't make any contact. And then in 1967, I came again to Zambia, and again in 1969. And then I came to Zambia to work. In 1970 I tried to go to Botswana and fetch my children. I applied for visas, they would refuse. And then Professor Matthews died and I was in the ANC delegation sent to his funeral in Botswana, and I thought that I would make contact with the children. But the Botswana government – which was still very new – put me in prison for five days in Francistown. And I was mad! They said I had no visa, I had no right to come there. I was using Tanzanian travel documents at that time, and they just said, 'No. We don't want you here, you are coming to cause trouble. We know you.'

I continued applying for a visa; continued going to Botswana, but every time I got there they would take me straight to the central police station and search me. I never got to see my children. And then when my children were there and I was here, I tried to get a visa to visit; they refused to give me a visa. My sister tried too . . . went to the Minister of Home Affairs – they just refused. It was so difficult and I was really . . . I just thought I was going to go round the bend.

But there was a lot of help. I heard from the children that friends from Australia had sent toys; friends from somewhere, internationally, had written to my mother. Friends from London who knew my story had written to my mother, or to the children. And it became easier when you know there are people who care.

Then in 1972 I went to Botswana again – this time I had no problems. They were beginning to get used to the ANC and being independent. So I went there, and wrote a letter to my children, and I told them, 'I'm in Botswana. I'd very much like to see you. I'd also like to take you along with me, but this is a choice which you must make. You, the young one, are twelve, your brother is sixteen. And you must decide yourselves whether you are going to come with me. It won't be an easy life. But I really would like to see you. Even if you can't go with me, I'll be very happy if you'd both come and meet me.'

And they came to meet me. They just came. They packed their bags, crossed the border somewhere – they didn't come legally. They just came. And then they agreed to go with me.

But it was such a shock. I left babies, and you see grown-up people. Tall! My elder son was tall, sixteen, he was taller than me! And the baby who was two and a half was twelve years old, although he was on the small side for twelve years; but he was grown up. It was a real shock to see this. You don't imagine growth of children. No. You only see your babies, and you would like to receive those babies. I suppose it would

have been terrible if I'd met the children, still two and a half and still six!
After ten years! [Laughs]

But that's what I felt I missed. I missed my babies, that I could cuddle.
It was difficult, I mean we didn't know . . . or I suppose also it was not
so much that we didn't know each other. I think we were all so conscious
of the fact that I don't know them, and they also. I was not their mother,
I was their aunt as far as they were concerned. My sister had played the
place of mother for ten years. And my mother, their granny, those were
the people that they knew. I was a stranger.

I think . . . me, I suffered. I think I suffered more, because they had had
substitutes. I hadn't had any substitute babies. I now had grown-up children, who became my children as years went on. But I hadn't had any young
babies who became mine, who I could take as substitute for my babies.

I had to behave normally; I couldn't behave the way I felt. I couldn't
cry all the time. Couldn't cry in front of them as I felt like doing. And
they were so . . . you could see that they were a little restrained. They
were watching me, and I was watching them. But I think on both sides
we consciously built a new relationship. I'm like my sister, so they had
no problems in relating to me. And after some time, we just . . . we
formed a family, yes. They stayed with me in Zambia. They got into
school in Zambia. We stayed together as a family fortunately for several
years, until the younger boy left for school and until the elder boy left for
higher education.

For me, the hardest thing of my life in exile was the separation from my
children – to have missed the childhood of my children. I don't wish it
on anybody.

I have my children's letters somewhere. There was a time when I had it
all worked out. I was going to write a book which was going to have the
title 'Letters from my children – Dear Mum'. Because I used to feel very
moved by some of the letters they would write to me. And I've mothered
many children outside. I've lost many children, young people who died
from malaria, from a number of diseases. There was one who died from
rheumatic fever at a very early age, there was one who died from cancer;
then there was one who was drowned – he was one of the first. And then
there are those who have been successful – who came out, joined the
struggle. They've contributed . . . you just feel that it has been a full life.

Sometimes my people, especially the people where I come from say,
'Didn't you go to study?' And then I started to remember that having
been twenty-seven years out of South Africa, maybe I could have taken
the first seven years and gone and become a little bit more qualified. But
when I think back to those seven years, I feel that they were the most
important years, because there were very few people. There was a lot to
be done, and very few hands. And I feel happy that I was one of the
hands that were around.

Nomads and Pilgrims

The destinations of those serving their political organisations – where they went, how they lived – were subordinate to their organisation's political needs. They did not choose to make their homes in any particular country, in any specific town. They journeyed anywhere that they were needed, filling the airways as they attended conferences and seminars; appearing at United Nations headquarters in New York or at a small church group in a suburb of Oslo.

Their purpose was two-fold: to let the world know about the reality of apartheid and the dangers it contained; and to seek assistance in a multiplicity of forms, money, bases for operation, office space, training opportunities, scholarships.

But before the events of 1960 that sent people like Oliver Tambo into exile, men and women had begun seeking outside South Africa what apartheid denied them within. And as the range and severity of new apartheid laws grew during the 1960s – the introduction of house arrest, the 90-day law (that became the 180-day law and then became limitless) the prohibition on writings and speeches of banned people (including those who were dead, like Chief Luthuli, and those in exile) the life imprisonment imposed on the Rivonia trialists, and the establishment of the Bureau of State Security – so the exodus increased.

The exiles were prodigious travellers. The rootlessness, the restlessness of the disease of home sickness marked their lives; for whatever the rationale – a chance for further education, a new job opportunity, political expedience – many of them continued moving over the years from place to place, from country to country.

Wherever they went, the politics of apartheid went with them; whatever their original intention, even those who only wished to study for a while or to obtain professional experience overseas found return became difficult. Outside South Africa House in Trafalgar Square the Special Branch photographers snapped every placard holder, every leaflet dispenser, anyone who stood with a demonstrator even for a few minutes. In the files of the Security Police, diligent as the Stasi, were photographic records of every South African tourist who met by accident or design on a public street, in a cafe or pub, with a known member of the ANC or the Anti-Apartheid Movement. And for those who came as students, even when they were aware of this surveillance, ethics drove them to oppose apartheid. This involvement became a barrier to going home.

They were nomads of the late twentieth century, and like the nomads of old, they continued to move in search of something that they had been forced to relinquish and for which there would never be an adequate substitute.

ALPHEUS MANGEZI
Mazimbu 1989

'Being in exile means you are constantly on the watch. You are constantly thinking about home. Exile is a very expensive type of experience.'

Shortly before this interview, he had taken up an appointment as Director of Mazimbu and Dakawa. A well-built man with an understanding of life gained by living and working in many countries.

I was not directly involved in politics in South Africa. But the development of political consciousness starts in from early childhood.

I was born in the Northern Transvaal in a place called Rebola, where my father and grandfather lived and farmed. When I was born we still had something like seventy or a hundred head of cattle. My father could be described as a rich peasant; our fields supported us. But the Swiss Mission who had been given this land by the government put their own farmer there on condition that he run the church on Sunday and a school. We needed a school, we didn't need a church. The farmer also took the best land away, pushing our people out of the fertile and grazing land. The peasants gradually became poorer and poorer; and there was no protection for our cattle.

As herdboys we had the responsibility of ensuring that the cattle were well fed and well cared for. One night we drove the cattle into his fenced land, which was really our land. We were caught – I think there were about ten or fifteen of us – and brought to the public meeting. There he was, this big Swiss farmer, saying either our parents were going to pay fines of £1 each, or we had to submit to corporal punishment. We decided that we would submit to corporal punishment. For one thing, we knew that our parents didn't have money; for another it was the acceptance of responsibility as a herdboy – if you did something wrong, you account for it.

We were brought up to the understanding that if the enemy wants to hurt you, you show him that he doesn't. He who cries is lost. I must have been about nine because I had not yet started school. We were given something like ten lashes with the cane, and none of us cried. The farmer was really hurt. When I was much older, I saw this as my introduction to political action. Because we then constantly drove our cattle to his land to graze when he was not there – during the night and so on. He never caught us again!

My father and mother were both illiterate, but they were crazy about education. They wanted me to do well. My brother, to whom I was very close, ran a small grocer's shop in Alexandra. There were two gangs there, and they took protection money from shopkeepers. When my brother refused to pay, the head of the gang killed him. He was knifed, the knife punctured a lung and he died.

I was deeply frustrated. I was very, very keen on education. My ambition had been to become a doctor or a lawyer but there was no money to get me to university. So I trained at the Jan Hofmeyer School of Social Work in Johannesburg and became a social worker. While at Jan Hofmeyer, I visited a psychiatric hospital and decided that I would like to specialise in psychiatric social work. I found out that the British Association of Psychiatric Social Workers might be able to arrange for people to go as trainees to Britain. I just wrote to the Association, and they said they would find me a placement in Glasgow if I could find money for the ticket. And so, family and friends went around, literally bowl in hand, until the fare was raised. And in May 1960 I went to Scotland to specialise in psychiatric social work.

Glasgow – what a very strange place. I had never even heard of it! [Laughs] My supervisor met me at the airport and took me straight to the hospital where they had arranged accommodation for me in the nurses' quarters. I remember getting up in the morning, very early – to look for kilts. I thought all Scottish people will be wearing kilts! [Laughs]

My main work was to visit relatives of patients or patients who were being discharged, to collect social histories to enable the doctors to make diagnoses. So one morning I was to go for my first home visit. I asked my supervisor, 'Which bus do I take?' And she said, 'No, no. Don't worry, you will be going by car. It will be waiting outside.' I got to the car. The chauffeur jumped to attention – he was in a black suit and a hat – he knew my name although I never met him, said, 'Good morning Mr Mangezi.' And saluted. He opened the back door – I just stood there, frozen. Mr Mangezi! White chauffeur! Opening the door for me and bowing! What do I do? What's happened? The world had turned upside down.

As a social worker, I was introduced to some of the city councillors who told me of the problems they had in Glasgow. We'll show you the slums, the Gorbals. And after that we'll show you the new areas where we are resettling the people. We are doing our best, but you know it is very difficult to help these people. 'These people.' I was taken around, shown the slums, shown the new areas they called 'overspills', new housing schemes; and this man was saying to me, 'You see that telephone kiosk there – last week it was intact. Now the door is broken, the telephone will not be working. This is the problem we have with "these people".' I felt I was at the point of a big discovery. Then, 'You see that man on the third floor there, standing there, with a kind of a blank vacant expression? If you stand here, you will see him come down and take a bus – back to the slums, to the Gorbals. To drink, huh!' So I asked, 'Why go all the way to the Gorbals?' 'Ah, because we have no pubs here. This is such a clean place.'

In South Africa I was 'these people'. And in Glasgow I was on the other side. It was so clear, I've never forgotten. I will never forget.

I had to work very hard. I was learning how to interview – I had been doing it in South Africa. But the situation had changed – it was a question of class. Fortunately I had become conscious about that.

In social work there is a very strong emphasis on professionalism – the professional way of behaviour and so on. You don't accept a cup of tea from your client, because that is likely to interfere with the professional relationship. Even a cup of tea! Now, this was so foreign to me – not as a black person but as a person! It was so foreign to me I decided that when people offered me tea, I would accept it, or not, depending on the actual conditions.

There were lots and lots of alcoholics in Glasgow, particularly men living by themselves. They would be found completely knocked out, and be brought to the hospital by the neighbours or by the police or whoever. They would get treatment in the hospital with insulin and so on, so after two, three weeks, they look wonderful; clean-shaven, healthy, happy, OK. Then we discharged them back to the same little hovel. There is nobody there; the little hovel had not been cleaned since they left for hospital.

After two years he was offered a scholarship in psychiatric social work at the London School of Economics. He went on to work at the Brighton Child Guidance clinic, dealing with the problems of mothers and small children in a mixed population that included many immigrants from the West Indies and Nigeria.

In 1964 he went to Zambia and worked in Lusaka as social welfare officer in the Eastern Province. Then SIDA offered him a scholarship to study for a degree in sociology. He was admitted to the University of Ibadan in Nigeria.

The studies in Nigeria were OK, although there was too much emphasis on social theory about societies that did not exist. There was nothing about real society, very little. The purely theoretical thing: If you live in a society like this or that, then this and this happens; if people really interact, the more they interact the more they like each other – that kind of thing. And I say, 'You know, there are cases where the more you interact, the more you hate each other. Is that possible?' [Laughs] OK. So fortunately I had this solid background in social work in South Africa, Glasgow and London, and I was not really attracted to theoretical kite-flying.

Ibadan was a completely different experience from South Africa. I got there in September 1965, January 1966 the army took over. Then there was this Biafran War. And then – to me the most important thing – I met my wife. Nadja was in Nigeria as a volunteer from Denmark, teaching French in a government college; and I was a student at the University.

At the University all foreign students were told to leave, but because Alpheus had nowhere to go they allowed him to stay on. Danish volunteers were also advised to leave unless thay wished to remain at their own risk. Nadja decided to remain.

They met when they became involved in the problem of Ibo students who had been arrested by the army. They succeeded in getting them released, and then Nadja drove them to safety across the border into Togo.

We got to know each other – it's one case where more and more interaction . . . [Laughs] So when I finished my degree in 1968, we went to Copenhagen and we got married there. Then [Laughs] again, before I left Nigeria I had applied to go on a course in Holland at the Institute of Social Studies. So as soon as our daughter was born – she was nearly born on the plane – I left for Holland. And Nadja stayed in Copenhagen teaching Spanish at the University. She joined me later.

My Swedish professor invited me to Sweden as assistant research worker. So off we went, as a family, to the University of Upsala; and there I studied for my second degree in Sociology – Master's – while working as assistant researcher to my old professor.

Then we went back to the UK for a year. I got a job as a social worker in Tower Hamlets in London's East End, to do social work, particularly in their schools.

He then had a post as a lecturer in social policy. But his Swedish professor was urging him to work towards his Ph.D. So after a year, they returned to Denmark.

Nadja was there working, and I got a part-time job lecturing at the university in a new department specialising in the Sociology of Under-Developed Countries. So I was teaching part-time, doing my Ph.D. in Denmark and going to Upsala in Sweden for meetings and supervisions.

Our second child Temba was born in Sweden; and then when we were in Copenhagen, our last child was born there in 1974.

I finished my Ph.D. in 1976, and I was offered a job at the university in Maputo. So in December that year I went to Mozambique. Nadja joined me and we lived and worked in Mozambique for twelve years. I liked it very much. I sometimes toy with the idea that, when South Africa is free, we will then be free to live where we want to live – which means I may not even want to live in South Africa, and I could be able to go away without any feelings of guilt. And if I were to go away, Mozambique is one of those places where I would like to go.

We lived in great danger. Ruth First was my Director of Research. We worked very closely together. We were attending a UNESCO seminar about social science in Southern Africa, while mail was piling up in our offices – particularly in her office. When we finished the seminar, she took some of the visitors and some of our own people – including Pallo Jordan – to her office for a brief meeting. I went to attend another meeting.

Suddenly there was a knock on the door. Nadja is out there. And I can see that something is very wrong. I look at her. She says, 'So you have not been at the Centre – there has been an explosion! Ruth might be . . . '

We discovered that Ruth had not even had a chance – she was opening this letter, and the bomb went off right in her face. Ai! After that, there was the usual investigation. But we could see that this wouldn't come to anything, because the investigators had no experience whatsoever.

We organised the funeral – I was in the funeral committee. The condition of the mortuary was horrible – the Muslim practice of burying their dead on the same day is really so practical in the situation in Mozambique. But Ruth had been so smashed up it was literally picking up pieces. And we did that. I remember running up and down looking for sheets and so on, to arrange things as decently as was practical in the situation.

Samora Machel came to visit the office the day after the assassination. He was shaken. Samora was a very strong man, and if you saw him shaken then you had to know there was something very special. He had tremendous respect for Ruth. He looked at the office with the practised eye of a guerrilla, making an assessment of how things had happened. Eyeing this and this, pieces of flesh there.

So that is what happened. We never learned anything more than that. I worked very closely with Ruth – her passion for the problems of the peasantry was so stimulating. Then after we had done the research on migrant labour and written the report, it was proposed that a book should be published. But more material was required, particularly interviews, so she gave me that responsibility. I drafted a scheme where I included work songs. This was something that I liked very much about Ruth: 'Alpheus, I'm very doubtful about work songs.' And I looked at her and said, 'OK, I will do them all the same. So all right.'

I went and collected work songs. I was taken by car three hundred kilometres away from Maputo and left there. And I just walked around and talked with the people, and collected the material. I couldn't carry it all – it was just incredible. So I returned. I took my tape recorder to Ruth and put on a cassette with one of the most moving songs that I had collected. I said, 'You told me that you didn't believe in work songs. OK. Sit and listen.' And she listened, and she was moved without understanding what it was all about.

So I say, 'Now I will tell you. This song says: where is my husband? where has he gone? The rivers are full. In front of me the Nkomati is in flood, I cannot cross it. Behind me the Limpopo is in flood, I cannot cross. Where is my husband? Where has he gone? After the singing I had interviewed the woman: Can you explain to me what all this means? She said: I would like to join my husband – he left for the mines; but there is no way of getting there. The Nkomati is in flood. I would like to go back to my people. I come from across the Limpopo River, but lobola has been paid; and since he has not said he is divorcing me, I cannot go back to my people. The Limpopo is in flood, I'm stuck here.' Ruth looked at me. 'Take your stuff,' she said. 'Go home – go and sit by yourself and translate it!' [Laughs] So that book is full of that stuff, work songs and so on.

And then we planned another book, where she was going to simply make an introduction about the migrant labour system, and the rest was going to be interviews, work songs and pictures. The manuscript was finished and it was going to be sent to a translator. It has vanished . . . The theory was put about that when the bomb exploded some of the papers were burned. But that manuscript was not among them. One document that was there was an outline of an article she had asked me to write – Strategies of Survival by the Peasants. That was subsequently published after . . . at least a year after her assassination. When I got it back one page was burned. I took it and I put it in among my books at home – I couldn't look at it for several weeks. I think I have kept it somewhere.

After Ruth's death I remained working in the Centre of African Studies to 1987. But the Centre was never the same again. We had big problems of administration – and I was very, very unhappy, not just because of her death but because the whole situation was changing so much against us in Mozambique. We were always having to take special security precautions.

In 1987 I decided to leave the Centre. I worked with two Norwegian women from the University of Oslo, who had come to Mozambique to study the position of women before and after independence. We worked with peasant women and women living in the cities who were basically still peasants and were living their lives as if they were still in the countryside. The most interesting thing here was the clarity with which they defined the problem of women's emancipation; which contrasted very strongly with what you got from the women's leaders, who were more privileged and had got a bit of education, but who you couldn't describe as independent thinkers. They took the definitions given, and said: 'This is the women's problem in Mozambique.'

FRELIMO at that time was so strong and so overwhelming that in fact they controlled the way that the Mozambican women's organisation worked. During Women's Days it was not the Secretary General of the Women's Organisation who delivered the main speech, it was one of the top Ministers – all men, of course. And the Secretary of the Women's Organisation was left only with something like closing remarks. It was always like that.

In 1988 I was approached by UNICEF to consider a job at their office in Maputo, to start with a survey of Mozambican women who had been displaced by the war. So that was a very important job. It would also be the first time in my life that I was really going to earn money, because working in Mozambique for FRELIMO was solidarity work – we couldn't even survive on what we were earning.

But I had to go to Lusaka for a seminar on social welfare, and there I was asked to consider working for the ANC on a full-time basis. So I was in a dilemma. At the same time I was trying to write a book. I had got a grant from SIDA, I had collected the material, and I was going to sit down in Copenhagen and start writing. So I indicated to the ANC that I had this job in hand, and that I should be given a minimum of three months to be in Copenhagen.

But that didn't work. After I had been in Copenhagen only a month or two, I was urgently asked to come here to Mazimbu. So that work is still waiting. I moved from Mozambique to Copenhagen to Tanzania. And this is where I am now.

Being in exile means a great deal of waste, because you have very little choice of what you can do with your education. You are very limited in what you can contribute, because as a foreigner you are often cut off from the informal activities of the community about you. You are constantly on the watch, you are constantly thinking about home, you are constantly confronted with the problems of your fellow countrymen. I have seen big, big problems in exile, not just here in Mazimbu but in Europe in particular, where highly gifted South Africans have succumbed to alcohol and to drugs – but particularly alcohol. It seems to be the biggest disease that attacks us in exile.

In negative terms, therefore, exile is a very expensive type of existence. You are never happy. You tend to idealise what life was when you were young, or what life is at home. But that is a defensive mechanism. We tend to think that the whole world owes us something, always – which is another problem of being in exile. The mentality that we develop – like here at Mazimbu – is of living in a welfare state, where everything is free, and nobody asks where the money is coming from. But we demand all the time.

We South Africans suffer from that disease where we think everybody, every country owes us something. When you manage to reduce that kind of feeling, or eliminate it, then living in different countries is a very enriching experience. Here at Mazimbu when comrades talk about people, they are always grouped – Whites are like this, Blacks are like this. But when you have lived in different countries, you think different-ly. So I regard myself as having been very lucky in that I have lived in all these different countries.

There's a kind of resentment among exiles because they're accepting favours – and nobody wants to be put in that position. So in a sense they are antagonistic towards the people who are helping them. You have to hit back; you want to show that you are an independent person, you can look after yourself. And the very person who is helping you often gets a kick in the face.

You know, we have been taught colonialism did this and this to Africa, so colonialism must pay us back. Every child is taught that. I'm afraid we actually grow up thinking that if there had been no colonialism, all of us would have made it. There are lots of people who don't know they would have failed even if the best conditions were there.

JOYCE MOODLEY
Mazimbu 1989

'I'd cross illegally over the mountains, and I'd walk and have to put him on my back.'

> She is small and slight; a hard life has not robbed her of her ability to laugh. At Mazimbu, she often caters for visiting guests, and she started a handicraft group of women who make bags, collages and other things from any materials they can obtain.

I was born in a small town, just outside the outskirts of Benoni, called Modder B, now notorious for its jail. There was about sixty houses. My father was working on the mines and my mother had to do some washing. My father died when I was seven. Then my mother had to go and work in Johannesburg, where at least the wages was a bit higher. And she would come home once a fortnight to come and see us. So my auntie took care of us. It wasn't happy, you know, it wasn't nice. All right, it was my auntie. But it's not . . .

Now my mother . . . we would always sit and watch by the evenings when we know she was coming. And we watch and see her coming down,

and when you know then it's her, then we would run down to the gate to
go and meet her. Four years after my father died she decided to marry again,
so that at least we could be together. And then we moved to Benoni.

Benoni was such a different place. I never thought there was so many
different kinds of people – I thought it was just those people that were
living at Modder B. We saw all the different nationalities. And the worst
of all was this fighting, the struggle, the faction-fighting.

We stayed in a little pondokkie, about three, four, five families, and we
had two rooms. And there she did some washing. When she was pregnant with the first son from the second marriage, she lost her job, and it
was really very, very tough. She had to do some washing where she could
earn sixpence there and sixpence here. My stepfather, he worked, and he
used to get seventeen shillings and sixpence a week, so it was difficult for
us to survive. Myself and my sister Violet used to sell some vegetables for
an Indian woman; so now after selling them we get a few rotten tomatoes, soft tomatoes and a piece of snoek, so that we can make a meal.

Fortunately I went to school. I had to leave at the age of fifteen for then
my mother couldn't afford to buy my books. My mother got work in a
Germiston factory. So then I also got a job there. Things were much
easier but it was still very tough because my stepfather had one trousers
and one jacket he used for work. So Friday evenings we have to wash the
jacket and the trousers. Then Saturday the whole day he has to be in bed,
he couldn't get up! [Laughs] There was nothing else to wear!

My stepfather was always – you know – under the influence. Then his
behaviour got worse and worse. But he never interfered with Mary's
political activities – though sometimes he says: I wish you were dead. But
then it was the beer talking. And three months after his death Mary says
sadly, she says: I miss the old bugger, you know.

In '52, when Sophie Williams and Stanley Lollan started the SACPO,
they came to Benoni. They did some house to house campaigning. They
came into the house and just started talking. But you know we didn't
even allow them to finish talking, and we just said: Ooh, we want to join,
because we have been looking for this organisation and we didn't know
where to go. And that is how we joined the Congress Movement, ja.

I got a job at the New Age with Ivan Schermbrucker and Arnold Selby.
You know, and I still remember when we got into this building of New
Age we had no furniture. I started working on the floor, and I had to do
my filing, everything, on the floor there.

You know, there was just something about Mary. She was so powerful,
and she had a way of convincing people. Ivan used to say: I don't know
what's wrong with your bloody mother. You don't even get enough for
your own family, but she always picks up bloody stray dogs! And that
was it – she always used to feed stray dogs, anybody ill, homeless. One
slept under our kitchen table when there was no place. It was just her.
I'm very proud of her. I can never be Mary.

In the 1960 Emergency, Mary was arrested with everyone else. I was fortunately not. I remember when Mary came out, the whole location came out to greet her then. There was just something I heard . . . mmm . . . mmm . . . mmm I ran out, and there is a car. Bram Fischer and Molly brought my mother. And I was the first one and I just screamed Ma! Ma! Ma!' you know. People – everybody – came out. Oh it was such a beautiful reunion, and everybody running, the kids and my brothers and sisters and everybody around the house, you know. Do you know what she told me, Mary? She said she was sitting by herself on the stone floor of the cell, and she was feeling very depressed and sorry for herself. And then suddenly she said: No, it's no good – so she just got up and danced. That's what she said! [Laughs]

I think the first . . . my happiest days were at *New Age*. It was meeting people, all different people. Oh, I really miss, miss, miss those days. It was my best days, I was just so happy those days. And Ivan was just like a father to me.

I remember once when we were in the office in Progress Buildings, there was one raid, ja, when the police went everywhere, in the lavatories and everywhere. It was like troops.

It happened now – ja, that was now in '64 – there was this other Emergency, ne? Then everybody was arrested, you remember? Ivan came to me. He says to me: Cocky (he always called me Cocky), you know what? We're going to be arrested. And he wanted me to leave, and you know I just could not go. I told him, no; I don't think I want to go. During that time everybody, so many they were arrested. Reg [September] and his wife were hiding out somewhere in Benoni. So when my mother was arrested, Martha Singh came and she says to me, 'Joyce, you're Mary's daughter. You have to see now to these people, it's your problem.' And I said, 'Oh God, what am I going to do with these people, I can't have them here – I have a husband that's an illegal immigrant.

The only person I could go to is Auntie Christina. So I went to her and says, 'Auntie Christina, there is trouble! But we can't have the people being arrested.' Auntie Christina talked to her daughter and the husband McClipper. He says, 'No problem, we shouldn't worry.' So he took the Septembers across into Botswana.

So then is it when my troubles started. So that is how I became involved, you know . . . arranging escapes for other people, yes.

Then August '64 I was arrested, yes. It was a Sunday morning when they took me. They interrogated me, it was almost a whole day. It's early in the morning, I think they picked me up roundabout eight o'clock, and I was there in that room for almost a whole day until the evening. The Special Branch said: I don't want to know what you did. I want to know something that we don't know. And I didn't know anything, you see. So he gave me a big file, you know everybody's pictures, and: Who's this? Well I know this is Ruth First. What did she do? I don't know . . . she was a journalist, she was taking photographs and she was writing. Don't tell me nonsense – you know, rude – don't talk shit to me! Tell me the real thing! What about Hilda? I just told him that, you know I am not very educated, and they spoke very high English that I could never understand what they were talking.

He says: So you are trying to be a hero? So he calls this other officer, he says: Take her. Take her away and lock her until she rot. That time, I really thought I was going to die. You know I felt I wanted to faint, I couldn't even stand properly. They took me to a cell – it was next to male prisoners. I think that was the worst thing that could have happened to me, because they were on the one side, and when they saw me I could never sleep or just rest, because you would find them hanging on the window trying to get in at night. They would start hitting on the wall. I was a nervous wreck there. I thought I was just going to die of fear – not of the police, but of the prisoners.

They would ask: Why do you get special food? Why do you get food on a tray? And I would tell: Me, I'm a political prisoner and that is why. I couldn't even eat all the food, and I would ask the police if one of the prisoners could just come in to help clean my cell, so that I could just give them the food and I would talk to them why I am there. When they understood they says: No, you are one of the people who are working for us. And so it was OK. Then they started being friendly. It was August, September ja. I don't think we finished the whole ninety days – I don't know.

My husband, he was from Mozambique – I got married in 1959. He was not very political. But he gradually became involved, helping here and there. And he was very scared. Then he got deported as an illegal immigrant. He got deported twice but then he returns back. Then he was deported again, and he decides to stay in Mozambique.

So I have been in and out of Mozambique since 1972. I was without passport – I would cross illegally in the mountains. Oh, I think it was one of the most horrible journeys. I would start from Komatipoort, yes. And just go on foot. I remember when I went with Abdul, he was about two years and I was pregnant with the second one. Then over the mountains you know, and I'd walk, and have to put him on my back. So I gave him a 50 cents, I say: Now you walk. So he walked. But then after a while he says: You can have your money back! You put me on the back now; I just can't do it any more. [Laughs]

Agh God! It was about three times – three times I crossed the mountains like that, ja. And then I said: No more! I rather just be arrested – but no more! Then in '74 I joined my husband there in Lourenco Marques.

He had no work. I started doing a little bit of teaching English at home. I had some classes in the morning for the children and in the afternoon I had adults. This kept us going, I was very cheap, but that kept us going.

I worked with the FRELIMO during that period to mobilise the people,
I was helping the preparations for the independence. FRELIMO had a lot
of confidence in me. Since '74 I had been working for FRELIMO with the
women; and I later got a job in an office there, and I taught some of
the women some handwork, some knitting.

So afterwards more South Africans came. I loved it there in Mozambique. It was nice working with the people. You know it was like my
mother at home – I was not just Joyce there; I was doing social work –
all the people around there with all their social problem.

Until the Nkomati Accord. Ja, that is the time that really broke me. It
was painful you know, after all the ten years that I had been working
with FRELIMO, that that happened. The way they handled our people I
just couldn't take. I was standing on my verandah and you see the police,
the soldiers just surrounding the houses, all of this AKs. And, Everybody
out!, and searching the place. It wasn't nice. It wasn't nice. But that
evening, after the raid when they raided all our houses there, there was
an announcement, a report on radio – Republic of South Africa but in
Portuguese – that I was also on the list that South Africa don't want in
Mozambique, and that I have to go. And that I escaped arrest because
when the soldiers came there, I wasn't there.

A lot of our comrades felt that I shouldn't have left. But even when I
left on the airport, these Mozambicans who I worked with, they stop
and says to me: Now Joyce, we don't want you to go; you've been
working all these years with our people; you've been doing so good,
doing so well. And I says: That is just it! After this ten years that I've
working with you, that is the way you treat my people! I mean, what am
I going to do, you take all my people away?

I had my sons with me, but me husband no. We were separated because
he couldn't leave. I mean, he is the only technician doing this installation,
and he just couldn't come. So we left and just separated. And I came
straight to Tanzania, to Mazimbu. And I've been here ever since.

Well when we came, there was no work. But I found work to do. Five
– it's about five years now. And I've seen the place grow very much since
then, ja.

LINDA MVUSI
Harare 1990

'South Africa is multi-cultural, it's almost non-ethnic.'

> Her flat, opposite Harare's beautiful park, is light, compact, mod-
> ern; and she is also compact and modern, an attractive, sophistic-
> ated woman of diverse talents.

I left South Africa with my parents when I was five years old in 1961. We came here when it was still Rhodesia; and then went to Ghana at the time when Kwame Nkrumah was there, and we were there for four years.

I would say I grew up in exile and I've always been a part of the South African community wherever I've been. I don't think I've ever been where there wasn't a South African community. Ghana was one big hodgepodge melting-pot, and the concerns of the South African community were also the concerns of the Ghanaian community, not just the government. So it gave one a chance to be not just confined to South African issues but also to engage in and be part of the development of what it means to be a free nation.

So at a very early age one did escape the sort of ghettoisation which can occur with a community in exile, which gets ingrown.

When we moved to Kenya, it was more or less the same again. This was the time of East African community so the borders were pretty open to Uganda and Tanzania, it was like one country in a sense. The boundaries in Kenya between Namibians and Zimbabweans and us were very few. I remember as a child, growing up in an exile community with security. People never had surnames, so that if anybody asked you as a child, you couldn't say 'Mr so and so' or 'Mrs so and so' – everybody was uncles and aunts. And all these aunts and uncles came from different places. It's been part of the surprise of being in Zimbabwe, finding that a lot of these 'uncles' and 'aunts' who have had a very real input into my life, are Zimbabweans or Namibians, not South Africans. Coming to Zimbabwe has been an integration of one's past and one's present, in that one's finally come to a country where people regard you as at home. Which is also a painful thing because one's not really at home, one's South African. But to the extent that it happens it has implications beyond liberation in South Africa. It begins to look at a sort of post-Nationalist perspective. Perhaps we are Southern Africans. Yes, ja.

My background is art and I found West Africa very sympathetic in the kind of confidence that they have in themselves as people, in their culture and their history. Which is somehow akin to how South Africans feel about themselves. There's an enormous confidence in South Africans which I think is what helps us to fight. In West Africa one lived in cities where the centre was four hundred years old. You lived cheek by jowl with a modernised tradition as well as history. I found that very healthy. I found it easier to think or even to design in West Africa. There were less divisions, class divisions, for instance in West Africa. People happily introduced you, or introduced themselves – you were happily brought into people's family backgrounds, and the family, as an extended family, worked as one unit. There were no differences. Which I think is also similar to South Africa.

It was very difficult for me to adjust to Kenya, because there are very stark differentiations which even divide families. Tribal, class, yes. And both are strong, so that it's difficult to make links outside of a particular sector of the population.

Originally I'd wanted to be an artist, a painter but I was rather intimidated by my father's work, so I did architecture, which was a cop-out. And I went back to Ghana to do my degree.

She did her degree in four years, worked in Zambia for two years with the Danish architect Hart Lawrence, followed by two years in England at Newcastle, where she did her second degree.

She went to work in London for the GLC-funded architectural services to the community. The clientele was immigrant, poor, aged, 'all the disempowered' – a design service dealing with the community. It was a co-op of architects that 'validated my conviction that in Africa we cannot sit and design precious buildings'.

This was followed by work in Chicago which 'was also trying to empower communities across racial boundaries . . . and New York which was trying to reclaim parts of the city for everybody'. Then back to Africa where 'bureaucracy and the infrastructure is so entrenched that you're back fighting basics'. She decided to work in the private sector. Her clientele tends to be groups of people coming together in co-operatives, and she often finds herself advising people not to build – 'working against my own interests!'

Linda Mvusi won a best actress award for her part in the film *A World Apart*.

When I was in Zambia, I did work with Tequiza Theatre; we were a group of twelve, and we were absolutely sick and tired of Shakespeare in the middle of Africa, that type of thing! [Laughs] We have to support indigenous Zambian theatre and ja, we did that for two years and then I went to University.

They'd been looking for someone to play the part of Elsie in the film. Chris Menges, the director, was worried about the part; he had the names of professional South African actresses suggested. I don't really know what happened to them.

I saw the script and I liked it very much. But Elsie was written from one perspective. In the script she was not her own person, she was an image of the child. And I agreed to take the part if Chris would give me the space to develop the Elsie character within the film. And he did. [Laughs]

I saw the film for the first time at the premiere in New York. He absolutely refused that I should see it before it was on a huge screen. And afterwards, he sort of said, 'Well? Was it OK?' And I said, 'Yes, it was, it was'. I thought it was a really good effort on his part.

How did you enter so fully into this role of Elsie when you'd been so long out of South Africa?

Well, that's probably the strength of the exile community outside; I'm really thinking of the community which left in the Sixties, their culture is also very much Fifties when the film was set; the norms and moral expectations and even the language is very much of that time. But also I suppose in an exile community you spend a lot of time watching, you watch your national hosts because you're different. You watch your parents' generation because they're different from you. You go to an ordinary school and they're always talking about South Africa, so you're a part of it but, in a sense, you also have this perspective of voyeur. There are still parts of the Xhosa language which I find hilarious. And with my brothers, it's like a ticklish joke, because we love the language, it's an emotional link for us, so it's never really an ordinary language, it's like eating icing all the time! [Laughs] It's just delicious. It's also been a different language from that in daily use. English is very ordinary and if you really want to express yourself artistically, you have to search Xhosa . . . you know that is the language of poetry.

I imagine if you live in South Africa, you take the language for granted. Whereas for the film, because of the distance between myself and a South African domestic worker, one was conscious of the amount of work that had to be done. I don't think I could have done it on my own.

And the accent?

The accent is always there! Oh, my goodness, I must have about seven accents in my head. I have a working-place accent, an accent to intimidate people, because in my profession I'm a woman in a man's world. I speak differently if I'm in a boardroom and I have to get my ideas across a whole bunch of white male contractors or whoever. I also have this language which comes from Xhosa, that influences my English if I'm speaking in an emotional or social setting – my English is quite different from what I'm talking with you now. At the same time, my thinking accent is quite different.

I've always felt South African. The only time when I began to doubt it was when I had to return to South Africa for my father's funeral. He died in a car accident in 1968, yes. And then again when my brother was killed. Because I've always lived outside South Africa it was an incredible validation from not just the extended family, who were spread all over the mountains, but as far as they were concerned, there was no difference in a sense. I've always felt like a South African.

In South Africa itself, it's such a mix of cultures – Malay, Indian – but you can tell straight away an Indian from South Africa and an Indian from East Africa for instance, and it has very much to do with this sense of openness, of acceptance and accepting people the way they are.

In a sense, now this is the test for going back home, having lived the last thirty years with this impression that South Africa is intrinsically an open society. It's multi-cultural . . . almost non-ethnic to the extent that the differences are our strengths. I wonder how, when it comes to the test of living there, as opposed to going back to visit, this will actually stand the test of time. We're not a tribally conscious people, but at the same time, we're so integrated into each other, that people will speak with three-four different languages, all integrated into one sentence – that's the extent to which we are joined together. And one has been at home in societies which are like that and extremely uncomfortable in societies which are not.

I think apartheid has failed. The purpose was to divide us forever, but there is a tangible South Africaness to all of us which actually transcends our differences of race. It still must be articulated and still has to be defined. I think part of the outpouring which we saw on the screens when Nelson Mandela came out was actually a visual image of that – that there is this South Africanness which I don't think we've fully understood. I just have this dead certain feeling that even without apartheid, there would have been a convergence. It's still going to flower. I get so optimistic – all of a sudden, it opens up! [Laughs]

> Linda's youngest brother, who had left South Africa with the rest of the family, was also studying architecture.

He was a student in the USA attending university in Greensborough, North Carolina. It was in 1982. There had been outbreaks of racial violence, because the town itself is a stronghold of white Klans people, KKK. And the college was like an island, geographically it was an island within.

Apparently there had been quite a bit of friction between the predominantly black college and Greensborough, which is basically made up of poor whites. It was probably quite typical of Deep South politics of the US. The year before, four black students had been killed in racial violence. He wrote to us about it. I think there was that sense that not being black American, one was not subject to this.

He was quite active in ANC/Black Consciousness/anti-apartheid movement. I don't think as a family we had any indication that there was any danger. His close friend was also part of the movement. They were more involved in South African politics and raising consciousness, but I presume in the American context, there's very little difference if you're a member of the Klan, between anti-apartheid South African politics and black Americans trying to assert themselves. And . . . whoooo, why do I find this difficult . . . ?

There are two stories. First of all the police were not willing to investigate what had happened. He was missing for about three days; and when his body was found, he was found lynched from a basketball goalpost, which was a signal that this was a political killing, not a criminal killing. What we did know was that he had gone to see a movie and he'd gone alone, so he must have been attacked or set upon after he left. He'd used a short cut through a racist neighbourhood and so somewhere in between having left the cinema on that day . . . But as to how or what happened we were never able to get any indication that the police investigated. The university students went on strike because the police were not willing to investigate the case. And the sponsorship bodies had to put on their own detective to try and trace what had happened; but without police co-operation, there wasn't very much the detective could do.

The student faculty took time to write to us family members about what they thought had happened; and when I was in the States, quite a few of them came to see me and to tell me what had happened. Well, that is basically how he was killed. What I understood traumatised the South African community in the US was this sense of defencelessness. Because if one had been a citizen of another country, your country would have come in to seek satisfaction from the government of the US. You're abroad, you're in exile, there isn't anyone to speak on your behalf. The ANC is a liberation movement, it's not a government. There's nothing much you can do if you're up against an institution or a set of values which are inherent in the society. And the Ku Klux Klan is very much alive in the US. This is in 1982, September, ja.

This was his third year. He was also studying architecture. I think it's been very easy for even our supporters to focus on apartheid as the symbol of racism and forget that racism is international, it's universal and if you really want to fight it, fight it in your own backyard first. That's how I would put it, yes, I would accuse supporters, especially in western Europe and in the north, of being very ready to move their shares, to disinvest from South Africa, but not as willing to face up to racism, even on their street. And this sort of brought the message again back. I mean, it's a very cruel way of learning it.

RUTH WEISS
Harare 1990

'We never, never integrated into the white society.'

A smart, grey-haired woman, a professional journalist – a percept-ive observer. She discounts her own abilities by talking about 'luck'. Now she wants to write – not for the demands of editors or publishers, but the things she wants to write.

Yes, I suppose I am an exile in a way, unless you want to say that I have no roots left at all. I was born in Germany, in 1924. The Twenties generation of the Germans, they were the people who fought in the war, the ones who carried that whole period really. They either were members of the Hitler Youth or they were members of the Young Communist League.

My family background is very *petit bourgeois*, very ordinary Jewish, orthodox, small-town. I come from a little place near Nuremberg. Nuremberg was the centre of this whole Nazi period. And because of that we felt the impact from the age of nine, which was how old I was in 1933, until we left in 1936 when I was nearly twelve. We literally grew up overnight.

The Jewish children had to leave their various schools fairly quickly, and were all put into one Jewish school, in enormous classes in a very, very small school. It had been a boarding-school for fifty boys; we were probably between five and six hundred children. But we had the best teachers, because the Jewish teachers had also been expelled. I was with people who were professors and writers. My arithmetic teacher was a physicist – I've never before or since had such fantastic education.

My father was employed by a non-Jewish firm, so he lost his job fairly early on in 1933. One of our family had emigrated to South Africa in the early part of the century; he wrote to my father's eldest brother, and said, 'We believe that there's some problem about Jews. And so, if anybody wants to come, I'm enclosing a ticket.' My father was given this ticket and he went to South Africa. I remember when he said goodbye to us and walked down the stairs in this little house in Furht. I was sitting there between my mother's legs and wondering where he was going, whether we would ever see him again. We grew up very quickly.

We were beaten up; there were one or two incidents – it was absolutely nothing to what happened later – but as a child I knew what it was to be ostracised and discriminated against on a day-by-day basis. There was an immediate connection between that period and South Africa. My father was no businessman, and he didn't make any money in his corner shop in South Africa. But eventually he sent for us and we came out by boat, my sister and my mother and myself, in 1936, and we settled on the wrong side of the tracks in Mayfair, Johannesburg. And we were very poor, really poor.

We went to the local school, in an area where there were mainly Afrikaner miners. And in the Thirties, during the Depression, the sort of experiences that one had in that tough area were immediate. And that's what I meant about having been able to make the connection.

We weren't in Johannesburg for more than three or four days when a black woman – I later realised she would be called a 'girl' – came on the stoep. She had a baby on her back. She untied the baby and put it on her cloth. My sister and I played with the baby, and my mother picked the baby up like any normal woman would. Within an hour, three women came from the neighbouring houses, very well-dressed, all Afrikaners.

They said that they weren't very sure whether we knew what the local customs were. We couldn't speak English; my father came and translated. And there was this peculiar conversation about their customs.

That was when I realised. And I said to my parents, 'You know, in Fuhrt they wouldn't play with me because I'm Jewish. And now here I'm not allowed to play with another child because it's black'. So there was never any break. We were never, never integrated into the white society.

My father went bankrupt and my sister left school so that I could do my matric. I got a scholarship on the strength of my matric results – I wanted to do BA. LLB., but couldn't do that because I didn't have the money. I discovered that although I was German on paper, I was stateless in fact. And I couldn't get a loan because I was German.

I was terribly lucky and got a job at a law firm as an articled clerk. But after six months, when the firm wanted to sign my articles, I found out I couldn't do that either because I couldn't swear allegiance to the King.

> Ruth found a job in a bookshop and continued to study at night. The bookshop was run by two men, one of whom, Hans, she later married. Then it closed down.
>
> 'This is where I really struck it lucky.' She got a part-time job with an Afrikaner who ran his own insurance company. He took her on as a bookkeeper/secretary, because 'his father had told him that the Jews had never cheated him when he was selling his oxen; and because I was a woman, he could show weaknesses in front of me which he couldn't show to any men'. Within six months she was company secretary. 'He started as an agent and just made a fortune, he was a millionaire.'

I always wanted to write. I have been writing since I was a little girl. Hans said that I didn't have the talent – I didn't have a big talent. And it's true, I haven't. But he didn't recognise that I had a little talent. I'm a good reporter. He himself was a journalist. And he said, 'Forget about trying to write the best poem or the best play or the best novel in the world. You're just not going to make it.' And he was right, I wouldn't and I didn't.

So I didn't write for ten years. He'd been freelancing since almost immediately after the war. And then, when he became ill, I literally picked up the pen or the typewriter that he dropped, and I ghosted for him for a while without him realising. And so I slid into journalism, if you like.

I had a ready-made career, because I had already been writing under Hans's name and occasionally under my name. Because of my business experience and the little economics that I had learned, I got into business journalism – which was very unusual for women. So I was very lucky.

I was introduced to a group of German exiles. They were all either

writers, artists, ex-politicians, or simply politically committed people
like Hans. And they formed something which they called the Independent Culture Association – UKV – typically German. And this is
where I first discovered the actuality of what it is to be exiled, because
that exiled group, they were so sick – I don't mean mentally sick – but
they were so torn about what they had left behind, particularly the
politically active ones like my late husband, and the artists. And many of
them were lost.

My husband was one of those people who was just simply lost. He left
Germany in 1933, on the day after the Reichstag fire. He was one of the
only two witnesses who could actually swear that the Nazis had started
it. It's an incredible story.

When I met him he was in his early thirties and had joined the
Communist Party when he was still at school. He came from a grand
bourgeois background, very wealthy parents; and the day after he sat
what one would call in England O levels, he left school. He was thirteen;
and he left home.

He had a fairly chequered career; he was a real Berliner. He landed up
eventually at the *Berliner Tageblatt*, which was a liberal paper, very
famous. He was working in the political department as a reporter. He
was on night duty together with one of his closest friends, Wolfgang
Brettholz, known as Brett Holz. They got a phone call to say that the
Reichstag was on fire. They went into the street, Friedrichstrasse, saw
the glow and they realised it was true. There was a fire! They hadn't
believed it because there'd been a lot of these hoax calls. When they got
to the front of the Reichstag, there were hundreds of people there,
milling around. They could see the flames, but the police had cordoned
off the area. They waved their press passes, saying, 'Press! Press!' and a
policeman made a way for them. And he said, 'The Reichstag has been
set on fire by the Communists! We already have the man who did it –
Van der Lubbe!'

Hans said, 'That's not the story! Let's go and have a look at what's
going on at the back.' They went round to the back of the Reichstag.
There was a gate where lorries come through. At that moment the big
gate was flung open, and about a dozen young men started running out.
They weren't dressed in uniform; but Hans and Brett could see the
jackboots; and above the jackboots they were wearing the trenchcoats of
workers and caps. They ran, jumped on to a lorry and the lorry drove
off. So they actually saw the Nazis who started the Reichstag fire.

Back at the newspaper office, Hans and Brett wrote up the story.
They were playing with dynamite. The paper refused to publish it.
They realised that the Nazis would learn from their supporters
in the newspaper plant that these two had an exclusive story – eye-
witnesses to a Nazi crime that the Nazis were trying to pin on the

Communists and Van der Lubbe. Hans and Brett realised they were in mortal danger.

Hans left the next day. He went to Prague and from there to Paris, where he lived for a while. His wife of that time – Hans was married several times – had a South African background. They went from Paris to South Africa. They got there the same time as we did – in 1936. Hans took one look at the country and said, 'I can't live here! This is a backward political country.' It brings you back to what I was saying – that Hans died politically the moment he came to South Africa.

Politically he rejected the Communist Party of South Africa, he felt that they were out of touch. He didn't believe that they had the correct line on the African problem. He opened this left door for me. But the moment I wanted to join the Party, he stopped me because of his own disillusionment. That was the unfortunate thing, because it meant I had no political home. I was floating. And I have been floating politically ever since.

By this time I was writing, not only ghosting for Hans. We'd invented a pseudonym for ourselves and that pseudonym, John Merlin, is still today known in Germany for the first anti-apartheid reporting of that period. People who look up what was written in the Fifties and Sixties would find that, yes. So in that sense we were involved. We were reporting on the current events.

The more that was happening around me, the more I wanted to leave. Hans was in Germany when his office in Johannesburg was raided, and I sent him a message to say that we should leave. But he came back, not because he was so fond of South Africa, but because he was fond of somebody else.

Then there was a pretty dramatic and traumatic separation and parting and divorce.

I finally left South Africa knowing I was pregnant – not with Hans's child. I went to England for the birth of my son. Tiny. I came to Rhodesia with the intention of settling here with Sasha. I was here for two years. I met a number of people who were prepared to tell me how sanctions were being broken. So I started writing stories about sanction-busting. I knew it was dangerous. What I didn't know was that I was not only being watched, but I was being betrayed by my secretary – although in the final stages she probably saved me from arrest by telling me, and I was able to leave.

So that if you ask about exile: I left South Africa because I was politically unhappy, and I knew that sooner or later they would find out that John Merlin was both Hans and me – later on, only me. In Rhodesia – where I wanted to stay – I couldn't stay because I was writing sanction-busting stories, and getting fairly close to the banned parties. So I was deported.

I went to London and got a job on the financial pages of the *Guardian*. My editor wanted me to come back to cover UDI. I wrote a letter asking for certain interviews in Rhodesia, and in reply I received a Prohibited Immigrant's order, which said that I wouldn't even be allowed in transit – I would be immediately arrested. So that was the second exile. And through that I seemed to get on a black list in South Africa, and lost my South African passport.

I stayed in England for three years. Then I took a job which was offered by the *Times of Zambia*, as the financial editor, coupled with the post of correspondent with the *Financial Times*. So I was in Zambia for the most interesting years, 1970 to early 1975, when all the liberation movements and everything were based there – Angola, Mozambique, and of course SWAPO and ANC; but the ANC at that time were not that prominent; it was more ZAPU and ZANU, and I was more involved with the Rhodesian story.

So Zambia, if you like, was my third place of abode. And although I was writing about economics, which was my area and my job, I was constantly also covering the political angles. I never really lost touch with the Zimbabwe story.

I left again because of Sasha, because of schooling problems and other considerations. We went back to England together, and there I started to freelance.

I had a group of Third World journalists with whom I was friendly, and I was hoping in England to build up a kind of freelance agency. All were exiles from their own countries. We were a Third World group, working on Third World issues for Third World media – as well as for the First World media which gave us our money.

But then Lancaster House* happened, and after independence the Zimbabwe Minister of Information asked me to come back, and I said I would like to but my son had just started his O levels. But if you still want me in two years' time, I'll come back. And I did. After two years I came back.

From which country do you feel that you are an exile?

Definitely South Africa. I never really felt an exile from Germany. I felt like an emigrant from Germany because of the experience. I felt that I had been evicted, if you like, from a place where I happened to be born, but where it had been made very clear to me it was not my home.

When my father died, my sister sent me something which I still have: his Iron Cross, second class. It was a memento of something which was obviously important to him, of the First World War. He was a good German; he just happened to be Jewish.

---

* The talks held at Lancaster House, London, between Smith's Rhodesian government and the representatives of the black organisations that brought about the end of the war.

But I didn't feel German. I speak it fluently. That's where my market is, and I held the passport for a long time. But when I went back, there were so many things there that had nothing to do with me. I can only say what a German Jewish writer said in the title of her book: 'This is not my Country'. That's how I feel about Germany. It still isn't my home.

And South Africa, where I lived for thirty years – 1936 to 1966? That's where I grew up, where I had my deepest emotional experience. Quite apart from the country, my emotional development and my political development happened there. So that is where my home is – if I have any home.

And when I came back to Zimbabwe in 1980, I thought what a wonderful country it is. But it isn't mine either. I'm sure one could spend a wonderful retirement here, but I wouldn't feel that I'm involved. I can contribute something on a professional level, and perhaps I have done in a little way. But it's not for me to build up. It's for Zimbabweans. I'm not a Zimbabwean.

I've convinced myself over the last ten, perhaps twenty, years, that I would never ever belong to any country any more. And when people have asked me what I feel, I always say I feel a Southern African. But no: I've never ever thought that there would be a chance of going back to South Africa.

And now that there is, I'm very tempted. We were talking yesterday with colleagues that, as soon as we clarified our respective different passport situations, shouldn't we go down to see? And I was talking about buying a little flat in Hermanus to look out over the sea. [Laughs]

FREDDY REDDY
Norway 1990

'I was always in some kind of trouble . . . We just started walking and walking and walking.'

> He is a psychiatrist and group analyst living in Norway. In 1957, with little education and no money, he set out from South Africa to walk six thousand miles to England.

I left South Africa in 1957, because I felt I had reached a dead end. I was working as a porter in King Edward VIIIth hospital in Durban and I was attempting to go to night-school at the same time. I only had Standard 5.

We had very low wages and poor conditions of work. Trade unions were almost illegal. We formed the so-called 'King Edward VIIIth Social Club' and used this as a pretext for meeting. We decided to petition the administration with the fact that wages had last been reviewed in 1904 or 1906. My wage was less than £10 a month. And that was the final rate if I worked there for the next twenty years. Just paying bus fares used nearly £3 of that, and by the time I paid for my room I had nothing to spend on myself, my clothes, or a book for that matter. The only way I survived was by wearing the hospital uniform – the wages included uniforms – with large stamps saying King Edward VIIIth Hospital. It almost meant my whole soul was of King Edward Hospital.

The Social Club started long drawn-out negotiations with the management. Delays were endless, years passed. One day a filing clerk discovered a letter to the hospital from the Provincial Administration authorising an increase in wage rates. The letter was then already a year old. Reddy photocopied the letter. At a subsequent meeting, when the hospital management denied that any wage changes had been approved by the Province, he accused them of lying and produced the letter. The workers were finally given the back-pay due to them – all except Reddy and one of his colleagues. Their pay was reduced to the lowest scale and they were threatened with an investigation.

They wanted to know how I had got the documents from the highest office. I knew that if I stayed there, one way or other I would never get a job again. The best thing was for me to leave South Africa.

I thought I would become a lawyer, and then go back to South Africa and fight apartheid. I had to leave immediately. I planned to make for London; but I had no money.

I had no idea how to get there. I thought of getting a job on a ship. I went to the dockside, and found that there was a whole mafia there – you paid money to get certain documents before you got hired. I was very naive. I used to go to the dockside and wait in the queue, but it turned out that only those who had the right connections and the right payment were allowed to get seamen's papers. So I abandoned that idea.

Next I went round to rich Indian shopkeepers in the Durban area asking them for help, saying I would pay them back when I had returned from my studies in England. But I had no real connections with people with money.

Then I hit on the idea of trying to buy an old car or bus and driving through Africa. Five or six chaps decided they wanted to go; we could go as a gang. After some meetings it transpired that it was hot air; they were too scared. But there was one, a teacher I hardly knew. I decided well, if I can't go that way, I was going to walk to England, yes. And this chap said he would hike with me.

I got a rucksack, bought with money that the hospital workers collected – they collected tickies and sixpences and gave me £8, which was a lot of money for them. That was all the money I had with me. And I started the journey through Africa, going to London. Didn't know any routes, just figured that we go and ask on the way. I don't think we even had a map in our possession. An English doctor from the hospital helped me to get a passport. When we arrived at the Transvaal border the fellow looked at it and said, 'No! you'll have to go back to Durban.' Indians were not allowed to cross the provincial boundary into the Transvaal, and I didn't know that at the time.

So I pleaded with this border guard, a Frenchman working for the South African government. He was fighting with himself whether to call the immigration police or to let me go. I saw him walk into the other room, pick up the telephone, put it down, lift it up again, put it down, lift it up again, put it down. And he finally came out and grabbed me by my shoulder, took me to the border post and kicked me, and said, 'Don't ever come back.' That was the first lucky break we had.

The first leg of the journey had been covered by an Indian wedding party who gave us a lift from Durban to the Transvaal. And from then on it meant walking. In those days there were hardly any roads to Mozambique. The journey took about two days. We crossed the mountains to get in. From Ressano Garcia we went through the whole of Mozambique, and then Nyasaland, Lake Tanzania, Tanzania, Kenya, Uganda, borders of Sudan. Sometimes we got lifts, but most of the journey was done on foot because in those days there was not much traffic.

We slept anywhere. We slept under trees, sometimes in churches; sometimes we found a school, sometimes African people gave us a place to sleep in their room – they were very generous and helpful. And wherever there were Indian workers, they helped us. For instance, in Nyasaland they put us up in their barracks; and in Kenya we stayed in Sikh temples. There was always some place or other; sometimes we just slept on a shop verandah. And food – sometimes we got food from the people who were living around. Sometimes it was a trading store, right in the middle of nowhere. In Africa you find these tiny shops, bartering beads and biscuits and peanuts. We could pick some fruit on the way. And in that way we finally reached Uganda.

The journey from Beira to Nyasaland was through very, very dense forest country. The people advised us not to attempt that, so we went to the station. The engine-driver was an Indian; we travelled in the baggage car. The next morning he took us to his barracks and allowed us to stay. We thought in a day or two we would be on our way, but the police came and picked us up. Although our passports were stamped, they told us we had no right to be there because we didn't have any money, and that they would deport us back. I said, 'My god! to come all this way and be deported back!' So I lied, told them my father was rich, and would be able to sign. We stayed in jail, I think a week, when an Indian came. He was from South Africa, living in Nyasaland. He had something to do with the legislature and came to investigate who we were. I managed to convince him we were genuine in what we planned to do.

In the meanwhile the Indian train drivers living in the barracks brought us food. Some days later, the legislator came back. He had paid a deposit to the government so that we wouldn't be destitute and become a burden. So they released us. And the railway workers found out that they could buy a ticket for us on a cattle boat across Lake Tanzania.

Oh, what a journey that was! I didn't know lakes could be so tumultuous and dangerous. The waves were just as high as that, and the cow dung and the stink – ! I vomited, I really got sick. It took about four or five days to cross from one end to the other, criss-crossing to deliver cattle, take passengers and so on. But before we left, the man who had deposited £20 with the government for us gave us £20 each, so that we shouldn't get into such difficulties again.

We went to Mbeya in Tanzania; this time we just went to the police station, they took us in and stamped our passports. And then we decided to just start walking as quickly as possible so they wouldn't arrest us.

I can't remember. We just started walking and walking and walking. We came to Iringa, yes, and there again we met another train driver, he was an Ismaili, and he took us in and organised another trip in a train. I think we went as far as Dodoma by train. Then from Tanzania to Kenya, from Kenya to Uganda, and from Uganda to the Sudan.

The fellow on the border post was a young Englishman who had never heard of anybody hitch-hiking from South Africa to London. He got caught up in the drama of it, and he didn't ask us whether we had money or not, he just stamped our passports. But there was this civil war, and it was impossible to get any kind of visa or travel document.

We were arrested three times because we didn't have money to pay our way through. There again I used tricks of my tongue, and lied. From the Sudan, back to Uganda. We were unable to go further because we had no money. We met a student leader in Uganda. When we were arrested there, he and his friends came and took us out of prison, and suggested that we should go to the local schools and tell the students how we came to that point, two or three thousand miles from South Africa.

I went and addressed them – I'd never addressed a crowd in my life before – and they passed a hat around. The Indians who were in Uganda were very rich – this was before Idi Amin. The papers wrote up about our journey. One man had a brilliant idea. He would arrange for me to address the annual meeting of the Njinja National Indian organisation – the whole Indian community. My knees were jelly, but I managed, and three or four days later they had given us money enough to pay for our passage to England. I found out that my companion had been travelling around and pocketing the money he collected from the schools. So I left Uganda alone for London, nearly a year after leaving Durban.

In 1957, if you had a passport, you could get into Britain – I said I was
a tourist. I knew nobody in London, so I went to the YMCA and stayed
one night. I had 17s.6d. left in my pocket.

At the Labour Exchange he saw posters advertising jobs for porters
on the London Underground and for miners in Wales. He went for
a job on the mines, but found he couldn't get a job there unless he
was a member of the Mineworkers' Union, which he couldn't join
unless he had a job on the mines. London Underground offered him
a job provided he could supply a permanent address – the YMCA
was not sufficient. A student he met took him to his landlady, who
gave him a small attic room when she heard his story.

My desire was to study; but I worked a three-shift day. But the first six
months gave me a chance to get my bearings and save a bit, wearing
London Underground uniforms, boots and everything, so I didn't have
to spend money on clothes.

Other jobs followed, and for two years he worked at a factory and
managed to go to night classes and take O levels and A levels.

Soon I came into contact with other South Africans and began to work
with the Anti-Apartheid Movement, with Vella Pillay, Mac Maharaj and
others. I think it was David Ennals who told me that there were possibilities of studying in Scandinavia; so I wrote to the Norwegian Student
Association and told them my story, what education I had, and that I
wanted to study law. My contact with the police in South Africa had led
to two or three times when I won my own case. I thought, therefore, that
I would make a brilliant lawyer!
But they said they didn't think that would be the thing for me to do,
because Norwegian law was different from other countries. As I had
worked in a hospital, I ended up by suggesting that I study medicine.
They said, 'OK. We'll let you know.'
Those months of waiting were real torture. I was getting older, but
finally I got a reply – I was accepted, I would get a stipend and could
study medicine.
In 1961 I left London for Norway, and that is where I studied and
finished my medical examinations, oh, with a lot of difficulties, including
language difficulties. But I learned the language within eight weeks. Yes,
I really put myself to the grind and worked at it. I didn't have a high
school certificate, so I took the whole high school examination in two
months. I never had a basis in mathematics, physics or anything like that
before. They didn't know that. And when I got my result it was forty per
cent – only just a pass mark. They said, 'No, you can't study medicine,
your grades are too low.' The people who were marking the papers

didn't know that this was done in only two months, and in a language foreign to me.

But I had become friendly with a girl who lived in the same student flat with me. She was finishing her medical degree. I met her two or three months after the examination and told her the medical faculty wouldn't take me. She said, 'Look, if you want help, I'll help.' So even if it went on to three o'clock in the morning, she would explain mathematical questions, and help me. She said, 'No, I think your pass was what one-third of our students achieve after a three-year course.' Her fiancé was on the student council, so they took up my case and explained my story to the faculty. Oh boy, within a month I got a letter saying I was accepted. And that is how I started studying medicine, a six and a half year course.

I was still political. I started an organisation inside Oslo, an anti-apartheid group which for the past twenty-three years has made Norway aware of what has been happening in South Africa. While studying medicine I used to go on tours and address students. I was talking about things they'd never heard about – the missionaries, colonialism, about racism.

Although he was a foreigner, he was elected president of the student body.

I did my housemanship, and I wanted to go to Zambia. But I had married a Norwegian girl, my wife was pregnant, and I was biding time for the baby to be born; so meanwhile I took up a position in a psychiatric hospital. I found the work stimulating and exciting. This was a new challenge. I didn't know psychosis, or what happened to people under psychosis. I saw how the human being suffered from malnutrition, depression, family problems, and so on. And reading new literature, new things, new dimensions came into my mind. Suddenly I saw how this was going to fit into our South African situation. It would mean nothing to be a doctor giving penicillin injections when they're going to go back to the same thing in a week's time. So I decided to become a psychiatrist.

My son was born, and a daughter. During this period I was elected as a city councillor. In 1972 I completed my practical and got a specialists' licence, and from then until 1979 I worked as a psychiatrist.

By then there were ANC people coming backwards and forwards to Oslo, and they told me about some of the conditions in the MK camps. The ANC Medical Health section was asking doctors to come and help them in a crisis situation, but they couldn't afford to pay the doctors' air tickets. I was in practice and could afford to pay, so I decided to go to Lusaka to investigate. I went through all the camps, saw the conditions, and wrote reports. The ANC president, OR, asked me to stay permanently. But I knew that that would have been disastrous for me. Because of the working and housing conditions, and lack of transport, sometimes I had to sit for two days and wait, doing nothing. If I didn't have enough work, it would ruin me. So I came back to Oslo and arranged to go on a yearly basis, which is what I have been doing up to this time.

I was divorced in 1972, and lived with another Norwegian woman for a time. But since then I have been a bachelor. My children are grown now, and I see them regularly, they are wonderful children and I have a very good relationship with them, and that's the story until now.

I intend to go back to South Africa this year to see, to talk with people, to find out what I can do. But now I am nearly sixty years old, and I think it is time for me just to live my life. I've been loyal to the movement, but I think for a short time before I become a pensioner, I could go back and work for a few years. I have patients in Oslo who I can't just leave and go away. It means weaning them, explaining why I am leaving and arranging someone else. All these things must be attended to before I embark on a new programme in South Africa.

If I had not left South Africa, I would undoubtedly have been in jail. I was very aggressive towards any white person, and never accepted the white man as superior to me. I was always in some kind of trouble with the police. And I wouldn't have gone very far without education. I don't know what would have happened, But I do know that I would not have been a free person.

ES'KIA MPHAHLELE
Johannesburg 1992

'I said to myself: This is all the more reason I should go back so that I don't just write from memory. I must come back.'

He was a teacher and Secretary of the Transvaal African Teachers' Association. In 1949, the Eiselen Commission set out to produce a blueprint for 'Education for Natives as a Separate Race'. Its recommendations were embodied in the 1953 Bantu Education Act.

Es'kia was dismissed from his post. For a while he taught in an independent community school; then that too was closed under the Bantu Education Act. He worked as a messenger in a lawyer's office, then as a journalist and in 1955 as fiction editor of the South African weekly *Drum*.

He did not like journalism. In 1957 he decided to leave the country, and went to Nigeria.

I was married then; took my three children, ja, four, seven and ten. We started in Lagos in a high school, went on to the University of Ibadan. By that time I had done my Master's here, as an external student of UNISA. So we lived in Nigeria for four years, from 1957 to 1961.

In 1961, I was offered a job in Paris, to be Director of the African programme of what was called the Congress for Cultural Freedom. It was really set up and financed by the Americans. It also published *Encounter* magazine and several other journals in Europe – an American kind of outreach activity. Taking charge of their African programme took me to a number of African countries, setting up writers' and artists' clubs and organising education conferences and writers' conferences. I had to learn French, but I mastered it – at least conversationally – and I could read French.

After two years I became restless, and I felt I really wanted to go and teach, go back to the classroom. At that time the Congress of Cultural Freedom was eager to establish a physical centre in an African country, and I chose Nairobi because I had been there before and had talked to people like Ngugi and other budding writers about establishing a writers' organisation there.

We moved again, and set up a creative centre there where we did theatre and music and writing. I was running writers' workshops around the country. Nairobi turned out to be not such a pleasant place – the people were not really welcoming, and a thing like a creative centre was a new concept. They were suspicious too, right? But I think they were really ignorant about the kind of benefit they could get out of a centre of that kind. And they were just not used to Africans from other countries coming into Kenya – and this we found was an endemic attitude throughout Africa, except for Nigeria. Nigeria and Ghana are the most welcoming places we ever lived in.

We arrived in Kenya in 1963 and stayed until 1966, so we saw their independence. We began to realise this is not the place where we would settle. I left the creative centre in the hands of somebody else and went to the university to teach – but they wouldn't give me a permanent job, and so I decided I'd better just move. I met an American there who introduced me to the University of Denver where he had come from, and where I wanted to do my Ph.D. So we packed up and went to Denver, Colorado, yes.

The children went to school to re-adapt to a new culture and a new climate, I did the Ph.D. in two years, and Rebecca upgraded the diploma she had got at the Jan Hofmeyer School of Social Work here in Johannesburg, and did her Master's. We both had exchange visas, which meant that we couldn't stay longer than the period of our studies; and no matter what we did we couldn't succeed to change into immigrant status. So we had to leave the country.

Which is how we came to the University of Zambia in 1968. I taught there in the English department. Rebecca worked for a United Nations outfit, natural resources – something like that. We stayed in Zambia for about three years. Then in 1970 I was invited to come back to Denver as

Associate Professor of English. Right. We packed up again and left. We stayed in Denver for another four years, Rebecca working for the Red Cross, social work department.

In 1974 we decided to go to Philadelphia. We were drifting slowly [Laughs] and Philadelphia would be the last place before we went home. By that time we'd been talking about returning, and saying to ourselves: You know, we have accumulated as much as we really need to on education, and we really need to go back. We really felt very homesick.

We started to write to those in authority here, to find out if we could come back. We had British passports but we were not British citizens. We had that kind of passport that the British had given to Indians in Uganda and Kenya – you had a British passport but you were not allowed to migrate there automatically. And according to the South Africans, we had lost our South African citizenship. Correspondence went back and forth, and the thing dragged on for five years, by which time – this is 1977 – they said we could come back as long as we live in Lebowa.

Lebowa, of course, was designated our 'homeland'. It was not independent, it was still just called 'homelands', right? My family originally – the Mphahleles – are people of Lebowa although I had left that area when I was eleven to come to Pretoria. They said I should look for employment at the University of the North. So we went to Lebowa, found a house there, and I applied to the University of the North. The Appointments Committee appointed me, but the Minister of Education vetoed it for their own political reasons. These universities were very strong centres of ideological control, and they didn't want people coming from outside – they thought I might be a threat. So that was it.

And then Wits [University of Witwatersrand, Johannesburg] offered me a job. The University of the North was under Bantu Education, but Wits was then under the Ministry of National Education. At Wits I was doing a research job into oral poetry in the African Studies Institute. I had a contract for three years, at the end of which they asked me to set up a Department of African Literature, the first of its kind in the country. Which I did – that was in 1983. I started the African Literature Department and worked until 1987 when I retired, right?

After we came back it took us something like another five years to resume our South African . . . to become South African! [Laughs] So we then became South Africans and our children could also automatically become South African citizens. One effect all this wandering had on our children was to enlarge their own experience and mental horizons. They could easily adapt to different cultures – African, American and so on. That was the positive side of it – and also a better education. The negative side of it was that, because they were displaced, wherever we moved we really didn't have community in the way in which one has in this country. You have community, you have relatives, you have people that you can always call upon to be assistants if a child goes wrong;

you've always got an aunt or an uncle; there was this kind of extended family in addition to the neighbours, right?

We didn't have that extended family wherever we went, even in African countries. Because of that displacement, they were developing certain unsavoury habits, being absorbed by the environment, and having to live by its own rules and the rules of their peer group. It was a constant battle between us and the peer group and the influence they have on them. This was the painful part of it. While we recognise it was the only way they could survive, we also felt uneasy about the fact that much of what the peer group was influencing them into was just not right. We felt we were not in control, that there was no way as parents in which we could modify their behaviour.

We have different ethics, different ways of addressing your elders, different ways of addressing your parents. Especially in America it was absolutely difficult, yes. And things were not getting any better as time went on. We, as adults, were at ease with ourselves; we had roots and we had a certain sense of control of our milieu, right? They didn't. They went with the flow and we realised that this was going to create conflicts all the time. That was the negative effect that exile had on them.

Only our daughter is back here. And now she feels very restless and wants to go back to America because . . . well she's been out of a job now, for the last year and three months; and she has a Master's in mass communication, and there is just no place where she fits in. Having grown up in America – she left here when she was seven – she comes back at the age of thirty-six. Her attitude of mind has changed and doesn't fit in. She has tried very hard to adapt, and it has just not been easy.

Our four sons are still in America. They are Americans, yes. They are Americans. We have lost them [laughs] though we still keep in touch one way or another. And so that is the toll it has had on our lives as a family. It is such a complex relationship that we find ourselves in. Even between Rebecca and me, we find in spite of the fact that we held our own as a unit, we've come out different people. The biggest advantage we find is restoring, rediscovering that community which we didn't have all these years of exile; feeling that there is a job to do here, something worthwhile, and we're self-fulfilled.

Rebecca is running a pre-school in Lebowa and I have been involved in community education here side-by-side with the Wits job; and that has restored for us the sense of place, the sense of belonging, yes. I don't regret leaving, no. I wish we could have come back a little earlier, maybe five years earlier. We still feel that it was good to go out and do the things that we couldn't have done here, yes.

Now my plan – when I finish this project – is to join Rebecca in Lebowa. I've got a committee going there to set up a community education centre, and we are now in the process of shaping it up. And this is what I'll be doing, side-by-side with my writing.

I've done so far . . . let's see . . . seven full length books – three novels, two autobiographies and volumes of short stories and poetry and essays. I've written countless articles, all Africa-centred. I was still always writing about South Africa, in the fiction and in the poetry. I could never comprehend the American human landscape. I couldn't feel it, I couldn't smell it, I couldn't comprehend it – and I never tried. Despite all the years in between, I was resisting being sucked into the environment of my host country. As long as I resisted that, I wasn't going to be able to assimilate its life sufficiently to write about it, right? I wrote one novel set in Zambia, and then the other novel *The Wanderers* was all over. And then the latest novel and the short stories are set in South Africa.

So then I said to myself, 'This is all the more reason I should go back, so that I just don't write from memory. I must come back!' Three things were working inside me. First, that ancestral bond one feels with one's own land of birth, and being a traditionalist in faith – I'm not a Christian – that had a strong hold on me. That pull I could feel all the time. Secondly, I needed that kind of community to work in; and as long as I was outside, I was not contributing anything to anything. Just a vague feeling that, as a professor, what are you contributing to the human environment wider than the university campus? And third: that I wanted to get back to the land which I want to write about, always.

And Rebecca is very happy. She feels that she's able to function competently. She does keep on about the fact that all her old friends are now so different . . . such different people. Because she's also so different, and she would have liked to have found them as she left them. [Laughs] Yes. And I always say to her, 'Well I feel the same way too. But we've got simply to understand that we are different, and they are different, right? And they haven't moved much from where we left them. But we have moved a long way, yes.'

I'm sure there are those who surrendered to the fact that they now have to live as exiles for good, and that's it; and the idea of coming back can become untenable, something they can only dream about. There is that rift. And one can never say it's a totally negative thing to have happened to one, or a totally positive thing.

I was a very bitter person when I left, because I had been dismissed from teaching which is the profession I loved and which I felt was my calling. I was thoroughly really bitter. But even then it didn't occur to me that I should leave for good.

BETTY DU TOIT
London 1990

'I want to die in South Africa.'

> She was a fearless and dedicated leading trade union organiser and
> political activist, working both among poor Afrikaner girls who
> came to the towns and also among blacks.

My mother died of a miscarriage when I was eighteen months old. My
father died when I was four.

Our farm was outside Johannesburg – I think it bore our name for a
long, long time. The most vivid memory I have of my father is standing
with him while he held my hand, and cattle were milling all round us;
and I was very very frightened. I must have been about three or so; and
he held me and said, 'You must always stand when you're frightened;
stand firm. Never, never allow anything to panic you when you are
frightened. Stand, see; nothing will happen to you.' I think it strongly
influenced me throughout my life.

The farms were sold up – I think there were two – and my brother and
I were sent to boarding-schools. My brother turned into a strong nationalist, almost fascist, with very racist attitudes.

I was also very racist . . . oh yes, very . . . That was my biggest problem;
and I knew that I had to fight it, even when I was a member of the
Communist Party. If I was stopped in the street and spoken to by an
African, I had great difficulty in standing there I was so embarrassed.
That was a big problem that I had to face and fight. And I only realised
that I had overcome my racism when I attended a Trade Union Conference. I wanted to ask H. A. Naidoo, who was secretary of the Sugar
Workers' Union, something about sugarworkers. To attract his attention
I moved from where I was sitting among other white women delegates,
over to where H.A. was. And there was an African sitting between H.A.
and myself. So I stretched across the African, pulled H.A.'s sleeve, and
spoke to him.

Agh! Some time later, a white miner got up; and the whole theme of his
speech was me, and the disgraceful way I behaved. Not only did I sit next
to an African, but I leaned across and pulled the sleeve of an Indian!
None of the men there – white men – wanted to talk to me or associate
with me. At the dance nobody wanted to dance with me. But I was very
relieved and happy, because I realised suddenly that I had no racial
prejudices any more – that I had been completely unconscious of what I
had done. So that's how I got rid of my racism.

And was then banned – I was the first woman removed from the trade
union movement for life. I was banned and confined. I had organised a
co-operative trading society in Orlando township, and I had handed it

over to the African membership and looked around for other work. And I saw an organisation called Kupagani, which means 'help yourself'. They'd given themselves that name because the Strijdom government had declared that the Africans lived on the backs of the whites, and never did anything to help themselves. Strijdom had taken away school feeding from the African children, whereas the white children were being given ice cream and delicacies for their school feeding. The African children who were starving, had nothing. So Kupagani decided to organise school feeding for the African children.

Dr Martini, the head of Kupagani, said, 'If you're prepared to work for two months for nothing, let's see what you can do.' I said OK and I went out to organise. I never told a soul what I was doing – I was afraid they would talk and I would be discovered, because I was banned from meetings with others.

In six weeks' time I had organised twenty-six schools. We gave them a very good protein soup and a slice of fortified brown bread, for which they paid a penny. We had to charge, otherwise the government would have said that they were again living on the backs of other people. I think this was for me the happiest time of my life in South Africa – working with those lovely, lovely children. They used to call me the protein lady, because I used to lecture at the same time to schools. The teachers were wonderful – it was really the teachers who helped me to organise. The children would gather the sticks, and we made fires outside, boiling paraffin tins full of water and put this high protein soup powder in.

The kids were terrific, and I noticed how much better they began looking. Their hair was no more so red – it was going beautifully black, and their skins were so black and shiny. Oh, it was a most thrilling time. It was wonderful.

I used to take a little basket of food along with me for my lunch, and go down to the Co-op and eat there. One day at the Co-op, suddenly I heard a white man shouting, 'Where's Betty du Toit?' I came out. They were Special Branch. They had passed my car on the road and recognised the number. They said, 'What are you doing here?' The Johannesburg Municipality had given me a pass into Orlando, day, night, anytime. I could go in and out of Orlando with this wonderful pass. But it was in an assumed name.

When the Special Branch said: What are you doing here? I couldn't think. I said I'd got a pass to be there. They said, 'Show it.' I wasn't going to show them the pass with this false name of course. I scratched around in my bag, and then I said, oh, I hadn't brought it with me. So they said: Get out! Get out! They waited there while I got in the car, right out, left Orlando.

I went down to Kupagani and I said, 'I'm sorry I can't work with you any more. The Special Branch have caught me in Orlando, and told me to get out.'

On her way home, Betty stopped at the local Municipal offices, and completely by chance, overheard a conversation about 'that communist woman' that the police were 'coming to get' that night. It was the time of many detentions under the 90-day law.

I thought, oh God! I walked straight out of the place, into my car; and I sat for a long time, not going to my house, sure to be somebody there waiting for me. Now, while I had been working at Orlando I had met an English woman, who had stopped and said: I always see you surrounded by masses of children – who are you? So I told her what I was doing and she said, if you're ever in trouble, come to me. And I suddenly remembered her – I had kept her address – and I went to her. She was married to an Afrikaner. She put me up in her loft.

She posted letters for me – one to Maulvi Cachalia and one to Nadine Gordimer. I told them what had happened. Nadine kept in contact with me and Maulvi too. I didn't know what to do. But Maulvi said, 'Betty, you must leave! You must leave, because if they get you they'll make mincemeat of you. I'll organise for you to get out. There's some Indians leaving, they'll phone at each little town, and find out whether the police are watching.'

So this is how I got out, with these Indians. We stopped at every town, phoned, spoke in Gujarati, and travelled to Botswana – Bechuanaland it was then. Maulvi had got money through to some Indians – I think Nadine had given it to him. But I had nowhere to go.

I didn't want anyone to know I was there, because I thought I would infiltrate back to South Africa. But someone told Rica Hodgson, who had left South Africa, that I was there. So she took me to her flat and I stayed there. There was a German there, he had a small plane; and he flew Michael Harmel and me . . . I think this man wanted R300 to get us to Tanzania, so we paid half and half, and I got to Dar es Salaam.

Later I went to Ghana and worked there for over three years. Wonderful! I was very happy there. I lived in an area where I was the only white among all the Ghanaians, and it was lovely. It really was. I was very happy there.

When I flew to Ghana Nadine Gordimer kept in close touch with me. Nadine has been the most amazing person. She has really taught me the meaning of friendship. When I was in trouble in Dar es Salaam, Nadine flew up to me to try to help. Whenever I've needed money or help, Nadine has given it. When I was in prison, she always came; when I was worried about her being associated with me, she would say to me, 'What one must do when one's friends are in trouble – you must see them.'

The trade union movement in Ghana gave me a research job for six months; and at the same time, I was writing articles on South Africa for the Ghanaian Broadcasting Association. When my six months was up, they decided to give me work – research and working with young writers. I was becoming immensely happy because I was researching on Africa, a continent I adore; and I was becoming an expert on Africa.

I used to swim a lot. One afternoon it was very hot, and I took Violet Matlou and her daughter to the beach – I was teaching her to swim. A storm blew up. I don't know if you've ever seen a tropical storm. It's the most beautiful thing. The clouds are sort of . . . you feel you could just stretch your hand up and feel these black clouds. And fork lightning everywhere; and the huge seas! I was wet – I'd been swimming; and I said to Violet, 'Take Maggie and go to the car. I just want to watch the storm, the swaying coconut trees on the beach, it's a magnificent sight.' I thought: I'm wet so it won't matter if I sit in the storm.

Well, it did matter, because I got very bad earache. I went to an American doctor that I was friendly with, Roger Lewis, and he took me to an English doctor. This English doctor examined my ear and prescribed antibiotics. I knew I was allergic to antibiotics. Both Lewis and I said, no. I can't have antibiotics. So he said to Roger Lewis, 'Take her away, there's a good chap; and you give her something.'

Roger Lewis was acting as an agent for Roche Products, trying to market a sulphanamide tablet; and he gave me this sulphanamide tablet. I said to him, 'You're sure I can take it?' and he said, 'Yes, yes, yes. The American army are marching on it in Vietnam. You can take them every day for the rest of your life, and come to no harm.' So I took one sulphanamide tablet.

The next day I was feeling very, very ill. I went to the Mammy Market because I wanted to buy cloth to send to friends, and I felt as if I was floating. Dr Lewis was in the Cape Coast, so I left a note for him, saying: I'm very ill. Could you please come and see me. He came back quite late, about eleven o'clock that night, and he said, 'You've got an allergy.' So I said, 'Is it from the tablet you gave me?' So he said, 'No. It's not that. Just take codeine, take a codeine and you'll be all right.' And he left me.

Well, my eyes began to pain during the night, and I got up . . . Do you know on the farms in South Africa, if you had bad eyes, they made a weak tea solution and bathed your eyes in that. So I was getting up and bathing my eyes in tea solution; and nothing helped. I understand that I was running a temperature of nearly 105. And I must have been quite heady, because, in the morning, I walked out of my flat in a nightgown, bare-footed, and got into my car – the doctors wouldn't believe me – and drove to a Swiss woman, Mrs Hlube, who was married to a South African Zulu and ran the airport hotel. A lot of planes had come through that night, and she had not slept; and her husband was away. I flopped down on a bed. And she was so tired after working all night that she didn't notice me, and she flopped down on another bed; and she slept.

I was coming out in these huge lumps everywhere. I had become unconscious. When her husband came home, he discovered me there. I couldn't answer or talk. They sent for Roger Lewis, and he thought I had some terrible disease – I was covered in huge lumps. He wrapped me in a blanket and took me to Kalibu Hospital. So there I lay for six months in Kalibu Hospital. And the poor Ghanaian doctors had written on my chart: Drug Poisoning. So I lay there between life and death.

Then some Hungarian scientists came there and they took some of my blood to examine. And they came back and said, 'She has Stephen Johnson Syndrome. She must have had some form of antibiotic.'

The Stephen Johnson Syndrome is named after the two doctors who discovered it. It's a completely new disease that attacks people who are allergic to antibiotics. It attacks the eyes, the mouth, the vagina and the rectum.

In those early days, nobody knew very much about Stephen Johnson Syndrome, least of all in Ghana. I should have been given massive doses of cortisone – evidently, if you give cortisone you save the eyes. But unfortunately they didn't really know about Stephen Johnson Syndrome. Even here in Britain nobody knows much about it.

Another American doctor came in. He said: You must find steroids; she has to be given steroids. I believe that I looked terrible. Friends have said to me, Betsy, if we didn't love you so much we couldn't have borne to have seen you; we've never seen anything so revolting. Blood was pouring from my mouth and my eyes. They said my eyes were the size of tennis balls, they reached out of my head like great lumps. I had scabs that were falling off. My face was sort of black stains; when I came to Britain I still had them.

Once I was on the cortisone I began improving. Everybody thought that I was dying – but there you are, I didn't die. I was given the cortisone – and I have never known such pain in all my life. I couldn't bear a sheet to touch my body. I was alone in a room, lying naked, because I couldn't bear anybody to touch me. I screamed if I was touched. It . . . ooogh, it was something I . . . And how anyone could have lived going through that I don't know. I slowly began recovering. I survived.

My eyes were then covered in ulcers, and the pain was still excruciating. By this time all my mucous membranes had been destroyed, so I had dry eyes. Oh, these made the eyes so red and painful. I said I wanted to come to Britain to save my eyes. But in Ghana, I had no money. I had to pay my fare – almost £1,000. Again my Swiss friend, Mrs Hlube, came to my rescue. She had a Swiss friend who was a chef and had earned quite a lot of money in Ghana before he'd left the country. Mrs Hlube held this money on his behalf; so he told her to give it to me. And that's how I got my fare to come to Britain.

I went to the Royal Eye Hospital – wonderful, wonderful little hospital. They got some new stuff from America that I could use to keep my eyes moist, which helped a bit. By that time I had lost one eye, and the sight of the other one was almost gone; I had a tiny, tiny little bit of sight. I went to see a special doctor who I was told may be able to help me. This doctor then said to me, 'Look, you've got a little bit of sight. Are you prepared to take a chance and have this operation, which may improve your sight or not?' I said, yes, I'll take the chance.

Now had I known more about Stephen Johnson's I would never have agreed – because I now know that it just never leaves you, no matter what the doctors say. It surfaces on any occasion. However, I had the operation; and some days later one of the stitches came loose. So they took me to the surgery and said, 'We'll have to undo all the stitches.'

It was wonderful! Slowly, as they were taking the stitches out of my eye, I could see. And I shouted, 'I can see!' Sister was there. She said, 'What have I got on my head?' So I explained what she had on her head. I ran to the window. I saw motor cars, lawn, I could see everything. It was most . . . Oh, I was so excited, it was wonderful. They said, 'Oh well, you won't be able to see now, because we're going to fill the eye with ointment.' So they filled it with ointment, and then they said to me, 'You can go home for a weekend, but you must come back again.' I came home, and I could see light! Even with all the ointment and stuff.

And suddenly – pitch black. I phoned the hospital and said, 'Everything's gone black!' They said, 'Come down right away.' I went down and they did another operation, they did the same operation again. And after? I can't remember, it was all so horrible; the days that went by, I can't . . . Anyway, they took me into the surgery one day, looked with the light and said, 'It's finished.' The retina behind the eye had all fallen down. They couldn't touch anything. It's finished, it's gone. No hope.

I just fainted, hit the floor. And that night Freda Goldblatt came and fetched and brought me home. She was quite wonderful. I stayed with her for six months, she was carting me up and down to hospitals.

I spent at least ten years in Britain, in and out of hospitals, in and out. I never knew whether I was on my feet or my head, I hardly knew what was going on around me. And I was still in such an enormous amount of pain all the time and anxiety about how I was going to earn my living, what was going to happen to me, where I was going to go.

I found out how to manage on my own, as a blind person. I had to go to the Home Office every six months or so, asking for extensions of my visa to stay in Britain, because the medical treatment was still continuing. For almost ten years! I was doing nothing but going in and out of hospitals. One day, when I sent my documents to the Home Office, they wrote back and said, 'You can stay indefinitely. You can open a business, do what you like.' I was so astonished; it was quite wonderful. I could have National Health – legally – and I could work. All these things. So that was fine.

Then I began learning Braille. And I was teaching Braille – teaching elderly people. The hospitals were sending pupils and I was being paid for doing it, so it was fine. And then of course Maggie Thatcher came into power – and, yes, money; that's right. Money stopped. So the teaching was stopped. All the social services were cut, cut, cut, left, right and centre.

I went to stay with an English woman who I had helped in South Africa when she was in trouble. She heard I was here and was very ill; and she searched for me and found me in hospital, and said to me, 'Betty, please come to me. You can stay as long as you like.' So I was very happy.

I stayed with her for over three years; and then she had to retire. Nadine heard that I was going to start looking for somewhere to live again. She and her husband came, saw this little flat and bought it for me.

I survived, but I've got a very bad back and my legs are becoming troublesome due to the back . . . it's again Stephen Johnson's that has attacked all the nerves of the spine. And my doctor said to me the other day: Well, I've spoken to all your doctors. And they all say that you should have been dead years ago.

A hard, dreadful experience, I wouldn't wish it upon anyone.

So here I am now, waiting and hoping to go back to South Africa. I want to die there.

The Insurrection: the 1970s

16 June, 1976, was the second watershed in South Africa's contemporary history.

In 1960 Sharpeville ended the long era of peaceful protest against apartheid, bringing a fundamental change in methods of resistance. But it brought also outlawed organisations, detention without trial, torture, and secret killings. It brought a long decade of silence and suppression.

After Sharpeville the trickle into exile of those seeking either an education or to establish an overseas base, became a flood. Many were seeking escape from arrest, persecution, even death. The young ones were searching for military training, so as to return to their country and fight with arms instead of stones. Most of them believed they would be out for only a few weeks or months.

The Sharpeville massacre marked the end of an era – for the ANC the end of forty-eight years of legal activity and protest, the end of legality of almost all peoples' organisations, and of whatever justice had survived under white law.

But the Soweto uprising marked a new beginning – the beginning of insurrection, of a new time of resistance and defiance, of a struggle that in the following decade would crumble the very foundations of the apartheid edifice.

For many years there had been a hiatus in the struggle against apartheid, and a mantle of silence over past political struggles. The children were politically ignorant. Their revolt was against the immediate frustrations imposed by Bantu Education and specifically – the spark that touched it off – the enforced use of Afrikaans as a medium of instruction in schools.

If the introduction of the inferior Bantu Education into all the country's black schools set the youth rebellion smouldering, and the insistence of the use of Afrikaans as the general medium of instruction touched off the explosive fuse, it was Black Consciousness that empowered the youth insurrection that followed.

Steve Biko, the charismatic young leader who abandoned his medical studies to found the Black Consciousness movement, believed that blacks would only achieve liberation when they broke the chains of psychological inferiority – an inferiority ingrained through decades of colonial repression.

In 1969 Biko led a breakaway of black students from the white dominated National Union of Students (NUSAS). Black Consciousness (BC) grew from this core. It rejected white liberalism, which Biko believed to be an agent for fostering the values and purposes of the white society. He was demanding not an equal place within that society, but the creation *ab initio* of a new set of values and purposes of the indigenous people. This meant that BC would – and generally did – claim not to be anti-white. But it excluded whites from membership, and advised those in the white community who rejected apartheid to organise amongst their own. In this atmosphere there was a period when would-be anti-apartheid whites felt themselves excluded from the black liberation struggle, and without a political home – as Barry Gilder and others testify.

Many progressive and radical young whites rejected apartheid; but feeling themselves rejected at home, they left and went into exile. There they made contact for the first time with that older and earlier generation of South Africa's freedom fighters in the exile ranks of the ANC and the SACP. Here they found the acceptance and the comradeship they had been unable to find at home.

BC was an urban movement, based almost entirely among students and the black intelligentsia. From the universities and high schools its ideas of self-pride and self-assertion spread rapidly to the schools, and awakened a generation who were not prepared to remain quiescent as their parents seemed to be. The children's uprising of 1976 was not planned. It simply burst the bonds.

On the morning of 16 June, 1976, several thousand Soweto students began to assemble in a demonstration of protest against the enforced use of Afrikaans as the medium of instruction in schools, and against Bantu Education. Their procession was heading towards the Orlando stadium, when they were confronted by police vans and cars.

A white policeman drew his revolver. Someone shouted, 'Look at him – he's going to shoot at the kids!' A single shot rang out. There was a split second's silence, then pandemonium. Children screamed. More shots were fired. At least four pupils fell, and others ran screaming in all directions.

'For us it was an adventure,' says Mpho Mmutle who was a first-year high school student. 'It was an adventure and we were very happy. Though at some point we suffered quite a lot of casualties, some young children died. But otherwise for me, it was – it was an adventure more than a conscious activity or struggle.'

A black journalist described the events:

I remember looking at the children in their school uniforms and wondering how long they would stand up to the police. Suddenly a small boy dropped to the ground next to me . . . they were shooting into the crowd. More children fell. There seemed to be no plan. The police were merely blasting away . . . Out of the blur of dust and fleeing children, stones began to fly at the police.*

Colonel Johannes Kleingeld claimed responsibility for the first shots, 'in front of and above the crowd', he explained. 'I then started shooting with a Sten gun, because this had a more demoralising effect than a pistol shot. My men also started to fire . . . '

One young student described how the police arrival had been greeted with 'peace' signs and shouts of 'Peace!' As soon as the first shots were fired, the front ranks – mostly young girls – picked up bricks, stones and bottles and pelted the police. Within minutes a well-ordered demonstration had been turned into a riot.

That night Soweto was in flames. In their fury, students set alight all administrative offices, beerhalls and liquor shops. They attacked any building, vehicle or person that they associated with apartheid.

Nobody knows the true number of children who died in the days and weeks that followed. Some quote the figure of 500 killed in the first few days. Allister Sparks, describing how the violence spread to 160 communities, states that within a week 176 people were dead, within a year more than 600; others state that by the end of the year there were 1,000 dead, and 5,000 casualties.

Within a month, a trickle of refugees began to arrive in the neighbouring countries of Botswana, Swaziland and Lesotho. In three months the trickle was a stream; by the end of the year, a flood.

The uprising lasted for seventeen months before it was finally quelled in another wave of repressive action, with the government banning twenty-two Black Consciousness organisations. By the end of 1977 Biko was dead, his movement outlawed, thousands of young activists were in prison and 14,000 people had fled the country into exile abroad.

Allister Sparks,
The Mind of South Africa

Inside the country repression increased as acts of sabotage, first begun in December 1961, became more successful and widespread. Laws permitting detention without trial were a licence to torture. As political trials flooded the courts more and more went to jail.

* Quoted in Alan Brooks and Jeremy Brickhill, *Whirlwind Before the Storm*, IDAF, 1980, p. 9

Some who had served long sentences chose to remain in the country after their release, but many found that harsh bans and restrictions made it impossible for them to do anything at all, even to earn a living, and they chose to go into exile.

The trauma of flight was too often preceded by the trauma of arrest, detention and interrogation with a wide range of mental and physical torture. Most of the detainees – some of whom were kept in jail for years – were never actually charged and put on trial. Some of their stories appear elsewhere in this book. Here are five that are typical of many others.*

THUSO MASHABA
Dakawa 1989

'I felt that those people who leave the country are cowards . . . I was forced to leave. It was not in my plans.'

Like many other young people who left abruptly, he is very emotional about leaving. He speaks softly. Physically and psychologically, he has not recovered from what happened to him.

During our exams in June, when we were about to write our Afrikaans paper, we decided to take to the streets and say that we are not going to write Afrikaans, that we do not recognise it as an official teaching medium.

Mainly it was a peaceful demonstration. We called for peace. Even in our placards it was indicated that we are not fighting, we want peace. But on our way to Orlando, we were intercepted by the police; and they responded violently. They shot at us. One of the first victims in our march was a young boy of thirteen years then, Hector Pietersen.

We also responded to that violence with violence. Very emotionally, we started now burning police vehicles. And that's how the whole thing started.

I was a leader of the school, and even before that I was active in the activities of the BPC. In my school a large number of our senior students then were members of the BPC – and some of our teachers too. I was forced to stay underground. Somebody confessed, a student in our school, not very, very active; he's the one who pointed me out, and they found me sleeping in a house in Alexandra.

* Many exiles have written their own account of their jail experiences. See *Bandiet* by Hugh Lewin (Barrie and Jenkins); *Island in Chains* by Indres Naidoo (Penguin); *The Jail Diary* of Albie Sachs (Harvill Press); *Escape from Pretoria* by Tim Jenkins (Kliptown Books); *Robben Island: Hell Hole* by Moses Dlamini (Spokesman).

They dragged me, beat me up. When I left the house I did not have clothes on, only my underwear; all my clothes were at home. Beat me up, I was bleeding. I also tried to fight back very stubbornly, but they had batons and some electric prods. They handcuffed me, even on my legs. There was a chain with a big round ball which is very heavy – even if you are not handcuffed, you can't run away with that. Inside the car, from Alexandra to John Vorster Square, I was beaten up. There was a dog inside, and the dog was trying to attack me. When I arrived in John Vorster Square, I was unconscious.

In the middle of the night when I woke up I was in an office, sitting there with a lot of white people looking at me, so . . . And then they started asking me questions. They kept on trying to interrogate me.

They beat me up; electrified me in my private parts and so on. It was painful. I would collapse, be unconscious. But really I didn't know . . . I didn't know really; I can't say much about it. There's a chair. You just sit down on the chair, and then you are handcuffed to it, and then on your leg again, you are also handcuffed. And they ask you to talk. I've seen one comrade, she was beaten with a baton on her forehead because she refused to talk. And she died instantly, and she was taken out. I don't know where she came from – we just met there. And they told us that if you don't respond, if you are stubborn, then we are going to do the same to you. We were, of course, very frightened.

That interrogation room it's full of blood, mainly on the wall; and you see that some of the blood, it's still fresh. We could see that somebody has been struck there, with the head hit against the wall. No, but they tell you that your blood will go on to the wall if you continue to be stubborn. But the mistake they did is that they kept us in the same room where they were beating up these people. You are brought in together. You sit together here; and the other one is handcuffed on the chair – we can see her or him. Yes, they want us to watch so that we are frightened.

And all of us we said, 'Whether I talk or not, the same thing is going to happen to me.' So the comrades decided that no, we don't do it. We don't talk. If you are going to talk you must know that you have betrayed all our struggling people in South Africa. And so you take a decision. So we all said, 'We are not going to talk. We know nothing, we know nothing. You can kill me, you can do anything. But I know nothing.'

They took us out, and some of the comrades we never met any more after that – we don't know what happened to them. Then myself, I was taken to Barberton prison after three months.

They just left me alone there. They just bring food; they just come and see me. 'How are you?' 'No, I'm fine.' Sometimes they would tell me, 'Come! Somebody wants to see you.' I would see this one police we used to call Devil Eyes – he was quite notorious in Soweto for shooting students. He came there. He said, 'Are you still maintaining your stand?' I said, 'Yes, I know nothing.' He said, 'Don't be stubborn, because I want to help you.' I said, 'I know nothing, I know nothing.' He came after two weeks again or three – I can't remember – and he asked me the same questions, and he said, 'If you don't want to talk then you'll rot here in prison.'

When they took me, I was only left with my underwear; they gave me khaki trousers and a khaki shirt. I had to wear the same thing, all the time the same thing. Wash them at night, wear them in the day. They never let me out except in the last two weeks in Johannesburg. But in Barberton I think I only went out for exercise once in about four weeks. Altogether I was detained for two and a half years, ja.

From the very beginning my parents did not know where I was. They made a lot of enquiries because the people in Alexandra told them I was picked up by police. They went to John Vorster Square. The police pretended to be checking in their files if I was there, and said: No, he's not in our books. And I remember very well when I came there I was taken to the charge office where my name and my address – all my particulars – were taken by the police.

Then one day I was just told, 'You are going home now!' I was in Pretoria. I didn't have money. I asked for a paper that would show I've just been released from prison, so that I'm not arrested again for not having a pass, and also so that I can board a train free. But they refused me. They just sent me out in the street, sickly as I was.

I was afraid to talk to anybody. So when I saw one old woman – an African – I asked for money. I was very frightened. She asked me, 'Why? Where do you come from?' Then I said, 'You know I'm from prison, I'm a student. I stay in Soweto. I'm just released from prison.' She said, 'OK. Come to my home.' 'No,' I said. 'I want to go home, my parents are there so I don't need anything else. I want to go home.' Then she gave me four Rand. I bought a single ticket to Soweto, I went straight home.

And when I arrived home I found that Mum was sick, she was in hospital. She had a heart problem. I'm the last one of four brothers. And my elder brother – the third one – I found that he was late. I did not know. He was shot in 1978, ja, at a demonstration. It was on a Saturday.

I was ill. I had a spine problem – I think mainly it was the lack of exercise, and because my cell was too small – I couldn't stretch all my body to sleep on the floor. My upper body, from the spine would go up against the wall, and my legs were just enough to stretch that way. It was like a cupboard. I couldn't stand upright. I could stand, but bend my neck a little bit. So I've got this spinal problem – even now I still feel it, but it's not so bad.

The other problem I have, it's my eyesight. I think mainly because of lack of light, never seeing light for quite a long time. My eyesight became poorer and poorer. I suffered from severe night blindness, couldn't see at all at night, and even during the day my eyes got severely strained. So I had to get special glasses and special treatment for my eyes.

I stayed home sick. After four weeks I recovered. I had to contact my colleagues, only to find that some of them had left the country, some of them are late – they were shot; some of them their whereabouts were unknown since they were taken by the police, when they disappeared. I still don't know what happened to them. They might have been killed and no report was given out.

My mother is going to hospital, to Baragwanath, all the time for treatment. My parents did support me very much, very much, advising me to be very careful with my work. But I felt I just can't sit. I was still sick, but I felt I should meet my colleagues and see how far they have gone, what they are doing. Those friends I managed to meet, they told me that they are working on the formation of a Student Congress. But I couldn't go back to school – they wouldn't accept me. So I began to travel to Cape Town, travel to Durban, to Pretoria, meeting students in schools, introducing ourselves, trying to organise ourselves as students.

I left home again, stayed underground until such time that the ANC itself issued out orders, 'No, my friend; it's too bad for you. Come! Come out.' So I was forced to leave.

It was unplanned. It was not in my plan, because at that time I thought that those people who leave the country are cowards – they are running away from the situation and leaving us alone. This is how I felt. I was asking myself all the time, 'Where are those comrades who left in 1962? Why are they not here and come and help us?' And the comrades were saying, 'No, they will come!' I said, 'Let them be here; we want them here – they are trained.' I said, 'I won't go out, I will die here.' So this had been my stand before I was arrested. I said, 'Comrades, go! I'm not going.' Then I was arrested – and now I myself was leaving!

It was not good the way I left. Mummy was sick, very, very sick; she was lying all the time in bed. But I didn't tell her I was going – she told me. Around ten one night she called me. I went to her bedroom. She said, 'My son, I know that one day you will leave me.' I said, 'No Mummy, I won't do that.' She said, 'No, I know one day you will leave me, like so-and-so did, like so-and-so did' – you know, in the township parents know who has left the country. She said, 'I know you will leave me. But please, should it happen that you leave, please go to Lesotho, because I know in Lesotho there is somebody who will take care of you.' My Mum is originally from Lesotho, so she's got her sisters there, she's got her brothers there.

But on the very same day my Mum spoke to me, I went to town to buy some groceries. And when I came back I found my Mum crying, and everything in the house was in a mess, upside down – the cupboards, everything. She said: The police were here, and they were looking for you. It's bad, my son. That's all she said. She was crying, she was beaten up by police. Yes, sick as she was.

Then I had to take a decision immediately. She asked me several times if I love her, if I have that love for her. And I did say yes. I did promise her that I love her . . . I haven't seen her since. I've met some people . . . I heard last time that I was in Lusaka that she was admitted in hospital, and I want to make a follow-up to see if she's OK.

In Lesotho he contacted the ANC. They arranged that he go to school to complete his Form 5 with assistance from the United Nations.

He managed to contact his family and tell them his good school results. Then he left for Tanzania, where he is the Deputy Co-ordinator in Dakawa. He is hoping to obtain a scholarship to study international relations.

I feel sometimes, ai, I've left South Africa. What hounds me is how I left my Mum very sick. And I don't have information about what is happening there. I don't know how I would react if they tell me . . .

My brother died, I was in prison. I wasn't there during the funeral. I'm alone now in exile, no brother and no sister, so I don't know how I will react really. I don't want to hear about this, that she is missing or what . . . It's been very tough of course. It's been very, very tough.

But I'm optimistic about the future. Very confident that we are going home. It might not be next year, but we will ultimately go home – to build that new society.

ZOLEKA DILIMENI
Mazimbu 1989

'I told them I've already told you the truth, so don't know which truth now do you want.'

She is expecting her first baby. A seemingly vulnerable young woman, quiet and gentle, as though she could never have been the twelve-year-old who slept in the forest to escape the police.

Early in the sixties my father was arrested and was sent to Robben Island. He was involved in the ANC activities. And then after they released him in about 1972, he was taken to the bantustan in Ciskei, at the place called Dimbaza. We were also forced to move from Port Elizabeth to join him in Dimbaza – myself, my mother and five boys. And then when we arrived there in Dimbaza, we find that the conditions of the houses they gave, they were so bad that we couldn't stay in those houses because there was no floor. It was just the ground; and the soil was wet because it's a damp place, that one. And there was no ceiling; it was just . . . this asbestos, you see. But it was very cold; and because it was almost winter-time by then, the wall was wet almost all the time.

So my mother told my father that no, it's not possible for me to stay in those conditions. My mother went back to Port Elizabeth and worked. My mother is a domestic worker, so she was sleeping at her work. My father was looking after me and my brothers. He used to get money from, I think, the ANC and other different organisations. Also the Christian Council of Churches was supporting us with school uniforms, books, and paying fees at school.

Mostly Dimbaza was a place where all these people from Robben Island they were dumped in. So mostly we were children of those political prisoners. In 1977, after the death of Steve Biko, we had a meeting with other students discussing about the conditions of Dimbaza, also the conditions of our schools. Because you find that the classrooms had no windows; and most of the time you will find that you are sitting on earth banks, not proper chairs. So we said no, we should demonstrate, and have a thing with those who were in charge in Dimbaza – to talk with them to at least give us chairs and desks in our schools.

So all the students from Lower Primary to Secondary school, we had a demonstration. But it happened that I was regarded as ringleader of this demonstration, although I was too young by then. We destroyed the cars of the government, and the shops. We went even to the factories to take our mothers out of the factories. And then after that, the offices of the government we destroyed them, burning them. All such things.

The police wanted me – many attempts at home. My father used to tell me that the police were here; they want you. I said, 'Why should they want me?' because I was not alone. And by then I never thought that they can arrest a young kid, because then I was only twelve.

There's a forest next to the place where we were living, so we used to go during the night and stay there the whole night. And then in the morning we would come back at our homes, and stay there. Again late in the evenings we go and sleep there. But my father told me that it was so dangerous for a young woman like me to do that thing. So he told me to stay at home, and then he should know where am I.

And then the police came in the evening. They kicked the doors, shouting that we should open. Then my father opened, they all got inside. They started to ask, 'Where is that Zoleka Dilimeni?' Then my father told them, 'It's that one who's sleeping there.' They woke me up with clubs, so . . . the other white man said, 'No, but I don't think this is Zoleka, because this kid is very young to be a ringleader of these things that have happened here.' Then my father said, 'I've got no other daughter except this one. This is the only Zoleka Dilimeni I have here in this house.'

I was pushed inside the van. They took me to the police station in Kingwilliamstown. It was late in the evening. They took me in the cell alone that night, so I stayed there in the cell alone. They didn't give me any blankets or mat so that I should have a place to sleep.

And then the following day they took me to other officers. They asked me some questions; since my father is an ANC member isn't he involved in those activities of ours? So I told them no, it was only students who were involved. There were no parents involved. We just told the parents to go out of the factories, to go to their homes. They said, no, I'm telling lies. I told them, 'No, that is the truth I have.' They said, 'No, you are telling lies.'

So they start beating me. They were wearing this combat uniform. Another white man, a very huge man, just clapped me, clapped me, clapped me; and then I start bleeding with my nose with a clap on the face. After that I was taken to another office. Inside there was guns on the table, and some long sticks. On the wall there were two photos, the photo of Vorster and a photo of Kruger.

They said I should stand in between those photos, so I went and stand there. They said I should tell them the truth otherwise they are going to kill me. But I told them I've already told you the truth, so I don't know which truth now do you want. Two soldiers came next to me wearing these combat uniforms. One was on my left-hand side and another one on my right-hand side. They said I should talk. I asked them what should I talk, or what should I say? They said, all what had happened. So I told. The thing that I know is that we went out of the classes; we were singing songs; we went and destroyed other places. They said, no, it's not enough. I should tell them what they need. I asked them, What do you need from me? They said, Who was involved? Who was telling you to do all such things? I said no one has told us, but the conditions has forced us to do such things. They said, Oh, you are clever, hey? Your father told you not to tell us the truth. Then they started clapping me. One will clap me; when I turn this side, another one will clap me. They were doing like that, both of them. So I started screaming. They said I should not scream, otherwise those guns on the table they are going to use them.

And then they went to the table and took these two sticks, one with one stick, another with one stick. So they beat me with these sticks on the face, so my face got swollen, you see. And I was busy crying. After that there was something like a written thing. They said I should sign there. I said, 'I cannot sign something that I do not know.' And I was crying with all that dirtiness, because I was bleeding and I was swollen. So they said, 'Now we are going to deal with you accordingly. You should sign.' I said, 'No, I'm not going to sign.'

One soldier was angry, saying that I'm very stubborn. Just came to me, starting beating me until I fell. They kicked me. They were white soldiers and there's one black soldier, also used to interpret what is related to me; because by then I used not to know how to speak English. And also not Afrikaans, I used not to know how to speak it.

So I was trying to run away from them. I fell. Another leg went forward and another one backward. So one just came and stamped on my leg, ja. You see.

So seemingly my leg had a crack after that, because he was wearing this soldier boots. After that, they said I should stand up. I couldn't stand up. I was screaming. I was really screaming. It was really painful. So I was taken to the hospital after that.

When I went to the hospital, there used to be a soldier all the time – a police in fact. My father and other fathers in Dimbaza, they tried to argue it out that I should be taken out of the hospital after they have put the cement on my leg. But after they took me out of the hospital, they took me back to the cell. My father used to come and talk with them, and say, 'No, you can't just leave a young kid in jail, and with that cement. Please allow her to go at home. She will come when it's time to go to the court.' Then they said, 'No. We are not going to do that.' They totally refused it. Then I stayed there. I was arrested about at the end of September, and then I was released in November – with that cement. I went back to my mother in Port Elizabeth. December they came back again. I was arrested for the second time, and I was taken back to Kingwilliamstown.

Then they said I've burned somebody's house who used to work for the government – we used to call those people 'sell-outs' at that time. I was not there. I totally refused that I was there. You see, the police they forced other children to say . . . ja, to say that I was there. Then those children in court they told the magistrate that no, we were forced to say that Zoleka was there. But we do not know anything about that thing – because even themselves they were not there. I had a lawyer, and I was found not guilty.

After from there, I was supposed to go back to school. I was told that there's no space for me. In fact there was no school wanted me. So I was taken out of Dimbaza. I went to school in Somerset East.

Mostly, outside urban areas the schools are not good, you see. So the students had demonstrations. So I happened again to be regarded as a leader of those demonstrations, boycotting classes. I was arrested for the third time, in July, 1980.

I was sixteen. Again there we were beaten. I was taken to an old building, and there were only two people. They said, 'Oh, the child is very young! And if you do not tell us the truth, you know you can be killed or people can do something else to you. So you'd better just tell us the truth.' So I said, 'If the truth is what I know, then I will tell you.' Then they said, 'OK, tell us what you know.' I told them that no, we just felt as students that we should boycott classes because of the conditions in our classes; and you know that in our school there is even no tap to get water – there's only a tank. If that tank it's empty, we won't get water – we should go to the village and ask for water. So such things they are really bad. And we have been saying to the principal that they should put taps in our schools, and change at least the conditions of our school.

They said, 'No. It's not enough. Tell us who was telling you to do that.' I said, 'But there's nobody who told us to do that. We just felt because of the conditions that we should do that.' They said, 'No, but we know that the Principal is involved, and the Vice-Principal.' I said, 'No. It's not true that they were involved; in fact we were demanding them to do what we wanted them to do.' They asked, 'What was that?' I said, 'We told them that they should go to the councillors and talk with them, that the conditions of our schools should be changed.' They said, 'But it's not enough; tell us another thing.' I said, 'That is all.'

Then that one white man left. I was left with that black man. That black man told me that – you know what? – if you want me to save you in these conditions, you should fall in love with me. I said, 'How? How can I fall in love with you, whilst I did not even know you? And secondly, you are too old for me to be in love with you. So how can I do that?' He said, 'No, but I want to defend you from this.' I said, 'No, I don't need to be defended, because I felt that what we did it was correct; so why should you defend me from the correct thing?' He said, 'But you know what? We are going to start beating you.' I said, 'OK. If you are prepared to do that, you can do that.'

Then another one who was wearing this soldier uniform came – there were two again with the black man who was there. So this black man came to me, started to beat me. They really beat those two, with that soldier. They were kicking me, using their fists, doing everything. The way they kicked me, I even bleed, ja. I started to menstruate immediately. So after that really I couldn't do anything. I was taken to the hospital. I was given the treatment in the hospital. I was taken back to the cell again.

The following day they called me again. I was just swollen, you know – having blou-oog – you call it, ja, black eye this thing. Again they started to beat me. And after they beat me they take you under a cold shower. Imagine being taken under a cold shower. So after taking me under a cold shower, they are going to take me back to the cell. So they continued.

Of course, there were some others who were also arrested. They did the same even to them. But since myself I was taken as a leader, so they did it worse to me, saying that I should say things that I do not know.

And then the lawyers came – lawyers the Christian Council of Churches got for us. So those lawyers, we told them; and they could see in fact how I was, and I told them that after they kicked me I started to menstruate and it was not my date to menstruate. I was crying when I was telling them. So when we went to court, they asked the magistrate, 'Is this the way that the children should be treated when they are being arrested? Just look that one who's having a black eye, who's swollen with big mouth, all such things.'

The magistrate, he told the lawyers, 'You do not really know if they are being beaten by the police. Maybe they fought in the cell.' He doesn't have any evidence that we were beaten by the police. The lawyers told the magistrate: 'Look and see these kids! If this one can even get a black eye, swollen face and mouth, all such things?' The magistrate said, 'No, they could all beat her, all of them. It's possible.'

We were taken back to the cell again. We stayed there. Then it happened one night there was another girl who was sick. So we were shouting, calling the police that they should run and come, because there's this one who was fainting. When they came, they said we are making noise. They were all having these sjambok [a rhino-hide whip]. They came with those things – whips – those policemen, so they started to beat us. They even beat even that one who was sick, fainting there. We are crying, 'No! But we are calling you because this one is sick!' They didn't . . . they beat us. Even now I still have the mark of that beat.

We were about fifteen females. So after they have beat us, they went to the boys' side. They also beat the boys. So the following day, we told ourselves that we will be on hunger strike. We didn't want food. So we stayed there – stayed without eating. The first day, second day, third day people got . . . others started to faint, others felt weak. So these were taken to the hospital, one by one, every now and then. Until the lawyers came.

We were brought to court, and they said we had destroyed things – beerhalls, all such things. Some of us were sentenced one year, others two years. I was expecting that I would be sentenced maybe years, because 1977 I was given three years' suspension, and it was not yet finished. But fortunately myself, because of the state witnesses each saying things that were different, all of them, so I got free because of that.

I was released. And when I was out, I found that my father was dead. You know when he came back from Robben Island, he came back with some illnesses. He was not really fit. He was there for seven years. So he was always sick, having high blood pressure, all such things.

So I went to bury my father. And it's then that I thought of going to exile, because I was really getting arrested many times and now my father is being dead. So I was thinking, 'Whilst I was arrested my father used to come and see me in jail. Who's going to look after me?' All such things.

So I said I should leave South Africa.

I was taken out of the place by these other fathers who were also from Robben Island. My mother didn't know that I was going. I only told her when I was in Lesotho, because I ran from South Africa to Lesotho. Even now my mother doesn't know where I am.

My father used to tell me that you must know the results of what you are doing. But you know, when you are really there you do not think, oh, what if I am arrested? Seriously, I was even younger, so I never thought of how is jail. I couldn't imagine it. We were angry, and we were enjoying what we were doing. [Laughs]

I think I'm really pleased that I've left South Africa, because by now maybe we will be talking about Zoleka who's already dead or Zoleka who's in jail, if I was still in South Africa. After I was in Lesotho, I came straight here to Tanzania. I've been in SOMAFCO since then. So here in exile I'm really free and relaxed, especially here in Mazimbu. We do not think of the Boers all the time. And secondly, that I've managed to do my O levels. And I think I did it very well, because when I was still at home I used not even to know how to construct a sentence in English.

I think I had the courage from my father not to sign the paper when they were beating me.

VICTOR MATLOU
Lusaka 1990

'I used to write poems . . . and I even started writing a book. But they just destroyed it and put it into the toilet. That's the greatest loss I had in my life.'

He feels acutely the burdens of life in exile. 'We have never accepted it – we are forced into it.' At home, he says, even if you are oppressed there are possibilities of a normal life. Now he is separated from his wife and child. He accepts the necessity of it – 'but in terms of lived minutes, I don't accept it'.

I was detained under Section 6 of the Terrorism Act in 1975, and I stayed there in jail for thirteen months. I was not charged.

They said I was recruiting for the ANC. And they went on to question me. The first thing that they do was what they called softening up. That was just plain assault. And then after that they used the towel – wet towel to strangulate me. And the third one was actually trying to push me through the window – that was the tenth floor; what we call Timol Heights* of John Vorster Square. The fourth one was electric shocks. For the first five months they were constantly taking me out and torturing me. From the cells to the tenth floor; and then to some cell downstairs where they do electric shocks.

The Security are just brutal, they don't use much thinking. But BOSS people used sophisticated methods. Sometimes they don't assault you; they just make you stand at one point and throw questions after questions; and they go in relays of sometimes two hours, three hours, and you are standing there. One group comes, and goes; the other one comes, and asks the same questions a little differently – you know, to catch you

* Ahmed Timol died when he was thrown from the tenth floor during interrogation.

somewhere within the matrix of your answers. And that is more painful than just being assaulted.

I was in solitary confinement mostly all the time during the interrogation period – the first five months. Naked, except that I had my 'onderbroek'. Otherwise I was not allowed to put on any other clothes. First, it's to humiliate you. Secondly it's torture by the temperature, because it's very cold. You had cold floors there, and generally South African prisons are very cold. And if you are naked it's even worse. You are naked to their whims and caprices, you know. And that is part of torture. It's a process of dehumanisation. It is. It is. Because you are not human any longer; you are just like an animal walking around naked.

Sometimes, to keep myself occupied I used to write poems, and memorise them and be able to recite. And sometimes I used to talk to myself. You know, after some time you can manage to get some ballpens from common law prisoners, sometimes even from the SAP because some of them hate the Security because the Security look down upon them. Things like that. And I even started writing a book, using the toilet roll to write on.

I had a mat where I used to put my writing. And they took off the mat and collected spools and spools of my writing. And I felt so bad in fact, I asked them to take it to Security, hoping that one day, whether I'm alive or dead, these things could be published after that. But they just destroyed it there and then, and put it into the toilet. That's the greatest loss that I had in my life.

When Black Consciousness started, I was at a tribal university. Though at the time, I had mixed feelings because I come from a family which – particularly my father – did not accept that concept of the separate tribal colleges. And that was my political upbringing from home. I had left when these universities were supposed to be 'autonomous', but I wanted to take a teacher's diploma, so I went back. In 1974 then I joined BPC.

BC had a great influence on young people of that time, particularly the students. I think it played a very positive role. It did, tremendously. Because at that time the ANC was working underground, and it was so difficult for the ANC to come from the underground to above-board type of politics. So Black Consciousness served as the above-board politics.

When it started, I remember Vorster – he was Minister of Justice at that time – actually welcomed the emergence of the black South African student organisation. In the Afrikaans universities they have this Afrikaans Studentebond, so he saw BC as a Studentebond vir Kaffirs, he thought it went according to the principles of apartheid. But I think he was mistaken because, through that, you had vocal, organised students speaking for themselves. And if you are a student you see the University as part and parcel of the manifestations of apartheid.

We never accepted voluntarily to go to these ethnic universities. We had no choice. In itself, to go into the university that you hate, was a political move. And as you stay there for a whole year, you hate even yourself; you despise yourself for being there, and that teaches you to take up a stand. You reject your own university. So you have this rejectionist philosophy. That's why Black Consciousness was rejectionist in character. You are rejecting everything. Sometimes we even rejected positive positions – for instance the concept of working together with whites was a problem to people who were really bigoted Black Consciousness personalities.

This also affected the attitude towards women. We really wanted women to get into politics. But we rejected everything that was white, European, and so-called 'un-African'; and one of those un-African positions was one-man-one-wife. We tended to espouse going back to the tribe, so-called traditional roots, where it was not a problem to have more than one wife. I think that as far as that is concerned, we were very chauvinistic. It is one of the blemishes of Black Consciousness.

We even adopted an economic policy called Black Communalism – I think the women fell within that. Black Communalism's characteristics are not only that men were the head, but the woman was subservient to the man. And that was accepted in Black Consciousness. It was.

It was necessary to make black people feel themselves as being powerful as individuals. For the first time, people said I AM – a concept that was not there, not prominent, particularly in the late Sixties. But people started saying I AM. And it helped for some time. By 1975 to '76 the trend of I AM was becoming a problem, because then I said I AM – and so what? And so what?

In 1977 I was addressing a meeting at Tembisa. We were trying to start a BPC branch, and we were in a private house. We were about twenty-five young people there. One young guy stood and said, 'No, here you are our leader here. What will happen if the Boers just walked in and arrest you? What can we do? We can't protect you. Do you think we must go on saying: Black is beautiful; black is powerful? Because if they arrest you here, black will be weak. What must we do?' And that I think was the beginning of starting to realise that, apart from saying black is beautiful, you must do something about it. And thus people moved into the underground of the ANC.

Around 1977, the ANC was very, very active within South Africa, and its ideas were coming out. We came to accept that, at one point or another, BC people will have to join either the ANC or the PAC. And the more bigoted ones thought of the PAC; and the people who had some influence from the ANC, even if they were not members, felt they would have to move towards the ANC.

There was a lot of criticism, for instance, on some personalities within the Black Consciousness movement who wanted to practise Black Communalism, who wanted to practise polygamy. There was a congress which was planned for December 1977, that was supposed to solve those

problems, where the Black Consciousness movement could have moved
to what we called the positive aspects – towards the open-minded positions of the ANC. Unfortunately the BC organisations were banned after
Steve Biko's death. And Black Consciousness remains what it is in the
pages of history.

It's unfortunate to some of us that we were banned before we could
realise our goal in December 1977. But the influence of ANC infiltrated
a lot of pamphlets, magazines, though it was not as influential as it is
now. But we got the trend.

But once we left South Africa, outside the sky was the limit! You know,
the first time you get into the ANC house, you find everything that is
banned in South Africa. And we read these books religiously. I am not
reading like that now, but at the time you swallowed everything that you
came across, and that helped. Including discussions, with ANC members
and the international community.

But some of the people that came out during that time had not met the
ANC in South Africa. They had heard of it somewhere, but they didn't
see it. It is not that easy to change positions of that nature. I think even
now we still have problems in terms of male chauvinism, including racial
chauvinism we still have behind our backs. If you prick hard enough, you
see Victor Matlou coming up as a male chauvinist! [Laughs]

After I was released I was supposed to report to John Vorster Square
whenever I left Johannesburg. But what was worse, they would come to
my house every now and then, and harass me. It would seem that they
wanted to arrest me again. So I left – July 1977. I crossed the border . . .
yes, I walked for seven hours in the night to Swaziland.

From Swaziland I went to Maputo and then to Dar es Salaam. I did a
six-month journalist course; then I worked. First I was a radio journalist;
then I became the ANC deputy director of information and publicity, in
charge of what was then called 'internal publicity'. That includes everything that went home. I was in charge of it until 1983. Then I was sent
to Nigeria as the ANC Chief Representative, until last year.

In Nigeria we are only similar in terms of colour. We have quite
different cultural backgrounds, and perspectives. The average person is
a black racist who hates whites. And when you come with the position
of the ANC, it becomes very difficult to explain that a white person can
be your comrade.

Your starting position in Nigeria is . . . it's money. And they don't
understand when you're offered something and you say: Look, I can't
take this. This should be for the ANC. They can't understand that, or
when you tell them that you do not have a salary – things like that. So
it's quite difficult in a sense for the ANC person to work there.

The majority of us were very young when we left home. You were
under the custody of your parents, very very protected, but also fighting
a very vicious regime at the same time. And when you left, the protection

is not there. And you find that you don't always meet an African who understands your situation.

Sometimes they say, 'You people cannot fight.' We fought for over three hundred years. Some countries under colonialism let go in less than ten years. These are the people who say, 'Hey. You people have not fought!' And you think about the wars of resistance that you know went on in South Africa for at least a hundred years, a hundred-and-fifty years, yes! Then you find you react in a manner that can only be described as South African chauvinism.

In exile you are in a community that is not a normal community; but you want to live a normal life. But it's not possible, and you are not equipped to handle situations like that.

You have to accept the separation from families, that as well – as with me and my wife. It's not that she is separated from me because we wanted to get separated, or the movement wants to separate us. You find that this person must do a job there in West Germany, she has to be there, and I have to do something here. I will try now and then to go and see her – like next month I will pass through there. But that's not enough; and we have a small child there. Two days ago they phoned me and she was the one speaking. You know . . . I just felt like I should not be here, that the whole thing was a miserable time. And I said, 'Why am I not there? Why am I not there?'

After some time, intellectually you accept that you must be separated. But in practice you don't accept it. There lies the dilemma. Intellectually I know that she is supposed to be there, I'm here. But in terms of the lived minutes of time, I don't accept it. And that's the dilemma within that type of relationship.

But in terms of the totality of the problems that we have, these difficulties are not central to our struggle. In fact, sometimes they encourage us to move ahead.

JOHN SCHLAPOBERSKY
London 1990

'I think they were trying to play on my instability to get me to kill myself.'

A tall man, his dark hair receding, he is a psychoanalyst who works at the National Foundation for the Care and Treatment of Victims of Torture.

I guess what's remarkable about my detention was that my experience lasted for only two months. I was arrested on Friday 13 June 1969 at Witwatersrand University. I was a student there.

They approached me in a very thoughtful way for what I presume were two reasons: that I had a British passport, and that my uncle was the mayor of Johannesburg – there was the big headline 'Mayor's nephew arrested under Terrorist Act'.

At the time I was arrested, I didn't really know what was going on. I wasn't even a member of NUSAS. In May that year they started arresting black leaders such as Winnie Mandela and Joyce Sikakane. They were out to create some kind of show trial. And subsequently all of them were acquitted, re-arrested and re-prosecuted, and acquitted again. It made it clear that they were beating a virtually non-existent organisation.

So they were hunting.

It was the Sixties, students were full of radical notions. If somebody had shown me how to get involved with the underground, I'm quite sure I would have done so. But in fact nobody had shown me. At Wits, I came across several young people from Alexandra and Soweto with whom I became close friends, mostly because they were, like me, writers. I used to write a lot of poetry.

After the arrest of Winnie Mandela, Joyce Sikakane and a number of others, there was a second wave of arrests which took in my friends; and my arrest came as part of that second wave.

My family lived in Swaziland, but there was a family flat in town which was used sometimes; so at five in the morning, the police went to my mother's flat. Bashed the door in. Nobody was there. That morning I got to the university and while we waited in the lecture hall for the lecturer to come in I was called out by the administrator. I went racing out thinking something had happened to my family – and ran straight into two Security policemen.

The administrator had delivered me into their hands and then scarpered. And these blokes took me out of a back entrance of the building. Nobody knew where I had gone.

They said, we want you to take us to where you live now. Four policemen got out at my place. There was an old shed in the garden at this big old house. At that time we were running a soup kitchen for street urchins, children who sold newspapers at night; and they all lived in this old shed. I shouted out to the children in Zulu, run away kids, these are the police! and the children just scattered. Then they took me inside. And they took the place to pieces.

They loaded my typewriter, a whole lot of books, bits of paper into the one car and me into the other. I remember feeding the dog and giving it some water and closing the door, and that was the end of my life in South Africa.

They took me to Pretoria Local Prison, where I was stripped, searched, and was sent into a cell, naked and the clothes thrown in after me. It was very casual. I got dressed. And then they came back and they took me to Kompol Building, back . . . back, and into a little ante-room, with no

windows. There was a whole gaggle of men, chief amongst them was
Swanepoel, who terrifies just by his appearance. He's in a state of
relentless and perpetual pursuit, of chronic rage. The aggravation is right
there, rumbling, all the time. He's kind of red inside all the time. I said,
'Can I see a lawyer?' They thought this was hilarious.

And then Swanepoel took me by my shoulder into a little room like a
large lavatory. I subsequently learned that this was Paul Kruger's old
safe, the vaults of the Transvaal Republic. It had a safe door. He said,
'Stand against that wall!' Then they all came into the room, yelling at me
in Afrikaans. I replied in English, I said, 'I don't understand Afrikaans',
and they couldn't accept this. Born here, been to school here, university
here – what do you mean you don't understand Afrikaans? And I replied
in English, 'I don't know what you're saying.' And they got angry and
that's when they beat me.

I can't remember how many there were, but they made a lot of noise,
they punched me, they grabbed my beard, they grabbed my hair and they
hurt me. They were determined to make me as frightened as possible. It
went on for thirty or forty minutes. I'd done secondary school Afrikaans
and I knew enough to follow exactly what they were saying. It wasn't a
calculated move. It was just, I will not speak to them in Afrikaans. I was
uncompromising about that, but I didn't realise what advantage it actually gave me. I'd never been with so many Afrikaans people in my life
before; I just knew to fear them and to hate them. They then talked
openly in front of me about the interrogation and I could prepare myself
for what was coming next. I knew what they were looking into and I
could forearm myself.

Swanepoel and his mate started a shift of four hours of interrogation.
They were then replaced by another two who did a shift from midnight
to four in the morning, and then another shift who did from four to
eight. At which point Swanepoel and his mate came back. Three teams
of two, working on a four hour shift.

Swanepoel produced a brick. He put it on the ground very quietly and
said, 'Now you're going to stand on that until you tell us what we want
to know.' And there was enormous relief because at least nobody was
going to beat me up with a brick. So I stood on the brick.

That was Friday evening. I was in that room from Friday evening, five
or six o'clock, until that sort of time on Wednesday. On the Monday
night they gave me a stretcher and I slept in the ante-room, but they
actually managed to keep me awake from Friday evening until Monday
evening. But it was a very strange state of wakefulness, because by
Sunday I was hallucinating and I didn't really know where I was, I didn't
really know who they were. I didn't know the time of day, I didn't know
. . . I didn't have a sense of place. There were periods when I was
convinced I was in a school laboratory, bare desk, bare walls and a
dripping tap behind me. They would throw water at me, to keep me

awake, or they'd tell me to drink, or they'd tell me to wash my face. They would bang a table, they would shout at me, they would keep me talking and they would keep talking in front of me. There was no opportunity to withdraw, to reorganise, to reflect.

I know that the others, my close associates who were under interrogation at that same time, were very viciously assaulted, in all sorts of different ways, compared to which my own physical beating was nothing. But they weren't kept awake for nearly a week. They had two or three days of pounding. The interrogators got whatever they could, and then threw them into a cell somewhere. In my case, it was nearly a week of systematic exploration.

At one point, early on, Swanepoel looked at me and he says, 'So you're an angry one, huh? I like them when they're angry. It's going to be more interesting this way.' He assumed from the outset the kind of paternalistic patriarchal fundamentalist position, a righteous position. I was a wrongdoer. He yelled, he reviled me, he humiliated me, he called me *die klein Joodjie*', the little Jew, like they referred to *die kaffertjies*'.

They said they would prosecute me for every book they had found. That for every time a black person had stayed in my house, I would be in prison for years. They said they would arrest my girlfriend and bring her in. They said they would make my parents prohibited immigrants in South Africa. They . . . just threatened and reviled me.

The Friday night was lucid and combative, really fencing. The same on Saturday on the brick; I think my own sense of fighting them became much less obvious by Saturday night. Sunday, my feet swelled up. They were like balloons really. I was in a lot of pain. By Sunday night they let me take the brick away, so I could stand on the floor. That was a great sense of relief. But one of the interesting things that had happened until then was that every time I got back on the brick, I would say to myself, 'This is my brick and I'm going to climb up on top of it', as if I was doing something heroic.

My girlfriend had come to the house on the Friday evening and, finding the house in total disarray, realised something dreadful had happened. They'd not allowed me to leave a note or a message, nothing. She rang my mother, my mother went to a lawyer, but the police insisted that they hadn't arrested me. My mother and girlfriend did a tour of all the hospitals in Jo'burg on the advice of the police, to see if I was on their casualty lists and also the morgue. I guess when one hears about kidnap squads and death squads and how they operate, this was the beginnings of it. My mother got the British Ambassador up in the middle of the night. He obviously got through to somebody because by Saturday morning Swanepoel had been spoken to. He came in demanding to know how I got a British passport, and he was furious. He brought in a Dr Venter who said, 'I'm just going to take some blood from you' and he pulled out a syringe. I got in a terrible panic. I wouldn't let him come near me. He said, 'I understand you've got infectious hepatitis, we want to take a blood test.' Gave me a very thorough examination and he said, 'No, this hepatitis is long gone.' Then he turned to Swanepoel and said, '*Daar's niks vekeerd, ry hom.*' At which point Swanepoel said, 'Back up on your brick, sonny boy!' That's another moment of terrible rage, medical complicity and collusion in torture. They'd obviously been told by Venter that as long as they kept me well fed, they wouldn't damage me medically. And I think that's why they didn't manhandle me more brutally and that's why they used a psychological approach rather than a physical one.

On the Sunday evening, as I said, my feet swelled up and they let me off the brick. On the Monday, I can remember walking into walls. I would start walking in this tiny room, dashing into the wall and wake up with a terrible fright and hurt my face. And I can remember them . . . little clusters of them standing at the door, looking at me, laughing at my confusion. On the Monday night, not only my feet were swollen but also I was very oedematose in my thighs and when I went to the toilet, I could hardly get my trousers down and I was very frightened to look at the size of my feet.

I think it was Tuesday morning that they woke me. I was more confused than at any other point. I wasn't sure if I was dreaming or awake. Or who Swanepoel was. I couldn't really keep a clear picture in my mind of who was who. They would engage me in discussion, while one was talking to me, the other would be writing down everything I said. It wasn't a matter of making a statement. They made a written record of everything. Question and answer. What was asked of me, how I replied. This pad got longer and longer and longer. I can't really remember what happened on the Tuesday and the Wednesday, because that's when I was slightly crazy. But in the weeks that followed I was able to reconstruct in my mind what I had and hadn't said.

One forms barriers in one's mind; you forget that you know these things in order not to disclose them. And there was a whole range of things which in the weeks afterwards, I agonised over and would think to myself, 'If they come back for me now, would I manage to protect these people, that information?'

I had hidden a pen I picked off their desk and hid it between my legs. So then on the Wednesday evening, towards the end of the day, they put me back in the little car and took me back to the prison and put me back in the cell. And when the door banged again, I can remember crying and crying and crying. I'd been determined not to let them see me vulnerable at any point. But then I just cried, for a long time.

But I got this pen out and I picked off a piece of loo paper and I wrote a letter to my girlfriend. Every day I would take one square of toilet paper and write a diary and then roll it round the pen and hide the pen in my blankets. And I held on to myself and maintained my own sense of resolution and self-discipline.

They would come every morning, take me for a shower. And after some weeks, when I got back to my cell, the loo paper had gone, but the pen was there. And I was lost. That was really a most terrible moment.

They allowed me a razor, but no blade. But the day after they took my diary, when I got to the washroom, there were two razor blades, stuck against the tiles on the wall, over the basin they knew I would be using. I pointed it out to the guard. 'Oh,' he said, 'there's obviously a mistake with somebody here.' And he took the blades and made a big fuss about it all. The next day the same thing. Every morning. As if they were saying, go on, do it, do away with yourself.

But questions were being asked in the House of Commons about British passport holders held in South Africa. There'd been big demos at university about this administrator who'd given me up to the police. They realised that they'd taken me for all they could and got nothing, that I couldn't be prosecuted. I didn't know enough about anybody to be used as a state witness and was actually a huge liability. I think they were trying to play on my instability and get me to kill myself. So from then on, I couldn't sleep, because I would be waiting for them to come in and cut my wrists with the razor blades. I became very acutely anxious and very frightened they would kill me. Six months before there had been a great tumult in the press because a man named James Lenkoe died in detention and they said he had slipped on a bar of soap, bashed his head and died. I was sure this was the very place he had been.

A month later, out of the blue, they called me out for a visit. It was my mother; and I couldn't actually speak. I had become very withdrawn, incoherent, I couldn't express myself and I couldn't relate at all.

They wanted a statement. I was collected from prison and taken to Kompol building and introduced to Coetzee. And he had this ream of paper with everything that I had said during the interrogation and he drew this up into a statement, which I signed. Some days later they said, 'You can sit in that cell and wait there until the trial [of Winnie Mandela and others] is over and that might be a year or two, or we are prepared to take you to the airport and see you out of the country. We want you out of here during the trial.' It was clear that they were worried that I would disclose information that would compromise the trial of the twenty-two.

My brother was at that time a soldier in the Israeli army, so their plan was to put me on an aeroplane to join my brother. Israel would set me straight. I would join the army like him and it would all be short back and sides, just like them. I was given a chance to think about that.

My mother had asked for me to be released to England and Swanepoel had said, 'No, there'll be a reception committee waiting for him and he'll be a hero when he gets to London and we'll have none of that.'

I was taken from Pretoria Local Prison straight to the airport. I was given an hour or so to say goodbye to my family and put on an aeroplane. I had been in Johannesburg on a British passport as a Swaziland resident. And that was a condition of my release from prison, that I agree to voluntary deportation. What I don't think I appreciated was that by agreeing to those terms, I accepted a life of exile. Because five years later when I needed to go back in an emergency, my mother was thought to be dying, I discovered that I had become a prohibited immigrant and I would not be allowed in without a special visa.

In London I furnished Defence and Aid with all the information about my own interrogation. The story was published in the *Observer* shortly before the second trial was quashed, and I guess I put it there to make my own contribution to the release of the people at home.

ELEANOR KASRILS
London 1990

'I put my escape plan into practice.'

> Eleanor at fifty-four is a young-looking, blue-eyed, fair-haired grandmother. Her husband, her daughter and son-in-law are part of the movement that has at last brought the rejection of apartheid, even by those who constructed the system.

My father was born in South Africa, but he went to Scotland to serve an apprenticeship. He met my mother there. They returned to South Africa just before the war when I was six months old. I never knew myself as being Scottish, but always South African. And now there's this anomaly: I've got a British passport, and it says 'Born in Scotland'. But in fact I am South African.

My parents were anti-fascist, and interested in mixing with people of different races. Their politics changed later. I think they became scared when the Nationalists came to power. They became involved in business – my mother had to consider things like government contracts. So when I became politically involved, she became very hostile.

It was post-Sharpeville. Durban was a stronghold of the Liberal Party, and most of my friends were Liberals. I attended things like the Film Circle; and that's where I met Ronnie.

I joined the Congress of Democrats. We had a small group in Durban. At the time I met Ronnie I was divorced. I had a daughter, Brigid, and I was living with her in our own little flat. Eventually Ronnie moved in with me for a brief period before he went underground. And I got more and more involved. With MK activities as well. It became very dangerous – obviously – which led to the present situation of exile! [Laughs]

They began arresting people. I came to Johannesburg to get money for Durban, because we'd become a bit cut off. We had no funds, and people were underground, in hiding. I came back to Durban with this very large sum of money, went straight to hand the money over, and went home to hear that the police had been in contact with my parents about a property they had at the Kloof; and the police wanted to know who the people were who were staying there.

That was one of our main bases for hiding people. So that threw me into a complete panic. I volunteered to go to warn them because I knew that I was going to be arrested anyway; I mean, I absolutely knew it! So I went to warn the people who were staying there.

I got there about four hours before the police. In that house had been Ibrahim and Ronnie and Bruno Mtolo – they were an underground unit. Bruno Mtolo had been picked up, and blown the whistle. So that night it was only Ronnie and Ibrahim. Ibrahim went one way; and Ronnie went the other. And Ibrahim got picked up, and Ronnie wasn't. It was just one of those flukes.

I went into hiding. But it soon became very clear that I served no useful purpose underground; in fact I would be more of a burden on the people in Durban. So I decided to go back to work and carry on my life as normal.

I was arrested at work by the Special Branch, who told me that they were merely taking me in for questioning. I would be held for a day, and then released provided I satisfied their enquiries. Well, what happened from then on was a very different story. It was very clear that they didn't have any real knowledge of what I'd been involved in, but they wanted to find Ronnie. And they knew that I had been in contact with him. And they seemed to think that I knew where he was. Which I did. Although there was nothing on this earth that would have made me reveal where he was.

They took me that night to Durban Central Prison. They were showing me that they were very reasonable. It was a very simple thing they wanted from me. I had got involved with the wrong people; they knew I was from a very nice family [Laughs] and that I needed to get rid of this Jewish person who was influencing my life. The strong anti-semitism in my interrogations, which became quite obscene at times, upset me. They concentrated on the fact that Ronnie was Jewish, and the fact that I was separated from Brigid, and that they could provide Brigid with a decent home that she could be proud of – not living with a terrible person like me. Those were the two things that really upset me during the time that I was at their mercy. Which wasn't for very long. Because I immediately refused to eat anything. I refused to co-operate.

I was being held in a prison, but the prison authorities resented the way the Special Branch used the prison. They also didn't like the fact that I wasn't eating and that I was very unwell; and they refused to lock my cell door and said that I could come out and see them if I needed anything. I remained in that prison about a week to ten days – I can't remember now. During that period I didn't eat.

I was looking for an opportunity to escape. I was absolutely determined to escape because, during the interrogations, I realised that while they knew certain things, other things they didn't know. And I felt that I should get out and warn people, and tell them what I knew from the interrogations. It made me absolutely determined to get out. You start thinking – well, there is all that money that I brought down from Johannesburg, maybe someone can give one of these warders some of it and get me out. You know, you think all sorts of things. But I knew it was hopeless.

They brought the prison medical officer, then the prison doctor, and eventually a psychiatrist to interview me. Let's say I exploited the situation. I found I could cry very easily. I just had to think of Brigid and I burst into tears and wept, yes. I'm not a sort of weepy person at all, but I knew that I had to get out of that prison and I was determined to. The psychiatrist recommended that I be moved to a hospital immediately. I thought they would move me to the prison hospital; but in fact they didn't. They moved me to Fort Napier Mental Hospital in 'Maritzburg. Into the most insane ward.

There were seventy-four patients there, and I was in a lock-up cell, a sort of padded cell. They were all patients who were beyond all hope. The only people who had any life were the alcoholics, and there were about five or six of them. And they were wonderful. We used to sit on the lawn every day, drinking cups of tea. They gave me the newspapers – which they weren't allowed to, and they had a radio, which I wasn't supposed to listen to. I had quite an incredible experience in that hospital.

But during all this time, I had kept some extra clothes. As detainees, we could wear our own clothes. And I hid them under the mattress, and no one ever saw me wearing this particular dress. By very difficult means, I managed to communicate with the outside, with my comrades. I sent a letter out which eventually reached Johannesburg. They thought that I was trying to tell them that I'd written the letter under pressure because I misspelt the word Lieutenant, so they ignored that first letter, which was terrible – I was so upset when I heard.

Then I wrote a second letter, asking permission to escape, because we had all been told – I'm sure you remember this – that we had to sit out the first ninety days, and that we weren't under any circumstances to do any deals with the police, or come to any arrangements for exit permits or anything like that. So I felt that there was no way I could escape without permission! [Laughs]

That was taking it a bit far, I suppose. But you were so isolated – you were so totally isolated, you worked through things that you thought were logical.

I hadn't had any psychological examination or consultations, because the only person that the police agreed could see me was the most senior person at that hospital and he was involved in a murder trial in Durban, and was not available. I met him once, only once. The railway police came to interrogate me about some sabotage on one of the railway lines.

We sat with these railway police in his office, and he said, 'Right. Well, I'll just leave you now.' And I said to him, 'These men are monsters. Stay here with me. You're a doctor.' But he said, 'No. It's quite all right. I've given them permission to talk to you.' But I hung on to his arm and his coat. He got terribly embarrassed and eventually they just gave up and left. So that was the only contact I had with him.

Anyway, after about five weeks, perhaps a little longer, the Sister came, and said, 'The Special Branch are coming to take you back to Durban.' So I said, 'Oh yes. When?' She said, 'Well, it's either tomorrow or Friday.' So I thought well, that's it! I'm not going back.

It wasn't an easy place to escape from; I was actually watched most of the time. I put my escape plan into practice. And . . . one minute I was inside that place, and the next minute I was outside.

I had assistance. From inside, ja. I had had a bit of time to make contacts and I also stole from the alcoholics. I stole a basket and money just to get me into town. And then I walked into 'Maritzburg. There were only a few Indian shops open. It was very early in the morning – changeover time from the night staff at the hospital to the day staff. So I walked into a shop and asked if I could use the telephone, and the person in the shop said yes. I only had a note, I said I had no change, but he let me use the phone. And I phoned one of our people who was absolutely horrified!

I said, 'Hello. It's me, and I'm out. Come and get me quickly!' Because I was in such a state I gave him the wrong street. He jumped into his car in his dressing-gown and slippers, drove into 'Maritzburg. Couldn't find me in the street I said I was in, and then had to patrol up and down. But already the police were out looking for me, and the hospital ambulance was out. So I kept hiding in the shop, fingering plastic raincoats and things, until he found me. I lay on the floor of his car, and he drove me to his house.

The local people decided they had to get me out as quickly as possible. They made completely wrong decisions. They decided to disguise me as a man, and they went out and bought me clothes, cut off all my hair, dyed it. They hired a car, and drove me into the countryside to a contact that I had – who I don't think was terribly pleased to see me. And I lived on a farm for about three weeks.

This is an area I don't really want to talk about very much. I'm changing it slightly. I asked this person to take me to Johannesburg which he did, about three or four weeks after I escaped. I had expected my photograph to be in the papers; but they hadn't put it in the paper because they didn't want to say that a detainee had escaped from a mental hospital – I never thought of that at the time. He managed to get me clothes from a person who must have been about four foot eight, [laughs] yes. My hair had grown a little, and he got me a doek to cover my head; and he drove me to Johannesburg, and dropped me in Hillbrow and just left me there, I didn't want him to know where I was going.

I went into a milk bar. I was so excited! [Laughs] I telephoned another contact who got absolutely horrified and said, 'Get off the streets immediately! Take a bus to this suburb, this number bus, and get off at such and such a stop. And go into the house opposite the bus stop and wait there until I come from work.' I did all this. I went to this huge house – I don't know Johannesburg at all; and I sat on the steps of this house out of sight of the gate. It became apparent to me that there was somebody in that house. The curtains were drawn; but it was very strange. I became very suspicious, and I walked round the house. Then I called out, 'Is there anybody there?'

And there was Ronnie! In hiding! [Laughs] And we hadn't seen each other since about June. He came out, and he said, 'Well, it's wonderful to see you. But I've got bad news for you. I'm leaving the country tonight!' [Laughs]

But in fact he was delayed. We were put in a flat together for a couple of weeks. Comrades were trailing that road to the Botswana border, checking roadblocks, and waiting for the opportunity. And we left the country together. The person who drove us to the border was Babla Saloojee, with a couple of other people. They were all Indian, so therefore we had to be disguised as Indians.

I wore sunglasses to hide my blue eyes. The sunglasses had a big crack in them; and also, we left at about two in the morning! [Laughs] They brought Nescafé which they mixed with Panflick, put that on my face; and every time I smiled I got white cracks round my eyes. And being very nervous and tense, I kept laughing all the time. I had a Punjabi dress with glitter all over it, and white nylons which I understood one of my male comrades had worn for the same purpose. And the same wig – a black one. Make-up! I had make-up on my hands and I was wearing a blue cardigan to cover my arms. I had a bag of clothes with me, because they wanted their disguises back immediately I got out of the car.

We had been told that there would be a car waiting for us on the border. Anyway, we drove. We broke down twice on the way to the border, which made us even more tense and nervous. We changed cars, I think at Mafeking. Anyway we got to the border, and stopped in the middle of an African village early in the morning. We got out, looking like something out of a fancy dress party – all dyed, plastered with make-up. And I ripped the wig off my head, pulled my clothes off in front of all this village of people, jumped into whatever clothes I had.

They said, 'We've got to go! We've got to go! Look!' We looked back, and on the road was a dust trail coming. They said, 'Go quickly! Lie down behind the rocks!' The people in the village seemed to be milling about, not paying very much attention to us. So we lay down. Our car drove off. And sure enough, the car that came racing past about a minute and a half later was one of these wire-mesh police cars, with a huge aerial; which we heard later chased them for ten miles and stopped them.

And then we got up and went, crossed over the ladders of the border – you know those high fences? There are ladders all along the border. We just said good morning to everybody in the village, and climbed over and walked. And sure enough, like magic, as we walked up this hill, the Land Rover drove up and stopped. And we drove to Lobatsi.

We stayed in the black township in Lobatsi. And then it became too difficult for them, and they took us out rolled in blankets. We registered in one of the hotels. I was very ill, and we stayed in our room playing cards while we applied for political asylum, and while arrangements were made to get us out to Tanzania.

So that's really how we got out, and we stayed in Dar for two years. I worked there in the ANC office. Ronnie went away for a year. We got married in Dar, had our wedding reception in Mendi's flat – he was ANC Chief Rep in Dar; and I then became pregnant.

But I was seriously ill. I had malaria, malnutrition and anaemia. So the hospital recommended that I should be moved to Britain. I was on special diets and things. It was all arranged by the ANC. They moved me. I was taken care of. I came to Britain, and Ronnie followed on a few months later.

Andrew was born in London. We camped on couches for about four or five months, and eventually, in the January we found a place to live. And we've lived there ever since. For twenty-five years.

For the first seven years, I was at home looking after the two boys. Then once Christopher went to school I did a course in geology which gave me some skills; and since then I've worked as a technician with the local authority.

Ronnie left London for Angola in 1977. In fact he's not lived at home since 1977. It was extremely difficult in the early years. The boys were – I think – eleven and thirteen when he left. I think it destabilised them quite a lot, because they were very close to Ronnie. He used to take them to football every weekend. And that just ended, abruptly. So I think it was quite a traumatic thing for them. And I don't think we really appreciated at the time how extensive it would be, the stress created by this separation.

Andrew had a difficult adolescence. He became very wild and unmanageable, and we had all the difficult things that parents face, but I had to deal with it myself. At times I felt very depressed and frustrated at having to go through all this on my own.

Exile has not been easy for me. When I left South Africa I had to leave Brigid behind. And I never saw her from when she was seven until she was seventeen, because my ex-husband would not allow her to leave

South Africa. He had guardianship, and my parents colluded a bit with that, so I had a very unhappy period in my life where I had no access to Brigid. I did communicate with her. But with young people, things like letters and the discipline of writing letters . . . I mean, I'm very bad myself; and she was guided by my mother who in fact used to censor my letters. And if my mother thought the letter was unsuitable, she didn't give it to her. I know that this happened on a number of occasions.

When Brigid was seventeen, she was told that if she got a first class matric, as a reward she would be given a ticket to come to London to visit me. And she came. We had a holiday together and it was very nice; it was very strange; it was very difficult. I didn't even know what she looked like. I had a very bad relationship with my parents at this time. I totally blamed them for the whole situation, because they could have influenced my ex-husband. And so I had no photographs of Brigid. The only photographs I did have was when she was young; and they were too upsetting for me. I asked Ronnie to put them away – I didn't even know where they were, because I found it too heartbreaking to even look at them.

So when she did come, I didn't even know what she looked like. I remember rushing up to the wrong person at Heathrow, and it wasn't her. And then I realised she was with my mother and I knew my mother! [Laughs] But it was dreadful. When I did see her, I got such a shock! I didn't know that she had braces on her teeth! And there was this smiling face, just a mass of silver! [Laughs] So all these things, you know, are really very upsetting.

I think she related very well to me and she related very well to Ronnie. And she related very well to the boys. We went for a lovely skiing holiday in Austria. And then I said to her: the important thing is to go back and go to university and complete her studies; she had given a promise to her father that she would go back. So she went back.

She had told me that she was involved with somebody at that time – that was Garth. I don't know whether the visit unsettled her, but she never settled down at Cape Town University. She became quite seriously ill and when she was convalescing she had terrible rows with my parents and with her father. I came back from a summer holiday in Cornwall and found a telegram in the hall saying that Brigid would be arriving in Britain, and it was over to me now to look after her. And so that's how she came to Britain.

I think our relationship has had a lot of difficulties because . . . well, ten years is a long time; but I really don't want to talk about that. But we are very close, very close.

Britain politically is actually quite an easy place to live in if you've got a job and a home. And although one does put roots down here, I've never regarded myself as British, I've always regarded myself as South African, and remain close and involved with the movement.

When I wrote to my mother the other day, I said: You know, I've been totally thrown by the fact that there's a group of exiles here, and we've all been together for something like twenty-five years. We're a very close-knit group in some ways. And suddenly it's all over and we're all going to be dispersed! And there are people who are really important to me, close comrades; and suddenly they're going to be . . . one's going to Johannesburg; one's going somewhere else; and I just feel very disturbed by the fact that I might not see some of these people again. I hope that we do keep in touch. We'll probably have something dreadful like reunions! [Laughs]

I don't feel it's been a waste. It would be terrible to review your life as a waste. I feel it was a commitment I made. Ronnie didn't just go. We discussed it fairly extensively, and we knew that he was making a commitment, and that I was making a commitment agreeing to him going. They've all been political decisions that we've taken. And although it's been hard – and very hard at times – I don't feel it was the wrong decision. For him it was the right decision at the time. It's been extremely difficult at times to just keep it going, and it's still happening now – the stress and the difficulties and the separation within the family.

PART TWO

Living on the Frontiers

The Road to Education

The Mazimbu Pioneers

The students who fled the country spilled over the frontiers, crossed borders at night, 'footing' illegally into the countries bordering South Africa. They did not know where they were going. All they wanted to do was to get a gun, learn how to use it, and go back across the border to liberate their country. For some it was exciting, an adventure, particularly for those who left in groups. For others it was a desperate, terrifying plunge into the unknown.

These were not people fleeing in families from war or famine, but young people who had never before been separated from their families. They were refugees too young to be independent in countries too poor to care for them. They entered countries that lacked facilities for their own people, some already straining to host refugees from other places.

Both the African National Congress and the Pan Africanist Congress now had missions outside South Africa; there was the United Nations Refugee Fund. Those students who sought out the ANC became the responsibility of that organisation. They were told, 'You can choose between two roads. You can choose education or the army – to go to school or to join Umkhonto we Sizwe.' Some were determined to finish their education. But most wanted to join the army. Many of them had to be dissuaded because they were too young. It was thought better that they finish their education first, and then their chance might come again.

The Solomon Mahlangu Freedom College – SOMAFCO – is the high school established by the ANC at Mazimbu in Tanzania in the years following the student uprising. The original intention was to build a school for the students, with the necessary support structures: hostels for the students, housing for teachers and administration and other workers. Within a short time Mazimbu developed into a complex, with nursery and primary schools, workshops and small industries, a farm and a horticultural centre. The Tanzanian Government granted the ANC a second site at Dakawa, which was developed as a vocational and reorientation centre to absorb the increasing number of people – adults as well as children – forced to leave South Africa. It also received those who were compelled to leave Mozambique after the Nkomati Accord.

'Mazimbu' became a generic term that is used loosely in ANC circles to refer to the whole Mazimbu-Dakawa complex, or to Mazimbu alone, or to SOMAFCO.

OSWALD DENNIS
Dakawa 1989

'I tried very much not to integrate. Because I knew that if I did it's going to be very difficult to uproot and go back.'

Everyone calls him Ossie. He is in his sixties. He was working as a civil engineer in what was then the German Democratic Republic when he received a call from the ANC. They wanted him to come and build a school at a place called Mazimbu.

I was born in Umtata in Transkei. After completing my Standard 5, I worked as a bricklayer apprentice for five years. It wasn't an official apprenticeship because at that time Coloureds were not even allowed to become apprentices.

I met up with a contractor who was doing a lot of work around the Transkei, and I started working for him. I worked myself up to become his general foreman. After the Nats had won the election in 1948, they were bringing down to Natal a lot of the Boer families from the Transvaal and the Orange Free State, ja – poor whites to work on the railways. This contractor was employed to build their houses. So I shifted back with him to 'Maritzburg. I was just a normal coloured artisan, working and earning a relatively good wage compared to some of the Africans, but certainly not as much as the whites were earning.

In Pietermaritzburg my boss started tendering for work also for government, but a foreman had to be a white man. And this started creating conflicts, because they were bringing one white man after another – and I was usually much better than them. So while I was doing the work, he was sitting in the office getting all the money. There was a lot of work in Swaziland at that stage, so I gave this job up and migrated to Swaziland.

Things were very much better. I worked myself up to rank of general foreman in Swaziland on a housing project. I also started meeting South African refugees there – ANC refugees. I was married at that time – my wife came and joined me, and our house became an open house for ANC people coming to Swaziland. Then in 1960, during the South African State of Emergency, ja, a lot of people came. And I really became involved. I became a member of the ANC in 1962.

Then the Swazis took away my work permit. People felt that because of my involvement with the trade unions and also with exiles in Swaziland, it might be dangerous for me to go back home. Perhaps I should go on a trade union course, and then be infiltrated back inside South Africa. So I was sent to the Trade Union College in Berlin, GDR. The course was one and a half years, yes. After that, the ANC representative informed us that the relationship between the ANC and the Tanzanian Government was not good, and we were advised to stay in Germany.

I had no idea whatsoever that I would be away for so long – it had been intended that as soon as I completed the trade union course I would make my way back to Africa; and from there, since I was not well known, a way would be found to send me back inside the country. But the situation deteriorated. It became more difficult to send people back.

I was in communication with my family in the beginning. In fact there had been a plan to get Emily and the children out of the country to join me in the GDR. That failed. And then Emily moved from where she was to somewhere else, and our method of communication broke down for a number of reasons. And it was not re-established for a long time. It was only re-established I think in 1978, ja.

I lived thirteen years in the GDR. I liked it. I had to work very hard because I had left school in Standard 5. I still wanted to work as a bricklayer, but the GDR people thought it would be better if I learnt something more but related to building. So I was taken into an office to learn draughting. I learned on the job. And while I worked, I was doing adult education that brought me up to a level to enter technical college. In technical college I did a three-year diploma in civil engineering, yes. So I got well educated in the GDR.

In the town where I was there was only one South African; and about twenty kilometres away there was another. Our other comrades were in Leipzig and Berlin, three hundred kilometres away. It was very lonely sometimes, very lonely. I tried very much not to integrate, ja, because I knew that if I integrate it's going to be very difficult to uproot and go back. And I wanted to go back. I wanted to go back, ja.

After completing civil engineering I worked for five years as a site engineer. We specialised in building schools. And I got decorated twice with a medal for my work. So I did quite well there.

In 1977 I had a call to come immediately to Berlin. Mendi Msimang was our representative there. He informed me that, since 1976, hundreds of South African children had been leaving home, and many had been sent to Nigeria, Sierra Leone and other places. Things were not working out well. So the ANC urgently needed to start building a school for these children. I should come to Tanzania as soon as possible.

I packed up and left. I landed in Dar es Salaam in July 1977. I still did not know where Emily was, and she did not know whether I was still in the GDR.

It was very frustrating. I was told to wait for Thomas Nkobi, the ANC treasurer, to come, and he would take me out to Mazimbu. It was one week; it was the second week; it was the third week. It went on for almost eight weeks, ja. I then got fed up. I said, 'No, I'm not waiting for Thomas.' I packed my stuff, and I came through to Morogoro.

A group of comrades were building a piggery about ten kilometres from town. So I joined them, building the piggery and waiting for Thomas. Thomas still didn't come. After we had got to know each other, we decided that we are trekking to Mazimbu. At Mazimbu we moved into the old house we called Congo. And when Thomas came that November he found us living there.

Mazimbu used to be an old sisal estate. But it had been abandoned – there was no more sisal there. Everything was dilapidated, overgrown. It was just bush, the road leading here was just a track, with some sort of a wooden bridge over the river. There was nothing! These old houses – the windows and doors, even the ceilings and fittings had been taken out.

There were eight of us. The only tools we had were a hammer, a saw, a hoe and a few nails. We brought some empty bags to cover the window and door openings, and a bucket and disinfectant. The first task was to nail up window and door gaps, and to haul water from the river and scrub floors. We lived this way for six months. During these months we completed the renovations for a students' residence. We made cement blocks near the river, we knocked down some walls, installed window and door frames and ceilings, and dug a pit latrine.

We slept on stretchers – there were no tables, no chairs. We didn't even have money at that time – we had to get all our money from the Treasury in Morogoro. Then slowly, slowly, our Treasurer General started buying a chair here and a table there. [Laughs] And I became friendly with the former manager of the sisal estate who was still living there; and he gave over to us some office furniture, tables and things.

When the first students arrived they had nothing. Nothing. All they came with was their stretchers and their blankets and their pots and braziers, ja. Everybody was cooking with braziers – there was no electricity, nothing. At that stage the students who were post-matric were teaching the others. Qualified teachers only began to come later on.

The ANC never gave me a brief of what type of a school they wanted. They just said, 'Build a school!' I kept on asking, 'What type of a school? Must it be a boarding-school?' They say, 'Yes, the children must have place to sleep.' 'Classrooms?' 'Yes.'

So I had to sit down with whatever people there were, to try and work out something. And then I was introduced to a Danish architect working as a site supervisor at the Lutheran Seminary outside Morogoro. His name was Lars. I brought him out here and showed him the site, and he was already bitten by the bug; and he [laughs] ja, he thought it was a wonderful idea and a big challenge.

So we used to sit down and plan and sketch and sketch, and walk around and walk around until eventually we chose this site for the school buildings, ja – that was in the beginning of 1978. And by the middle of 1978 I started getting telexes from headquarters, full force: 'When are you throwing the first foundation?'

The funds started coming round about the middle of 1978 – and not from the ANC! We got the first funds from the Dutch – they were then donating 500,000 guilders a year towards the building of the school. And then came a million. It carried on increasing like that – and then the Norwegians later. And we didn't even have a banking account!

With a lot of hard work, we were able to throw the first foundation on 8 January 1979. At that time there must have been about eighty students, girls and boys. The boys came out first while the girls were staying in Morogoro. We fought very hard to get the girls here, but the ANC, being what it is, were very reluctant: 'You can't send girls out into the bush. What is going to happen?' And so on. [Laughs] So we had to fight and say, 'No. They belong here, not in town – these girls are wasted in town. They should come and assist here.' And eventually they were brought out here in late 1978.

8 January 1979! This was really a very big occasion – one of the best days for voluntary work ever held here. Virtually every ANC member in East Africa participated. Morale was very high. Members of the Central Committee of the CCM (the Tanzanian National Movement) were there as guests – but they ended up also working and assisting us. We all did labouring work. Ja, we had dug the foundations for the first block of Unit 1; and that day most of the people – the healthy and strong people – poured concrete, while the rest were digging the trenches for the next block – dormitories. Other people were cleaning the surroundings. It was really a fantastic day, a very inspiring day, ja!

Eventually, an administration was created and a director appointed, so life became more organised. In a way, being more organised also created a bigger bureaucracy, which somehow stifled the initiative of people, especially the students. The students had been very motivated. I remember a time when we did not have enough trucks and we did not have money to hire more. But we needed cement, so trucks had to be off-loaded and turned around without delay – we couldn't keep workers waiting. So we had an arrangement with the students that whenever a truck came after working hours, the students would off-load them. Sometimes the truck would arrive at night, nine o'clock, ten o'clock, loaded with cement. We would go up to the classrooms and ask for volunteers, and the whole school would come out, singing and toi-toi-ing. In half an hour the truck is off-loaded, and they're singing and toi-toi-ing back to the classrooms.

Those days are past now. It is more of a traditional school now. Perhaps that's got its advantages. But it has also got its disadvantages.

Now we are building five villages at Dakawa. And we are offering technical training in four skills – carpentry, bricklaying, electrical installation and plumbing. We have a textile print workshop; we have a field crop section; husbandry – mainly dairy cows; we are working on a poultry unit and a big horticulture section.

During the first ANC National Educational Conference that we held here, Comrade Tim came from Swaziland, and I found out that my family was still in South Africa – I had lost all contact with them. He promised to try and trace where my family were. He did that, and he wrote me a letter to say that they had been traced.

So I wrote a letter and made direct contact now with the wife and the children. Well, [laughs] I told her I was still alive, and hoped that they were still alive, and that I hear that the children are grown. I was very surprised. I got a letter with pictures of the children. And of my daughter's twenty-first birthday. Ai! When I left home she was ... I think she was seven years old, and the younger son was only two-and-a-half years old. He's a big man now.

So in 1981 we made arrangements that I should go down to Swaziland and meet them there – they would come from South Africa. So my family joined me in 1981.

I was very fortunate, because when children are away from their parents for so long it takes a long time for them to get to know each other again. But it was not the case with any of my children, because Emily had kept my image so clear that when I met them it was just like I'd been away for a week or so. Ja, ja.

Well, exile life is not easy. I never dreamed I would be away from South Africa for so long – it must be twenty-five years now. I remember in the Sixties discussing, and saying: No. By the beginning of the Seventies we'll be back home – it can't last so long. Well the Seventies came and went. And we said, 'Well, the Eighties.' But it does look more hopeful now, ja.

BABU (DENNIS SEPTEMBER)
Mazimbu 1989

'I've been footloose ever since I left South Africa ... Now I'm part of Mazimbu.'

His grey hair is tied back in a pigtail. He could be an Indian from the Canadian reservation where he once taught. He is the principal of the Mazimbu Primary School who, more than anyone else, has held the hopelessly over-crowded and under-staffed school together. He loves the children, and they feel it. They wander freely in and out of his house and its garden filled with flowering bushes.

My mother's mother was a Mozambican, and her father was a British soldier who had come to South Africa to fight for the British in the Anglo-Boer war. And the offspring of that first mixture is very interesting, there were very dark ones and very fair ones. My mother happened to be the fair one of the lot. But because of the hair texture it wasn't possible for her to cross over the colour line.

My father's grandfather was French from the time of the Huguenots. My own father came from a very large family, seventeen – the Septembers are very widely scattered in the towns and fruit-growing regions of the Western Cape.

I am midway in the colour. There are three brothers who are fairer than I, and two who are darker. All my sisters are fairer, although only one crossed over the colour line into the whites. We lost track of her. She just disappeared from home overnight. That's always been very hard for me to accept – that I had to lose members of my family in that manner.

I had been harassed by the police since 1951. Now that was the time that all those vicious laws were enacted. And the one that we in the Cape worked on particularly was the Population Registration Act that compiled a race register for the whole population.

A lot of people left the country at this time. We said to them, 'Where they ask for race on the form, you put "Human". And that's it! And you don't explain anything. You just say that is what you are, and that is how it's going to be.'

Well, the people were asked who had told them all these things and they said it was the little teacher, September. So they came to visit me. And I just stood firm, trying to convince them that that was the only answer. The result was that I was never ever counted in that registration, and was never issued with that coloured card which people had to get.

It was very difficult for me, from then onwards, to do anything which required the assistance of the government. My son, who was born in 1956, the youngest boy, he was never ever registered because I didn't exist as far as they were concerned. [Laughs]

Around that time I became involved in very small things in Athlone, like the incident of a little boy being knocked down by a bus, and I called the ambulance. When the ambulance did arrive it was a 'Whites Only' ambulance which wouldn't pick the boy up. And I argued the point with this man, and I was taken to jail. It was from then onwards that I really made up my mind that I'm going to leave this country, one way or another.

There was a shortage of teachers all over the world. I applied for posts all over, in Rio, in Australia, I could choose wherever I wanted to go. So I left and went to Canada. My family joined me a year later. I taught from 1960 to 1967, and by that time I had a passport as a Canadian citizen.

But there was an urge always to find roots, because there were really no roots for me in Canada. So I decided to come back to Africa. I took work with the volunteer organisation called Canadian University Service

Overseas (CUSO). I was really coming for two reasons – to find out what was happening; and to see what I could do. CUSO gave me the opportunity to move across borders, and I got to know ANC well at a time when they were extremely hard pressed. I was a courier on many occasions.

I came to Zambia as a teacher in 1967 and taught for a short while. Then CUSO asked me to take charge of their programme in Zambia. I became Education Adviser to CUSO in East-Central Africa, and I went on safari very very extensively, covering Uganda, Kenya, Tanzania, Zambia, Malawi and Botswana. I did that for three years.

After five years in Africa my wife Hazel wanted to go back to Canada because the children were there. We went to the far north in Canada, and lived on a godforsaken little place called Cross Lake for three years – an Indian reservation. Canadian version of a bantustan. The only thing is that they seem to accept their fate, although there are moves now among young people.

The situation on the reservation is extremely depressing, virtually ninety-nine per cent unemployment; the people live on federal welfare. They are entirely dependent on the little work that there is from the Hudson Bay Company. You also have a system of migrant labour, whereby the Indian young men leave the reservation and go to the big cities to seek employment.

But a large number of them do not fit in there. They become the lowest of the low. Native Indians are lowest on the totem pole in Canada. First the whites, then the Asians from Asia, then the blacks from Africa, then the blacks from North America. And below them all is the Indian. They do not find any kind of family and social life in the cities; they are always in trouble with the law. As late as the Fifties, just before my arrival in Canada, the Indian people carried passes to leave their reservations. It was not very much different from South Africa.

On the reservations there is nothing for the people to do. They stand around the Hudson Bay Store waiting for the welfare cheque, and spend most of it on liquor. And for the next three or four weeks they are drunk most of the time.

The suicide rate was exceptionally high. The school drop-out rate perhaps higher than I have met anywhere.

I spent three years in Cross Lake, hoping that I could make some kind of impact. I had hopes of doing something through education, but after three years Hazel couldn't stand it any longer. She said, 'You are bashing your head against a brick wall; we just have to get out.' I stayed there too long. There was nothing really that I could do. Then I came back to Winnipeg.

Babu was approached by Indians in a reservation in Saskatchewan to help them launch an education project of their own, but he fell foul of the Indian Affairs Department. He went to work for the school board in Winnipeg. When the ANC unit there received a circular in 1979 asking members whether they would volunteer to teach at Mazimbu, Babu and his wife volunteered. It was 1981.

I came to teach at the secondary school. At the early stage there were no plans for a primary school. That school started accidentally only when certain comrades who came here saw young kids just playing around. So the idea of a primary school began.

But we had difficulties. There were children of thirteen, fourteen, fifteen, who couldn't read or write. We never had enough qualified teachers. The ANC had the idea that only South Africans could teach our children in exile – I don't agree with that. Afterwards they had to agree to teachers from other countries, and now volunteer teachers come for two years.

When I came here, the fifty kids were still in these old houses together with the nursery school. And by the time they decided to build a primary school there were about a hundred and fifty. But when they completed the building where we are now – that was in '85 – there were two hundred and eighty children and the school was already full. Now we have over four hundred, and more all the time!

I've been footloose ever since I left South Africa. I think that's the reason I've been all over the place, and this is the nearest I've ever come to settling down. Now I'm part of Mazimbu. Whatever has gone wrong, our problems, our mistakes – basically I remain optimistic.

JANE DUMASI
Dakawa 1989

'In my mind I said, "My own children and the children of the ANC, as long as I live they should not live the life I experienced." '

Softly-spoken, self-effacing, she is a gentle and loving woman in her forties, deeply concerned about the needs of the children in her care.

I was involved in the 1976 uprisings. That very day I was going to work at a job in Roodepoort. My friend and myself we were going towards a bus stop. These hippos came. So unfortunately they mistook us for leaders of the students in Roodepoort, and then we were chased. We had to climb fences and go from yard to yard, and then we escaped.

Unfortunately my stepfather is a policeman also, so he was visited by those police – and I was not on good terms with my stepfather. So I just had to escape without saying anything.

I stayed underground, just with friends; and sometimes sleeping in the open air – it was just a month before I got married. My parents were not involved. My mother is somewhere else, where I don't know and we were staying with this stepfather who was brutal. So the church prepared the marriage, and then we got married in 1976.

Just a year after, my first daughter was ten months, I was just living like a trapped bird – police this side, hunger and everything. I wasn't a leader; I wasn't anything, though practically I suffered all the experiences the students and all the children were suffering. I just had to leave, leaving my husband behind.

I just said I was visiting friends in Botswana. You know, it's not very easy, but I had to leave. I didn't want to leave my child. I didn't know exactly where I was going. But I said to myself: Whether it is in the bush, under a tree or in the mountains, I will live or die with my child. And I knew that somehow I would get to the ANC, and if I get to the ANC and I get a chance, when my child grows a bit older, then I want to get to go to MK.

I went to Botswana and after a while I got to the ANC Office, and that was nice. They bought us everything because we had nothing – the clothes that we came in and that's all. It was just fortunate that I had a lot of milk and my child just breastfed throughout. Otherwise we had no food, so the office in Botswana had to buy everything. And then we were sent over to where the other comrades from the ANC were staying.

My mother also suffered – she had to leave me when I was ten days old. I didn't know the reasons, but as now I'm a mother, I know. I think she had no way of keeping me, you see, because she had no job; she had no home; she had no husband. So my grandmother took me – throughout my life I've known my grandmother and myself. I didn't know my mother for a very long time, until 1962 when she appeared with this stepfather and she called us to stay with this stepfather and herself. She thought, now she's got a family.

But it didn't take six months – the family was broken and she disappeared again because of this man. She disappeared, and we started our life. Mostly it was not a life – it was just a life of sleeping under verandahs, stone verandahs. In the morning we play on the ash heaps – you know the ash heaps at home called 'emathikithwane'? That is where our playgrounds were. And then we got our food from the garbage bins in the markets.

So in my mind I said, 'My own children and the children of the ANC, as long as I live they should not live the life I experienced.'

So in May 1980, we were sent by the ANC to Tanzania, where I stayed with the other young ladies who had small children – in the first Charlotte Maxeke Creche. And that is where I started getting the idea of starting a nursery school for ANC children, so that all the other children – whether inside or outside home – should not grow as I grew. Not in ignorance, without you name it – not the same as I.

At Morogoro where we were staying, there was a garage, and that garage was renovated very nicely, and then everything was organised. And then I got one teacher, Fike from Holland, who assisted us, one from Denmark, and then other comrades from the Charlottes. Comrade Dennis organised everything for us. Even clothing – the uniforms were sewn by Emily Dennis. So we started to take care of the children. And we started the nursery school on a very good foundation because everything was there.

The ANC was very co-operative. Even now I haven't found any problem in my work, because whatever we need for the children the ANC says children are the first preference. So since I've been in the ANC, I've enjoyed working with children.

Before they built the main nursery school at Mazimbu, they renovated an old building and we moved there until the new buildings were ready. We started with eighteen children in 1980; then when we moved to the renovated building there were thirty-six; and then the number grew. We now have thirty-six per unit – and there are about three or four units in Mazimbu.

In 1983/84 I went to school to take the Pre-school Teacher Trainers' Course in Ndola in Zambia, and then 1985 I went back to Mazimbu. Then I was asked if I would come to Dakawa. I am happy here, although there are problems. But I feel that the problems are just growing problems, everyday growing problems, which are necessary to give our cadres experience for the present, and for the future of our country.

My experience of exile has been a good one. If it was not for the ANC it would have been traumatic. I had the experience of seeing refugees in Botswana – those who had come from non-aligned countries without an organisation. It was not a good experience. I think what I needed at home I found in the ANC. So you see, for me being in the ANC it's being at home. And when the ANC goes home, I'll go home with them. I will!

I would like to tell you about my experiences of exiled children – of those children who have been dramatically separated from parents at a young age. It is very difficult for them to adjust to exile life. They are too young. They are still dependent on their parents. So to be just isolated from their families is very traumatic. That is why we have so many problems with our children.

When they come here, there are buildings, there's food, there's clothing. But there's no family. They don't have that family experience. There are no mother substitutes or father substitutes in our day care centre and nursery schools.

We don't have experienced, trained people, who could play this part of being a mother substitute or a father substitute, you see. Our people are afraid of taking this course, because of their hang-ups from home – that people who are taking care of children are nannies! Because this is what is happening to our mothers and our sisters, at home – they are nannies of the whites, yes. So they have an attitude towards this course. People should know that this is also a course for a professional, just like other courses. It is necessary in this movement because we have now so many children.

Our children have been arrested, detained and brutally tortured. The children need psychologists, they need doctors, they need people who have been specially trained to be mothers, they need special teachers. So if the organisation and the international community can assist us to get those people we need so much – because we have hundreds and hundreds and hundreds of those children who have gone through those tortures – those children can be helped to live a normal life.

The problem won't go away when apartheid is changed. It will take many years to change that base, you know, so we really need many, many people who are going to concentrate on children. Especially in our case, because those children have been forced to lead a life of a grown-up person at an age of seven or eight. They are forced to fend for themselves at a very early age.

They are very restless. They are tense. You know, when you hold a child the child is so . . . how do you put it? It's like stone, because the child is all knotted up. And sometimes, when you approach that child for the first time it is very difficult for that child to accept you – he imagines you as one of those adults who are going to hurt him. Other children have nightmares; other children just become very, very unruly or rebellious towards all adults, because adults they come across as very brutal to them. Other children have a tendency to become very cruel. We have cases where a child feels very satisfied to see another child crying, or to see blood coming from another child. So those are tendencies which are dangerous and which have to be curbed. And we cannot curb them now because we have none of the professionals.

We have three or four groups of children. The first are those children who have run away on their own. The second are children who came out with one parent. Then there are children who came with their parents – those ones are very few. And then there are others born in exile.

Some of our parents leave their children while they go for training or to school, because they have to get skills and get professions. So those children have to be left at day care centres – usually at the age of two, ja. Two years! The pressure is so much on people to get some education that they are thinking, 'Now if independence comes and I don't have a certificate, what will happen to me?' The situation now demands that our comrades go for training.

This is my personal feeling – if we don't get some help I don't know what is going to happen with those children, or with the many more who are still coming.

DUNCAN MANZINI
Dakawa 1989

'I was there, I saw it myself, all that happened. I was not told, I saw it personally with my own naked eyes.'

> He is in charge of the cobbler's shop at Dakawa, where they make and repair shoes, and also produce leather goods such as travel bags. He speaks little English, and we speak through an interpreter. He says he does not learn from books; what he knows is in his blood, he grew up with it.

I had no education. I started working on the farm when I was about fourteen years and worked for four years. I was working under a farmer called Danie Steyn. I used to look after the sheep of that farmer, and cattle – I used to milk the cattle. I left the place, I went to another place, I worked there for two years. Then the other one he demanded me back, so I went back there again to Danie Steyn and I worked for three years.

The political life I was taught by my father. He told me about the ANC – I did not know it before. This stayed in my mind. My father was a migrant worker, and he used to tell us about everything that was going on about the ANC where he was working.

I worked in this farm place for a long time, until my younger brother grew up. Then I was relieved – he took my place at the farm. Then I requested for a letter from that white farmer, to release me to go and work in Johannesburg. He refused. I stayed there, but I realised that it was useless because the money was so little – I used to get 15 cents per day working with an uncle, building houses for the whites.

This younger brother to my father he's the one who taught me to be a shoemaker, to make shoes, even also to be a builder, bricklaying. I worked with him for three years. Then at last I was relieved – my younger brother took my place so that I could go and look for a job again, and rest for a while from that. I never got a chance of going to school. I then went to Germiston.

I went to the Pass Office looking for a job. Then there in the Pass Office they told me to produce my pass. I showed them. Then they told me that I don't have permission to come from Amersfoort. I told them that the farmer who I was working under, Steyn, he refused to give me permit. Then they refused – they said they cannot give me a permit to work in Germiston.

So I left the place, I went to the farms, and I worked in a dairy. I was milking cows. I worked there for two years before the dairyman could fix a pass for me. Then he took my pass and he fixed it. I worked there for six years further than that.

It's then that I really got what my father used to tell me about the ANC. Because there in that farm, in that dairy, they used to talk about the ANC a lot – the political life. When I took my day off, I used to go to a township, Dugatole. That's where there were men sitting, discussing about the ANC, where I used to sit and listen. And sometimes I contributed my views.

When I left that dairy, I started working in a firm called Power Steel Construction. Eh, I worked for a long time, about fifteen years – I left that place around 1959. Then I started working as a shoemaker working for myself, as a shoemaker for a long time. That's where I really realised that politics was inseparable from my life, because during this time – all my life that time – I used to try to find a job. Finding a job sometimes I would get arrested, because they would tell me that my pass, dom pass, is not signed because these people I used to work for they didn't fix my pass properly.

1960 – that's when I joined the ANC. That's where I realised that politics was very important in my life, and our people as a whole; that it was necessary that we produce together and we share together, and not just to be producing for other people. That as we Africans were poor, it was better if we produce and share as family of the whole nation.

That's where I understood that it was important and very good that, as we are workers, we should work and satisfy all people who are living in South Africa, black and white. That's where I realised that those who are already at the upper stage of the ladder, he could help and assist the one who is at the lower-most rung to come to the normal level in the society.

When South Africa was declared a Republic in 1960, there was this strike which was called by the ANC, saying that people should just sit, boycott. And there was a response. Then Verwoerd said to Luthuli: If you say you want freedom, you will never get it peaceful. We got this South Africa through arms. We spilt our blood. That's what Verwoerd said. He said: You will never get it just without blood.

Then all the people, I mean who were normal people in South Africa at that time, they raised and opened their eyes. They realised that there's something wrong here. We realised that our feelings of not liking war and that we should love one another and help one another and live in peace, it was being threatened. Ai. We realised that there was no love in that government which was ruling at the time. He does not rule the country with love, with peace, with patience, but he rules the country with a whip all the time. We lived and worked under that whip all the time. As far as I'm concerned, it was those words that Verwoerd uttered – when he said they got that land through armed struggle – that means even ourselves – people of South Africa – we will only get it back with violence.

Then we formed Umkhonto. I was there when Umkhonto was formed, when Mandela was arrested. It was really a tragedy but . . . well I stayed. I didn't leave the country. I stayed, though others ran away.

In 1976 I was in Soweto that day when this uprising started. I was there! I saw it myself, amongst those children who took part, who were protesting. I saw it personally with my own naked eyes. I realised that now these people are really fighting against us, it's better if I should also join my comrades outside. I saw it exactly when children – in front of me – children dying in front of me. Seeing dead bodies in the street. One of the police shot his son, his own son, the police. Many dead bodies, children. I saw it with my own eyes, because I was there that place.

I don't know even myself how I survived. I saw the need that I should get out of the country and get arms and get ready. Because I realised that we protested peacefully, but we are answered violently, with arms.

In 1960 I went on a visit to Swaziland, I find comrades there. They said, 'You should go to Lusaka.' I said, 'No, I'm still going back to South Africa.' And I went back. But it was now my conviction that the only thing that we can do is to go out and get arms, and overthrow the dictatorial regime which is ruling our country with blood.

At the time he left the country he was married and had three children. He has not been in touch with them since. 'It's tough, it's hard. But when conditions don't allow, you have no choice.'

When I left South Africa, I went to Swaziland and then from there to Maputo. I saw a new life in Maputo, where people were having a different life from the one I was coming from. I stayed there in Maputo for some time, then I went to Angola for military training. Then they wanted me back in Maputo to come and do some work. I continued in Maputo, until Nkomati. Then we came here to Tanzania. We stayed well. We were working, we were happy. There was no government amongst us who could raise the whip and whip anybody. We were working. And that's where we realised that we should work with love and patience and full of initiatives, working for a new South Africa.

Here we are one – black and white. We are working. We are working happily. If even at home the Boers they did the same thing, recognise one another – black and white and whatever colour might be – as normal human beings, it was going to be very good. I'm saying this because all nations they have one and the same blood. Among the cattle there's a black, brown, whatever, they'll never discriminate one another to say, 'This is a black cow. This is a white cow' – like that. They live together! [Laughs]

In Tanzania, I went to stay and work in Dakawa. It was a naked place, a totally bush place, where there were no houses, no tents, whatever. Just a forest. Then that very same day, we started putting up our tents. It was raining terribly. We were sleeping on water, literally on water! [Laughs] OK?

The first work I had to do here was to start a tailoring and shoemaker. There was a small room where we used to have a store. I shifted it, put everything in a corner, then I had a little corner myself where I was able to work. I realised that when the children came from home, their clothes were torn and shoes were already gone bad. So I saw a need that I should start doing this because I'm able to do it. I worked there until the beginning of 1985. I used to teach others.

Then we were called to sew school uniforms for SOMAFCO. We sewed that and finished it. Then they requested me to head the cobblery. I worked there for a long time. I tried means and ways of getting material. I went to Dar es Salaam factories, glue factory. I got the skins of cattle that we slaughtered here. Then we wrote a requisition to Lusaka and machines arrived from Finland. And the Finnish people, who sent us those machines, are the ones who even built the factory.

They sent us three teachers – one teacher is for the cobblery, the other one for the garment factory and the third person is a mechanic to look after the machines, yes. They are trying to show a lot that we did not know. They are sharing their experience with us. The job is going on well and normally – I would say almost perfect, although we have a shortage of manpower.

For the future I wish that all the children, they should learn, not only academic but even the work, the handwork for their future. I see that as something that would be marvellous for us, if that could happen. We teach them all skilled work, handwork, academic, science and everything that a normal human being can do on this earth. That is my wish which I really cry. And I feel that, if that thing it happens, all the time my heart will be at peace.

Even here, I feel that I'm contributing, because here outside South Africa I'm the father of all the children outside. They should see what I'm doing, because I myself I'm following those people who are leading me and my people generally – copying good examples from them. It's about the future.

I have nothing else to say, except I wish the children should open their eyes and ears and see what it's happening not only here, but the world over. Because now the dawn is approached. It's beginning to be brighter now about home. Soon something will happen!

People of Mazimbu

Many exiles came to Mazimbu. Most of them were students, for whom the school, SOMAFCO, was built in the first place. Others came as teachers, as administrators, and as workers on the farm and in the small industries.

Some students stayed on when they had finished high school, working in the various departments of what grew to be a large complex. Others scattered through a dozen different countries in Western and Eastern Europe, in Africa, in North America. They studied wherever they could obtain scholarships or sponsors, mastering difficult languages, learning different social attitudes. Many of their stories appear in other sections of this book.

I interviewed many of the students and teachers at Mazimbu and Dakawa. Their stories were remarkably the same. They described how they were drawn into school protests and youth activities, followed by arrests and detention, often by mental and physical torture, always by beatings and cruelty; and then, after that, of being debarred from going back to school, of constant harassment, living in hiding away from home, being on the run from the relentless persecution of the police, and finally deciding to go into exile. Like the exiles in the Angola camps, they deserve a book to themselves. It was only possible to include a few of these interviews, to indicate the varied backgrounds and experience of the people of Mazimbu.

MEISIE MARTINS
Mazimbu 1989

'Oh, I'm having home disease.'

> She looks far too young to have six children. She works in the
> Mazimbu Clinic as a medical assistant.

I was fourteen years old when I got pregnant. We couldn't get married until when I was eighteen years. By that time I had already four kids, because he used not to believe in contraceptives. He didn't want I must take them. Since I was still young, my mother took the kids; she brought them up.

In 1976 – that was when I had my third-born – when the June uprising started, I also took part together with my schoolmates. We were together in the demonstrations. I was scared to inform my parents that I also took part there, because there is an incident whereby I nearly got injured – I was nearly shot.

We were demonstrating; and we were attacking a shop when we looked back and we saw that the hippos were coming, and they were coming right up to us. I ran into a house. There was an old lady, she was doing some sewing on a machine. I simply ran into her house, and I ran into the room and hid under the bed. She started shouting at me, 'What do you think you are doing? What are you doing there? Come out!' And I said, 'Just look out of the window', and she looked. And these hippos were passing, and they were chasing the children and picking them up. And the soldiers came to her house. She said, 'I don't have any kids here. I'm sewing and I'm all alone.'

I then peeped at them through the window and this is what I saw. One girl – she had twins – a girl I knew, she had twin babies. I saw them shoot at her. She just floated up like this [lifting up both arms] and then she fell down; she was in pieces, in pieces. It was before my eyes. It was very sad. She left these two little babies. Somebody had to go and tell her parents.

And then on 30 June 1976 my mother passed away. She had a heart attack. I couldn't understand what happened to my mother – her death, you see, because she was very healthy; not ill, nothing. It just happened suddenly. She passed away. Then I stayed home until December 1976 – I had to look after the children. At the same time, I never knew that I can fall pregnant again while I was still breastfeeding.

When my mother died I was scared, because many of my friends they were already arrested. And I was scared also to inform my husband because he was not political. We had friends in Mozambique – we used to spend our December holidays there – so I decided to tell my husband that I want to go and visit in Mozambique for a while; I was under a bit of stress.

Then I went in December to Mozambique. That was 1976. I was about five months pregnant with my fourth child. I left with my children with the car. I had learned to drive when I was at home, although I didn't have any licence. Then I just decided suddenly that I like the place, I would like to stay there. I phoned my husband. And I told him that, no, I was thinking of just staying for some time. He said, 'OK, if you like to stay there there's no problem. But I haven't plans of leaving South Africa.' He had a hairdresser shop in Jeppe Street. He said, 'You know Meisie, it's going to be a long process to close up the shop and just to move suddenly like that. You can stay there, I'll be coming and visiting you, OK?' He used to come and visit me every weekend.

Just before being delivered I went back home again with all my kids, three of them. When the baby was three months old, I returned to Mozambique; and by that time, I told my friends to look for a house for me, and I decided to stay there.

I did not really think what it meant, having four children by the time I was eighteen. I was feeling OK. He was giving me really tender care. And before I went to stay in Mozambique, he was also helping me with the kids. We shared the work. And he had this hair salon. Before my mother died – she really brought up my first and my second-born – she said to me she is still young and she wanted the children. And she used to say, 'These kids are your brothers and sisters because you are so young.' In fact the children used to call me Sister Meisie, and they used to call their grandmother Mother. Only afterwards, when we came here to Mazimbu, did they start to call me Mother.

I started changing in 1977 when I went to live in Mozambique. I felt: my mother has died, and there is no one left who can help me. And the other thing which made me want to leave the country was the demonstrations. I was scared that if my husband should discover that I was taking part in the demonstrations, there would be a problem. But by the time my fourth child was born, I decided to use contraceptives without his knowledge.

In Mozambique I met my uncle, who had been on Robben Island. And I met many South Africans, they told me about ANC. Then I joined the ANC and I started working together with them, attending meetings; at the same time schooling, because I had interest in secretary work.

In 1979 we were moved from Maputo. I came here to Mazimbu; and then it's where I started to have interest in medicine field. I went to the OAU school in Morogoro, I learned my nursing there, for three years, from 1980 up to 1983. My children were in the Charlottes.

When I finished with my nursing, I made an application that I want to go and learn midwifery and childcare. I went to the GDR. We were about ten students from the ANC and ten from SWAPO; the Minister of Health in the GDR decided that the whole group should do one course, which is medical assistant's, which is above nursing and midwifery and child-care. I studied there from 1984 until 1989, where I also included a specialisation of surgery. Then I returned back again here in Mazimbu, and I found my kids. They were very big, grown-up.

During my stay at school in Europe, all the kids used to write to me they wanted to know about their father. Then I replied to them that I think this thing need a proper explanation when I come back.

So when I came back here, I called them, sitted down with them. Then I told them – related the whole story what happened, and since their father is not a politician, he is a businessman at home, I left him to live in Mozambique. After a while he stopped to visit me in Mozambique. When I was in Mozambique he used to send me money, yes; food, everything, clothes, what I will need for the kids, yes; I even had my own car. Later I just heard from my friends; they told me that, no, he came once – that was 1980 – and he was looking for me. They told him that I went to school. Then he said, 'Oh well', and went back to South Africa. I think they related to him that I am a member of ANC, so he decided to go back at home, and he got married to another woman.

But I don't feel any regret about him, not at all. Moreover I have learned many things from the ANC. When I was still at home I couldn't understand how people were living. The only thing – I was still young – it was only that infection of demonstrating, 1976 when schoolchildren were shot at and so on. But now, since I joined the ANC it's where I got a clear picture about what we are fighting for at home.

In the GDR in 1984 it happened I was having a new boyfriend. We were in love and we made an application of marriage to the ANC. We got the reply from the headquarters in Lusaka that we can get married. And then we got a baby girl.

He is studying medicine. He started last year. This is his second year. We were studying together the medical assistant course. When I returned back to Africa, he continued. I couldn't continue due to the problem of the child, since they don't allow us to get any kids during studying. So I had to come back.

So I've got six children now. They are all here at Mazimbu, studying.

When I was two years, my mother and my father parted so I was brought up by my stepfather. My real father got married to another woman. So my half-sister came into exile, and she never knew she had a sister. Neither of us knew. When she came here people asked her, 'Ah, your name is Martins. Are you related – there's another Martins here?' And she said, 'No.'

I was at that time in the GDR. Then she met my kids and she wrote me a letter and introduced herself. When I came back we met and I said, 'Is this your exile surname or is it your surname from home?' And she said, 'It is my surname from home.' I said, 'It is also my surname from home.' She told me her father is a boxer. And my father was also a boxer. And then I asked her about her mum, and she told me her father and her mother had separated because her father used to beat her, he had a very short temper. And that was why my mother separated from him, he used to beat her as well.

So after that we realised that we are sisters and we were very excited. I even felt cold – I didn't know what to say. My sister had left in 1985. She was in a group that was caught up in the school struggles of that time.

I don't regret leaving South Africa. Because if at all I was still at home, maybe I couldn't have the degrees which I am having now; and also the experience of life that I've gained here in exile, compared to at home. Moreover my former husband, he never bothered himself that I should use contraceptives; every time I was getting a child. Maybe at this present moment I should be having ten kids, I don't know! [Laughs]

He never liked that I must go and work; I should just stay at home and look after the kids. But since I came here in exile, I decided on my own that I want to learn. Moreover this pain it was still there, because I wanted to know what was the cause of my mother's death. And when time goes on, I had to understand that a shock can happen to anybody. Maybe my mother was very worried about me, or something like that, since I'm the only child.

I am also feeling that my children, they should learn hard and get a proper education, proper qualifications. I asked them what should they like to be. One said he wants to be a pilot, one wants to be a doctor, one wants to be a lawyer. So I hope that in future it will be possible for them to achieve these ambitions.

My husband knows my background. I told him and he never regretted to get married to a woman who is having five kids. Also we are the same age – I'm thirty-one, he is also thirty-one. And he loves me, I also love him. I think in future we will go back in South Africa, being a good family. And as doctors we will help our country.

Life here in Mazimbu, it's very difficult. But I think since I arrived here, I got used to being with my people. Even when I was in Europe, I used to say, 'Oh! I'm having home disease' – and I meant Mazimbu. I still have that picture of South Africa, but I was thinking about the people which I stay with here, people who are taking care of my kids.

It's difficult really to stay without a family, and to bring up the kids alone. But the ANC, I took it as my mother and my father; they brought up my kids, and they also brought up myself, because when I came I was still young. I grew up with my kids. While they are studying I am also studying. And now I've got some qualifications, they are also big. So I don't really regret.

JABULILE MAPHISA
Mazimbu 1989

'Never, never play with politics . . . You will never, never, never beat the Boers.'

> She ran away from home after hitting her stepfather with a chair. She never knew her real father. From this background she emerged with a single purpose – to get an education.

I was born out of wedlock. When I was one year old my mother left to look for work in Johannesburg as a domestic worker, and then I remained with my grandparents. When they passed away – I think I was three years old – that's when my mother came to collect me and my brother; and she took us along to Johannesburg. I stayed with an aunt until I was six years. Then my mother rented a room in Soweto; she bought a sewing-machine and she was working at home to make a living.

I don't know my father. We were called by my mother's surname, Kunene. I was twelve years old when she met somebody who decided to marry her. She was by herself – well, occasionally we would see somebody who we used to call Uncle. We never asked many questions. And then she told us that now she was getting married, and that she was now getting us a home. This man had two children – his wife had passed away.

Life was OK in the beginning. My mother had money. But as time went by, this man started drinking. I think this happened when my mother was having the second child with this man – twins. I remember very well when she was being beaten when she was seven months pregnant. I remember running away to my aunt, to tell her that he was beating up the mother.

We could tell that life wasn't OK now in the house. But it went on and on and on until my brother passed away. He was stabbed. It was

Christmas Day. I must say that he had started drinking; and then he was stabbed during this fight in the township. And when my mother came back from work, I told her. We went to look for him, only to find that he had been rushed to Baragwanath Hospital. But when we saw the sheet that he was wrapped with we gave up, because it was just full of blood. The wound was right in the heart.

Now I left that house after I hit my father with the chair. I remember, it was one of these quarrels between my mother and my father where I couldn't help it, but had to . . . there was a small chair in the kitchen. So when this man started fighting, I just hit him with it. And that's how I left the house.

I stayed with my aunt. Then there came June 16; I wasn't active in politics then, but we were told we shouldn't go to school. We should protest against Bantu education. I didn't join the march, but in class we were singing revolutionary songs. But still in my mind I was there only because everybody was there. And I was listening, and I liked the songs. And that was it.

All I wanted myself was to go and further my studies. My mother had very little education. So she would always tell me that I must get education – that I mustn't be like her. And I must never have a child before I get married – to suffer like her. So these things were always ringing in my mind. I never troubled my mother, I must say, about having boyfriends and all that. No. Until this incident happened, where I had to hit this man, run away, stay with my aunt, until my mother made arrangements that I should go and stay with an uncle in Swaziland, and at least finish high school. So I left for Swaziland. I was seventeen. That's the last time when I lived with my mother.

While I was at school in Swaziland, several times I skipped to visit my mother. I used to cross the border without a passport. Ja. I was already used to that fence! The last time I saw my mother was in 1980, because after the exam I skipped again to Johannesburg. She was working as a domestic worker, so I would sleep there with her in the room, avoid policemen because I don't have a pass. So I just used to sneak, hide – that was my life. And then I had to go back to Swaziland to check the exam results. That is the last time I saw her.

Paswana was my teacher in economics, commerce and accounts. And I was his best student – I got a prize for being the best student. He was very concerned about my future. He would always tell me that I must go and study in the States. He got his Master's there, in Colorado.

But I did not have a sponsor. So finally he said, 'There's only one organisation that can help you to have an education, a home, everything. It's a very good organisation.' So I said, 'Oh, I would love that!' [Laughs]

Then he took me to Ba'Maseko, who told me that this organisation is the African National Congress. Then I . . . it dawned to me. I knew all about Bo'Mandela, all this group that was arrested. You see, I knew there was such a thing as an ANC, but something far away, because my mother didn't want politics; so she had an influence. She would tell me, 'Never, never involve yourself in these things. Where is Mandela today? Where is Govan Mbeki?' She would call them, 'Where are all these people today? So you must never, never talk about these things.' [Laughs] 'Look at what happened to Uncle! He had to run away, go to Swaziland. So just stay away. Get yourself educated. Then you see when you come back, you get a job. Never, never play with politics!' Ja, she would be shocked.

I remember very well the Silverton siege, when there were three or two MK combatants who were shot at the bank, Volkskas. When we saw it in the paper, my mother said, 'You see! You see, my child? You see what's happening now to these people who leave the country to go and train? They will never, never, never do this thing – beat the Boers.' That was her thing: that the Boers are strong, they are powerful. 'Now you go, you think with that little . . . with those two guns they could do something.' [Laughs] So that was my mother. She didn't want anything to do with politics.

Anyway, I made up my mind that, no, I will . . . I'm going! I had no way. I only regretted later that if I had known how it was like, I would have even brought my younger sisters. Ja. I didn't know where I was going, so I sent a telegram to my mother. I just said I am going to school, to a place which is far away – I wrote it in Zulu – and she should come and see me before I leave. I wanted her to come so that I explain that this is the position I am taking. But unfortunately she was working for a Boer who was very strict; that man didn't want to release her during that weekend. And I had to leave . . . without seeing her.

So I left. And I'm told she came the following week, to discover that I had gone. And she was told that the person who had helped me to leave was Paswana the teacher; and she went and said to the police, 'He must tell me where my daughter is!' So I'm told there was a big problem there after I had left, because my mother was crying, 'This man must be arrested.' He must tell her where is the daughter, where is the daughter? You see, another thing – she was relying on me; I was now the eldest in the family. She had hoped that at least, after finishing Form 5, I'll go back home, maybe get some job, and help her.

This was the last time I heard of her. I've never heard of her since then, never. My uncle in Swaziland, they tried. Her elder brother died. When there was his funeral, they made an announcement through Radio Bantu that she must come. But she was nowhere to be seen. So that's the last time I heard of her.

I told Tim Maseko that I was ready to leave, and once again I skipped across the border. We arrived at night at the Mozambique border – I was with others – at Namaacha. We were collected there and taken to a house in Matola. I found people sleeping on the mattresses, with those – you know, at home there's these very cheap blankets used by very poor people – grey blankets. So I said, 'Ah, so this is the life here?' Eh, I got scared I must say. I was told to open my suitcase. They checked the suitcase, they checked, they checked; they didn't find anything. Then they gave me a new name – Togo Mayema. I said, 'Fine, I'm Togo Mayema.'

I was the only woman around seemingly; I was shown a bed, but I couldn't sleep – I was scared. Now on the very night, this person whose bed it was had to be on guard – you know they take turns. Here comes somebody throwing an AK on top of me, just like that, not knowing that it's another person there. Wasn't I scared! Ai-yai-yai! You know I had never been so scared in my life. No, I feel this thing here on my legs. I was afraid to move. I thought, no, maybe they test you when you arrive here [laughs] to see if you are not a coward! I couldn't move until, I think around four in the morning, when they removed that heavy thing. Then I was relieved a bit. And in the morning that's when I saw comrades. Then I was introduced, I was told that my job would be to cook with another comrade. I used to be in the kitchen cooking porridge in the morning, sorting rice – everybody would take part in sorting rice. I used to cry for the first few days, ja. I used to cry. I missed home. I missed my mother. I knew I could not go back. But the only consolation I got was Bo'Maseko wrote me a letter, told me he was arranging a passport for me, and that I would soon be leaving. I should go to school. I shouldn't worry.

But of course, as time went by, I realised . . . you know they politicise you bit by bit. [Laughs] There used to be political discussions; and then I started reading some of these books, although some of the discussions would bore me. There was this thing they called philosophy . . . cause, effect . . . I used to sleep there . . . [Laughs] I just found it so boring. What I enjoyed were revolutionary songs. When we were singing, I liked that. And then . . . my first poetry was there. I must say I liked poetry from that time.

There were these nurses there, they would come to me and tell me that I must take contraceptives. So I would say to them, 'Why? I don't need them.' They didn't understand. 'No, no. You are the only girl here, there are men.' Sex was something which was very far in my mind, even at school all I wanted was just books, books. My mother used to tell me, 'Your friends are books until such a time that you finish school.' So now I was angry that these women were telling me that I must take contraceptives, so I said, 'Look. I'm going to stay until I leave – no boyfriend. Don't worry about me.' They didn't believe it. [Laughs]

I stayed there about three months. Then I came to Tanzania. When I arrived here at SOMAFCO, only Unit One was complete. We were using it as a school and as dormitories. I had done O levels so I didn't have to go to school. So they said now I was going to do what they called

Development of Society and a history of the struggle. At the same time they asked me if I could assist in the primary school, teach. So I was a teacher and a student at the same time, until I went to Addis Ababa for further education.

I was doing accounting. I had got busy in economics, accounts and commerce. I preferred to study in English, so this is how I went to Ethiopia. And that is where now life started.

We were a group of eight South Africans. This is when I started having a boyfriend for the first time! [Laughs] I was twenty-two ja, ja. That's when I . . . unfortunately I fell in love with one Zimbabwean. I was crazily in love with this man – I don't know if I should mention this! It was my first boyfriend, and he wanted to marry me – this is what I believed. OK, the very first man to touch me, it will be the very first man to marry me. This is what I thought. And – eh, but you know things didn't go that way.

Anyway, we got engaged . . . so I wrote to the ANC. I was madly in love, blindly. The chief rep was trying to stop me, saying that look you can't do that. But I just felt no one can stop me. So I wrote to the SG that I wanted to marry this man. They didn't say no. They just said, 'Finish your studies. When you are finished your studies you shall have made up your mind by then. So wait a bit.' The ANC did well by not granting me that permission. Because I realised later it was not going to work out.

But I stayed there for four years, ja; I was doing this degree. It turned out that this man disappointed me anyway. Somehow, he broke my heart, let me put it that way. I finished my studies in 1985. Then I came back here to Mazimbu.

I've been here since. I am doing a course – they call it Certified Accounting. I'm doing it in Liverpool. The sponsor, WUS, has placed me there.

When I was leaving Swaziland, I really didn't know where I was going. All I had in mind was that there was this organisation somewhere, and it will take me to school. All I wanted was to go to school. And I was sure that I would just go somewhere and then find myself in the plane to the UK and . . . [Laughs] I didn't know what it actually involved. I only got to know about it in Matola when I was told, 'Well, there are two roads. You go to the army, or you go to school.' And I was clear that, no, I would take this one. But when I completed school, I wanted to take the other road.

In fact, when I completed school and came back here, I told them I wanted to go straight to join Umkhonto we Sizwe. The problem now, they told me, was that they don't have anyone for the treasury. Even when I went to work in the treasury, I told them that, 'Look: I am on the way. I am going to the army.'

But then I met Martin Maphisa, my husband. He is working in Dar es Salaam as an ANC education officer in UNESCO. He is remaining behind when I go Liverpool because he doesn't have anybody to replace him at the moment. My daughter – she's two and a half – she's coming with me.

I remember when the time came for me to take the other road, I was already in love with Martin. So I didn't go. I wanted to take the other road; and then – [Laughs] circumstances changed, ja.

CAESARINA KONA MAKHOERE
Mazimbu 1989

'I'm not going to serve these five years alone – the prison staff is going to serve it with me.'

> She spent six years in South African prisons, where she carried on an unrelenting campaign of single-handed protest and struggle, undeterred by constant punishment. The full account of those years is to be found in her own book '*No Child's Play*', published by The Women's Press.

My mum was a domestic worker and my father was a policeman. My mum used to take us to her place of employment, where there were two fridges full of food. We didn't have any fridge at home. We didn't have any electricity.

Not far from there they had a playground. I said to my Mum, 'Momma, may I please go and play with those kids?' She said, 'No, you can't go there because you will be arrested – it's not permissible.' I said, 'Why?' She said, 'No, it's only white kids who are supposed to play there.' And at my age, eleven, I wished I was white. I felt that to be white, you are more privileged. When I grew up I realised that it was true. So I had this inside me.

I went to Vlakfontein Technical High where two-thirds of the teaching staff was white, and most of them were Afrikaner – only a few were English-speaking. For a white person, an Afrikaner, to teach at a black school shows that they are the rejects, because if they were good they wouldn't have come there.

Apartheid was seriously practised right inside the schoolyard. For instance, they had a white staff room, and there was an old black man cleaning it. It was very clean. And there was a black staff room which looked like a toilet, and the man who was cleaning the white staff room was not supposed to go and clean that one. We didn't see the need of them having two staff rooms; why can't they share the staff room? In fact, because the black teachers were afraid of being labelled as communist, they never said anything. But we, as students, we felt offended by this type of situation in the school, and we used to complain.

When the 1976 disturbances took place in Soweto, I was already doing typing in Afrikaans, I was doing mathematics in Afrikaans. So by the time when the Soweto students protested about being taught in Afrikaans, it was a long time that we had been taught in Afrikaans. But you felt that this our brothers, this our sisters, we must have solidarity.

The disturbances continued, and at one stage I realised that we were being shot at, students were dying, others in prison unnecessarily. I went to other students and I recruited them that we should go for military training, to come and revenge – when they shoot, we shoot back. I wanted us to join Umkhonto and get military training. We were not experienced about these things; one of the people I recruited was arrested, and he revealed everything I said to him. And then I got arrested, ja.

When they arrested that student, I ran away from home. I went to stay with my aunt. Apparently they came to my home looking for me. Because my father was a policeman, they were threatening him. He was just about due to go on pension the following year. So they made him go and look for me, and they said if he doesn't get hold of me he's going to forfeit all his benefits, and they are going to lock him up. He took them from one relative to the other, until they found me at my aunt's place.

I was taken to Mamelodi Police Station. I stayed there for a night, and then I was taken to Kompol building in the centre of town, where I was seriously beaten. There were two whites and two blacks, four hefty men. They took their jackets off. They were hitting me with their fists all over the body, and put that black thing over my head. And that time I decided they are going to kill me.

There was this sadist Selepe. And then they said to him, 'Selepe, you know how to deal with these people.' And Selepe was so excited, he dived at me, punched me all over my body, screaming, cursing me all the time, 'You won't get out alive!' It's always the same when white and black policemen work together – the black police are more vicious than the whites because they are trying to please them and prove that they are really genuine in their working.

Selepe was saying he used to be in the ANC, and he knows everything. It was true that he was once an ANC member. But to be honest, he was a real sadist, ja.

Interrogation went on for almost six months. I was detained in October, charged in May. The interrogations were just sporadic – they would come and pick me up and continue the interrogation. I was in solitary confinement, always alone except when I was being interrogated. I was sleeping on the floor. I developed a heart problem.

To keep myself sane, I used to sing. Religious songs, protest songs, folk songs, even though singing was prohibited. Then they removed me from Pretoria Prison, they took me to Silverton Police Station – and I used to sing very loud. Then the commander of the police station came and said, 'You are making noise – we are going to move you out of this!' And then

I was so happy that now they are going to move me away, that I sang louder than before! [Laughs]

At Silverton, my ears were so tuned to the keys. Just a little click and I would just know that now they are coming. Even the footsteps, so when they opened the next cell I would just time it, and then when they go I knock. Bang on the wall, so that I can at least talk to somebody. That's how I used to keep communication, and speak with common law prisoners who were arrested for pass laws.

They used to give me stale pap in the morning, lunch and supper – without anything. So what these common law prisoners would do, they had the opportunity of cleaning outside, washing the cars and all that. Then they'd be able to buy some bones, cook them, and smuggle some to me underneath my pap and at least I'll eat something. I really respect them for what they used to do, because the diet was very terrible. I was so happy that people knew we have been fighting for their freedom. I got real support from them, ja.

I was charged under Section 2 of the Terrorism Act with recruiting people for military training, organising school boycotts, and leading an assault on white teachers – those were the main charges. I appeared in court many times. A full year after my arrest, I was sentenced to five years on the charge of recruiting. I was found not guilty on the other charges.

My father and mother both attended the trial, and brought me food and clothes. When I was sentenced, my father was sobbing. My mother led him out of the courtroom.

I was taken to Kroonstad, I stayed there for two years. And then from Kroonstad to Pretoria for two years, and from Pretoria to Klerksdorp. All this moving around was because they said I am causing trouble for them. In fact, when I was sentenced I thought, I'm not going to serve these five years alone – the prison staff is going to serve the sentence with me! How are they going to serve the sentence with me? And I made it a sure case that life became unbearable for them.

I think what really gives you courage is knowing that you're right. I knew that. And I still know it. And if I was to give in, then I don't see any reason why I was opposing the apartheid regime when I was outside. So there was apartheid, and there still is apartheid inside South African prisons: why should I keep quiet when I'm in South African prison? So I must keep on resisting, keep on saying no to whatever they're doing. Because if you don't, then it shows that what you are fighting for is a failure – you'll indicate to them that they are successful, that by keeping you in prison they are able to close your mouth. But if you keep on resisting, even in prison, they end up not knowing what to do with you. Like they did with me. Mmm.

When I was released I went straight home. My brother and my sister-in-law came to fetch me because I told them I would rather walk to

Pretoria than be in a police vehicle. Because now I was going out of the small prison and into the big prison, I don't want any prison car to escort me. So they came and fetched me and I went home.

I was very active, very active. I was thinking about my comrades inside. Successfully, we were able to form the youth and the women's movements, and revive the Congress of South African Students. We even formed Mamelodi Parents-Teachers Association involving teachers, students and parents. I worked for the Black Sash, I was running an advice office in Mamelodi; and I was also in the executive of the Federation of Transvaal Women.

I was told by some reliable sources that there's a plot to kidnap me and assassinate me. And that was highly possible. So I went into exile.

I left with one friend, and with my son who's now studying at Mazimbu. I knew where I was going – the comrades were expecting me and there was no problem with accommodation or any other thing. I went to Lusaka, and from there to Angola. I joined MK.

Caesarina spent months undergoing military training in the camps in Angola. Eventually, she came to Lusaka to discuss publication of her book, but encountered a great deal of delay and bureaucracy. Instead of returning to Angola, she was sent to study in Nigeria, and stayed there for two years. She intends to continue studying for a degree in Britain, and to become a writer.

MA-MERCY MNTAMBO
Mazimbu 1989

'When my father died, my education was doomed. I had to go and work for 25 cents a month. I was fourteen years old.'

She walks with difficulty on swollen legs, and her sight is not good. She is one of Mazimbu's pensioners, now in her seventies. Physically, she carries the burdens of her harsh life.

What made me to leave South Africa it's because, you know, I had my children, these three children. So I thought: if they grow big in this small house, it's better for me to go to Swaziland. So I went to Swaziland with my three kids. I was separated from my husband by then.

I had no relatives in Swaziland. But because people were being taken to the bantustans and I didn't want them to push me anywhere, I wanted to get a place of my own. I didn't want to go to these bantustans. So I went to Swaziland. They told me that they cannot give us a place to stay, and oh! it was just too bad. But somebody gave me a place, and then I stayed there with her. She had a big house. She gave me one big block of rooms, then I stayed with her.

I had some Provident funds and other things that I was supposed to take with me; but still I said I just forget about it, and leave South Africa. I had some few pennies with me, as I had been working in the factory.

Then when my children were getting big now, they wanted to go back to Johannesburg again. The young one was much too much of a problem to me, Sesiswe – she wants to go back. So I went to my brother to go and try if we can go back. They say no we can't. After we have left South Africa for five years, we are not entitled to go back – because I was going to take this young one to go back to my brother. So we couldn't. We stayed there.

We stayed until 1976 when there was this uprising. So we were just getting these young fellows and girls from Soweto – they were passing there all the time. And then this young one of mine one day say, 'Mama, I think I better go where all the other children are going to, so as to get the key to go back to South Africa.' Oh! And then I said to myself, now what's happening? I said, 'How can you go there?' He says, 'Yes Mama, I'm going there.'

I said, 'OK. Go then with the other children.' He went. Then after that the other one again, the elder one, says, 'I'm also following.' [Laughs] So I said, 'Well, OK then.' He also left. Then I was left with one girl, the eldest one. So I stayed in Swaziland; I went to the ANC residence. I went and stayed there.

While we were there then, we had some problems when the Swaziland police came; they came and raid that residence – that whole community. They found some things, arms – and I did not even have the permission to be in Swaziland yet. Then they asked me how did I come to Swaziland and all this; and I just told them any old thing.

And after that they release us. They say we must come every morning. Because my daughter had a small child so they could not arrest and keep us in jail there. They were not too sure about these things they found, because they found them outside. I said, 'I don't know what is happening outside there. I don't know. I am staying in the house here. You didn't get these things in my house, in my room where I stay.' They said, 'But you must know about this.' I said, 'No, you can't say I must know about the things that are outside, what is happening outside at night or any other time; it's not my fault.' So then they released me.

After that, the organisation said that I must come to Tanzania, to come and look after these children; because these young girls were getting children, and they had nobody to help them as a mother or anything. So that is how I came here to Tanzania. That was in 1979 then. Then we started these Charlottes. That was in Morogoro. It was me and Mabel Choabi – she came to show me how to start. Until 1987, when I had to leave there because of my ill health.

My daughter, she did come with me, she is here in Mazimbu. The one son is in GDR studying music. And the other one – I was just too cross with him. He doesn't write to me, but he is around. He's sometimes in Lusaka, and then he goes ... You know, he is working underground for the ANC. That's the young one.

When I was a child we had to move from the Free State to Johannesburg when my father died. When my father died, my education was doomed. I had to go and work for 25 cents a month – that's two and sixpence in those days – working in the kitchen, domestic. I was fourteen years by then. I had to come and clean the kitchen, and sweep outside; and they showed me how to put everything there, to cook oatmeal and make coffee, and set the table for them. Then sometimes I go out with the two kids, the *klein-basies* that they had, then bring them back again; and then I go home. Then the next day again, I come. Then the end of the month I just get the two and six.

Then the third month, they gave me five shillings. So it means that when I was working for this two and six – that's thirty pennies, nie ja? – so I was working for a penny a day. Then after three months it was tuppence a day. Those days, that's how I worked.

My mother wrote to her brother in Johannesburg, tell him that she has lost my father, and she would like to go back home. So they sent my mother money; we went to Johannesburg. Then I started to work in the white homes in Mayfair in Johannesburg. There I started with ten shillings – I thought it was plenty! [Laughs] But it was a lot of money. Then that went up, fifteen shillings. Then after that I went and worked in Turffontein, and then I was getting one pound five shillings a month. That was 1933. It was a lot of money.

We were staying in Pimville; the room we had we were paying eight shillings per month. It was before I was married – I was still young then, yes, still with my mother and my little brothers. I had to pay the school fees for them, and see that they have got clothes to go to school and everything. And pay that eight shillings and so on. But everything was very cheap then, yes, because we used to get a loaf of bread for sixpence, and you could get a tin of condensed milk for a tickie then. Even coal, what ... half a tin of coal for tickie, that's three pence. [Laughs] Everything was cheap, very cheap. So I had to live that way.

I went on working in these homes for a long time. Different places. Oh, you know what kind of a person I used to be? Because I never liked to speak Afrikaans; I never used to like it. So sometimes when they call me Annie, then I say, 'No. I'm not Annie. I told you that my name is Mercy.' They say, 'Oh! *Sy is so parmantig!*' She is so cocky. [Laughs] Then I say, 'I can't speak Dutch' – I never used to say Afrikaans. I used to say, 'I can't speak Dutch.' They say, '*Waar kom jy van af – jy sê jy kannie Afrikaans praat nie?*' (Where do you come from that you say you can't speak Afrikaans?) I say, 'I can't understand what you say.' Then they get annoyed, you know. And then if they don't like me, then I just walk out and just go.

And they tell me that I must have a different food from what they get, and all things like that. Then I used to say, 'No I don't! Because you give me little money you must just give me good food. Don't tell me that I must eat mealiemeal, and take this dog's meat. No. I'm not going to have that!' They say, 'Hoor wat sy sê? Sy sê sy kan nie eet pap nie. Sy will nie pap nie; sy wil ook nie daardie vleis wat daar is nie. Sy sê dis vir die hond.' [Do you hear what she says? She says she won't eat pap, and she won't eat that meat. She says it's for the dog.] I rather stay without food if it's like that. Ja. I used just to be like that. I was right. It's my right they must give me proper food, because I'm working for not a lot of money, ja.

But what I wanted is that they must treat me equal, ja. That was in me. I'd never met the ANC or any other people who are talking like that, to now tell me what rights must I have. But it was just out of my head then. I never had any education. I was never educated.

It is a good thing that I left South Africa. The children would have been in jail there – I don't know how to put it. Because when I left South Africa, my aim was that – I know these children are going to grow big, and they will leave me. Here in Soweto, I don't think I can really be sure that I've got a home for my children. 'Look now,' I said. 'I'm staying in a two-roomed house. These children are going to grow big, they must have their bedroom, they must have what, what. You know, a home. But here I'm just in a matchbox.'

Then also, they will send me to the bantustans. I was really just scared about these bantustans. I want to choose my own place where I want to go to. That's how I had to move to Swaziland.

I think it is all right here in Mazimbu. They give us all the best they can, food and clothing and everything. I'm pleased with what they give us, because if they haven't, then they haven't. All what we get here it's what it's been given to us from all other countries. So I'm satisfied.

I think about going to South Africa one day. But it has to change. I like South Africa, it's my home. It will always be. It will always be, mmm. Even if I die here, it will just be too bad. [Laughs] Then I would want my ashes to go back to South Africa, ja. I'm still praying like that.

Students in Other Places

From Zambia or Tanzania, students in search of higher education spread out to colleges and universities in Europe, east and west, in America, in Cuba, in Australia; and some to African countries.

You would think that students from South Africa would find themselves more at home in other African countries than among strangers in cold climates speaking outlandish languages – in Germany, the

Soviet Union, Bulgaria, Italy, Sweden. But it was not so. The toughest experience was in Nigeria. The Nigerians established a Commonwealth scholarship scheme that operated through the South African Relief Fund of Nigeria (SARF). Somehow the ANC students found themselves waging a silent war of nerves with SARF. In 1989, eight of them were expelled from the country. According to SARF officials they had proved to be stubborn and ungovernable. The students themselves presented a different view.

The Nigerian government had decided that the ANC and the PAC should unite. ANC students resisted this unification. They argued that the government should assist the struggle against apartheid, but not impose a leadership policy on its liberation organisations. From that time on, they maintained, everything went wrong. Their stipends were withheld. Their universities and polytechnics demanded fees. Not only were the students unable to pay, but they were not receiving money for food, to sustain themselves.

Here are the experiences of three students who studied in very different countries: Cuba, Nigeria and the USA.

GLORIA NKADIMENG
Tanzania 1989

'Let me be exemplary.'

> She went into exile when she was fourteen, separated from her mother who she did not see again for nearly ten years. More than most, she is able to articulate the experience of a student growing up in exile.

The very same year on which I was born – 1963 – my dad was arrested. Well, we had to move as a family, because you know in Johannesburg a black woman couldn't own a house just on her own. So we moved to where my mum came from – a farm near Pretoria. My mum was working in Johannesburg. She used to come from time to time to see us. We were living with a grandfather, and my eldest sister used to help to look after us. She was still very young, about ten years old.

My dad came out of prison after four years, but the Special Branch made him move to Diepkloof. They wanted to isolate him from other ANC people. He was banned for five years, he couldn't be in the company of more than two people – and he was not supposed to move to any other area, except to town to his work, and back home. And they would check on him, maybe twice or thrice a day during the hours when he was at home.

But we were so happy to be reunited with my father! At that time, my political understanding was none, I didn't know what was happening. I just used to be surprised when there were these policemen visiting my dad. I didn't understand anything. I didn't know what the ANC was.

My father didn't really tell us anything, because he didn't want us to be telling other people in the streets about it. He used to drive a station wagon and the Special Branch used a station wagon also. So the people in the street used to think he was a policeman himself. We used to say, 'Yes; he is a policeman' when they ask us. [Laughs]

When his five year ban was finished, we were about to make a party. Mum was cooking a big supper. It was a celebration, and when people had already gathered then the Special Branch came and they took my dad away. And they kept him for some days. And when he came back . . . well he told us that they had banned him again for another five years.

So I used to question my mum about some of these things, but she also never used to want to explain anything to me – maybe she used to think I was still very young. I'm asking her, 'What is this ANC?' She'd say, 'It's a liberation movement.' But I would never understand much of it in any case. I used to ask, 'Why is it that when we go to places, we can't go with my Dad?' My mum would say, 'You know your dad can't go because he's banned.' Well, I used to understand that. But not the real thing, the core of the reasons why he has got to be banned.

He didn't get to complete those second five years, because he left the country.

My political realisation came with the student uprising in 1976. My mind opened, and I started witnessing many many things. After the riots we couldn't go back to school. I used to like schooling a lot, and I wanted to become a doctor. I think most of the schoolchildren who were really serious about their schooling wanted to go back to school; but all of us were serious about the conditions in the country. That's when I started hating the country. Our family life certainly changed a great deal. After he left my Mum had to start looking for a job. And she had to try to find a sponsor for us to go to school, because we no longer had a breadwinner in the family.

I was still doing Form 2 when the riots erupted again – demonstrations and many other things. That year the repression was worse. The policemen were using a new type of teargas which affected your eyes and your nose, and most people couldn't get over the after-effects. Many schoolchildren were dying. They imposed a new rule whereby you were told which school you were to go to. I was very sad about it, because our new school was ready by then, and it was one of the most beautiful schools in Soweto, because we raised funds on our own and we built it with our own money. But we were not allowed to go and study there. I was forced to go to another school. We would see police cars passing by the school. At any time they would shoot at you, even if you are just sitting in class.

There was this English teacher who used to like me very much because I used to be one of his best students. But after my dad left, he started questioning me about my dad's whereabouts. Most fortunately I truly didn't know where my dad was. I didn't even understand people when they told me that he has left the country; I thought he was going to come back.

So there came a time I'll never forget because it really depressed me. You know in the black schools in South Africa you have to buy your own textbooks. Well, you bring money to them as a class, and the teachers go and buy a bunch of textbooks and they give the books to you. So we gave this teacher money for a book and after the teacher bought them, he gave everybody in class the book. But he left me out.

When I went and asked him for my book, he said, 'I'm not going to give you your book until you tell me where your dad is.' I didn't know what to do. I was very worried, because I also wanted to start studying with the book and preparing myself for the final exams. The teacher kept on refusing until one time he had the book in his hand, saying, 'I'm not going to give you this book until you tell me where your dad is.' I grabbed the book and ran away. [Laughs] I didn't want to tell my mum about this problem, because I used to think she had enough troubles in her life already.

When he was about to evaluate us, he said he was not going to evaluate me until I tell him where my dad is. I just burst out crying in class. So all these things, you know, they're just troubling our lives. Even in the streets some people used to ask us where my father had gone; we were scared to tell them that my father was a freedom-fighter, because that time people in South Africa didn't have that understanding. They used to take freedom-fighters as terrorists. I was also feeling bad about that. I didn't want people to know that my father was a freedom-fighter.

Finally a message came from my dad. He wanted us to come out of the country so that we could live with him. I was very happy but my mum was a bit reluctant. She didn't know what to do about it. That was about 1976. And she ended up doing nothing, until another message came again in 1978. That time, my dad had sent people to just take us out of the country, without passports or anything.

My mum had agreed that I can leave with my elder sister and brother. She could join us later. I was fourteen years old. So when we were supposed to leave, she started crying, and saying I must remain behind, I was still too young. I really felt bad. I was split into two. I wanted to remain with my mother, and on the other hand I wanted to leave because I felt I was losing so much time not studying. I wanted to go and continue with my studies, so in future I could help my parents. If there is one thing that I've always thought in my life, it is that I wanted to do things for my parents – give them that happiness that they have never been able to have. So I finally decided to leave, feeling bad as I was. But I left.

We took the train which travelled for the whole night, and then got to some place. We got down – it was a deserted place, no station. It was not a populated area, and we had to start footing it from that place until we got into Swaziland!

It was the first time that I walked for such a long distance – it was seventeen kilometres. It was around twelve in the morning when I started walking, but we got into Swaziland at about 7 p.m. We avoided the border post; we crossed the border in a certain area where there was just a small stream. The fence there was broken; maybe it was already prepared so that people could cross there – I don't know. All I know, I was just scared that something was going to go off from somewhere – because I used to hear about bombs, people being shot, and what not.

In Swaziland another comrade, an elderly, who was waiting for us in a car. As soon as I got into the kombi, I slept until we got to the house we were going to. It was already dark – I think it was past eight or nine. I was so tired! So the first thing I asked – I was very shy by then – I just asked my sister, 'Is daddy around?' When she told me no – oh, I was really really disappointed. I didn't know anybody in that house. They just told us my dad would come some time.

We stayed in Swaziland those first two or three weeks without seeing him, and nobody to explain anything to us. I was missing home a lot. I wanted to go back because seemingly my dad doesn't love us; he left us in South Africa; now he's not there when we come to Swaziland! And things were really hard because we couldn't walk freely, we didn't have political asylum, so we had to stay indoors all that time. Except me. Because of my age, they used to send me to the shop sometimes. But I was very very lonely. I never used to see people of my age around, and I was not doing anything.

Everybody was just living underground . . . there was always somebody there, twenty-four hours of the day, watching the house with binoculars.

My Dad came back from wherever he was – I saw him at last! And I was very happy. But he had changed a lot, because he never used to keep a beard in South Africa. By that time when I saw him with a beard, he had grown fat. Ah, I was shocked to see him!

So I kept on asking him when was he going to make sure that my mum comes this side? He told me I shouldn't worry; she was going to come. But I was eager for her to come over because I was much closer to my mum – I had not lived a lot with my dad that time – so I always felt freer with my mum. I thought we were going to live as a family in Swaziland, with my dad and mum.

I used to ask my Dad for things when he came back in the evening, 'Can I have this and that? Can I . . . ' because we had left all our clothes and our things in South Africa. He used to give me small things like sweets. But one day he spoke to me, saying, 'All these children who are here are my children. I think you should stop asking me for little things, because when I buy sweets I must buy for all of them. And if I just give to you, it's not nice for those who don't have anybody who they can ask for things.'

From that day I . . . I just closed myself up, and told myself that I no longer have a father. I thought that maybe my dad doesn't like me very much. He's much more in love with his cause than with us, his children. I felt like . . . some sort of hatred towards him. I mean, I didn't really hate – I felt distant. But not really hatred.

My mum didn't come. And it was arranged that I should leave for Mozambique. I didn't know what to expect in Mozambique, but because my dad didn't care for me, that's why I said I wanted to go to Mozambique, and I wanted to go back to South Africa and fight. And that time I felt that I was not scared of death. Even if I died, it didn't matter, because I didn't feel that life was worth it. But I really felt politically inspired by my father's life, otherwise I don't know if I'd even thought of going back to fight and things like that, but without the love of my parents.

I got to Mozambique. I was with my sister and brother which made things better for me. But I didn't really feel much, because as a kid I was . . . I would prefer to be in a family situation with parents around that I can confide my problems to. And I just felt my brother and sister were still too young also for me to be troubling them.

We were interviewed and I told them that I wanted to go to MK because I didn't want to stay in exile any more! I wanted to go back to my country and fight, so that we should be free. [Laughs] Everybody was shocked. And they were saying, 'No. We can't take this kid to our military – she is still very young. She must go to school.'

I remember then one weekend my dad came to Mozambique. They asked him what does he think about my case. He said he doesn't think it's proper for them to ask him; because he is a parent to every child who comes to exile whoever they are. So he doesn't think that he must decide for me; there are children who don't have parents in exile to be asked what should be the fate of their child. So he didn't really answer that question.'

So the comrades in Mozambique just decided I was to go to school and I was brought to Tanzania.

At that time SOMAFCO had not yet been established. The few children there were were housed in some old buildings left over from a former sisal plantation which had occupied the site.

Mazimbu was by then still very rural. I found there were very few people of my age; but we lived together. That time, Ai! I was just depressed because I wasn't going to school; neither was I seeing my parents, I didn't know what was happening. I didn't know whether I could ask anybody in the office what was happening to us – so I just waited. We were about twelve girls, some my age – we were the youngest. And there were boys in the other houses. The boys, at least some of them, were much older.

I learned a lot of things when I came there, because it was my first time to be in contact with political books, which I read and I was very inspired. And well, there were political discussions which were held weekly. We had cultural nights, where we used to rehearse things like Ndlamu which are things I didn't know when I was in South Africa, because maybe we concentrate on western civilisation. I really used to enjoy all of those things. We also used to have classes. It was thought that if we are left all this time without doing any schoolwork, we are going to be really outdated by the time we go to school.

I was really worried, because all that time that I lost of school really counted to me a lot. But finally, in 1979, we were told that we would be leaving for Cuba to further our studies. I didn't know anything about most countries in the world. But I was willing to go anywhere as long as I was going to study; because after I came to Tanzania, I never thought there was any going back. I never thought I could go back to Swaziland and live with my dad.

I hear my mum was very hysterical when she discovered that I'd gone to Cuba – so far away that she wouldn't be seeing me. When she finally left South Africa for good with my kid sister and brother, I was already in Cuba.

Around forty of us went to Cuba, some from Angola and some who were from Zambia. It's because our parents were in the ANC, that's why we were there. I was still very reserved by then. Cuba – it's still a Third World country, it's got its own problems, and it's underdeveloped. But when it comes to education, medicine, it's far ahead of most of the Third World countries.

We started having our Spanish classes. I used to miss home a lot, the country was just too far for me. But my dad had explained to me that I'm in exile now, I have to put up with many, many things. There are many things that he can't offer me as a parent who's in the ANC; so I have to accept the little I can get. So all the time, I just used to think of those words – even if Cuba is difficult for me. I used to think of his words. And I used to tell myself that, well, I have to understand my parent's situation. In the liberation movement he doesn't earn a salary of his own. And here's this country that's trying its level best to cater for us, so I must also try my best, and study.

We did about five months of classes of Spanish. After that we were taken to a Cuban secondary school, where I went into Form 3.

I was really impressed about the way they treat other people. They really made us feel at home. Our school was a boarding-school – the dormitory was right in the school. We used to spend every day there, even weekends, although the school rules allowed us to go to town. If you had a friend in town where you could sleep, if a Cuban took you home it was OK. But we didn't know the language well, so we just used to keep to ourselves and we didn't have lots of friends of our age. Even if they would invite us to their homes, we used to say we didn't want to go; because we couldn't talk properly. And we were just a bit, you know . . . awkward.

I used to study very hard, very hard. There was this friend of mine, Nosizwe Mbembe, whose father was a member of the ANC – he died in Lusaka in 1975, killed by a bomb. She was also very hard working. We used to go to class at all hours . . . study until twelve at night. I remember one time we woke up very early in the morning. We wanted to go and study; so since we couldn't put the lights on in the dormitories, we decided to go to the dining-hall. Behind the dining-hall there is a kitchen, and this kitchen has this big, big generator for the freezers that made some funny noises.

So we sat with our books, ready to study. The fridge kept on making these funny noises – I think it was three or four in the morning. We just kept on looking at one another, until both of us grabbed our books and ran up to the dormitories because we were so scared! It was dark outside. When we got to the room, we went into our blankets with our clothes on. We didn't even undress! And we slept. [Laughs]

But we really studied a lot, and we passed at the end of the year. The Cuban authorities thought it was better to take us to the Island of Youth. On this island they have many schools for boarding students.

Well, it was an adventure for us. It was a good place for a high school student, because there is no room for nice time. You have to work, you have to study, and it's not easy to go into town. The schools are really out of town, very far; public transport is very very little;, and then the only way you can go is through the school authorities giving you permission, and transport to town.

My friend, Shaun Naidoo, he asked me what I wanted to do. I told him that I was confused. He told me, 'When you are good in science subjects, I don't see why you don't want to be an engineer.' And he lent me a book on careers. I liked mathematics, chemistry and biology. So finally I came across this career that dealt with computers. I thought computers very fascinating – I didn't know much about them. I just knew they were something new in life.

Towards the end of our holidays that year, we were taken out of the Island of Youth to our different universities. It was yet another phase in my life, because then I had friends that I'd lived with since I went to Cuba – from the first year until that day, like Nosizwe Mbemba. We were very, very close friends and we had a lot in common. Nosizwe took electronics – she was taken to another university. I was taken to the university called Instituto Superior for the Technico, San Antonia

Achievaria. It's a very beautiful university. And big. I was nineteen. We were two foreigners in class – it was me and Mark Shope's son. We used to move together a lot, because we were in a class with Cubans and I never used to be very sure of my Spanish. I used to think I was going to have a slip of the tongue and say something wrong. I think I miss those days – but I was really eager to finish up my career. [Laughs]

There were some in class who were very, very nice to me, aways eager to help me. They wanted to take me to their places every weekend. They used to understand that I'd been away from my parents for so long and I don't have anybody there. That's one thing that made me be able to stomach everything in Cuba, because the people there are very warm. They are very warm.

Sometimes if I was sick, I would just feel that I didn't want to stay in Cuba, and I would tell them that I think I've had enough. I want to come back home. My mum was very worried about me. She would say, 'No, come back any time you feel like coming back. We don't want you to stress yourself, to overtax yourself. If you feel it's too much, come back.'

But I never used to. You know, every little step I used to take I used to think of my dad. I think he's gone through a very difficult time, and I just thought I always had to do my best to help him, to make his life much easier for him; I shouldn't be a trouble. So I used to feel I should put up with anything that came about. And the only gift I could give to them is finishing up my education.

So I decided I had to make it through. It was interesting, and at some stages I really had fun and enjoyed myself. I didn't only learn academic things – even life itself; how to cope with many things on your own; how to help other people. In South Africa I never had an opportunity of mixing with people from different walks of life and different countries. There in Cuba I met up with so many people, and I learned a lot about their histories, about their way of life.

I think it's in everybody's blood to think their own country's the best. And there I learned that everybody has got qualities, and everybody can be the best at any time. [Laughs] So I think it was a great experience, you know. A really great experience.

I had a five-year course as systems analyst. I finished in 1987; by the time I finished, I was so eager to come home! But my dad came to Cuba twice. I was very happy to see him in Cuba. I always asked if my mum couldn't come, but I think it was difficult. I accepted it. I didn't want to be a pest! [Laughs]

While I was in Cuba, one of my brothers was brutally assassinated in Botswana – that was in 1985, May. He was newly married. They only had three months of marriage together. They used to go to work together – but on that particular morning he left alone. A bomb was planted into the car he was driving. It blasted him to pieces. He had left the country in 1976, and he's the only one in the family that I didn't see after I came into exile. He was an MK commander in Angola. He used to write inspiring letters to me, telling of how much I have to study because I was the only one in the family who went to higher education. My elder brothers and sister had gone to train in MK, and they didn't have the opportunity I had. My brother told me he had wanted the opportunity to study; but he feels that he has got to do what he is doing, so he can't give it up. I used to think well, since I'm the first to have this opportunity, let me be exemplary to my younger ones.

So at last I finished. I came back home.

But not really home. Not to South Africa. She returned from Cuba to Tanzania, and went on to Zambia where her mother was. They had not seen each other for over nine years.

She was totally different. She had changed so much. Her voice, everything about her, was different. And then of course I know I also looked very different – when I left South Africa I was just fourteen. My sister had also grown a lot. Everybody was different. And it was a new life altogether.

But I was glad of what I saw. I was happy the way my mum was living and my dad – at least they were together. You know, since I was a child when we were still in South Africa, my parents could really spend very little time together. So at least I found her happy – although she was not completely happy because we were exiled. But she was in a comfortable home and she knows that we are safe wherever we are, and we can come and see her from time to time.

Gloria returned to Tanzania to work in the SOMAFCO electronics and computer laboratory and teaching students who had problems with mathematics.

I'm just happy that I finished my education, which was one of the things that I wanted to succeed in. But somehow, after all the difficulties, I have expectations now in life and I feel I have to go forward, I have to go forward. There are things that I have to do now. I want to make my own software, to be able to invent something that has never been made by anybody else. And – well, the past is gone.

Cubans used to always ask me which country do I like better, South Africa or Cuba? And I would tell them, 'Home is home! There is nothing more than home whatever the case. You cannot even understand because you've never been away from your country.' You know, the time when I wanted to leave South Africa I felt I hated it. But I knew shortly after that that there's nothing more than home.

I think the only time that my soul can settle, it's when I'm in South Africa.

LUNGI DAWETI
Mazimbu 1989

'I thought that in six months' time I would be back in South Africa; even three months, into a new South Africa.'

His student experiences have been traumatic, and he says he is hardened now. But his manner is mild, even hesitant, and the scars inflicted by exile will always remain.

I was schooling in Soweto. I was doing my Form 4 then. I didn't have a very clear political consciousness. It was only on 15 June 1976 that I saw some headlines of newspapers: Soweto Students About to Strike, about Afrikaans being imposed as a medium of instruction. Afrikaans was already introduced in our school, we were doing subjects like geography, history, mathematics in Afrikaans. But now there needed to be some solidarity with students in other schools.

On 16 June we all got to the streets, demonstrating against this imposition of Afrikaans, ja. I did take part. Well the demonstrations were led by different schools, and we were coming from behind because we were very far from the centre. So the shooting started while we were still coming. And then later on, the students retaliated by burning all property that belonged to the government.

I started seeing helicopters coming and shooting now. And teargas. That's when one could see that everything was just serious. I didn't belong to any organisation then. On 23 August, a demonstration was planned in Johannesburg where all students were supposed to meet. Well, I took part there; I was caught by the police. We were three, but one of us ran away and only two remained. They didn't take us to prison, they took us in their cars, they went with us to the mines. That's where they started beating us, ja. With fists.

Well they were moving in three cars. The car in which they were carrying us was the first one to arrive there in the mines – it was Crown Mines. So when the other man who was arrested with me saw them coming, he started running. And this other cop who was beating me asked, 'Do you see what he is doing?' I said, 'Ja, I see.' And then he told me, 'You'd better do the same, otherwise we are going to kill you.' That's when I started running – but I was thinking perhaps they were still going to shoot, and maybe say I was running away that's why they shot. I don't know whether he was saving me or what. But fortunately that's how I survived.

One day when I came home, my mother told me that she saw some police car standing outside, and they were pointing at our home. But nobody of them entered the house. So that's when I thought that it's real danger now. I started now sleeping out in different places, changing houses. I was not actually thinking of escaping. I had relatives who were very politically inclined. I would listen to their discussions. That's when I thought there is that possibility of one maybe being able to . . . well maybe arming himself in a better way to change South Africa.

It took something like two months . . . ultimately I happened to meet with someone who arranged for us – I was with a friend – to leave the country.

I didn't tell my family. I went to my granny's place and told them that I was going to Zeerust to mobilise other students, and we would be coming back in two weeks' time. But I could see that there was some suspicion that I might be leaving.

My mother was working in a clothing factory, and at the same time she would sew clothing for people to raise money for the family. My father was a heavy-duty driver. They had separated in 1965. Well, I believed that I was not leaving them for a long time, ja. I thought perhaps that in some six months' time one would be back in South Africa, even three months into a new South Africa! [Laughs]

I couldn't see my mother the last day when I left. I used to come and go to the house, but not waste time; when I came there, my mother is at work, so I can say maybe some two, three weeks before I left I last saw her.

We were about nine students who were leaving that day, though we never knew one another. We left Soweto at night; we arrived at the borders around seven in the morning. Then we had to stay on the South African side, in the bush, and letting the car pass into Swaziland. Then around twelve during the day, that's when some message came we could jump the fence, and behave as if we are people who are just living around there.

In Swaziland I arrived in the hands of the PAC. Most of the people who were there were my former classmates, who I had thought were still at home. But now this PAC – I didn't know anything about it at home. I thought I have landed in the wrong hands. So a few of us we decided that we should find the ANC. And found out. It was arranged that we should go to Mozambique.

We had to walk across the border, no man's land, you know. In Mozambique that's when now we had some political discussions – understanding the ANC policy and strategies and tactics and all that. That's when one understood that there is a need to get further education, and also that need of going for military training for those who opted for it. I decided that I'd like to go to school first. And we were brought over to Tanzania, while the others who opted for the military training were taken straight to Angola.

We were about sixty who were sent to Nigeria to study there. Nigerians are also people, there are good and bad amongst them. But the conditions for us there as South Africans were just too different from the ones we were coming from. Food ja, and everything – different cultures and maybe standard of living. And also the fact that one was in exile, so it was difficult. Fortunately I had relatives who were in Nigeria. They were teachers who had volunteered to go and work there. So during the holidays I got to them, ja. And that's the time when I got a photo of my mother. I could ... ai, I nearly cried even, when I was given this photo. I didn't want to take it. But my aunt also was saying that if I don't take it, she's not going to take it. So I took it.

Well, I decided on my own that I wanted to go and study further. We were asked which countries we would like to go to. I thought maybe in the Soviet Union there would be a lot of things I would learn – it has been the first country where socialism was practised. And I wanted to see if we could be taking examples from what I'd see over there.

In the university I was the only South African until maybe at the end of 1983, when another girl came. Ai, there were times when you could get homesick, and you couldn't even find someone to speak your own language; that's difficult.

I happened to fall in love with a Russian girl – I intended marrying her. I made an application to the ANC through the General Secretary, but I didn't get any reply and then she was pregnant. The Students Union discussed it, and they decided against me marrying her, ja, and she was also believing that I am not intending.

The mother talked her into making some kind of abortion late in the pregnancy. It had a psychological effect on me. For some time I could not go to school and be close to her. Well, the authorities at school tried to console me, talk me into going to school. And friends too. But it was just too difficult, up to an extent that it was suggested that I should just come back to Tanzania.

I was sent to Dakawa. It's a tough life there, ja. Anyone who comes from school without completing the course is to stay in Dakawa two years, one year in the rehabilitation centre, and one year working. I stayed in the rehabilitation centre for one year; the other year I was working in construction, building houses. And later on I was in the kitchen staff.

After three years I went back to Nigeria again for studies – journalism. The course was supposed to take one year. It was supposed to have started in 1986, September, only we were sent there 1987, February. So we were told that it's better that we wait for the next session. We could attend classes but we wouldn't be writing any exams.

But now, when the new session came in September we were told by the authorities that our sponsors had not paid our school fees. And we could not start with the classes until they had paid everything! So we waited until February 1988, when it was said, 'OK. [Laughs] OK, you can start now studying with the other students.'

But now it was more of a problem. During the year there had been some student strikes and the university decided to extend the session. And we were supposed to pay for that extended time, but the sponsors had not paid for it. Just when we were about to write the exams, the university authorities came to our room, took our mattresses, and told us that they were going to lock the room the next day if we did not pay. In fact we were being sponsored by a body that belonged to the government; and if there was such a problem, it was not for us to come and pay, but for them to liaise with the sponsors.

So, ai . . . one wrote those exams in very difficult conditions. We were not the only South Africans who were sponsored by that body in that university. But the manner in which they reacted only applied to us. You could look at the differences – the PAC was not affected, but the ANC was affected in that manner.

I wrote. I passed some exams and others I could not. I was told that I could still do them again. But with all the problems that the sponsors were giving us, and the political problems that the government was giving, I thought I could not continue in Nigeria.

It was a time when there were some countries which were trying to form what they used to call the third force in South Africa. The idea was that the students can lead the whole revolution. The government itself was pushing a line of uniting the PAC and the ANC. Because we were resistant, they started making life harder for us. They wanted to deal with us one by one – not as a group, not as the ANC. I think the authorities tended to believe that we were fighting against them, because there's just too much that is in common with what is happening in South Africa and what is happening within Nigeria. For instance: the Nigeria Labour Congress were very much in support of us. And when we talk about the conditions of the workers in South Africa, it sounds as if we are talking about the conditions in Nigeria. And the government was very much pro-PAC.

Ja, we had about sixty students who went to Nigeria. Among those people who were in Nigeria, I think about seven of them got mentally disturbed and had to come back here. But realising the conditions that were created there then, I should think that is what disturbed them.

It is chauvinism. The Nigerian leadership take Nigeria to be the biggest black nation in the world, therefore it must be the one that leads the revolution against racism and all that. And they want to monopolise all these bigger bodies, the UN Anti-Apartheid Committee, the Liberation Committee, the OAU and all that.

I thought I can't stay in Nigeria. And I came back to Tanzania, to Mazimbu. Here I have been working with our paper, News and Views, and then with the Radio Freedom recording studio in Mazimbu.

I left the country thinking I was going back soon. And now it's been a long journey to Nigeria, to the Soviet Union, to Nigeria again. I think I'm hardened now.

I don't know how to put it. But if I had stayed in South Africa, one can't believe whether you would still be alive right now. But I believe one would still be involved – I mean in the struggle. On the side of the people. I'm convinced on that.

THABISILE VIKALALA
Los Angeles 1991

'When we left home we were very angry at the older generation who had left before us. With time we've come to appreciate that they had already paved the ground for us.'

> She is an engineer in aircraft maintenance, an unlikely profession for a small woman – less than 5 feet, weighing 100 pounds, and looking as young as when she left home at the age of seventeen.

I left with my cousin without telling my parents. She had been expelled from school for involvement in student boycotts, so I left with her because the police had been to my place three or four times, and I thought next time they will catch up with me.

The first time they came for me I was there, but when they asked for Thabi, I realised they didn't know who I was, so I said Thabi wasn't there. They left a note saying that Thabi should report to the police station. But of course I never went. We took a train to Mafeking and then we hitched a ride to the border with a nice old Botswana man and when we got across he was still waiting for us. And he knew some of the ANC people in Botswana and he just took us there.

I joined the ANC there, and then they sent us to Tanzania. I went to SOMAFCO – we built it actually, I was there when the foundation was being laid; but I left before it was finished. I got a scholarship and went to Cairo and I finished my high school and then I went and I did aircraft maintenance. I've always liked fiddling around with radios and stuff like that when they are busted. When I was in Egypt in our apartment, I used to fix my TV when it stopped, and things like that. At home I wasn't doing very well at maths, but when I got to Egypt a gentleman from Lesotho used to give us tutoring; and after this tutoring, I realised that I can understand mathematics better than I could at home where we didn't have good teachers. I found myself enjoying it and so that's why I decided I'm going to stick with it.

Initially it was hard, it was very, very difficult. I don't know how to explain it to you. It's very difficult in Egypt because the Egyptians are like . . . they are racist a lot. Oh, very much so. The black Egyptians don't have good positions; most of them are porters and waiters. They look down on blacks, so it was very hard, you know. And even the life there, the heat and everything. But overall I did like it because I learned a lot.

Initially when we went there, we were eleven South Africans; but some of the students were not doing very well so they had to be sent back to Tanzania. Eventually it was only me and my cousin. I qualified in aircraft maintenance, avionics, public address systems on airplanes, stuff like that, installing those things. Then I wanted to do an engineering degree in electronics, so I tried for a scholarship and got one here in the USA.

Now I've done my degree and I want to go home! Ja! Although I am not sorry I left. I think that I've learned a lot, for one. Sometimes when I call my home, some of my old friends are at there. And when I talk to them then I realise how wonderful it's been to have been outside, even though it wasn't really my choice. But I've really learned a lot. I've learned to see things not just from my perspective, but I've had to interact with different people from different countries; and learned different things from a lot of people.

Even politically, I think my perspective is very, very different since I left home. I was very, very naive, because I was young at the time. When we were demonstrating in 1976, we thought that oh, we're going to just demonstrate, and then come out, train, and go home and change everything. Ja. Then you go out and you grow up, and you realise that it's not only a question of somebody giving you a gun to go home and shoot everybody. South Africa is not an isolated place. We are linked with other countries, and whatever happens in other countries has an effect on us and our struggle. When we left home, we were very, very angry at the older generation that had left before us because we did not realise the things that they had to go through. And now with time, we've come to appreciate that actually it made things a lot easier for us; they had already paved the way for us, and we did not have to endure some of the things they've endured. We've been able to get a lot of assistance from other countries which we would not have gotten without them.

I appreciate what they have done and what I have learned in exile. Even though it's been lonely and I have been homesick and sometimes I wish I hadn't left. But overall I have grown up to be a better person because of it.

Of course, the way of life here has influenced me. There are so many things that you can do here, that I wasn't able to do at home. When I do go home I'm going to have a problem, because I'm going to be hindered in so many things. I think the American way of doing things can spoil a person in a lot of ways. When I was in Egypt I was so much abreast of what's happening all over the world. But here you forget what's happening around the world, which is a very, very sad part about the situation here.

Ja, when I first came here, I used to think, Oh, I don't see how Americans can be so indifferent, not have much knowledge about things outside. Now I've been here, and I cannot make the same criticism because I've been a victim of the society here myself, and it has happened without me being consciously aware. Before you know it you are just part of it. The system here is geared that way. You are told you can be anything you want, but you are not encouraged to do anything. You have the television, there's Dynasty and all these things they are bombarding you with, that removes the time for you to do anything else or to see things any differently. Ja.

I left South Africa when I was seventeen. I'm thirty-one now. I haven't changed much from seventeen. It can be very funny sometimes. The male students at school, they think I'm their dolly, want to pick me up all the time. I've been pondering a long time how I will relate to a very male-dominated society when I get back. It's going to be very difficult for me. I admit that and I don't know how I'm really going to handle it, because I seem to have problems dealing with our guys that just came from home – even some of the guys who have been here for a long time. It does get frustrating, and I can get very short tempered. I get annoyed very easily with someone who thinks that they can take advantage of you because I'm small, and a woman to boot.

So I just hope that I'll be able to have the patience. But I will be going home next year.

The Military Road

Violence is the Rubicon of revolution. It is the crossing point at which civil disobedience, remaining within the political system and striving to reform it, becomes a revolutionary seeking to overthrow it.

Allister Sparks

Of the young people who fled South Africa in the 1960s, those who chose the military road joined MK. They were sent for training in a number of African and European countries and after training they went back to camps in Angola. There they stayed for months, then years, waiting to be infiltrated back into South Africa. The long trail back home was barred by a ring of countries – Rhodesia, friend of the apartheid regime; Namibia (South-West Africa) completely under South African occupation; and the former British Protectorates, beholden to South Africa's economy and cautious of antagonising their powerful neighbour.

Angola paid – and is paying – a very high price for supporting the South African and Namibian liberation struggles. South Africa trained, directed and equipped UNITA, and sent its own troops into cross-border raids and large-scale incursions. The camps were bombed, the MK recruits forced to move deeper into remote and isolated bush country. In addition to the physical hardships of their lives – the shortage of food, the extremes of climate, the prevalence of illnesses such as malaria – they had to endure years of boring and repetitive camp life. They were urban people, accustomed to a more sophisticated life-style even within the limitations of Soweto from which so many of them had come. Yet many of them assert that in the camps in Angola they had some of the happiest times of their lives.

The planning of the Wankie incursion was an attempt to begin some sort of action, to break the stalemate. In 1967, in a joint operation with ZAPU – the Zimbabwe African People's Union – an attempt was made by MK to fight its way through Southern Rhodesia to Botswana, and through Botswana to South Africa. It was a colossal undertaking. The distances can be gauged by looking at the map; but the map does not reveal the wildness of the African bush and forest, the hazards of the terrain, nor the fact that the support groups that were essential for their survival at their destination did not at that time exist.

About eighty ANC and ZAPU men crossed the border from Zambia into Rhodesia in August, then split into various groups. They crossed the Zambesi river in wild bush country and entered the Wankie area of Rhodesia, a game reserve near the Botswana border. Some eventually reached Botswana, where they were arrested and sentenced to fines and imprisonment. Graham Morodi was among this group. Others were captured in Rhodesia, tried and sentenced to death. These were members of the ANC and of ZAPU. Among the four ANC members was Isaac Maphoto.

Angola: In the Camps

GWENDOLINE SELLO
Tanzania 1989

'I got myself into really serious problems.'

> A vigorous woman, she talks rapidly and freely, tracing her journey from being a gangster's moll in Alexandra Township to becoming a doctor, specialising in gynaecology and obstetrics.

My mother died when I was six, and my father when I was seven. From there . . . well I had hardships in growing up, because I had to be brought up by my brother who was then sixteen. So it was a bit rough really.

I was fortunate because my father had left a bit of money. So with this money I got that little education until Junior Certificate, and then did nursing. After qualifying, I nursed for four to five years. Then I started facing political problems.

The hospital where I was, Edenvale Hospital, was near a ghetto, Alexandra Township. It was the times of Msomi and Spoilers – these were gangs in the township.

The Spoilers were a bit progressive. We used to work for Spoilers in a way that we didn't realise at the time. But they would let us trick policemen. Maybe when in the evening the police are guarding the prisoners there, we'll just make maybe an orange squash; and then you put two Valiums; the policemen sleep and the prisoner will escape. We didn't know then that some of our patients, they were political prisoners.

So that's how I really got into this gang. At the beginning I was unconscious of what I was doing – it was just a game! [Laughs] The real problem started when it was found out at the hospital this thing that we were doing under the command of some of . . . ja, the Spoilers. We as young ones, we never knew; but later on – as we discovered – that was a very dangerous game.

And me, I was on terrible terms now with the Catholic priest. I was a staunch Catholic, baptised and confirmed. So the then priest, Father Coleman, was very angry with me. I was called to order really strongly – that if I don't leave this game I would land myself in serious problems and even be struck off the roll of the church. So I had to decide now whether I continue with this or I leave my Christianity. But then that game was too nice for me you know! [Laughs] And I couldn't leave really. So I just continued now with the Spoilers. As a result, my first baby is even from that gangster, the chief of the Spoilers.

Well, I continued like that, doing this and this and this, given different missions now I was a full member of the gang. And then I was told now I can't be a proper Catholic, because I must confess my sins. But I didn't confess everything, because if I confessed everything I'm putting my people in problems. So I continued with them. And that's how I left the church, ja.

Then my boyfriend was arrested; he was chained and sent to Robben Island because he had escaped from Leeuwkop maximum prison. And then that's where my real serious problems started.

After he went to jail, I was arrested. They wanted me to be a witness against him. So I was put in Krugersdorp Jail for about two months. I was seven months pregnant when he was arrested, so I couldn't stand trial because now it was the time when I was supposed to give birth to my baby – the first one. Baby girl. Well, the Spoilers had a lot of money, so they organised a bail for me; after I got the child I was released.

I went out; but the case was still going on and on. It was a long case, because they had done one of the biggest robberies in South Africa. They got away with a big amount of money. So then I had to continue with this trial, but I couldn't now give them away.

So you know what I did? I escaped from Johannesburg. I went to the Free State. I was hiding in the Free State, and then I got myself a job in a mine hospital near Welkom. I worked there under a false name, false everything, ja.

There I got myself in problems again. I enjoy my life in the Free State, I have forgotten about Johannesburg. I'm only having communication here and there. These people in Welkom there, my uncle is a doctor, we are nurses. We are dancing, we are playing tennis. I didn't know that these people were working for SACTU, until one day all these people got arrested. [Laughs]

This time it was a different gang – the trade union! I didn't know, really! [Laughs] I just heard in Welkom there was a big raid. But how come my friends are all gone? Hai! No, it's impossible.

Then I went to my uncle, and I ask, 'Uncle, what happened to all my friends? What is this trade union?' 'No, don't ask me any questions. Please go, go.'

And after a few days the police came. Questions, ja. 'You know these people? There were about ten or twelve?' 'Ja, I know them all.' 'How do you know them?' 'No, they were my friends; we were dancing together; we were playing tennis; we are going to places – to Bloemfontein, to Welkom, to here, there.'

'Oh no!'

They took me, and they started investigating now. Oh! then I was in real serious problems. That's why then, after that, I was struck off the roll. 1973.

Well, then I was on the street for two years, doing this and this, working in the kitchens. For two years, 1974 to 1975, on the street. And then ja, my family started to think this is very, very unfair, so they tried to collect some money. And these people – progressive people like Dr Jassat who I worked for in a private surgery for some time, he said, 'No, nursing is not the end of the world. Why don't you study again, and do something – maybe be a social worker?' Then I said, 'Ah, but I only did my nursing JC. How do I do social science, because one must have a university entrance?' So Dr Jassat – again I didn't know that they were ANC members – they just told me, 'We are going to help you. We are going to give you some money, you buy some lectures from reputable college; and then you study. You write your National Senior, after that you go to any University – Turfloop, Ngoya or anywhere – and you do your social science and become a social worker.'

So I went back to Johannesburg to study. Just after I had completed my National Senior I was supposed to start social science, then it was Soweto – the children's uprising. But I was gradually understanding better now, because I had seen Sharpeville. When I saw Soweto, I thought: Ach, it's too much now really. And what can I really do now in South Africa, because I'm struck off the roll. I'm no more a nurse.

Then I got myself into really serious problems now. Because some nurses, friends of mine, they stole instruments from the hospital and we were helping the wounded children, but using my bedroom you see. That was the most dangerous thing I did, because now, when we were discovered, I was the one who was in most serious trouble. I was re-arrested again. And when they found that I was struck off the roll and I'm still doing this nursing, all these funny things, it was just terrible. Really I thought I was just going to get a long, long sentence. So I decided to leave the country after I got bail.

In Botswana I had joined the ANC, and then I joined MK and went to Angola. I knew exactly now what was I doing, because inside the country there were places where we could listen to Freedom Radio. And I used to ask, 'What are these mothers with green blouses and black skirts?' 'No, they are Congress.' And then they told us that Congress, it's coming to liberate us, ja. So I grew up hearing about this Congress, ja.

In Angola, it's when we first arrived – ah, it was real tough. You know most of the women – most of us from that first lot, the first fourteen, really I always look at them, because we used to wash with a half bucket of water – fourteen of us! Ja! Because we were given one mug. Whether you brush your teeth, whether you wash your face, whether you wash your body, whether you drink it – it's your only one. Look out!

Ja, those were tough days. But it was only in the beginning. We later became twenty-five, twenty-five women among five hundred men. It was just a small Benguela transit camp. Ja, there it was really tough going. We used to eat these oats – I think maybe it was leftovers after the Second World War. [Laughs] It was stale! It was . . . ones were moving by themselves, up and down, ja. And the brown beans that we were eating . . . There was this soup . . . we used to call the ants – the small red ones – the Red Army. So we just cook it with that Red Army, you can't choose. You can't separate the beans from the Red Army because the Red Army is right inside the beans. You know they have bored small, small holes, and the Red Army's hiding there! [Laughs]

In Angola, we lived in the camps. The women did exactly the same training as the men. Exactly the same. Drilling, handling weapons, topography . . . everything.

We used to live in tents when we first arrived, but later we had a very nice camp really, where we were attacked in 1979. This attack was three weeks in succession. They started with ZAPU – ZAPU was still in the bush. The following week it was SWAPO. And then the following week it was us. Oh . . . I think it was an inside job, because they came with the data. They came one morning. Usually we used to assemble for news at about quarter past seven in the morning. So they came exactly that time.

I don't know if I was unfortunate or fortunate that day, because on that day I was supposed to go to Benguela to collect some medicines; because we were just in the bush, and conditions were tough. In the bush, how does one store these anti-snake serums for instance? . . . Ja, that kind of a situation. And then that morning it's the morning they attack. Myself I never saw it. I was on the way to Benguela which was about eighty kilometres from where we are.

They bombed our camp completely down. We were a bit lucky, because we had learnt from the previous experiences of ZAPU and SWAPO, so we were out already. When they came to bomb the camp it was only a few people cooking for us – kitchen staff. They killed two of the comrades – the commander of the kitchen and the officer on duty; and one Cuban who was the typist of the Major. And eight were injured. I saw them at the hospital because by the time when I reached Benguela it had happened already. Communication was very fast from that place, so I was sent to the hospital. And when I arrived there, they were still very fresh, bleeding . . . in fact, they were just in the casualty.

So we were moved from that camp – it was in the deep south – to the north. Our camp couldn't be used again because it was completely demolished. By then I had long completed my training.

It was not difficult there, it was nice. We were under Cubans. We used to eat nice food. They used to celebrate even collective birthdays – you know, like me I'm born in March and all the people who are born in March will have a collective birthday – and then we used to celebrate their day, the big demonkada, you know. They would slaughter pigs and then cook nice food, their traditional rice with this brown beans and meat, and that and that and that. Even our days – like 8 January, 9 August, 26 June. Ja, ja, all! And we'll drink, even beer, even Havana cigars! [Laughs]

I lived six years in the camps, but not in one place – moving here and here. And in between, well, going to seminars, like in 1981 I was in Yugoslavia for about two months to a Red Cross Seminar. And then in between I would fly our fracture patients to Tanzania, and our psychiatrics to Lusaka. So really it wasn't so boring or one monotonous pattern of life, ja.

In 1982 I came to get married here in Dar es Salaam. But we were never . . . most of the time we were never together, because he was fighting most of the time in the front. We stayed together for two years, but only for two years.

And then I went to school. I studied in Germany. I've learned medicine, I've specialised in gynaecology and obstetrics. Oh, it was nice. It was very good – except the weather. It was . . . oh! it's cold in Europe! [Laughs] I didn't really adapt to the climate, not until now really. Every time in winter I must remember Africa. Ja, really. But well, it was nice. Food was OK, I never had problems even with my asthma. I was completely healed there. And I learned German.

I was seven years in the GDR. I didn't see my husband until 1987 when I came back from our Second Women's Conference in Angola. Then he joined me, only for two years again; and then I left him there when I came back now to Tanzania. Now he's in the GDR. He's doing stomatology technique in German. [Laughs] He'll come back in two years.

I have two children, both of them while I was with the Spoilers. Oh, it's another different story. You know, Spoilers used to operate exactly like the Mafia. Because when you are having a boyfriend there, when he goes to jail you must continue with the other one from the gang. You are never allowed to go outside. So both my children . . . both my children were from the gang.

They're in Lesotho now. They're big – but they are well looked after. I hear my daughter – she's eighteen – she's going to do a BSc when she finishes high school; and she wants to do medicine like the mother. And my son wants to do BA and International Law. If everything goes well, I'll go down south, because my people there are prepared to buy them tickets to come to Zambia – where we can meet for the first time after fourteen years. After I've seen the children, I'm going to come back to Mazimbu. I'm going to work here. They need doctors here, especially gynaecologists.

You know, when I was in Botswana, some senior members in the organisation wanted me to go to school first. But I said, 'No; I'd strongly like to go to the army first, if I'm given the opportunity, when I'm still young. And then after that, I'll go to school.' Well, I didn't know that it would take so long, but . . . it did. But I don't think I regret really, because it was a worthwhile experience.

I keep working. I'm learning more and more and more, until freedom day.

ZEBULON XULU
Berlin 1991

'It was winter, everything was dry, no water, no fruits, not anything. So that even to get water we used to dig and dig and dig.'

> He is a good-looking, well-made man, with a fearsome head-wound, as though a hammer-blow has crushed in the bone. Beneath the hairline there is also a hole that goes right through. He has a deep furrow down one cheek. These are the visible wounds. He has others that are not visible. He is serious, speaks well; but English is not his first language, and the constructions are sometimes confused.

For long years, our people were struggling through peaceful forms of struggle, and this did not bring about the change which our people needed, which is freedom. And our people were daily killed, they were not defended. So I wanted to go and join the people's army. If needs be I can lay my life for the freedom of our people.

I was twenty-four, ja. Someone inside the country, he showed us the way. We went in Lesotho crossing by the river, and we struggled to reach for the contact in Lesotho. We managed to get contact, and we were in the hands of the African National Congress. We waited in Lesotho, and after some time we went to Tanzania. We were more than ninety-five or so – we were moving in groups – and from Tanzania we went to Angola in 1985.

There in Angola there were some times when we used to not get the normal food, but we understood that we are people who are dependent upon solidarity. The commissars at the camp they stressed the need for understanding that, in exile and in the camps, one lives an abnormal life. But since one knows what has brought him or her to Angola, then one accepts everything. The hardships were secondary. What was primary is that one gets the training. And after the training, going back inside the country and fighting that mission given by the movement.

I was once a commissar at a place in the very southern parts of Angola, where we were sort of an outpost. In that area UNITA was everywhere to be found. On 26 June – South African Freedom Day – we went very deep inside the area of UNITA, hunting for meat. Moving in this area we used to see the footsteps of UNITA where there are no people, because it is an area used by UNITA. And then the commissar said, 'No, OK. Let us go forward, because last night we hunted and hunted and did not have enough.'

Crossing this sector it was difficult for the car to move, so when crossing this small river we had to dismount from the car, and then we went and hunted and hunted and hunted. On our way back, right in this place where we were crossing, UNITA has ambushed us there. So we fought and fought; and we lost two comrades, the commissar and one FAPLA captain who was also accompanying us. Others went this direction, others went that direction. So myself and comrade Aaron we found it difficult, because we did not know the area.

I said, 'Aaron, it will not be proper to move out of this area during daylight because maybe UNITA has sent some sentries to check us.' There was a bazooka – we are hearing the boom, boom, boom! After six days we managed to reach the camp. We took such a long time because we were having an argument about using the Southern Cross. Aaron was long in the army, but me I was fresh from the camps so I knew what topography was about, saying that when the north is in this direction, the east is in this direction. After moving one and a half days in the direction which he thought was the south, he said, 'No, man. It looks like you were right.' And then we struggle again to go back where we were coming from.

Oh, it was very, very bad. It was winter, everything dry, no water, no fruits, not anything, so even to get water we used to dig and dig and dig and dig, up to the time when you come to the muddy water. But since one is very much thirsty, one is just worried to quench the thirst, nothing more.

We have taken the decision that when we confront UNITA we fight and fight and fight, till one leaves one bullet for himself so that one cannot be captured by UNITA. Our feet were very, very swollen – mine were at least stronger, but the comrade was very, very bad, ja. He had sores on his feet, and since we were wearing boots it was difficult. And then hunger, plus very hot sun, and thirsty – even our weapons were too hot.

At last we managed to see some lights there, and we thought that maybe this is the village of the peasants, or maybe of UNITA. We discussed and discussed about this, and then we decided to come closer. Maybe the people they will show us the direction, because we were dependent upon the Southern Cross. We managed to reach the peasants who were very familiar with us, because the people of Angola they share our suffering, and they assist us in everything which they are capable of. We just find very, very young children and very old women. UNITA when attacking a village, it takes all the fit boys and the girls and the young men and women, and force them to go and to train for UNITA's unit.

We were met by women, they gave us food. They gave us funge – myself I did not think before that I can eat funge, which is the Angolan food – like pap but prepared in another way. Takes some time to be dried, and then rolled out, and then to get dried out, and thereafter again same process. But it is too much elastic – you can cook and cook it for many hours, but it will remain as if it is not well cooked, ja. It's rubbery substance.

Well we ate this funge, some. The Angolans are very much strong in cooking fish, so then we were brought some fish there. Myself I had never imagined that I can eat the head of a fish, but – well I managed to eat and eat; and then they brought us some oranges, they brought us everything. Then they told us that we can sleep. We told them no, it won't be proper for us to sleep; we were not sure enough of staying in that area because of UNITA.

But in any case, they were very much peaceful to us. And then some few old men went and showed us the direction, and we managed to reach another village. And then we said: OK, we must sleep. We must rest now, it's too much. We were warmly welcomed; we ate and ate and we were satisfied. And then we slept. Someone was sent from this village by bicycle to tell the commander that we are here, and we waited until the commander came and fetched us, and took us to the camp.

In 1987, on 25 June, we were in the northern front. We were moving on patrol in two trucks where UNITA mines the road, booby-traps the trees, booby-traps everything. I was in the front truck. Hardly five kilometres from our camp we detonated a mine. We dismounted. We took to cover and observe the terrain, but there was no fire from UNITA. So we thought, maybe this is a warning signal that UNITA is not very far from here, this could be a signal for UNITA to know that, ja, we are coming. Maybe on our way we will be ambushed. Aah, it was difficult.

So we communicated to our camps using the big weapon called Mzekezeke, so that they can know that, ja, something is happening. They take a long time, but ultimately they came. The commander said: Yes, we are going forward. But you must be vigilant and be combat-ready; the driver must be very much observant. But because it was rainy season we could not see whether here was what or what or what. And when we were in the first curve, we were ambushed by UNITA!

We were seventeen in this first truck – or fourteen, I'm not sure of the figures. We dismounted. We heard the sound of the bazooka, right? And then the bazooka hit our truck, and splinters bazooka hit me here! I fell down unconsciously, without knowing what is going on. It was just a very bad situation.

After some time, I thought that there is the sound of a weapon. I was hearing the shooting, boom, boom, boom. I realised that: No man, it looks like we are in an ambush. And then came the consciousness that, well of course we are in an ambush; and I was looking to see what happened. I've got no weapon; where is my weapon? It has fell down. I just managed to crawl forward, crawl forward, crawl forward, until I met one comrade who was late already, and then I took some of his magazines and I armed myself. I took his weapon. I dragged him under the coffee tree, and camouflaged him there, right?

Rolling back now, I met some two of our comrades and I told them that there's Mowawa in front, but he's already late – I've tried my first aid but it does not help. There was also a medico who was with us, and he said, 'Let's crawl forward.' I insisted, telling them, 'He is late. There is nothing we can do.'

And then, while we were crawling forward, there appeared UNITA from the left, right. Well, I opened fire there, but this UNITA were in a unit, and they were advancing, thinking that they have finished us. I heard Paswa say something – meaning the enemy he's dealt with me. And then I was hit here; a bullet grazed my cheek. Since I was now hot, I thought maybe it was a falling leaf.

I could not see – it was totally bleeding. I was only using my right eye. And then I was hit also here in the leg – even today my leg is in a very bad condition. It was very difficult. When you roll this way, you see that the leaves are falling; and then when you roll the other way, you find that the bullets are digging this end. And then you see it's totally no chance of doing anything – and you are just lying. My AK had been hit and could not fire.

Then the medico, Bali, came and took me out of the enemy sector. The radioman was phoning: We are under fire! We are under fire! But there was no response, till he was also killed.

After some time the reinforcement came, and we were taken to Quibaxe. The doctor came and asked me what had happened. When I told him, he said, 'Ah, no, I wanted to test whether your memory is still serving well, because the nature of your wound is very much serious – it's like you've been hit with a brick here in the face.'

By this time it was very difficult even to move by truck, so our comrades in Quibaxe consulted FAPLA, and we were organised to move by helicopter with some Angolan people who were hit, because UNITA was hitting at this village, hitting at this village, hitting at this village. So now we could get only two of our comrades in this helicopter of the six who were injured. And we went to Luanda.

There our doctors organised to send us to other places for further treatment, because the Angolan hospitals are all full. Money is used for defence, so some other things, medical supplies, are not obtainable. We went to different places for further treatment. We were four who came here to the GDR.

I came here in 1988. The doctor said it won't be proper if they operate on my injured right knee – it is very sensitive and the capsule inside and the ligament is destroyed. But the knee will heal by itself. In my head they took out some splinters. And then my head bone here is destroyed, so when the pressure is low it opens up – you see here a hole? It goes very down deep; and also the paining is very much bad. So now the doctors have told me that, when the wound heals from inside after one or two years – when it has completely healed from inside they can make something like a plastic surgery and repair. And also to fix my face as well.

So now during that process of waiting for my other operation, I'm trying to do something which will further contribute to our people's struggle when I come home. I'm trying to study male nursing, and I would like to work in an old people's hospital. Where I'm presently in, there is a hospital of the old people, and I find it very much necessary to help. You find someone who is laying twenty-four hours in bed who is dependent on the help of others. So I think it will be proper when going back home that I will have two things – first my health to be OK; then I to be having something to contribute. And then I will be able to go back home.

Now, I'm doing the three-year practical, but I've got problems with the language. It is very difficult to study, because I've got too much pain.

Another thing: the government changes here have brought some negative effects upon us as well. The Solidarity Committee which was supporting us, collecting money from the people, now forget about us, and some comrades went back to Africa, because now the money and the scholarships is not available.

And racism here is on a larger scale. Now there are the far rights here, who, when seeing the black man, use this insulting word 'negra' and shout, 'Auslander raus'. Now they are more free to do anything, they also now turn against us. Even when you are seated in a train, you are lucky if they don't beat you. It's very bad. Sometimes they will beat you and throw you out of the train.

It is worse when you go with a German girlfriend. Aah! They insult you. They start with the girl, 'You girl! Are there in Deutschland no men, that you got a negra?' And then they start hitting you. So it's very bad there, this racism. This is just the same fascism which was practised by the Nazis; and also which is taking place at home in areas like Welkom and Boksburg. This is the same racism. Sometimes, you are just lucky, you don't know how you survive. But it's not good to walk during the night and during the weekend. But on the other hand, there is a young group of Germans – the group called Antifascism – and in every demonstration for foreigners they are there with support. They also demonstrate against this far right actions.

So I think for me it will be proper that I continue with my studies. And when the time is ripe, when the amnesty has been granted also for the MK combatants, then I will think of going home. But what is basic is that I can finish this course in the GDR.

GLORIA MEEK
Mazimbu 1989

'We had high hopes of going back in six months' time, and fighting!'

> She is thirty-four years old, born in Johannesburg – Kliptown – into a family that is very racially mixed.

My father's father is a German, and my father's mother was a Zulu. My mother's father is Asian and my mother was a Sotho. So we are really mixed – we even have Chinese and Indians all mixed in with our family. There are five children in the family. I went to a multiracial boarding-school in Natal. We had German and Irish nuns taking care of us. It wasn't an easy life being far away from home and the nuns were quite cruel.

When I was fifteen my mother decided to withdraw us from that school, so I continued my schooling in Johannesburg. Things were quite different then at that school because we were used to mixing with all the races, to mixing really with everybody, and all of a sudden we find ourselves exposed to all kinds of segregation laws and things . . . well, it was not easy to adjust.

When I enrolled at UNISA for a course in social work I started getting involved in student politics, and I ultimately found myself in SASO. I was the secretary for some time in our area, Eldorado Park. We were continuously harassed by the police – myself and my brother – picked up, detained time and again, released, picked up, detained, without ever being charged.

I only managed to get to my second year when I was detained again; I was held for six months in solitary confinement – that was in 1975. They just kept me there, and they used to beat me up. At one stage they even beat me up at the back of my head with a baton or a pistol. And they used to make me undress and stand naked in front of them for hours on end. Sometimes from the morning until late at night I would stand there. I was expected to incriminate some of my fellow students that I was active with in the Movement.

They used to question me for hours on end. They had documents already written out, and they wanted me to sign these declarations against. They told me they wouldn't let me go until I am prepared to sign, and appear in court as a state witness. I refused. I was prepared to stay there for as long as they wanted to keep me. I was not going to get people into trouble, and have them exposed to the same kind of thing that I was being exposed to.

There was one particular time when they had some metal in the shape of bricks, which they would plug into some electrical device, and these bricks would freeze. They made me stand on them for about twelve hours. They were beating me, pulling my hair out by the roots, and doing all kinds of things to . . . to humiliate me. And all this time I was naked, you see, so I really felt terribly humiliated. Then I finally collapsed, I couldn't stand it any more.

I was pregnant, but they didn't care a damn. Because of the beatings I had a miscarriage in the prison cell – and I had to clean up everything myself. I was in my third month, ja, and I informed them. But I didn't get any medical treatment after that; and when I was released I did have some gynaecological problems.

During the time I was detained, they picked up my youngest brother, and one evening they brought him to my cell. He was terribly beaten up, bleeding all over. I couldn't even see his face, he was so bleeding and swollen; and they warned me that they were going to kill him if I don't speak. They were going to kill him and leave his body in the cell with me. Well, both of us vowed that we were not going to say a word – we were prepared to accept anything that was coming our way.

During the time that I was in detention there were twenty-seven coloured boys who were detained, also students; they were on the top floor, I was right under them on the ground floor; there was a policeman who became used to all us detainees, and we would write each other letters on toilet paper. But ultimately this policeman was found out, and he was killed there, right in John Vorster Square. They just shot him through the head, ja, the minute they found out that he was helping us to get out information to the outside. They just killed him.

When ultimately I was released, it was on the condition that I would report to John Vorster Square at six o'clock every evening. And if I don't do that I would be redetained. So life really became a hassle. I didn't feel like going to report, and that is when they started going after me again. They used to come to my home, and I wasn't home. And they used to go to the place where I was working. I was sleeping at different places every night trying to avoid them, and at the same time trying to organise to go out of the country, because I didn't want to become a 'system vegetable' – that's what we used to call people who had been detained and tortured to a point when they are totally useless.

In the end I left home with another girl, she's in Canada now, and some boys. We had intended to drive as far as the Swaziland border and then from there skip the border at night into Mozambique. But unfortunately on the way, the car had a breakdown near a game reserve near the border of Swaziland. Then two of the guys who were with us had to go back to try to organise another vehicle. So we stayed in this game reserve – there was a holiday resort there. But after three days, when they didn't come back, we realised that something must have happened to them. And so we decided to move on, three of us.

It's a good thing that we did. Because, back home, these two guys were picked up, and the police already had the information that we were escaping across the border into Swaziland. We walked from Barberton, right into Swaziland. We used the mountain route – a long distance. We walked for hours, climbing steep all the time. One night we slept – we didn't even have a blanket; we had to huddle closely together; it was very misty, right on top of the mountains. We slept there until about five o'clock in the morning, then moved on again and got to the border around midday.

We met a little herd boy. He told us that at three o'clock every day those border police there go out and drink, so if we want to cross we should cross at that time. We were just waiting patiently for three o'clock. We didn't have any food or money with us. The border gate was right at the river, and we crossed the river round about half past three in the afternoon, and we were in Swaziland.

We were afraid of reporting ourselves to the police, because we knew that some of them collaborated with South African police. So we just hid amongst the bushes there, near the river until about six o'clock. Then we decided to look for a mission house, and tell them we are students on an educational tour of Swaziland. We asked some people where the nearest Catholic mission house was. One man was so kind – he had took us to the mission house in his Land Rover . . .

When we got there we were all afraid to go to the priest! [Laughs] We didn't know if he would suspect us of lying or something like that. But he was very kind – apparently he was used to helping people who were escaping from South Africa. He understood our problem, ja. We all had a hot bath, and he gave us a lovely warm supper.

The next day they went to Mbabane, and eventually crossed the Mozambique border with the assistance of an ANC underground agent. This was 1975. The ANC had not yet established an office in Mozambique, so they were accommodated by FRELIMO in their army headquarters. There were other South African refugees there, and people from Kenya, Southern Rhodesia and Malawi. Gloria and her friends were anxious to get in touch with the ANC. But before they could do so, all the refugees were removed to a place up north, in the Mampula area.

We travelled one day and a night to this place, very far from the capital.

Oh, it was a terrible place! In all we were twenty-six, ten South Africans together with refugees from other places. And we were just dumped there. We were given a blanket each, and told this is where we were to stay. We were surprised, because there were no houses, not even huts or anything. They dropped us there with a bag of mealiemeal and a bag of beans, and they just left.

We had to sleep out in the open; it was during the rainy season, and that place was so wild! Elephants were passing by. You could hear lions roaring in the night, snakes everywhere. It was just a terrible place. We had to drink water from the river and bathe in that river – it was just a little stream. Oh, it was just too terrible. It was my first time to find myself in a place like that, and I couldn't understand what was happening. Even the people that were with us were hostile towards us.

We stayed in that place for about a month, sleeping in the open like that, eating that pap and beans every day. We didn't even have soap to bathe; we just had to get into the water, rinse ourselves, and get into the same clothes again, because when we went through Barberton we left all our clothes behind.

After a month they brought some reeds, and told us that we had to build huts. We had to cut some of the elephant grass and make a sort of a mattress that we can sleep on in the meantime. We stayed in this place for about six months. We used to make requests to go to the United Nations (refugee organisation) because now the ANC seemed very far out of reach; they never sent anybody.

Even the soldiers who were guarding us were very vicious. They said that if we want to eat we will have to grow food for ourselves. We didn't mind because we were tired of eating that pap and beans every day, and we had nothing to do. So we decided that we will start working in the fields now. We had to wake up at five in the morning, and they showed us a certain plot that we had to clear and start planting vegetables. That is how we passed the day, and this continued for about three months.

When the vegetables were ready to be eaten, a big truck came from the town in that district, and the official who was looking after this place told us that they are going to sell these vegetables so that they can buy sugar, tea and soap, toothpaste and all these things for us. They took all the vegetables and they never came back. They must have sold the stuff and shared the money amongst themselves. And we kept on living the way we were living – that pap and beans every day.

> Eventually the ANC did make contact with them, and brought them to Maputo. They were all given the option of going to school, or joining the army.

We opted for the army because that was what we wanted to do all along. From the time that we left home we were intending to go and join MK.

We were told we were going to Angola to start our military training. We were all very happy because that is what we had been wanting to do all the time. We had lots of high hopes of going back home in six months' time and fighting! [Laughs] Well, you know, at that time, how you are. We didn't understand many things.

We were flown to Angola. In Angola we were about thirty-six women and more than five hundred men. We were separated into two groups – the male comrades went to another training camp, and we were put in a house that was the former South African embassy. We spent most of the time cleaning, because training facilities were not yet available.

We stayed in the capital for two months, then went south to our first training camp in Benguela – a Portuguese farm that was abandoned. There was a cowshed and one building. We were twenty-two women and we slept in the cowshed – the men were sleeping in tents. There was only one bathroom and one toilet, but we had the privilege of going to bathe in that house.

We started having problems with the water supply. There was a breakdown in the generator, it could no longer pump, so water rationing started. You could only get a cup of water – to wash your teeth, your whole body and everything! [Laughs] We had to wash in that cup of water. So we collected a big tin and we each contributed our cup of water, and we all used to bathe out of that tin there! The ANC wasn't properly established – it was still new in the place, and we were having a lot of problems with food and clothing and all these things. The only thing we had to wear was our military uniform; and there was a time when we had to choose between soup and cocoa for breakfast, soup or cocoa for lunch and supper! [Laughs] If we had soup for breakfast we knew we were going to have cocoa for lunch. So it was like that for quite some time. We had some powdered eggs – we didn't have oil or fat – so we just used to dump those things in the boiling water and eat them like that. And it was terrible.

Things were quite tough during those days. It was a sort of semi-desert – the grass was hard and thorny, very dry. It was very cold in winter, very hot in summer. You had to crawl, and we would come back all bleeding, our arms and knees scorched because of crawling in the hard grass. But as time went by we got used to the training, climbing fully armed with knapsacks, and marching for long distances. We also had political classes – we argued about everything. We were still young, we were having wild ideas, but we learned a lot.

We stayed there for six months and then we moved to a new and better place. We travelled further down south, and we got to a beautiful camp, all prepared. There were barracks, there was just about everything there needed for proper training, so we settled down. There, at Lelutatenge, almost on the border with Namibia, we started our actual training. We did a one-year course under Cuban instruction – it was also quite tough, but we didn't mind – we just wanted to go back and fight. That was our only aim.

In 1979 the Boers started their massive raids into Angola, bombing villages. Every day villages were being bombed, getting nearer and nearer to our camp. And we knew very well that they were looking for our camp and we didn't have all the facilities to combat such a situation. So, as a safety measure, we used to leave the camp at two o'clock in the morning and not come back until ten at night. We had our breakfast at one o'clock in the morning! [Laughs] There were ten minutes given to eat your breakfast, and then we had to start moving out in different directions, far away from the camp – twenty to thirty kilometres away.

We did this from January until March. On 18 March, we were all in our hiding-places round about seven o'clock in the morning, when jets just came zooming from different directions. They started bombarding the camp. Three of our comrades were killed there – one Cuban, a comrade who was in charge in the kitchen, and another comrade who was on guard duty. Three people always had to be in the camp – we used to rotate every day. There were defence stations in the camp – dugouts where you could go and hide. But they thought that the planes had moved out before they really did.

The planes dropped more than five hundred bombs of different types; there was nothing left of the camp at all. A camp which we had built up with our own hands for over a year, razed to the ground in three minutes. There was nothing, absolutely nothing. Even the chickens that were there were burned to death, The comrades who were killed thought the planes were leaving and they came out; but the planes came back a second time and they were gunned down. You couldn't even pick up their bodies – they fell apart. We had to pick them up with spades, completely messed up all of them. So we just had to make graves and bury them there in the camp.

It was the first time it dawned on me that now we are involved in war. All the time it was just an idea. I realised that if we were in the camp at that time, there wouldn't be a single one of us that would have survived. And I realised how vicious the Boers were – really terrible.

We were moved to the north of Angola. We had to start again from scratch. It was just bush, it was just a wild place. We had to start chopping down trees, clearing the grass, and digging dugouts – because after the bombardment we were no longer going to live in barracks. We were going underground. It was really hard work in those days. And then, well once the camp was built, life returned to normal, daily routine continued. But we were more on the alert than before.

I became ill with malaria, coupled with other problems. I got treatment in Luanda and after recovering I didn't go back to camp, but went to college in Lusaka, where I worked in different ANC departments in Lusaka until I went back to Angola in '82.

Round about 1984 my boyfriend came back from his mission. We decided to get married. I fell pregnant. There were no conditions for married people at that time in Angola, so we had to come to East Africa. And that's where I find myself.

GRAHAM MORODI
Dar es Salaam 1989

'We fought and we did our utmost best . . . They have killed some of us, and we have killed some of them.'

> He is one of the men who formed the Luthuli Brigade of Umkhonto we Sizwe, and a veteran of the military incursion into Wankie. He joined the ANC in 1950, when it was still a legal organisation.

When the ANC was banned in 1960, I was already a branch secretary, ja. Then when it was banned there was this Residents' Association. I was also secretary of that – it was an underground cover for the ANC. I was working with recruiting to go outside.

One of my boys which I had recruited was in a group that was arrested at the border. And he knew my name – so they came to the house where I had been staying. I had recently moved. The police went to my next-door neighbour.

Then the police says to him, 'Can you tell us, do you know this next door of yours?' He says, 'I know him very well; we stayed fifteen years together here.' They say, 'Where is he?' He says, 'I don't know. He have moved last week, Saturday. I don't know where he has gone to.' They say, 'But you stay fifteen years together, he couldn't tell you where he's going to?' He says, 'Hai! I don't know.' They say, 'Do you have any reason why didn't he tell you that he's going?' He look at them and says, 'I think the only reason he had it's what you have come here for!' [Laughs] Then they give up.

> Graham was arrested at the factory where he worked. He was held for eighty-seven days, interrogated, released, and returned to his work.

I worked for a week or two. You know, the people were so respecting in the factory I felt, no, it's not right [Laughs] you know, everybody respecting me – including the white workers. Some time I got a taxi with one of my friends. He asked me: When did you come back? I say: No, I was just released last week from jail. When I got out the taxi and I want to pay him, he says: No. People who come from ninety days we don't take their money.

So you know, I thought I don't deserve such respect here in the factory. But my colleagues think I should go and organise for a trade union! So I became an organiser for the General Workers' Union.

In 1964 January, early in the morning, the police came to my house. Then they banned me for five years not to enter the factory, not to talk to any child except my child, only to be in the area of Robville, not to go to any township, for five years. Ja ja, for five years.

Then I felt I should leave. I couldn't do anything and my wife was working, getting very little money.

He went to Tanzania and joined Umkhonto. He was sent to Egypt for military training, followed by a year in the Soviet Union.

We came back in 1966. I was assigned to go to the front. But we come to Zambia, we stayed there till 1967, outside the front, doing nothing. First we were making charcoal, because at that time cigarettes, you used to get a packet once a week, and there was not much food that we were getting, even clothing. So we burn some charcoals because we are right in the forest there. Then we supply our comrades in Lusaka, in town, where this charcoal is very expensive. We make it so cheap so we can be able during the weekend to come together, have some cold drinks, and buy extra cigarette for all of us.

Then in July 1967 we were preparing to go back home, and Oliver Tambo came to address us. He says now, because of the death of our president, Chief Luthuli, he declared a week mourning, so we'll be delayed by a week to leave. And this detachment become the Luthuli Detachment.

Some of our men who had been sent through Botswana were captured, and they were beaten up and sent back. So we choose that we have to go through Rhodesia, so that when we meet people there – the police or the army – we can be able to fight, because it's not an independent African state and we know it's our enemy. So it was agreed.

We started leaving the end of July. We cross Zambezi in a very dangerous boat – the enemy could not believe that we have crossed there. We were using some rope – in fact we who are trained in Egypt were trained on overcoming obstacles mostly, ja. We used some rope, and it was very dangerous. President Tambo was there, Nkobi was there, Joe Modise was there. And Ndlovo of ZAPU was there because it was a joint venture with ZAPU.

Then after crossing, we are forced to walk about three hundred miles! [Laughs] Through the bush! We started crossing at eight o'clock in the night till eight o'clock in the morning. I was almost the last person to cross. Then we stayed there the whole day, and at five o'clock started moving. We came to a place where there was a chief. Some of the ZAPU comrades went there to find out can we get food. Then the chief says to them, 'Yes, it's very good that you people are here. And me I'm here not satisfied. The Smith regime they sent me without my consent and my people here to the stones. We can't plough. And after they put me here, they say I must watch for guerrillas not to pass through here, ja ja. So I'm also fighting against the Boers, I'm going to help you all.'

Then they give us some porridge and this spinach, and we ate. At night they cover us. We are walking the road, but they are bringing some cattle behind us so they can destroy our footprints. During the day we just sit there till the evening; then we started to walk. The next morning we're at Potgieter Spa, then we spent the whole day there. From there we move into Wankie Game Reserve.

Then we start to see the spotter planes, flying very high. We walk. We came to a river, we killed a buffalo; and we spend twenty-four hours frying this buffalo, getting water, washing ourselves, drinking. We decided to spend twenty-four hours because the terrain was very much in our favour. If the enemy comes, we know that we can deal with them. We took some meat with us, and started walking again. When this meat comes to an end, then we got a zebra. But at this time we didn't want to waste time. We just cut it, cut it, cut it and make fire and fry; take pieces and start marching.

We marched, we marched, we marched, until we come deep in the Wankie Game Reserve. That's where twenty then branch towards the east. Their mission was to go and blow a bridge, it's no more secret now, then we continue going ahead. We run out of food again, we keep on marching. And there was no water. We drink water with the elephant at certain times; we had these tablets to purify water, but at this time we didn't use them any more – we were so thirsty that you got no time to stop and purify the water.

There were some time, you know, two hundred elephants; there was lions; there was buffalo. But they were not an enemy to us. Ja, they were very friendly – they didn't care of us. It's for the first time I see that! [Laughs] They don't interfere. I think our smell too it was almost an animal, because we were eating these tree leaves. We stayed about ten days without food – we ate leaves from the trees. Because this other animals they were running away from us, we shot a dove. Between fifty we share that dove! [Laughs] We cook it in a little tin, then we make a soup. If you got a l-i-t-t-l-e leg of a dove you are satisfied! If you get the smell and drink the little soup, you are satisfied.

But we walked! In the morning then we came to a cattle post. We are very, very hungry. We sent two comrades from ZAPU – because it's their area – to go and find out if they can get something for us to eat, if they can buy a goat. When they get there they find an old man. He says: Today it's Sunday; and the men are gone home. I'm the only one left here. We have been told that when you come, we don't ask you questions – where you are going, where are you coming from. But we do assist you by giving you food. But now today there's no food; they will come back tomorrow.

So he give us four gallons of sour milk, a little drop of porridge! Then, just when we finished this drink we hear ta-ta-ta-ta-ta-ta sound of gun shooting. Our next section! When the shooting goes on, we heard they say, 'Surrender! Commandos! Surrender! Surrender! Apanazan shaida!' – you know in Shona apanazan shaida it means that you can't do nothing.

Then we started to fire back and they run away. They run away leaving their kitbags with clothing and food. It was the Rhodesian army, ja. White. They were white, mixed with blacks. We have killed about fifteen of them, they killed three of us from the first section. So they run away, and we captured this food. We were very hungry, I'm telling you! [Laughs] Very very hungry! And the first one I opened, I saw something like toothpaste. I open it. It was condensed milk. I drink, then Lennox he says to me, 'No no no. You know it's the law of the guerrilla anything that you pick up you must report to the commander – otherwise they are going to shoot you.' But I drink. Then he took another one and he also drinks. I said, 'Now they are going to shoot both of us!' [Laughs] Then we get together, we report whatever we have captured there.

We took out the spare uniform, we put on the Rhodesian army uniform. Others they found some lieutenants' uniforms, and they put them on. But we took off the badge, ja. Helicopters and spotter planes were flying very low. There is confusion on their side, and they just run, unorganised. We captured their radio – we are able to hear the helicopter signals.

Now we had this four-gallon tin which they brought the sour milk with. We went to this man to give him his tin, so he cannot be incriminated. Then he says to us, 'Don't go to the river there. There's a lot of them. They are planning an ambush.' And we are thirsty – after every fighting you feel very thirsty. We wanted to go there. Then he says: No. Don't go to the river; take this way. We continued, carrying a wounded man. I carried him for a long distance by myself.

Just as we walk – it was a full moon – we saw four black soldiers coming. And when they saw us they say, 'No! Don't kill us because we are also black.' We opened fire! We didn't waste time. We were afraid if we capture them then they are going to see our number and they are going to see how we are armed, and they may escape and give a proper report that side. So that it's best that we wipe them off.

Within two, three minutes, we hear firing at the river. What they did, they put one group of Rhodesians that side, and another group this side. Now they wanted us to come – when we get to the water the one group would be firing, so when we retreat the other one will finish us up. But they heard the shots when we shoot these four people. The one group, they think the other are shooting at us; and the other one also think that. So one group advances and the other also advances. And they start shooting one another. For fifteen minutes! We say, 'Hah! What is going on?' Then we continue marching. But our steps was very slow at this time, slow pace ja. We were tired.

In the morning, when we listened to the radio, they were giving to Salisbury a report saying that we laid an ambush, and that we killed the commander and fifteen others. But they killed themselves and fifteen others.

The next morning the helicopter started. Now we decided to rest where there's long trees to keep the helicopters not coming close to us. We eat and clean our guns. We sent two men – scouts – to go and reconnaissance. Our scout, he saw they got all their guns piled up like this; they were lying there and discussing the battle. They said, 'If we can meet those people and they fight like they did yesterday . . . I'll run, you see.'

> One of the Umkhonto reconnaissance group was spotted by the Rhodesian soldiers. There followed a pitched battle lasting an hour and a half.

We lost two men. But we killed a lot of them that battle, because we were very close, It's where the brigadier from South Africa who was an expert in anti-guerrilla warfare, he was killed. He left South Africa. When he gets to Salisbury they sent him straight to the front; and within an hour he was killed, ja. South Africa cried very much about that brigadier.

We are very fortunate because from the first go, we managed to kill the commander and the radio people – the whole seven. We killed them all and they kill only two of our men.

After this battle, we decided to leave early. We had captured seven radios but we had nobody to carry them. We captured a lot of arms.

We were aiming to go to South Africa. We are leaving others like ZAPU in Zimbabwe, but some of us were also going to be left there – like Chris Hani. He was the commissar. He have to go back to Zambia and report, so he can get other people to come and reinforce.

> Morodi and four others went to look for water. They found water, but could not find their way back to the detachment which had been forced to move. Cut off from the main body, his group of five crossed the border into Botswana, where they buried their weapons. They had no intention of doing battle with the Botswana authorities. They were arrested by the Botswana police, who demanded that they hand over their arms. They denied they had any, but the police traced their footsteps to where the arms were hidden. They were held and given food. The next day white police arrived, took them to Francistown, and charged them with bringing weapons of war into Botswana, and with entering the country without a permit.

The sentences was different. The other group, the group of Hani, they got two years, I got three years, and others they got six years, ja; for the same crime. When we appeal, those who were sentenced to two years they had the sentenced reduced to one year. And they find that they have over-served two days and they were released. I was left with about ten days to finish my sentence.

I was released in December 1968. I arrived in Zambia. I went to a camp where our people were.

We were asked to come and meet a journalist in Lusaka. Then he start to ask us the first question, 'What is this? Are you ZAPU, ANC, or you are together?' Then we say, 'No, we are together. This is ZAPU and ANC' – although we knew at that time we are only ANC. Then he started to ask us about the operation in Rhodesia. How do we feel now after this? We said, 'OK! We fought and we did our utmost best, and they were keeping on running away. And they have killed some of us, and we have killed some of them.' Then he says to us, 'Don't you think if you have to go back now, you must kill all the whites in Rhodesia in order to intimidate the Smith Regime to surrender?' We said, 'No. That is not our policy. Our policy – we shoot the soldiers, the police who are armed. Any civilian person we don't shoot.' In fact we told him that we met a woman and a man, white, in the bush, where they should not have seen us. But we left. We didn't shoot them because we don't go around like terrorists shooting everybody. Then he asked many questions, then took some photos, then he left. But only later we hear that he was senior CIA member. Ja.

I and one of my colleagues were appointed regional commander. We were both in the Wankie operation. We started to run the MK East Africa region. I was brought back to Tanzania, where I stayed about five months totally underground. Then I left for Zambia, where I was to cross the Zambezi into Rhodesia, and go into Botswana so I can do some underground work.

They set out to cross the Zambezi by boat. He was in civilian dress.

Then about twenty-five metres into Zambezi – I was wearing my coat and I had my shoes, I had my luggage with me – the boat overturned. And the current was fast. I don't know how did I manage to save myself, because the pilots who were crossing me they just left me and swim off. I found myself coming to sort of an island within the Zambezi. When I get to that, climb out, I discover that those people who were crossing me they are already on that island. I ask them, 'Why? Why do you leave me and I'm wearing greatcoats and all these other things and you are wearing swimming costumes?' They say to me, 'No, don't talk too loud because the Boers are just across there.' Then I kept quiet.

In that little place there were a lot of people; it was just a small place. Cattle was eating grass around us there. They asked me, 'Do you still want to cross, because you are wet?' And I said to them, 'A courier will be waiting for me other side.' They went to look for another boat. Then later, I was crossed.

You know, the Boers relied on the crocodiles and hippos, because that place is crocodile infested and they thought that we won't cross. But I crossed successfully – and I had two suitcases of hardware to take with me to South Africa, and I was dropped about the area where the courier is going to pick me up.

I stayed for three days. There was no courier. I had no food. That time I was smoking. I had no cigarettes because I couldn't carry Zambian cigarettes – I would be discovered. I had about eight hundred rounds with me. Now, there's no food. I see some monkey eating some fruits in a tree. I also jump that tree. I find the monkeys have eaten all the ripe ones up. I took one – very bitter!

> Eventually, he decided to try and find his way unaided. He was arrested once more in Botswana. He gave his name as Abraham Makgothi. The police brought out photographs of the men captured during the Wankie battles. The police said to him, 'Now tell us which name you want? You say you are Abraham Makgothi, and we have two other names for you, plus your home name. Which is your real name?' Then he said he was Graham Morodi. He was interrogated for ten days, fined as a prohibited immigrant, and went back to Tanzania. He worked in various countries, arranging the reception and organisation of new MK recruits coming from home. His work took him finally to Swaziland, where he worked in the ANC underground.

We were arrested on 16 December 1982 in Swaziland. We were twenty-seven – all ANC members, ja. We were all arrested and taken to the police college. We were questioned there. They take us to a place, they call it Mawelawela; this is . . . the prison is open. They said they were taking us for safe custody.

But it was close to the borders of South Africa. And we told them that the helicopter from Amsterdam (in South Africa) to here, it take two, three minutes, and can come and bomb us, or land and take us, so we are not protected there. We refused to get into that prison for three days, until the Deputy Prime Minister, the Police Commissioner, the Prisons' Commissioner, they are all gathered there, and we have a meeting.

Then at night, a senior officer came and says we must see that we are spoiling our stay in Swaziland, which is a tree that give us a good shade that we are sleeping underneath. After the meeting then we agreed to go into the cells because it was safe custody, with the promise that after 8 January we'll be released. 8 January, it's our national day. It's the day that we hit the Boers (at Wankie), and the Boers want to hit us too. There we got information that some Boers came in a car, armed, and the Swazi police intercept them and ask them, 'Where are you going to?' They say, 'No, we are going to our brothers there. We are also members of the ANC!' But they were sent back. They were sent back with their arms.

They carried on long and often heated protests against their detention by the Swazi authorities. Finally they decided they had had enough. They would defy the authorities and simply march out of the prison – a mass breakout. He made his way to Maputo, to rejoin his ANC colleagues, expecting to be returned to operations in Swaziland. He was sent instead to Angola, as a regional commander of Umkhonto.

He became ill. He was diagnosed as having diabetes, and sent away from Angola for treatment. He spent four years in Lusaka as ANC Chief Representative in Zambia, and then in Dar es Salaam as Chief Representative in Tanzania. But his health deteriorated. When interviewed, he was about to leave for Lusaka, in semi-retirement.

Was it all worthwhile – all those years of struggle and fighting?

Yes! Yes, I think it's worthwhile. Because really it is within the struggle itself, ja.

ISAAC MAPHOTO
Harare 1990

'Then they prepared the coffins and put them outside. Then the whole prison would keep quiet. When you see the coffins outside, you are going, there's no way out.'

A veteran of the Wankie incursion, he is one of those who was captured and sentenced to death. But 'they didn't hang us, we were given life imprisonment'. Now he is working in the trade union movement in Zimbabwe.

I started politics early in 1952. I've been a strong supporter of the Movement but I happened to work under the City Council of Pretoria. Now that did not allow me to attend meetings. But the Security discovered that I was a politician. So in 1957 while I was working in the Labour Bureau – influx control.

I had a brother-in-law who's a Special Branch, so he told me that my name was in the list of people who must be detained; I was accused of being a communist. 'You are going to be arrested.' So I went out to

Botswana in 1961, in March. I had thought I would be there for some time and go back. But someone from the ANC said, 'No, you must proceed.' So that's how I left the country for good. Then I went to Dar es Salaam.

Isaac wanted to go for military training, but he was advised to apply for a scholarship, and went to Beirut in 1962.

I was there for eighteen months – then I was not happy. I wrote a letter asking the ANC to allow me to join MK. So I was not recruited, it was from my own innermost soul that I became a member of MK.

I was in the first group which landed in the Soviet Union for engineering and armour training. My group was the first group to operate tanks in Africa – the first black South Africans to operate those.

Then we came back to Tanzania where we stayed for about two years and left to go to Zambia. We did what we called Saga training, to prepare us to cross the river. Then in August the first group – the Wankie group crossed. Then we followed, we opened the Sipolele operation. Now in that group of Sipolele we were a hundred, and twenty-four were ANC chaps, the others were ZAPU comrades. I was chief of logistics in a unit of twelve. I still honour them. I don't think I will ever respect any army better than that one in my life, because we were a hundred, we stayed in the forest for four months, and we don't have a record of anybody who misbehaved in that group. One thing which helped that group was their political maturity. They were highly politically-minded group, despite the standard of education, the differences of language and different terrain.

At first when we crossed we had food, there was a supply group which followed us; but later we lived on the wild food. In court – after we were captured – it was stated that we ate more than eighty-seven animals, including two elephants and five rhinos, and we had quite a number of zebras. Even vultures – we could eat a vulture.

The problem we had from the beginning was water. But when water came, it was rain so much. We were using very good shoes. Whether it rains or what, you sleep with them, you wake up with them, you don't change them. And our guns are very good – that's why we had an advantage on the enemy's side, because their guns – FM . . . what you call it – can't fire when it is raining; it jams. But AK doesn't jam even in the grass. We were fighting in the elephant grass area.

On 14 March the enemy spotted our tracks. We also spotted that we were spotted. A group of three were sent ahead. These chaps said to me, 'We may not meet again.' And we never met again. They all perished – in one battle on the 18th.

We decided to divide the people into groups – the fit ones and the weak ones. So I was fit, I left the main group.

We walked the whole night and the following morning, early in the morning, we discovered that we were spotted. There was no doubt. There were many planes surrounding the place, ja. Hardly ten minutes, air force came – from the east as if from Mozambique. We all thought now we are attacked by Britain, because we didn't think Smith could have so many planes. There were too many. It was no more a guerrilla affair – it was just a war. That war continued until 7 p.m.

In the area we were sixty-four; no one died – it's still a mystery up to now. We survived because we killed them first. Later in court, when Ian Smith's Colonel Chris was asked by the judge, 'How many men did you have in the battle?' he said, 'My lord, I had 5,000 men on duty, 1,000 vehicles, 6 air squadron, which is 48 planes. I didn't want to commit suicide, my lord, because these chaps were very tough.'

That was a real battle, where our comrades displayed their courage and determination. But we were scattered, because the area is so hostile that if you leave a man twenty-five feet away, you don't see him again – long grass, bushes, tall trees, that type of a thing. The terrain was very, very hostile.

On the 21st we fought a very successful battle, where we lost three of our chaps – they died in that battle. But that battle, that's where we really achieved, because we counted fifteen; they said they lost twenty-four, but we saw fifteen, ja. The same night we had another battle where one of our comrades was wounded, and Comrade Zelane – chief of communication – died there. There was war all over. At one time we found ourselves completely surrounded, and in a terrain which we don't know. It's in the game reserve, ja, where there are terrible animals. You can't sleep on the ground; at night these animals move – elephants and rhinos, they are too big, so we have to sleep in the trees. One time we uncovered a camp – we were seven in my group at that time – they ran away; we killed three. When they ran away we got food there, enough food after a long time. We didn't even take the precautions that in wartime you don't just eat anything you saw. But we were so hungry that we ate that food, we shared the tins, then we left.

Then I was captured. I went to a house where I used to get food – I had stayed there before for two days. Now I think they told the army that no, there is a chap here. Just when I entered there was such a fire – AHAHAHAHAH – that I don't know how they didn't shoot me. After some few seconds I heard, 'Come out!' Then I said, 'No, stop shooting.' They say, 'Are you not hurt?' I say, 'No I'm not hurt.' They say, 'Are you Ike Maphoto?' I say, 'Yes.' They say I must raise my hands, then I went out. Then they say, 'Lie down! We are looking for you, you are wanted, ja, you are wanted alive. We need you.'

White soldiers, ja, there were about fifteen. It was at night around half past seven. They say, 'You are Chief of Logistics, we know you; you come from such a place.' Then I said, 'What is your name?' He told me he was Mr Strong. I said, 'Mr Strong, look, tell these boys – meaning his soldiers – they must not kick me. I know I'm going to be hanged; so you have no right to touch me. You have captured me, take me to court and I get my certain sentence.' Then he said, 'How do you know that?' I said, 'There are two things in guerrilla warfare – you win or you lose. And if you are captured, then there's no other way out. I have lost my battle but not the war.'

The following morning, the Special Branch came to fetch me, they have captured thirty people before me, I was number 31; and they've talked much about me. And as a result I was never interrogated, no. They took me by helicopter; then a plane came, took me to the Hunyani Mission. There was General Boorman. He came to me and say, '*Waar kom jy van af, jong?*' I say, '*Ek kom von Pretoria af.*' He say, '*Waarvoor plek in Pretoria?*' I say, '*Ek kom van Atteridgeville.*' He say, 'There's no communists in Atteridgeville, ne?' Then I look at him, I said, 'I know you; *jy is Meneer Boorman.*' He says, '*Waar ken jy van my vanaf?*' I say, 'Valhalla.' He said, 'No, *die man hy ken my.* What is your position?' I told him that I was a chief of logistics. Then he told the soldiers that in wartime commanders are not beaten. To tell you the truth I'm the only prisoner who was never beaten for all these years in prison, from the day I was captured until I left prison. I was never beaten. I was their leader in prison for seven solid years, and I was respected. I was never beaten because Boorman said this.

We were taken to Harare Prison, appeared in High Court 7 July, and on 9 August we were sentenced to death. We were thirty-two. We stayed in the condemned cell for a long time. So we sent one of our comrades, Moto – he's still alive – to go and tell the superintendent that we are tired, we want to be hanged. They were shocked. At one time, they took a decision that hanging will start very soon. Then they prepared the coffins and put them outside; you could see them from the window. People were saying that we are going, then the whole prison would keep quiet. When you see the coffins outside, you are going – there's no way out.

But the international community was helping us. You know, we are the people who forced the judges to resign, ja, because we said, 'These people, they took an oath under the Queen, they were not supposed to work under Smith, unless you want to join Smith, then you must resign.' Then they postponed the case on Thursday and new judges came back on Monday, they declared themselves to serve the UDI government. The judges were forced to resign by the prisoners, ANC and ZAPU together.

They didn't hang us. We were given life imprisonment. We were transferred to Gami Maximum Prison. We served twelve years.

The prison which we were in was the worst. The food, if you put them outside dogs wouldn't eat. The type of blankets was bad, completely bad – blankets like that are not sold in town. We were in solitary confinement. They put me in cell 65 – five years eight months in one cell, without books. The only book which you get is the Bible.

We worked until 1971 in the same quarry. We used to work in the pits fourteen foot deep; and then you would get water here, you shave here, you bath here, they bring food here. Ja, all in the same pit. You see it was a very big pit; you go there, you'll be maybe a hundred, then you sit down and you will grind the stones, ja. It was terrible. That was the worst thing.

Amos Minangawa – he's now Minister of Justice here in Zimbabwe – he was a prisoner. And when he was released he revealed our conditions to the United Nations.

They used to deprive us of exercise – they can lock you up for three months without exercise. Punishment was common; beating was common. But they did not beat those who were serving life – we had 'life' you see, written on our clothes. So we were not subjected to such tortures. There was a young boy, he was thirteen years old when he was arrested, but when he actually joined the guerrillas he was twelve. The group who was with him were hanged; he's a small boy, he was not hanged. So they gave him 120 years! You know, he's still alive. He's a policeman now in the government here. [Laughs]

When the Lancaster House discussions started then they discussed that the political prisoners must be released. But they wanted to deport us to Robben Island.

They managed to get a lawyer, who stopped the transfer to South Africa. After the Lancaster House agreement and elections when Mugabe came to power, the political prisoners were released and stayed in Zimbabwe.

They said they can release us on condition that we are not going to take part in politics. That is why I was the last with George Dawu to be released because we refused the conditions. (Others accepted the conditions, then they left. They left us in prison. We remained in prison.) We were the last political prisoners to be released in Zimbabwe and in the end without conditions because our lawyer saw Mugabe; and then Mugabe said, 'No, those people they must get gratitude for this country, they fought for this country.' So that's how we were released.

I left South Africa twenty-nine years ago. I had a child . . . I've got a child at home. He's coming to see me in April. When I left home he was four months; he is now twenty-nine years old. He has never seen me, only he sent me the pictures, I sent him pictures. Yesterday I talked to him on the phone.

They always ask me, 'But what makes you to be so active after so many years, you still can run, you still can work effectively, intelligently; what is it?' Then I say, 'No, it's my conviction.' I feel no different, no. What I want is my country – nothing else. And under the proper administration of African National Congress, ja.

The Front Line

Many exiles who left in the 1970s went no further than to the neighbouring countries across the border; to Swaziland, Lesotho and Botswana. With the collapse of Portuguese colonialism in 1974, two more countries received exiles: Angola and Mozambique.

Then, in 1980, the seven-year war in Rhodesia ended, Mugabe was swept to power, and Northern Rhodesia became Zimbabwe. Many who had been living in more distant lands were now returning to these countries of Southern Africa that had become open to them, so much closer to home.

Life in the Forward Areas was hazardous. The South African authorities were well aware that members of MK were operating from Swaziland and Botswana, although the governments of these countries, pressurised and even punished by their powerful neighbour, frequently jailed and deported the militants. From the time of Portugal's collapse, Pretoria extended its activities to the more direct use of military power against all the Frontline States, as well as Lesotho and Swaziland. The cross-border raids were indiscriminate and citizens of the Frontline States were assassinated together with South Africans.

In addition to the military incursions the South African Defence Force set up a secret unit, the Civil Co-operation Bureau. As the journalist Jacques Pauw described it: 'It was an organisation that took upon itself to charge, try, condemn and execute people regarded as enemies of the state.' The CCB operated both within South Africa, in the Frontline States, and in Namibia; and also far beyond the borders, as far as Europe. They targeted not only those suspected of being MK operatives, but anyone who was a member of the ANC, particularly those with a high profile, such as Petros and Jabu Nzima, Ruth First, Joe Gqabi and Albie Sachs.

This covert unit of hired and professional murderers began to be uncovered when a member of one of the Death Squads, Dirk Coetzee, defected, left the country, and sought the protection of the ANC.

RONNIE KASRILS
Harare 1990

'We came back ready to march home – Che Guevara types, black berets, that kind of thing. Highly romantic. And then, of course, the frustration set in.'

He has the face and build of a medium-weight boxer, an unmistakeable way of articulating his words; a smile that is almost always there. And he has spent most of his adult life in clandestine and dangerous activities.

I was a war child, born in 1938. My mother had a passion for the cinema and she used to take me – I must have been four or five years old – and there was the Movietone News dealing with the war and Hitler. That used to freak me out, and I was full of questions about this and that. And, of course, the adults, the family, the relatives were always talking about the Jews and Nazi Germany.

I can remember asking my mother to explain. She was born in South Africa in 1908, and had no politics. But she gave me an explanation about what Hitler was doing to the Jews. And I said to her, 'But this is how we're treating the blacks.' She paused and she said, 'You're right.'

There were hardly any books in my house. There was no political discussion. At school I was just sports mad, and in the lower, sporting stream; and also girl mad. Late in school I had a history teacher – this is around 1955 – and he began to teach us about the French Revolution. I'd been bored stiff up till then with things like the Great Trek and the Tudor period, Henry the Eighth and his wives. I was a bit of a rebel, always out of sorts with the prefect system at King Edward's, the snobbishness and the authoritarian methods. Then this guy – a most wonderful history teacher – says, 'We're going to study the French Revolution,' my ears prick up.

I think for the first time in my life, I concentrated. Come the end of term, gives us a test – an essay on the causes of the French Revolution. I'm in Class D, and I've got A plus. And it goes up on the noticeboards, and all the Latin swots come running to me to ask me what have I been reading on the French Revolution! [Laughs]

I've got such faith and belief in the power of a good teacher to open one's mind.

I didn't know what the hell to do on leaving school. I went to look for a job as a writer, and finally ended up as a scriptwriter at Alpha Film studios. This is about 1959.

Sharpeville shocked me to the core. I looked at this multiracial sort of bohemian crowd that I spent all my spare time with, the rather cynical way they coped by drinking harder and smoking more dope, and I really looked at myself and said, 'Right buddy. You can't do it this way. You've got to do something!'

The post-Sharpeville State of Emergency had been declared, and political activists everywhere were going underground to evade arrest and detention. Ronnie was roped in to help. He left his job in Johannesburg and went to work in Durban. There he joined the Congress of Democrats and later the Communist Party. In 1961, when Umkhonto we Sizwe was formed, he joined and took an active part in many Natal sabotage operations. He was soon a member of the Umkhonto Regional Command.

With the passing of the Sabotage Act and ninety-day detention, the police came to arrest me. My wife Eleanor was much brighter and much more practical than me on how to prepare for such eventualities, and totally through her I managed to escape being arrested with my colleagues on the Regional Command. But for her, I would have been caught up in that round-up which was May/June 1963. They served twenty years! And that would have been my fate as well.

So I was suddenly underground – worked underground for some time. Things were very difficult. There wasn't such a great support system as now. People were very intimidated. Most of our few white friends were known to the Special Branch, and we had become so involved in the movement that we had failed to develop friends outside. So we found ourselves with very limited possibilities. But there were sufficient friends of friends – not so political and very scared – who were prepared to help one for a few nights here, a few weeks there.

We attempted to set up a proper underground residential base. I was working cheek by jowl with Bruno Mtolo; and he was arrested having left our hideout. When he failed to return within twenty-four hours, we began to get very jittery – that was Ibrahim Ismail who's now serving twenty years again, for the second time on Robben Island, and Abalani Duma who died recently in Zimbabwe. Bruno became the betrayer.

Eleanor had gone up to Jo'burg with reports and requests for vital monetary help. She came back to Durban, and fortunately visited her parents before coming to us at the hideout. The parents had already been contacted by the Special Branch, because Bruno had been picked up on a property they owned. She rushed to the place we had transferred to, and we left. We know that the Special Branch came a few hours after us. We got away by the skin of our teeth.

I was called to Johannesburg. Things were very hot. I was told that I was to be sent out of the country for training, and I'd come back after a year or so. Eleanor had by then been detained and had escaped from detention; she joined up with me. We were sent out the country by the underground, and went to Tanzania, where we worked for two years in the ANC office. In that period, 1964, I went for training with about five hundred comrades, the first really large MK group.

We came back ready to march home – Che Guevara types, black berets, that kind of thing. Highly romantic. And then, of course, the frustration set in. No underground base at home! No possibility for the leadership of getting such a force home. Thus began a long grind of exile, of exile camps, of leadership battling to keep the comrades in battle-readiness, dealing with problems, welfare, morale.

One way is to begin to infiltrate comrades through an underground railway, an enormous task. Dar es Salaam is so far from the borders of South Africa. An underground link run by Babla Saloojee and others had existed, but they were now in jail or dead.

All that had disappeared. Those in the camps, of course, had the problem of how to endure years of waiting. It was going to be a long haul. Despite their political maturity, they became impatient and frustrated; and I would say this is the key reason why the Wankie incursions took place in 1967.

I think, in the main, the comrades in the camps coped well. There we were at our main base at Kongwa in the outback of Tanzania, where we went through a pretty hefty regime every day: up at 4.30 a.m. Heavy exercises, drilling and arduous survival training, which we went to with enthusiasm, because we thought next month – and the second and third month – that the transports would be there and you would go home.

And after the third, fourth, sixth month of that heat and arduous training, comrades began to wonder: Are we really going home? There were rumblings and problems. The Movement decided then to deploy our forces in 1967, in that campaign in Zimbabwe – the Wankie, and then Sipolele in 1968. We would go into the then Rhodesia with our ZAPU comrades, who would go to their own bases and carry on their fight against Ian Smith; while our forces would carve their way through Rhodesia into South Africa, somehow establishing themselves as guerrillas of the bush, and carry out the good fight from within South Africa.

It proved to be impossible, although a task which, in historical terms, meant that the combat record of Umkhonto in full-blooded warfare and baptism of fire was opened. It had a profound effect on that generation who had that baptism of fire and became later the commanders of MK. Easy to say with hindsight it was impossible to try to send people trained for war, to carry out the war, without an underground base at home!

I was sent to London in late '65, to help try to create an internal MK presence and propaganda effort. My work was with Doc Dadoo, Joe Slovo, and Jack Hodgson – a very small group. It's accounted for in South African trials, so it's not a secret. We were trying to find likely recruits, which led us to a whole string of heroic characters – Tony Holiday, Ahmed Timol, David and Sue Rabkin, Jeremy Cronin, Tim Jenkins, Steve Lee, and many others. They were South Africans – and Sue who was married to a South African – who were either holidaying or studying in England. They went back to South Africa and they were outstanding, they performed a very important role between 1967 and say 1976.

I was able to recruit the kind of South Africans that we're talking about, together with outstanding internationalists, like Alex Moumbaris who had a Greek background; Sean Hosey, who has never been IRA as Pretoria and some Tories in Britain tried to claim; and many others who performed fantastic tasks for us, going in as couriers and helping us in all sorts of ways, organising the reception along the coast and reconnoitring landing places. I was involved in that kind of activity, into the Seventies.

The Soweto uprising in 1976 was the turning point for the Movement. Our lack of real dynamic contact with home was broken. A new generation had risen, and people were pouring out of South Africa into the neighbouring states. Our camps were being set up, training programmes expanded, etc., so I was asked to transfer to Angola to help with the political preparation of the young comrades. I was there from 1977 to 1980.

Our main political instructor was Jack Simons; in the secondary camp in the north, Kibashi, I was the political instructor. As things developed, I was made the political commissar in charge of the political life of all the camps including political instruction, cultural life, morale, and so on.

It was absolutely wonderful. It was only tough at the beginning, after ten years in relative comfort in Golders Green. But you know, the kind of rough aspect of it was so compensated by being with our people again, that it was no problem.

At first I thought, 'Well – Black Consciousness; how will they treat a white?' You know, our people have that kind of humanity that Africans – when they find whites side with them, then all problems just melt. One is accepted so quickly, and you're sharing with them. So it was just wonderful.

My problem initially was just the damp climate and the disease. I came down after a couple of months with malaria. And I couldn't believe it, because I was taking the damn pills. It took me a couple of years to re-adapt to that kind of harsh tropical climate. In my fantasy moments, when I had the most severe fever, I thought to myself, 'How can I get hold of Eleanor to send me crates of Coca-Cola?' In fever, craving for ice-cold drinks with high sweetening content. At the worst time I said to myself, 'You know, you're mad! When I get better, I'm just telling the comrades I've got to go back to London. I'm sorry.'

But the moment I was well, it was all over. And I was quite happy I was back into the thick of things.

The next decision was to transfer me to Maputo, because of the problems that we were still facing in 1980, in creating that internal political base, that underground, without which the solving of all other problems is so difficult.

In 1976 right through into the Eighties the emphasis was on sending in the trained cadres to carry out operations. We had to show that something was happening. And what we did was reflected in the ANC, Umkhonto, becoming so popular in the wake of those operations. But it meant that the development of the political underground base was secondary. Operations of the kind though weren't creating structures. In some cases comrades carried out the operations, but couldn't then survive; were either captured or else they had to get out of the country. So they weren't creating something permanent.

1980 the Movement recognised the need to strengthen the machineries of our Movement in Maputo, Swaziland, Botswana, etc. with the task of building an underground base to receive combatants and provide security for them, assistance for them. But not simply to play second fiddle to combat, because we always regarded mass struggle as primary. The underground structures we were setting up were to link with mass organisation inside South Africa, bring up propaganda, and help to create conditions to develop the armed struggle. So I was brought to Maputo to carry out that work.

I was in Maputo from 1980 to the Nkomati Accord in 1984, when, except for a very small group, we were all forced to leave.

Maputo had been the base, and from Maputo we had used Swaziland as access into South Africa. And I was the first person deported from Maputo into Swaziland. The first time that I went into Swaziland – coming from Maputo with its sub-tropical climate worse than that of Durban – up on to the plateau which is Swaziland, I suddenly felt like a salmon back at the place of birth. My body began to operate in the greatest efficiency. I couldn't believe it. I just felt happier than ever, and it wasn't psychological; it was physical.

Swaziland was very useful – now again this is all in trials and open stuff; it's not secret. I was just slipping in and out of Swaziland all the time. Very clandestine!

We had big problems in Swaziland. The South African Special Branch were very high profile there, hunting us down, and sections of the Swazi Police were working hand in glove with them. It was, from an underground point of view, more dangerous than being in South Africa; because you were in a pocket-handkerchief kingdom, with two towns of about thirty thousand people in each and a strip of highway forty kilometres long. There was a saying that after 10 p.m. only the ANC and the South African Special Branch were on the road. Even the Swazi police had knocked off, you know. [Laughs]

I remained in Swaziland illegally for that whole year and part of the next year. It was an incredible period, because several hundred of our people were put, heavily armed, across the border from Mozambique into Swaziland to evade deportation. I was now heading a structure in Swaziland that had been dealing with forty, fifty, sixty people, and we now had two hundred armed guerrillas on the run, who we had to accommodate and look after and find money for. And prepare to infiltrate them into South Africa.

1984 was the most hectic period there, in which underground ANC houses were besieged, in which shootouts occurred, in which our comrades, shooting over the heads of the Swazi forces, attempted to hold out or break out of that siege and just escape. Cases of comrades being rounded up and put in jail, and breaking out en masse. There was one breakout at Simunya where twenty of them escaped; cases of comrades being killed by the Swazi forces; one or two Swazi security people being killed; South African Boers coming in, and with the complicity of the Swazis, arranging a so-called escape from prison which was actually South Africans kidnapping our guys back to South Africa.

We managed to survive, managed to get a lot of comrades into South Africa, and keep an underground structure going through that hectic period, which was compounded by a power struggle within the Swazi ruling group between those who would sell out to the Boers for forty luka, and those who were a bit more patriotic.

In that period, comrades who were captured by the Swazis – and at one stage they had a hundred in their jails – were taken blindfolded to secret places, within Swaziland, barracks of the Swazi Defence Force, where they were interrogated ostensibly by Swazis, but really by South African Special Branch using physical and mental torture, and threats. Like taking the blindfolded, shackled comrades and driving them around for a few hours; and then telling them: 'You are now on the South African border, and the Boers are the other side of the wire. Unless you answer satisfactorily, we're going to hand you over!'

It was real tough stuff. And these young people, recruited post-1980, trained for only a year or so since we were now getting them back into the country quickly: they showed the most amazing heroism! Youngsters from all over South Africa. I had an incredibly high impression of them.

A house of ours was besieged by the Swazi defence force in a suburb of Mbabane. One of the comrades from that house had ended up the night before getting drunk up in a disco, and drawing attention to himself by fighting with local people over some Swazi beauty; and getting into a taxi and being dropped at this house, so giving the taxi driver vital information. We had some indisciplined cadres, and young people without maturity or experience.

But it was quite amazing that despite their inexperience and years, despite such lapses inside and outside South Africa, in fact three-quarters of the comrades behaved in a very firm and disciplined manner. But it's the tragic events and the departures from disciplines that hit the headlines. And of course affect the image that one then has of the whole group or generation.

By 1985 I was brought to Lusaka, headquarters of the ANC, and worked with the Political Military Committee here. I found it very difficult at first. Lusaka to the ANC is like Brussels is to the Common Market – the corridors of power, the bureaucracy, innumerable departments. And it takes some getting used to. It takes a long time. I have been living in Lusaka ever since '85, ja.

The long separation from my wife and sons, and from a normal, settled life is more difficult to relate, because now you're getting into one's emotions, and under the skin. Fortunately I've had a very happy marriage to a comrade who was political, who was committed, who understood it all and was prepared for the separation and the sacrifice because Eleanor understood that I wasn't escaping from her. We've had a good marriage and a close relationship. We're very close friends; which I think is important in a marriage. So Eleanor was prepared to carry that burden of bringing up two young sons in exile in London – together with her very big problem of a daughter in South Africa from a previous marriage to whom she didn't have access. That was really morale-sapping for her.

But the fact that I knew that my sons were stabilised and happy and being brought up the right way meant that I could concentrate on my work. And although I missed the family and missed seeing my sons grow up, I felt so lucky that I'd seen them grow to the age of twelve and ten, when I left for Angola. But nevertheless I missed them terribly.

As long as Eleanor could keep a stable family, I felt very stable myself. And the Movement was very good to me. Mzwai Piliso was the guy who took me to Africa. He had a wife who lived in Burnley with two young kids, and Mzwai had left them way beyond this period. So he understood this. And Mzwai organised my life so that twice a year I was back in London for a month each time.

This long period in exile – it's the autobiography I've got to write one day! It brews in one's mind and you never get down to it. So I'm going to be simplistic. I wouldn't have changed my life for anything. I'd take the same path. I would never have changed it.

I love South Africa. The Swazi experience, and going into places like Botswana which I've done on numerous occasions, have recreated for me something of my antecedents. And I'm just so looking forward to being alive and working in that country again! It's a country that has got such incredible quality. And it's all about the African people. You know, scenery and rocky coves and all that's so wonderful; and you love the climate, it kind of places you back in the womb. [Laughs] You kind of feel that that's where you come from as an embryo. Maybe that has some effect. But it's all about the people.

I think South Africans have got the most fantastic things to offer about life, because they've been living on the frontiers of life, the majority of the people. And those who side with the Africans live on the frontiers of life. So that life is so full of meaning, and the lifeblood of the oppressed and of the African people has got such force and power that it just inflames one. I think it inflames one to such a degree that there's no way I can believe that I've been outside for twenty-seven years. Because it's got that magnetic power and electrification for me.

As it had for me up to 1963. That's the kind of power created by a struggle against a real evil regime.

KATLEHO MOLOI
Toronto 1990

'It's mostly women who are supposed to be quiet. If you are angry, be quiet! If you feel pain, be quiet! If you're happy, be quiet! And I think it's time we stopped being quiet.'

> Together with her husband Peter she worked in an ANC counter-intelligence unit, uncovering infiltrators and investigating the assassinations and kidnappings of ANC personnel in the Forward Areas.

I had been going to Lesotho since 1978, backwards and forwards. In January 1981, after staying there for three weeks with some ANC members, I was arrested at the border on my way back to South Africa. They searched me, my bags, everything. I was taken to Ladybrand to these rooms where they are interrogating people – the sight was very unbecoming. There was blood, the rooms were dirty and quite dark. They made me have a bath in very, very cold water. And then there was the beating up. Then they were driving me around for long distances; it was very disorientating and confusing. I spent a whole weekend like that, just being driven around, not knowing what is going to happen to me. And being talked to nicely at one point, and being manhandled at the other point – psychological and physical torture.

I was charged with the possession of illegal literature. I got a lawyer and my mum sent money for bail. I went back to Lesotho and got involved again in the political life within the ANC. We were doing a lot of study of the history of the ANC, because many comrades who came straight from home didn't know our history, basically because so much literature in South Africa was prohibited material.

I had been doing a Bachelor of Science back home and I had to leave before finishing. But now I wanted to do military training. Some people felt that I should go to school and some people were encouraging me to go for military training, but I decided to take my own decision. I went for military training.

I was in Angola. It was a hard life in a sense. I was underground, so I didn't go to the camps where there were many people. In fact underground itself, it's like prison, and it was tough for me as an individual, because of my health problems, ja. I'm an asthmatic, so . . . ja.

In the house I was in, there were three women and around thirty-five men at a time, coming and going, going from our house to Lesotho, Swaziland and so on – what we called the 'forward areas' or 'the front'.

The military training I underwent was basically for combat, and the impression I got at that time was that, after training, I'm going to be infiltrated inside the country. Which was exactly what I wanted to do. I could just see myself in that situation. I guess I was still so angry, I was still so bitter. And political education and knowing exactly what's happening to us and to our forefathers gave me that push to want to go inside the country, and be brave and do underground work.

But, as it turned out, I didn't go there. I was still in Angola at the time of the Maseru massacre in December 1982. I was supposed to have gone to Lesotho a long time before, so the delay was a blessing in disguise. One of my friends died there, and it's a possibility that I could have died there too. I would say it did save my life.

I left Angola early in 1983 and went to Mozambique. I was recruited into the security department, I worked with Peter and his unit and was trained in security work, processing biographies and interviews. I went to Lesotho later on and I realised that the method that they were using in Mozambique was more efficient; there was less confusion in the way they were doing it. So I found myself using that experience.

It was difficult in my unit in Lesotho, because I was the only woman. And one thing I've realised – I don't know if it's within the Movement, maybe I could also say globally – but it's very difficult for men to take women seriously. If they don't undermine you, they're going to feel that you're a threat. I didn't understand that at the time. I knew I was very very sad because of the pressure I felt, and sometimes I would be so depressed that I'd just burst into tears for no apparent reason. I couldn't understand what exactly was wrong, and that created a lot of problems.

Later, all those things become clearer. I'm looking back on it now, I'm looking at what happened, my experience, and I see that this is exactly what it is. But at that moment you try and look within yourself, what wrong thing you are doing. And there's that part of you that says, 'You shouldn't have done it this way; you should have done it that way.' And then later on I realised that no, no, no; there's nothing wrong that I did.

I was working so hard. And then to find these obstacles . . . And you could see some of the things that you're not involved in. It's only men, who stand there whispering. And then they're gone; and you start asking yourself, 'Why am I being left out?'

I think one of the reasons I left Lesotho was because of that. I don't know, but I have a feeling that some of my comrades didn't like the way I was operating. But it's one of the reasons that I left and went to Angola, where I was supposed to be *en route* to Europe for a course – and that never happened. But I kept myself busy. I participated a lot. I assisted in the radio unit in Angola, and wrote some poems for the radio. I was writing about the women in the ANC and in the struggle. And then I wrote some poems for our journal, *The Voice of Women*, ja. I used to stay up late at night, covering the news and typing it up, getting it ready for the morning so that the comrades could read them, and analyse them later on. So that kept me going. My morale was not dampened because I felt I have to do something. Wherever I am, I have to do something that will be a contribution to the struggle.

And then, with some confusion, I went back to Zambia. I wanted to know from my department what was happening about my course. Still I was not given an answer. And with the same umph! I went to the women's section. I said: 'Do you want somebody to work with you? I'm here.' I started assisting them in the administration. Peter and I got married in 1985, I gave birth to my first child and I was still working with them. I regarded myself as part of the women's section – they took me seriously. And then they asked me to come here to Toronto to work in the office.

> Katleho and her husband worked in the ANC office in Toronto; but some problems arose with the then Chief Representative, and they felt they could not continue working in the office.

I have two children now, five years and fifteen months. One was born here in Canada. After we had differences with the ANC office, we had to look for a job. That was when the realities of the way Canadians perceive other people really did strike me. I'd look at the paper and see the advertisements and think, 'This I can do.' So I'd pick up a phone and call; and then the first question would be, 'Where do you come from?' 'Well, I'm from South Africa' – and you could hear from the tone of the voice that you're not going to get the job. After three calls you realise that that's a dismissal. And from then on, you'd be so discouraged.

And then about your accent. Some people will say positive things about it, but they make sure that they tell you that you speak differently. I remember going to speak in London, Ontario, and this little Canadian woman came to me and she said, 'Good speech!' And I said, 'Thank you.' And she said, 'Good grammar too!' Ah! I really didn't know how to respond to that. You're mobilising support for the Movement here, so you want to be very careful – you sort of swallow some of the words that you wanted to say.

And it's still going on. In my first job – I was working in a non-governmental organisation called Development Education Centre. I was helping manage the book distribution services, but there were the questions that I found very ridiculous. For instance, 'Where exactly did you learn English?' And then I have to explain that South African black children, from the time they start to speak some of those words will be English. We say one, two, three even at two years old – we don't even know that that's English, you know what I mean? That's how people speak at home – we speak English, we speak Afrikaans, we speak so many languages; but we don't know that we're speaking all this and that we're multilingual. If I say I know more than six languages they get shocked, because an Anglo-Saxon will most likely know English only, not even French.

When I came here, it was the first time I used computers. But I liked them so much, I was so inclined to the technology that I just was weaving through everything that I was doing. The job was mostly computer work. I'd produce a report from the computer and say to somebody: 'I think you will need this; it will assist you.' They would say: 'I didn't know you could do that!' And OK, the first time, I thought, well they didn't know that I could do that. But when it happens with three more people saying 'I didn't know you could do that!' you start asking yourself what exactly do they think I can do? [Laughs] There were only two of us doing computer work in our subgroup. The other person left and I was the only one who knew most of the things. But still the people who came after me – the people I had hired! – didn't expect me to do that! [Laughs]

I think it's because I'm black, I think so. Black and African. Because when they talk about Africa, it's about disadvantage, people who don't have opportunities. And even the capabilities are submerged under this no-opportunities thing. People do not realise that you might not have opportunities, but you do have capabilities. And once you're given the material, you're intelligent and you're capable and you'll work on it. Canadian culture has helped me to say: 'I AM capable of doing one, two, three.' In our culture you do things, but you don't blow your own horn – you don't say: 'I can do this, I can do that.'

But here you put yourself on the table, most especially if you're going to look for a job. Just writing a résumé, you have to say: 'Look what I can do!' I found myself in some interviews being very humble; and some friendly people would tell me, 'That's not how things are done here. This is how you do things!' And then after that, I knew that every little thing that I'm capable of doing, I must just put it down on paper or say it. And I'm still learning even now.

Now I'm working with the Jesuit Centre for Social Justice and Faith. Social Faith and Justice, wow! I've been with them for only four months and I'm learning there also, because one of the people who was interviewing me was saying: 'You've got so many capabilities and you don't write them down, so people don't know. You should. That's the way things are done here. You have to have more confidence, Katleho. You have to talk about what you know, your organisationÿo...)üHä'communication skills.'

Those are some of the positive experiences – things that I'm going to take home with me. More especially for women, because I think it's mostly women who are supposed to be quiet. If you are angry, be quiet! If you feel pain, be quiet! If you're happy, be quiet! You have to swallow all these things. And I think it's time we stopped being quiet.

I hope I'll have the opportunity to rally around other women to say, 'You know, this is the triple oppression that we said we were fighting. This is what I learned, and I think it's good for us.'

I do regret leaving South Africa, more especially when there's so much political activity going on I think my place is down there with the people. When so many people are dying, and not only dying but working and getting their gains and their successes, I feel I should be down there. It's not all regret. Even when I was frustrated and confused, I felt I'm a soldier. And a soldier makes the best of the worst situation and fights on. Even here; even though I have to wake up in the morning and bear in mind that I'm black, I still find a place for struggle, one way or the other.

I do hope to go back. Yes, I do. There are things that can never be finished in exile, like when my mother died. It's an open wound to me. It doesn't close. You see, those who were there they had a chance to mourn – and then they can start to live again. But me, I feel I haven't mourned. I am traditional inside still. There are certain rituals that we believe in, and I need to take part in them.

All the positive things that I'm learning here I'm going to take back. I take many things here as learning experiences. I live in co-operative housing now, and I look at it and I think: 'This is what people at home should get.' These are some of the things that people do not know about: the government grants, the loans, the this and that. Ordinary black South Africans will not know about these things.

So these are the things that we, who were able to go outside South Africa and live where apartheid is not written in black and white; where we can operate without being told, 'You're black! You're white!' – we should go back home and enlighten our people, and say to them, 'We went out there, and this is what we found out. Let's make use of some of these experiences that some of us got.'

FATHER CAS
Lusaka 1990

'To be a student in exile, a youngster cut off from your family, hey, it's the pits. It's really bad.'

> He was arrested in the so-called 'independent homeland' of the Transkei, where apartheid prison rules did not apply. His prison experiences must be unique amongst political detainees. He has a deep insight into the heartaches and deprivations of the exiled young.

The name is a Polish name – Casimir – and the surname is Paulsen, a Danish name. I shorten it to Cas for easy remembering.

I was born in Milwaukee, Wisconsin, middle of the depression. My mother was Polish. I went to a parochial school, probably there picked up the idea of being a Catholic priest, studied in a seminary. Started in 1949, came out the other end in 1962 as an ordained priest. Taught in the seminary. Our community was called Mariannhill.

I left the States in 1966, Martin Luther King had been one of my heroes. My first assignment in Africa, in Durban at the Mariannhill Monastery. And on my arrival at Jan Smuts, I really was shocked and horrified by my first encounter with apartheid – Blankes, Nie-Blankes. And watching the servility of people at that time, the gross injustice – things I had never noticed in my own city, or knew about. I really was unbelievably shocked by what I saw.

Was asked at Mariannhill to begin working with youth, the Young Christian Workers and the University Christian Movement. And moved from Durban to Cape Town to Jo'burg and back. Youth at the time were very vociferous. Probably a great majority wound up either going underground, or being put inside, or simply leaving the country. Steve Biko came to our youth centre, Stebeleni, asking to use the place to draft the constitution for what turned out to be SASO – South African Students' Organisation – which was then just an idea in their minds.

We ran into a lot of difficulties. We worked with a lot with groups, as people were beginning to be more and more aware of the unacceptability of apartheid. On the whole, the government wouldn't bother you if you talked a lot, but as soon as you began acting and getting groups together, that's when they got nervous.

When I applied to the authorities for an extension of my temporary residence, it was refused. I then applied for permanent residence – I had lived there long enough to qualify – they just reminded me: 'We didn't accept your temporary residence, so certainly we are not going to allow you to stay permanently. You must be gone by such a date.' I had arrived in South Africa in September 1966 and left in March of 1971. So it was just over four years. It was a very sad moment because I had expected somehow to stay my life there, which was the normal commitment we would have made. I went back home to the States, tried to find another place in Africa; and eventually wound up going to Zambia.

I stayed in Zambia for four years, really disconnected from the South African scene; had no regular sources of information, and was simply caught up with normal parish duties.

In 1977 I left Zambia – my contract had expired – went back to my community in Detroit, worked for a year for the Ford Motor Company on the assembly line. Then my community asked if I would return to South Africa, to the Transkei. They said: It's independent now! and we had a laugh about that. But we applied, and I managed to get in.

Again I was involved with youth work. Became a chaplain at UNITRA – University of Transkei – as well as chaplain within the diocese working with various age groups, and was given a parish that had nineteen outstations in the rural areas. It was really a no-win situation; there was no way you could meet everybody's needs – it was an impossibility. But I felt that youth were a prime responsibility.

There at UNITRA we had discussions about economics, about politics, about the common good. And if we call ourselves Christians, what are our beliefs? And if the basic belief would be to love your brother and your sister, how do you translate that into positive action? We had a Catholic Students' Association which was ninety-five per cent non-Catholic, but it was an alternative to the so-called Student Christian Movement who were the kind of very fundamentalist Christian believers who clap their hands and sing and praise the Lord, but when it came to doing something wouldn't want to get involved. Perhaps you have heard of Batando Ndondo, murdered by the Security Police? He was the leader of our group. Several others came looking for help because they were on the hit squad's list, and we managed to get them out of the country.

And then came my own turn.

In 1986 there was a young woman who was working with me, Nomondi Matiso, mid-thirties. They detained Nomondi in December, and – I didn't know this until later – they tortured her very, very badly. They beat her, they kicked her, they put a bag over her head filled with water, she couldn't breathe. Kept this up for eight or nine hours, trying to force her to give them information. She was the type of woman that would die before she said anything.

Well, they picked me up three days later, when they didn't succeed getting anything out of her. Tried the same drowning procedure with me. They were looking for names, names, names of people. Where's so-and-so? Where's so-and-so? People who were involved in the student movement. Thank goodness, I hadn't seen them for several months. My presumption is that they managed to get out.

There were the Transkei Security Police with the normal tactic – seven or eight all shouting different questions. You know: How old is your mother? Where did you go to school? Just to keep you confused so that you can't begin to reason. And the: 'All right, we'll teach you now!' and they introduce you to what they call the TV; they stick your head in a sack of water. 'What you didn't see before, maybe you'll see once you start drowning!' But that doesn't work either, because you can't say what you don't know.

The day that I was picked up – I don't know if it was my sixth sense, or instinct or whatever – I wrote a short note to the secretary at the Bishop's House in Umtata giving her the phone numbers of the American Embassy in Durban, and of my community in Detroit. It wasn't fifteen minutes later when I was on my way. Why I did that I don't know.

I was living with two Dominican Sisters who were parish assistants. When I didn't come home, they went down to the Security Police, where we had found Nomondi's car a few days before, hidden. And there they saw my car covered up with a canvas to try to hide it. So they told the

Bishop. The Bishop went with my superior to the police to say: 'We're a bit worried about Father Cas. Is there any report that he might have been in an accident or something?' And the Security Police played their game: 'Well no. We haven't heard anything. What's the name again? Well, if we hear anything, we'll let you know.' And the car was sitting outside. And the Bishop knew that because the sisters had told him.

My colleagues didn't know where I had been taken. I was in fact taken to Kei Bridge where there's a kind of a police compound, on the border between Transkei and the Eastern Cape. I was interrogated and tortured by these Transkei Security Police. The next day, two white Security Police came from East London – Van Wyk and . . . I thought I'd never forget the names! But one of whom knew Xhosa excellently, excellently. Then he played the gentle, be-reasonable, just lay your cards out, why do you want to go through all this? And the other one was going to put my head in the toilet and flush it, and kick me and I don't know what. The usual tactics.

Well I saw them over the next three months, regularly. And I knew they were also going to Umtata, interrogating others, so that it was quite clear that the South African Security were the ones who were really in control. They got the Transkei Security to collaborate and do their dirty work for them. But they didn't really trust them to do the hard work. Made it very racial – typical somehow – the attitude that blacks, they're too dumb to do anything. It amazed me that the black Security Police couldn't see it.

My community, the Bishop and whoever were trying their best but they never were allowed to see me. But the news got to my family – and that was pure accident. After about four weeks my aunt phoned from Chicago to wish one of the priests a Happy New Year. And he asked her: 'Have you heard any more about Cas?' And she said: 'What do you mean, any more?' And that was the first time my family knew. They were never told either by the State Department who knew from the Embassy in Durban, or by my community in Mariannhill – and my sister only lives five minutes from our place there in Detroit.

Then my family immediately got in contact with a Senator, and a huge bundle of people, Amnesty and just about every country you can imagine. They got schoolkids, karate clubs, union people from the factory where I'd been working – hundreds of thousands of letters coming to General Gawe there in Umtata: 'Let this guy go!' Some of the kids I had worked with managed to get a hold of his personal telephone number, and were phoning him, two, three, four o'clock in the morning, driving him buggy! [Laughs]

During that period, when I wasn't being interrogated I wasn't alone, and I'm grateful for that. We had a cell that was probably about three and a half metres by three and a half metres. And there was one other political prisoner there at the time I came in, and the first thing he did was tear his towel in half, say: 'There's the soap.' Because I came in just like this. And ja, this comrade, brother, I don't know what you want to call this terrorist, he shared whatever he had. And there wasn't much.

During the three months that we were there, there were two, three or four political prisoners at most. Over the weekends we got the local crowd – people who were pushing infangu – what you call dagga, grass, whatever – or drunken vagrants or so on. And then things got a little bit tight, because there'd be seven, eight, ten, twelve people in this very confined space. The guy that was sleeping next to me, for example, I'm sure he had TB. But then you got a look also at the rural areas; you just kind of got a feel for how, ever since independence, things got worse, not better – just by the local people coming through.

Being the Transkei, it had the advantage that there was no distinction between black and white. We were all in the same cell together. In fact I was the only white guy that was ever around there; and it gave me a chance to continue to talk Xhosa so that I wouldn't forget.

Because you had no watch you didn't know what time it was, but there was a kind of an unwritten rule that about eight o'clock, seven thirty – you gauge the time – you keep quiet now. You stop talking and you start thinking of tomorrow, because anywhere from eight to ten o'clock they'll come to interrogate you; and you want to have it quite clear in your head what you want to say if they ask this; what you want to say if they ask that.

The reason why you are there is because somebody mentioned your name. And if you mention names, for sure they're the next ones who are going to go in. So you tried to eliminate all names of people who might still be around; and you mention all the people you can think of who are already gone. And it irritates them to say the least. You try to leave out any people who in any way could be remotely involved. You think out what you have to say, what you know they know etc, until your mind works like a computer. And you didn't want to be disturbed.

In the morning, you had some kind of breakfast, porridge and some black whatever, you didn't know what it was. And then again quiet, because you knew any time now they're coming, and you want to be ready. Well this went on for a couple of weeks. It takes a while to begin to work out a routine. But you notice that once they have finished with their interrogating, they go out and check now what you've said. Then you just sit. Then it came to Christmas, and they didn't want to work over the Christmas and New Year's holidays. So you got a bit of a break.

I remember several things. I found a sleeve of a jersey that had been torn off, and I would clean the floor twice a day. You never got a chance to clean – the blankets were filthy, filthy; they had been puked on and bled on and you name it, so that they were crawling with vermin and whatever. You tried to shake them out. They had never been washed since they had been bought. You only had a cement floor to sleep on.

There was no furniture at all. No mat. You tried to get . . . if no one was around you took another blanket; then you put that under so your bones wouldn't knock on the cement. There was no water. There was one tremendous advantage – a flush toilet. And if you had any inhibitions, then you'd die of constipation.

So I got into the routine of cleaning the floor twice a day with that rag, slowly, meticulously, each corner, to use up as much time as possible – while these guys would be playing checkers. I got fascinated with cleaning my comb – eventually I did get a comb – and I could spend hours just . . . You know these tops they have on bottles? They have a little ring. Well I took the ring off and I used that piece of metal for cleaning the comb – just as a way of keeping occupied and thinking thoughts while you're doing it. I never realised that that could offer such a constructive time, somehow – cleaning a comb, for goodness sakes!

On Sundays I didn't want to impose my own feelings on them. But we managed to get hold of a bible – Xhosa bible to begin with. And I started reading from the Old Testament, the life of Isaiah and Jeremiah and Amos and some of the old prophets, kind of identifying with where they were; facing many of the same things because they too, in their day, were challenging the powers that be. I found it very supportive, so I would have my own interior service on Sunday to kind of nourish my own spirit; and would choose those kinds of readings from the scripture that involved this kind of struggle – Paul and Peter thrown into jail, and how they reacted and how they managed. I had never imagined before what it must have been like in a jail in their day. So these kinds of things were nourishing for the spirit. I don't know.

I noticed one or two things that were a part of keeping you psychologically under their control. One was, you got filthier and filthier and filthier, and you only had a shower about once every two weeks. In the meantime you had only this container of water – and you had to split that depending on how many people there were – so you might get a cup of water to wash for the day. Call it dry-cleaning. Eventually when we did get a wash rag, it was so soapy that it would almost slip out of your hand, and you had no way to wash it to get all that gook out.

And because now you were very dirty, and very conscious of it, they would come dressed up in a nice suit and tie, with some kind of deodorant or after-shave lotion. Purposely. Just to chat. They had been taught the psychology, that this has an effect.

Finally, in the third month, I was released. I was given twenty-four hours to leave the country. Went back to the States via Lusaka, and told the ANC I wanted to work now full-time for the liberation struggle. 'I'd like to be a chaplain for the ANC. I hope that my community won't object, I hope that the Catholic Church won't object. I think if they do there might be problems, because I would just go ahead anyway because I know that's what I have to do.'

They were all agreeable. In 1984 IMBISA – that is the Inter-regional Meeting of Bishops of Southern Africa – started a refugee department, and a Dutch priest was asked to take over as co-ordinator of the refugee service. But it was just at that time that he was drowning in hundreds of thousands of Mozambican refugees. He was very happy for me to take over that side through IMBISA.

The South African exiles' needs are quite different from those of the thousands in the refugee camps. They're urban refugees, with completely different approach to life, and probably the vast majority of South African exiles are ANC members. There are others – PAC, BCM in a comparative minority, and a few unattached or UNHCR. But for the most part they belong to the ANC, and are committed to somehow unravelling that system and going back home.

I went up to Mazimbu to see the place, and I found a bunch of my kids up there, in fact there were a couple I didn't know were still alive. I had taken them out of the country, two years had gone by, I had heard nothing. Well, we established contacts. In Lusaka, the same thing. Many who were just kids at the time I last saw them were now full-fledged members of the ANC. They'd been off to Cuba; they'd been off to East Germany; they'd been educated. It was like a renewal, old-home week. Coming to Harare the same thing, bumping into kids. One said: 'It was back then when you first brought those tapes of Martin Luther King – that was the beginning of thinking what my situation is about.'

I've been here in Harare since July 1988, feeling around how I can be of help from my Catholic priest point of view; trying to address the needs of the spirit somehow. Often we get so caught up in political economic things that you forget people are suffering on just a normal human level.

So anyway, ja, I'm working with Father Lapsley. We don't have a big fund, but we have big problems. Education, drink problems, all kinds of psychological problems. You have kids of Soweto; it's a township, it's humming, it's buzzing, you're active, you're on the run, you can't sleep in your house. And suddenly you get farmed out to Mazimbu. It's like going to the boonies! You were somebody there at home, they knew that you were one of those who was active in the Movement. And now you're just one among many. It's psychologically devastating. The number of scholarships that you need to be able to meet everybody's demands! And they don't come, and they don't come, and they don't come. The unwed mothers and the pregnancies and not knowing what to do now and having no norms or models to grow up by!

I was really impressed with Mazimbu. But beautiful as it is, when you talk to those youngsters who started out from scratch when it was just a field, and slowly built farm and houses and schools and whatever, you see that it's not the buildings; there's some spirit, quality, that's not there. And it's just so difficult to meet those needs. To be a student in exile, a youngster cut off from your family, hey, it's the pits! It's really bad. Well this I feel. And Father John Osmers and I, we have made a decision to try a couple of times a year just to get up to Mazimbu. To be what? An uncle or something? Just to visit, to be a friend, because you feel that tremendous need for just simple friendship from somebody from the outside who cares. We're free to do that. We don't have to concentrate on other things.

Then of course, marriage is under the extra strain of exile. Husbands and wives go to different places, are separated – ah, horrible, horrible. You try to influence the structures, to say: 'Try your best to keep people together, otherwise we are recreating the very same thing we've been criticising – you know breaking families to pieces.' But what do you do when you get a scholarship for one and you can't get one for the other? And I'm sure that they're aware of it and they try. But that's just a part of the tragedy of having to live in exile.

Stan Mabizela, who was the ANC chief rep here and is a Catholic, came one day and he said: 'Look, my son-in-law's brother-in-law just died. Would you mind having some kind of a requiem mass or something for him because the whole family comes from a Catholic background?' And I said: 'Sure.' So we all came together, and I said: 'Well, while we're here, let's remember the whole family.' And then his wife Dixie said: 'Well, I'd like to remember my mother because I wasn't able to be there when she died.' And Stan – both his mother and his father, he wasn't able to be there when they died. And so on it went. And you thought how painful that is – somebody as close as your own mother – and in African society your own mother! And you can't be there because of that block in the system. That's too painful to even imagine.

Another funeral. Every time there's a funeral I become aware of other aspects of apartheid that I had never thought of. Comrade Duma whose arm was blown off in Swaziland and was sent up here, and was what? – an elder to the youngsters coming out, a surrogate parent. He passed away. He had left his wife in South Africa – gosh, when was it? 1964 or something like that. He had had to leave now-now, and he couldn't say where he was going. At that time she had three children and one on the way. And when that one was born, the name she gave was Asinamali – we have no money. She had to raise those kids on her own. And for all those years! A whole bunch of people came up for the funeral – from the Durban area where he had grown up.

They said, here's his widow. Well, hell, she'd already been a widow for God knows how many years now. The implications of exile, of apartheid, mmm.

BARRY GILDER
Harare 1990

'Exile is the inevitability of being separated from your country, your family, your friends. Not a very nice way to spend your life.'

> He was at university during the Black Consciousness period, and he did not have any contact with black South Africans until he left the country. 'I would have joined the ANC if it was there for me. I would have done it with pleasure.' But he had to leave the country to find it.

I was called up to the army at the beginning of 1976 when the SADF had just gone into Angola for the first time. I was working at NUSAS Head Office at the time.

The debate about whether people should go into the army, and serve in order to stay in the country, was only just beginning. But I would be doing active service in Angola. And I just wasn't prepared to do that. The military police had come looking for me at my mother's place in Jo'burg, although I was in Cape Town. And she had phoned me on a NUSAS phone, which we knew to be tapped, so that they knew that I knew that I was called up. So I had to do something.

I didn't tell my family I was going. That certainly caused pain to my family. I wrote to my mother within weeks after I'd left. And she wrote back almost immediately, very, very upset – irrationally upset. But over the years she's got used to the idea.

I consulted my NUSAS colleagues. There was NUSAS work that had to be done outside, so the timing was almost perfect from that point of view. That made it easier. I told myself I was going on a mission – in a sense. And I guess it was only really when I got out that I realised that this was going to be a very, very long mission. And it's been fourteen years!

Part of my mission for NUSAS involved going to Geneva to work with the IUEF. I worked with them for about three months. Towards the end of that period, I attended a cultural conference in Amsterdam; which was where I, for the first time, met the ANC. I had been involved in cultural work in South Africa, within NUSAS and in my own right. I was very interested in cultural politics, and kind of gate-crashed the conference. When I arrived everybody thought that I was some kind of agent. Nobody knew me, I had no credentials, and some of the ANC people were very suspicious of me.

At home I used to compose and sing political songs – I was known as a sort of NUSAS troubadour. I got permission to perform on one of the evenings of this conference. The concert went on until two in the morning, and I had been sitting in the bar talking to Ronnie Kasrils, begging him to just come in and listen to me sing. I needed some sort of support. I sang, and it went very well. Ronnie came up to me afterwards saying, 'Comrade, are there any more like you at home?' [Laughs] So it was this cultural thing that opened the door for me.

Soon after that I moved to London. For about three years I was working for a British political theatre group, and in my spare time working with the ANC. I eventually left the group, and did a lot of work talking and singing on behalf of the ANC as well as other solidarity Anti-Apartheid groups. And I became involved in setting up COSAWR, the war resisters' movement.

At the time, there was a lot of debate among white comrades in London of my age and generation, that it was necessary to join MK if we were to really become part of the Movement. I felt very strongly that I should join MK. So I begged – basically I begged the Movement, until I think they got fed up with me and sent me to Angola for training. At that stage I think I was the first white after Ronnie to join MK.

It was fantastic. I arrived in Angola very apprehensive, both about being the only white comrade among all black comrades; and, of course, apprehensive about the training itself. It was a big decision for me. I had come from quite a privileged background. I had done my initial military service in the SADF. But this was not just military training. It was a commitment that if MK sent me to fight, I was going to do it. Whereas, with the SADF, it was just a duty and I was going to get out of fighting whatever way I could. So I was very apprehensive.

I was a novelty. Almost all the people in the camps had been imbued with the non-racialism of the Movement, but this was their first concrete experience of it. And the comrades were wonderful to me. I think that political acceptance made it easier for me to integrate. I told myself that this is not a symbolic gesture – this is something I want to do! And the longer I was there – I was there for about one and a half years – the more I felt at home.

If I look back on all my years in the struggle, those were really the best years. There were frustrations; there were problems; the conditions were not easy. But I think that period in MK was one of the most coherent and exciting periods. For me, it was the greatest time in the Movement that I've ever had.

After I finished my training there I went to the Soviet Union for further training, and then back to the UK for personal reasons. I had just got married and my wife was about to give birth to our daughter. I spent eight or nine months in Britain, working with the ANC office. After my sojourn in Britain, I was sent back to Africa – to the Forward Areas – to try and find the country where I could base. And that turned out to be Botswana.

When I first went to Botswana I was working as a journalist, in a news agency which was trying to provide alternative news in South Africa. In

those days – this was pre-June 1985 and the SADF raid into Gaberone –
Botswana was a much more politically open place for South African
refugees, and the ANC in particular. We had an office there. We had
various open organisations, cultural and other kinds, in which we involved local people. We lived much more openly, we socialised. Some of
the ANC community were not involved in underground work – it was
just their country of refuge. But there was also quite a large underground
community.

I was involved ultimately in the underground leadership structures in
Botswana. Our role basically was to oversee and implement the under-
ground activities of the ANC, covering the whole Western Transvaal,
Northern Cape and Western Cape. I was there altogether about six years.
I had my wife there for about a year and a half, ja, almost from the time
I moved there, and my daughter. After the 14 June 1985 raid, we both
decided that, for the kid's sake, they should move out. And as a result of
that we were separated for something like four years.

I was there during the raid. Fortunately my wife and daughter were
away at the time. I was woken up at about half-one in the morning by
the sounds of shots. I got up, looked out the window, and saw SADF
attacking the house across the road. I knew there were comrades staying
there, because I'd seen their cars. But I had just moved into my place
myself, so I didn't yet know who was who. I thought that I was also a
target, and I had no means of defence. I was alone in the house, and had
no way of escape. Both exits from the house opened right into the view
of the SADF soldiers who were about ten to twenty metres from my front
and back door. So I just sat it out.

The next morning when we took stock, twelve people had been killed,
quite a few of them locals or non-ANC people. About six ANC people
had been killed. This sort of thing had been happening in Mozambique
and Lesotho, and problems in Swaziland had been starting. But I think
we had told ourselves that Botswana was somehow immune, that the
Americans and the British would never allow the South Africans to get
away with something like this. But that didn't stop the raid.

It changed the whole complexion of underground work in Botswana.
It made conditions very, very difficult for us. The local people – who had
never had any serious struggle to attain their own independence and who
had never really been involved in any armed struggle – were extremely
frightened by that raid, and by subsequent smaller attacks that took
place over the years. People became terrified of refugees, and the government did not help by calling on people to report any strangers in the
towns and villages.

For about two years after that, it was very, very difficult for us to
survive, to get accommodation, to move in the streets. People have a way
of telling South Africans by the way that they walk, talk, dress and act.
So being underground in a small place like Botswana was very difficult;

THE MILITARY ROAD 197

and in those conditions post June 1985 it became, for a time, virtually impossible.

It got to a situation where we would frequently get arrested by the local police, jailed, held for two weeks, maybe more, deported to Lusaka. Lusaka's position was that it couldn't afford to send new replacements, so we got sent back illegally. And this carried on indefinitely. It was a sort of – I know it's a sexist term – a sort of gentleman's agreement. We would get arrested, deported. They'd know we would come back. And it would be a cat-and-mouse game, until we got arrested again; and they would say to us, 'We know you're coming back again.'

We needed to maintain some continuity of leadership in Botswana, so we needed the same people to be there. But the more often you got arrested and deported the better known you became to the local police and the more difficult it was even to go down to the shops for a packet of cigarettes or to meet people from home. Every time that you went to any public place you knew you were exposed. But when we met people from home, for obvious security reasons we could not use our own places; we had to meet in relatively public places; and every time you went to such a place you were literally shaking. So that the act of going out to the shops, meeting people, doing your work, created a lot of tension. You had the local police to worry about. They don't beat us up, they don't interrogate us very viciously, but it's not pleasant being in jail, even for two weeks. And the jails there . . . we used to sit in jail and compare them to South African jails. And South African jails came way out on top! [Laughs]

I'd been there a long time, and it was becoming very difficult to survive. I had asked for a transfer some time before. I'd been separated from my family for a long time, which ended in a divorce because of the separation. The relationship just ceased to exist. I really felt bad about my daughter, and I wanted to be based where she was – which was here, Zimbabwe. So I had asked for a transfer. It just happened that, on my last trip out and back, I got arrested again, and my chances of going back again became completely minimised. So in a sense it was fortuitous that I was in the process of leaving when they kicked me out. I came here to Zimbabwe.

I think for me as a white South African, going to MK, to the camps and spending a year and a half made a big difference. I've grown up in the ANC, for the better part of my time with black comrades, and that has wedded me to a South Africa which I didn't know when I was there. So that I've discovered my South Africanism – if I can call it that – outside. It's only through coming out that I was able to find a South Africa that I do really love. In a sense I'm scared of going back into a South Africa which still retains so much of the things I hated.

Exile is not a very nice way to spend your life. There are many personal aspects – my divorce for example, the separation from my family. My parents have grown old. I have sisters who have had kids whom I hardly know. I've got a young half-brother and sister who were five and three respectively when I left the country; I don't know them. It's not nice . . . not nice for anybody. Other comrades have had much more difficult experiences than I. But exile is just not a nice experience. Exile is the inevitability of being separated from your country, your family, your friends.

I came into the MK camp a 'kroesant', as we call it, a new recruit. And with all my university education, my political background in NUSAS as a leader of the white students, I went through the same shit that everybody else went through. And I saw attitudes of comrades changing from a theoretical political position to, ja. Here's one at least who does fulfil what our political instructors are telling us about: white comrades, who have been involved in the struggle and who have identified themselves completely with the struggle.

I think I'm lucky in the sense that my timing was right. But I was just the first of a generation of white comrades who did the same, and went further than I did. And it's that which is building the new South Africa.

Kidnapping

On 12 December 1986 a South African raiding party made a strike into Swaziland, killing a man and a fourteen-year-old boy and abducting five people, one of whom was subsequently shot and killed.

Those abducted were: Grace Cele, a Swazi citizen working for a Canadian relief agency; Corinne Bischoff and Daniel Schneider, young Swiss nationals; Danger Nyoni, father of the dead child; and Shadrack Maphumulo, a former political prisoner who had been living in Swaziland since 1979.

The Swiss couple were released two days later, after strong protests from their government. They described how the raiders had blown in their door and fired automatic rifles. They were dragged from their beds, handcuffed and blindfolded. During the drive Bischoff was shackled to Maphumulo, after he had been killed.

The South African Minister for Foreign Affairs said cross-border raids were in the interests of South African security.

This is how Grace Cele described what happened to her.

GRACE CELE
Ottowa 1990

'There is no place safe for South Africans.'

She was married to a South African who was working in Swaziland. Her husband died in 1980; she was left with five children, four boys and a girl. At the time of this interview her eldest son and her daughter were away studying in the United States. The three younger boys – Sipho, Mfana, Zanele, are with her in Ottowa.

I was living in Swaziland; it was in the night of 12 December. I was kidnapped by the South African commandos. My apartment was bombed – I thought it was an explosion from the refrigerator. I wanted to get up, but I didn't have time. I was pulled out of my bed and there were these men who asked me who I was. And I told them that I was Grace; and they said, 'Grace who?' And I said, 'Grace Cele.' I thought I was dreaming, I thought it was a nightmare. It was the middle of the night.

So they took me out of my bed, I was handcuffed. And as I went out I thought I was dreaming, and I called one of my children: 'Sipho!' and there was no response. So I was taken out, bundled into a car and it ran away. I was blindfolded. The car stopped – I didn't know where it was, until one of these guys – they were laughing then – he said, 'Please use your ashtrays to prevent forest fires.' Then I knew that we were on the road to Mhlambanyati, because there's a sign there in the forest, a man-made forest. They got out of the car and they were talking to somebody who was outside the car, and they were using these walkie-talkies. And the other one said: 'Oh, that was quick.' And the one said: 'Ja, it was quick. But next time they mustn't give us the same cars.'

And when they took off again we were just in a convoy; we were following other cars, two. And at one stage they tried to push me down, and one said: 'There's a truck coming.' You see, that road from Mhlambanyati it's used by loggers, usually during the night when there's no traffic. So they pushed me down and the other one said, 'No, they mustn't see that we've got something here.' So the truck passed. I was . . . I was defenceless because I was blindfolded; I had a nightie on, just my nightie, nothing else. My hands were crossed like this [indicating] just like this, and tied. And they were just . . . they were trying to touch me and I was trying to protect myself – I think if they had time they would have raped me and killed me; and they would have said I was trying to resist arrest. But they didn't have time, because they were saying, 'At such-and-such a time we should be at the border.'

Then they must have got lost, because somebody said: 'No. This is not the turning we are supposed to take.' So they reversed again, they followed, and we stopped somewhere – I have no idea where. And I thought to myself, oh, I think now they are going to kill me. But I heard . . . it was just . . . it wasn't a sharp sound . . . I don't know how to call it, but it wasn't sharp; no, it was sort of deadly . . . how do I describe it? No, they were shooting at something, but it wasn't sharp; it was as though it was snuffled, ja. Muffled. I thought, well they are shooting somebody.

I heard gates open, and the car went in. And next thing I was told to get out. So I got out and I heard this guy talking in Afrikaans: 'Is the gate open?' 'Ja. I have the key.' Now I assumed that we were on the South African side now. So he opened the gate and I was pushed through. Then I heard a Kombi, and it came this Kombi and I was the first one who was thrown in. And immediately when they threw me in, I was handshackled. You see this Kombi I think it was specially made to take people, because there were these bars where I was tied. My feet were chained on to the bars and my hands were chained at the back, and I was left like that. Still blindfolded.

There were others who were thrown in too. And it took off. On the way, I heard these people talking – I thought they were talking German – and the police, well, these bandits kept on saying: 'Shut up!' And then they would keep quiet; and then start talking again. Then I was trying to think, now what is happening because we have got Germans here; who are these other people? But they drove on and on and on, it seemed we were just driving for all eternity.

We came to a place I don't know where, and these two whites were taken out. And the lady started crying and they said to her: 'No don't cry. If you co-operate, we won't harm you.' So they moved them, put them into another car; and we proceeded. Later I met these two – it turned out it was Corinne Bischoff and Danny Schneider. I found that out afterwards.

So we just moved on and on. There was this man who kept on crying and saying: 'I want to pee.' And they kept on saying: 'Shut up!' But he kept on saying: 'I want to pee.' And I heard them say in Afrikaans: '*What van die?* What about this one?' They whispered to each other, and I heard them pull something; it was as though it was a sack, heavy sack of sand. Then I said to myself, whatever it is it must be dead.

Before we took off, when they had taken out that couple, I said to one of them: 'Excuse me, could you please make me comfortable' – I was all bruises because I was knocked all over the place. So they came, put me up straight; they made me sit this time and my hands were still behind me. So we went on. Then we came to this place where we stopped, and they took this guy out – the one who was asking to pee. And I was left there. I can't recall how long . . . it could have been for ten minutes, it could have been two, three hours or whatever. Just sitting in that van.

Eventually they came for me and they took off the foot shackles, ja, but my hands were still tied, and they said I should walk. I couldn't walk; I was swollen all over. So they picked me up – there were two – and they told me: 'Now, listen! We are going up the stairs now. Start walking.' So they tried to lift me up, up, and I went to the top floor whatever it was, and I was just thrown into a . . . I discovered afterwards it was just a long passage. I was thrown there and left there.

After some time they came again and removed the bandage from my eyes. And these two guys came again – I think they were the ones who had done this operation – and put me into a room. It was full of these Boers, and they were just hurling insults at me. Then I saw September. I was shocked when I saw him. September had been in Swaziland; I knew him as a refugee who had been arrested and put into Mangayane Prison. We had then heard over the news that the prison was broken into and some of the refugees were gone, so we thought they must have broken out. But it turned out the South African bandits came for these guys and took them over. I didn't know then that September was alive – I thought he was dead. He says: 'You're surprised I'm alive? I'm alive and I would advise you to just co-operate with these guys; they will give you a lot of money.' I couldn't believe it, because I thought, you know, September was a staunch ANC member. And I looked at September . . . I was confused. And I said, 'What?' He says, 'No, later on we'll talk anyway, we'll talk. But there's a lot of money involved, Grace. Just do as they say.'

By that time I was in pains; and one of the guys said, 'Ay, just look at her.' Now I didn't know what they meant when they say look at me – whether they meant how I looked; because I was bruised, the face, the head, I was swollen just everything. So I thought maybe he meant about my swollen feet, swollen hands, swollen face. And I heard the other one said, 'Oh, you'd better go and get her something to dress.' So one guy went; and they took me to a lean-to thing, and I was made to get in there and wash myself. That's when I was trying to take off my nightie that I discovered that I had blood all over my back, it was just a big stain of blood. I didn't know where that blood came from. But I learned later that one of the ANC members, Maphumulo, had been shot; he was taken from Manzini, put into the car. And I think he was the person I was sitting next to. Dead. It was that person they were pulling. It was Maphumulo.

I came back. They had brought me an overall; and they started asking me questions, 'Do you know ANC people?' Then I said, 'No. But I do have friends who are refugees.' They say, 'No. ANC.' You see, with the Boers if you say refugee, no, they don't want to accept that; you have to identify and say ANC. Then I said, 'Well as far as I know, my friends are refugees.' Then they said, 'Oh ja, we know a lot about you. And we are asking you, as a South African, to help us get these ANC people.'

Then I turned to September – you see I didn't understand. I said, 'September, they say I'm a South African now, but I'm a Swazi. I'm a Swazi citizen now. I know at home I've never been considered a South

African by the Boers, so how can I be a South African?' He says, 'You are not a Swazi.' So I kept on saying, 'No, I'm a Swazi'; they said, 'No, you are not a Swazi; you are a South African.' Then I said, 'Well, I'm a South African conveniently.' That's when they started beating me up. 'Don't talk! We are the ones who are going to do the talking. You only talk when we want an answer from you.'

So they left me. And September said to me, 'No, please listen. You see that one? He said I should talk to you because I told them that I know you. And he said I should talk to you, and there's a lot of money involved.'

But I was not interested then, I was in pain. They took me, put me in a cell, and locked me up there. After two days they came again. So they used to come . . . sometimes they would come every day, sometimes they would stay for three, four days, not appearing, and I'm left in that cell all by myself. All I see is people giving me food through the iron bars. I remember, it was the second day they came with a piece of paper, and this guy said to me, 'Oh sign here.' I said, 'What for?' He says, 'Well Colonel Verster says he arrested you at the border with a car full of arms of war.' And I said, 'No, I'm sure I'm dreaming – did he say he found me?' He says, 'Yes.' Then I said, 'No, I'm not going to sign that.' He says, 'Ek sal jou drap! I'm going to beat you up.' Then I took the paper, I flipped it over, and I signed on the Afrikaans side because they maintained that I didn't know Afrikaans. So at the back of my mind I was saying, Oh let me sign in Afrikaans. In case they ask me, then I'll say, 'This was Afrikaans, I did not know.' Then I said, 'Now what is this Section 29 you are telling me about?' He says, 'No, you were found with arms of war, and you are state security or something like that. How do they call it? Section 29 . . . '[Laughs]

I was asked to identify refugees – yes, they brought piles and piles of photos. And before he started, he says, 'Now Grace, I'd like to know where you are working, how much do you earn?' So I told them. He said, 'Now listen, that's peanuts. We can give you five times, seven times what you are earning. And we can give you, if you give us a big fish, a bonus for that. And we can give you a car of your choice.'

They told me where my children were schooling and they were asking me to verify. So I thought, no, I'm not going to lie because I don't know what they know. So I told them. They said, 'Ja, we can take care of your children, we can educate them, you don't have to pay anything.' Then I said to them, 'What about my place that was bombed?' They said, 'No, that was nothing. We can look after that; if you still want payment for that we can do that easily. But you can get a better place.' And September was harking, kept on saying, 'Grace there's lots of money, lots of money here.'

Then I said to myself, I know in Swaziland a lot of people have been killed by the system after they have done whatever they wanted them to do, and when now they couldn't give more information. So I said, 'No.'

This time I thought, I don't know how I'm going to do it God, but please help me. Because really I was at their mercy.

They beat me with fists, with clubs, what they call it, sticks, ja. I still have scars here on the legs and you can see some of them here, here. Ja, there are still some of them here and here; it's never been right since that time. I didn't know what I was capable of saying or doing. And at one stage, I don't know, I think . . . I must have fainted, or I can't describe it because there was a time when I couldn't feel pain. You know, during these beatings I couldn't feel pain, so I don't know whether I fainted or it was the body mechanism trying to protect me. I don't know.

They would come, sometimes three would come and get me, sometimes two, sometimes one. And I remember one time they said to me, 'You keep on saying you don't know these guys, but they know you.' I was confused now, when they say, 'They know you.' Who were they talking about? Were they talking about the people they kidnapped from Swaziland and who were trying to save their skins? I had no idea. Then I got a very serious beating when they said, 'Oh, they know you, and you say you don't know them?' Then I said, 'Ja, you're right. It's like the Minister of Justice Vlok, ja.' I said, 'It's like me saying I know Vlok; and when you ask Vlok he says he doesn't know me.'

And I . . . I decided then, that I'm not going to say anything. I didn't want to eat their food because of the stories we hear about people being poisoned. So I was scared to eat anything. And they would come and they would find the food stacked there. And they said to me, 'Are you on hunger strike?' And I wouldn't answer them because it wasn't a hunger strike, it was fear more than anything. And at one stage they asked me, 'Is your hair permed?' Then I said, 'No it's not.' Then I heard him saying to this guy, 'Ja, she's lucky. Because I was going to set light to that hair!'

I don't know what to say, there's so many things. Some time during my stay in the cell there were people in cells on both sides; and they would shout to each other, 'No, just get on the toilet seat.' They were not talking to me. Then I said to myself, oh boy, all along I should have done this thing – get on the toilet seat and look outside. But I went to the toilet seat and I look over, and I saw there were two Kombis, and children coming out of these Kombis. Then I said to myself, now, what are these children . . . what are they doing here? And I heard this other guy in the next cell saying, 'Oh, those are the children that have been taken from all over the country.'

One day I heard them opening the doors. Usually they used to give me food through the iron bars. They opened and I saw this child, he was about eight or nine. Then I looked at this guy who was bringing my food, and I said to this child, 'Hey, what do you want here?' And then he started crying. He said, 'Oh I was taken from Soweto. Please I want to go home, I was taken from so-and-so'. And this guy said, 'Shut up! You are telling a lie! You were trying to chop somebody with a machete. You are telling a lie!' He says, 'No, I'm not telling a lie. I've been taken from Soweto!' That's the first and the last time they brought anybody around, but sometimes I would hear people crying. I heard one crying and she says, 'No, I'm telling the truth! I'm telling the truth!' But they were just beating up these kids, just beating them up. She says, 'No, I'm not lying! I'm telling the truth!'

So the guy came again who was bringing me food. I said, 'Now who is this one crying? What is happening?' He says, 'Oh no; that one is mad. Ja,' he says, 'he's a mad person. He's mad.' But I could hear the beatings up.

One day I was taken to a doctor because now I was getting sick. The doctor says, 'Now you are very sick; you have got kitons in your urine because you don't eat. Right now you should have been in a coma, why aren't you eating? Are you on a hunger strike?'

I said, 'No. I'm not on a hunger strike. I don't know why I'm here; and my children have been killed.' They said, 'No, your children haven't been killed.' I said, 'I called to them when they took me, and they didn't respond; it has never happened with my children that when I called out to them, they don't respond.' The doctor talked to one of the police, said, 'Find out if her children are OK, are alive.' He went, came back and said, 'Oh, we called your house and there was nobody.' I said, 'Of course. You've killed my kids! Do you expect the ghosts to answer the telephone?' Then they said, 'Who can we get in touch with?' I remembered a friend of mine who was working for UNDP, so I said, 'Oh, call Doreen.' I gave them the number, and he came back and said, 'Doreen says the children are OK.' I said, 'I don't trust you. I'll only believe when I talk to Doreen.' But at that time I was hysterical, I was crying. They said, 'No, try to keep quiet; then you'll be able to talk to Doreen.'

So I spoke to Doreen. I was warned before, 'Don't tell Doreen where you are, what we are doing; just ask about the children and that's all. And don't cry.' So I said, 'Doreen, it's Grace.' Then she started crying over the phone, 'Where are you? What are you doing? Where are you?' Then I said, 'Are my children OK, Doreen?' Says, 'Ja, they are fine; somebody is taking care of them.' And then she said, 'Oh your cousin just called from Ermelo.' I don't have any cousin.

The doctor said, 'Now you can eat.' But I never ate a morsel of food for all the time I was held there. That was sixty-eight days, ja; and my teeth were sort of getting loose. And they called the doctor again and the doctor said, 'No Grace, you'd better eat.' And he prescribed some tablets. I was afraid again to take those tablets because I'd heard that people are given slow poison. They would bring these tablets and they would look at me, then I would put them under my tongue; as soon as they go, then I would spit them out! But when the doctor came a fortnight later and told them, 'I've given her these vitamin tablets but there's no improvement,' I nearly kicked myself. And after that, faithfully each time I would take these vitamin tablets. But I never ate their food.

During that time a number of people would come. One said he was from the Minister of Justice to ask if I have any complaints. And I said, 'You've been coming here I don't know how many times, asking about my complaints. I've asked you, and I'll still ask you: if I've done anything wrong let me be charged. If I haven't done anything wrong, let me be released and put back into Swaziland.' 'I'll convey your message to the Minister!' And another day there was one who came and said, 'I'm the Prosecutor here.' I said, 'Prosecutor here – where is here?' Says, 'Oh, never mind; but I was told to come and see if you have any needs and so on.' I said, 'Oh, could you please try and get me a toothbrush and some toothpaste, and soap.' Because they gave me a carbolic soap and I used it and I just got burned. But he never brought me soap.

Until one day, they just came and said, 'You are going home.' I cried all night. I cried all night because I was thinking: now home, it means they are going to kill me; it's their way of talking, they are going to kill me. So . . . that was Friday when they told me. Nothing happened. Saturday nothing happened. And they came on Sunday morning with a nailclipper – my nails were this long, I'd been asking for a nailclipper and they refused. But that particular morning, when I was supposed to go home, they brought a nailclipper, said, 'OK. You can cut your nails and make yourself presentable, so that they shouldn't think that we are ill-treating you.'

Just before I was told I was going home, somebody came and said, 'I'm sent by the Minister to check if you have any fresh scars and wounds. Did you have any beatings?' That's when I was told that I can go home. They came at about 5 p.m. and said, 'Now we are taking you home. But never ever utter a word to anybody where you were held, what we did to you, what we asked you to do for us. Because if you do, we know where your children are.'

I wasn't scared so much for myself. I was scared for my children. And I know how brutal they are.

So I was released. They said, 'You shouldn't be interviewed by anything – media, television, nothing, nobody. Because we will be watching you.' This is why, when I was released, I didn't talk to anybody. I asked my children, 'If the telephone rings you'd better answer it.' They would call and ask to talk to Grace; my friends would say, 'She's not in.' I kept quiet. I stayed away from the media.

But I was scared. And as soon as I got home I had made up my mind that I'll just organise my children and run away. But I didn't know where to.

I had been working for the USC – Unitarian Service Committee of Canada. On the day I was released, the Programme Officer, Andrew, was trying to make plans for the office. I said, 'No, Andrew. Better get somebody – I don't think I'll be staying around.' And he said, 'Where are you going?' I said, 'I don't know where I'm going, but I'm going.' That's when they asked me, 'Do you want to go and live in Canada?' I said, 'Anywhere where I'll be safe I will go.' So Ed Wheeler who was the Ambassador for Canada then, expedited things and gave us a Minister's permit within two, three weeks. He asked me, 'Is three weeks long enough, Grace?' I thought it was enough. But I found that that three weeks was like three years, because I used to get phone calls, I used to get followed, I used to get threats in the office. Somebody would come towering over me: 'We can kill your children and tell the press that these children were killed by ANC.' Even there, right in Swaziland, in Mbabane.

When this Minister's permit came, I just took my children and my bag and we left. Sipho was at university and Mfana was at boarding-school. So I told them, 'Just leave your things as they are, so that you mustn't show that you are leaving.' And we just went to Matsapa airport, got our tickets. And we went through the customs.

It was boarding time. We got into the plane and it started taxi-ing. But suddenly it stopped and there was an announcement, the air hostess, 'Grace Cele please report to immigration!' I went cold. 'Grace Cele please report to immigration!' I said no. I was so scared I said no. I said, 'No. I'm not getting out!' So she took our passports, went out to immigration, and it was about thirty-five minutes. Then she came back and gave me back our travel documents. And we went.

But without Sipho. He was turned back at the airport, because his document didn't have a Zimbabwe endorsement. So I tried to beg them, I wanted to stay behind. I meant to take every one of them. I said 'No, I can't leave you, Sipho.' If I left Sipho behind I wasn't sure whether he'd ever come and join us. I felt at that stage he grew overnight, because when I was taken he was a youngster with two other youngsters on his hands; he was eighteen then. So Sipho just looked at me and said, 'Mum, go!' I said, 'No, Sipho.' You know, I've never seen such defiance in a child. He looked at me, says, 'Do you hear me? I say go!' Then I got the message. I said, 'OK. Go to immigration tomorrow, ask them to endorse Zimbabwe; I'll call you at ten o'clock.'

So we flew to Zimbabwe. The next morning I called him. He said, 'Ja, I'm from the immigration; they've endorsed Zimbabwe.' So we stayed about a week or so waiting for Sipho, and then we flew to Canada. Zanele was eight then – I didn't tell him that we are leaving home for good. And in Toronto he just suddenly turned and said, 'I want to go home.' Then I looked at Sipho and Sipho said, 'Tell him, Mum.' So I said, 'Zani, it's not possible for us to go home now.' And then he started crying. I said, 'OK. You remember what happened at home when Mummy was taken? If we go home there is a possibility that I will be taken again or I may be killed. So we are running away from that so that it shouldn't happen again.' And he turned and said, 'No. I don't want to go home!' [Laughs] 'No, I don't want to go home.'

So we came over, and we got to Ottowa. We started getting calls. You keep on saying, 'Who's talking?' And then somebody puts the phone down. That's when Sipho and Ntombi and my friends kept on saying, 'Grace, we think it's best if you talk to somebody about your experiences, because now if anything happens, nobody will know. You'll just disappear like a lot of people who have disappeared.' Journalists had been calling our office, saying, 'We understand that Grace Cele, the refugee from Swaziland, is around.' You know I used to scream, I used to tell the children not to talk. But then Sipho kept on saying, 'Mummy, talk!' So that week I just went to this journalist Pamela Macrae. I said, 'Pam, I think I will talk.'

So I started talking; it was published. And for some reason, after that all those calls stopped. I don't know whether it's a coincidence, but it just stopped.

The life of an exile . . . it's difficult. You have been uprooted from your friends, from your family, from your culture. And you suddenly found yourself in a world where you have to start afresh. And you are constantly looking over your shoulder – because we've been brainwashed. So now, if somebody is trying to ask you about this, you think: it's still happening to me! Why is she questioning me? Ja, why is she questioning me?

The boys have settled down. But end of July I got a telephone call from the school where Zanele is – he's eleven. The teacher said, 'Zanele is suddenly falling asleep in class.' And that particular day she said Zanele should go outside to get fresh air. And when she went out, she just found Zanele sprawled on the floor. She suggested Zanele should see a social worker.

Two days thereafter I was called by the social worker, Penny, who said, 'I had a talk with Zanele. And information I didn't ask for just spilled out. He started telling me: "Mummy was taken by the Boers; and now I'm here – I never said goodbye to my aunts, to my uncles, to my friends. I just left them. I want to go home." Phew!'

Then I said, 'Oh Penny, I thought the child has adjusted.' She says, 'No, it's deep inside. But now, he's suppressing that by sleeping. Do you want your child to see a psychiatrist?' And that's the same story he's telling the psychiatrist, you know, 'My mother was taken away, and we came here and I've never said goodbye to my cousins and so on.' Then the psychiatrist started talking to Zanele, and since then I haven't had any complaint from school. But I don't know what else will come out again.

Sipho? He's adjusted, but at the same time I don't think he has adjusted; because last summer he took a baseball bat and bashed a guy who was six feet. So we went to court and this guy said, 'Ja, I provoked him.' And I said to Sipho, 'Now why did you do it?' He says, 'Mum, we ran away from a country where these remarks were the order of the day. We are coming to what is said to be the First World, and we are getting people who are racists, saying: "Go home you bloody immigrant!" ' Sipho's reponse to this guy was, 'Well, this country belongs to the Indians; it's not yours! We are all immigrants!' But then he kept on provoking Sipho, and that's when Sipho took a baseball bat and hit him, ja.

It's been difficult making a life in a strange country; difficult, yes. But not because of the children. You know what they say: *Inhlo icinwa mboko iyi* – the elephant does not feel the weight of his trunk. So no, I didn't feel it. Even if I did I had to carry it. I have to. It's part of me. Ja.

Death Squads

In 1989 Captain Dirk Coetzee admitted his involvement in at least twenty-three crimes committed 'in the line of duty' as a member of the South African Security Police. These crimes included six murders, attempted murder, conspiracy to murder, arson, sabotage, kidnapping and housebreaking. The story of one of the murder raids he led is told here from the viewpoint of the perpetrator, Coetzee himself. Later, in Canada, I interviewed his intended victims, Tieho (Rola) Masinga and his wife, Joyce Diphale. Coetzee's account is no less horrific for being matter-of-fact; while the trauma of that night and of the terrible period through which she lived is evidenced in Joyce Diphale's inability to speak for herself.

DIRK COETZEE
England 1991

'I was in the heart of the whore. I know the deepest secrets of this unit. I'm guilty of, or at least an accomplice to, several murders.' (*Vrye Weekblad*, 17 November 1989)

For five years, from January 1977 to December 1981, Captain Dirk Johannes Coetzee was a field commander in a Death Squad, performing illegal operations outside South Africa. He is athletic-looking, with brown hair, a strong jaw, and a wide smile.

I'm fifty-six years old now, I'm married, I've got two sons, Dirk Jnr and Kalla, fourteen and twelve. In the night of 19 October 1989, an ex-colleague of mine, Almond Nofomela, a police colleague, was on death row for a murder that he committed while robbing a farmer. Him and his brother were supposed to hang. He saw there was no way out – he was going to hang the next morning – so he said: 'Wait! there's other murders that I'm responsible for, amongst other things the Griffith Mxenge murder, a lawyer down in Durban.' So that night he blew the whistle on hit squads.

They then had a stay of execution, temporary, and they appointed the Attorney-General of the Free State to investigate these allegations. His story was published. Almond said that we had government-sanctioned hit squads in the South African Security Police and my name was in the papers. But everyone denied it, and an ex-colleague, white, still in Security, came to me and just said: 'Deny everything.'

I went to see Brigadier Jan du Preez at his house. He simply said I should deny everything. I then asked about Brian Ngulunga and Joe Mamasela, also members of the hit squad. He insisted: What does it matter if one or two kaffirs should talk? I should simply deny it.

I'm out of the police now, I'm a pensioner, I went off medically unfit in January 1986 as a result of sugar diabetes. And I thought, hell man, for how long still? I've been out of this system now, this security police system, killing activists and government opponents, eliminating them. But it stays with you. I mean all this killing and blowing up of houses and cars and innocent people being killed, it's in your subconscious. You live with it day and night. But how do you come to make peace with it? There's no way out. If you admit it, you're in for murder and you will hang, and you will hang alone, because you've worked in this rotten system.

And you can go nowhere. I'd never been out of South Africa – so where do you go? The ANC will kill you if they get hold of you. They knew of all the stories, they've got people . . . comrades that went back, that's been caught inside South Africa, and been working on Vlakplaas, the security farm, and then defected again, back to them, and told them stories. So I just said: Hell! There's no ways, it's no use running away from the ANC and the South African police worldwide.

Luckily Jacques Pauw*, a journalist on the *Vrye Weekblad*, who's a friend of mine since 1985, said he's got a way out if I'll be prepared to meet with the ANC and tell my story. I says: 'Hell they will kill me!' He said: 'No man, forget it. They're not that monster that you think they are.' He says: 'I've got a contact.' So he flew to Lusaka, met up with Zuma and J. J. Jele, two of the ANC National Executive guys, and they said, OK they will listen to my story. And if they're not happy with me, I must go back. And if they're happy, OK we can talk further.

I said: 'No ways! There must be a bottom line. You help me for four months to get on to my feet outside South Africa, and I look for a country

* Jacques Pauw has written a book, *In the Heart of the Whore – the Story of Apartheid's Death Squads* (Southern Book Publishers, 1991), which tells Dirk Coetzee's story in full.

where I can get political asylum.' First I decided to fly to Mauritius and I'll tell my story to Jacques, in case something happens on the road. So we flew out to Mauritius – the ANC put aside I think R50,000 for this project – and I told my story. Why? Because I knew if I stayed inside South Africa, they were going to make me a liar, they would say Dirk is mad. Because I was in the heart of this clique, and I knew sometime in future the truth will catch up with you, your past will catch up.

Well . . . I was confused of course, I was utterly confused, and I didn't know which way to go. I went to my brother, Ben – he's two years older than I am. He's been in the National Party. He's just the opposite that I am, very intelligent and can see things in the future very clearly. He went into the Democratic Party, and he's now a member of the ANC. And I went to him, and Ben said, 'Dirk, you just leave the country, you know what the system is going to do with you – you know it. Please, just get out. And we can talk again. But just first get out. Once you're behind bars and the case is put in camera again, you're buggered. Just get out! Fight the system from outside! Just get out.'

So it wasn't a case of fleeing from justice, but from injustice – which was clearly proved during the Harms Commission*. The Judge said I'm a psychopath, I've got psychopathic tendencies: 'How must I believe this crap?' It's the first time in history that a Judge in public, from the bench, there in the commission, used the word 'crap'! A Judge!

So from the start, I was up against a wall. I could just see he was just not prepared to believe my story. The few slips the police made, he just didn't look into it, he didn't comment on it. I would have been in it alone. Dirk Coetzee, lunatic, acted on his own, murdered for himself. And the big generals and the ministers would have been free.

I've written a letter to F. W. de Klerk and to the Minister of Law and Order, Kobie Coetzee, after invitations in the press to me that I must come back and stand trial. I said I will come back. But a fair and honest trial depends on a fair and honest police investigation; and they've proved themselves not willing or capable of doing that. So just give me the chance, I'll put my money where my mouth is. What are you afraid of? I'm a police pensioner; appoint me, temporary, in the police again. They do it daily. They've appointed ex-ANC members, the trash that ran away, that couldn't stand the exile life, couldn't stand fighting a cause. They are appointed as Askaris, and some ninety of them are fully fledged members of the South African police!

The task of the Askaris was to mix with the population at public places such as shebeens, bus stops, railway stations and taxi ranks, spot ex-ANC comrades, and point them out to qualified policemen . . . Three deserted back to the ANC during my stay and three were killed by us.

---

* A Government commission under Justice Louis Harms to investigate allegations about Death Squads.

Two landed in jail for murdering their girlfriends. All the Askaris smoked dagga. With a few exceptions they drink heavily. They know nothing about the law!

But they've got the power, through their appointment, to arrest you, to shoot you if you run away. Now, if you can appoint them, why can't you appoint me? I said I'll come back after that; and I'll reconstruct all these murders and explosions that we've done – blowing up of the White House, the transit house in Swaziland; and Rola and Joyce Diphale in Gaberone, which we shot at one night.

I left school in 1963, joined the post office, worked in the investigation section for six and a half years, investigating irregularities. I worked closely with police detectives. As a result, I joined the South African police force in 1970, went to police college, and I came out best student of the year. I went to the police dog school, I did a driver's course, then I went to radio control. I became a station commander at Volksrust, did border duty in Rhodesia, worked with Rhodesian guys in incidents with freedom-fighters, terrorists.

In the 1976 Soweto uprising, I was in charge of a lot of instructors and students in Johannesburg, guarding keypoints and the mortuary in Hillbrow amongst other things, where there was . . . just about 240 bodies stacked up under the tables and on the floors and in the passages and in the garages. We had to guard all these places.

Then after that I said, 'No. I want to think for myself. I don't want to be in a place where the brigadier says you must try this police student for being absent without leave and you must find him guilty. No. I want to think for myself.'

They drew me into security. And they gave me an option of Swaziland border-post command, or Oshikate, north of Namibia, the Koevoet contingent. Wife didn't want to go to Oshikate, so we ended up at Oshoek border post, near Ermelo and Mbabane, done a helluva good job there. The Ermelo Security that worked Swaziland drew me in slowly but surely; I just took over Swaziland. Jacob Zuma was there, Stanley Mabizela – I stole his car, his Peugeot; we had a big laugh about it in January when we met in Zambia! All the important guys that's now really high up in the ANC used to be in Swaziland.

I was helping to blow their houses up; their transit house, the White House, was wrecked, and the Impaka railway line to Mozambique to implicate the ANC. A lot of things . . . Bafana Duma used to work for a solicitors' firm there, and he'd collect their mail at the Manzini post office, and he used that box for ANC purposes too, so . . . Post office bomb. I also led a mission to bomb another ANC transit house occupied by Mawick Nkosi, who they said was the man who built false panels into vehicles to smuggle arms and explosives into South Africa.

I was in this Section C(1) Vlakplaas contingent. I worked directly under Brigadier Schoon. Now there's a need-to-know in security, so I won't be told every time: 'Brigadier Jan du Preez said that General Johan Coetzee said that Minister Louis le Grange said you must kill Marius Schoon.' Understand? He will say, 'Dirk, Marius Schoon is a problem for us, see Rudi Kraus of Zeerust – Zeerust security works Botswana; he will explain everything.' Then I know, OK. You don't ask questions.

I'm in that job because I was selected. My personality suited them. In the Harms Commission the advocates for the police said: 'You're a murderer?' I says: 'Yes.' Says: 'You're a housebreaker?' I says: 'Yes.' Says: 'You're a car thief?' I say: 'Yes, yes, but it's strange that I've done it only whilst I was in the Security Police – never before and never there-after; it's now ten years, isn't it strange?' So then they come and they say: 'Dirk Coetzee is a self-admitted murderer,' without explaining the details. So my personality suited them. You are selected, you grew up in a community where you were brainwashed, I was doing it for my country and these bastards! Hell, I mean I was just . . .

I thought, what was this all about? Why did I do it? What was the purpose thereof? I mean, what did I achieve by it? And in the end I was forced into a turnabout. But now how do you come to grips with what you've done? How do you make peace with it? How do you get out to the community and get it settled? It's impossible. I was forced into it when my ex-colleague Nofomela admitted, and then I had to decide. Forced! Well, I could have said no, and could have still been back in South Africa, sitting there put. Almond would have been hanged and that's that. And the hit squads, I mean they would have gone on like never before. But I just decided no, up to a point and no further. Just here, just here I'm going to cut it short.

I was staying in my mother and father's house, an old house up in the mountains . . . in Pretoria. So I left my wife and two children there. After I left, unfortunately my wife got involved in a relationship with a young chappie – she's forty-three – twenty-five-year-old little guy, which we believe is from military intelligence. Luckily I've got a helluva open relationship with my two boys. But that was my hardest knock. My wife was very dear, we know one another for twenty-seven years, married twenty-one years. That was my hardest hit. I've been in exile long, and you won't get me buggering around with any woman, I'm just not that kind of guy.

My roots is back home. My whole body and soul is back home. I can't imagine myself living in exile. I knew when I came out it would be a few years at least. But in February last year, when de Klerk made the announcement, I wanted to go back, you know, I wanted to go and clean up this mess for de Klerk, show him! And if we must go to jail, we'll go to jail. Everyone! From his previous minister of Law and Order down – whoever is involved. Because hit squads wasn't born in my time and didn't die after I left, it's been there long before and it's still going on, for sure. More selective, I should say. I don't know the record, but looking at this turmoil in the townships and this third force, it's obvious that it's going on.

That's my country, I don't know how I'll ever stay out of it.

In 1981 I was called to Durban where I was told to kill Mxenge. I was told to make it appear like a robbery because the police did not want another Biko case. I asked for Joe Mamasela and Almond Nofomela to be sent down. They were both healthy and fit and had the killer instinct. There were four of them. When I met them one Thursday night, Joe was wearing Mxenge's jacket and watch. They told me how they kidnapped him and took him to Umlazi stadium where he was stabbed to death. They also slit his throat and cut off his ears. The Askaris received R1,000 each for their good work.

When I went to the ANC they were very friendly. Hell, I mean I was so nervous telling Jacob Zuma about Griffith Mxenge – I was responsible for it; he was stabbed forty-four times and his throat was cut and his dogs were poisoned – and he was a friend of Zuma, close friend. And Zuma didn't wink an eye. I was very well-received, very well-looked after, very well-cared for. Up till now, this day. Hell, it's just beautiful. Hell, I can't complain really. So warm, so genuine, so human! You can talk to them, a human being. 'We know, Dirk, we understand, you're a victim of the system, like thousands and millions of other South Africans, black and white.' And that kind of attitude. Forgiveness, forget.

But you can't forgive and forget the past, if we don't know what the past was all about. Craig Williamson now, he's written open letters in the newspapers – No, Craig! Come out, come out you bastard! Come and stand here and say you killed Ruth First! You did the Albie Sachs bomb with Wal du Toit. The chap making those bombs is a personal friend of mine! The chap that sent me the headset bomb to kill me, who made it, was a personal friend of mine! So I said, we can forgive and forget, but then first we must know what it's all about.

In the Death Squads there's apartheid of sorts. I was handling the blacks in Botswana/Lesotho/Swaziland and South Africa, Williamson only handled whites. Him and Johan Coetzee had their little special reasons, why this one and why that? Agh, it's just so senseless. I don't think there's any sense, there's any logic in it. Why choose Ruth First? She was at the University of Maputo, why kill her? That's why Craig said once: 'You've got to be a controlled schizophrenic' – I'm probably cutting my own throat here. Well, only a schizophrenic can do such things, people that he lived with in exile. Why then Marius . . . Jeanette Schoon and her daughter? Why Albie Sachs? How do you justify it? How do you justify it? Apartheid! Because you're black and I'm white, you can't stay here, you can't sit with me in school. Why? But I accepted that all my life, I did. I did. Brainwashed. I believed in it. That's why it's gonna take a generation or two to get that out of the system. There's millions that's got to be educated, and it's gonna take a helluva lot of time.

I won't be able to live anywhere else, you know, even if it catches up with me. This is what I've said. This is my part in it, now make peace; give everyone political asylum, hang us all, do what you want now, but let's start, let's educate, let's try and get a stable country. Let's get it over! I'm just floating here, with a suitcase with two jeans and a few shirts, underpants and socks, and I'm going. So my roots is not here, my children's not at school here.

Dirk Coetzee's two sons came to live with him in England. I asked Dirk Jnr what he felt about his father's activities.

DIRK Jnr: My attitude was always to stand by my father, or to stand by the family, no matter what they did. But especially now . . . I don't say . . . I couldn't say it's wrong, what he did, because at home we were afraid . . . we were talking . . . we were afraid they were going to pin it on him, frame him.

But what about what he did previously, in the Death Squads?

I knew about it always, but I didn't think . . . Yes, I knew about it from small, and I didn't think about it. It was my father's job, he did that for a living. I just accepted it. It was nothing strange, and when he came out, it was nothing strange again. But then I started to go deeper into details, with the families, and we came out into Zambia and we saw the films about ANC people being blown up and the conspiracy against them, all that stuff; and it's only then that I started to think about these things. And well, I can't say it's right, but it was war. And that time my father was on the one side of the war, hearing only one side. That was his job, fighting for his country and blowing up the terrorists.

DIRK Senr: While I was on Vlakplaas, Dirkie went out with me, he was only five years. With Joe Mamasela, Arnold Nofomela, he went out into the veld up to two weeks at a time. I wouldn't take him if I went on special ops, but on our routine scrutinising of a border area, shebeens, stations, he loved it. Kalla was too young so I couldn't take him with me.

DIRK Jnr: I made big friends there, ate with them and had jokes . . . the whole day. My father never told us, you don't eat with a black and you don't go there to the lokasies, they stay there and you stay here. And it's only now when I came out, when I became aware of these situations where they live in a whole world apart from us . . . I thought they choose to live there and it's just . . . just a way of life. And because we were friends, Arnold Nofomela and David Chikalanga, all those people I was friends with, there was no difficulty in becoming friends with any black person anywhere.

I knew the ANC was the enemy, but I didn't even know they were standing for the rights of the black, I didn't have a clue what they were standing for. I knew that it was essentially a black army and they were bombing the whites and all those things, no.

KALLA: I almost knew the same, I was just more sort of innocent. I didn't know my father went to hit squads, I only knew my brother and my father was in the army, as I saw it, and they went to the bush together. A lot of times I was angry at my father, because I couldn't understand why I can't go with him. And every time my brother came home and told me what a nice time he had I started getting a little jealous. I didn't have much to do with them, I knew that my father was fighting someone, I don't know who.

DIRK Jnr: Just miss a few things. Like the sun. Gees, that's what I miss here. My friends.

The Raid on Joyce Diphale

This account is from a manuscript, giving details of the activities of his Death Squad written by Dirk Coetzee.

Colonel Schoon sent me to Zeerust to join up with Security there, for a mission into Botswana to eliminate the occupants of an ANC house in Gaberone.

During the early afternoon we congregated at a house near the Kopfontein border post, and were briefed on the location of the target house, and its layout – they had a plan showing Rola and Joyce's bedroom. We were told there was no garage, and that if the 1400 Datsun bakkie was parked outside the house, then Rola was there.

In the afternoon Joe and Almond went through the Kopfontein border post to reconnoitre the target house. When they returned, I went to familiarise myself with the surroundings, and after that I explained the details of the plan as we later carried out, except for a few opportunistic improvisations offered by the weather.

The border post closes at 8 p.m. At about 7.45 we sent Joe in again to ensure the road was clear of roadblocks, and to meet us at nine inside the Botswana border. The rest of the hit squad crossed the fence south of the border post. We concealed ourselves and waited. When Joe arrived, flicking his lights as arranged to identify himself, Paul took the wheel,

Koos and I got in the cab with Paul and Joe, Almond and Spyker mounted on the back. We left Rudy and Jan behind at that point as markers, and to guide us back to the fence.

About two blocks from the target house, we left Spyker and Paul under a tree with the bakkie, and the rest of us continued on foot. Joe was armed with a Tokarev pistol and Almond with a Makarov pistol. Koos and I each had an HMK sub-machine gun with silencer and a canvas bag attached to the side to catch empty shells. Koos had a hand grenade. Koos and I had blackened our faces and hands. We wore long-sleeved shirts and balaclavas to cover our hair and ears.

We walked along a road from where we would turn left into a side road to get to the target house. Just before the turn, Koos and I took up concealed positions in the long grass. Joe and Almond patrolled the street. We could see the bakkie belonging to Rola parked next to the back stoep of the target house.

We could hear a loud party going on across the road from the target house, and people were mingling in the street. There were dogs barking. A thunder storm was building up, and I decided to wait for the storm to break. This happened around midnight. The rain poured down, and there was much thunder and lightning, then the lights also went out. People were in their houses and the dogs were taking shelter.

We could then walk undisturbed along the street to the target site, and through the gate. Koos took up position near the bedroom window at the back. Almond, Joe and I were at the back stoep deciding how to get the door open. We looked through the kitchen window, and at that stage two women entered the kitchen from the passage carrying a candle, and proceeded to unlock and open the outside door.

There was no time to think or talk. The women spun around. Joe grabbed one from behind, covering her mouth. He shot at her point blank and she collapsed on the stoep. The other woman fled into the house screaming, while Almond and Joe fired shots after her.

I pushed Almond and Joe aside and ran into the kitchen. I sprayed bullets down the passage with the HMK. I argued that the women would be trapped in the crossfire with Koos firing through the bedroom window and hurling in the hand grenade. I ran out and shouted to Joe and Almond to follow. I could see Almond firing a last shot at the fallen woman. As I ran past Koos, I shouted that he should follow us. He asked whether he should shoot, and I realised there had been no crossfire. This was Koos's first operation of this nature. He then fired a spurt through the window and followed us, forgetting to throw the hand grenade.

We cleared the fence, then another fence, and ran through the gate into the street where Paul and Spyker were waiting in the pouring rain. We clambered in and sped off towards the border. The two soaked and anguished markers appeared in the road. We made our way through the veld to the border fence south of the border post, cut our way through three border fences and pushed the bakkie through the quagmire. We reached our farm base, tired, cold and wet, in the early hours of the morning.

According to the feedback we received later, the woman who collapsed on the stoep ended up in hospital, and did not die. The woman who fled into the house was Joyce, and she escaped with superficial wounds. The two women had dropped Rola at the airport that afternoon, and he was out of the country.

JOYCE DIPHALE AND TIEHO MASINGA (ROLA)
Toronto 1990

When she first arrived in Canada, interviewed on television she spoke fluently, expressively. Her face was soft, round, her hair in two little plaits that made her look very young.

Since then, she has suffered a stroke and lost the power of speech. With treatment, she is beginning to get a few words back. The interview was conducted with her husband, Rola; she intervened with gestures, became agitated at some points, and indicated strongly when she did not want certain subjects discussed.

Rola is round-faced, of medium height and sturdy build. He speaks slowly, thoughtfully.

ROLA: I was acquitted from a trial in 1978, the ANC trial in Pretoria. And as soon as the trial was over, the South African police wanted me to take a decision: whether to be inside South Africa to be killed by them, or to just cross the fence – that's the language they used. They said this to me just a few moments after the acquittal. But I didn't leave. And three days after my acquittal I was picked up again and put in solitary confinement.

I was kept in John Vorster Square for a few months and then transferred to Modder B prison. So after my release in late 1978, we did think of leaving, but Joyce and I thought that before we left we should do some work. We were involved in the student movement, and we planned the launching of the Congress of South African Students in 1979. We worked very hard – there were many things that we had to do. And then, I think just three months after getting out of prison, they raided my home. I wasn't sleeping there any more; but that was a signal for me to leave immediately. The launching of the student movement was well ahead.

Joyce had also been in detention in the same year as I, 1976. She too was kept in solitary confinement for two years. And her experience was worse than ours. We never knew where Joyce was. She was being moved from one prison to another, and she experienced a lot of torture which we believe led to a deterioration in her life, her health and loss of memory. And we assume that the South African government did in fact try to kill Joyce in Botswana.

Joyce and I went into Botswana and continued our work, working with Joe Gqabi and other student leaders, and with the ANC political committee. Joyce was in charge of the committee that was entrusted with organising the youth and students in South Africa, and this is where all her energies were devoted. The South African government tried to infiltrate people into the organisation in Botswana, and one person who was infiltrated was able to give them information about Joyce. That's why when they came to assassinate her, they knew exactly that she was going out that night to pick me up from the station, and they were waiting for her in ambush. So when she came out, they shot her.

The night when Joyce was shot, I had gone to Lusaka to discuss some of the issues with the leadership in Zambia. The very same night they killed Joe Gqabi in Zimbabwe – I only heard this when I was in a Botswana prison, because when I came back the Botswana government said it wasn't wise to leave me hanging around in a critical situation like that.

Joyce was badly wounded; friends from the Swedish Embassy took her to hospital, but she suspected these fellows were going to come and look for her in the hospital. So after getting treatment, she was taken somewhere in hiding; and then moved out of Botswana to Germany for further treatment.

I stayed in Botswana for a few months, working there – underground, and because there was a confrontation between us and some members of the Botswana Security, I had to leave Botswana. I went to different areas, Zimbabwe, Mozambique, just doing ANC work. And then after Joyce came back both of us went to Lusaka.

When the South African government failed to kill Joyce, they arrested her brother Mohabi. Two weeks after the attempt on Joyce's life, they took this young man – captured him in the street, and put him in the boot of a car. But because a lot of people saw it happening, they brought him back the same evening, then they picked him up again the day after in Soweto, and murdered him while he was in detention. We now know that this boy was not killed in prison. What they did is that they drove him to the border of Botswana, and they shot him there, then took him back to prison. And that, of course, affected Joyce a great deal.

We thought Joyce should probably leave Southern Africa. South African incursions were taking place from time to time, and we were living under such severe conditions Joyce was getting affected. Some of our friends who were involved with us had mental breakdowns. So we thought it would be better for her to go somewhere where she could be away from all these threats. Which was why she went to Nairobi.

We were members of the Lutheran church, ja, and Joyce joined the All-Africa Conference of Churches, where she became the head of the Youth and Women's Section. But in Nairobi there was a problem between the Kenyan government and the church there, and people like Joyce were not really welcome. They gave her forty-eight hours to leave Kenya. So friends who had been working on social justice issues with us, they thought we should come to Canada.

Here she started working immediately with the Inter-Church Coalition on Africa to mobilise support for Mozambique and other Frontline States. She had a tour to Mozambique and Angola, she had been going all over the place without any rest whatsoever. Joyce was working too hard. Just before she got sick, she was really working too hard! She was never home. Well ja. She devoted her time to that work. She wanted to do it. So it was part of our life – until she got the stroke in September 1989, ja.

She doesn't want me to talk about other members of the family, because she is thinking that Mohabi died because he was identified with Joyce. And now she's afraid for other members of the family, yes. That also is a liability, because they always continue to threaten the families, relatives.

After her stroke people from all over the country were very sympathetic. They did all kinds of things – I was never alone. It wasn't only our people from home, but you know, everybody who's involved here in the struggle, people who knew Joyce. They came in big numbers at the hospital, she was never alone. And that in itself was a therapy, because it shows what it is to become part of an important objective like that of liberating your own people. So that in a way has kept us going.

MARIUS SCHOON
Dublin 1991

'I feel as though you came back and you gave me an AK and I've beaten those monkeys. And the monkeys have gone. They'll never come back.'

His daughter, Katryn, was six and his son, Fritz, was two years old when the events described here took place.

I was in prison in Pretoria from 1964 to 1976, and was released with very stringent banning and house arrest orders which meant getting a job was absolutely impossible. In prison I had decided that when I came out I was going to concentrate my energies and my activities on the white left, which had revived during the previous five or six years, but was very ill-informed and very hostile to the ANC.

About six weeks after I came out of prison, I met Jenny Curtis a couple of days after she had been banned for her trade union activities. And Jenny and I spent the next nine months doing what I think is possibly the most important political work I've done in my life, we both ignored our banning orders more or less completely. We saw literally hundreds of people. We spoke about the Movement, we argued against the ultra-left positions that they were taking.

Then a problem arose. Before I came home the prison authorities put me on my own in the condemned cell area of Pretoria Prison – to rehabilitate me. At that time Breytenbach was being kept there. We were exchanging notes which were being carried backwards and forwards by a warder. Then Breytenbach was charged again with all sorts of things that this warder had led him into; and it became clear that I was also going to be re-arrested and charged with him.

Because it was illegal for us to see each other at any time*, Jenny and I had applied to the Minister for permission to get married. But we'd had no reply. So one afternoon Theo Kotze married us quietly in somebody's flat and that evening a comrade drove us to the Botswana border and we walked across.

We stayed there six years, teaching in Malepolole until 1981. Then we got jobs as the co-field directors of one of the IVS programmes and we moved to Gaberone. The bulk of their funding came from the British government. In May 1983 the General Secretary of the organisation flew out from England to tell us that the Foreign Office felt that the lives of British volunteers were being put at risk by having us in the programme; and that we were to be terminated immediately.

We were called in to see the British High Commissioner and he said, 'The Foreign Office have what they regard as excellent intelligence information that you are to be shot by the South Africans in Botswana. And I have been told by the Foreign Office to advise you to leave immediately.' We were very sceptical.

We discussed our position with the ANC Chief Representative, and within two or three days the office got a telex from Lusaka headquarters saying that we should move from Botswana immediately. When the dirt about the Death Squads first came out, Dirk Coetzee said that he had been given instructions to shoot me in Botswana, and was actually in the car in Zeerust when the orders were countermanded.

So we left very precipitately. I mean we packed everything into the Land Rover, dogs and two children, both born in Botswana.

We spent six months in Lusaka, working in the ANC, and then it was suggested that we should go to teach at the university in Southern Angola – the ANC had had requests for English teachers. So in December 1983, we flew to Luanda and went down south to the University of Labongo.

---

* Banning orders prohibit communication between banned persons.

It was very much a military zone, very close to the frontline. The South Africans had bombed the airport a couple of times; there was constant troop movement through the streets. The South Africans were starting a major assault on Angola. There was a time when we could actually hear the artillery. In 1975 the South Africans had captured Labongo and during that time they had built up some form of underground apparatus. It was quite scary. One would hear the shooting every night, the helicopters would be going over day and night; the bandits were clearly in and around the town.

As always with the ANC, nobody had briefed us on the situation in Labongo – it was actually craziness sending two young kids into that situation. We hadn't had one minute of learning Portuguese. There was nothing to eat – I mean literally nothing. We arrived just after New Year 1984. We didn't get ration cards until ... oh, sometime in May. The university arranged that we had one meal a day in a restaurant. Colleagues and friends were very good to us. But even when we got ration cards, one could basically get buggerall on them. The whole time we were in Angola we got a meat ration once – for the whole family it was half a kilo of meat. And there was nothing in the shops. Money was like Monopoly money. It just wasn't a place to send kids.

We had a flat; the lift didn't work because when the Portuguese left Angola they had taken some of the parts away. Water ran ... well sometimes for an hour or so a day; but basically never.

And then in June, when I was down in Luanda working with Chief on the development projects, Jenny and Katryn were killed by a bomb.

I was staying with Jane Bergerol; we'd had supper. Jane was upstairs working, she was studying medicine. I was sitting downstairs listening to music and reading. There's a knock on the door and there's the ANC Chief Representative with two comrades. He comes in and says, 'I'm afraid I've got very bad news. We've just heard from Labongo that Jenny and Katryn are late.' I was completely numb. I asked for details. He said, 'We have no details, all that we know is that there was an explosion.' And I still didn't understand. I kept on saying to him, 'I understand that Jenny's been killed. But Katryn? How badly is she hurt?' And the Chief said to me over and over again, 'Our intelligence is that both the comrades are late.'

Jane knew everybody in Angola, she'd been in Angola since the day before independence. It was decided I would fly to Labongo the next day. Now flying in Angola was not easy. You had to have passes to move from one area to another; getting on to the internal aircraft is an absolute shambles; they sell as many tickets as people want, and you take chances about getting on. So Jane took the Chief to see a very senior airforce officer and we were given some passes to get on to the flight.

When we arrived in Labongo airport the Angolan head of security was waiting on the tarmac. As we came up to the arrivals hall, through the window, I could see one of the ANC comrades with Fritzy in his arms.

I rushed over and took him, and he was absolutely rigid. He just put his arms around me and he only said two things to me. In fact, I thought the child was never going to speak again. When he put his arms around me, he said: I thought I'd never see you as well. And then the comrades from the students' union came to fetch us and we went into town in the Land Rover, and he sat on my lap with his arms around my head and he whispered in my ear, 'Marius, you know the enemy didn't kill Jenny, they just broke her apart.'

They took us straight down to the flat. Our street was cordoned off, there was no traffic. The whole street was covered in glass. It was a four-storey block of flats and the explosion had blown virtually every pane.

We went upstairs to the flat and it was terrible, Hilda. It was terrible. On the floor of the flat, there was a heap of blood mixed with flesh. And that had clearly been Katryn. And then across the one wall, the whole wall was just absolutely covered in blood. And that is where the explosion had thrown Jenny. I mean it was too ghastly. [Pause]

There was a memorial service for Jenny and Katryn at the university. The university was closed for the whole day, everybody was absolutely shattered. Just before the service a young airforce officer came up. The Angolan government had put a military aircraft at our disposal. So immediately after the memorial service, we went with the two coffins out to the airport and Fritzy and myself and comrades from Labongo were flown up to Luanda.

As soon as we got back, Jane said, 'OK, you've got a lot of phone calls to make.' Making phone calls then in Luanda at that time – I mean, Luanda just wasn't functioning. The Portuguese had buggered off taking most parts and plans with them, nobody knew where any . . . you couldn't fix the telephone system because the Portuguese had taken the plans of the cables. So making international phone calls – you'd sometimes take two days not to get through.

Jane had a friend, Celestine, who was an international operator in the telephone exchange. It was late in the evening, half past ten, she drove round to Celestine, came back, said, 'OK, she's going back to work now, she will put you through to wherever you want.'

And you know, it was this sort of spontaneous warmth. Eventually Jenny's parents and her brother came into the country on South African passports, no visas, straight into the VIP lounge. The government and the ANC couldn't have done more for us. And this is something I've got to make myself remember, because there are times when I'm so irritated with various things that the Movement does. But I will be grateful forever for the support and comradeship which I received during that period.

Fritzy was in pieces. Putting things together from remarks he's made subsequently, he was clearly in the room when the explosion took place, so he saw everything. It is miraculous that he wasn't hurt at all. His ears were a bit . . . he was deaf for a couple of days. And as I said, the first day he didn't speak at all, and the next day hardly said anything. I was frantic about him. All he wanted to do, he'd just sit next to me. And then his granny and his grandfather came and gradually he started relaxing, started playing a little bit with the other kids.

Jane had a little girl and there were three lovely Angolan children who stayed just three or four houses down, and they were in and out of the house all the time; and he started playing and he started being a little bit more himself. And then, after three or four days, Fritzy said, 'I'm going to play with the other kids.' I said, 'Are you OK? Shall I walk down with you?' And he said, 'No I'm going to walk down on my own.' I thought, Jesus, that's grand! That's grand! This was the first time that he'd actually been prepared to leave me at all.

He'd just gone when I heard him screaming. I rushed out; he was in front of the other house, and there was a monkey that had come in from the bush, sitting on the lintel above the door, leaning down and grabbing at him. He was absolutely terrified. His granny and I had to spend three, four, five hours before we had calmed him down. It was just absolute hysteria.

Then we came to England. We were with a friend and driving down to Jenny's sister in Devon. And OK, this is the worst day of my life. This is actually worse than the day arriving in Labongo. We get into the car; Colin is driving, in a very lovely London street with leafy trees all along the side of it. And as we get into the car, Fritzy looks around and he says to me, 'Marius, the trees are full of monkeys, look at the monkeys, look at the monkeys!'

Now we rode to Devon, what – four and a half, five hours and there were monkeys all the way. 'Look at the monkeys, the monkeys are in the road! Stop, Colin! Stop! Chase the monkeys! Marius, why are the monkeys here?' And it went on for a solid five hours with these fucking monkeys, hey? The monkeys had clearly come to represent all the horror and all the bloody ghastliness.

We got down to Jenny's sister and the cousins were there and there was family routine and he calmed down a bit.

We drove over to Ireland, in the car, got the ferry to Rosslare and then a long drive to West Cork. Fritzy had been sleeping in the back of the car, and very late at night we got to the village where the landlord was waiting up for us. This farmhouse in Ireland, old trees all around it; and as we get out of the car Fritzy looks around and says, 'The monkeys are here! Monkeys are here!' It took an hour or so, then he calmed down and went to sleep. He'd be OK at a place that he actually knew, but every time we'd go somewhere, the monkeys would be there.

We went to Dublin to spend a little time with Louise and Kader Asmal. So we drive up from West Cork to Dublin, and as we get to the house of Kader and Louise, he looks up and he says, 'The monkeys have followed us! The monkeys are here!' And every time we went to a house he didn't know, the monkeys were there.

Gradually this wore off. Then just after he was three, we went down to Mazimbu. We arrived in Tanzania, we haven't been cleared, we have to spend something like two and a half, three hours in the airport before they get us cleared and he's absolutely dropping. We get given lunch and while the others are finishing I took him to the Kombi – we were driving from Dar es Salaam to Mazimbu – to see if he would go to sleep. He's sort of dozing and then he looks out and he says: 'It's monkeys! There're monkeys, there're monkeys, they're coming through the window! They're on the bonnet! They're on the Kombi! Marius, look at the monkeys! Marius, close the window, they're coming in!' Oh, Jesus! And then when we get to Mazimbu, the monkeys are there in Mazimbu too.

And then the monkeys gradually go away.

In June of that year, I go back to Luanda for the unveiling of the tombstone on Jenny and Katryn's graves. But I didn't want to take Fritzy to Luanda, so I left him with comrades in Lusaka for the week. We'd arranged that when we came back from Luanda, we would all go down and spend four or five days together at the Victoria Falls. So we come back, we fly down to Livingstone, we're staying at the hotel and there's a swimming-pool with a big patio around it, beautiful trees. And Fritzy and I would go down and have breakfast next to the pool; and then I'd swim with him. It was very nice.

And we're sitting there one morning and I'd just buttered toast for him, and a real monkey comes out of a tree and grabs his toast. And I think, agh Jesus! It's all going to start again! And he says to me, 'That monkey took my toast.' I said, 'That's right, Fritzy but we'll get you more toast, don't worry.' He says, 'You know how I feel?' I said, 'How do you feel, Fritzy?' He said, 'I'm really glad you went to Luanda because I feel as though you came back and you gave me an AK and I've beaten those monkeys. And the monkeys have gone. They'll never come back.'

A child psychologist friend says that, to her, the most significant thing about the monkeys is that it began with reality and it finished with reality. And if it hadn't fortunately finished in reality, he would possibly have it forever. But I mean, that little boy's courage – and he actually knew he'd beaten it, ja? And he was only . . . at that time he was four.

He virtually never talks about Jenny and Katryn any more. I don't think he really remembers them. I mean it happened . . . he was two years and three months. But there must be things going on inside him. He's not all that well, he's got epilepsy and it's very worrying . . . he just goes away, he just goes away. It lasts quite a long time and it's very worrying.

We spent almost three and a half years in Mazimbu. But I didn't want Fritzy to go to school there. I really wanted him to have a more adequate education than I think the people were getting in Mazimbu. So then we came back to Ireland about four years ago and we've been in Dublin since then.

I've never really thought about how my life would have been if I'd stayed in South Africa. I think at the time it was right to leave. We made decisions which we thought were right, and one thing leads to another. Now I have a certain ambivalence about going home. I really feel that in the last two or three years, for the first time in my life, literally, I've got a stability and a security that I've never had. I'm actually enjoying the security that we have at the moment. I would like to go home for two or three months with a return ticket and make up my mind if that's what we want to do.

I was at the South African Embassy on Wednesday. They gave me the forms to fill in, and I started to apply for a passport, and to get Fritzy's birth registered late so that he has citizenship. I just looked at the bloody forms and they made me angry. It's my country! I was born there! Why should I have to fill in on a passport application form what my race is? And I thought to myself, Jesus, you've been away from all this nonsense for so long and it isn't going to disappear overnight. I'm going to go home and friends of mine are going to be living in Soweto and you'll be living in Yeoville or somewhere like that and will I ever see them? And that sort of thing isn't going to change overnight.

I've had lots of things from the ANC even if I'm sometimes critical of it. The ANC has given me a great deal; it's given me a sense of dignity which to a white South African is an enormous generosity. Warmth and friendship – things I value most. But I think at home perhaps it will be the same bloody nonsense – that we see each other at funerals.

Massacre at Maseru

Maseru is the capital of Lesotho, a small mountainous state completely surrounded by South Africa territory. It is economically dependent on South Africa, but was committed to granting asylum to South Africa refugees.

At one o'clock on the morning of 10 December 1982 five helicopters of the South African Defence Force flew across the border – the Caledon River – and dropped a force of about 100 soldiers, whites with blackened faces, into the city.

The commandos' task was to seek out and destroy ANC members living as refugees in Lesotho. Forty-two people were killed that night; thirty were South African refugees, and twelve were Basotho citizens, all of them shot in their houses.

The commandos did not discriminate. They slaughtered men, women and children. Phyllis Naidoo, Bunie Matlanyane Sexwale and Nelly Marwanqana (Ma-Mia) were among those who survived.

PHYLLIS NAIDOO
Harare 1990

'If politics doesn't encompass people – if it's just a matter of ideas – then I don't want it.'

> Her politics has always been irradiated by her warm humanity and her care for individuals, poignantly illustrated in the concern she felt for the mother of the man who murdered her son.

My grandfather came to South Africa at the turn of the century. My father was born soon after they got here. I think the predominating thing in their lives was they wanted an education for their children. They thought that would get them out of the poverty. So that when I got to Standard 6 and should have stopped there – that was the norm – dad said, 'Nothing doing! You have to go on.' And I found that there were three girls in Standard 7, two in 8, one in 9. And I was the only one in 10.

We were a family of ten children, and in 1938 my father was earning £12. And I keep thinking of how they managed feeding... [Laughs] and we had an aunt with five children, grandparents, and an unmarried uncle – all on £12! I know the rent was £4!

When I was sixteen in 1946 I went to this meeting where I saw Dr Dadoo speaking on the back of a truck, and I came back and I said to dad, 'I'm going to go to jail because I think this is the only way to do it.' And my dad said, 'Do you think I've educated you so that you'd go and spend time in jail?' [Laughs]

> Phyllis didn't go to jail – not then. She went to work at FOSA, a TB settlement. She was appalled by the social conditions. After they had been cured patients came back reinfected. She did a variety of jobs, went to university part-time, and sharpened her political ideas in debate with students who followed the Unity Movement. In December 1956, 156 leading people of all races from the Congress movement were arrested and charged with treason.

On the day of the arrests, I said to these Unity Movement fellows at university, 'There are lots of kids without parents – like the Shanleys picked up and their three children left. Shouldn't we offer our homes to these?' And they said, 'If you want to do welfare work, you're welcome.' And I said, 'But if politics doesn't encompass people – if it's just a matter of ideas – then I don't want it.'

I found out that the children were being cared for, but that money was needed. So that Christmas period was taken up with a whole lot of money-raising events. Always, I wasn't on the stage – no speaking. It was just doing things.

I was a member of the Natal Indian Congress, and the Human Rights Group. We took care of all the banished people in Natal. And then we took up issues like pensions, welfare grants for mothers who were stranded, divorced or whatever. A lot of that. And in fact my base was more on that sort of level – dealing with people. Old ladies would phone – pension hasn't come. We look into those things. Quite a lot of that we did. I think once or twice I spoke at meetings; but mostly it was welfare of comrades. I mean – I've taken fifty-seven meals to the jail for detainees – that sort of thing. Rushing around.

There was a magistrate who was checking on detainees. We used to go to him and say, 'Anybody dead this week?' And he said, 'Oh shut up!' And I says, 'No. Babla's dead, don't tell me no!' So he says, 'No no, Phyllis. It's all right.'

But you know, that relationship we set up helped save Ibrahim's life. Because that magistrate phoned me one Sunday morning, and told me go to Point Prison, because Ibrahim Ismail has been detained. For twenty-three days he hadn't had a wash, he hadn't had a change of clothes. He was in a cell as big as a toilet, and whenever they opened that cell, it was offensive.

I came running home, and I phoned a fellow and I said, 'Get some clothes! You're a Muslim! This fellow's a Muslim! I want some clothes, man!' And got it. I got food, got a taxi. I had fare to get there, but no fare to come back; I was broke. And I said to this taxi man, 'Look. My child is in prison; there's his food; there's his clothes. I just don't have busfare to go and see him.' He took me. I was terrified. He said, 'Get in!' And I thought I was going to be raped – I'd never ridden in a taxi before. And I went in to see Ibrahim. And he said, 'Hey Mom: you made it!' And that name 'Mom' has stuck.

So that sort of work was my forte. Nothing catching the limelight. Defence and Aid in the Sixties with Alan Paton and all these guys – terrible working with liberals I found. You talked about liberals, you intellectualised them, and then you worked with them – it was a very sharp experience for me!

For instance when all the sabotage trials came up. There was this woman Professor Ellen Hellman. So she said, 'No! This committee can't deal with sabotage cases.' You know that argument that went on – we don't deal with anyone who engaged in violence? And Alan Paton, George Singh, a whole lot of the people said OK. And then I said – and I was the baby of the lot, politically and otherwise – 'Hey!' I said. 'You know Vorster is better than the whole bunch of you because he gives comrades a chance in court to be heard! He doesn't condemn them before he charges them. But you!' You know, they were so ashamed.

So that sort of thing – but always nothing public.

Then in 1966 I was teaching, and they banned me from schools. Oh, it was very stark right at the beginning, very difficult. I was banned on

1 April; my daughter was born at the end of May; and my husband MD was picked up about two days later. Not that MD earned, because as an advocate he was very poor with all these banning orders and all that.

So we did a whole lot of things, like selling newspapers. My kids used to go and sell chips at the football matches and earn a rand, sell hankies in the arcades on Saturday mornings. And a rand was a helluva lot of money. And of course the international community sent us – nothing big, but it was very worthwhile, sometimes gave us some eggs, some milk and bread.

And I studied at the same time. By that time I had four children, ja. This was my second marriage. I first married in 1949 and that marriage came to an end in 1950, and there was a child there who was mainly taken care of by my mother, so he never called me mum, he called my mother mum. So quite often when I say three children, I have to think again, and remember no, it's four. The three kids were with me.

I had to leave – well it was underground work. We were taking people out of the country, organising for people to come in; and people who came out of Robben Island establishing things. Lots of details – but I don't want to tell you that story.

And then our unit got picked up – and I didn't know. I was going to work that morning, I get a call, 'Don't go!' And phoned the office, and Rita who answered the phone said, 'Oh, we're all waiting for Mrs Naidoo to come in. The office is packed – even the Special Branch are here waiting for Mrs Naidoo.' She was talking to me! Well, we had to move! I couldn't get back home. And I had to make arrangements, because the Law Society might get into my office and find something wrong; and I didn't want them to do that. I was a practising lawyer by then.

So I went into hospital. You see, this constant travelling got me bleeding – and I had been told you'd better go and get that womb removed. So I phoned the doctor and said, 'Admit me and make arrangements to remove my womb!' He said, 'No, the theatre's being repaired and we can't do that.' I said, 'Well just admit me.' And he did. The Special Branch grilled him afterwards.

But that gave me about two days to fix up my office and all the papers. Then I stayed in an old shack in Claremont for two days. There were holes in it, and I had to make sure that I didn't move so people wouldn't see me. And they gave me a potty to do my thing in; and someone brought me cocoa. And these were so poor people – oh, it was beautiful, the sort of beauty that makes you want to cry!

By this time, Phyllis and MD were divorced. He had custody of the two boys; she had custody of her daughter. Some one came to pick her up. They drove to Lesotho. Phyllis was left on the side of a mountain, somewhere in the countryside. She was making for the capital, Maseru. She had to make her own way down the mountain and cross a river.

The river wasn't very big. The water was up to my hips and I could walk through, but my clothes were all wet and I lost my shoes. Ja. I was freezing with cold. And when I got to the road – it was about six o'clock – nobody would pick up this miserable wretch with all these wet clothes. Then I went to the location there and asked them for directions to Maseru; and the woman said: Sit down. And she made me tea in an old jam tin – this is all they had. My teeth were chattering. She sent her daughter to fetch a pair of stockings. They were full of holes.

The poverty over there was stark. There was no bread, no pap, nothing. The soil it was just hard rock – and all the huts were perched there! I don't know how people lived there. But they took me to the road to Maseru. I waited for an Indian shop to open. I asked to use the phone, but the shopkeeper was unfriendly. He says, 'Get away from here! We don't take care of people who cross the river.' But then he let me phone a lawyer in Maseru, who said he would come and fetch me.

He took three hours, and I had to wait in the cold. He wouldn't let me stay in the shop. He wouldn't give me a packet of cigarettes, so I went and grabbed it and I said, 'When Kulaki comes he can pay you.' And I sat outside shivering – even when the sun came out. I'd never been so cold. Kulaki came at eleven, picked me up and took me to Maseru. My feet were all eaten up with frost – I couldn't walk for weeks.

Lesotho was wonderful, because I was able to receive the children – I MEAN children; ten, eleven . . . coming from home. Oh, they came in droves in those days. Kids were going away, leaving – and there were lots of kids coming through. I saw to the kids that were going to school and staying. So you had to be mother. And none of the kids had anything until they got to school; then United Nations used to give each one R30. They would walk to the town and see a lovely pair of sandshoes or something for R27 and buy it; and sort of starve for the rest of the month! Being a mother, I knew that kids are liable to do this.

So I had a pot of beans boiling with some meat or bones – whatever I could muster. And around four loaves of bread I used to buy daily, and the kids will come and eat. Some of them wanted to have a bath, because I had a lovely home, and they lived in a camp with about twenty or thirty from time to time.

That's when I met an Anglican priest, Father John Osmers. He was wonderful to our children. He was out at Masiti, and the first time I met John he had taken some refugees home, and his telephone bill went up to R200 – and he only received R45 as a stipend. And I said to him, 'John, you know, lock the phone or do something. These children are so wanting to get in touch with their families, and you leave the phone there – of course they're going to use it. They want to talk to mum; they want to talk to sister, grandmother, whatever.' And I said, 'Don't apply your middle-class ten commandments here – thou shalt not steal, thou shalt not . . . ' All his food was finished in a weekend – the food for a month! 'You can't apply those things to us. Thou shalt not steal means nothing. We've had to steal to live. So you have to be gentle, understand what our kids are all about.'

I mean, he'd feed them for lunch, lots of rice and lots of bean stew. He was very poor, John. And about the only thing that made him better than us was that his church gave him a car. And so he had use of that car for so many things. John used to go and visit them late at night, and they used to be cold in winter, and he'd come and say to me, 'You've got two heaters here; give me one for the kids.' Or, 'Have you got some blankets?'

Kids would be crying, 'I want to go home, mum.' And then there were other things. Like John happened to go there one day to the camp, and the kids were trying to burn somebody. Had poured paraffin on him and they were going to burn him, or threatening to burn him. And John picked him up and brought him home. So I said, 'What happened?' He said that he wanted to see his parents, who had come to Ficksburg. So he crossed the river and went to Ficksburg. And somebody saw him there and reported it – and these guys were going crazy. I had to go back to the camp, and I said, 'Just tell me. Who isn't missing home now? Just tell me! Who doesn't want to go home now? If there was some way you could go home, will you all go? Yes!' And I said, 'You were going to kill this child because he went to see his parents, hey?' That sort of hardness, you know – trying to do the right thing, as they said. But it was very difficult. Kids were heartsore without parents.

There was a child who had lost his mother on 16 June 1976 – Senti. How pained he was. He used to phone his dad; and his dad used to drop the phone when he'd hear him: 'I don't want to hear you! You know you've done something terrible! You've left the country!' All that sort of thing you had to smooth over for children. And John was absolutely wonderful.

John was getting copies of the ANC magazine *Sechaba*, and the Boers got to know because it came via South Africa. He got *Sechaba* one day in 1979 and he was rushing to my house; it was nicely parcelled up. And we didn't think! We should have, because by then Max Sisulu had had a bomb in Lusaka, and Dube had died from a bomb. But we didn't think about it.

I was trying to open it. And I couldn't. I was getting late for work so I said, 'You all do it,' and I turned away. And John cut it and blew the whole thing up, ja! It was awful! We were six in the house. I had taken some refugees home to have lunch. And we were bombed there. John lost his hand, Andile some fingers . . . there were white fingers and black fingers lying there . . . oooh. I think the bomb was intended to injure, because my bum is still full of lots of shrapnel, ja; and nails and things like that.

John was taken by the church for treatment. And eventually the ANC took me out, and I was sent to Hungary where I met my boy, who was studying agriculture. And when I returned, it was the next year.

And then in 1982 one of the most traumatic things in my life happened. That was the raid in Lesotho on 9 December. You know, one of the things that happened with the bomb was that my eardrum was gone; and so hearing on one side becomes impossible. If you make a noise here, I can't hear a thing.

So throughout this night – it was a beautiful moonlit night – there was lots of noise and bombs and things like that. And I was alone. I thought it was the Lesotho Liberation Army (LLA), because they used to come and fire bombs and things. But it was more that night, and I couldn't sleep; so I took the pillow and put it on my ear. And then, four o'clock, it was quiet; and I got up and looked around.

And then there was a loud knock. I was still scared from the night before; and I went down. I looked through the door – it was my comrades. They said, 'Mum! Thank God you're safe!' And I opened the door and I said, 'What's happened?' They said, 'There was a massacre!' I said, 'Hold on!'

I put on my pants over my pyjamas and I went with them. Oh, I saw Gene! I saw Zola Nqini, and he was just riddled with bullets – his face, his body, his pyjamas was holed. And Zola was the gentlest of our comrades, so gentle, he wouldn't talk. He was our Chief Rep at the time, Zola Nqini. And in the room were two other comrades dead; and somebody else lying on the floor, with the tape recorder still moving. And nobody else. From that house a comrade escaped, I found out later.

On that night they killed forty-two, thirty of whom were comrades. Twelve were Basotho. And the terrible thing for me was Gene. Gene was a comrade – ooh! The ANC must be so proud that they can produce giants, articulate! You know – ideas, arguments, he'd take you on. Work his butt off! You know – joining ideas and work together; Gene combined the two. Gene Gugushe.

Gene and I, we worked in what was the propaganda unit. At a meeting that evening Gene read out his paper for Heroes Day. And it was a beautiful paper! And I was cooking and listening, and I said, 'Ten out of ten, Gene! Ten out of ten!' And he said, 'Oh mum, you must be tired because you never say ten out of ten. You must be tired!' 'No,' I said, 'read it again.' And he read it again. And he said, 'No full stops, no commas, no punctuation. Are you sure?' And I said, 'Yes, it's excellent!' And he folded it and put it into his blue shirt.

That was the night before. And the next morning he was dead. He was the fellow that shot at them, and eventually dropped three stories and broke his leg. And he was moaning from the pain of his leg when this black soldier came back, and says: '*Daar's hy, baas! Daar's hy!*' And they peppered him. Got him – oooh . . .

They said we must leave. But I didn't – I wouldn't go. Because we are older and I think we are necessary for the children. And the youth need whatever strength we can give them. We all needed to be held at that time, supporting each other. I stayed on for another year. But the Boers were threatening Lesotho. And eventually they said to the government, 'If Mrs Naidoo's here at seven o'clock on Saturday morning – which was 9 September – we will kill her.' And they came to me and said, 'We can't protect you. Please go.' And in twenty-four hours I had to leave.

She went to Maputo, then to Lusaka, and finally to London to see her daughter who was studying there. Then she received permission to stay in Zimbabwe, and made her home in Harare.

I went to Hungary after I was bombed and having treatment. My son Saren was there on a course, studying agriculture. I said to him, 'Why did you choose agriculture?' We couldn't grow a plant in our flat, they just died on us; and people made us gifts of plants and I said, 'Don't! These things just die on us.' And he says, 'Well, I wanted to do brain surgery, mum. And then I found it was fifteen years, the course. And that was too long. So I looked around. What does South Africa need most? And I decided it was food, and that we had to create that food.' He explained it to me as though I was a child – I was in bed and I was looking up and watching this seventeen-year-old at the time, telling me this story. And then he said, 'So I did agriculture.'

My son completed his agricultural course in Hungary in 1985. He came to me for a month, one precious month, and then went to Lusaka. He was managing the ANC farm at Chongela, and I saw him once or twice.

In April this year we'd talked on his birthday. A week later the Chief Rep came in to tell me that he had been killed. It was only with searching and investigating that they found out the fellow that shot him was an agent, who had come to us in 1978. They tell me that my son was very fond of this fellow Tex. But Sha told me that Tex used to come in with his gun while he watched TV every night – he said he was nervous – and that was the gun that he used on my son. The comrade who was in charge of all the ANC vehicles was also shot and killed.

Mmmm . . . they tell me my son did a marvellous job of work. I like to think that he gave his best to the ANC. He was fascinated with his studies. And the way he worked at Chongela . . . get up at four o'clock in the morning – Oh you know, early hours – he wasn't working by the clock. He gave his heart and soul.

After this Tex had murdered Saren, TG came and he said, 'Agh Phyllis, your son, your son! Ah, what a boy, what a boy!' You know, I was so proud of him, so much so. I said to TG, 'Have you informed Tex's mother? She doesn't know what's happened to her son – she thinks her son's with the ANC. Have you . . . ?' And TG said to me, 'I want to put my hands around Tex's neck! Don't ask me to do silly things, Phyllis. I can't. I really can't. You go and tell his mum if you want to.'

I think that sort of thing can happen to anybody's child. And I think we have a duty to inform parents who think their children are with us, in our ranks. If we're a country, if we're the government, we have to take on these things. But we didn't.

I was in a terrible argument in Lesotho where a comrade had murdered somebody – seemed like the gun went off. Whether it was deliberate or not, I'm not sure of the facts. But one comrade shot another, and was arrested and put in jail. And nobody would deal with him. And I said, 'This is not right.' But they said, 'We've been instructed by Lusaka not to touch him.' Right! Now I don't believe in that sort of thing; and I had to go and see some Basotho lawyers and say to them, 'Please attend to him!' I think we have to fashion some method of justice, or our whole legal system is nothing.

I was torn away from my children. Before I left, when I went to that hospital in Durban, they were on my hospital bed and I was saying, 'Polish your shoes for school on Monday.' And I knew that I wouldn't be here on that Monday – I'd be gone. That was very hard, being parted from my children.

I was fifty plus when I came into exile. But so many times in Lesotho I've stood on this side of the river and looked at that sandy valley which is Caledon River, and wanted to cross. And remembered so many times Bram saying, 'Much rather a South African jail than exile in England!'

We've never felt safe anywhere. Quite often when I forget, I look out of the window; and I think, 'There's a gun!' Quite often when I'm watching, I have to stand here just in case someone's pointing a gun at me. You have that at the back of your mind. When your children are here, you don't want to show them that you are afraid. So you go on living as normally as you can.

It was very painful. But the pain was tempered, in the sense that there were so many around you also pained. Who we laughed with, we . . . You know, a young boy from Natal came in. And when he knew that I was from Natal, he said, 'Let's ride for a bunnichow.' He'd say all the things that brought us together: let's ride Possie, *ek se* – you know, just those things. Then we'd put our arms around each other and the kids would cry. And after a while I said, 'I can't be seen to be crying if I'm going to be of some strength to these people.' And I did cry.

She is back in South Africa, working for the Natal Lawyers for Human Rights.

NELLY MARWANQANA (MA-MIA)
Mazimbu 1989

'It's better if me, I die altogether with my children. Ah, why those Boers left me alone? It's better to kill me.'

> She is a matron of Unit 6 in Mazimbu. Despite all that has happened to her, she is pleasant, relaxed, a substantial, motherly woman. English is not her first language, but we speak without an interpreter.

I stay in Port Elizabeth before my husband, he's put in jail. My husband, he is going to Robben Island, political prisoner, six and a half years. ANC. My brother, my big brother, he's together with my husband in Robben Island; another one is still in Port Elizabeth.

When he's come back, they say he does not want my husband must stay in Port Elizabeth any more. He chase my husband to Queenstown, to Bantu place . . . Bantustan, Linge Township. And my husband stay there, together with me and my children. It's four, my children is four, and I got . . . I'm granny already! Two, ja, with my daughter. And my husband work there, is work hard there; he's dig trench only his pay R16 in a month. You see, this money is not enough, he's go to work in furniture shop, he's work there.

And then he's taking my husband again to jail. In 1979, then he catch my husband again, eight month. He's bring back again when he's finished eight month. That time I'll have baby, my small baby Pumalane, he was small that time. And he's bring back my husband. Then he's take again; one year – third time now. One year in prison now, only he's not charged, my husband. He's keep there . . . till one year. Just detained, ja.

When my husband is come back in jail, he say, 'Now, it's enough now. I'm tired to stay away in my house; I'm never staying together with my children. I'll think now I must leave South Africa 'cos I'm suffered.' That's why my husband leave South Africa. He's come exile. He's leave South Africa in 1982, December.

I tell like that 'cos I know he long time is want to kill my husband, since in South Africa. I know my husband a long time he's worked for ANC, and long time is want my husband. I think when he's hear this thing, the Boers, he's glad when he hear my husband is in Lesotho there. No one know me, I'm there in Lesotho. All people at home think me I go to Port Elizabeth 'cos all time, December holiday time, I like to take my children and go there. This parents of my husband is there.

I leave together with my husband and my children. Ja. I leave with passport, 'cos I'm say I go to holiday, ja, in Lesotho. Only me, I know my husband is not going to holiday, he's goin' leave South Africa. Well, I couldn't say to they when I cross border, I couldn't say: No, I'm people of ANC, I not like to stay in South Africa. I say: No, I go to holiday only. I leave South Africa in 5 December 1982.

Only when I came to Lesotho, I stay only four days – and it is attack on Lesotho. For four days only. Four days only, then this attack is come. Ja. In the night, one o'clock. We were in house with other people, it's not a lot; it's only . . . my family, it's family of eight people, together with my children, my husband. And in this house, in this house of Mavimbela two more people only. All together, ten people. Is killed five and leave five. Leave me and my big daughter and my three children, Maunde, Pumulane and Pumese. And baby Yolanda. And me.

Is killed my husband; is killed my daughter; is killed my son; is killed another man Mavimbela and girlfriend.

I hear . . . I hear . . . I hear somebody outside, only I'm not looking window 'cos my husband said, 'If you hear something, you mustn't open window, you know.' Only I wake my husband. I'm say, 'Something outside!' 'cos I feel something that do-do-do [imitating sound], like a big motor car. I say to my husband, 'You must wake up' – 'cos I hear something outside. And this girl – this one is killed – is call, 'Dadada! Is something there outside!' I think today must die, you know. And is break this . . . is break this front door already when she call.

Is white, I see white men. This one is shoot my husband, white man. They just came in with guns and say, 'Where is Mavimbela? where is Mavimbela?' When he's pushed this door – my husband pushed this door – and me I wake up already. Only me I say to my husband, 'No, you have no life, you have nothing. Only you must ready to die 'cos this people is carry big gun, big lot thing you know.' I see this white one he's put black thing on his face [Gestures with hands drawn down her face] and put this hat . . . balaclavas you know, ja. And put on this brown blanket, you know; and put big pin there, ja. But I see really, I see this hair there is white man, is not black people. Only I see one black people, he stand there.

Now we are in passage. Only before he shoot my husband, he do like this already. [Aims] He say to me, 'OK you. Now you must *voetsak*, take this kids and go out in this room.' I think he's shy to kill my husband in front of me. Only already he's take this gun and ah, before he shoot my husband he say me, 'You go out, take this children and voetsak.' Me, I take my children, and this big one is there in my room already. When he's want to go in under this bed, me I'm saying, 'No my child, you mustn't go to there. If this one want kill you, he must stand there and kill you.'

I go to bathroom. Only when we are there in bathroom, he shoot my husband and he shoot this one. Go to another room now, only this she my girl, Thandiswa, mother of Yolanda. That time Yolanda is a small baby, six month old, yes. They shoot her mother. Only her mother say to me, 'Mama, please look after my child.'

This man, he's run, he's run, he's go through to this room of Mavimbela. Me only I'm going to take this small one when he's finished to shoot. This one is crying, you know, the little one. He's feel something is happen. He's small, but he's feel something is happen. I go to take this one. Oh, when I take this one he is full of piece of glasses in the head, ja. He's try to crawl and run, you know. He's small, only I take this one, I clean.

I go to this room, I see he's kill my husband. I go to this room of Mavimbela, I see he's killed Mavimbela. And I not see this girl, my girl, this mother of this young one. I start to go dining room, I say, 'Ah, where is this . . . where is my boy? You are still . . . you are asleep? People is dying! You sleep?' – me, I'm say. Well . . . then I enter the room. Ah, this one is finished already . . . Mmm. Only me, I'm not thinking he is dead, because that's why I'm say, 'Ah, you're still asleep; people is dying in here. You still asleep?' Well then me I see, hah! He's shoot there. He'd be eighteen at that time, eighteen years.

Then is just go out. Is go out, ja, leave this bodies. Only police and me. I say to this my big daughter: You know you must carry this one. Me I carry another one. I leave this big one Maunde go herself. Only me, I've not found where is my daughter, you know. I reported to another man, I say I not see this mother of this young one. I don't know if is run away, or I don't know where 'cos is not know Lesotho. 'Oh,' he say, 'OK. You mustn't worry, I look after where she is.'

Another two is came to this house, is call me. Is say, 'Ja, I found five people is dead there.' Me, I'm say, 'Ah, another one?' He say, 'Come, Mama.' I go, then I'm see Thandiswa, this mother of this one, over the wardrobe, is lie like this – I think is shoot there. Only I not see nothing on her face because is very pretty girl. I'm see blood ja, right down there, (indicating her heart) 'cos is put long nightie, Mmm.

When it's finish to bury this people, is fix my passport, whole thing, I come to Maputo. I'm not stay in Lesotho, I think I stay three weeks. I come to Tanzania, Mazimbu, since now. When I came Mazimbu, I stay there first in the Charlottes, I wait there 'cos me, I carried this baby of my daughter. I work there, I think I work two years there. Since then I work here in Mazimbu, matron of SOMAFCO. I look after girls. My children get education.

I take child, Yolanda, I bring her here, yes. Is big girl now. Is nearly finish eight, ja. Is big girl now; is in primary school. Is not a baby any more. [Laughs] Is start to tease me now, is say, 'Ja ja, you're not my mother; you're my granny.' Me I'm say, 'Hah, why you say like that, 'cos I you take when you are small?' She say, 'Ja, my brother tell me; he say I never suck in your titties!' [Laughs] She laughed at this, she say, 'You my granny.'

My name she is calling me Ma-mia. My name is Nelly, ja. Only Billy call me Ma-mia; and this young one like to call me Ma-Mia, ja. She is saying, 'You are matron of SOMAFCO. You're my granny, you're not my mother.' Me, I'm say, 'Ah, you not say I'm your mother. You never know who's your godmother or me I'm your mother.' I like to say that. [Laughs]

So they destroyed your family?

Yes. People is not understand really, 'cos they didn't see that. But I'm there. You know, they ask, 'Were you there? Really, that time?' Me, I'm say, 'Yeh, I see myself, it's me wake up my husband, say really he's come to kill you, you wake up.' Then I come back into room and say, 'Alfred, Alfred.' Only he's quiet, he's not sleep; I take blanket, I cover my husband. I go to another room, I see Mavimbela, he's kill already and break lot thing in room of Mavimbela, is break wardrobe. I see another girl is shoot there under this bed. I'm see her face, it's got big blood, you know. I not see mine, I not see Thandiswa is there, 'cos I look, only I see my husband and this two and my son, Mzukisi, you know, I'm not see Thandiswa. I'm not see my daughter. That why I leave this house and I leave this people is died here. Only when me I go, I hear is still shooting there.

Thirty . . . thirty people of ANC, twelve people of Lesotho. forty-two altogether. Oh is big funeral, big funeral and Babu Tambo is there. Mmm.

That time, I say, it's better if me I die all together with my children, you know, it's terrible. Ja, you can't think that time when this people is burying; me, I'm say ah, why these Boers left me alone, it's better to kill me and all this family of Marwanqana must be finish. This thing I think that time; but he's not do that. Then I'm say ah, I must look forward. Yes, yes, yes. And my children has grown nice. Is attend school, I have no problem. I have no problem of clothes, OK.

I'm there in house, only is not kill me. Ja, is better now, somebody look after children, ja. Only when . . . when something happen, he kill, he die, you think, ah, it's better if me I'm not there together with my child at all, you know. Better I also die. But I'm not saying now 'cos I look after my children. [Laughs]

Alfred Marwanqana was fifty when he was assassinated. His daughter Thandiswa, mother of Yolanda, was twenty-one. His son Mzukisi was eighteen. They had arrived four days before, and were staying at the house of Phakamile Mpongoshe, also known as Sydney Mavimbela. Mavimbela, also a former Robben Island prisoner, was also killed, together with a Basotho national, Florence Mateseliso, who was also in the house.

BUNIE MATLANYANE SEXWALE
The Hague 1990

'I have to live a life of having to justify why I did not die.'

> She has lived and studied in the Netherlands for some years now. She
> has researched the lives of women migrant workers who leave Lesotho
> to find work in South Africa, and is now teaching other women, in a
> development course on ways of organising women for change.

I was born in Lesotho. The history of the two countries divided families
and left some on one side and others on the other side of the border. I
have sisters and close relatives who have been born on the other side of
the border, and some of us have been born on the Lesotho side. So I feel
I am as much South African as I am Lesotho. I feel I have never left South
Africa. To avoid Bantu Education I did all my education in Lesotho
where I was born and where I feel I rightfully belong.

I have not been able to return to South Africa since 1978. And I didn't
feel that I was in exile even after that. You live in Lesotho – you have
contact with everybody; I feel that I am at home in Lesotho. I only felt I
was in exile when I had to move away from Lesotho after the Boer
Commandoes raided Lesotho at the end of 1982.

They came in the middle of the night. I can never put an exact time to
that. We had been having a women's section meeting in the house and
my then husband had another meeting with ANC comrades he was
working with.

All I remember is taking a shower and going to bed around twelve. I
remember having slept for a short time and I suddenly heard this big
sound WHAH! I thought that Mathabatha had forgotten his key and
was trying to break a window to climb through; that he had tried to
knock on the window and I had not heard. But then I realised he was also
starting up, and he immediately said, 'Cover!' So we both took cover.

It was actually the turning point of my life, of my family life, of my
political life, of my academic life. We had a very low bed. We just lay
there next to it and I will never forget the anxiety I felt there. We knew
what was happening. Already there were sounds of people talking
through the house, in Afrikaans, a bit of English and also Sesotho, but
mostly in Afrikaans. Giving orders like in the army. It's easier to relate it
thinking back. But as it was happening, I just remember this sense of,
'Oh dear, what about the children sleeping next door?' And we looked
at each other and we knew we were thinking about the same thing: what
shall we do about the children?

It's easy to relate these things as if you had time, but it was all
happening at once. And before I knew it, there was shooting in the
passage. Now the house we lived in was fairly big and it had this long

corridor leading from the living-room to the bedrooms, and it was this corridor that the noises were coming from. But at the same time there was the noise of shooting and other war noises from outside of the room next door to us, and that was the room where the children were sleeping. We just heard this terrible noise, commands and shooting, coming very close to where we were.

Well, it's you or . . . We had to defend ourselves. And it was during this that I think that they saw that there was need to retreat. So after some shooting and counter-shooting, they made an order and they retreated. They went out, and all I heard was just a pushing sound as if they are dragging someone or some people.

Then the attack concentrated on the outside of the house and at that time, the two children flew into the bedroom where we were. I just remember this sense of relief and just hugging them. It was Nomagqabi, a child who's now studying at Mazimbu, and my last daughter Kananelo. I just hugged them and I told them, 'Listen, just take cover.' And they laid there next to me, you know just laid, with nothing else to do. And up to now I wonder what went on in their minds.

But my second daughter Matsobane was not there; my sister-in-law who was sleeping in the other room was not there. I remember this sense that we both had, communicating just by looking at each other; and I think our conclusion was that they have been killed.

That commotion lasted for a long long time. It could have been an hour or two hours, but it was like a lifetime. They had been concentrating the attack on this bedroom where the two children had been sleeping. That was the main bedroom so that's where they thought we had been sleeping. Anyway, after a long time they gave an order to retreat. My first thought was to take the children I still have and deposit them somewhere outside and dash back and find out what is happening to my other daughter. And immediately I clasped them, Mathabatha just gave a sign for me to wait a little bit and we lay there for some time.

Then after a while they re-attacked, so I think he guessed that was a false retreat. They re-attacked, they gave another pause; re-attacked. They gave a third one, and after that we heard footsteps, people going, going, going. And at this time there were incredible noises around the house. I don't know what they had thrown, I don't know about military weapons – they must have thrown things there that started exploding. So we crawled out through this passage that was by that time just a scene of war, to the kitchen which was the only room which was not burning, and tried to look through the window. And the only thought I had was, 'Are these two alive?' I have to go and find out what's happening to my daughter, and I see this fire coming – the thing that drove us out of the house was the fire catching on to the rest of the house. We thought this may be also false pause; we have two choices: to be shot trying to run out, or to burn to death inside here.

I couldn't just think of running and leave my daughter burning in there. So he just said, 'Wait – I will try and do something.' And he went in. I'm all the time thinking of these two people, trapped in there, who can't move, can't do anything. So he went in; and after a while his sister joined us, and after what seemed like a year he emerged with my first daughter. No injury! I should say no physical injury, because I think in retrospect there has been a lot of psychological damage done which I don't know how to deal with. I talk very little about that time; but when I start talking about it I can take a whole year, talking just about that.

We left. We took everybody. We crawled. There was a policeman living in the neighbourhood, and Mathabatha went to see if he'd take us in; and he said, 'I am sorry, I love my life, I don't want to be involved.' There was a man living in a shack – you know these kind of pondokkies, like Crossroads; he started shouting to us, 'Come over, come over!' He lived in that shack with eight children and his wife, and he was the only person that night who could open his door to us. As we were coming in, he said, 'Listen, I have been watching it all. If they come back and attack us, I think I'm as much a victim as you, so I am prepared.'

So we stayed for a while there. My house was blowing up, I don't know what they had thrown but it kept on just BAM! BAM! continuously from different parts of the house. We used gas in the house, so I think it was also the gas blowing up. Zinc sheets were flying around, and we were afraid that it might affect the shack, so we decided, all of us, to evacuate the shack. We went to his garden and lay down in furrows in the garden, and stayed there for some time. Then from the other side of the shack a neighbour came out and started shouting, 'They have killed my wife! They have killed my wife! Don't stay there in the garden! Just come here and stay with me. I can protect you – I cannot protect my wife. So please come over!'

And we went there. True indeed, his wife was dead. She had woken up suddenly and turned on the light, and then went straight to the window to see what is happening. He said, 'She was so fast, I could not warn her, and yet I knew she was heading for death.' So as soon as the light flickered, whoever was outside our house just turned back and went BHAH! and she was gone. One shot, she was gone.

I remember feeling you know, OK; I was involved in the ANC, and if you can attribute blame for the attack, we are the ones. But what about this poor innocent woman just sitting there? The only crime she committed was the love of her neighbours, to see what was happening in the neighbourhood, that is all! That is all!

That night it was many, many other houses raided – at the time we thought ours was the only one. Come daylight, we decided to take the children to a neighbour, Hi Popholo. On the way to his house, we started seeing bits and pieces of my papers from the university, bits and pieces of things that we had in the workshop; and so we could trace the trail of that part of the Boer mission. I had this urge: I must find out about other comrades, but I had in my mind first to inform Comrade Zola, our chief rep, that we are OK.

Hilda, I will never forget the sight I saw at that house that day. Outside the house, the so-called servants' quarters, I found this comrade with a three months' baby, sitting, looking so hopeless. And I said to her, 'Busi, how are you?' A stupid question to ask. And she couldn't answer, she was just helpless. And I said, 'Where is your partner?' and she just shrugged. I went inside, I looked. There was nobody in her rooms, there was no . . . there was some drops of blood but there was no sign of anything else. I just remember pushing through the Lesotho police to go inside the main house. I don't know, I would never choose to just go and view dead bodies. But they kept on telling me, 'Don't go in there, because dead bodies are still lying there.' And I just pushed, I just pushed past them.

And there I found these comrades lying there, together with comrade Zola, lying in a pool of blood, lying in a pool of bullets. They had obviously shot them, shot them, until they could not die any more, and they still continued to shoot in them. You could just see holes and holes and holes. And just blood. And it is only at that time that I began to realise how lucky I was to have survived. By the end of the day we knew forty-two people had been killed that night, both people of the ANC and also some Lesotho citizens. And some people who had just come out of South Africa, visiting.

This was the turning point of my life, a new chapter in my life of exile. They said that we must all go out; and I thought I could resist and just say, 'Listen, I'm not a refugee here, so I don't see why I should be chucked out.' But in any case, we left soon after the funeral of the forty-two people, and went to Mozambique. And after some time, I went to the GDR to take care of this other child who'd been injured by the fire that night.

I do wish that people in the Movement, when they look at physical wounds, would think of psychological wounds, mental wounds. Nobody ever asked us about, nobody took care of that. And I do realise today that definitely something has happened to these children. Anyway, we got very good treatment in the GDR, and we went back to Mozambique afterwards.

There I was worried because the children were not in school, so I went back to Lesotho for a while. It was impossible to live there. It was hell. That was the real beginning of exile for me. Part of 1983 and the whole 1984 I lived in Lesotho, and I felt I was an exile from one of my own countries – exile inside your own country, living always with this fear: where shall we sleep tonight? What have they seen? All that tension all the time.

That's one side of the story. But the other side is that we had to think of their safety in that school. There were my children and there were also the children of Comrade Chris Hani there. I remember this sense of anxiety if they were even just five minutes late. From the window I could see them walk from school through a field next to the Maseru Club. I used to stand there by that window until I see them coming, and only when they entered the house would I feel relieved.

By the end of 1984 it began to be a security nonsense to live in Lesotho any more, so I sent them to Swaziland, and a month later I followed them. I had been working on a research project on migrant women workers of Lesotho who go to work in South Africa, and NORAD gave me a grant to travel, to try to form a network to get people in touch with each other. So I used to stay in Swaziland for about a month with my children; and then for two weeks, three weeks, or a month I would be away in one or other of the five SADCC states.

UNHCR had started this effort to resettle all of us who had to leave Lesotho. We would go for interviews. I went for an interview for possible resettlement in the USA. At the American Embassy they showed us the photographs of our house, of the shooting that night. And they started saying, 'The papers have asked you how you survived, and every time you said that God helped you. And you, a communist? But none of us is playing games here. Bullets do not go in zigzags. The only people who could have been shooting and who could have made this dent on this wall and this kind of mark must have been shooting from your side. These huge holes are Boer bullets that are used for aircraft attacks – so we know that you were armed that night.'

So we were rejected. Then on the strength of their rejection, the Canadians wouldn't take us, although they had sent word that they would. Then Australia, the same story on the strength of that rejection.

At this time my marriage was breaking down, exacerbated by the fact that when I went back to Lesotho we lived apart. He had to stay in Mozambique, ja. So for something like a whole chunk of 1983 and the whole of 1984 we were separated. So ja, it was very clear anyway to me that it has reached an end. Good things must end also! [Laughs]

So I came here as a student to do an MA. It was a way of getting out. I learned that it is possible also to do things here, and to be on terms with your exile by continuing the struggle. We didn't even have an ANC office here, but I just arrived and jumped into activity, ja, and just continued my political life.

The children are here. They are no more children now, they are women. [Laughs] They have been here since summer of 1986. It's not easy to summarise these years out of Africa. One side of it has been a period of finding myself . . . finding myself as an African, finding myself as a black person in the world. I have learned a lot about the common-alities of racist oppression through living here. Never have I been so aware of racism. It is one thing to talk about racism as part of apartheid – everybody's focusing on that institutionalised level. And we forget personal relationships. Living here I have known racism through personal relations, and it hits you hard.

I have learned what it is to be a black woman also in this situation and it has shaped my perception of being a black woman in Southern Africa. I have learned also about the strength and weaknesses of our Movement. I have learned to survive. I have to live a life of having to justify why I did not die! Instead of people celebrating life, you have to justify why you did not die. Martyrs are those who died.

This has been the most painful period of my life. It has been a very strengthening experience. I have been very close to a serious depression; I learned how to pull out of that. I learned that psychiatric treatment is not only for the ones who are raving mad, but everybody who is involved needs that kind of attention. I could not go to the traditional psychotherapist. There were alternative circles here, there were women's circles. They were frank with me, they didn't want to experiment with me. They have a very simple answer: 'We see you need help, but we don't think we can handle people with your history.' So I have learned to . . . I don't know, to bear the pain and to work it out myself without professional help, because people feel you are too much for them.

Whose problem am I? I don't know. We have to go inward, find our own resources. I have learned to separate individuals from the Movement, from an ideal. I did not join an individual, I joined a Movement. I was attracted by an ideal, a vision; and I have learned that in the process of struggling for that vision, there is a lot of rough road. There are beautiful people also, don't let me depress you! [Laughs] I've learned a lot from people. I've learned also from you. I have learned that to be human should be number one on the agenda – to just think of the human element of our struggle.

Building this human element, that has been my struggle and that has been my experience in exile.

PART THREE

Beyond the Frontiers

The Anti-Apartheid Movement

One of the most important consequences of exile for South Africans was the generation of a uniquely powerful solidarity movement in the cause of South African freedom; a solidarity movement that has had a tremendous influence over the policies of governments and ultimately over international policy. That, I believe, is one of the basic pillars that help to explain the transformation of South Africa in the recent period, towards the liberation of the African people.

Vella Pillay

The British Initiative

The genesis of this 'uniquely powerful' movement was a small group of South Africans who had come to London to further their studies. They all believed they would soon return. This small group of students was soon joined by ANC members such as Tennyson Makiwane and Mazisi Kunene. Together they were the pioneers. Years later, when South African exiles came to Britain, there were well-established organisations: the ANC's external mission; the Anti-Apartheid Movement, a British-run organisation with branches all over Britain and in the universities; SANROC, organising the sports boycott; and the International Defence and Aid Fund.

There was little interest in South African affairs in the Fifties, and no knowledge of apartheid. The massacre at Sharpeville was the catalyst that brought the solidarity movement to life. The British government maintained a highly ambivalent attitude; the Cabinet bent over backwards to avoid condemning the South African government, and Prime Minister Macmillan told colleagues to 'avoid lending support to the view that the recent disturbances were the inevitable result of the racial policies of the government'. When a motion was tabled at the United Nations condemning the massacre, Britain abstained.

Four of the first to launch the Anti-Apartheid Movement in Britain which later spread to many other countries were Vella Pillay, Kader

Asmal, Abdul Minty and Ros Ainslie. They had not come as exiles; they intended to return to South Africa when they had finished their studies. But their lives were irrevocably changed by involvement in the anti-apartheid struggle.

Vella Pillay left South Africa in 1949 to continue his studies at the London School of Economics, after completing a first degree at the University of the Witwatersrand. 'I did not go back after I'd done my degree because I got heavily involved in anti-South African activities, organising demonstrations against the apartheid regime and in support of the South African liberation movement.

'There was also the problem of my marriage to Patsy. We got married in South Africa – before the Mixed Marriages Act. It would have been difficult for Patsy and me to live together under the Group Areas Act.'

Abdul Minty had attended a government school for Indians in Johannesburg. In conformity with apartheid plans in the Group Areas Act, the government decided to move all Indians – and the school – to a special area, Lenasia. So the Congress movement started a private school. 'That was the first non-racial school in South Africa in terms of staff. We were taught by many who were banned from teaching in government schools. Many of us were influenced by that.

'When the police started arresting teachers and detaining them, we got engaged in the fight in defence of our teachers. It wasn't politics in the normal sense of the word. It was simply that we wanted education.

'It became clear that I couldn't study there very long. So I left South Africa and came to England to finish my O and A levels. I arrived in October 1958.'

Kader Asmal left South Africa in 1959. He had been a teacher, but he wanted to go to university to study law. Under Verwoerdian legislation of 1957, the white universities – Wits, Cape Town, Durban – were closed to blacks. 'So I got my teacher's pension money back from the Natal Provincial Administration, and I came to England to study law. I thought of England as a counter to the South Africa we were living through at that time – a kind of symbol of freedom.'

Ros (De Lanerolle) Ainslie left South Africa to do research for an MA and to live in Europe for a while. When she became involved in student politics she met and later married a man from Sri Lanka. 'Following the Mixed Marriages Act it was not possible for us to live in South Africa, but I didn't see this as a permanent condition. "Things will change soon" was what we used to say, always. When we were asked earnestly how long it would last, all of us always said: Five years. After five years had passed if anyone asked, it was still five years. [Laughs]

'So I didn't see it as a permanent choice, but I was very torn about whether I should go back, or stay with Achah. I stayed. I think the energy that went into the political scene came out of that conflict. South African students began associating with students from Nigeria, West Africa and Commonwealth countries who had their own organisations in London. The African students formed a Congress of African Organisations (CAO). Frene Ginwala constituted herself an unofficial member of this organisation.'

In 1959 the president of the ANC, Chief Albert Luthuli, called on the world to boycott South African goods.

ABDUL MINTY: We formed the boycott movement at a meeting on 26 June, 1959. Julius Nyerere was in London for constitutional talks and I went to ask Trevor Huddleston if he would speak. We ran an intensive campaign for boycott. Our whole case was that unless the outside world supported sanctions, we would have violence in South Africa on a very big scale. And in March 1960, less than a year after the prediction of violence, came the shootings at Sharpeville.

KADER ASMAL: Sharpeville was a traumatic event. It transformed the boycott campaign into a very popular movement with tremendous demonstrations up and down the country, and outside South Africa House every day, every night. Sharpeville was a seminal thing and galvanised everyone.

In January 1960, we set up the Anti-Apartheid Movement, and all my undergraduate days – apart from one month studying for my finals – were devoted to the AAM, five or six hours every day. Ros Ainslie became honorary secretary.

ROS AINSLIE: I was still working for Anti-Apartheid from home five years later. Then more ANC people arrived, Mazisi Kunene and Mzwai Piliso, and they became part of the campaign. I really think it's important to stress the African base of this thing – people too often forget it. To say nothing of the women! [Laughs] No, without Frene it would never have happened – to say nothing of me! That's women having a bit of imagination; and Vella had some imagination. The rest of them behaved like a lot of old fuddy-duddies. It's true!

KADER ASMAL: Apart from Canon Collins, it seemed that very few British people knew about apartheid. And I think it is the abiding triumph of the campaign that we were able to reveal the meaning of apartheid right across the country. The motivation came from the ANC, consciously, as part of the externalisation of the struggle – not simply as a humanitarian thing.

Of course the Boers helped, with things like the killings at Sharpeville. There were much worse massacres around that time in other parts of the world, so why did Sharpeville have that impact? One can still ask that question, and maybe we can't find the answer. But the impact of that single day of massacre did more than anything else to alert people here. And alerting Britain was very important in alerting the world. The sanctions movement started in Britain. The consumer boycott started in Britain.

VELLA PILLAY: We were running campaigns on every issue that emerged out of the South African freedom struggle, right? But centrally focused on the need for international sanctions. We were continuously organising demonstrations outside stores up and down the country to stop them from stocking South African products.

The anti-apartheid campaign was given great impetus by the arrival in 1960 of people like Oliver Tambo and Yusuf Dadoo, and an increasing number of other exiles. At that time Tambo and Dadoo were relatively unknown to the non-South African world. They lacked public status and recognition, and their movement at home seemed to have been stopped in its tracks by a State of Emergency. But their leadership proved crucial. They played a central role in setting the direction for the anti-apartheid movement abroad.

The first substantial victory for the sanctions campaign came in 1961 when, with help from Kwame Nkrumah, Pandit Nehru, and the Prime Minister of Malaysia, South Africa was excluded from the Commonwealth. So the whole Anti-Apartheid Movement's campaign for isolating South Africa began to take shape.

In 1963, Abdul Minty on behalf of the South African Sports Association persuaded the Olympic Committee to expel South Africa. The AAM and later SANROC ran campaigns against South African sporting links with Britain; cricket and rugby tours were cancelled as the sports boycott which began in Britain spread elsewhere. And in the 1970s the United Nations lent its support.

Abdul Minty became something of an international ambassador against apartheid: 'In 1962/3 we suggested that there should be a permanent body at the UN to monitor South Africa – some of the UN officials thought we were being very impertinent. But anyway they established the UN Special Committee against Apartheid. And after Sharpeville, when South Africa outlawed the ANC and the PAC, and embarked on a big arms build-up, AAM campaigned for – and got – a Security Council embargo on the sale of arms to South Africa.

'In 1963, during the Rivonia Trial when it was believed that the Congress leaders might be sentenced to death, we set up a World Campaign for the Release of Political Prisoners. I was in charge of running the office. The Secretary General of the UN wrote to Verwoerd to say that, if the South African courts imposed death sentences on Nelson Mandela and others, sanctions would be imposed by the international community. Verwoerd wrote back, listing the kind of disreputable people who were behind the sanctions movement. I was on that list. So it was quite clear that I wouldn't be able to return.'

Kader Asmal was working closely with Oliver Tambo. He applied for a renewal of his passport and was refused. He too realised that it would not be prudent to return to South Africa.

Ros Ainslie and Vella Pillay had both acquired high profiles in the whole anti-apartheid cause. Both had problems about returning to South Africa because of marriages across the colour lines. Ros Ainslie recalls that an incredible amount of energy went into the AAM campaigns: 'But our energies come out of the conflict between what you've left and where you are. The conflict produces the energy – it's all an attempt to resolve your problem of being in exile.

'Anyway, I made myself into an exile by all this. I think you can't really claim to be an exile because you happened to marry somebody who's not acceptable to South Africa. But it was as a result of all that campaigning in the 1960s that I was put on a banned list, and then it was impossible to go back.'

Abdul Minty had given up a promising academic career to work in the Anti-Apartheid Movement: 'I got swallowed into Anti-Apartheid, like getting onto an escalator. Chief Luthuli made his appeal for boycott, a few of us South Africans here felt we had to respond. And once I got into Anti-Apartheid I had to go on.

'In all my life I lived only seventeen years in South Africa. When I became twice that age, thirty-four, I would still say to people, I'm South African. But you're not. You've only kept one foot in South Africa.

'When I left it was not a permanent goodbye. I thought I would come back in a year or so to visit. And now: to go back? I don't know how I'd settle.'

Vella Pillay says that if he were to go back to South Africa 'I have to relearn some forty years of history of which I have only an academic understanding; not the feel, not the touch, not a knowledge of the realities of life. And that is the problem.'

Kader Asmal's greatest regret is that he was not in South Africa during all those years to do, to create, to build. He regrets what the country has lost by denying itself years of contribution from people like Mandela. 'Regret arises from apartheid's role in denying us the right to be creative, to be developmental in our own country. They don't have that much talent, the whites. There are some remarkable emerging Afrikaner writers, but the level of intellectual and political output among English and Afrikaner politicians, even academics, is not high. And yet we have remarkable people who could have contributed to artistic, political, economic and social development. 'We've lost these thirty years. Thirty years that could have had such an impact on our society.'

(Kader Asmal has since returned to South Africa. Abdul Minty's home is in Norway, although he still travels a lot. Vella Pillay has been back to assist with economic developmental plans, but remains based in Britain, as does Ros Ainslie.)

International Defence and Aid

The impulse for setting up the Anti-Apartheid Movement in Britain came in the first place from South Africans living in exile. But the organisation could have no validity unless it was rooted in Britain. South Africans were the generators who brought AAM to life, and whose energy and single-minded commitment spurred its growth. The consumer and sports boycotts, the disinvestment campaigns, the demonstrations and pickets involved tens of thousands of people in Britain, the USA, the Scandinavian countries, and many distant places such as Australia and New Zealand. AAM drew to itself students and other young people propelled by their hatred of racialism and their recognition of the inherent dangers to their own countries of the ideology of apartheid.

At public meetings and demonstrations the local officials always shared a platform with speakers from the ANC. The two organisations worked together closely in an ever wider range of activities – 'solidarity work' that created an informed and increasingly powerful lobby against the apartheid regime.

A third organisation, the International Defence and Aid Fund, was established by Canon John Collins with the aim of providing financial aid for defendents in political trials, and of assisting the families of political prisoners. The organisation was established at the time of the first Treason Trial in 1956, and when it was banned in South Africa it continued to operate from its headquarters in London.

One man symbolises this active relationship between South Africans in exile and their host country. Archbishop Trevor Huddleston, born in Britain, exiled from South Africa, became President of AAM and chairman of IDAF.

ARCHBISHOP TREVOR HUDDLESTON
London 1991

'That period of my life in South Africa was not just a honeymoon period. Everything I really understood and learned came to me there, in those thirteen years.'

His tall, lean figure and long-jawed face is familiar through countless TV interviews and public appearances. At seventy-seven he has lost none of the conviction and outrage that has fired his life-long opposition to racism.

I joined a religious order in the Anglican Church, the Community of the Resurrection which has its motherhouse in Yorkshire. But it had always been a missionary order. We set up secondary schools and teacher training colleges in Rhodesia; and then in the Transvaal we took over all the primary education of the Anglican mission schools – about one hundred schools stretching right along the Reef.

When I joined the Community I didn't know whether I'd be sent to South Africa or not. I had to do my training as a novice, then be professed, that is, take the traditional vows of poverty, chastity and obedience.

Towards the end of the war I was sent off to South Africa, to take charge of all our work in what is now Soweto – Orlando it was then – and to be based in Sophiatown, which was the most marvellous place in the world to be based. It was a place of absolute vitality; and it proved itself through the quality of the people who came from Sophiatown. Nearly all the best journalists and lots of the best musicians and all the rest of them lived there.

Sophiatown was always exceptional because it was a freehold township. That was the reason why, when Sophiatown was removed as a 'black spot', it was such a terrible thing, because it destroyed one of the two urban areas for Africans that were freehold. And it was . . . oh, it had a terrific quality about it.

I arrived in Sophiatown on a Thursday morning, when there was the school mass. We had an enormous church – Church of Christ the King. It dominated the whole place because it was right on the top of the hill, with a great clock tower. People used to set their watches by our clock, if they had watches to set. Our primary school was the largest in the country. We had two thousand kids. And I arrived just as they were coming out of church, and I thought, 'My God, am I ever going to know any of these kids?' It was just a sea of black children, laughing and doing all the usual things.

Sophiatown was the nearest black township to the centre of the city. And all our people were working in the city, in various parts of the commercial and industrial areas; and the women were nearly all doing the washing for white mums in Johannesburg. There was a terrific lot of rack renting, building of shacks in back yards. The population was about sixty thousand, and it shouldn't have been more than about ten thousand.

It was, I think, about a year after I'd got there that I was invited to attend a meeting of the ANC one Sunday . . . I knew some of the ANC leadership. I knew Nelson and, of course, Oliver Tambo who was on the staff at St Peter's Rosettenville. It was a mass meeting in one of the central meeting places in Johannesburg – I've even forgotten which one because I went to so many after that. And it was a sort of challenge moment for me. I knew that I either had to take the one side or the other. And I threw in my lot on the black side.

So I never looked back after that. I was highly political anyhow, although I was not mature enough in England because I'd lived a monastic life. But when I was about eighteen at Oxford, I was committed to Christian Socialism, as I call it, by the hunger marches. So I had a strong political bias. But it wasn't until I got to Africa that it really meant anything – that I really had the chance to try to practise what I preached.

In 1955 the removal of 'Black Spots' was part of Verwoerd's great grand apartheid plan. And Sophiatown was the very first. That was where I really met and worked with and spoke to Nelson Mandela, Walter Sisulu, and all the others. And in the same year was the Congress of the People, 1955. I was asked to be there for the Congress – I've never forgotten that weekend and the launch of the Freedom Charter. It was also, for me, a very momentous thing, because the Isitwalandwe Award was supposed to be given to three of us: myself, Yusuf Dadoo and Chief Luthuli. Neither Luthuli nor Dadoo could reach Kliptown – they were under government restrictions – so I was the only one of the three actually present. It was a terrific event! I saw that as the background to my removal from South Africa.

The Church, for its own reasons, decided that I was too politically involved, much too radical. I believe it was Father Raynes, as the Superior, who decided to recall me; and I can only really believe that it was because the Archbishop of Cape Town found me unacceptable. But I was under a vow of obedience, you see, so my conflict was an internal one. There's no point in taking a vow of obedience if, when you're told to do something, you say, 'I'm sorry chum, but I'm not going to obey.'

I just knew I had no option – I couldn't otherwise live with myself. It was in 1956, the year in which my book was published, *Naught for your Comfort*. That was the beginning of my exile from South Africa – it was, in every sense of the word. And I really felt that I'd never see Africa again. It was devastating!

After two years in Britain, he was invited to become Bishop of Tanzania. The then Archbishop of Canterbury – extremely conservative – refused to consecrate him for the post. So the Tanzanian congregation elected him as Bishop of Masasi. He was there for eight years.

My job there in Tanzania was really to prepare the way for a black successor, a Tanzanian. I thought it would take ten years, but it took eight. And suddenly, out of the blue, the then Bishop of London said, 'Would you come and be Bishop of Stepney?' It seemed to me, as I'd done eight years, as I'd Africanised all the posts I could except my own, it would be the right thing to do.

I did ten years in Stepney. It also brought me into an area where, again, there was this vast immigrant community from Bangladesh, having a terrible time with Paki-bashing, the police and the Sus law.

So I did ten years there and got more and more involved in Anti-apartheid. And when Bishop Ambrose Reeves died, they elected me President of the Anti-Apartheid Movement. And around the same time, Canon John Collins, who had founded the International Defence and Aid Fund, died, and they elected me Chairman of that. So those were the two focal things – and it was a heck of a lot of work to build them up. And that's what I've been doing ever since.

But then – out of the blue again – having decided to retire at the age of sixty-five, I got a delegation from Mauritius, saying, 'Our first Mauritian Bishop has just died; he was only a Bishop for six weeks, had a heart attack. And we haven't got anybody. Will you come?' I said I would do a maximum of five years. I did five years, first as Bishop of Mauritius, and then, after a couple of weeks, I was made Archbishop. So I had Madagascar, the Seychelle Islands and Mauritius. And that was enough to keep me busy.

I came back to London. But, you know, for me that period of my life in South Africa was not just a honeymoon period. Everything I really understood and learned came to me there, in those thirteen years – everything I really understood and learned about human relationships, yes. And about the necessity for political commitment if you were going to do a job as a Christian leader. That is really literally true.

I've done more travelling in these eight years since than I've done in my life, I think. The Anti-Apartheid Movement started when apartheid was not even known. And by the time I came back from Mauritius, there were anti-apartheid groups all over the world, virtually in all countries. And so I was needed. And I was asked to speak on apartheid all over the world.

He was the instigator of a conference in Zimbabwe on the treatment of children in South Africa.

I've always believed, naturally, that children are the future of the whole country, of South Africa. If they are targeted, as they were after the Soweto uprising and then on through the last seven years, the world must know. And the purpose of the Harare Conference was in fact to enlighten the conscience of the world on what happens to children under apartheid.

For the first time we were able to get delegations from children's rights organisations all over the world. And to let them hear for themselves what was happening to the children. We had there some of the children – and a lot of the parents of children – who had been tortured and detained without trial. Having it in Harare made it very much easier. It also enabled the ANC and Oliver Tambo himself to come to the conference; and the lawyers that the Defence and Aid Fund had employed in South Africa. So the world community could hear, really at first hand. This is what impressed . . . well, more than that, it converted them really.

People tend to think apartheid is already finished – although we haven't even started. So there's plenty to do. I'm seventy-seven. So, assuming I can get to eighty, I believe that I'll see apartheid dead before I am. I think there's a good chance of it.

I identified with the struggle of people in a conflict which, for me, is a moral and absolute conflict between good and evil. Speaking as a Christian, I believe human rights rest on a theological fact: of God creating the world in which every human being has a place and a place of privilege; of God the Creator and we are his creatures; or God the Father and we're his children, or whatever you like to say.

But we go further, we assert that God has actually come down into humanity – has shared it. Therefore every human being has an infinite dignity, so that an offence against that dignity is a blasphemy. For me, it's a blasphemy. Now that took hold of me in Sophiatown and therefore I never lost touch with the people in South Africa. I saw and see the struggle to end apartheid as an exact equivalent to the struggle to end slavery. You can't accept it. The sort of Thatcherite political statement, or the Bush and, of course, the De Klerk too, that apartheid was a mistake, that it was a political error of judgment. Not for me, it wasn't! It was an evil! And it is an evil that should be wiped off the face of the earth.

The fact is that de Klerk has been part of the system, an active agent in imposing apartheid all his political life – until now. I know that he's been converted because he sees there's no future in apartheid. But I'm not at all convinced that he's converted to the essential evil of apartheid. He's never said so. There's never been a single word of contrition or penitence about apartheid – only just that it's been a 'political error'.

Therefore, I say they've got a helluva long way to go before they can persuade the majority population in South Africa that they are genuine.

It's this anger against the evil of apartheid that has kept me going all these years. Truly I think it is. I did express it in my book. But I long ago decided I'm not writing another book. And I've also long decided that to debate apartheid is a waste of time. There's nothing to debate. It is evil. Full stop. Therefore you've got to find the best ways of getting rid of it quickly.

So, in a sense, though I left South Africa so long ago, South Africa never left me. Never left me, no. Not for a moment.

HORST KLEINSCHMIDT
London 1990

'I've been able to do what I think most exiles would love to do – which is to remain in touch with the issues as they develop.'

His father, a convinced fascist, was leader of the Hitler Youth Section in South Africa. From this unlikely background Horst grew to become the discreet and responsible Director of the International Defence and Aid Fund for Southern Africa.

I found myself involved – probably the very last link in a long chain – with ANC people who were taking action against the impending so-called 'independence' of the Transkei. In those days – the 1970s – it was very difficult for blacks to hire cars; and all I was doing was hiring cars for them. Someone by name of Magalies Ramagadi from Alexandra would use these cars. He didn't drive them himself, but I know that some of these cars went to Swaziland. I can only speculate as to what they were used for.

The group who were working with Ramagadi were arrested – two of them were kidnapped in Swaziland and taken into South Africa. That was what later on became known as the Pretoria 12 Trial.

After the kidnap Ramagadi told me that he was going to stay and go underground. He stayed on for quite a few months, but then they caught him. He had already served ten years' imprisonment; he served another seven years. Now he's back in Alexandra Township.

I was detained. It was at the time of the arrest of Breyten Breytenbach and that whole episode. I was simply picked up one morning at home. I was constantly asked about OKELA, which was the organisation that Breytenbach was involved in. I knew absolutely nothing about it. It turned out that Breytenbach had me on his menu of contacts to visit. And they assumed that I had been contacted by him. But I hadn't.

I could not work all that out very easily. One night, in Pretoria Central Prison, I heard someone whistling an English tune; and I assumed anyone with an English tune must be a friend. So I whistled back, and found that we could whistle the tune of 'We Shall Overcome' together. We had established contact.

I put my one water bin on top of my toilet bin and climbed up to the top grille, and shouted, 'Who's that?' It turned out to be someone I knew quite well: Gordon Young. I said, 'They want to know all about OKELA. I don't know anything about it.' And he said, 'Thank your lucky stars you don't know – keep it that way.' [Laughs]

They realised very soon that I wasn't knowledgeable about OKELA. But they used it as a way to deal with everything, including my connection to people abroad, to whom I was sending information about foreign investment in South Africa. The French documentation, it turned out, went to Breytenbach. So there was a sort of link.

I had been working for the Christian Institute of South Africa, compiling lists of detainees, and also supplying information to the Defence and Aid Fund in Britain. The Christian Institute from time to time had money which we passed on to people who were standing trial; or their families. The Security were interested in all that.

I realised that I'd been in their sights for a long time, because I was presented with three or four photograph albums of people leaving the front door of my house in Melville, Johannesburg. The man opposite was a railway policeman. They had built a camera into his door; and so they had a record of everybody who'd come to my home. And there were lots of things I couldn't talk about.

It was a bad time . . . so solitary. I was caught out with this Gordon Young incident, and they moved me into a wing of the prison where I was entirely on my own; and I would not hear a voice, or anything other than the chirping of a bird flying over the prison.

So the 'solitary' was a very tough thing. I didn't find it easy at all. I don't think I feature as a hero in that sort of situation at all.

I was threatened with violence, but it was never inflicted. They merely would come into the cell – four, five of them – and shout, and force me into a corner, and then they would hit the wall next to me. But in honesty, they never hit me physically. The same happened in Kompol. And you just are aware of the blood-splatter on the walls around the sink, and you anticipate. Spyker van Wyk used to keep me awake at night by just switching on the light, and locking and unlocking the door, saying, 'Just checking if you're OK!' which was just a way of wearing me down.

Two and a half months. And then came the end of Breytenbach's trial. After he was sentenced, they released everybody of that group who had been picked up more or less incidentally.

I went straight back to the Christian Institute, and spent six months there. But those were miserable months for me. I was quite traumatised by the whole thing. I wanted company, and yet found all company extremely difficult. It took me years to overcome the feeling. I think that the worst part of my detention was a sense of not really feeling anything;

not feeling any solidarity, not feeling a great sense of companionship. I was not associated with the group who were detained with me, nor did I have any sense of a broader political comradeship, because of the period through which I grew up politically.

It was the high point of Black Consciousness; whites were, in a sense, excluded. My peer group in age were the Black Consciousness people whom I knew prior to SASO and BPC being formed. And I remained close to some of them. But I was also very aware that, as a white, I was not particularly appreciated for whatever I was doing.

In those days, the Christian Institute – which after all was mainly white – was steering clear of trouble with the police. And, to my view, was veering away from any real challenge to apartheid. I was aware that Black Consciousness people were saying in public, 'A white man in detention leaves us cold, it's got nothing to do with us!' And that's a sort of central theme of what I felt at the time. It was a lonely experience, and I wished very much to have a sense of association.

I was born in Namibia. My parents were both born in Namibia as well, but of German descent. On my father's side it goes back five generations. The first missionary who came in 1842 married a missionary's daughter whose mother was black, Griqua, by the surname Baum. And this I only mention because it features strongly in the political orientation of the family: trying to hide and deny the black side of the family altogether, and destroying photographs of relatives in the first part of the century, because many of them would have crussy hair. They wanted to pass as white, and not be reminded of this skeleton from the past.

Most of my relations deny this fact altogether, and pretend that it's something that I have invented.

My father was chosen to go to the World Hitler Youth Festival in 1936 in Germany, and, upon his return, he became a foremost leader of the Hitler Youth in South Africa. My father despised the church completely, and espoused racism in many ways: anti-semitism, and also this sort of Aryan belief that he was really a cut above the Afrikaner too. That's what I grew up with. Through my father I didn't grow up with any religion at all.

We were whites who weren't quite making out. And so in spite of being white, the family never owned a house or a car or anything that would materially signal 'white'. That resulted, I think, in my father's alcoholism; drinking was a big factor, which resulted in me and my brother clashing with him very severely at an early age.

We lived in Johannesburg in a suburb, Highlands North, where all our neighbours were Jewish people. We went to the Johannesburg German School; and there, luckily for both my brother and myself, there were teachers who challenged the views that kids brought from their homes. They were Germans who had come to the school on contract, but they saw it as their task to challenge these views. And that changed my views –

initially not on apartheid issues, but certainly on this sort of whole German cult issue. And that was the first step.

I was the first one in our family who ever went to university, because I got a scholarship. It was a bad period in the late Sixties, when the universities were being closed to blacks. I found that Wits was in a turmoil of liberal politics versus conservatives. Ian Robertson, NUSAS president, was banned at that time, and I got involved in a demonstration against his banning. That was my very first engagement ever. I just saw it as a moral issue, which became a confrontational issue with my father since I was living at home.

Through liberals at the university I got invited to the NUSAS conference, and there I met Steve Biko. I happened to sit opposite him at the last dinner of conference. It was traditional for NUSAS to sing 'Die Stem' [the national anthem]. And Steve didn't stand up! And then, when it was finished, he stood up alone and sang 'Nkosi Sikelele' with his fist clenched. And I just thought there must be something quite remarkable about him, and was intrigued. I spoke to him and became friendly with him. He was in his first year at Natal University Medical School, ja. He was not in any way, at the time, involved in black politics. He was politically ambitious, but at the time through the medium of NUSAS.

I didn't find it easy to make a friendship with blacks, but on the other hand I didn't actually find it very difficult. I began to reject the affluent whites I was with at Wits because I couldn't keep up with it. And I found the black people who were poor – I found it very much easier to get on with them although they were much poorer than I was. It was a class issue, not only economic but also cultural.

A few months later I was elected to the NUSAS executive. I was Regional Director for the Transvaal on the NUSAS executive, and I actually managed to bring all the black educational institutions of the Transvaal, every one of them, to a NUSAS conference in Cape Town in 1969. This was a major achievement for NUSAS – it was always accused of being *de facto* white. But that time the vote was 45 per cent black for the first time ever. Of course it only lasted for about ten minutes, because then the black delegates banded together, and broke away to form SASO in a caucus outside the conference room. [Laughs] And they were right! They were absolutely right, because they were being manipulated and dominated by the liberal establishment.

So I supported them. When they walked out, I agreed with them. There was good contact with Steve and myself for many years after that, and we were colleagues in a Christian Institute project later on.

Just after I qualified as a teacher in Afrikaans and German, I was elected NUSAS Vice-President – a full-time job in Cape Town which I accepted. But the College of Education would not defer my teaching service. So I had effectively broken contract, so I could not teach after that. And so I never taught. I've never been a teacher.

After a year and a half as NUSAS vice-president I was unemployed. I became disillusioned, and thought: Where do I really belong?

I was approached by the Progressive Party which was collapsing. They thought their Youth Wing should be expanded. I accepted the job for a year. On the night that Ahmed Timol was murdered by the Security, I was one of I think 350 homes raided right through the country. The police found banned literature in my possession in Cape Town, a copy of the *African Communist*. I was charged for that. And the Progressive Federal Party didn't want to be associated with me, and bid me farewell.

I was then offered a position in the South African Christian Institute. I said to Beyers Naude, 'But I'm not a Christian; I'm not a church-going person at all.' And there were many members who challenged my appointment. But Beyers just said that he, as a Christian, had more in common at that time with people who are not Christian than with those who profess to be, and so he'd got no problem with employing me. He took that further. He employed Muslims and Jews as well; my wife was Jewish and she also worked for the Christian Institute.

I started working on what were called community programmes, and for a year and a half I was in charge of the white programme; and Steve Biko was in charge of the black programme with Benny Kwapa.

We had a meeting near the end of that project when the white project was in total disarray and failure, but the black programme was doing quite nicely – until it was banned. Four of us staff members met. Steve Biko testified that if he were ever exiled he would join the ANC. Benny Kwapa said if he was exiled he would join the PAC. The discussion went on round issues of socialism. Benny Kwapa said, 'I have no truck with socialism.' And Steve said, 'I have.' Peter Randall, who worked with me on the white side, said, 'I side with Benny Kwapa.' And I said, 'I side with Steve Biko.'

Then I was detained, and when I was released the police were making life very difficult for me; they pursued me everywhere, very openly and very overtly. So much so that friends said, 'Look, every time you turn up, so do the police – so just don't turn up!'

I decided to leave. The story of my getting out of the country is described in a book of Cedric Mayson's* – a priest who also had a pilot's licence. He persuaded a rich businessman to lend him an aircraft which was scheduled to fly to Kimberley. Instead he overflew his mark and dropped me in Botswana. So I left in a very, very elegant way.

I managed to get asylum in Holland. I was appointed by Beyers to represent the Christian Institute there.

I ran the operation quite well for a year and a half. Then the Christian Institute was banned in South Africa, so that effectively ended my task

* *A Certain Sound: the Struggle for Liberation in South Africa*, Epworth Press, London, 1984; Orbut Books, US, 1985.

in Holland. Just as well, because an unbelievable row erupted between the members of the Christian Institute and the Black Consciousness movement. Many of the Christian Institute staff were in the Black Consciousness movement, including Sharleen Pokati. She was interested in developing Black Consciousness as an external movement to challenge the ANC and PAC. She wanted to start her own army, and she collected some ragtag band of priests who were willing to start this army in Holland. I totally disagreed with that. My allegiances were to the ANC.

Her thing never took off, of course. But the process that it unleashed was an unfortunate one for me. I had been invited to the UN to address the Security Council on a big thing – the banned organisations. In the very brief eight-minute slot that I was given, I said that I believed that the legal organisations have now been forced to a decision: they have to go underground. And if they decide to go underground, they've only one choice, and that is to join the ANC.

Well, most of the people in the Christian Institute disowned me after that, including churches and support groups here in Europe. The furore lasted for over a year before the offices of the Christian Institute were finally closed down. Many coup attempts were made by BC elements to take over the resources of the Christian Institute in exile, because of its money, power, influence, connections in Europe. They wanted them – and I prevented it. In the end they didn't get them, but I was left with nothing either.

I was once again unemployed, and was offered a job here at the Defence and Aid Fund. That was 1979. And I've worked here ever since. I took over as Director of the organisation in 1983.

I feel today very happy that, yes, it's been a worthwhile job, and I've been able to do many things . . . providing aid to thousands and thousands of people in trials; at this very moment we are looking after over four thousand trials that are still hanging in the balance somewhere in South Africa. Twenty-seven thousand accused still have a charge hanging over them, and we are providing – solely – the support for all of that. And we're providing support for the families, another community of between twelve to fourteen thousand people. So through this work here, we reach thirty? forty? forty-five thousand people every year.

In spite of the banning of the organisation in South Africa, last year alone we commanded £10 million, of which 90 per cent went into the country despite. We had a network of law firms – over a hundred and twenty of them in South Africa – acting for the defence. Many of them didn't know about IDAF at all, but were in contact with law firms in Europe who would instruct them.

Through go-betweens we supplied people in South Africa with assistance like clockwork, regularly every month, month after month, some since their spouses were imprisoned in the late 1960s. I think it's quite a record.

We built up a network of people all over Europe and Canada who acted as correspondents, not aware in most cases that there was an IDAF identity to this at all. This remote control arrangement worked very well. Now, of course, we can work openly. It's a new era for us. People can ask questions now. We have to be accountable.

It was very difficult to raise money when we weren't able to tell people what it was for, or how it was being used. Very difficult. In the beginning Canon Collins went to sympathetic governments, and said to them, 'Will you fund something that is effectively secret? We'll tell you what's going on, but don't tell anybody else.' And of course those governments had enough at stake not to allow this to leak out. And they haven't over the years, although we have support on a regular basis from at least fifteen governments; and on a sporadic basis from many, many more. And through the UN Trust Fund and the EEC, there are between fifty and sixty governments who regularly contribute. It's a very, very big network, a very large operation.

I feel I've been fortunate, I've been able to do what I think most exiles would love to do, to remain in touch with the issues as they develop. That's my daily bread and butter, and it's a very fortunate position to be in.

I've no doubt in my mind about going home. These operations here need to be dealt with responsibly; we cannot foresee when and how they will end. IDAF here is actually close to its end. And I think that's good.

(Horst, together with the IDAF structures, has since returned to South Africa, although British Defence and Aid for Southern Africa still operates in Britain.)

The American Committee on Africa (ACOA)

In the US there was no national Anti-Apartheid movement as there was in Britain. An American Committee on Africa had been established by George Hauser in 1953. Two South African exiles, Jennifer Davis and Dumisani Kumalo, went to work in it, and gradually the work of the committee came to centre more and more on South Africa.

Jennifer Davis had not chosen exile. Her lawyer husband had gone to America and decided to stay. So she joined him.

'I moved into doing some kind of support work very quickly. And the people I found to be most coherent and organised were in the ACOA.

'I set up a research programme to systematise all the information and to feed out the kind of publications that were readable to Americans – anything longer than four pages was not a good idea, because people wouldn't read it. What really worked for us was that we stuck to an issue for a very long time. Nobody in America sticks to anything; it's instant everything.'

Dumisani Kumalo was a journalist. 'In 1977 they were going after the Union of Black Journalists and anybody involved in the Black Consciousness movement. I had been one of the founder members, so they came for me. And I left. I did not tell my family I was going. No! No exile ever tells his family, no.'

He had been to graduate school in Indiana five years earlier, so he came to the US and went to work for the ACOA. They persuaded Federal governments not to invest in South Africa. One of their most spectacular campaigns was the Unlock Apartheid Jails campaign at a time when thirty thousand were in detention. They collected keys from all over the country – 'boxes and boxes and boxes of keys. And we took these keys and threw them out in front of the South African Consulate in New York, in front of the Embassy, with the slogan "Unlock apartheid jails." '

'When I came to this country they did a poll about how many people knew about South Africa: 2 per cent of the people. They did a poll just last year, and it's gone up to 38 per cent – larger than the number of people who vote for the President. I can say, we've done that. We've taught people about South Africa, and we've taught them what they can do.'

Jennifer Davis would like to return to South Africa, but her children are unlikely to go. 'They were only five and six when they came here. Like many people, they're not entirely American, but also they're not South African. I think I could return, yes. I'm not sure how, when, where, because if you work for an organisation like ACOA you don't earn enough money ever to retire.'

Dumisani Kumalo is not in a hurry to return. He will wait and see whether South Africa becomes free. 'But South Africa will always be my home. And you see, I have no problem about my identity. You can't be Dumisani Kumalo and be Irish! So that takes care of that – right? I'll always be South African; what else am I going to be? I'll always talk with a funny accent; so it will always be home.'

The Wider World

Beyond Southern Africa, beyond the Frontline States, the exiles scattered throughout Africa, Europe and North America. They set out on un-mapped journeys, travelled with the uncertainty of unknown destinations, found ways to pilot themselves among the confused streets of anonymous cities, mastered difficult, often obscure languages; tasted a variety of cultures, learned to modulate their voices to a European pitch, to adjust their eyes to the foreshortened landscapes, the diminished skies. And knew they were never again situated in the normal. 'We're always temporary,' said one exile. 'You don't belong.'

There were many fissures to be bridged. The first, the definitive one, had been crossing the frontier, whether with passport or exit permit; or illegally, secretly, dangerously.

The distances that had to be travelled were not just between places – continents, countries, towns. There was the rupture with home and family, the break with a total environment, being in a strange, even alien milieu; the different domestic patterns and social conventions; the reverse of the seasons in the northern hemisphere, the cold dark days, the loss of the sun; a loss that was more than a change of climate, but embraced a whole way of life.

Leaving the old was conjoined to learning the new; there was no time for mourning, no space for gradual growth. The urgency was finding a place to live, a new job. For some, finishing and extending an aborted education, then trying to make a connection between their skills, their new ways of life, and the love and the loyalties from which they were severed. And overcoming the barriers placed before the non-native, permits to live, permits to work, green cards.

But for those in their forties or fifties, professional people many, the task was of beginning again in middle age, trying to slot in to unfamiliar structures, like sportspeople who could still play the game but find the rules have been changed. No longer knowing exactly who you are, nor having the old confidence in one's skills; having to seek out and construct a new identity. Learning how the cities of the West demand that you subdue your enthusiasms, respect their sense of privacy; learning to conform to protocols in different societies, to accept customs grown from a different history, to understand rituals based on different traditions.

Some bridged the rift by finding a place in the structures of the external missions established by organisations banned at home, or by slotting in to local groups that had related ideals and objectives. Some gave up their studies, relinquishing hopes of professional careers to work full-time, low-paid, for the ANC, AAM, or other organisations. Others combined jobs or professions with unrelenting extra activities; or managed to join the two in their careers, as did writers, artists and musicians, who found their own ways through creative work to draw from that fertile source from which they had been sundered.

Apartheid had been very selective. Those who left were generally people who held more developed views on racialism and injustice, who engaged in community activities, people with a social conscience who were courageous enough to put their own freedom, their jobs, their very lives at risk. It was these people who in exile built the powerful movements of solidarity in many different countries at many different levels, and who organised the extraordinary successful IDAF. The energies that went into all this were part of the process of bridging the rift between 'what you've left and where you are'.

Living among people with whom they had no common background, no shared experience of the past, and with whom they did not plan to share their future, they were living in the stasis of an external present. The past was elsewhere, the future was elsewhere; but the past was their only justification for being in exile, for having severed themselves from home, family, community. The only thread of constancy was their struggle against apartheid. This at least provided the solace of continuity, linked them to their past, vindicated their present, and gave hope for the future.

The years rolled on. Their status changed. 'It wasn't meant to be exile,' says Hugh Masekela. Whether they had left under pressure or not, exiles believed they were only temporary sojourners wherever they stayed. But wherever they stayed, the essential routines and necessary implements of daily living imposed a permanence they did not wish to recognise. However much they resisted, exiles put down roots. You have to live somewhere, find work, communicate. You need companionship, friendship, love. Your children have to go to school, be part of this different society. You have to construct a new, a separate, a present life. You don't intend to, but you learn a different way to live. The unhealable rift grows between the self and its true home.

PETER (HAPPY) MHLANGU
Toronto 1990

'Canadian culture has been built for individuals – you are the one, right? Anybody else comes second.'

His real name is Happy, although he is known as Peter. He has a cheerful, buoyant nature; but understands the extent to which life in exile has changed him, his outlook, his ethics and values.

I came to Canada four years ago as SACTU representative. Before then I was in Zambia for about a year after having been in Angola, after having been in Tanzania, after having been in Swaziland, after having been to Bulgaria. So those are some of the places that I've been to.

I arrived back in Swaziland in 1982, two years after I left home. We were just operatives who were building the trade union movement which culminated in the formation of COSATU in 1985, so I used to work with people coming from different unions and different plants in South Africa; more especially from Natal, which is where I come from.

I used to transport people across the borders back and forth from Maputo, very early in the morning. We used to carry guns and ammunition and stuff like that. I did a number of trips, sleeping in the bush and then going the following day so that you are not detected by the Swazis.

I did that until 1984, when the Nkomati Accords were signed. We in Swaziland were affected by that; we were harassed, thrown in prison, first for about three months and the second time for about six months. Then I ran away from prison. Basically, the Swazis argued that it was for our own safety. They rounded up people, under the pretext that South Africa was going to bomb Swaziland. They said they were protecting us, but actually the guns were pointed AT us. We were prisoners of war to a certain degree.

So I jumped prison and I worked underground for another six months. After which, the comrades complained that my presence in Swaziland when I have escaped puts a lot of pressure on them. So I had to leave again to go back to Zambia. I worked at the SACTU office for about six months then I went to Angola for retraining.

I was in Viana and Pango, which is the north of Angola. When I got there, it was the time when there had been mutiny; and it was still very fresh, to an extent that in the first camp that I went to, there was still fresh graves of people that had been killed by the mutineers. To be honest the atmosphere at that time was very fluid; people couldn't talk about things. The atmosphere was very tense, very, very tense. I used to sit around with all the comrades who have been there for years, and you could feel that there were things that they were not prepared to talk about, because they didn't trust the people amongst themselves. The place was fraught with dangers.

To add to that, the food situation was really very critical. Usually when there is food people don't eat their oats, so it gets rotten and gets full of worms and stuff like that. We used to eat those oats. But we all got used to that. We used to eat rice with bananas, exchange with the peasants there; sometimes rice with avocado pear. I got quite nourishing food. But that was just a desperate situation.

There was frustration in people. You can imagine! South Africans from township life living in the bush – to them it's something totally exceptional. There is no entertainment, there are few women; now and then people get wine during special occasions of the Movement, or beer – you would be entitled maybe to three bottles of beer – and people used to be drunk silly, to pretend you are entertaining yourself.

But one of the amazing things was when they used to call 'M'china' – which means 'recruitment' to go to the front. The Chief of Staff, Chris Hani, used to come there, and then certain people would be called at night to prepare for the front. So the excitement and the anxiety as to who was going to be pulled by this M'china was amazing. These young men – I will say men; there were some women, but mostly it was men – the determination, the feeling of going to the front to make this sacrifice, was amazing! One day maybe I will write my own book about individuals that I sat down with and talked about how cruel the Boers are, and how they have bought people over.

But that kind of spirit of comrades saying, 'I want to go home and make a sacrifice.' They even used a term in Zulu, *Uglahlesenta*, meaning, 'I'm going to throw away my testicles.' They would say, 'This time around I don't think I will come back. I think I will throw away my balls', which means, 'I'm going to die.' But even that was like in a joke! But the determination and feeling of people who want to go there, it was amazing. For me, up to today, I still can't imagine how young people of that age would want to go and die and joke about it, that they may not come back. Accept it. Amazing! An amazing thing. Made me reassess my own commitment because when I was there, I never thought in those terms. I never thought of dying. I thought well, now that I'm equipped with the knowledge of killing, those people will be dying, not me! You know what I mean? But I was amazed at people who acknowledged the fact that it could be them.

I was in Angola for about fifteen months, and then I went back to Zambia. I came here to Canada after about five months. I met my wife in Zambia; we got married in 1987; she came here and joined me the following year. We are together now, but have lots of problems. My wife is very insecure. She didn't have good education at home, so she wasted almost fourteen years of her life in exile without anything that she could look back to. And the way that things happen in exile, the behaviour of

men and some of the things in terms of relationships . . . She was not
really a happy person. She left home when she was only about sixteen,
so she doesn't have that background of love and care; and this has had a
lot of problems in terms of how she relates to me. I think very strongly,
it has to do with exile.

I come from a family where my mum wouldn't allow you to insult or
look down upon other people. That's how I grew up. Very strict woman,
my mum. She taught me that you don't hate people and you don't gossip,
you don't say bad things about people. I think in the Movement, there's
a lot of gossip, there's a lot of hatred. Here we are in a liberation
movement, supposed to be comrades and supportive of one another; but
you have a situation which is not like that. I attribute all these problems
to the life in exile, the jealousies, the insecurity of people, the wasted
lives. All the things that you can think of are exacerbated by the fact that
people are not home, so they long for home.

Leaving home has changed me to a very large extent. My philosophical
outlook, my values and ethics and everything has been influenced by
leaving South Africa. When I was at home people who were outside
South Africa used to be referred to as Makwerekwe – a derogatory name
for anybody who's not a black South African. Now having been to those
countries and interacted with those people, I realise that we have to think
differently about other people. In Tanzania, for instance, I've never seen
such warm people in my life. Very warm, unassuming people, down-to-
earth human beings, who have no problems with anybody. This
prompted me to learn Kiswahili. Within six months I could communicate, almost with no hindrance. I fell in love with the language, I fell in
love with the people.

Bulgaria shocked me. They were advanced in terms of their industrial
complex. But they had no clue of other peoples who were not Bulgarians;
they didn't know how to interact with them. Very, very racist. You
know, on the streets, calling blacks monkeys. A very beautiful country.
In six months I had learned enough Bulgarian and understood very well
what they were saying, but still there is no way you can communicate.

When I came here to Canada, the kind of sophistication at every level,
the decadence, the ignorance! But people are very . . . to a certain degree
warm and willing to talk. Canadians are very generous people, but they
will hide their feelings, which I don't like. But then it is Canadian culture,
the culture that has been built for individuals . . . You are the one, right?
Anybody else comes second. And I guess that's the culture of North
Americans – you know, the Reagan type. You are number one! Which
causes a problem if you have to work in a collective, because you are all
number one, then . . . [Laughs]

So I've learned all those things, and I've come to grips with them. I even
understand the sophisticated racism in this country and the discrimination
against women. There is a lot of racism: 'You blacks must understand

that we can do things for you but . . . and you have to comply because you are not in a position to articulate your own positions the way we can.' That is racism, although nobody says that you are a bloody kaffir, or, 'I don't have anything to do with niggers.' Very subtle, and very difficult to deal with. Very – what's the English expression – condescending?

My own attitudes about women have changed since I left South Africa, a great, great deal. When I grew up I had lots of girlfriends. I think that was a way of feeling you have some control – that you must be known for something. When I look back now I think it has a lot to do with apartheid, in the sense that you cannot aspire for anything else outside your community, outside yourself. You cannot aspire to learn and become something. You never have control in your life, so you tend to have control of things that are not necessarily helpful in society. It gives you status.

I think I've learned a lot. I'm very much conscious that there should be equality. It should start in the house, it should start in the education. We cannot talk about it at the level of politics when in the house women are still made to be subservient to men. So that's my general outlook. But I never even thought like that when I was in South Africa, and I left when I was more than thirty years old. Never, ever. I thought of women as being good to sleep with, to entertain you. There are lots of things that I noticed. When you talk to another man, you are polite because that man can beat you up; it's inbuilt in you by society. But when you talk to a woman, you are talking to a weaker species, so you're very aggressive.

I will find it very difficult to go back home and settle at present, much as it's something that I want. Because I cannot live in a township where by six o'clock I must be in bed because there are no lights, I can't read; that on weekdays, I have to drink four bottles of spirits as entertainment. I cannot bear, for instance, people beating up women in the streets, and I don't know how I'm going to cope with that. It's a daunting task for me as to how I'm going to be able to integrate myself, because I've outgrown those things now.

But I chose a path. I don't regret it, not at all, not at all. It's just that, having done that, I've been exposed to a lot of new teachings and my whole attitude has changed. I'm not motivated a bit by having a drinking binge . . . a drink or two, that's fine with me, but it's not something that I live for. But I hear a lot from South Africa – so-and-so has died, he was drinking too much. Almost all my friends are no longer there, or wasted. I no longer have the same values as my friends at home. So how do I go back to those people and become friends? Except maybe to say, 'Let's go for a drink' – because that would be good for them.

ESTHER LEVITAN
Tel Aviv 1991

'I am as much in South Africa as the day I left.'

> Although she feels as alien in Israel as the day she arrived there, she
> manages to involve herself in many political activities. She is a
> vigorous grandmother with an exuberant personality.

I had been in detention, and I came out March 1982. There was a lot of
harassment of white political activists at the time, and my very first night
back in my apartment a stone came crashing through my window. I live
alone, and the effect of this – the noise and the shower of glass all over
my bed on my very first night of freedom – was absolutely terrifying. My
telephone would ring in the middle of the night: sometimes there would
be somebody there, other times it would just be silence and heavy
breathing. Garbage was dumped on my front doorstep; the windscreen
of my car was broken while it was in the garage; this kind of thing. It
wasn't constant. It was very erratic. Just when you thought, oh well,
they're going to leave you alone for now, it would all start up. That was
one of the things.

The other thing is the effect that detention had on me as far as political
activity was concerned. Before I went into jail, I was only too flattered
and happy if anybody asked me to do anything, I would do it gladly and
willingly. And now I heard myself saying, 'Do you mind if I think about
it?' I was afraid I would end up doing very little. So that was another
factor.

I missed my children who were living overseas. I didn't have a passport. So I would never see my children – well at least until I got a
passport. And that was still another factor.

There was also the question of money. I didn't have a lot of money, but
I had some. And although I'm not an expert on economics, I said to
myself: the situation in this country is going to get worse; and at some
stage the rand is going to become so valueless that if I ever do leave, I
won't have any money. It was all these factors.

I had never intended to leave South Africa. Way back in the Sixties
when people were leaving – our children were small – Jack and I talked
about whether we too should leave. And we decided that we were not
going anywhere. This was our country, and we were not going to send
ourselves into exile. And we never discussed it again. Even after Jack had
died and my children said, 'Come and live abroad with us' I never ever
considered it.

But now the circumstances had changed. I was alone. I had been in jail.
It had affected me physically, mentally, psychologically – in every way.
And I came home late one night – I think that was what finally decided

me to go – I came home late one night and I found that the lock on my front door had been smashed in. And I really got into an absolute state of panic. I turned round, took my car and went to spend the night with friends.

Well, I couldn't spend that night and the next night and the next night with friends, so I had to make some kind of a decision about going home. My windows had been smashed again; I moved from the bedroom into the spare room, which had no frontage to the street. I was being harassed all the time. And then I started thinking about leaving.

My detention came about like this. In 1979, three white political prisoners escaped from Pretoria Central maximum security prison. A friend of mine, Prema Naidoo, had to find a safe place for one of them. If he'd been black it would have been no problem – they could have just put him anywhere in Soweto. But there were not many places they could find to hide a white man, so Prem asked if I would keep him. Steven stayed with me for about ten to twelve days until they got him out of the country. And I was told – strict instructions – to forget all about it and blot it out of my mind. And I did.

In 1981, when hundreds of people all over the country were picked up and held in detention, I was in England visiting my daughter. I heard that Prema Naidoo had been picked up. Because I had, as instructed, wiped that whole episode out of my mind, it never occurred to me that Prema in the clutches of the Security Police constituted any kind of a threat to me.

I came back to Johannesburg in January 1982. And the following morning they arrived at my office and arrested me. I asked them why and they said, 'You will be told at John Vorster Square.' We went to my flat, and they searched it for about two hours. Then back at John Vorster Square I was taken to Major Arthur Cronwright who was then the head guy there. He asked me if I knew Prema Naidoo, and I said, 'Yes, I know Prema Naidoo. But what does he have to do with it?' Then he showed me a copy of Prema's confession.

They had done everything bar kill him to get that confession. I have an affidavit of Prema's which he gave at Neil Agate's inquest. And the torture that was inflicted on him! They held him in solitary in Modder B, and brought him to John Vorster Square to torture. They inflicted just about every kind of humiliation and pain and torture that they had devised. He eventually made a confession about his activities in the anti-SAIC campaign; and then he kind of went on talking – the relief of getting everything off his chest. Almost involuntarily and unconsciously – I hope I am remembering it correctly – he started talking about my harbouring Steven Lee.

Cronwright said to me, 'What would you say, Mrs Levitan, if I were to tell you that Naidoo has implicated you in a very serious crime?' And I said to him, 'I think I would say you are lying.' And he said, 'What if I were to show you a confession?' And I said, 'Show me!' He had a thick sheaf of papers in front of him. He flipped over the first section and let me read the latter part. And there was the story of Steven's stay in my flat, and how they got him out of the country.

So I said to Cronwright, 'You've got a confession. What do you need me for?' And he said, 'Because a confession has to be corroborated. And we want a statement from you corroborating Naidoo's confession.' So I said, 'I have to think about that. I can't just give you a statement, just like that.' I was very arrogant at the beginning – I'm naturally arrogant I suppose. And he said, 'Take your time, Mrs Levitan. We have plenty of time.' Which gave me a little cause for anxiety; but not much.

The first week I got ill. I was very lucky. I was ill not only physically but mentally, hallucinating, hearing voices telling me, 'Make a statement. Make a statement.' And I kept saying, 'One more day, one more day'; if Prema could hang on for all those weeks and months, I can hang on for one day. I used to be taken up every day to be asked if I was prepared to make a statement. And every day I said, 'No, not yet.'

After a week, they took me to hospital because of my condition. That gave me a kind of respite, though still in solitary and under twenty-four hour police guard. But I was away from the cell. I was kept in a private ward with a bathroom. I opened the door – I didn't realise there was a mirror in front of me – and I saw a grey woman; grey not only hair – I actually got grey in detention, I wasn't grey before – but grey skin, sunken eyes. I looked like somebody from a concentration camp. I had lost twenty pounds weight in the first week, and was not only a physical but also a mental wreck.

I thought: those bastards! Look what they've done to me! And this is only one week. I had been taken in under Section 22, in terms of which they could hold me only for two weeks. And I thought: I've only got another week to go. This was the turning point. I evolved for myself a programme for survival.

I had to get out of making a statement. I thought about it. After all, what had I done? I had accommodated a young man in my flat a few years ago. And in South Africa that was not yet a crime. For all they knew, I could have been running a bloody brothel. So if I do not admit that I knew the identity of this young man, there's nothing that they could do to me. Or Prema for that matter. I would not corroborate his statement. He asked me if I could accommodate a young man. Yes I could. I had a large flat. He brought this young man to me, and he stayed for ten to twelve days; and then one night he left. I don't know where he went. I don't know how he left. It was not my business, and I did not ask. So that would form the basis of my statement.

When I went back to the cell I still thought: only a week! Come on, you can hang on for another few days. And another few days. It was only on the thirteenth day that Cronwright called me to his office – shouting, ranting and raving that I hadn't made a statement. And then, like an act of vengeance, 'Now Mrs Levitan, I have to inform you that your category has been changed. You're now being held under Section 6 of the Terrorism Act and you can be held forever!' Which horrified and shocked and frightened me. But at the same time it made me angry. And I thought, 'You can bloody well wait for your bloody statement now. If I'm going to be here forever, I'm not going to make a statement yet.'

I think it was about the third week – you lose track of time, you know. You have no watch. I don't know how long I'd been in when I finally sent a message: 'OK, I'm prepared to make a statement.' I told them: 'On such and such a date Naidoo phoned me. He came to see me; he'd got a friend who needed somewhere to stay.' 'What was the name of the friend?' 'I don't know.' 'Didn't you ask?' I mean, it took me three weeks to make that statement, because it was obviously not a statement. It said nothing except the bare things – a young man came to stay with me, he stayed with me for X-number of days. What did you talk about? they wanted to know. And I said, 'He was a young man about twenty-two, twenty-three years old; I'm a middle-aged woman. What do we have to talk about? We didn't talk about anything. We hardly ever saw each other. I work, I have a social life.' 'Didn't you ask him what kind of day he'd had?' I said, 'I might have, but I don't know if I did. The fact that he was staying with me, did not entitle him to my company or my conversation.' I'm very proud of the way I handled that. They never got me to admit that I knew who it was. Never!

My explanation was quite simple. I've got plenty of room. Naidoo comes and asks me – he's got a friend. 'Why shouldn't he go to a hotel?' 'If he could go to a hotel Naidoo wouldn't have asked me. Maybe he can't go to a hotel – he's got no money. I don't know why.' 'Didn't you ask him?' 'No, why should I ask him? I mean, why should I ask him?' The name is what freaked them out. 'What was his name?' I said, 'You know, I don't remember.' 'Didn't you ask him his name?' I said, 'I might have done; but it was so unimportant to me, that I never really remembered. I mean what if his name was Smith or Jones or Van de Merwe? Would it make any difference to me?' I'm a good actress! [Laughs]

The violence to me was not so much in this interrogation, but before. They would rush me up to the tenth floor and keep me standing, facing a blank wall for what seemed like hours, hours and hours. I don't know because I never . . . you're not aware of the time . . . hours and hours and hours, doing nothing. Aches in your legs, pains in your legs. And the kind of humiliation. The humiliation of having your fingerprints taken. Why it should be humiliating to put your hand on a black pad I don't know, but it is. Or the photograph, with a thing across . . . your name across your chest. The rushing you for no reason, not allowing . . . If I'm sitting and waiting for the key, being kept waiting, for hours . . . they'd rush you upstairs, and then you'd sit, looking at a wall.

The most effective instrument that they have, the most difficult thing to cope with, is solitary confinement itself – your total vulnerability. One night, for no reason, the toilet started gushing in the middle of the night – a constant flow of water. It was the only thing that was in my cell, the toilet. And you can't call anyone. There's no one around. You can scream your head off; you can bang your head against the wall. But only the Security Police can let you out of the cell.

I don't know about other places, but in John Vorster Square there's an outside steel door to the cell which the police and the wardress can open. And then there's a steel mesh door that forms a sort of a cage which only the Security Police can open. And the second or third night it occurred to me that, if there's a fire or an emergency, nobody can get to us because the Security Police are not there twenty-four hours a day. And the police have no access – they obviously don't trust them with detainees.

At the end, ten days before I was released, I had an attack – I thought it was a heart attack. I was lucky . . . I was lucky in so many ways. All the wardresses were black. As soon as you thought you'd identified one, a new one would arrive. But one of them was always on duty – every day she had an eight-hour duty – and she was very good to me. She became my friend. Shortly after I arrived she said, 'Mrs Levitan, you are in jail because of what you've done for the likes of me; and if I were to help you I'd probably only end up in jail with you.' And I'd say, 'I don't want anything from you, except to come and talk to me sometimes.' And she did. She'd stand at the door and we'd have a little chat about her day and that kind of thing. Some kind of human contact other than the police.

I was just lucky that the attack happened just about when she came on duty at ten o'clock at night. I'd decided that I'd be less likely to die of this heart attack walking than if I was lying, to be on my feet rather than on the bed. So I was walking up and down the cell in excruciating pain, when the outside door opened and there was this wardress. 'Hello Mrs Levitan. How are you?' I said, 'I think I'm having a heart attack.' Oh my God! And she rushed off. Came back with a young policeman who asked what the trouble was, and I told him. He rushed off. If it hadn't happened then, I could have been lying there until six o'clock the following morning, because although they claimed that they checked up on me every hour, it's not true. I'm a bad sleeper – they certainly never checked up on me.

For instance, the night that the toilet was gushing. At six o'clock in the morning an enormous man with every medal that you can think of – looks like Goering – would open the door. Any complaints? And before you could tell him whether you had complaints or not, he'd be gone. And that morning after the incident with the toilet, I said, 'Yes, that bloody toilet was gushing all night.' 'Why didn't you tell anybody?' I said, 'Who was there to tell?' And he said, 'They check upon you every hour.' I said,

'That's a lie, nobody checks on you.' So you are totally and completely without any kind of insurance, any kind of life insurance. No contact.

There's a guy calls himself a magistrate, who comes once a week. 'Any complaints?' 'Who are you?' He's a magistrate. I said, 'If I have any complaints, who do they go to?' 'They go to the police.' But the police know about me. They know the kind of treatment. So why do I need to tell them about the kind of treatment they're giving to me? The whole thing is farcical. It's got a kind of legality – but it's really weird. You complain to the magistrate so he can tell the police exactly what they already know – because they're doing it.

Anyway, like I told you, I had this heart attack – well, it wasn't a heart attack – at about ten. At about midnight the pain went away. So I decided to go to sleep. And about ... well, I know it was after midnight, another man arrives, clatters at the door and says, 'Levitan, I've come to take you to the district surgeon.' I said, 'Who are you?' 'I'm Lieutenant something from the Security Police.' I said, 'Well I'm not going to the district surgeon now, because the pain has gone away.' 'Oh no?' he says. 'It's Sunday! They drag me out of bed. I've come to take you to the district surgeon, and I'm going to take you to the district surgeon if I have to carry you!'

We sit in the charge office and wait. Finally there's a squad car – vroom vroom vroom – and in trips a pretty little thing in a crimplene dress; makes a grand entrance, smiles at everyone – that's the policewoman – and we all get into the squad car, me at the back, locked in. They always locked you in. And there's three of them in the front. We tear through the streets of Johannesburg on a Sunday night, in the middle of the night when you don't see even a cat crawling. Through every traffic light with the siren blaring. I thought, if I didn't have a heart attack in my cell, I'm certainly going to have a bloody heart attack travelling like this!

I heard later that at that time there were fifteen detainees in the Johannesburg General Hospital alone. I was there under observation for about ten days. The wonderful thing about being in hospital, apart from sleeping on a bed with sheets and pillows and pillowcases – you were allowed one hour's visit a day. Also – wonderful thing – people other than police.

We were under twenty-four hour police guard, three shifts a day. And do you know, they do nothing! They sit and stare at a blank wall for eight hours a day. They don't read. They used to chat and giggle and play, until I put a stop to it. I complained. I said, 'This is not a playground; you're not here for fun. I want peace and quiet.' I also complained to the lieutenant in charge that they walked around with guns. I'd say, 'This is a hospital, there are patients here. Look at them walking around toting bloody weapons!' After that they sat, silent, for eight hours a day – and that gave me pleasure.

About the tenth day, another man arrived – they're always strange men – and gave me a paper to sign. It said: State vs. Naidoo and Others.

I wasn't prepared to sign it – I thought it meant that I was going to be called as a state witness. He said that in due course I would be called, 'and then, Mrs Levitan, you can decide whether or not you are prepared to be a state witness'. And I said, 'What happens now?' 'Now,' he says, 'you can go!' And I was released. They never charged me. And that was it.

I applied to the Brits for political asylum. They granted me permanent residence with all the rights – I can work, I can live there for the rest of my life. Nevertheless, it took me two years to decide to leave. I tried again to get a passport, hoping to be able to travel and come back. They would not give me a passport, only a one-way exit permit. So I took an exit permit and I came to live in England.

Being in England was like being on a holiday – all the theatres, all the friends, all the comrades, talk of home; my daughter and her family. And then winter came – and I went underground. I never moved out of the house. The house was nice and warm, there was no reason why I should go out into that cold and wind and wet and the grey skies. I looked at the newspaper and saw that the sun was shining in Tel Aviv. And I thought: aha! I'm going to spend the winter in Israel.

I stayed six months in Israel, came back to England for the summer, got cold again. I never felt that I was really permanent anywhere – so I went back to Israel. And probably would not have stayed there, because it was very alien to me – the country and the people – except that an apartment was offered to me. I thought: oh well, while I'm hanging around here I'll move into the apartment.

It was towards the end of 1985. I'd made acquaintances, and met people from the left in Israel who notified me every time a demonstration was held outside the South African Embassy. There were always various parties and groups, and one day I said to some man standing next to me, 'How is it that the people who hold these demonstrations are so divided? One week it's Mapam, the week before it was the communists, the week before that the civil rights movement, the month before whatever?' And he said, 'Because that's the way they operate.' I said, 'Isn't there any anti-apartheid organisation in this country?' And he said, 'Where do you come from?' And I said, 'South Africa.' He said, 'We've been waiting for you. You start it.' So I did.

My biggest problem was to get the left wing parties to talk to one another, because they don't. I spoke to each group separately: OK, you can kill each other about Israeli politics. But I'm not interested in Israeli politics. You don't have any argument with one another about your attitude to South Africa. And that's all that I'm concerned with. This is an anti-apartheid organisation, and has nothing to do with Israeli politics. And so gradually I got them all to send representatives, and we started Israelis Against Apartheid.

It was a very good little organisation. If we called a demonstration, the parties and groups would call on their members – mostly the kibbutzim, the civil rights movements and the communists. We had a tremendous launch outside the South African Embassy. We marched from the Town Hall through the centre of Tel Aviv to the embassy. We got financial support from the parties and the groups.

Our last event was 12 December 1987, commemorating Human Rights Day and Freedom Day. We had a seminar in the morning and I showed a video in the afternoon: 'This is apartheid' – it was excellent. A few days later the Intifada erupted. And that, unfortunately, put an end to Israelis Against Apartheid, because all the people who were anti-apartheid had a struggle going on in their own front garden, never mind back yard. And the South African struggle – quite rightly – had to depend upon the South Africans. Israelis have their own struggle.

The moment I first arrived at Heathrow airport after I left South Africa, I realised that I had made a terrible mistake. Exile is not for me. Maybe I'm too old. Maybe I left too late.

I feel like an exile. I don't feel at home in England, although my family and some of my dearest friends are there. In Israel I feel as alien today as I did the day I arrived five years ago. I don't feel it's my country. I don't feel I belong there. The people are strange to me – I'm probably equally strange to them. I feel that because I'm living in a country where there's a struggle going on, I should do something about it. But the fact is that I don't feel any kind of passion. It's not my struggle. It's not my country, and therefore not my struggle.

I am as much in South Africa as the day I left. Whatever happens in South Africa is mine. Perhaps I wouldn't feel so passionate about it if I was living there. But when the announcement came that the ANC and the Communist Party and the other organisations were unbanned, I went hysterical. And I had no one to share it with! And when Nelson was released . . . oh, then we had a champagne party outside the South African embassy!

I was interviewed at the champagne party, and the guy who interviewed me said, 'This is a great day.' I said, 'Yes, it's a great day! And I should be celebrating it at home and not on a street corner in Tel Aviv.' And he said, 'Where is home?' So I said, 'Where should home be? Home for me is Johannesburg! And Cape Town! and Durban!' I mean, that's home. I said, 'What am I doing here, celebrating something like this?'

And he headed his article, 'I want to go home!' Because that's exactly what it is. I want to go home. To me, that is home.

SIMON DUNKLEY
Amsterdam 1990

'That force of separation has given me the freedom to break patterns I had in South Africa.'

His black leather jacket is cracked and worn, his hair tied back in a pigtail. Blue-eyed. Wearing a faded shirt.

I come from a background where I was taught to critically question my environment and what was around me. I went to Bishops, a fairly good school. I was never one of the team, I rejected team sports. I was a rock climber, and spent my time in the mountains.

I had great problems with school cadet corps. We used to have camps – three weeks out in the bush to be trained by the army. The last one of those, I actually went into a kind of a breakdown, a rebellion breakdown; I literally couldn't move. I couldn't get up and do the exercises in the morning, and I just went down, down, down to a point of non-co-operation on anything. It wasn't political, it was coming from a rejection of mindless authority, and of the things I was expected to do with no reason. I would have done them if they could have provided an adequate reason for them, but they could never do that.

I went to university, studied architecture, which opened me to people in student politics. But that wasn't really where I broke from my so-cialised pattern, it was becoming a dagga-smoker [laughs]. That broke a lot of barriers for me, because it's what first took me out of a white environment into a black or coloured environment. You make friends and you're both illegal, and that breaks down certain barriers. So my kind of knowledge of the country came from the street in that way.

I had to do my practical year in 1983. I had a Zimbabwean girlfriend so I went to do my practical in Zimbabwe. I lived on a co-operative commune outside Harare. There were maybe twenty people there, mixed races, mixed nationalities – European aid workers, black and white South Africans and Zimbabweans, Australians, British, some skilled, some not, some people who worked with farming and that kind of thing. That was a very powerful experience for me because we ran everything democratically.

I was there for about a year, and then I travelled to Europe – hitch-hiked about forty thousand kilometres from Turkey to Scotland, up and down and round and round, sleeping on the streets. I was earning my money from street painting – you know, with chalk on the pavements and things like that. On my way back I got to Johannesburg on the day that Nelson Mandela's daughter Zinzi made her address at Jabulani Stadium: 'My father's freedom is tied to the freedom of his people . . . ' I'd never been to Soweto before. That was a powerful experience because

I realised how isolated the whites are; there were diplomats from European countries in Jabulani Stadium, and scarcely any other whites.

I hitched back to Cape Town, moved into a house where this friend of mine was working as a news stringer for ITN, a cameraman. He asked me if I would like to help him as a sound recordist. I said, 'Yes.' It was the beginning of 1985, and four days later, before I'd even registered for my course, they started clearing Crossroads*.

We had to come in from the police side. Crossroads was just screened off. First traffic wardens saying the road's closed. Later military roadblocks, then later the police barricades; and then you see the people. We filmed the situation but from the police lines. This really angered and frustrated me. You'd have these waves, like a frontline of people, and the ground littered with shells and cartridges and rocks and burning tyres and all this kind of thing. And people in the frontline looking at me and seeing a white with a camera or a recorder standing next to or coming through a group of police. And I was just saying the whole time: I'm not these people.

My cameraman went to get a helicopter for an aerial shot. I had no press card and no experience of what a journalist was meant to do. I had a small instamatic camera and this huge sense of outrage. I was running around like . . . The police would come charging in in a sort of armoured convoy of Land Rovers, shooting at people; and these people would flow through the shacks like that. The police would take this piece of ground, but what could they do with it? They'd man it for a while and then they'd have to withdraw; and the people would flow back again. It was constant thrusting, and taking land but not taking people and not taking people's minds, just taking this little piece of land. And there was I, running along behind the police, taking photographs with my instamatic camera.

And then there was a stalemate; the line of people here, and the police drawn up there, and there was a kind of no-man's territory. It was a sort of pause in the activity. I was still standing on the side of the police. I had this feeling, 'This is South Africa. You've got to take your side now. You've got to make a statement. For myself, find out where I stand.' So I started walking out across this like no man's land. Later that whole year we worked every day, every day, three stories a day; tear-gassings, shooting. But that first experience for me was the key moment. I subsequently realised that things happen like that – a journalist can film the story, but sometimes the journalists are the story. And one person can be the focus of everybody one minute and then they can be invisible the next.

I was the focus at that moment for the police and for all the people standing there. Here was this young white guy walking out across this bullet- and rock-strewn territory, across the line. The police were all shouting at me saying, 'You're taking your life in your hands' and 'We're

* A squatters' camp outside Cape Town that was destroyed by the police.

not going to help you.' And I'm trying to ignore them. I got to a certain range, the rock range, and there were kids on the other side in the mass of black faces, saying 'Come! Come over – we're not going to hurt you. Come and speak to us.' I thought, 'I've got to go; there's no question about it, I have to do it now, I have to!' And I went; and the moment I got within range, a shower of rocks came at me, and these people were all stoning me.

And that for me was the whole situation – that I wasn't allowed to cross. Do you know what I mean? I retreated at that point because I'm not a fool, I'm not going to walk into a rock on my head for some sense of my own identity. But the moment had flipped in my head.

We carried on going back, back, back, every day; and we built up contacts until we were being smuggled through roadblocks, through to funerals, with comrades sitting on top of us; we'd have to dodge between patrols; and . . . incredible things – like a house dismantled and rebuilt around your car, so your car would be concealed in like SNAP! [Click of fingers] A whole house, tarpaulins attached to the side, and then a fence and bushes attached to the fence. We needed cars inside to get out with stories. One comrade would drive five cars through a police roadblock and they wouldn't recognise that he was the same person driving the cars. That kind of racism, of seeing just the colour and not the person at all.

So that gave me a lens into South Africa that I never had before. But it also ripped me apart in terms of seeing how news is exploited, who is telling the story, why they're telling it, what's it for, who's distorting it. Seeing incidents happen, going to Parliament and seeing the response of politicians who didn't see it; then the press responding to politicians' statements; and people responding to the press. And how the whole thing became so distorted, with stories going out to the international media and being twisted again.

So I lost all faith in anything but one's own experience.

Ja. But that first day just remained with me. Because if you want to ask, 'When did you confront that point of who are you in South Africa? Where do you stand?' it was that, you know; it was that pure moment.

I didn't finish my degree. That incident was on the first day. Then it was getting worse and worse and worse. The first day nine people were killed and hundreds were shot and wounded; second day was eighteen dead; then twenty-two dead. And it still hadn't hit the press, because the press wasn't covering it. It was all contained like that.

On the fourth day I had to go up and register for my fifth university year. And I was coming out of this reality where people are not going to work, they're forming human barricades against bulldozers coming to flatten their shacks, and the police trying to clear them. Then you go up to the architectural faculty where people would be talking about housing! It was so intellectual and so removed from what was happening just down the road. I walked in and I registered because otherwise I would be called up to the army. And I started asking people, 'Do you know what's happening down there?' I was still smelling of teargas. And I'm sitting on Jamie's Steps looking straight out across the Flats towards Crossroads. There were just smoke plumes . . . it was burning, and there was just the smoke; and if you looked carefully you could see the police helicopters just circling in the smoke. And I'd say to students, 'What do you think that is?' They'd say things like, 'That's the municipal rubbish dump – it's always burning.' And I'd say, 'Do you know where Crossroads is?' 'Yes, it's out there.' 'But where? Is it at the bottom of that plume of smoke? . . . '

I walked off campus that day and I never returned.

I came to realise things that were happening in the coloured townships that people in the black townships didn't know about, there wasn't contact between them; I realised that everybody's fragmented. Every community is fragmented. I couldn't relate to my own community. People would be coming over from the beach or work, and we were like the bearers of bad news. You'd walk into a room and people would see you and they wouldn't want to speak to you.

When we went out, we would go into areas where people didn't know us, and we'd be stoned. At first you put your foot flat on the accelerator to get out; but then you reach a point where you'd stop the car and ask, Why are you stoning me? It was just like an urban warfare situation. We'd turn street corners, we'd be following Caspirs, monitoring, filming them as they were shooting; you'd go down through burning barricades, maybe twenty, thirty in line on a street, turn the corner and you'd come into a cul-de-sac or blocked with barricades; and you're faced with a choice – now what do you do? And you're white, you're in a car, you're a target and you're scared – because it's all an act of faith, the whole thing. At that stage you've got to stop your car, you've got to get out, you leave your camera in the car, and you go and speak to people. And people respond to you 100 per cent differently because they see, here you are, you're unarmed, you're unexploitative. So you're safe and you're actually at their mercy. You know they've been stoning cars, burning, throwing petrol bombs and everything; but they want to see who you are, they don't actually want to burn you and destroy you.

Finally we got arrested. We went to cover meetings in Gugulethu, and we got picked up because there was a State of Emergency, we weren't meant to be there. I had been banned from all the townships in the Western Cape and if you contravened that you'd go for a six month detention. And that six month detention would have just put me straight into the army. I was terrified that I would be arrested and transferred from a civilian jail to a military jail and come through the back door into the army.

Four days before my call-up was due, we just put down everything we were still working on, and jumped on a plane to Amsterdam. I would have gone to Zimbabwe had I been allowed to. But I've always tried to stay out of organisations. I couldn't say I'm an ANC member. I was going as a white South African and I couldn't get a work permit. That was the beginning of 1986. So I came to Amsterdam.

I'm still not a member of the ANC and I probably will never be, because I don't want to be a member of any organisation.

I'd like to go back. I'm really pulled. I grew up on the beaches and the mountains, because that was my only place of peace in that country and I need that. I've also got a child now from a German girlfriend. I'm not allowed to acknowledge that he's my son, because I was a refugee with B status at the time of his birth. And three days later when I received A status, I could've acknowledged him. But because we're not married he was German by then. So in a way, I haven't been pulled into the society. I'm on the outside but I'm comfortable with it. I don't feel it's a problem any more – it's where I want to be. I can't identify with this population group or this religious group. It's people I relate to, not groups. I've come to see that organisations are represented by people; but people don't always represent organisations. I believe that you can be jailed and free; and you can be free and jailed.

It's a personal thing. For me, separation has given me the freedom to break patterns I had in South Africa. Apart from the alienation, you actually have a chance to choose how you come back into that society. Exile has given me that freedom to create my own life when I go back. And I'm going to be more free in that country than I would have been if I hadn't had an enforced break. Because it's an exciting place and that's what I've missed most here – the energy.

JOHNNY NCHABELENG
Amsterdam 1990

'I knew what I wanted . . . and I've had to fend for myself.'

He holds a doctorate in philosophy, which he taught until three years ago when he had a stroke. He was instructed to be still, not to read or lift anything. This he could not do. He began a programme to rehabilitate himself. He reads, he drives a car. He is quick, with nervous, restless gestures. He is on a disability pension, and not allowed to work. He needs to work, he cannot be idle. His seven-year-old daughter goes to the Owl School in Amsterdam, where philosophy is part of the curriculum.

I was expelled from school, and told that I wouldn't have a place in any South African school.

My school was Kilnerton in Pretoria. We were just in the middle of a white residential area, and we always had to fight with white boys; we were always in trouble. We had to defend ourselves somehow. Some older people who were members of PAC and ANC started what they called Young Africans Improvement League. After school we'd go to these meetings just to learn how to improve ourselves.

My father at one stage was treasurer of the ANC branch, so I already knew something of the ANC. At school we were doing chemistry; and it was very nice to learn that if you added an excess of this, you will get an explosion. So we thought, OK, we could start. But we were found out.

My mother – she's a very sweet lady – didn't understand what's going on. She had three sons in that school, and all of them in trouble with the police. We were first suspended; then you had to come in with your parents and answer questions. She said, 'Na, you're so small, but you're not afraid of the white people, especially the police.' They tried to get from you names of people you thought were leaders. If you refused, or if you didn't know and they didn't believe you, then you were expelled. So at one stage, eighty of us were asked to leave school.

I read in a newspaper that there was going to be a new school opened in Swaziland, and I applied. I was invited for an interview and a test. I did quite well, and then was taken to Waterford, a multiracial school, ja. It was a new experience to me, because, to tell the truth, I really did not want to have anything to do with white people. And there I was, at school with them. I was there from my Form 2 to my A levels, which is from 1962 to 1967.

My father died in 1961, ja, and then I could leave the country. I was fourteen and a half then. In 1967 I went to America on an exchange scheme. I didn't like it, even from the first moment. It was an Anglican boarding-school, ja. They were celebrating their hundredth anniversary and they wanted to open up to black people. They came down to Swaziland where I was interviewed, and they thought, OK I could survive. I really was frightened of a huge place like America.

The students' attitude towards life was so alien to me. Those of us who went through South African schools, we respected authority. But these children came from very rich families, and it was like their parents owned the school; and their children could say anything to the teachers, even threaten them with suspension.

For the American students it was something new. They'd never met an African, they'd always seen Tarzan pictures and all that. And there I was, could speak English, I could do mathematics, and they hadn't expected that. But I got on very well with them . . . well, it was because I was very good in sports. So that helped a lot, ja.

I went back to Zambia where I spent four years at the university doing a BA in sociology and French. I was taught by Dutch people who arranged for me to come here, that was in 1973, November. I've been here ever since, studying, and then working at the university.

When I first came here I was rather annoyed that people tended to treat you as a invalid; they want to do everything for you. They were not used to black people, let alone people from South Africa. They thought we couldn't talk, we couldn't do anything. I can't say it was just racism, because it was not the type of racism I was used to. People were ignorant and naive; they just had to be educated. And those who actually stayed with me have become great friends. We share things – the relationship is mutual.

My BA was not recognised, so I had to start from scratch, and that's really taken a lot of energy. My wife found it quite different, but not difficult to adapt. It is a very open society, and you're rarely left to yourself. You really have to fight for the right to have time on your own, and again that takes energy.

I only regret the way in which I left home, without my family's knowledge. When I went to Waterford I just skipped, ja, because I wasn't living with my family; I was staying alone. My mother was in the Northern Transvaal. So I just took the opportunity to go. That caused a lot of trouble, especially for my mother. It took me about twenty-seven years before I could see her. We didn't communicate in all those years, because I didn't have any way of getting in touch with her. I wrote letters, which she says she never received. There was no way of phoning.

I didn't feel the loss of my family that much when I was in Africa. I only felt it when I was here. I was doing all right, and I just really wanted to share that with my family – that I'm working and earning well. My mother is old, and I thought, well, part of the money I earn I think should go to her. So my father-in-law helped my mother get some papers from the Boer government, then drove her to Lesotho – I was working there then.

As a family we really bottle up our emotions. I mean, it was just a question of extended hands and sitting down and talking; but no huggings, no cryings, nothing – as though we hadn't seen each other a week or so. But it was nice for her to see me. The only communication we had before was just before I got married. She just said, 'Hello boy.' I said, 'Hello.' She said, 'Well, the only way you can come back home is through fighting – I don't see you coming home just like that.' So what was happening, that's a surprise to her. To me it's also a surprise, and an anti-climax.

I was privileged in that I'd always been independent and been able to fend for myself. I knew what I wanted, and the ANC made it quite clear that you just find your own way. So I got all the scholarships myself. I went right through their Candidates to the Doctorate within a very short time. It takes too long to get a degree in Holland. In five and a half years I went through the Candidate and the Doctoral and Doctorate. And then I could actually fight for a job.

Three years ago, 1987, I had a stroke. It didn't handicap me a great deal – just that I cannot co-ordinate well, especially when I have to write. Writing becomes very difficult. My memory has improved; in the beginning, it was very, very bad, ja, the first year was very difficult. But I think I'm luckier than most people. First the doctor said, 'Well, you should have died, but you didn't. And you are not even paralysed; and that is something that we don't understand.' And then he told me one of the blood veins burst, and they've just clipped part of this out of circulation. And that's what's bothering them – that if anything goes wrong around that clip then I might just get epilepsy. The chance that I'll get another stroke is there, but very minimal as long as I don't exert myself in anything. And that's what I'm doing.

I work for the office of international relations of the Free University. I recently had the experience of meeting two South African professors, one from Stellenbosch and one from Rhodes. They didn't understand how a black boy could come to Europe and be as comfortable with the culture as I am. I didn't tell them I was South African. They said, 'Ah, but our Africans are not like you. They cannot learn the way you can learn.' At one stage they were talking to each other in Afrikaans. I smiled. Gerber said, 'No, look, that's not Dutch, that's Afrikaans.' I said, 'I can speak Afrikaans. I was born in South Africa, I'm South African.' That really shocked them.

I've just met colleagues from the University of Western Cape, and they said, 'You belong to our university.' But I think I'd like to go up north to my home area – University of Turfloop. That's where I'd like to work, simply because I belong there. In a democratic South Africa, much as black people have to learn a lot, the white people also have to be educated to be able to live with black people. That is going to be very difficult – it is already difficult.

When I was young I could jump a fence at the sight of a policeman; but now I'm too slow. All the brothers have knife scars – you have to learn to adapt. The country's big; and so many people – it's really frightening. That's why I say I'd like to go back and stay right up in the north with the tribal people – not because I want to be better than they, but I feel that I'll be safer there.

And it's not money that one wants. You just want to be comfortable with the people around you. And to be able to work.

CLIFFORD SHEARING
Toronto 1990

'Part of my project is to explore the extent to which you can create a system of policing which doesn't inevitably lead to a misuse of power.'

As a sociologist in South Africa he 'looked at things but wasn't engaged'. Only through studying in Canada did he find his way back to his own country, to which he has returned to work on his project of policing in a democratic society.

I trained at Natal, and then went on to do Honours; and I wanted to go to the US to become more of a sociologist, I suppose. I'd actually had a job with Hilston Watts before I completed my Honours. It was a liberal institute, but clearly part of the apartheid system in assumptions, context. The first work I did there was – the title actually reveals it – 'Blood donation among the Bantu'.

I'd just got married; my wife would be unable to work in the US, although we could both emigrate to Canada. So I applied to a school here, was accepted, and came to Canada as an immigrant with the intention of improving my skills and returning to South Africa.

I got a Research Fellowship at a new Institute of Criminology, which I knew nothing about, and began to spend some time in that. Did an MA here, did a course for my PhD in the US, came back to Canada again and was offered new attractive fellowships at this Institute of Criminology. I suppose I stayed there because I found that the real subject of criminology was the exercise of power, the provision of order and the creation of hierarchy. And the creation of dominance. And I'd had a lot of experience of that as a South African! [Laughs]

So in a sense my South African background sparked an interest in power, dominance, inequality; how it was exercised, how it was resisted. And my main area of attention began to be 'policing'; began looking at public policing, and then began to be interested in more blatant forms of policing, less obvious forms. Became interested in corporate policing and private policing, and various embedded forms of control.

I was brought up, as I suspect English-speaking whites in my class in Natal were, to a really *noblesse oblige* view. I had a dad for whom the worst offence we could ever commit – and this was part of the power – was to be rude in any way to, or show a lack of respect to our domestic help or any of the blacks who worked for my father in his chain of grocery stores. And we were required to tip our caps at primary school to the charwomen and all of this.

So I grew up with this wonderfully English embedded sense of power that comes through kindness and respect because of the great inequalities. This is a very insidious form of power and oppression – certainly the epitome of the iron fist within the velvet glove. That was my apartheid, my experience of oppression – laced with kindness, but patronising; totally secure of its position and power, and absolutely unforgiving when the norms of inequality were broken.

So here I became interested in that form of power. It had this reflexive effect – I began to see my own society now within these terms. And see the extent to which the oppression and the dominance was so pervasive and so all-encompassing that any liberal discussions and dialogue I'd been engaged in were part of this structure.

I was almost completely uninvolved in South Africa, except on a social, family level. I looked at things, but I wasn't engaged. I wasn't like so many other academics who make South Africa their international subject, their professional material. I did that, but in a much more generic way. I made forms of policing, power and oppression a topic, but didn't look at them in that particular country.

And very soon, I couldn't go back to South Africa for two reasons. One I've just enunciated, which is the sense of how all-encompassing this power and oppression was, and how impossible it was to get outside of it. And another, somewhat contradictory, was the feeling that, given this perception, I could only come back in a very destructive capacity. I'd have to be undermining everything – but if I lived in South Africa, I wanted to be constructive, to be able to build, to be able to contribute.

I retained – as many Africans do – an enormous nostalgia for place, and for the knowledge and comfort that comes with childhood familiarity. No matter how well I got to know North Americans and Canadians, no matter that I liked them very much, I never knew them as intimately. So when I returned to South Africa on visits, I found not that I liked the people particularly, but I knew them very well. 'Show me a hand and I would see the person.' I knew how to act. There was a level of comfort, of security which I missed. When I returned to Durban, every street corner, every part of the town, of Berea, was just charged with meaning. Here's where I walked with my father; here's where I did this with a friend; here's where I was with my brother. No matter how long I stayed in Canada, I never had that same sense of belonging, of being a part.

So here in Canada I was in this sort of schizophrenic existence, having become in a way an exile but being very careful not to call myself one. I saw a lot of South Africans coming over for what I thought were largely instrumental reasons, becoming instant exiles on arrival as a way of legitimation. And I was nervous about that. So for most of my time here I had a great nostalgia to go back, but feeling that I could not do it because of the sense of not being able to participate in any directive way.

And then in 1985, I decided to take a sabbatical in Natal. I wanted to go and spend time there – not to work, but to put South Africa under my analytic microscope.

And so I went back to Natal, and was really taken up with the life of the university, in a way that I had not anticipated. The sense of energy, the sense of struggle that was there in 1985! This new phase of struggle was beginning, and I became involved in a lot of small constructive ways, motivated – to use a South African expression – by the idea of a social-legal institute at the Law School that would begin to anticipate what a post-apartheid legal system might look like; what principles of justice in a post-apartheid society might look like.

And I am very pleased to say that it is up and running, and doing well; with a major labour component to it – a discreet little project. And at the same time I kept asking myself and everyone I met, 'Where is South Africa going? What is happening here?'

I came back and wrote my first piece, interestingly enough published in a Canadian journal – a piece called 'Policing South Africa' that looked at Botha's reforms as a policing structure. And I tried to expand the notion of policing, in my academic world, to include major political structures; and show how apartheid itself was a particular kind of policing structure that engaged people in policing themselves. I began to see how I could make a small positive contribution, trying to understand some of the activities of the struggle that was going on all around in the black towns.

So I decided to engage in a project on black struggle within the context of policing. And on its anti-policing strategies. I began a project where I asked black law students to tell me about the struggle in their home towns. And – as always in research – I was taken aback and amazed by the responses I got, both in the way in which those lives became real, and in the wonderful, articulate analyses that came out. But I saw something in it that was quite unexpected to me: the notion that struggle is drama – living drama.

What they told me were stories about dramatic events. People would say things like: Struggle began in our town at three o'clock September 4th. And I was just astounded by this, because obviously we knew the struggle had been going on for a long time. And I thought: this is a very different notion of struggle to the one that I had anticipated. What kind of struggle was this? I realised what they were saying was: The drama of this particular struggle – the curtain – went up at this particular time.

I began to see the struggle in South Africa working exactly along Biko and Black Consciousness lines. I began to understand the struggle as a struggle for consciousness, for subjectivity; a struggle for a way of seeing the world and for a way of being in the world. And I began to see this as incredibly astute and telling, because it got to the heart of apartheid – which was a system for creating a consciousness, a subjectivity, a compliant way of being in the world, that engaged you in your own oppression.

It struck me that the problem of struggle is ultimately a struggle of consciousness. And this is the problem: how can you undermine that system of power when you are the person that is being built to reinforce the system? In the sense: if hegemony is like a piece of paper covering a desk, where do you find a corner to lift it up? And how do you deconstruct such a consciousness?

I began to see policing as a symbolic ordering, where the symbols that kept this consciousness in place were continually reinforced so that you created compliance. And this compliant way of being was the heart and soul of the 'good' policing system and a 'good' system of oppression. The struggle was about dramas that lifted one, as it were, above this world; gave one a perspective on it to see yourself as an object engaged in this activity of compliance.

And I saw how rational and clearly-ordered were things that were presented in the process. Mob activity: I got descriptions of house burnings of collaborators, and I saw how carefully structured, ritualistic they were. And how the house burnings were living, symbolic, spectacular analyses of apartheid, and of how to respond to it. They were analyses that could be participated in – not by a sort of Leninist elite, but through practice. I remember one description in which every other line said 'total destruction', 'total destruction'. The burning of a house was the demonstration for people of two things: that there were collaborators who supported apartheid, who created oppression; and that apartheid could be destroyed through the destruction of the system of collaboration.

And so what I see here through these dramas is what any great drama does – a wonderful, sophisticated analysis, which uses a poetic as opposed to a linear logic.

But I'd spent my whole time learning about linear logic. What did I know about poetic logics? What did I know about drama? So I had to stop seeing culture as I had done – as a recipe book – and see it as a story book being able to understand what parables were, and what allegories were, and what myths were.

Well, for someone steeped in a kind of Galilean tradition of science, this was a big job. I've had to learn about literary theory and all of these other things – post-structuralism and post-modernism. And only now am I beginning to know what it is that these everyday struggling black youth and black workers knew intuitively all along.

If I make any contribution in this particular work, it will be simply articulating the knowledge on their behalf to create a more explicit understanding of it. But they can't themselves put it within the theoretical framework. So I'm hoping to do that, without doing any injustice or violation to what they're doing. I see this as being the opposite of an advanced intellectual elite, and rather a rearguard description of what the elite have in fact been doing. A whole new vision, for me too. It's changed my whole intellectual life.

So I've actually spent the last few years writing very little on this, trying to comprehend just what this means, and what kind of activity's going on. What it means to look at social life as drama. Not that 'life is like drama', but that drama – that form of theatre – is like life. It's not using drama as a metaphor for life, but saying that drama simply takes up the features of everyday life. And so I've been struggling with a paper on this, and trying to understand this for some years now.

And while all this was happening, along came the de Klerk speech of

2 February – the anniversary of my arrival in Canada. And there, for the first time, there opened the possibility to me anyway of becoming involved constructively in South Africa, and becoming reborn as a South African; to participate in the country not by making South Africa my topic, but by doing something quite different – making South Africa the place in which I, as a South African, would contribute not only to South Africa but to international debate.

I suppose this brings me to the end of my story. Because I then got an invitation from Dullah Omar to come out and – as I understand it – explore, for the African National Congress or whatever democratic government would be, ways of building a new policing and ordering structure in South Africa. One that would grow out of and would support structures of equality, as opposed to structures of inequality. It so happens that this really is the international problem of policing too. And so I've agreed to go back for at least two years.

I was also offered the Chair of my old department at Natal University, which is a wonderful honour. So I had this choice now between taking on a project, and leading an institution. And I decided to take on the project.

You can have all the constitutions in the world, and Bills of Rights. But sheer practice is essential to turn it into reality. What I want to do is to engage in a process of community consultation, especially with the people who are usually not listened to – women and youth and workers – as to what kind . . . what images of policing, images of justice, images of ordering and processes they have.

I've got a couple of ideas for exploring it. One will be to use the struggle that's been going on as a series of experiments in ordering, which I can tap into as kind of experiments in popular policing. What I want to do is to describe the models for policing which have emerged outside of state structures. And then articulate these; return them to the communities in which they took place, and ask: What were your experiences with these models? Where would you see them going? And then taking the responses and seeing how they can be integrated with macroscopic concepts of justice, constitutional rights etc. And so, get a kind of up-down linkage taking place. And then, as a final thing, bringing this to the international community as South Africa's contribution to ordering and policing more generally.

We have a crisis, I think, because the Marxist ideal of a utopia without power has crumbled. So we cannot simply engage in a critique of all systems of ordering and all systems of power, in a utopian belief in a society without power. South Africa is at this critical point in its history at exactly the time where this utopia has crumbled. So that it's not enough to talk about a 'free South Africa'.

We have to articulate what systems of power, what systems of ordering and what systems of justice we want. And that places South Africa at a very critical point globally – because that is the global problem. That is the problem that we're seeing, in a sense, in Eastern Europe – when you think there's going to be a vacuum, in fact you create other systems of inequality just as terrible.

Part of my project is to explore the extent to which you can create a system of policing which doesn't inevitably lead to misuse of power. I don't know whether such a system is possible. I have a hunch that it is – but tempered by the very experience of South Africa; that experience of warlords; of totally decentred, fractured systems of power, with no more general state-type system of control or accountability to turn to. The warlord experience is the classic example of the use of protection, of the use of regularisation to create inappropriate use of power for exploitation or self-engrandisement.

I think we have to find ways of creating a system that integrates far more local autonomy, far more local input in the design and control of this, so in that sense more radically democratic. But incorporate that and integrate it with a very strongly enforced, limiting framework of rights and protections.

I think what will happen in South Africa is going to be critical to what happens in the whole of Africa. And that I see as the challenge of South Africa, and very much an international challenge, because we have two things happening here at the same time: one, the move that is breaking down national boundaries through economic integration; and an opposite trend towards a clearer definition of ethnic differences, a wanting for greater wealth autonomy. Our challenge is to find an answer to this question of the misuse of power.

I'm hoping in the methodology for my project to actually try this out in one small way, beginning with the local. I want then to hold a series of consultations at an international and very national level that says: given what we know about the dangers of local autonomy, given our best understandings at the moment about constitutions and charters and rights and all the rest of it, how can we build in protections that will allow these local initiatives to work in ways that will not foster vigilantism and warlordism and all these other things? I don't know whether it's possible. But it seems to me the challenge that we have to address ourselves to.

I've always seen myself as a South African who happens to be living in Canada on a one-year basis, year to year, always renewing my time here for another year. I've been living in Canada, I haven't been a part of Canada. It's a pity – I realise now what I have been missing. But that's the journey I've taken in a little over twenty years in exile.

And I feel now as if this whole exile has been preparing me – maybe a very arrogant, egocentric way of looking at it. But preparing me to go and make a contribution now as a South African. And perhaps, through being a South African, to make an international contribution.

AMOR STRAUSS
Amsterdam 1990

'I never actually knew where I belonged. I was this Afrikaans-speaking girl in an English church, being raised by a black woman speaking Sesotho.'

She is a small, compact person with short, straight hair. Very direct. She believes that women should study religion so they can develop their own kind of spirituality.

I was raised by a black woman. My mother was widowed quite early, and because she had to raise me and my brother she had two jobs. She was a teacher and she was badly paid. And so I had a black mother and I got a black name, and I spoke Sesotho. Because of this, I had this . . . it was a sort of – what's the word in English – schizophrenia, that I had a black mother with whom I had a very good relationship. When I started menstruating I shared that with her; when I had my first boyfriend, my first kiss, she was there for me, because my mother was always too tired from these two jobs.

Then she remarried. My stepfather was extremely racist; he's an AWB orientation; and I then learned to become the master of blacks. And I couldn't accommodate this. On the one hand having this enormous power of hiring people and firing people, and on the other hand recognising that through the love and affection of this woman, I grew into a human being. It tore me up.

My home was in Welkom in the Free State. I always felt myself at odds with the community. My own father committed suicide, and in the conservative religious community – Gerevormerde Kerk – where I came from, that was a no-no. I mean it was absolutely out! So because he didn't die naturally, we were ostracised and actually kicked out of the church. Then, because my granny's English-speaking we became Methodists; and the people started looking on us as foreign. You've joined the *rooinekke*. You know. That battle is still fought in Welkom, even up to today.

So I never knew actually where I belonged. I was this Afrikaans-speaking girl in an English church, learning their values, being raised by a black woman speaking Sesotho. It was to me, up till today, a complete schizophrenia. And the struggle for me today is to find my identity as an African.

I left five years ago. I was becoming uncomfortable with my situation as a white in South Africa. I felt that I had no right to the country. And I got a bursary and I left.

At that point I was working in community development in Crossroads. There was no way – with the means we had at that time – that we could change the situation and I could see it becoming more desperate day after day. And it depressed me. I think that's a typically white kind of reaction – just to turn away from it, because you have other choices.

I always wanted to study theology. I was angry for the church at the way that they treated my mother. I thought that they had no right to make the rules by which things should be played, and I wanted to change that. I thought I could do that by studying theology.

Because of the situation of women in South Africa, I was never allowed to study theology thoroughly except through UNISA, so I studied sociology. But I was still interested in the role that theology plays in empowering or disempowering women, especially in developmental situations. So that is what I studied for one year in Utrecht and then we returned to South Africa. I'm married, I have a husband and a child of six years. And he's a theologian, so we're at loggerheads as well with each other.

We returned to South Africa to find a terrible situation. Almost all my family was in the Security force – I never knew that. I knew they were in the police force, and I knew they were sometimes 'civvies'; but I never knew that they were in the Security Police. On my return, an uncle of mine whom I later discovered was very high up in the Security Branch, told me that he had been told to keep an eye on me; and as I was particularly embarrassing to him I should rather go back again. And then he tipped me that they were looking for me and my husband.

My husband had done his two years in the army. They had a lot of theologians and the army couldn't handle them, so they distributed them all over, to the Lugmag [the air-force] and the police. And in the police he was stationed at Hoofkantoor in Paarl; and there were a lot of things going on there. If you walked in the building, you could hear them interrogating – the Security Police. You could hear people shouting and screaming, agonising; and he asked questions about that, being a pastoral worker in the police. And because of the critical questions that he was asking – and he even wrote articles in the police paper or whatever – they thought that we were starting to constitute an organised form of trouble, ja. Subversion. And they in fact called us communists.

On our return, he heard that he was being called up again for a camp in some God forsaken place, which was highly irregular. It was a signal that they were looking for us. He left immediately. I had to stay behind for another three months trying to tie up the knots, selling things, clearing out the house. And in that time, the Security Police were looking for me.

I was living at a farm in Franshoek, and just behind Franshoek, you had Victor Verster Prison; only a little hill and a mountain dividing us. And a lot of convicts used to escape. So living, a woman alone on a farm . . . well you never felt safe, because of everything that's been written in the papers and because of your own paranoia. You never felt safe.

I woke up at nights. They had a two-man police station in Franshoek, Groot Drakenstein, two people who manned the office; and they used to take their van and put the lights on and sirens, and drive around the house to harass, ja. And I became extremely scared because my child was a baby at that time, he was two years old. There was no way that I could go to my parents; I had no money. The Afrikaner community has kicked us out – more likely vomited us out [laughs] – there was nowhere that I could turn to then for help. So I led this life of pretending to my white friends that everything was OK; and I did not have enough contacts in the black community to secure me either. It was agonising. So after three months, I left and came back here.

But living in Holland, it's just sort of a continuation of the schizophrenia, but another kind now. I am a migrant. I speak the language – that's one of the things that I decided to do: I'll beat them at their own language. So I studied the language and it has given me some comfort, and I studied their society a lot.

On the other hand, I still see myself as a *buiterlander*. And you have this strange thing, that you long for home. And now when the situation is that you actually can go home, you're scared. You don't know whether you can fit in. So when the reforms were made, I went on holiday, I went back home; and I found that it was a different society altogether. I found the Afrikaners so *verkrampt*. There's no way that I can even contemplate going back to the Afrikaner-speaking community. It was impossible before, but it is now even more impossible. There's no way that I can communicate properly with my family. It's a joke in our family, we've decided that we won't talk about politics, and we won't talk about religion; and we don't talk about sports, because then the inter-racial sport things come up again; so we talk about the weather and in South Africa the weather is always good, so it's quite boring!

You have this terrible sense of *vervreemding* – estrangement; we sit there at the table and I look at these people, and they are my blood family and I've got nothing in common with them. And I go into the black townships where my friends are now, and somehow I sometimes belong and sometimes I don't.

You know, living in Holland has been easy. You sit here in a country you don't really settle in. You meet people who align with your struggle, but you don't really make friends. You still think of home as home, so you plan your life for a year or two or three, and you stop beyond that. And when the end of the four-year period comes, you get this agonising situation – that you have to consider another four-year period, or something like that.

I was very glad that I came to a foreign country where I had to teach my son a second language. It was quite funny that I never taught him Afrikaans. Only now, having lived here for four, five years, I'm beginning to see that as an Afrikaner I have rights too; that I have the right to teach my child his mother tongue; and I'm now doing it. But I find it sad he's living a life without grannies or grandpas, without that extended family with family parties. Christmas is terribly lonely.

I welcome the openness of the Dutch society. I find South Africa very . . . not tight, *versmorend*, suffocating, yes. It suffocates people, especially children, and I'm glad that my child won't have that. But on the other hand, what does he have? He has these parents flying up and down, running to and fro from meetings, and he has to find his own way. He's actually growing up Dutch. He speaks Dutch fluently. He has Dutch mannerisms already. He doesn't speak any English yet. He's actually Dutch. And I look at him and on the one hand, I'm proud that he can walk so tall in the society, being a child, and on the other hand I think well, I don't know. I really don't know.

The positive side of being in exile is that he doesn't have a grandfather and a grandmother who will actually impose apartheid on him – which they do when we are there, ja, forbidden to swim with the black children, forced to call the gardener 'boy', and things like that.

Here he doesn't learn apartheid. On the other hand, Dutch society has apartheid as well – very subtle, but still there, ja. *Buiterlanders uit!* Especially now, with young people not able to get jobs, the first people they want out is foreigners. We get less racism because we are white and we speak their language fluently. But that makes me doubly uncomfortable, because I do not want yet again to be put in the position of privilege just because I'm white and speak the language properly. It still stays schizophrenia, whether you are there . . . here or there.

I come from a Gerevormeerde Kerk tradition, although I've moved a bit to the Methodist side. They ordain women, you are allowed to preach in the church, although I do think that the church concepts of women, their definition, is still a very conservative one. In South Africa in the Women's Section of the ANC there's this fear of feminism, because they say that it's a bourgeois Western Europe kind of thinking. I don't believe that. I have met a lot of strong women, especially in SADWU, the Domestic Workers' Union, who had no formal training but knew from their gut where things were going wrong. They had a very strong basic kind of feminism which I adhere to.

I strongly feel that women should find and study religion so that we can develop our own kind of spirituality. We have this vast richness in African spirituality, forms that we can introduce, and we can create a whole new religious culture by which people could be liberated. It may seem a sort of naive, far removed concept, but I really believe that religion is one of those aspects where you can thoroughly enjoy your liberation, and I would like to see that.

But we get a lot of problems because men see the women's struggle as opposed to the national struggle. And I can see a situation where women again will be oppressed, and we will have to find our own language to express our oppression. For very long they said that even though we are women, we are still in one struggle. I think they are seeing their mistake now. You still get the situation where white women oppress black women and coloured and Indian women oppress black women; and yet we have this euphoric view that we are all in the same struggle. But we have never been sisters. We have never been. We still have to create that sisterhood.

I do not consider myself to be European. I do now see myself as an Afrikaans-speaking African. I don't know whether my child is that. Born of an African – does that make him an African? But I do consider myself to be an Afrikaans-speaking African.

When I went back in January, I found the situation very tense. When I left the first time, I saw the police on the streets, but I never felt the tension on my skin. When I got back in January, I was more liberated than ever as a human, but I felt more uncomfortable than ever. The way people moved on the streets made me uncomfortable. It was as if, when the eyes met, it was war between the two races. And there's nowhere that I can get out of my white skin and yell: I'm one of you!

I don't know. I don't see myself in South Africa yet. I know that the skills that I have can contribute greatly to the struggle. But you have learned to hold back. You don't want to be on the forefront, imposing your skills yet again. I don't know. I don't know. I really don't.

M'AFRIKA NODUMEHLEZI
Amsterdam 1990

'All the countries, whether you enjoy or not, there is one thing which keeps on coming back to one's mind: that is, you are not a citizen of this country; you belong somewhere else.'

A sturdy man, of medium build, with the typical small African beard. He trained as a lawyer.

I was at the University of Zululand where I was doing an LL.B. We had formed SACPU – South African Congress for People's Unity. It was an underground movement within the university, the aim of which was to sensitise the people politically – when you wake up in the morning, maybe you would find slogans painted somewhere; you wouldn't know who has done it. We also sent some of the people out of the country with the aim that they should train, and bring some weapons back inside the country.

We wanted people to be aware that you are black, that you have to be liberated psychologically. But I expected them to go further – not stop at that point. That is why, when I came out, I was surprised that there are people who are still members of the Black Consciousness Movement. I never expected that! [Laughs]

I went to Swaziland. The border was being patrolled. Ja, it was being patrolled but they were foolish because they were rigid – after every thirty minutes, you will know! [Laughs] They kept to a timetable. But I did ultimately find out how to cross – well, it was through the help of the people who are there. I had to pass through mielie field and I found myself on the Swazi side of the border.

But all the other SACPU colleagues were picked up, except Mzala and myself – so we were safe. The rest were detained for thirteen months. There was still that belief that I was within South Africa, and it is for this reason that I did not go to the press, I kept quiet. I wanted them to keep on searching for me in South Africa! [Laughs] Well, when they discovered that I was outside, the trial of the others started after thirteen months of detention. I was supposed to be Accused No. 1! There were nineteen accused. They were acquitted, the State could not prove its case. Mmm.

I stayed for five years in Swaziland. I joined the ANC. I was working there with the underground. Because I'm also a teacher I was teaching there – I was teaching English and History, ja, at a high school.

There were conditions of tension there. For instance, the Chief Rep was using a certain car. He had just acquired a new car, a car that was not known by many people. We assumed that the police knew only the old car. But the following day, having come with this car, he was blown up with his wife. It was Nzima, ja. He was blown up with his wife. Early in the morning. So I think someone who was maybe working close with us planted the bomb there in that car. Not many people knew that. That was what was bad about living in Swaziland. Even the way Ablam Duma lost his arm; he went to collect the mail from the post office; and when he opened the post box, the device went off. It must have been planted from inside the post office. It was booby-trapped from inside because the box itself it exploded – not a letter; the box itself.

One day, some people came to my house early in the morning, at about five o'clock; and I knew one of them as Pieter Malans. I knew that he was working for the Security Police. Later on we got this man, this Piet; he's with us. We eventually got him because after that episode when he came to my house, and I beat him up, he actually decided to work for the ANC and be a double agent. [Laughs] And he was useful to the ANC, ja, until the Boers suspected him. He had been responsible for abductions – Shadrack Mapumulo for instance was killed when he was being abducted; Shilanyanda was abducted; Ibrahim was abducted. This man was part of that thing, ja. But then the Boers had discovered that he was working also for the ANC. They wanted him to perform the last task, so that they could kill him thereafter. Someone tipped him off. He never went back – he came to the ANC! [Laughs] Ja, there was that tension in Swaziland. Swaziland has been very bad.

The late Comrade Mabhida came and said, 'South African children are suffering in Mazimbu, they don't have teachers. Would you like to go there just for a year and help?' So I had to go there for a year. But well, the year was very elastic, because it had to be stretched! [Laughs] One year became three years, ja.

What I noticed there were the psychological effects of exile. I felt there ought to have been maybe a social worker working with the people who were in exile. People adapt differently to stressful situations, I think that was the main problem. And the idea of living in a close community also contributed to this stress. That isolation did not remove that idea of being in exile. Instead it reinforced it, such that only the strong could survive.

But I also think that the political education that was given really helped most people. Otherwise we would have had many many cases of people breaking down. You would find people dying there, sometimes under mysterious circumstances – you don't know what has killed them. That was worrying, that was very worrying. It increased the anxiety of the community that there are enemy agents. And it was still not clear whether South Africa will ever be free, so people were thinking that they will be permanent exiles. They were staying with those who came long ago, in the sixties. Mmm.

We had very young children, children who should have been under parental care. They came out. All of a sudden, no parental care. They needed parental love and attention – they never got that. That was another problem.

But going outside was necessary. People really benefited from all these traumatic experiences which one wouldn't have encountered in South Africa. People became stronger. It built their resistance. There were opportunities really for anyone; there was even adult education for those who never went to school.

After Mazimbu, I was called to Lusaka from the beginning of 1986. The ANC was setting up a new Department of Legal and Constitutional Affairs. I am in the Legal Affairs section and in Justice. The Officer of Justice deals with discipline and the protection of individual rights of the members of the Movement, even those who have been found guilty of certain breaches of discipline, and those maybe who are discovered to be enemy agents. We have a Code of Conduct, and people are given a trial. When we try them – even enemy agents – each person is defended by a member of the Legal Department of his or her own choice. They have the right to defence, they get the indictment before they are brought to trial – at least fourteen days before – so that they can consult with their own legal counsel. It is organised just like a formal court. But the Officer of Justice must ensure that people are not ill-treated, people are not tortured. He has to visit the places where these people are kept and take complaints from them; and if ever there are complaints, then something is definitely done. This has been done because of the ANC's belief in the protection of human rights.

I'm still posted in Lusaka – I've just come here to Holland to get a chance of writing this book I'm working on, on the constitutional developments in South Africa, basing myself specifically on the five-year plan of the Nationalist Party. We are looking for solutions for a future South Africa.

All the countries, whether you enjoy or not, there is one thing which keeps on coming back to one's mind. That is: you are not a citizen of this country. You belong somewhere. Your country must be liberated. But with me – I don't know with other people – I wouldn't say there's a country where I was ill-treated, that I didn't enjoy. People have been good. Tanzania, the people were good. Zambia, the people were good. Even abroad, Soviet Union, GDR, and other places – no, people have been good, they have been good. But you still know that you can't exercise all the rights you are having, because you are a foreigner. You are not part of them.

We learned quite a lot. The problem has been . . . what? Languages, maybe; because you have to learn a new language. Then you go to another country, you will learn another one, [laughs] you go to another one, you learn another one – such that when you go back to South Africa, we will be having many linguists, many linguists from the ANC. Ja.

I think I did the right thing by leaving – it was a correct decision. I am far better than I was or I would have been – this is what I believe – had I not left. Because being outside has exposed me to many people, conferences, discussions, ideas and the like, which are not available under the apartheid regime.

FATIMA BHYAT
Toronto 1990

'I have a lot of problems personally because of my views on feminism . . . It's going to be a struggle that women are going to have to fight for a very, very long time.'

She is familiar with every type of Toronto life through her work, which takes her into the best and the worst parts of this clean and orderly city.

I was seventeen when I left South Africa. I wanted to study physiotherapy, and that was a job that was reserved for whites only. It was only being taught at two universities: Witwatersrand and Cape Town. I had applied to them both and was accepted at Cape Town. But being of so-called 'Indian origin', the Minister of Indian Affairs refused permission. Witwatersrand simply said it was a job for white people at that time, so that they couldn't admit me. So I went to Britain.

I still laugh over my first arrival in England. My cousin took me to meet some friends at Charing Cross station. He went off to buy tickets, and I was standing and waiting for him. And an Australian woman tourist approached me; I was just so scared I ran off. I would not speak to this woman! [Laughs] He found me some time later, cowering behind one of the ticket things! [Laughs] You see, I'd never spoken to a white person in South Africa on a one-to-one basis, and I thought I was in trouble or something. This poor woman was quite upset because I was so upset, I was physically shaking. She was simply asking for directions [laughs]. I can laugh now. But at that time I was simply . . . and I think that's a stark reality of apartheid – that we didn't deal with each other on a one-to-one basis.

Part of the scholarship deal was that I return to South Africa to work, which I did four years later, but I had difficulties obtaining a job. There were three non-white hospitals in 1969. The only one that offered me a position was Baragwanath Hospital; they had a shortage of physiotherapists. The salary for white physiotherapists was R120. They offered me R30, which I accepted; and I was to start work on Monday.

When I arrived on the Monday I was told the Minister of Indian Affairs had refused permission for me to work – again, because they didn't have separate toilet facilities and a separate staff room, and I couldn't share the staff room with the white physiotherapists!

My cousin was working at Baragwanath Hospital at that time – Dr Asvat, who was killed recently. He organised some of the black sisters and nurses, and they agreed to share their toilet facilities with me. [Laughs] But of course, the Minister again refused. I couldn't share their toilet facility either! The irony of all that was that all the white physiotherapists in South Africa had been British trained, as I was. They had never had non-white physiotherapists in the country! [Laughs] But they had to register me, because they had accepted the other British trained. So they registered me, but still I couldn't work. Coronation Hospital simply said it was a job that was reserved for whites, and they weren't willing to do anything about it. And the same thing at the Johannesburg General Hospital.

As a new physiotherapist, new graduate, I couldn't very well open a private practice; I simply didn't have the experience. So basically I was forced either to try something else or to leave the country.

At that time Farouk and I had decided to get married. So three months later we did that, and I came to Canada. I had been involved with the ANC in London, but very peripherally, because I had wanted to go home. But now I could join the ANC here in Canada, which I did.

I didn't have any problem at all finding work. However, I have had problems with patients. I guess they hear my accent on the phone – I've been told several times that I have a British accent – and they expect somebody British. And then this brown face arrives! And they're quite put off by that. But I'm in the position of authority, I'm basically telling the patient what to do, and I'm helping them, so they're very willing.

Canadians right now are very many people of various colours, ethnic backgrounds and whatever else. The original Canadians feel really threatened. Racism has gotten worse. They see themselves as losing their jobs, unemployment has increased. So brown people are a visible minority – the brunt of the problem. It's an economic thing. But I find people who are racist don't expect you to confront them. And when you do, then they back off.

In 1978 Farouk and I decided that we would like to return to Africa and do something in the liberation struggle. Farouk decided that he had first to brush up on his geology; so we spent two years in Holland while he was doing his Master's degree. I wasn't allowed to work in Holland at that time, so I spent a lot of time at home with Dutch women at the universities. Farouk was at an institute where people from so-called Third World countries studied. They had a lot of professors' wives who thought that it would be a good thing to introduce all these people from the Third World to the Dutch way of life. And so we would have coffee parties; they'd take us around visiting Holland, and explaining. So some of us started learning the Dutch language, and interacting with people in Holland.

Although we have this image of Holland as a very liberal country, in reality women were to be in the home. Dutch women would throw out, literally throw out their mattresses and their bedding every morning at 7 a.m. to air their home totally. The emphasis on women doing the wifely household thing was tremendous – it bothered me enormously.

I got into Dutch society, worked with some of the anti-apartheid movements which are very visible in Amsterdam and Rotterdam. I think that Dutch society has an unwritten law: you don't speak about religion or politics. So when you were asked where you were from and you said South Africa – that normally elicits a lot of response from people – it didn't with Dutch people. In some instances, I felt perhaps it was a guilt reaction, until I learned that this was an unwritten law, religion and politics can be very confrontational, and they don't want to discuss anything that's confrontational. However, when we did go collecting for the anti-apartheid movements, standing on the streets with these bins, you could collect 700 guilders in a matter of half to three-quarters of an hour. So they were obviously aware of the situation in South Africa, but didn't want to discuss it.

After we left Holland we spent some time in Botswana waiting for our visas for Mozambique, where we had applied to work. When they did not come, we applied to Zimbabwe and were accepted as independents. We both worked in Zimbabwe for five years.

Zimbabwe had merely thirty physiotherapists for the entire country, so I had absolutely no problem. I'm fortunate in that I have what I call a recession-proof job! [Laughs] The worse things get, the more I am needed. But it's a position that's a female ghetto; in remuneration, we're at the bottom of the rung.

I worked with the ANC. We had what was called a safe house. I did a lot of things, like meeting people coming in. I was able to get through the airport security, because I was treating the children of two of the security officials. So I was able to get to people at the airport who weren't allowed to come into Harare because they didn't have visas and things.

After five years, we went back to Canada, because of Farouk's position. He's a geologist. We would have loved to have stayed there. But there were a lot of Zimbabwean geologists being trained, and it's right that their people get priority for work, so within perhaps three or four years, Farouk would have been unemployed in Zimbabwe. And that's the reason why we came back.

Naaema who was six when we went to Zimbabwe, was not aware of race at all, because we'd brought her up where she has access to all kinds of people. She was not aware of race, but when she went to school in Zimbabwe she would come home crying, because Zimbabwean children were telling her that she was Indian, not Canadian. And in Canada, where she was born, the kids told her she was Indian, not Canadian. And she had a problem dealing with that. We had to go into the aspects of racism, and make the child aware of why she was being called Indian, and why she had to insist on being called a Canadian. She's born and brought up in Canada. And she has every right to be a Canadian.

In Canada here I've worked with women's movements, and the Women's Caucus of the Ontario Federation of Labour. What we're fighting for is affirmative action for women in terms of pay and employment equity, and also fighting for women to be regarded as persons. As I was driving here, I was listening to a programme that said that Canadian society is now beginning to see itself in a post-feminist era. [Laughs] I don't see any society being in a post-feminist era. It saddens me to think that fifty years from now, our children and our granddaughters will perhaps still have to be fighting for what we are fighting for. I think we're still in the thick of fighting for women's rights, and we have achieved very little.

Within the South African struggle, I have a lot of problems personally, because of my views on feminism. Until very, very recently the South African movement and the ANC Women's Section has put the emphasis on national liberation; and I've had problems dealing with that myself. They're now saying that we are for women's liberation, and we want women's rights. I'm not sure. I've met people coming over recently, particularly males; and I don't think that they're supportive of that; so I think it's a struggle that women are going to have to fight for a very, very long time.

I'm ambivalent about going home. I've always had this hankering of going home, and I think being in Zimbabwe got some of that out of my system – although I loved being there. I got a lot of self-satisfaction in terms of my work there, as well as just being with the people. I felt really at home there. I think I'd like to assess the situation in South Africa a little bit more. As a woman, and as a liberated woman, I'm going to find it very, very difficult working within an Indian society in South Africa. If I go, I'd like to work in a rural area. Some of that is my own feeling of getting away; some of it is also my feeling that I think I can do a lot more good in rural areas in terms both of my work and of the women's struggle. Rural women are the most downtrodden in South Africa. And I think the work there is going to be quite exciting. I look forward to that somehow.

Farouk has a joke about what would have happened to me if I'd stayed in South Africa. And although I don't agree with him, in the back of my mind [laughs] although I won't admit it to him, I half agree. Within the Indian society, you have these arranged marriages, and yes, some of these people had approached my parents; and I absolutely refused. I had already fallen in love with Farouk and wanted to get married to him. But yes, I would have probably got married to one of these fat-cat businessmen, doctors, lawyers, or something of that sort. And had twenty children. And been a typical woman! [Laughs] No, politically my horizons have really expanded.

People I call my friends are mostly non-South Africans. I work with people from South Africa, work with South Africans in the political sphere and in other respects, but South African males do not relate to me. In some sense they're threatened by me. So I have built up quite a network of friends through my trade union activities, through women's movements.

The labour movement has been somewhat cagey about support for the ANC, because of its alliance with the South African Communist Party, and they didn't think the ANC was important. So the mainstream labour movement have tried to find alternatives, looked for speakers of other movements. We have had to push at grass-roots level to get through various resolutions and campaigns on South Africa by the trade union movement here. I've been quite pleased with that.

I think we're going to have to spend many, many years eradicating apartheid's effects on people. My mother was here two years ago. She arrived one day, and a fire started in the house at three the next morning. The alarms went off. I simply got her and Naaema out of the house, and then called the firemen – they were there within two minutes. It was minus 25°C outside, and I could only throw a coat over her. We were all standing outside while the firemen were dealing with the fire. But my mother kept on insisting on going back into the house. We had to physically hold her down. She wanted to go in and get her passport! Because in South Africa, without your documents you're a non-person. I was not relating to this, I was simply keeping her out. When the police and the ambulance came, my mum was almost hysterical, and shaking with the cold. So the policeman put his arm around her and says, 'Let me take you to my car and you can warm up.' At that point, my mother just went to pieces. The police in South Africa are so threatening and here was this policeman taking her away to his car! [Laughs] And again, I didn't relate to this, until I talked to her afterwards. It really struck me how I had lost touch with some of the realities of South Africa. A totally different perspective now.

So it will be difficult to adjust. It will be very, very difficult. [Laughs] I think I've been away from home too long.

EVERT CILLIERS
New York 1991

'It was a painful country for me to be in. I was an odd man out.'

He is an Afrikaner in exile from his own family and his own culture, as well as from apartheid.

I was going to a church religiously, my mother went to church religiously; my father never did. I must have had about three short and revealing conversations with my father in my entire life, and I once asked why he didn't go to church. And he said, well, he felt that he could do more for his soul sitting on the stoep and watching the birds than listening to a reverend tell him how to conduct himself. I knew what he meant: that the reverend is not as clever as he is; my father was very clever. So it was an intellectual snobbism which kept him out of the church. In terms of his status in the Afrikaner community, it really hurt him; he was never invited to join the Broederbond.

I will tell you two stories. I was in a school . . . the first year in this school. Our teacher starts telling us in a gentle way about his plot of land, and that he's got eight guns, and he oils and polishes them because when you have guns, you have to look after them. 'Because the first nigger to step upon my plot of land, I will shoot him stone dead and I can't wait for that day.' And he goes ha ha ha, snigger-snigger, and I'm sitting there . . . I felt like alone, because these people think this is jolly talk, and I think this is really terrible, because he meant it! And so that was one reason I wanted to leave.

The other reason was a cultural reason, I read *The Future of an Illusion* by Freud, which is about religion. It blew my mind, and I left the church because of that. I wanted to read things that could change your life, and I very quickly got to the end of the number of listed readings. But I couldn't read *Why I am not a Christian* by Bertrand Russell. It was banned.

So when I was an adolescent, after going through an intense religious experience, I read myself out of religion. At the point where I was to become a member of the congregation, I told the reverend that frankly I thought the Bible was a collection of fairy tales. So that was a very big split between me and my own Afrikaans household and Afrikaans friends. This is how my exile happened. It was an exile from my people, which I have always in some way deeply regretted because it stopped me becoming somebody in that group. That was my internal exile, you may say.

I went to an Afrikaans university, and I was a king of the rebels there. I joined the English theatre group and I became English. I went to work in Johannesburg and my first girlfriend was Jewish – in fact all the girlfriends I had in South Africa were Jewish or English, bar one. It was very strange with that one, because I had to say all these things that you say to girlfriends in my own language, and it was unfamiliar to me. I was in exile from my own language. It was a strange and novel experience to say 'I love you' in Afrikaans, which was really my language. So I became an anglicised Afrikaner.

I wanted to be a film-maker. In South Africa, if you're any way culturally inclined, you always look to the rest of the world to get your apprenticeship. Look at all the Afrikaner writers – they've always gone overseas and returned. I always knew I was going to do that. So I got a degree through correspondence and then left. Spent two years in London, which was a very, very, very happy time. I was living on money I earned as a copywriter, and I was going to school – being the eternal student is a wonderful way to live. And there were forty-seven nationalities at this college, ja, so I met a lot of people, Jews, Arabs, Persians, a priest from Hong Kong.

I went back to South Africa, and stayed, I think, four years. South Africa was stranger to me than England and I wanted to get out. And I was going to go to LA when I met the woman who became my wife, Dunja, and she was going to New York, so I just said well, that's it, I'd go. I got off the plane in New York, I felt at home. There's something about New York which really suits me and I've never felt any different.

I'm a cultural exile as much as a political exile. I don't think I would have been able to write the novel I'm writing about South Africa if I had been in South Africa. In New York you just imbibe a number of worlds and a level of sophistication which I now understand. This is a place that implodes on you; it enriches you. And I know I would not have been able to write the sentences or think the thoughts I think about South Africa and create the characters if I were there, in the country. So there is a dichotomy between me saying I never want to go back – and that's not exactly true – and saying I'm happy to be here. Yet what am I doing here? I'm writing this massive novel about South Africa, the place I don't want to go to. South Africa is the subject that I lived as an Afrikaner. So I think I can bring a unique perspective to bear on it. But only because I'm outside. I can look at South Africa from New York, the world city.

There are great things that you get from South Africa, even when you decide to leave it; such as a political sense you cannot get if you live in any of the social democracies. The first second I saw Reagan I could smell that the guy was a bull-shitting fucking fascist, just from watching twenty seconds on the box. I thought, Oh, my God! No, no. Why? Because he spoke like P. W. Botha, because he spoke like Vorster, it was the same fucking shit! And you know I could look at Carter and I could see he's an honest man, he may be confused but he means what he says. But I look at people like Bush, and I know – because Bush and Reagan would have been great Prime Ministers of South Africa! You know it! And if you haven't had that South African experience of politics, you don't.

Do you hanker after anything from South Africa?

The only thing I hanker after from South Africa is Mrs Ball's Chutney. I have a bottle now and it's my last bottle. I had three, right? And it's down to the half, and I'm beginning to use it real sparingly because that chutney . . . it's just the most amazing stuff. I love it! [Laughs] The scenery, the place? No. Because I got estranged from my own people in South Africa. It was a painful country for me to be in. I was an odd man out . . . and I used to in some sense glory in being an odd man out. But somebody like me is accepted in New York. Every strange, weird, ambitious or bizarre person in the whole of America comes here if they don't go to San Francisco or LA. But most of them come here. It's like living in a beer-keg, it's fermenting all the time. And you don't really get that in London. I arrived in New York with my South Africanness still clinging to me, all right through me; and I became a New Yorker.

It's a challenge that South Africa never was . . . [Long pause] I was upset about the political situation and I never . . . did anything. I never joined . . . I never laid my body on the line, I never had the . . . the courage of my convictions. I guess I'm a writer. I feel that writing this book about South Africa . . . Somebody's gotta lay out the struggle and tell what happened; so maybe an ex-Afrikaner like me could have a go at it. And that's really what I'm trying to document, the black struggle. And I don't feel in the least shy that I, a white man, presume to do that; it's a bit like Robert Graves writing *I Claudius* about the Roman Empire. What the hell did he know? He just did it. So I think I can do it, and I hope with sympathy, but mostly with truth.

So I'm still tightly bound to South Africa. I think I always will be. I would definitely want to be home, if I thought the big change was coming. I would be there like a flash, because you cannot be a South African and miss that one.

I went home for two days. I spoke to my mother for an amazingly long time – our last conversation face to face. She tried to get me into an argument about politics. She would go, 'But the blacks can't really run the country, you know.' And then I was out of there – WHEW! Out, as quickly as I came in. And then, many years later, my mother died. So forced by social conventions, you have to traverse oceans and land in planes to see your family there. And your father looks like he wants to cry, which moves you tremendously; and it looks like, oh fuck, this is going to be one of those crying disasters.

But then we sat there and my father just talked and it was absolutely wonderful. And the thing that will always stay with me . . . Here's a man who in a sense was in exile from himself, in exile from his real self, his entire life. Ja, he is, my father. He was just basically a poor boy who was very, very clever and went from nowhere to become the chairman of the South African Agricultural Union. So he was a big deal. He used to know all cabinet ministers. He said, in the course of this talk, two things in his life that he really regrets; he's being very open in talking about this. One, he would absolutely jump on people who worked for him if they ever made a single mistake, but he never ever praised anybody for doing something nice or good or right. And that he really regrets.

But the most important thing is that he had never told anybody that he loved them, only my mother a few times; he very much wished that he could have done that. This guy was a goddam South African who travelled long and far, and now he could only talk with regret because he could never divorce himself from his South Africa.

ANNE LOUW
New York 1991

'He must have thought about doing that a long time ago . . . He took all the kids, all three of them . . . I never found them. Never, never, never.'

> She is short, quiet, pleasant; classified as 'coloured'. She came to the USA with a South African family, the Sagovs, for whom she was working. She still works part-time.

I was very young when I was given away to work – eight years of age. Eight. My mother worked for people from London, from England. Well, they're dead now. And they wanted my little brother; and my father said, 'No, I'm not giving my son.' So they gave me . . . he was five, I was eight.

So then I went and worked there. Well, this is how I was going, on my elbows and knees, you know, doing domestic work, yes. I lived in the house. Dressed up . . . they dressed me beautiful, because they didn't have any children. I was always dressed up like a little princess and they treated me like their own, you know. But I worked hard. I worked, I worked hard. Very hard. My mother also worked there.

This woman had a son in England. She left the son there, she came to live in South Africa and she married in Cape Town. She married a Malay man, and he had the brickfields where they make all the bricks; and that is where I grew up. So the son came when I was thirteen, nearly fourteen. He came for a holiday, and I didn't know about him, nobody did, and his mother she never told us anything about him.

I used to go with them on Fridays, when they used to go and play bridge; I used to always go with them. But that particular Friday, she said to me, oh, he will have a little party and would I like to stay? So as a child, I said OK, I would like to stay. They were playing records and dancing and all this music what's going on. By twelve o'clock the youngsters started to leave and I went to bed. And he raped me. I didn't even hear him come in, I just felt when he was right on top of me, and he raped me. Six weeks I was in hospital and came out of hospital and I was pregnant.

My employers knew, ja. They knew it was their son because that's the only two of us that was there after the youngsters left; and they came and found me in my bed. I was unconscious. He bruised . . . my body was absolutely bruised. I didn't fight. I couldn't fight. I didn't know what was going on. I was only so tiny and he was a big man, he was twenty-three, I was only thirteen, not even fourteen. I was still out when they came. They never wanted me to close the door if they go anywhere, so I leave the door on a little hook, like that, and when they come in, they look if I'm sleeping, cover me up, and then they will close the door because my room was next to my employers. So that time when they looked in and came to me and they touched me and I didn't wake up, that's when they knew something was wrong. And when they opened the blanket, I was covered with blood.

Well, then I went to hospital and I had this baby. So this child, Peter, my son, he grew up with us for about a year, until he was one year old. And he's still alive. He is still in South Africa, married. And that was that.

My employer, he used to take him for a walk every morning, every afternoon and every evening. With me. We used to walk together with a big pram and he in it, and he was just like a little . . . you know, like a doll. And me the same. I didn't dress like a domestic, nobody would have think that I was working because they dressed me up so nice. And I had everything; there was nothing short that I didn't have. But the only thing, I had to work. And I wanted to take Peter to my home to his grandma and grandpa, because he would be starting to call them mum and dad and I wouldn't like that to happen. We called up my father and my mother and said, could I bring the son home, I would like they will take him. So my father took him, he said, 'Yes, you can bring him. But I don't want you in my house.'

So I gave him to my parents and that's where he grew up. He didn't know I was his mother until he got married, and that was just a slip of a friend's tongue. And he was so mad that he could kill me. He said why did he have to live with a lie all his life? and that was not my fault. That was my mother and father's fault. My father blamed me for the rape. Yes, it was not my fault.

But I didn't know anything about those things at that time. It's not like the kids are today. How could I say, people are more open with their kids, especially in this country. People even in South Africa, they are nowadays open with their kids, let them know what is wrong and what is right. But that time I wasn't told this was right, this was wrong or anything like that.

I had a hard life. My brother was stabbed to death by tsotsis. You know what tsotsis means? It's like gangsters. My mother say he didn't feel like going to work that day and my mother didn't know why. But he said to my mother he just had that feeling to be with his kids. And he took his kids to the store and he bought them just whatever they wanted, my mother said, that day. And afterwards he was sitting in front of where he stayed, and the kids was playing around him. And then another woman, a friend came and ask him, 'Isaac, would you like to go to the store with me?' He said, 'But I just came from the store, why should I go back there again?' And she said, 'Oh just to take a little walk, it's such a nice evening.' So they went over to the store.

And that was just the last. That was when they just attacked him, three tsotsis coming out of the store. They asked him for a cigarette, well he wasn't a smoker and he said he hadn't got a cigarette. So they said to him, 'Don't lie, we know you have cigarettes,' and that's how they stabbed him. They pulled nearly his whole heart out, my mother said. The way my sister scream, my granny said to her daughters, she said, 'Something must be wrong because that's Isaac's children screaming there.' And it was on account of that, that they were screaming like that. When my mother came to him, he was . . . my mother was just grabbing him and lying with him there; the people who told me – I wasn't there – they said, when they came to my mother, my mother was just pulling in, like this – you know, like a chicken lying there. They had to come and give her an injection so that she can come right again, when she saw my brother there.

Well, that has happened a long time ago. But I had another son Harold, and he was also killed. Harold was stabbed there three years ago, also by a gang, yes. The ones who stabbed my son dead now, three years ago, that is coloured gangs. You don't know where they came from. He just came out of church and they attacked him and they attacked my sister's son-in-law, so both of them were killed on the same day. The son-in-law still had a chance to run to the house, and he said 'Mother, don't leave the door open, close the door because they're after me still.' And that was his last words, then he died. And he said, before he died, he said, 'Go and look for Harold, go and look for Harold,' he said that three times. 'Go and look for Harold, go and look for Harold' . . . and then they knew something was wrong. But they had to wait until these gangs left; and then they went across the street and there Harold was lying dead. They said they stabbed a dagger right through his body, right through his body, so long it was.

I had three other children. I don't like to talk about it but I'll tell you about it. After my child was born, Peter, and I brought him home to my father, as I said, I stayed by this people until I was about eighteen/nineteen. Then I looked for a job to go and work in the ammunition factory. They don't take people in until you are twenty-one. So I had to make myself older, to get into there. And working there a year, met this Irishman and left with him to Johannesburg.

We were not married. Well, we were like lovers then. Put up a home, had a nice home, beautiful home and I had three kids; went to work every day. He didn't work because why? he was a big gambler. Ja. He used to take me to bioscope and book two seats in the bioscope, nobody can come and sit there at that seat, because it's booked for him and me. But I sit, and he go away. But nobody can come and sit there, see. Then he comes back and pick me when the bioscope's out. He used to go gambling all that time. He had money, he had money. He was from Ireland somewhere, I don't know which part from Ireland, but he was Irish. Very nice at first, you know. He was very nice until I had my third kid. The third child was just a year, just a year . . . there was one three and a half and one two, and this one was just a year.

So I went to work . . . I was at work. There was an old woman – she was an old Zulu woman – she looked after the kids in the day. And when I came home I didn't see the kids on the stoep, because every night they will stand there and see me getting off the train and come out, and they will be standing there waiting for me, and she will have Diana on the arm. And that night it was strange, because I didn't see them. I thought, why they are not on the stoep tonight? What is happening? And at that time I got a funny feeling in my body, something is wrong. And I went inside. Nobody! Not even the old lady was there. Not even Martha was there. And I went over to Martha's house and I said to Martha, 'Martha, where's the kids? Where's McCorley?' She said, 'He gave me off for the day.' I said, 'He gave you off for the day? He said you could just go?' She said, 'Yes.'

He must have thought about doing that a long time ago, because everything was so well arranged, that I didn't even have a picture of the kids to go on. There wasn't a picture of the kids in the house, there wasn't even a picture of him in the house that I could go on, looking for them on that. But as what the police said, he must have gone away by another name. Because they were looking into this at the airports, all over, but there was no such name of McCorley. So he must have left with either a woman, he couldn't have got away with nobody with him. The two could walk, but the other one could not walk yet. He took all the kids, all three of them, I was . . . I couldn't think for that moment, I ran to the police station and I said to the policeman, I said, 'My kids has gone with the husband, all their clothes, everything, there's nothing!' They came over to the house with me, they looked around, they could not find anything that can give them a lead, not a photo, nothing! He swept it all away. And this must have been planned for weeks and weeks, which I didn't think about. I didn't think about that. Nothing!

I don't know why he did that. I don't know why . . . I mean, I was a good mother, I was working and I was with them, I never used to be away from them after I come from work, I used to be with them all the time. Oh, it was terrible! I was off my head for months. I never found them. Never, never, never. Never found them.

That happened years before I came here. So I just worked in Cape Town. And then I went to work for the Sagovs. Then when they wanted to come and live in America, they asked me to come with them. I worked for them for thirty years, and they were always good to me. I loved them. I wanted to come with them, because I felt like the Sagovs were my family.

I'm living quite a nice life now because since December I got my flat and I'm quite happy there. I can be happy. But to get old in this country, that is the problem. I can't get old here when I have my family back home. Nobody looks after nobody here. Here you cannot go to a friend if you're sick and just go and knock on their door; you've got to be invited. You've got to make a phone call to ask if you can come over, and that is only weekends, you cannot go during the week when everybody works. And even when you go there, they will tell you, But there was no appointment made, we are busy working. And that is terrible. We don't live like that in South Africa, we don't. We can go and knock at anybody's house, any time, and the house will be open for us to go, friends or no friends.

And if you get sick in the street, there's people that will . . . but here I see people just walk on. People don't pick people here. I've seen that, I could just stand and cry! One day I came from the hospital to see one of our church people. And this old lady must have been about . . . say about in her eighties or over eighty. Then it's like I see there's two men still walking in front of me, they pass me; and this old lady was one step away from me and they just push her down and they grab her handbag and they ran through the park. I called out to these two men, I said, 'Hey! you bastards' – sorry for the word – but that's what I said. I said, 'Hey you bastards, what are you doing to this poor old woman?' But they didn't even look around, they just ran off. And I picked her up. And she says to me, 'They must have followed me from the bank because I went and get some money to pay my rent.' And I said, 'But why couldn't you bring somebody with you?' She says, 'Well I have nobody, I stay alone and that is what happened to me.'

But I was crying the whole way home. When I came to Dunja's mother, she said to me, 'What is the matter? Why are you crying?' And then I told her what happened. I said, 'Oh my goodness, I can't stand this.' I said to her, 'One day, before I get old, I must go home.'

The War Resisters

COSAWR – the Committee on South African War Resistance – was set up in Britain, with a branch in Holland. Its purpose was to assist young white South African males who had left their homes to escape conscription. Conscripts are liable for two years' service in the Citizen Force, followed by operational service in annual camps for up to three months, for a period of twelve years. There is no conscription for blacks, although many joined the army as volunteers. Military service could be deferred for full-time students.

Hundreds of young men went into exile to avoid military service. Many had already served a period in the army, but were called up for further service when South Africa invaded Angola, and when the SADF was being used to suppress township unrest. COSAWR helped draft dodgers to obtain political asylum in many different countries. Those who refused conscription but remained in South Africa were arrested, tried, and subject to a jail sentence of six years. Within the country, the End Conscription Campaign was set up in 1983.

GAVIN CAWTHRA
London 1990

'I ended up squatting in a very run-down old house in the East End.'

One of the early war resisters, he worked for COSAWR for five years. He is the author of a well-researched study of the apartheid military machine and its effect on the destabilisation of Southern Africa, *Brutal Force*, published by International Defence and Aid.

I left in December 1977 – it was just after the banning of the Black Consciousness movements and after the death of Steve Biko. I'd been called up to the army, and I saw no option other than leaving; or making a stand against the army, which meant imprisonment, but when I came out of prison I would have been called up to the army again. I decided to leave.

I suppose I didn't have the personal strength to face indefinite periods of prison. The whole War Resistance Movement, as it's called, was just starting. There was no network that could have created political support for the stand of an individual.

I was opposed to the South African army for various reasons. I'd been at university and involved with NUSAS, so I had become politically aware of apartheid and the oppression of the black people in South Africa. I'd also become peripherally involved with the trade union movement that was just starting in Durban after the 1973 strikes. South Africa had just carried out its invasion of Angola, and the army had been involved in supporting the police suppress the Soweto uprising.

I would have had to be part of the armed oppression of the South African people, as well as aggression against neighbouring states. I'd been in touch with black South Africans and come to understand their attitudes and feelings about the South African Defence Force.

To me, it was totally untenable to take up arms in defence of apartheid. My brother went into the army. He took the opposite decision to me, although in many ways he shared my views. He simply didn't get it together to raise enough money to leave the country. My parents accepted my decision. I think by then they realised there wasn't much point in arguing against my decision or political attitudes, and they also accepted my brother's decision to go into the army. They let us make up our own minds, and they sort of sat on the fence about it.

I left as a tourist. It was the first time I'd ever left South Africa, and the first time I'd ever been in a plane, so it was quite a tense experience. I couldn't discuss it with anyone. In those days the question of avoiding military service wasn't discussed openly. I'd mentioned it to a few of my best friends, but there was no question of discussing it in a sort of comradely atmosphere. And the people I did mention it to, I think, didn't really believe that I wasn't coming back.

London was the easiest and cheapest place to get to from Johannesburg. I had no idea what I'd do when I got here, but I was young, and I thought something would pan out. I actually hadn't prepared myself at all. I knew absolutely nothing about London.

I can remember getting to Heathrow, going through customs, and asking the first bloke I saw in a uniform where London was! [Laughs] I'm not sure if he was a policeman or a customs officer. He told me to get a bus to Earls Court. That was before the tube was built, all the 'colonials' went to Earls Court, ja. He thought I was an Australian or a New Zealander, I'm sure. And I got to Earls Court and I can remember being horrified at the greyness and drabness of it all. This was mid-winter.

I spent the first few weeks just being miserable in Earls Court, staying in a very cheap bed and breakfast place, and finding that the cold virtually froze my brain. I was incapable of even thinking. It was, in fact, a very cold winter and of course I'd lived in Durban most of my life so I wasn't accustomed to cold at all.

I had enough money to live for a couple of months, so I wasn't terribly concerned about money. And I lived cheaply. After a week or two, I had some addresses – not of people I knew, but someone's sister and friends and so on – and I went to visit. They turned out to be South African exiles who were politically involved, more with the PAC than anything else. And while I was visiting, a bloke called Jimmy Corrigal, who is a member of the ANC, also visited them occasionally.

He took me under his wing. He was involved with a small group in the ANC who were trying to set up a committee to work on this question of draft-dodgers who were leaving the country after the invasion of Angola. He invited me to a party at his house. I arrived at the party with my backpack! [Laughs] And after all the guests had left, I told him that I had nowhere to stay. He had a room for rent in his house, so I moved in with him and that of course put me straight into the network of the Anti-Apartheid Movement and the ANC.

I think they probably thought I was a bit of a nutter, [Laughs] because although I'd been quite radical and militant, I very much came from the Black Consciousness period, and my attitude to the ANC was quite disparaging. I regarded the ANC as a bunch of has-beens. I remember saying to Aziz Pahad, 'I'm very interested in hearing your perspectives, your views as the ANC.' And he said to me, 'It's not my views; it's the views of the South African people.' Which I thought was enormously arrogant! [Laughs] But at the same time it was very educational for me.

I came to realise that the tradition of the ANC was a very important one, and that the ANC still existed inside the country. So my political views moved very quickly on from the sort of Black Consciousness views to pro-ANC views; and I soon became involved in the Anti-Apartheid Movement as well.

I got a job which Jimmy arranged for me at Central Books. It was a pretty shitty job – it involved working in their warehouse in Southwark, which was incredibly Dickensian. And we used to off-load these books into this ancient warehouse, standing in the snow. It was snowing constantly. [Laughs] I didn't have a work permit, so this was all done illegally.

I had to do something about my status – I was still a 'visitor'. So I applied for asylum in Britain, and was in fact one of the first war resisters to do so. Eventually, after about eighteen months, I was given what they call 'Exceptional leave to remain' – which was just an annually renewable work permit. After four years that converted to refugee status.

I got support from fellow exiled South Africans, people like Dulcie September who was very supportive. But in general, there was very little support from any of the British people I met, and little understanding. It was very hard to make a living. We weren't allowed to work while we were waiting for asylum; one could go on the dole. So I ended up squatting in a very run-down old house in the East End in conditions of poverty, which I wasn't accustomed to being a white South African. The weather and the dreariness of London became very psychologically oppressive, and I think the only thing that really kept me going was my commitment to the South African struggle, and the support I got from my comrades.

Shortly after I arrived, in conjunction with the ANC and the Anti-Apartheid Movement, we set up this committee, COSAWR, with the aim of helping people who'd arrived in Britain to apply for asylum; and also putting the whole question of resistance to military service in South Africa on the political agenda of the world anti-apartheid movements, and indeed of the ANC and our structures at home.

So for the next five or six years, I worked full-time for COSAWR. We built it up into an organisation. We probably assisted a few hundred people who'd come to us for advice – not all of them applying for political asylum. We mobilised people into the Anti-Apartheid Movement and we saw some of them go back to South Africa. I think we contributed to establishing the climate in which an organisation like the End Conscription Campaign could develop there.

I knew I wasn't able to go back. For some reason the Security Police were extremely interested in me. People who visited me in London were often interrogated when they got back to South Africa. In fact, one person who was questioned when she went back was shown photographs of herself meeting me outside a pub in Charing Cross Road. [Laughs] So they'd obviously been monitoring me. I think some of it had to do with Craig Williamson – he'd left shortly before me, and saw me at an ANC meeting in London soon after I arrived.

I've been out for thirteen years now. I was tremendously excited when de Klerk unbanned the ANC, and I was kind of tempted to get on the first plane back. But things are a bit more complicated than that. I've been working for IDAF, I've been organising COSAWR, and I've been involved with the ANC. So I've got certain commitments here. I wouldn't want to go back to South Africa without being able to contribute positively to the struggle.

Then there are personal questions. My partner is English. I've got a five-year-old kid who's just started school. And I certainly wouldn't want to send her to a segregated school. And yet I'm opposed to private education. So there're a lot of practical difficulties. Not to mention money. I can't impose upon my family by insisting that they go and live in South Africa. But it's always been my objective to return.

I suppose if I hadn't left I would have gone to jail – unless my will had failed and I'd gone to the army. And either probably would have done me a lot of psychological damage. What has happened to me has been a process. By the time I left the country, I was quite committed to the struggle, but really my commitment wasn't so great. But after a few weeks abroad I began to itch for the old involvement. And my commitment has, if anything, grown over the years.

I don't feel any less committed to South Africa – for having been outside of it for thirteen years.

JOHN BASKIND
New York 1991

'Since I was sixteen the world was wrong, and I wasn't going to have any part in making it wronger.'

> For several years he used a great deal of ingenuity in trying to keep out of the clutches of the army. In the end the only way was to leave.

Everybody who turned sixteen in the school would be taken to the assembly hall and the army would arrive. That's where we had our initial physicals and determined which branch of the service we would have to go to when we finished matric. And I chose to go into commandos.

Commandos is like the American National Guard. You would do a month of training and then six months later do another three weeks, then you come back once a year for a month in camps. With commandos, you would have to do your initial period of service and then you could to all intents and purposes drop out of sight. There were three of us at school in Pietersburg in the Northern Transvaal who decided that commandos would probably give us the best ability to avoid service, so we thought. And in fact, that's how it turned out to be. We were in Kimberley during our basic training, and once we were in the army we learned how it was done.

Since I was sixteen the world was wrong, and I wasn't going to have any part in making it wronger. That's all. My whole life in South Africa, as an adult, eight years before I left, was concerned with trying to make the world right, if you like, and at the same time, keeping out of the clutches of the bloody army, because to me that was a kind of moral death. I knew damn well that there was a lot of nonsense about defending the country. We weren't defending the country against anything. Nobody was about to attack the country, it was too strong. And I knew that what it was all about was keeping apartheid in place.

So I did my basic camp, went to Wits University, and did my next camp in Port Alfred six months later; we ran up and down the dunes and played soldier in the bush for three weeks, which I have to say was a great deal of fun. So I had some fun and then I put the plan into action.

For a time the plan worked; he dropped out of sight, had various jobs, some connected with a theatre group, Phoenix Players. But the army eventually caught up with him. Then he feigned illness, but was found out, and sent with the army to Northern Namibia. There he witnessed assaults and brutality.

I found myself on guard duty from eleven o'clock straight until three o'clock which was the sort of graveyard shift, in the prison camp down the road in Oshakati. I was stationed above the interrogation tent. It was the most horrific thing I have ever experienced in my life, because really it was like the jaws of the devil. I mean, there was nothing I could do. I used to have to stand guard at night in the prison camp and during the day I was in the hospital. There one day they brought in this guy who I had to guard because they decided he was a terrorist. He was riding his bike home one night and some army kid had shot him three times in his buttocks. And so I had to sit there for a week and he would stare at me. He wouldn't say anything; he would just stare at me. He stared at me with such hate! And what to say, 'Look, I don't want to be here either?'

Next door to him was a kid who'd played with a phosphorus bomb. He was burned over seventy per cent of his body, third-degree burns, his penis had been burned away. He'd been blinded – a black child of about seven. He was just a mass of suppurating sores. His father was in the bed next to him. His father had tried to smother the burn. But phosphorus is a terrible thing. It just eats into your flesh and just keeps going and his whole chest was covered with third degree burns. This kid was being kept alive with pipes and . . . I mean he was completely . . . there was nothing left of him except a brain and he would cry all the time. They – the soldiers – used to just roll phosphorus grenades out to the kids, say, 'Come, play!'

I got back in September 1976, and I couldn't get a job.

The army started chasing him again.

If there'd been an ECC in those years, I would have known that there were other people in the same boat. It wouldn't have been such a terrifying thing. But everybody that I knew had found some way to accommodate the situation. I just . . . I couldn't do it. If, by virtue of the colour of my skin, I had to be involved in that kind of criminality, I couldn't. I wasn't going to do it, I just wasn't going to do it. The penalty then was five years; and I was just too frightened to go to jail. In a lot of ways, since then I've regretted that I didn't.

If I had been able to rationalise my life as a South African, like so many of my family have been able to do, I could have rationalised my way into believing in the communist menace. But I never could – none of it! It was a lie, and by the time I was seventeen or eighteen, I'd become convinced that ninety per cent of what I was being fed was a bunch of nonsense. Ja.

I was beginning to feel absolutely hemmed in. I didn't know what to do, and I did not want to leave. I'd grown up in Rooiberg in the bush there, I had wanted to come to Jo'burg and work in music. I'd been able to do that for a while, and I was happy. I had my life and I didn't want to go and change it. I just didn't know what to do. I didn't have any money and I didn't know how to get out, and I couldn't go to Botswana to the ANC, because I believed that they wouldn't want me there once I'd been in the army. I didn't know what the hell to do.

So I became a Zionist! And I went to work for the *Zionist Record*, selling ads. I worked for them for about three months; and . . . the second month, I experienced a conversion, as it were, and decided that I was going to become a Zionist pioneer and go and live in Israel. There was good reason for this conversion – the Zionist Fed. would pay your ticket to Israel. So I did it, and they gave me a ticket and I left. And February 1978, a week after I left, my call-up papers arrived.

So I went to Israel. I was going to live the socialist ideal. And it actually was. I don't know whether it could be replicated anywhere else, but it works on a kibbutz. So I was there, and I met Julie, and we decided that we were going to get married. And just at that moment my mother phoned and said, 'Come home, your father's dying.'

My father died and I was almost paralysed at being back; and where am I going now? So we decided Julie'd come and stay for the summer and then we were going to go back to Israel. But her parents – they're American – got really upset with her for wanting to marry me, because I was a farmer and because I was South African and they had never met me, so we came here. And I thought it would take six months and we'd be out! [Laughs] That was ten years ago.

It took six months to get a job – at Carnegie Hall. I started off as the office manager and nine months later, I was programming concerts at the hall and producing their fancy concert opera series, and was given my own series to produce, fifty-two concerts! So better than Israel! [Laughs] And what's the difference? I mean I wasn't home, so what the hell!

In 1985 I started an organisation called the World Music Institute which presents concerts of other cultures. It's financed by state support and by grants from individuals and by membership. For the last three years, I ran a thing called the Jazz Composers' Orchestra Association, which worked in new, experimental, improvised music focusing mostly on Africa. And I set up a company to do that on a commercial basis here. I'm working with Blythe Mbityana, who's also an ANC member here in New York, and we're planning a school for kind of hands-on training in music and in theatre arts and so on. We'd like to set it up somewhere at home, and so we've started looking for funding for that and hopefully we'll get it and we'll be able to go and do it.

I miss South Africa terribly; maybe it's because I grew up in the bush. I didn't really ever adjust to living in America; I always felt like a foreigner. I am lucky that I have a community to live with here that are South Africans, that I do relate to. But, ja.

In a funny way, nobody really has a stake in America; everybody's immigrant and there's no real root. There's no real basis for who you are. I know I'm a South African, I know I am. Americans don't necessarily know they're Americans and they hate each other virulently. And the only thing that I regret about the work I've done is that I haven't been able to do it at home.

Freedom of expression is something I've learned the value of. I've learned how good it is to be able to say exactly what you want to whom you want to and not have any fear of a knock on the door. That's an amazing thing, and that's something that I would hope will some day grow at home.

And working with the few people who I know in the ANC here has taught me something else. I've had a kind of fellowship, I suppose comradeship in the real sense of the word, that I have experienced very rarely in my life. As my friend Enoch says, we've proved that we can live together here and there's no reason that we can't do it there. We depend on each other totally. I just never had that there, I had to find it here. [Laughs]

Last February when the big day came I phoned my brother in South Africa and he gave me the de Klerk speech off radio as it was coming from parliament. It was morning here. I cried all day. I walked around the streets of Soho where I was working and just cried. I just . . . I didn't know why I was crying. I thought I'm so happy that things are finally . . . But it wasn't happiness. It was just . . . so many years of bitterness and anger and everything, just pouring out. I was walking around, just . . . people looked at me as if I was completely mad, which they do in New York. You know, you've got to conform, you never know who the next nutter is. And then when Mandela finally went free, I was sitting right there, from about six o'clock in the morning, waiting to see what was going. It was a real catharsis of so much pain.

The next day, I started thinking, gee this is a nice place! I'd never thought that before, I'd always been bound up with this: Got to go home and this is temporary, and that kind of feeling. Now it's different, I feel free-er, I breathe and think it looks good here, with interesting places to go. I'd never thought in those terms. I had always been stuck in the bitterness of the way I had to leave home. And ja. So now it's not a bad place to be actually, New York. Now that I'm going to leave! [Laughs]

So I'm planning to go back – no question. It's where I'm from. New York's a great town and it's as hard as hell. It's full of exotic, wild, interesting people. But Jo'burg – with all the problems and all the running away and all the hiding – is a fantastic place. Jo'burg's got more energy than New York; it hums, it's buzzing, it really is a cusp. In South Africa culture has always been the vanguard for change. It's always been music and art that's carried the message. That's traditionally African, that your message is carried through music. I think that there's real work to be done there, and I hope that I'm going to be able to get a chance to do it.

Artists in Exile

The source of material for artists is in the immediacy of their surroundings. The substance of their work grows out of the language, the sounds, the landscapes. No other occupation is based so specifically within the context of place.

> The problem of being in exile is that one is away from the material basis of one's imagination. You need to be in that bus, to hear that phrase being used by a people quarrelling or laughing or whatever. You need to be near a factory to hear those little things that set the imagination flying. Those images that one encounters when one is walking about, those gestures, that laughter – you miss all that when you live in exile. Using a certain language, you miss a situation in which you are interacting with the new developments in that language.
>
> Ngugi wa Thiong'o, during a discussion on the role of culture in the African revolution

The exiled artists took with them the images of their own town and country, the local idiom and the songs of the streets. But locality is the substance, language is the essence; and both are part of what has been left behind. And memory can be a misleading source, for memory is stabilised at the time of departure; the trees grow, the aspect changes. More than in normal societies apartheid, through its grand plan of total separation, bulldozed towns, transformed landscapes, shifted three and a half million people into the Bantustans. The exiled painter or photographer has never seen the massed settlements of KwaNdabele, the exiled writer has never heard the women's voices around the communal taps in the region of Dimbaza; the exiled journalist can write about the situation, but has never been inside Sun City, or witnessed the destruction of Crossroads.

> Of course one might say you do take your languages with you wherever you go – but it is rather like carrying the bones of your

ancestors with you in a bag: they are white with silence, they do not
talk back.

Breyten Breytenbach, *Random Remarks on Freedom and Exile*,
Paris, 1972

In the Sixties a number of talented young writers and musicians,
mainly from Johannesburg's black townships, left South Africa in search
of opportunities to utilise and to improve their skills. For many of them,
this was a fatally destructive experience.

Some of them stayed in neighbouring countries – Botswana, Swaziland –
where the rural life provided no scope for their urbanised, sophisticated culture. A few went to Britain or America to study, where some of
them succumbed to the depression of alienation, the inability to identify
with a different country and culture, and simple homesickness and loneliness. It was a time when the Western world was unreceptive to music,
writings and art from Africa. It had 'discovered' the bronzes of Benin,
but it did not recognise the validity of contemporary work or appreciate
the painting and the music for what today is most prized – its ethnicity.
The small South African exile community lacked support structures. The
ANC operated from Morogoro in Tanzania. In London, even more in
New York, the exiled artist was a stranger among strangers; some died
young, through alcohol, suicide, or by simply losing the will to live.

For those who survived, exile bestowed rewards. Jazz musicians were
among the most successful. Being an abstract art, music did not depend
so intensely on the immediacy of the local scene. They had opportunities
for study that had been denied to them at home, and they were able to
meld the influences of Western music with their own cultural patterns.

The situation gradually changed as the exile community grew, and as
the anti-apartheid movements began to focus world attention on South
Africa. The artists were no longer so isolated. Many worked in communities and with local populations, as in the Medu ensemble in Botswana.
They became 'cultural workers', attuned more closely now to the cultural
upsurge within South Africa where especially in poetry and the theatre
resistance to apartheid fired work of great vitality and originality. Cultural
festivals – Culture and Resistance in Botswana in 1982, CASA (Culture
in Another South Africa) in Amsterdam in 1987, and Zabalaza in London
in 1990 – brought artists from all disciplines within South Africa
together with the exiled artists from countries all over the world. They
strengthened the bonds between inside and out and established the vital
importance of the arts in the struggle against apartheid.

Exiled artists succeeded in making a mark on the world stage. But the
price was high, and the greatest loss in the end was not to individual
artists but to the South African people. Exiled writers drawing on their
experiences of South Africa were banned; their work could not be
published or circulated in South Africa. Thus a new generation of

writers, journalists and poets were robbed of knowledge of the work of
their immediate predecessors; there was a break of continuity in development, a void where the stories of Alex la Guma, the poems of Dennis
Brutus, the biographies of Bloke Modisane and Todd Matshikiza should
have been; while for three decades the banned writers, poets, playwrights, musicians, photographers and other artists were removed from
their vital source, and dispersed throughout the world.

ESMÉ MATSHIKIZA
London 1991

'Exile inflicted a great tragedy on me and my family by taking Todd
away. We miss him to this day, and ever will.'

> Her husband, Todd, was a gifted musician and writer who died in
> exile in 1968. His account of coming into exile is in his book
> *Chocolates for My Wife*, first published in 1961 and banned in
> South Africa. It has recently been republished by David Philip,
> South Africa.

My educational background is Methodist missionary; Todd's was Anglican missionary, with Lovedale and Fort Hare thrown in – which is a
very English traditional education that we had, all the way through. We
met in Johannesburg when I was a student of social work.

Todd studied music formally at Adams College in Natal. He comes
from a long line of a musical family. His great-grandfather was a great
dancer, a kind of witchdoctor dancer, who was extremely well known in
that part of the Cape. The word 'Matshikiza' in fact means 'the Dancer';
'Ukutshikize' is to dance; and 'Umatshikiza' is 'the One who Dances'. So
with his reputation as a great dancer he used to attract people for miles
around; and was given the name which has become the family name.

The whole family is extremely musical. His older brother, Mickley
'Fingers' Matshikiza, was a highly recognised jazz musician in the
Cape. He taught Todd the piano and introduced him to jazz, so that
before he went to college he already had a musical background not just
of classical music, but also of jazz. And he listened to a lot of American
jazz music, so he was influenced by black American musicians. His father
was a church organist in Queenstown, so the church also had an influence on his development.

We got married three years after we met, and we had our daughter
fourteen months later, and then our son, John, two and a half years after
that. The year before John was born the South African government
passed the Bantu Education Act, 1953, and this was the point at which

we decided that we had to try and get away from South Africa. We knew that we could not possibly let our children go through that system. All kinds of ideas came into our heads – Botswana, Rhodesia, Swaziland, but nothing actually gelled. We didn't do anything. Then came *King Kong*.

King Kong was a musical based on the true life story of a boxer, Ezekial Dhlamini, nicknamed King Kong because of his size and lethal punch. Gangsterism was a feature of township life, and gangsters always attended boxing tournaments. They also attended jazz concerts and dances. King Kong fell foul of the gangsters and was sentenced to life imprisonment for killing a girl who had stood him up for a gangster. In the dock he demanded the death sentence; and not long after being imprisoned, drowned himself in the prison farm dam. From this material, the musical King Kong was created.

With Todd as the exception, the production team was all white, the performing team all black. Todd wrote all the music, but except for two numbers, was excluded from writing the lyrics and the musical arrangements. He was a great poet and a much respected journalist, and had been a teacher of English at Lovedale College for many years. But with the exception of the overture, 'Sad Times, Bad Times', and the song 'In The Queue' – both in Xhosa – he was not given the chance to write any of the lyrics. Race prejudice is not the exclusive preserve of the Afrikaner and the Nationalist government.

The production, which opened to segregated audiences in the Great Hall, at Witwatersrand University in February 1959, was ecstatically received. It then toured the country for about a year, receiving rave reviews wherever it went. In 1960, Todd collaborated in another musical production, *Mkhumbane*, staged in Durban. And two months later we left for London and exile – permanent for him. *King Kong* had made us a bit of money, so we were able to pay for the tickets.

London, May 1960 – a real life fairy tale. Strange. You walk in the street and nobody seems to wonder what you're doing here. You're called Sir and Madam. You can walk into any restaurant, any pub, and order what you like; into any clothes or shoe store and try on anything. No Whites-only buses or trains or park benches. Not even an 11 p.m. curfew? You're not forced to carry a pass and produce it on demand. You can go to a nightclub or visit friends undisturbed.

The magic of Piccadilly Circus and Eros – who in those days had heard of drug dealers, junkies, rent-boys or the homeless youths? The wonder of Soho and its night-life where London never sleeps. The theatre, cinema, opera, all unsegregated. Our children being able to sit in a Lyons Corner House restaurant, swivelling around on bar stools, little legs flying free, undisturbed. The underground train system – now that really was an extraordinary experience, being confused at interchange stations. How do I know which direction I'm going in? Or where on earth I am? Deeply mysterious and puzzling, but exciting. Arthur Letele, the Secretary General of the ANC, took the Tube to call on us during his first visit to London, travelling everywhere with a compass – it didn't help him. He couldn't understand why he was travelling east on the Northern Line.

This was London in the spring and summer of 1960, a time when there was full employment, and bus drivers and others with required skills were still being recruited from the Caribbean, and blacks still felt welcome. Among the many strange sights were white men, faces covered with black coal dust, bent double under the weight of coal-filled bags; or white labourers, covered in mud and grime, working on building sites. Or to become aware, while sitting on a bus or train, of a particular kind of body smell which back home was called a 'native smell', when we were the only blacks there and we knew that was not emanating from us.

We felt happy and relaxed and unfettered and unghettoed for the first time in our lives. You will not understand. You have not had our particular kind of South African experience.

So those were magical days in London. Both children adjusted easily to school. Marion was eight, and soon her teacher was comparing her work with that of her class mates, wondering why an African child, straight from 'out there', should speak, read and write so much better English than some of the natives.

But house-hunting was something else. So was job-hunting. Todd had one disappointment after another. He had a job lined up at the BBC. But he took an ANC concert party to perform at the independence celebrations in Algeria; and when he came back they asked him why he had gone to Algeria, and told him the job was off. A bitter blow, from which he never recovered. He did part-time work for them, and the odd freelancing journalistic work. Our many English friends were helpful and supportive; but there was nothing for someone like Todd in a cultural environment where the school or university to which you went determined the type of job you were, or were not, able to do. This was Britain of the 1960s – warm and welcoming and available at one level, totally insular at another. Todd could not adjust to this culture, nor could he be reconciled to exile. His soul started to die then.

His cultural environment was totally different and foreign to the cultural, musical environment here in Britain – to anything that people understand here. If Todd had lived, he would be far better understood now than he was then. Then the musical world was dominated by people who had never really understood, or tried to take in influences from other people's music – music from other cultures. Now young people on radio and television are very heavily influenced by the Far East, by India, and particularly by Africa in the past few years. They would have understood what Todd was all about. And I think he would have worked in a very much happier cultural environment.

The process of decline accelerated when we moved to Zambia in 1964. It became clear to him that home, as he knew it, was left behind when we left South Africa intending to return after a few years. Events had overtaken us all, and what had begun to be set in motion was threatening to change the country for ever.

Todd was born before his time. It is conceivable that, if he were alive today, his music would at least be understood and appreciated by serious students of contemporary music. And that he would feel encouraged to be creative in a way he found impossible in the 1960s. Yet I say this with reservation – I'm not sure how well he would take to the present climate of ruthless exploitation, particularly of African art and music.

He became more and more upset. He lost . . . he didn't lose his musical ability, his ear or feel for music. But the ground wasn't fertile for his kind of imagination, and didn't take any root whatsoever. His imagination used to be quite, quite colourful – he was a very colourful, very interesting and very talented writer. And a very talented musician. He really lived his writing and his music. But in Britain it was a totally different culture, and he simply couldn't find root. So it was a great excitement for us to be able to go back to Africa, to go to Zambia. And we felt that we are back home. Almost.

But it isn't home. [Laughs] Although we got on extremely well with the Zambians, again Todd, culturally . . . his music and writing simply was not what he was able to project or bring forth from himself in a place like Zambia. He worked for the Zambia Broadcasting Corporation, and he did quite a good job at that – a very good job. He's still, to this day, very well remembered and well loved for the work he did for Radio Zambia. But it wasn't easy at all. And very very gradually, Todd went into decline. Because he just missed home.

He was drinking. Yes, he just missed home. Then one brother who was very, very close to him, died, was killed by lightning in the Cape. And then his older brother, the one who had been his jazz mentor, also died. And Todd just went into steep decline after that. He just couldn't bear the thought that he was never going to see his brothers again, and maybe that he was never going to see home again. And when he was on his death bed, he just kept imagining that he was back in Queenstown – all the time he was just back home. He really pined for it. He really wanted to be back home. He died in Zambia in 1968. A most powerful experience for the children and myself.

I stayed on in Zambia, and later married a Namibian and went with him to Namibia. I left there in 1983 – I needed to get away. I didn't want to live there any more. I could not endure the political and the personal circumstances. So I came to Britain. I was divorced at the end of 1984. Since then I have been living and working in London, as a social worker for the London Borough of Lambeth. My daughter is married to a Congolese and lives there. And John came as a student in 1974 and has never really left London.

Our children are what they are today because London enabled them to develop their personalities fully, without the constraints imposed by South Africa's race laws. They had the opportunity to compete on an equal basis with their peers within a fair system. Given the inequalities with which the society is now riddled, things might appear different. But in the 1960s they were able to prove the obvious, that colour is no barrier to learning or to achievement.

But exile inflicted a great tragedy on me and my family, by taking Todd away. We miss him to this day, and ever will. But my mind has been considerably broadened since I left the stuffy, destructive confines of our apartheid prison in May 1960. Exile has opened my mind to the best and the worst of other cultures. I am satisfied with my children's and grand-children's development. They are able to stand up for themselves.

WALLY SEROTE
London 1990

'Exile is an assault on creativity.'

He grew up in Alexandra Township, a black ghetto nine miles outside Johannesburg. Alexandra was almost unique in the age of apartheid; its residents could buy and own property in freehold – which was impossible virtually outside the Bantustans. It grew as black people came from the rural areas to work in the towns, bringing with them their community traditions, their extended families, their sense of independence.

He recalls the political rallies in Freedom Square led by Chief Luthuli and other ANC leaders. And the bus boycotts, when the bus company, PUTCO, with the only transport into Johannesburg, put up the fares by one penny, and the people of Alexandra walked nine miles to work every morning and nine miles back for six weeks rather than pay that extra penny, starting as early as four o'clock in the morning. Whites living in the suburbs that lined the main road to Alex – Louis Botha Avenue – would wake to hear the shuffle of thousands of feet in paper-stuffed, worn out shoes passing by their suburban gardens. But nobody rode the buses until the old fare was restored.

He is a poet and a novelist.

For me, the fondest memory of Alexandra is weekend when there was this continuous buzz of music – the throb of music throughout its length and breadth.

Music was practised very fervently in Alex. The influence came from the Afro-Americans especially, although musicians also found their own bases – Morabi, Mbatlanga and many other forms.

We had a weekend which began on Friday. It was a continuous moment of celebration when people were not going to work, were with their families; and within the community and part of the community. The whole of Alexandra buzzed with music – record players, live performances both traditional and modern, choirs which were organised for birthday parties, for weddings, for funerals.

But of course there is another side to Alexandra – abject poverty, crowded houses, where a family of thirteen people live in one room, throat to throat with each other. Unemployment was very high, crime was very high, the apartheid system manifesting itself through Pass Laws and the repressive machineries of the state, the police. Alexandra was a very very poor ghetto.

One of the teachers at school absolutely captivated my imagination. He read novels and poems to us. He related this to our daily lives. It became very clear to me that this is what writing is about – about how people live. I remember telling my mother that, when I left school, I wanted to be a writer.

I was fortunate. I had begun to have friends in the white suburbs, which means I had crossed racial barriers and also had access to their books. I became sharply conscious of the contrasts, and I could not answer why it was so except to keep saying: Some people are white, some are black. Those who are black are relegated to this dustbin of life. Those who are white must have the best. And deeply in me this was absolutely unacceptable. One must do something to fight against this. At that time, I really committed myself to the idea that the only way to do this was through writing. I wrote a lot – poetry, short stories, essays – which never were published.

I was young – nineteen, an age in the township where, whether you like it or not, you are forced to make a decision. Many of my friends made decisions which eventually destroyed them – became professional thieves, learned ways of killing people, became part of the street. I was part of the street, but my point of reference was different. I had this craving for writing, craving for knowledge. And fortunately it was accessible.

I really lived in two worlds. During the day I would be there at the university in the white suburbs, reading. At night, I would come back to my friends and we would go to the shebeens and actually live the life of the township.

I worked in the underground of the ANC at that early age; and of course we were arrested eventually, in 1969 under the Terrorism Act, Section 6, which meant indefinite detention. It's another story that. I spent many months in detention. I was interrogated, I was tortured. I was in solitary confinement. The only social contact that I had was with the Security Branch. I was aware that every contact that they made with me was a deliberate, conscious action to destroy anything that was human in me.

I remember at one point realising that I had been standing, not going to the toilet, not eating, I realised that the people who were interrogating me had changed their clothes; they were wearing different suits; they were smelling fresh. I must have been there for several days without being aware.

Under those conditions certain senses seem to become more developed. One is very keenly aware of the meaning of different sounds, for instance, and they tell you what is happening around your cell with absolute precision. When I heard the sound of a truck, I knew that there were pass offenders being brought to prison. I would take the toilet bucket to the window to climb up and watch as they come out of the truck, as they have to undress in the yard outside. As they searched every little part of them, made them dance, the Tauza dance. This went on for – what? three, four, five hours.

This makes one understand what apartheid is; the fact that I was in prison, that I had to witness hundreds and hundreds of people each day who were being criminalised the way they were, who were being brutalised, beaten, searched in their private parts in broad daylight. And this was legal! So one finds ways and means to survive under those conditions.

One resisted to the last. But in the end, they recruited me. All they say is, 'Well, you buy your freedom. If you are going to work with us, we'll set you free. If you don't agree, we'll keep you here until you die.' They used to bring me in and out only to say this; many times. At one point I said to them, 'I have no problem, I'll work for you. I agree, I'll work for you.' And I thought, if I get out of here, the first thing that I do I go to the reporters and tell them why I am out.

But then, first day passed; second day passed; third day passed. I changed my mind. I said, 'No no no. I must not do this, because I know now what they are doing. I can't be responsible for bringing anyone else to this condition. I would like to be a free person. But if it means doing that, I'm sorry I can't.'

I left Swanepoel's office, after having told him there is no way that I can work for him; and having to accept the fact that I may be in solitary confinement for the coming five, six, seven years – wondering in my mind what that meant. And trying to come to terms with it, and the thought that I may never be a free person again.

I believed they might keep me forever. There was nothing to tell me that they wouldn't. Absolutely nothing. When I was there, Benjamin Ramotse – one of the stalwarts of the African National Congress – had been there three years. Some comrades from SWAPO had been there four, five years – nobody even knew that they were there. There was even somebody from Tanzania, I don't know how he arrived there, he was already beginning to speak Zulu, Afrikaans; and he was there three, four years. So I believed this was my fate.

The day they released me, I went through the process of signing documents, getting your belt, getting your shoes back. This had happened before. But this man walks outside and says, 'You can go home.' I was absolutely startled. I stood there. I did not know what to do. I thought, perhaps they want to kill me; it is not possible that I'm free. But then something told me the best thing is to run the fastest way home – if you don't reach, just too bad.

So this is what I did. I was not ready to go out, I was unkempt. I remember how people looked at me – I must have absolutely looked like a mad man. I carried my suitcase and there I was, running from Commissioner Street, to North Street to catch a bus and go home. As I was running, somebody recognised me, and gave me a lift, and took me home. [Laughs]

I wanted to work in theatre with Barney Simon, and Barney got a scholarship for me at Colombia University – this was nine months after I'd been released. I applied for a passport. They refused. Time after time I applied, they refused. Then one day, for no apparent reason, they gave it me, and I left.

For three years I was in New York. First I tried to study writing; but discovered that in fact I couldn't learn anything about writing. I had done as much as I could in writing. I was already a published writer by then. The only thing that was left for me is to know what I wanted to write about, and I was not going to learn that in any university. So I switched on to film-making which I really enjoyed. I studied film-making at the University of Colombia.

I was coming into contact with African-Americans and understanding their condition. I also began to understand the role of America in the world. If there is any education that I got there, it was that.

Before I left South Africa I had read extensively about America, so I knew where I was going. But knowing and actually experiencing are two different things. The experience was very traumatic – to see how such a highly industrialised capitalised country can devastate people; reduce them to thinking about nothing else but themselves as individuals, and relating only to the dollar. This is how life is led to a very large extent. This is the cruelty of America, where people become deaf, blind and mute to other people; where the only relationships they make are relationships linked with the dollar. This is what people live for. Nothing else.

After my three years in the US, I went to Botswana. I could have stayed in the US for ever, but I made a conscious decision that I must leave because of the events at home – the 16 June 1976 events. My intention was to start a film company and begin to explore Southern Africa in terms of film-making, which I saw could give access to peoples across language barriers and the divisions created by the bantustans.

In Botswana, there was a large number of young students who had just crossed from South Africa, and these kids had nothing to do; they were there in the streets. And because of this, there was beginning to develop a very negative relation between South Africans and the Botswana. I started a theatre group – there were about four of us. We called in all these young people and discussed with them their experiences from the 16 June uprising. We also discussed our vision of what we wanted to do. The first play that we produced explored the events of 16 June, and tried to project into the future what would happen.

Once the play was produced, we were faced by another thing. Botswana does not have infrastructure for theatre. How are we going to take this play to the schools, to tour the villages and the towns of Botswana? Which then led us to think that instead of just doing a theatre production, we should be thinking about creating an organisation which can address different aspects of cultural production. The first organisation that emerged we called the Pelindaba Cultural Unit. 'Pelindaba' means 'We are finished talking'. We moved into action.

We divided this organisation into various art forms. We said we'd deal with film, photography, theatre, painting, writing, dance and music. It became a very big organisation. The first funds we got were from the IUEF based in Geneva; they gave us about . . . what? Ten thousand pula or something. That was the outfit in which Craig Williamson was operating. We did not know then . . . but they gave us money to rent premises, to buy a Kombi for transport, to equip ourselves with basic administrative requirements.

But political problems began to emerge among ourselves. ANC, PAC, BC were meeting in this cultural organisation. We could not contradict the positions of the ANC, other people could not align themselves to the ANC, so the split happened. We wanted this organisation to do several things: engage us in cultural work that will contribute to the struggle; and create proper relations between us and the local people. We needed people who were qualified, who had training; and the only way to do this was to incorporate the ex-patriate community there, because among them were people with the necessary skills.

It worked out very well. So in the new group, which was called Medu Art Ensemble, we had South Africans, Botswana, and ex-patriates from the US, Europe and other places, and people from other African states. For the first time we were consciously, and in an organised manner, trying to identify the relationship between politics and cultural work. It kept us a united force.

Medu Art Ensemble started in 1978, with about eighty people. We were able to experiment in various art forms. We started a journal through which we wrote about political and cultural issues, and about the regional arts. We could not start in filming, because it is so expensive. We were able to travel the length and breadth of Botswana, and even overspilled into Zambia and other countries nearby where we took our productions. We were beginning to enter Southern Africa in an organised manner, searching for solutions to our problems, and looking for what we did not know about those countries, because South Africa had been so cut off from the rest of Africa. Medu gave us access.

Consistently we produced, experimented. This built confidence among us. But we felt that it was very important for us to address one major issue: how do we link with cultural workers in South Africa? It was this thought that brought about what I think was a very important event. We organised a festival-seminar in 1982 in July under the title 'Culture and Resistance'.

There was a great response from inside South Africa. About a thousand cultural workers from different parts of South Africa, from different art forms, came to this ... a thousand, yes! Black and white. In addition, South African exiles came from Europe, the USA, and neighbouring African countries. We raised two questions there: how can we ensure that cultural work becomes part and parcel of struggle? and how can the cultural boycott be intensified?

By about 1984, our work in Botswana was entering a different phase. The signal for this was that one night, in a house where our comrades stayed, a bomb exploded. It was followed by a car bomb which killed one of our comrades and then that massive South African Defence Force raid into Botswana, when twelve people were killed – nine ANC activists, one Basotho and two Botswana.

At the time of that raid, I was not in Gaberone. When I came back, very early in the morning – about three in the morning I drove into a roadblock put up by the Botswana Defence Force. They told me that there had been a raid. Within an hour I knew exactly who had died, which houses had been hit. And of course, very very dear comrades that I knew very well, whom I'd worked with, had been killed.

In 1983 I had become head of the ANC Department of Arts and Culture which gave priority to internal mobilisation in culture – that was why I was working from Botswana. But after the raid it was very obvious, for our survival, we had to reconsider. I was posted to London as cultural attaché in the ANC office.

One of the main questions that had to be dealt with was the cultural boycott. A new situation had arisen in South Africa; a culture of resistance. An anti-apartheid culture had begun flourishing, with powerful plays and poetry, and with groups coming to perform in the Western world. The boycott was not directed against them. How was it then to operate? Who would make the choices?

These were among a wide range of problems that were discussed in Amsterdam in 1987 at the CASA Conference – Culture in Another South Africa – which brought exiled South African writers, poets, artists, playwrights, choirs, every field of cultural activity, together with 150 cultural activists from within South Africa itself. And among the things that people discussed outside the formal sessions was one of great interest to me personally – what happens to the writers, painters, actors, film-makers and photographers when they try to carry on their work in conditions of exile?

Maybe I look at it from the art form that I'm more familiar with, which is writing. Although I'm known primarily as a poet, I've always written essays, short stories, articles, plays; and I've written a novel. When I was working on the novel, *To Every Birth Its Blood*, I depended a lot on memory. I wanted to locate it within an environment that I knew best: Alexandra. I was very troubled, knowing that Alexandra was in the process of being drastically changed, that demolishing and caterpillar tractors were always present. Which corner is still at the same place where I left it? I did not know. Which house, which tree, which street-light? So you worry . . . you write, and you feel extremely worried that you may not be reflecting the actual geographical situation. That's one aspect.

Another is that people also change. When I left the United States and got to Botswana, I met these young people from the age of thirteen and maybe the oldest being . . . what? twenty, twenty-six? I realised something had changed about young people from South Africa, I did not know what it was. These 'June Sixteeners', really young boys and girls, are people who had been face to face with death continuously, had confronted the hippos, had dodged the bullets; thrown stones against people armed with guns; had had to sleep anywhere, everywhere, because they were in hiding.

These were people who had been tempered almost by war. They did not recognise the rules that we still adhered to. This is what I had to deal with, to understand – that in one way or the other, the culture, tradition, temper of my people had changed because of the struggle that they'd entered. Even if we were there on the spot, it would take very long to absorb, explore, understand and then produce material on this, even if we lived minute to minute with it. I know that I was very confident when I sat and wrote *To Every Birth Its Blood*. I don't have the same confidence if I approach a novel now. I feel that if I were living at home, I would listen once. But now I have to listen five times to make sure that what I'm hearing is correct. I'm making up for the distance between me and the life of my people.

So exile is an assault on creativity. It's very criminal to be in exile. And of course, the full blame for this goes on to the apartheid system which forced us out.

The ANC has made it possible for me to keep close contact with South Africa by meeting people from home. It has given me the chance to understand the issues of people in exile. So being an ANC activist has been also a continuous important education. But I cannot remove the fact that I know that I should have been an ANC member living in South Africa. I would be much richer if it were so.

So it is fortunate that somehow, in ourselves, we know that we can go back there. And many of us who are creative people are contemplating this. I'm sure, many times we are thinking about this, how we are going to handle it. Because of the stature of the ANC, we have had access to different parts of the world. We have learnt a lot from other parts of the world, and this is what we are taking back to our country.

We'll make up. I think the conditions are right for that. We will be able to make up. I think so.

JONAS GWANGWA
London 1991

'The evolution of music, of our culture in general, has been greatly affected by apartheid. There's been an onslaught on the culture of our people inside South Africa.'

A musician and South Africa's best-known composer. He composed the music for the Attenborough film *Cry Freedom*; for *Destructive Engagement*; *Land of Dreams*; *South African Blues*; and many others.

I was one of the products of Father Huddleston, from whom I got my first instrument. Trevor Huddleston was at St Peter's School, and there we formed the Huddleston Jazz Band. Then St Peter's was closed down, and I transferred to another school which was in what was called Western Native township, next to Sophiatown, and that way I was able now to meet professional musicians over the weekends. And that's how I got exposed to show business.

I started playing with singers. I was picked up by a group called the Boston Brothers, they wanted me as a back-up horn player, which opened up a whole lot of avenues for me. Domake, the composer, he had a group then called the Jazz Dazzlers, and he incorporated me into the Jazz Dazzlers where I met the big guys, Kipi Moketsi, Mzala, Zoltlas, all the people. That was how I got launched into the business itself.

You couldn't make much of a career of music in South Africa because it was not regarded as a job. You were a vagrant because you didn't have anybody signing your pass, so most of the musicians had day jobs, except, of course, the Jazz Dazzlers. They did not take any day jobs, they were full-time musicians. But it was very difficult, it was very hard. I managed because I was still living with my parents. I started getting more into music, playing nightclubs. Once in a while you know you would play a nightclub – white nightclubs. You wouldn't even do a run of a week; you'll have just a day, and that's it.

We had formed another group, Jazzapiso, with Kipi, Dollar Brand, Hugh Mackay, Joe Ncwana, and Johnny Gatse. There was to be a festival in Switzerland and they wanted some musicians from South Africa. So we were picked to go out there. We rehearsed in Cape Town for this Switzerland thing and we really got one of the best jazz groups at that time. The festival unfortunately fell through.

Jazzapiso had to disband because of the State of Emergency after Sharpeville, when no more than five Africans were supposed to be seen together. Well we were already six, so we were illegal [Laughs] . . . we were already illegal, ja, without even performing. I remained with Kipi and Dollar Brand when the Emergency was lifted. But then the musical *King Kong* came about. I was in the orchestra in the first run in Johannesburg, and when the show came to Britain, I came with it. So I left South Africa years ago. I left the show here after about five months and went to the United States to study. I had acquired this scholarship to the Manhattan School of Music, New York.

I was very excited about going to the United States, but it wasn't what I thought it was, of course. Hugh Masekela was there, and they received me at the airport . . . there were automatic doors and that puzzled me a bit [laughs] – I was impressed. But then the taxi went through Harlem and right there . . . phew! It was like deflating. This is America! Ja, it's a slum, you know. I said, 'Ah! So this is New York?' [Laughs]

I adjusted gradually; I liked the place there, but it wasn't very easy as a student; I went through some hardships there, and with my health also. My passport had expired – that time they used to give us one year, and you have to apply every year through the Consulate. I just stayed on. I was playing in groups. I was writing, composing, arranging, that's when I did Belafonte's album, which was a Grammy Award winner, with Belafonte and Makeba – I arranged and conducted that. I also did *Pata Pata* with Miriam which was a big hit; and I went into various things, I even started directing some dancers. I had a group of my own. I wrote some music for a play, for Brown College, and I just kept on, finding out different fields. It kept me. But it was not like that all the time. It was sparse and far between.

I could not move, you see, because I did not have a valid document or even a visa to stay. I was advised by Immigration to apply for asylum which they refused, but I just stayed on. So Miriam Makeba, who had been in touch and working with the Guinea government, organised something and I got a Guinean passport.

Then in 1976, I was invited to do a national tour of Botswana, and at the end of the tour I decided to stay on. Just said, 'No, I'm staying behind.' I hadn't seen my mother those fifteen years I'd been gone, my daughter . . . so I regularised my papers in Botswana and stayed on.

And then there came more ANC activity. In 1977, there was this big festival in Nigeria, Festaka, and the ANC was invited. Contingents of students, professionals, choir singers, dancers, poets, writers, musicians, were invited from all corners of the world, all of them exiles. We all go to Nigeria. But this was so big an occasion that I suggested that we make one show that had all of these singers, dancers and musicians, all these different disciplines, ja. Put them into one show. Thabo Mbeki was leading the delegation, and he said, 'Well, OK then, we will listen to Jonas here. We will put him in charge.' So I put together this programme, making a show. It was difficult! [Laughs] It was difficult, just having to explain it, because you're not dealing with professionals – even the poets were there. But we succeeded, and we made the show.

It was a very powerful success. We toured Nigeria, Tanzania and Zambia. Then it was decided in the ANC that there should be a standing group, a cultural group in the Movement. I was called back to draft a memorandum for forming a Cultural Department. I was working with Lindiwe Mabuza. Then in 1978, there was this Student and Youth Festival, a World Festival in Havana; and a contingent went out to Cuba to represent the ANC. We assumed the name that we had used when we came from Nigeria, Amandla. In 1980 it was felt by the young musicians that the music was not indigenous; they wanted something that was more South African, and I was called to come and give direction to the music. I realised that there was some talent, latent talent here, so I decided I've got to make a show. I've got to create something theatrical. So I went back to what I had done in Nigeria: that format where we started choreographing dancers, and then we had some poetry and choir and songs. And I put together this thing, wrote a little script; and we have the present day Amandla. To this day, Amandla has toured about thirty-four countries, ja; and doing something like between ten and twenty cities in each country.

Amandla performed in documentary style – just the history of the struggle and the history of the ANC. And so some facts stay that way. It's just in presentation that we embellish that a little bit. What changes is towards the end, where we keep abreast with what is happening inside the country.

Amandla is growing. Now it's not strictly a musical, it is not a musical review, it's just unique, in its own slot. But we refer quite a bit to what is happening at home and try to get people who have some fresh ideas. I've been adding in traditional dances as we get new members, try and ask people who have just come from home, what kind of dances they know, and how we can incorporate them; because we have this medley of traditional dances at the end of the show. They only had this Zulu dance, so I added Xhosa dance, Sotho dance, Pedi dance, Shangaan dance, Venda dance, and try to encompass everybody.

But you don't really have roots; it's almost like seaweed, just reflota-tion. People always ask me, 'Jonas, where are you based?' I say, 'No, I'm country-shopping. I haven't found the right one, I'm still looking in the windows.' But you see, fortunately with music, people can keep in touch with what is happening inside the country, through records, tapes and television. You tell yourself that you are playing jazz. When you are at home, yes you are playing jazz. But just like speaking, you get to America and find that there are some differences. It's like jazz with an accent. So ours is a South African accent on the jazz.

I have a lot of material that I wrote in my earlier years. Some of the music in *Cry Freedom* I wrote in the Sixties, ja, some of the themes. And I have a lot of those. And it's always a challenge to try to maintain the indigenous character of the music. But then you say, 'Well, is this the music of the time?' Things have evolved at home too; but the evolution of music within the country, of our culture in general, has been greatly affected by apartheid. There's been a definite cultural onslaught, on the culture of our people inside South Africa, effected through the media.

You see, you water down the music by dictating to the artists what to play. If you don't play this, you'll not get any acclaim. So a lot of music doesn't get acclaim – only a certain kind of music. If you get to be indigenous and play the music that our people always like, only new . . . it won't get acclaim. The bubble gum music that is at home, is something that has been created by the media and recording companies. Our people have always liked American music, like anybody else; but we have always had our own music. Now a fusion of the two could be done by an artist, but if you take that and make that the music of South Africa, that's wrong. But the media will control that. All the restrictions they had with censorship affect the artists – censorship in terms of your lyrics being read before they can be played on radio. That has forced the recording companies not to even record. I was told once by a guy in a recording company, 'Jonas we can't record you. You're just not going to be played in South Africa, with ANC and everything, so we can't waste money on you.' And that has been with many companies. They don't want to touch me. It's there. So that's how they control everything.

In America it used to happen, the same thing, where you had a white artist standing there and miming, and the black guy singing behind the curtain, that happened many times. Ja. So the control of the artists has affected the music. They've directed the music and . . . I wouldn't even say watered it down, they really have changed it a lot; and it's made meaningless, because it's the kind of music that you would have a hit today and by the end of the week, it doesn't mean anything. You know the kind of music you and I can't listen to. It doesn't linger, it doesn't last. So that's the kind of thing.

I've had so many invitations to come home now. I would like to have a peep. It's unfortunate that I have to go to hospital now, to attend to my leg. You can see I'm limping; this was a car accident. Actually I've had three accidents on the same leg – as a driver, as a passenger and as a pedestrian. [Laughs] All three versions. Ja. So I have to have an operation, but otherwise I've been invited at home. I've just made a record; they wanted me to come for the launch. And there are various shows and festivals. I have to go and see what is happening. It's not easy from what I hear.

HUGH MASEKELA
Johannesburg 1992

'I think when this becomes a human community and we have a democratic way of life, South Africa will probably dominate the music world.'

He is internationally the best-known South African musician – a virtuoso jazz trumpeter who ranks among the world's best. For most of his exile he has lived and performed in New York, but has now returned to South Africa.

I started as a musician very young. My parents thought I had a gift because I used to sing with all the records, the 78 rpms from the Forties. By the time I was six years old, living in Pimville Township, Springs, there were piano teachers that taught rudimentary sort of classical stuff. You started with nursery rhymes like 'Lavender's Blue, Dilly Dilly', and I became quite proficient at the piano. Then we moved to Alexandra Township which was not a place where a boy played piano or tennis, unless you wanted to be beaten up or bullied around; they were looked at as sissy sports. So I got into soccer.

But I followed music very closely and I had idols who became role-models; people like Louis Armstrong and Miles Davis and Dizzy Gillespie and Clifford Brown and Duke Ellington . . . people who had come from very humble and poor beginnings; they seemed to have pulled themselves up and gotten not only the attention of the world, but they brought the attention of the world to the sufferings of the African-American as individuals, as human beings. That amazed me. They were in a country that at the time was worse than South Africa, where they were being lynched. You know, the only problems we really had were with the police, and they were quite rough. But it was not like the American South, where it was a free-for-all on African peoples. So they really amazed me. And I figured that if they could do it, I could.

When I was thirteen, I was in quite a lot of trouble at school. We'd gone to play a school called Kilnerton Training Institute which always used to beat us. I scored three goals. And afterwards they took a whole lot of us off into the village to celebrate, because it was the first time St Peter's had beaten Kilnerton in ages. So they bought a four gallon tin of sorghum beer and half a bottle of Gilbeys and I was sort of carried on the shoulders. And we drank – it was just camaraderie. We always travelled with two teachers, but when I got into the bus I got very sick. If you were found drinking you were expelled and you couldn't go to any other school. I tried to make it outside, but everything just came out on the back of the science teacher. I was one of his favourite students, so he asked everybody to try and give me a break because I was so young, and there would be no future for me otherwise.

When you had broken everything, they sent you to Huddleston – Bishop Trevor Huddleston, who was sort of the hoodlum's priest at St Peter's. And he said, 'You know the monks are complaining, the nuns are complaining, the prefects are complaining, the monitors are complaining, the teachers are complaining about you. What do you want to really do?' I had just seen a film about a trumpet player called *Young Man with a Horn*, and I said, 'Father, if you get me a trumpet, I won't bother anybody any more.'

So he went to Polliack's music shop and spoke to a salesman there, and he sent me with a note, 'This is the boy I was talking to you about.' And I picked out a £15 second-hand trumpet. And he got me an old man who was the leader of the Johannesburg Municipal Native Brass Band – they worked out of Jubilee Centre in Eloff Street – to come and teach me.

After about five or six Saturdays I started to play tunes. And other students got interested. Huddleston was very buoyed up by it, and started to beg instruments from everybody. So we formed the Huddleston Band. Musicians started taking us under their wing; and during the holidays, in Springs where my family spent a lot of time – I played with the Merrymakers. The greatest trumpet player then here was a man called Elijah Mkwanyana, who died from TB a year after I left. He sang very beautifully, and played the smoothest trumpet. He was my biggest idol – and I still try to play like him. My township style is directly from him and another man called Bunzie Pangane, who was his friend.

By then I was crazy about Clifford Brown, who was the greatest trumpet player that ever lived – you know in his proficiency and his lyricism – and Miles Davis. I just felt that what was available in South Africa was not enough for me. Although the political atmosphere bothered me a great deal, I was obsessed with music – my whole life was around music – and I wanted to be as good as Miles Davis or Clifford Brown and them. And I knew that I couldn't get a chance to do that here because, even if I was white, there was not that kind of opportunity and teaching.

Things were getting tighter and rougher here, and I started feeling even politically I had to get out. I was a very successful musician here, but my real urge to go was to get the kind of teachers that my idols had had an opportunity to get. At the beginning of 1960, when I was at the highest pinnacle of my career here, we formed a real pioneering band called the Jazz Epistles, with Jonas Gwangwa and Kippie Moeketsi and Dollar

Brand and Johnny Mackay. And we were doing really well; we were planning a national tour, and were about to take off.

I had been waiting for a passport almost for three years – you know it was really hard in those days – but it seemed like I would be getting it soon. Huddleston and Menuhin and Dankworth had been able to place me at the Guildhall School of Music, so I had got all the necessary papers to get a passport.

And then Sharpeville happened. Whenever I had late lessons and it was too late to go back to Natalspruit, I'd stay at the Bermans'. So one night, shortly after Sharpeville, they came to collect Monty for detention; and I was sleeping on the couch in the living-room. Of course, they wanted to know what I was doing there. I tried to lie – to say my aunt works there so the boss was good enough to put me up for the night. They actually phoned Spengler*, you know, and said, '*Luister, ons is hier by Berman; daar's 'n kaffir in die huis.*' And Spengler said, '*Vok die kaffir. Waar's Berman?*' So they took my pass number and they said they'd get back to me. They got back to me – I think three months after I had left. My mother said the Special Branch had been there to look for me – they were not as fast or as sophisticated as they became later.

About six weeks after that my passport came through. It came through on a Friday, and the Monday I was on a plane and I was out of here to London. It was one of the saddest days of my life, because I hadn't wanted to go away with a feeling that I might never come back – that the Special Branch might be looking for me.

And then, of course, when I got to London, I found a very big anti-apartheid movement community. And with the atrocities that were going on here and the jailing of people and the Treason Trials – not that I wasn't politicised before – I started getting very activist about the situation.

By the time I came to the States, it was the height of the Civil Rights. And Harry Belafonte was one of the people – and Dizzy Gillespie – with Miriam Makeba who had helped me to come to school; and they were very deeply involved in not only civil rights for African-Americans, but also very, very involved in the cause of the South African people. By 1962, I think, Miriam and Belafonte were formally banished from South Africa.

I still had my passport. I planned to come back home because I had finished at the Menuhin School of Music, and I thought I was equipped enough to come back and impart what I had learned. I was really proficient, not only in classical music but also technically. I already had like three albums out. But Belafonte kept insisting to me, 'Listen. It is better to build your name, so that when you talk about South Africa it will have clout; and so that if you do go back, people will notice what

---

* Then head of the Transvaal Security Police.

you say and you won't be as . . . you will be a little more untouchable than you are right now.' I said to him, 'What guarantee do I have that I'll get famous like you?' And he said, 'Look. You just have to try it!'

And then my passport was about almost finished, and I sent it in for renewal. Of course, I never heard from them again. And by then we'd become very heavily activist. We'd done an album with Jonas Gwangwa, called *An Evening with Miriam and Harry Belafonte* which was all protest songs. And then Miriam gave a speech at the UN General Assembly which was, I think, the first time that anybody at an international level really got to know what was happening in South Africa. She was really officially banned then.

All the time we lived in the States we lived under surveillance by the security agencies, especially the FBI. We were aware of it. There was a car always parked outside my flat. There was a time when the State Department was fighting for the souls of Africans, especially South Africans, so they were always worried that, as an independent student, I could say what I wanted to say; it didn't depend on the State Department's charities. I became more and more activist especially when Jonas came to live with me, and we became involved in starting South African students' associations. And we were very involved in the Civil Rights. Miriam was doing a lot of fundraisers, and I started to play professionally and to talk a lot about South Africa.

So by 1965, I had given up the idea of coming home, because by then everybody was put away in Robben Island. The situation had become draconian. I think Verwoerd was killed the following year and I thought things might change; but they just got worse. And I got more and more activist, and I couldn't go away from the States because I didn't have a passport, although I had a resident's permit. When I went to get my resident's – I was married to Miriam by then – they had a secret file. And the first thing my lawyer asked is, 'Why is there a secret file?' But the person who interviews doesn't know either: 'Gee! It says here that your client is a communist, that he'd been arrested in a communist home and blah-blah-blah.' And they asked me if I was aware that I had been under surveillance all the time and I said, 'Yes, sure.'

1972 I decided to leave the States, because I had like peaked there. When you're successful in the States, besides Civil Rights there's nothing much that you can do. Except conspicuous consumption. Success there is a very different situation. I just felt that I owed something – a great deal – to the people at home; and wanted to be closer. But it was difficult; there was a war in Mozambique, war in Angola and war in Zimbabwe. So I opted to go to West Africa where Miriam was living. I lived in Guinea, then in Liberia and in Ghana. And in 1980, an old friend of ours from the townships persuaded Miriam and me to come to Swaziland, Botswana and Lesotho. But the Swaziland and Botswana Governments cancelled our shows because they said there was cholera there.

But Lesotho didn't. So we went there, and we played for 75,000 people on Christmas Day. It was amazing – in a little place like Lesotho! They came from South Africa mostly, and from the border you saw cars parked for miles – there was a traffic jam and people were leaving their cars and walking in. And the country ran out of commodities – they had to send away to Bloemfontein; the army vans had to go and fetch stuff.

I was going to stay for a week; and I stayed for three months because I was so close to home. It was the first time I saw my folks and my friends. I decided that I was going to come back and live in Lesotho. And then an old friend, George Pase, called me from Botswana. He said, 'Listen. On your way back to the States, please come and visit me; don't just pass by.' And I said, 'Damn Botswana.' I knew it as a desert with railway sidings and a little town, so I stopped there. I was supposed to stop for a weekend, and I stayed there for six weeks; and decided I was going to come and stay. Wally Serote was there at the time, and they were preparing for this big festival. So when I came back for the festival, I stayed. I just had a hope that soon things would change there in South Africa, and I wouldn't have to travel so far.

And then in 1985 there was the big SADF raid. George and his wife were killed; and I had to leave again. It felt like stepping backwards. I lived in England for three years because my record company was there. And then Mbongeni Ngema wrote *Sarafina* which I helped him with, and it was a big success on Broadway. But before that I was with Paul Simon and did *Gracelands*; and that moved me back to the States.

And of course, in July of 1990, my sister Barbara and Miriam called from Johannesburg and said, 'Come home!' I said, 'Come on, you're kidding! This is a joke!' They said, 'No! We're calling you from Johannesburg. It's for real.'

So in September I came back. And I'm like a sponge here, because there's so much work to do. I had always kept close to the musicians and the people at home on a day-to-day basis. I was away physically, but spiritually I was always here. I always had a hope that I would come back – but I didn't think it would be in this century. I thought I'd come back in a wheelchair maybe one day. So it's really fascinating to be here.

There's an insurmountable amount of work to be done because there's been so much damage done. I hope in my lifetime I will be able to be part of the effort to remedy some of the years. South African popular music, our urban music, has always had a lot of its roots with African-American music – which is the most popular music in the world. I mean we all come out of jazz, you know, even the lifestyle of the townships. The role models for us were African-Americans who came out of the plantations to forge a way of life that was really unique. But it affected the way people dressed, the way people walked, the way people sang, the way people cooked all over the world. So it's an amazing achievement for an oppressed people – to have that much influence over the world.

I think this common feel makes South African music very digestible to the international popular music-buying audience, as was proved by Paul Simon. I think that when this becomes a natural community, a human community and we have a democratic way of life, South Africa will probably dominate the music world just as much as African-Americans did. If not more because we'll be able to do it with the support of the whole country and the whole fabric.

I have never imagined having music of my own. I've always looked at myself as an antenna or a transmitter for the feelings of the people of South Africa, and I've tried to stick as close as possible to what I was nurtured with. We all started in township and mbaqanqa bands and it's like my ABCs.

My mother was a social worker, my father was a health inspector. Before that, they were schoolteachers, and before that he was a clerk in the mines – a lot of my family is working in the mines, so I was very involved with the lives of miners. And there are a lot of songs that I write that talk about miners – one of the most popular songs is the 'Coal train' (stimela) song. People overseas don't know what this means but it's still the most requested song.

I left in 1960 and first returned September 1990. So I was away thirty years. And some change, ja! I feel that my return was long overdue. I wish I'd returned maybe twenty years ago because of the work that has to be done. Yes, I'm back for good. I plan to spend eight months of the year here at home. I do a little teaching, I do a little fundraising just for music and arts education; and I'm part-time co-director at a Centre for Jazz and Popular Music at the University of Natal. And I'm working on a film with Mfundi Mvundla, who was also an exile and an ANC guy, and became a fabulous screenplay writer. And I have been working on starting a record company.

So I'm going into the fields, professional and business, that we were never allowed to go into. So I think I've bitten off more than I can chew to work on, and I wish I had more time. I wish I had forty-eight-hour days.

CHRISTOPHER HOPE
London 1992

'I grew up in a kind of Catholic enclave in a Calvinist city in an African country . . . Wherever the centre was, you were a helluva long way from it.'

Since the publication in 1974 of his first book of poems, *Cape Drives*, which received the Cholmondeley Award for poetry, he has written thirteen books, a number of which have won major literary prizes: *A Separate Development*, his first novel, was the winner of the David Higham Prize; *Kruger's Alp* was awarded the Whitbread Prize for Fiction in 1985; *White Boy Running* won the CNA Literary Award in South Africa.

I left in 1974 and my reasons were very mixed. I wasn't forced out, so I've never seen myself as being a political exile. I was not under threat, though I'd had a certain amount of difficulty with my work: my poems had been banned by the local broadcasting services and so on. But it was that I simply didn't see how one could go on being in that place, in that way, any longer. To that add the fact that I wanted to write a book, a novel about the place. And the great difficulty for me about South Africa is that there's always great heat and very little light around. If you feel apartheid is one of the most colossal absurdities, indeed a wickedness, it makes you quite incoherent. You cannot live in Africa and detest Africans – it is a nonsense of the very first order – nor can you live in Africa and pretend to be living in Europe. And because I wanted to write, to record, I didn't think I could do it close up. So I went away to France thinking I would probably never return. And I went away in particular to write.

I was over thirty, and I flew into Paris as the first European city which I had ever visited. I had family, but they stayed in South Africa. So for the first three months I was on my own. I spent, I think, two or three months in France, and then went to London. As an English-speaking South African one imagines that because you share a language you have something in common with British people. It is a discovery many people have to make – that it's the language alone which links you. You are in a foreign country. It was something of a shock to discover that the natives of the British islands are far stranger than the natives of France.

I am talking of a voluntary exile – not of emigration, of deliberately choosing to put yourself in a place from which you cannot then go home. The effect, I think, is rather like bereavement. It can be got over, but it takes a considerable time, and some people never get over it. Exile becomes a condition, almost an affliction.

I think I went into exile before I left South Africa. Africa is a kind of political concept, a geographical convenience. It doesn't exist as a place. It exists only as an expression of political will. Where South Africa is depends on who's running it at the moment, so unless you happen to be among those running it, your own location in the place was always terribly vague.

There was only one thing to do with the system – you couldn't change it – and that was to buck it. And to record the fact that one lived in a kind of asylum, an institution in which everything had been reversed; in which – I've used this metaphor before – the patients have taken over from their keepers; that one lived in an asylum run by people who should have been in the asylum. And I was determined to register that fact.

By coming away I got enough distance between myself and the place to be relatively cool about it, which is essential. And as a writer it was useful. All I suppose I did was to retreat and take up sniping positions on various hills. [Laughs] You see, anger for me is something which is very difficult to come to terms with. And my way is to write stories about it, not so much wishing to set the system to rights as wishing to subvert it entirely.

My first novel set in an unnamed provincial town in the mid-Fifties was published in South Africa, and promptly banned. It was banned, I was told, because it made people laugh, and they lost no time at all in removing the book from the shelves. So I knew I must be doing something right.

My grandfather was an Irishman who ran away from home when he was about fifteen and went to South Africa during the Boer War. He came from a very strong Fenian family and so he was a supporter of the Boers against the British in the war. After the war he stayed, settled down, and so my family was very strongly Irish.

I grew up in small towns. I was raised as a Catholic, principally in Pretoria – a Roman Catholic in a Calvinist city. It was like living on a shrinking island surrounded by wonderfully lethal trout. If there was anything they hated more than black people, it was Catholics. There was the 'swart gevaar' – the black danger – followed very closely behind by the 'Roomse gevaar' – the Roman danger. So I grew up in a kind of a Catholic enclave in a Calvinist city in an African country. So that was an oddity. Wherever the centre was, you were a helluva long way from it. One was a displaced person to begin with – exile was just an inevitable step.

At the time I came out – 1974, 1975 – South Africa was seen as entering a kind of thousand-year Reich. John Vorster was the Prime Minister. It seemed as if the age of granite was going to go on for ever; nothing was going to alter. I still have strong connections there, not so much with the people or the ideology but with the spirit of the place. And the capacity of that country for moving from tragedy to farce and back again in the blink of an eye, deserves recording.

I think if one has kept any sense of anything by coming away, it is the abhorrence of the uses and abuses of power. What one realises in Europe, with a certain amount of despair, is that there's a lot of racial detestation and discrimination about. The absurdities of seeing one group in some emphatic way other, different, lesser than, is widely spread. And because you have such ridiculously acute antennae as a South African, one does register those things in France and in Britain now, the spread of what is called in dignified terms 'nationalism'. It's nothing of the sort. Any South African in one and a half seconds will tell you what it is. It's the sort of thing we more or less invented – a wish to put into place a distance between 'us' and 'them', without the apparatus to do it. And it's widespread.

There was in the Fifties a generation of black writers. But it is as if they never were. They wrote in Sophiatown; they were associated with the magazine *Drum*. One by one they were banned, expelled, or went into exile. The banning of a person's work is a highly effective form of suppression – the person and his work simply disappear. And indeed so did these people. So a generation later, in the Sixties and Seventies, nobody had ever heard of perhaps five or six of the best writers that we have produced. It was as if they had never ever been. And the loss not just to the culture of the country, but to the *joie de vivre* of the country, to its essential liveliness, has been lethally effective. Simply not being able to tolerate their own poets, their own novelists, they inflict great damage on themselves.

In my case I've written the exile into the books, and I hope I've recorded something of the absurdity. The images may be tinier for the distance involved, but they are sharper, it seems to me, than they would have been had I been in it.

I try to think of the uses of exile or the compensations of distance. And one of them of course is to discover that there is indeed a world out there. We were raised, many of us in South Africa, to believe not only was the world flat, but if you moved too far forward you'd fall off the edge. One heard of the outside world so often disparagingly, that one began to wonder whether the outside world existed. One was never entirely sure. So it was good to go and check it out and find that it did indeed exist. And indeed that people who did live there weren't entirely different from the sorts of people that one had grown up amongst.

The present government have been in power since I was four years old – I'm now forty-seven. And there they are, still there. So I'm staying firmly in exile because I wait for real change. I have yet to see it. I see great changes, and yet I see no change. I see the same people who ran it when I was a child are still running it.

LAURETTA NGCOBO
London 1991

'From that time on, once I understood the children, I understood the parents, I understood everything. And that was a great cure for me. Because I think all the pain I suffered really was my weakness, my own problems, my own legacy of being South African. Yes, I had taken it all with me.'

She has published two novels: *Cross of Gold* and *And They Didn't Die*; and edited a collection of essays by black women writers in Britain.

How did I find myself living in London? Such a long story! [Laughs] Such a long story that really one can't say it in a few sentences.

My husband, A.B., had been in prison for some time. I was politically very aware when I met A.B., but I didn't get involved in the actual creation of the PAC. In any case, at that time most men felt that politics was for men; you were part of the discussions as long as it wasn't official, but official circles were for men.

In 1956, A.B. was in the first Treason Trial. He was involved in endless meetings with other Africanists, Sobukwe, Cele and others, which resulted in the formation of the PAC. I married him during the Treason Trial, so later when he was imprisoned, it was not a violent shock for me.

I was a teacher at the time that young students were just awakening to what was actually happening. Sharpeville, 1960, was a real shock for many of them, and in their questioning, they focused on the one person who was around. Here I was teaching them, with my husband in jail; they wanted to know more. I did see my role as that of helping them understand, if not politicising them, which was very dangerous in that climate of the early Sixties. I got to a difficult point where parents would ask me, 'Why are the police after you?' The police were going to the homes of these young people, they were questioning them about what I was teaching them, how I was teaching them, they were asking them to bring home composition books, so I knew from the parents that the police were encircling me.

A.B. was in prison and I would go to see him in Pretoria. Sobukwe too was in prison at that time. A.B. would give me messages for different people, and I would pass them on, often verbally. But in a few cases, the people were far away and I had to write letters. Although I was very careful, the police began arresting a lot of people around me, and bit by bit they did make the connection. One of the police, an African, told a fellow teacher – they used to drink together – 'At last we have got it clinched, we're arresting her this week.' This man went straight to my friend, she came and told me, and I had a restless night trying to decide as to what to do.

I thought there's no way I was going to leave. A.B. was in prison. My children were very young, and my mother was retired, there was nobody to look after the children; so I had decided that well, if they come, let them come. I was in the bus to school when I suddenly just questioned myself: why should I let this happen? Why should I, a small link, go to prison? What contribution is that, to my family, to the politics, to A.B.? It just dawned on me that this was not the decision I should take.

So when I got to school, I packed away everything, and cleared all my shelves where most of my secrets were, and threw it all in a great big rubbish pit, and left that afternoon. Left my key on the table and didn't tell anyone except this friend of mine. I had taken my elder daughter to my mother when A.B. was imprisoned, and the little one, too, until I could get someone to look after her during the day. It was the first weekend that I was without my little girl, which is why I was able to leave at a moment's notice. She was about two and a half at the time. It was one of the most painful things I've ever done. I had felt terribly lonely anyway when she went to my mother for that week. But just leaving them with my mother, not knowing whether I would ever be able to see them again . . . It was another two years before my daughters could join me.

I went to Swaziland. And A.B. came out a month later and joined me there. That was a very difficult time for all refugees. They arrived in a strange town not knowing where to go. They were hanging around street corners. Women were coming in with their children. One woman, Italia Dlamini, used to work for the Roman Catholic hospital, and there were one or two rondavels on the hospital grounds. She just collected all suffering South African women with all their children, three, four. And of course husbands couldn't join them at all, they used to live way out in Moneni. It was a very difficult time. No food; I was fortunate because I got a job in St Michael's where I became sort of a semi-hostel matron to look after the girls. It was very, very little pay, about £10 a month; but I just needed money to send for milk for my children at home. That's what I really wanted more than anything else, I felt if they got milk, never mind anything else, then they would be all right.

In that job, too, I escaped the starvation that the others suffered, and I was able to feed a lot of them; because these schoolchildren left a lot of the food uneaten. And so instead of throwing it away, I used to collect it in buckets and take it down to the women at the Roman Catholic school.

But the sisters at that place were strange! A.B. arrived and he had to live at Moneni, a distance of something like three miles, with no transport. I was told clearly that he couldn't come and join me where I was staying because it was a girls' hostel. He couldn't even come and visit me at night, and what made it so painful was the way they used to snoop around. There was just no way of us being able to sit down and talk about what had happened to us, and what to do next. We needed to be able to talk. We got to a point where he would wait until perhaps after midnight and then creep to see me. And they would still find out that he came! [Laughs]

Another painful thing in Swaziland were the South African women who had emigrated and were working there, comfortably well-off. They reacted to us refugees with so much arrogance and annoyance. They wouldn't come anywhere near us. I think they felt we imperilled their own position with the Swaziland government. We were an inconvenience. We were poor, we didn't have any food, we didn't have anything and we needed all the basic things, blankets, everything. And they just were not going to put themselves out.

A.B. left in six, seven weeks' time. We just hadn't had time together, we were in such a mess. Then I discovered I was expecting anyway, in spite of all the prohibitions. I moved to a Catholic school outside Manzini, where I was offered a teaching post and had my baby.

I had never associated with Catholics, I've never been one, but the Catholics in that school were marvellous to me. They didn't have much in the line of material things, some of the conditions were ghastly, but they were no worse for me, as a South African refugee, than they would have been for any other person.

Then I was to leave. A.B. had arranged for me to go to Zambia.

Several attempts to leave were thwarted by outside interference. Finally pressure was brought on the South African government to allow her, and some of the other women refugees, to fly via Jan Smuts airport to join their husbands in Zambia. She was taken with her children to the airport in the morning, to await a flight in the afternoon.

We were supposed to board the plane about twenty past four. I had the children nicely clothed, everything had been taken, packs full of nappies and chamberpots and whatnot! And right at the end, round about four o'clock, they picked me from the line, they just said, 'You, come out!' I thought, well this is it; and I took the children and followed them. Instead of going into the main building, they took me to a place on the side where there was a lot of rubble, out in the open, and said they wanted to search my luggage. I opened everything out – everything! All the ironing of weeks, carefully washed and packed, everything, on that dusty ground. They took out everything.

The baby had a strange knack of knowing when I was unhappy, she used to cry until nobody could hear what they were saying. She began screaming. And when they had taken out everything, searched handbags, the lot, and they hadn't found anything, they stood up and left it all on the ground – nappies, chambers, clothes. It was that kind of heat, the baby's crying, the children are here, the plane is leaving me. I just turned and left everything where it was on the dusty ground, and went into the plane. I didn't think I would find my case again. I couldn't care less. That was one slap on the face that I got from the South African police.

And I went into Zambia.

There's a strange feeling once you are out of your home that you're in the world. This thin line between inside and outside; once you are not inside, you are outside. It just didn't occur to me that there was any other border in the world, or that I needed a visa. So I just arrived with my children. They wanted to put me back on that plane. Fortunately, after a lot of wrangling and arguing and phone calls, they said I must wait. I sat at the airport, oh, until well after midnight. They were looking for a PAC man, Masimini, and he was up and about enjoying himself on a Saturday night; in the end they found him and he was able to come and claim me and take me to where he lived. Anyway, there began my true exile, ja. In Zambia.

I got a teaching post within weeks, and then things were looking up. There was quite a struggle finding accommodation with a family, so we shared this one little house, a little four-roomed thing. This was called a PAC house. Everybody was there, men, women, children, the lot! There was quite a large body of women who were leaving South Africa, not because of political involvement, but to get better jobs and adventures. People who were coming through Botswana experienced far worse things than I did in Swaziland, living at Gazangula for weeks and months with the lions roaring around them, in wild conditions.

Although A.B. was based in Tanzania, he was hoping to join his family in Zambia where the PAC was to set up its headquarters. But political problems arose in the PAC, and feeling that he might himself be contributing to these he decided to step aside. Through Defence & Aid he obtained a scholarship to study in Britain. This was their first opportunity to live together as a family.

Coming to Great Britain was another thing for me. I had never lived with white people. Meeting a white person or a white child was meeting an enemy. Then I had to come to Britain and live with these people. What hope had I of understanding them? To get over that took a long time; and it took the white children to help me over those hurdles, and I got over them through teaching.

English children are so naughty. They're so different from the children I knew. I knew African children. White children, I had seen as enemies. They did all sorts of things, spitting – all sorts of things, so I just accepted that they were evil, like their parents, and that was it.

I was teaching primary section, you know, eight to eleven. My nerves were raw, I literally used to count the hours in a week. I think I had got into a bad school anyway. Then two new teachers came along, a young teacher from college and another more mature teacher. I knew that the young one was having a very raw deal in her classroom. But this other teacher was apparently a very confident person and just made me feel here is a teacher who knows her job. And one morning she came into the staff room and just collapsed on a chair and broke into hysterics. Phew! what was going on? It turned out that the children were really nasty to her. What! nasty to HER? So it's not a racial thing!

It was the first time it occurred to me that the children were nasty to all new teachers. And once it wasn't me as a black person, once I knew that they were just being silly, I said, 'Children! I know children!' And as I walked into that classroom, I wasn't in enemy territory. I decided to go for a short retraining course and was able to come back, oh so confident.

After that I was just at home and I was in full control and enjoying teaching, and the children liked me. When we moved down from north London to the south, I was able to change schools, and immediately became a deputy head.

From that time on, I just knew there were very good people and very bad people and some very innocent weak people who need as much help as I do sometimes. Once I understood the children, I understood the parents; I understood everything. And so that was a great cure for me. Because I think all the pain I suffered really, was my weakness, my own problems, my own legacy of being South African. Yes, yes, I had taken it all with me.

When I started writing, I was trying to retrace my steps, to find out if there'd been different choices I could have made. I felt coming to the Western world was the greatest mistake of my life. So there was a lot of internal speculation, trying to find out exactly why ... why I had really ended up here – I must have made some big mistake? South Africa had been such a pain because of white people there, and now I had sought them myself to come and live here. In fact, one good thing about Great Britain was the anonymity it gave me. I was able to sit in my little house and nobody worried about me, nobody sought me out, I pottered around, I made mistakes, I made little successes, I overcame problems, but that anonymity was new and was wonderful for me.

Even then, I wasn't writing for publication. I just piled it and piled it and it was a great big bumpf like that. It was a friend of mine who one day looked through this pile [laughs] and said she felt there was a lot that was good in it; she took it herself to publishers and finally I had it published.

And now, what about going back?

I wish you had asked me this question four weeks ago. I have just come back from South Africa. I had to rush there for my mother's illness. We had been very excited and ready to go almost right away when things first changed. Except that two weeks later we suddenly were very quiet – both of us just suddenly stopped talking about it and talked about other things, but not about going home. And it came out slowly; well, what do we do about this, what do we do about that? But really the main question was, when we had said 'home' all these years, what we were really saying was your mother's house, or your sister's house, or who-ever. Now when you say home, suddenly it has a new meaning. It means you must have a house. First of all when you first go to South Africa with all your luggage, where do you go from the airport? You know, those questions are very real.

The children are grown-up now and they can make their own decisions. They are quite excited, they are looking forward to going home.

But it's not in the same way – they're not as anxious. They can stay here as long as they like. Whereas with A.B. and me, it's an immediate issue. We want to go . . . we want to go home, but is it the right time to be going home now, especially in view of what's going on there? What's the point of selling this house, going and building a new house and get it burned down to ashes? In a strange way, I feel like an outsider now.

I think people are ever so eager to meet us there, they are overwhelming with their joy and our own joy at arriving home. But this stream . . . you feel as though this stream has cast you aside. Even when you have tried to drift on, you feel as though you are at the edge. You know how, at the river, you can see at the edges, a lot of pieces gathering on the side? That's how I feel. I feel that . . . I don't understand everything fully. Things are so topsy-turvy that even if I can mentally explain what I see, understand what I see, I do not understand it with my whole being.

Another thing – this may sound arrogant – I don't know whether it's me that's outside, or it's them that have been so enclosed that they can't think more broadly. I don't have another way of putting it. I know that I feel like a terrible outsider; but I try to follow, I want to learn, I want to understand. I suppose perhaps they are just as confused. Just what being a South African really . . . has meant up to now; how raw, how harsh the system has been on the development of our people, because now we're looking at ourselves with different eyes.

MAZISI KUNENE
Los Angeles 1991

'I want people to know that, yes, it is not demoralised people who create masterpieces. It is their spirit that revolts against their demoralisation and marginalisation.'

Mazisi Kunene is the leading South African poet writing in his own language, Zulu. His works have been published in Zulu and in English translations. He left South Africa in 1959 with a scholarship from Christian Action to study in England. But he went with the feeling of responsibility towards the ANC. Within a short time he had abandoned his studies and was working full-time for the Movement. He played a pivotal part in the difficult early years of propagating the truth about apartheid and establishing anti-apartheid organisations.

In London I quickly teamed up with Tennyson Makiwane. We used to speak at sometimes five, six, seven meetings a day and so on, in different parts of the country. At that time, very few people knew where South

Africa was. They only knew that . . . oh, maybe is it near Nigeria? So it meant we had to do a lot of ground work, very raw kind of description, a map, show where is it, write notes and so on.

The mood gradually changed. People like Rosalind Ainslie and Vella Pillay participated – Vella was crucial in our effort, though he was working full-time. Eventually I gave up my studies because the work just got too much. I had been depending on a scholarship from Christian Action. Fortunately Canon Collins understood. He said, 'I fully support what you are doing.' I hope one day Makiwane's name will be rehabilitated because he contributed a great deal. We were pioneers, both of us. Canon Collins was really the pivot, the stone against which we leaned. The Committee of African Organisations gave us a base.

The following year, 1960, there was Sharpeville. All the activities and the demonstrations that we had been having in 1959 and all the vigils around South Africa House paid off, there was an immediate powerful response, not only from the newspapers with whom we had cultivated very strong relations, but also from people throughout the country. The response was very strong.

We changed from Boycott Movement to Anti-Apartheid, to broaden our campaign, to encompass the whole idea of apartheid itself, not just a boycott of fruit. It's one thing to be organising at grass-root level, appealing for action against South Africa because it has done some atrocities and passed laws that are unacceptable. It's another thing to see the actual laws in operation. So every event influenced the change, especially Sharpeville and the Rivonia arrests in 1963. These changed the quality of our campaigns and the response.

The ANC had decided on internationalising the boycott movement and the whole solidarity effort, so every event that happened after that had a corresponding impact on inside and outside. We had to create anti-apartheid committees in all the different countries, to appeal to workers' organisations, to intellectual organisations, academia, create committees to which each sector could respond. It was a lot of travelling, in fact that's when I developed my terror of flying. Because we were flying so much, I would take my case, put it down today and tomorrow get the next plane. We did just about too much travelling to various parts of the world. But it was a responsibility. Others were engaged in other more fierce activities inside, others were in jail. So travelling itself was minimal compared to our desperation for those of our comrades who were inside.

We developed a programme of scholarships for our refugees, and created the World Campaign for the Freedom of Political Prisoners. Had a huge exhibition to support political prisoners. Artists from all over the world participated in this exhibition. Then Tanzania became independent and they allowed the ANC to open an office there. Tennyson Makiwane went there and I remained in Europe.

I was in Europe from 1959 to 1976. Through many of those years I was the Chief Representative of the ANC, not only in the United Kingdom but also for Europe and the Americas. There were no other offices there. The scope was quite vast. In the Sixties, I used to come to America, come and talk, organise here and so on and make contacts with many people – Martin Luther King, Michael X, oh, numerous people who were here. Spoke at meetings with Kennedy etc. etc. – there were a lot of activities in the whole area. The only area that I didn't effectively cover was South America, because it was just a bit too much.

Later, I was given the position of Director of Finance. My idea to make the ANC financially viable was that we should actually go into business, without the name of the ANC being directly involved. But the feeling in the ANC was that we are not a business organisation, we are a political organisation. That was in my opinion an unfortunate attitude because then it did not give the ANC the kind of speed in some cases, which came from utilising its resources.

It's just the right of every member of an organisation to criticise, and discontent is inevitable, especially after we'd been outside so long. I was not working with any particular group myself. I was always suspicious of people who worked with a group just for individual ambitions. I am glad that I will not go down in history as having been the person to have broken up or divided the ANC. I was said to be in cahoots with the 'dissidents'. I think one must avoid this kind of damaging labelling of people because it doesn't build the organisation. We were all outside, we were all in very difficult conditions. We were dislocated from our own base, the resources were very limited, we had to take care of many people who were refugees. We faced a lot of problems.

> The differences of opinion gave rise to difficulties; Kunene felt that his dissension was unjustly condemned.

I must tell you the truth that, as a result of the differences, I was very broken. I felt that I had not been treated very fairly. My spirit was low. In fact at that time, I was thinking it will be better really to die with others who had died – I had many friends who had died. I thought well, maybe I should also just collapse and go. It was at that time that Mathabo came. My wife.

I'd known her in South Africa, she was my student, a young student when I was there, and now she was in London, a grown woman. I was not in the mood to talk to anybody. But she came to the apartment where I was. She said, 'Oh, I've been sent by your ancestors to come and rescue you.' It was so appropriate that she should come there in that spirit. I was deep in a doldrum. I could only sleep by drinking wine, drink wine and sleep. I couldn't sleep normally. I was really in a terrible condition and it was bad for me because I was not a drinker. It was very bad for me.

So my wife-to-be, she said, 'In this condition, you will not survive in this place. What you need is just a break.' And then I listened to her. I thought yes, maybe that's what I need. And I went to Tambo and said I would like to go for leave to a place where I can write.

I started writing poetry at the age of nine. In fact, I started when I didn't even know it was poetry. It was a certain head teacher at school said, 'Oh, hau! You wrote this?' And I said, 'Yes.' Then he said, 'Oh, this is wonderful poetry.' My home was on top of a hill – we did not grow up in the city – and I could see the ocean this side and the mountains this side; and it always disturbed me to see the sun just emerging from the ocean. One day I decided just to say something about it, and that's when I began my writing. Yes. I was published – just some short poems at home in South Africa, in anthologies.

So in setting out to write, I did not set out merely to produce little booklets. It doesn't matter to me whether I'm published or not in my lifetime – I know I shall have given the next generation a heritage which is really worthwhile, which they will be able to celebrate.

I write in Zulu because that's my language. Yes, I write in Zulu. Sometimes I'm persuaded to translate. I translate because people ask me ... but I think it's not necessary really. It's only necessary for me to translate especially the two epics, *The Anthem of the Decades* and *Parashaba the Great*, to make a point, because people might think that oh, he's writing in Zulu, maybe he's not so great; this Zulu, it's a native language, or a Bantu language, or tribal ... all that kind of mentality and attitude. I want to straighten it out and I want people to know that, yes, it is not the demoralised people who create masterpieces. It is their spirit that revolts against demoralisation and against their marginalisation. So I see that responsibility.

I'm not writing just for my own people. It's just like somebody who is English and the bulk of the population in the world is not English. Nobody suggests that everybody should write in Chinese, because there is the biggest audience. But I believe that if you are born with a hundred people, it is still your responsibility to record their experience, to dramatise their experience, their way of seeing things and so on. The language is very controversial sometimes, because people are trying to cross the borderline of occupation. I'm not. I didn't feel occupied, my family didn't give that idea that I was occupied by foreigners. It actually taught me to despise foreigners. I could not understand the attitude of those people who were writing in English. I just couldn't understand it.

But in writing in Zulu, it's not out of a kind of sense of nationalism or Zuluism. I'm very clear myself: if there's any nationalism, it's a commitment to the African continent, to the renaissance of the African people, so that with their energies, they are able to participate in the world as it changes, as it develops. They have got their own contribution; they have done so in the history of the past, and they should continue to do so. I'm not a Zulu poet, I'm an African poet. I speak Zulu, I write in Zulu, it is the language that I can control better. If I was Yoruba, I would write in Yoruba. If I was an Ethiopian, I would write in a language that is most common in Ethiopia, whether it's Amharic or any other language.

I came to America to look for a job. My wife had gone to her home, because according to our tradition the first child must be born in her home. I was invited to Stanford University as a visiting professor. Stanford wanted me to stay, but I went to UCLA because it was a tenured position. I've been here ever since.

One cannot be happy away from one's home. I am not. I always ask myself the question why am I here? Then I realise that if I was anywhere else, there would be a lot of digression, diversion in my task – namely to write. Not only poetry but many other texts that need to be written: philosophies and cosmologies, that belong to our regeneration and renaissance of our continent. That's very important. Being here, I'm isolated from political activism, but there are enough things that I can do, that I have done here. I've got good relations and fortunately my wife is very active herself, so she has done a lot here. And as you see, I've also trained my children to be involved in everything. It's no use just merely talking about South Africa when you have no sensitivity about the condition of people where you are. So involvement here there is. I know that if I was in another place, in New York for instance, or London, I would be more engaged in everyday organisational politics. But, as I say, isolation is highly creative because I have been able to do a lot of work.

Are you thinking of going back?

It is not a question of thinking; I will definitely go back. It is my home. I will go back when the time comes. It's not an issue because I'm not American, I'm African through and through. There's no question about it, I'm an African. It will just happen. I will just go. When Mandela came out I was invited by BBC to go, but I felt that I shouldn't go at that time. I just felt that it's enough for other people to be there to celebrate the occasion, and for us to celebrate here the release of Mandela, Sisulu, of many others. It was a very great event. I went to a press conference, and I left and I was alone. I was very greatly moved by the occasion because it meant so much of our history; so much of the things, the campaigns that were done, the demonstrations, it was really a point of change.

ANTHONY SHER
London 1991

'I very quickly found I didn't want people to know I was South African; I didn't want to be identified with it, to the extent of actually losing my accent.'

He has a distinguished career as an actor, a writer and an artist. Not exactly an exile, yet not entirely an emigrant.

When I look back, my degree of ignorance about South Africa while I was there was staggering. I had never heard of Nelson Mandela, I'd never heard of the ANC, I didn't know blacks carried passes, I didn't know about the townships. I knew absolutely nothing other than what I needed to know, and what was comfortable around me.

I think the majority of white South Africans then, and maybe even now, are not aware of the implications of being South African. It's a society that closes itself off to people thinking about the context that they're in. It's a society that reassures you all the time, isn't it? It's a society that . . . that gives an illusion of well being to the whites. And that's entirely how I was brought up. The servants in our home fitted in with my vision of the world: that we were superior forms of life, they were somehow inferior forms. And both sides were happy; we smiled and joked and were polite to one another . . . them, of course, saying 'Master' and us referring to them as servants. And so the illusion was of a happy world, luxurious for us, with them not being particularly troubled by it. I don't think in all the time I was in South Africa did I experience a black person expressing any other kind of view.

I suppose my first consciousness of being an outsider in any sense, was as a Jew. You know, just in the banal ways in that at school you're aware that you're having other holidays than the majority of the kids. We were orthodox Jews, in that kind of middle of the road way, without passionate belief, but enough to make one be aware of it. So I think maybe that, and an awareness from quite an early age of being sexually different. I can actually trace my homosexuality back to as early as I can remember. So I suppose the Jewish and the gay thing, although still very kind of unformed, must have given me some sense of being an outsider myself and must have connected, even subconsciously, with knowing to some extent what the black and coloured people were experiencing. Knowing what it was like to be the disliked group, the disapproved of group. But purely subconsciously, in no logical way.

It's very difficult to imagine what would have happened if I'd stayed. Sexually I knew I was different.

That sense of being an outsider did surface again when I did nine months in the entirely white army. You were quickly formed into status ranks; the best thing to be was Afrikaner Dutch Reformed and then the next best thing was English-speaking Christian and then English-speaking Jewish – a third-class citizen. And that was, I suppose, my most intense experience of what it was like to be a second-or third-class citizen in South Africa. You were very aware that racially you were not the right thing. It wasn't anything like what black people experience, but it was enough to shock you as someone who'd led a very privileged life up until then. You're now away from home, and you're suddenly aware of being called *Jood*, of this constant word *Jood, vokking Jood*, coming at you. That is shocking.

But I think my move to come here was a combination of all sorts of subtle things rather than a very direct, very definite thing.

It had always been the idea that I would leave. Initially it was to come to art school, then it changed to drama school . . . But either way it was always overseas, that wonderful word 'overseas'. I was eighteen or nineteen.

So I came over and my parents came over with me. My parents had booked one of those 'Europe in Ten Days' by coach trips. And we discovered that our coach was entirely filled with a large Indian family, the Patels. My parents started behaving very oddly. My mother went to try and get our tickets changed, and I suddenly felt an extraordinary sense of fear and confusion; and suddenly a sense of . . . that we were no longer in cosy South Africa, that we were in a world where we could be with people of a different skin, for whatever reason. It was causing my parents distress.

When they couldn't change the tickets, they considered cancelling the trip. But we didn't. We went on the coach with the Indian family and, of course, it was fine. Except for a day when the head of the Patel family asked my father where he was from. And I remember going cold because my father said South Africa. It was just a sense of fear, it's the only way I can describe it. A sense of unpleasantness.

I very quickly found I didn't want people to know I was South African, I didn't want to be identified with it, to the extent of actually losing my accent. I suddenly realised I was part of a despised minority, and I wasn't going to buy that. It was more complicated than being Jewish, being gay, because I wasn't sure that I wanted to disown those things, although I spent many years pretending not to be gay. Whereas with being a white South African, I knew very quickly it was something I wanted to disown. Of those three groups, that was the one I instinctively knew was wrong. Now I'm happy to be gay and although I'm not a practising Jew, I'm happy to be thought of as Jewish. But I absolutely will not stand by anything white South Africa has done. And that I knew early on. I don't know why. That led to a certain deep shame that grew as I stayed in London and found out more about South Africa. A sense of shame.

At the time of finishing drama school in London, I was determined not to go back to South Africa. So I did a postgraduate course, partly as a way of buying some extra time. Then I was here to stay.

I've spent a long time not being South African and trying to be a British actor which I suppose I've succeeded in. But I find life much more stimulating and satisfying now that I'm no longer doing that. Since I've become involved politically about South Africa, I feel South African again; and indeed a lot of my recent work, both writing and acting, has been related to my background, either in terms of South Africa or from a Jewish point of view. I now feel quite passionately about it being virtually impossible to suppress one's background, one's upbringing. It sneaks up on you in the strangest way. When I went to Kenya a couple of years ago, I found I was so moved just by the smell of the earth, the colour of the air, the bushes that I recognised from the Karoo. During a sunrise one morning in Kenya I realised that I was undeniably African and that it was very, very much in my blood.

Black culture is not something that I can really be part of. I'm fed by it, but it's not a culture that I could imagine myself contributing to. I feel South African in my blood; I feel it undeniably in my blood. I think it is contradictory, I think it is a struggle for me in identifying myself.

I have a career as an actor and as a writer which is based in this country. To throw that away is not something I'd want to do. I think as well it's to do with being a gay – I feel more comfortable in this country, it's still something which is illegal in South Africa.

I'm writing a novel about . . . you know, the breed of white South Africans who left simply because they were fearful, who because they had the money to get out, have gone out. And that's the sort of central character of my new book. So it's South African centred, but with the experience of being in this country and indeed, dealing with a lot of the things that we're talking about. Of seeking identity, denying identity.

When I wrote my first novel it was all about my family history, roughly based on my grandfather going to South Africa at the beginning of the century – that was a time of me facing up to my background; and through the medium of art, of writing, confronting the question of roots and cultural identity. It changed my lifestyle. It led me to this new feeling of that's what I am even if I don't live there now.

Of course, being an actor, you are changing identity all the time anyway. But I do know that on the few occasions when I've played South Africans, I found that my whole body had gone Whoooff with relief, even if one isn't anything like the character. I did the Athol Fugard play, *Hello and Goodbye*; the character in that is a poor white from Port Elizabeth, which I'm not, and yet there was still such wonderful relief and joy in being able to do that accent. And quite recently on the BBC I played a Jewish South African living here, very close to me. That was the first time that I was actually speaking in the accent that I brought over twenty-one years ago, and found that just the most delightful relief, to finally do that.

It's such an interesting question – the idea of my family being in Eastern Europe as the century began, then making that huge journey and growing up through the century in South Africa. I find it absolutely related to the South African situation, in that it seems to me that Jewish people like my family had to bury their own experience of persecution, in order to become blind to what was happening in South Africa and become persecutors. For the persecuted to become the persecutor, they had to forget; they had to wipe clean. And indeed my family, my parents know no stories about Lithuania although three of my grandparents came from there. When I started to research my previous book and needed some information, they knew nothing; their parents had told them nothing, they didn't carry their stories with them. That intrigues me. I'm doing a play at the moment about a survivor of the holocaust and the whole theme of the play is about whether to forget or remember traumatic experience. And in this play, the character chooses to forget and subsequently becomes a monster himself.

I feel . . . no, I don't feel shame, I feel a terrible sadness for what my family have gone through. Terrible sadness that they never educated themselves to understand. That people bury their own experience of persecution, and don't relate to others. And not just the Jewish people, but the Afrikaners, who suffered terrible persecution, and have simply learned the worst habits of their persecutors, the British.

I know that when I go back to South Africa that there's something intensely moving and reassuring, strangely enough, about that land mass that is Africa. In England, however beautiful it is, and I've been very moved by those fields and all of that Cotswold landscape . . . But Africa! And yet I'm not . . . I'm probably Lithuanian and probably before that, I could be – whatever! [Laughs] . . . It's very bewildering.

AUDREY KGOMOTSO MOTAUNG
Hamburg 1990

'Black people who have lived outside, we've gained more than the owners of the countries where we live. They don't know us; but we know them.'

A professional singer who composes her own songs, for her exile has not been negative, despite the bad times. If she had never left, she says, she would not have been able to develop as far as she has. Black people, she says, are joyful people, 'We play a lot. We laugh too much.'

I was trained as a teacher, and I felt: I'm just a liar. There was nothing good I'm doing to the kids; I was just giving them this kind of education that the government wants me to give them; to feed them with wrong information – not actually broaden their ideas, giving them knowledge of what's happening around the world. We knew more about the Voortrekker history than our own history, than the world's history.

On the other hand, I was making music and I tried to study music. Those possibilities were not there in South Africa for us black people who were interested in art and culture and all that. It was really closed up. So I joined up with a white group. These white musicians, they are the ones who actually helped me to get out of the country. Alone I wouldn't have made it.

I went to England with the group, and to my surprise, I think people were still not yet open to the fact that there was a black and white South African group. I was singing with this group – 'Hawk'. Some in England, mostly blacks, looked at it with some kind of sceptism. Maybe she's a sell-out? She must be working as a spy, working with the government! How did she manage to get out? – and all that. That really disturbed me, this kind of attitude mostly from my own people. I thought I was making a statement that we are liberal people, the blacks in South Africa; we do want to share our lives with the whites. But I was regarded with suspicion.

Things were starting to shape up a bit, with a contract with a British company. But there was a turmoil. In this group it was six whites and four blacks. So there was this kind of things: 'Aah yes, they are exploiting you.' I came out of South Africa saying, 'Now I'm going to show the world that black South Africans are capable of living together with the others too, we are capable of doing something good. It's not only fists high every time saying "Down with the whites, down with this and that". We can do creative things, work on the creative side with the white South Africans.' I was shocked to find so much suspicion, because I wasn't expecting it.

The whole thing just got spoiled. The black members got out of the group, and I was in the end the only one left in there. [Laughs] And it's obvious – then the suspicion grows. Ah you see! The others are gone; so she's the one; there must be something wrong with this one.

When the group broke up, I was faced up with a real hard time. So you had to look for a job, just working . . . scrubbing floors, forgetting that you are trained teacher, you've studied – these kind of things. You really forget them at that moment, because you want to survive. You want to get money to live, pay your rent and have something to eat – that was the most important thing. I used to do some petty jobs, like singing in jazz clubs – which is also good in a way, because I learned to know some jazz musicians I'd only heard of when I was in South Africa. But nothing could quench my thirst of wanting to make music further. So I left

London because I didn't see any progression at all. I became frightened. Would I end up being in the streets? I think that's what made me really run away from the country, searching for a better peaceful place.

I just thought maybe Germany . . . they went through a lot of things: the first world war, second world war; and they started both wars. So I said, 'Maybe this time they've learnt much more; they won't do anything like that.'

So I came to Germany. Here in Hamburg there were some people from South Africa and one family gave me a place to live. I was sort of a nanny for their family, so that I could make ends meet. Then after a while I thought: oh well, why not try America? You've never seen it, you've never lived there, you just hear about it. Why not? I went to America.

I was there in Pittsburgh for almost a year. It was devastating, it was depressing. I didn't think it was like that. We get the wrong information that America's the greatest, America's the best artistically, musically, economically, industrially. So one thinks, 'Oh, this seems like it will be heaven on earth.' And when I got there it was OK. I was really excited now; oh, I'm living in the States. Until I really found out what it meant as a black to live in America. It's really hard. You have to have good qualifications, you have to have a good job, money, to survive. As a South African you see it.

I was able to sing, but most of the time in churches. That was good. It gave me much more power to keep on hoping that things might be good. That church singing, it has so much influenced my music. You know that if you sing for almost a year in the church, this Gospel music, this Baptist Church music, it becomes part of your life. So it was like blooming. It was just beautiful. And every time, even today, I still sing church music. I still sing Gospels.

That's a part of America that I could never forget. It always will keep living in my heart. But the other part of it was not what I wanted. So that's why I left it, and came back to Hamburg wanting to go to a music school, having no money. And I had a child at that time. I was not married, so it was difficult to make ends meet. Did odd jobs for over three, four years, any job I could find, until I got a job at a department store. I learned, worked myself higher until I was able to lead a department for myself. For ten years I did that. I really had a hard time; I had to take care of my kids. I have four children – a sixteen-year-old girl, a fourteen-year-old girl, and two boys, nine and five. I had to be a housewife, I had to work in the department store, I had to compose songs, write my lyrics, make music, sing in the churches, singing in clubs. So it was quite . . . it was a hard time.

Then I came here to my present work. It's Festival des Frauen – it's a platform for women, creative women. It gives women a chance to express themselves artistically – women from all over the world. We don't deal only with German women. There is a festival every two years.

My job is in communication, calling artists, talking to them, trying to win them for our festival, being polite [laughs] – that's very important with artists; you have to be polite because artists are very sensitive. And I do a lot of translation of letters, German to English.

I still perform – this work here gives me a chance to perform. If I say to my Directorate: 'I have to do a show tonight, I have to leave earlier', I can leave. There's a lot of flexibility in this kind of work. It's artists working for artists. Our director, she's also a conductor in an orchestra, classical music. Artists doing something for artists – run by women. We do have men working with us, we can't do without them; we do need them for some more technical things.

I haven't only developed musically, I think I have a better vision. I can see things much differently now. I think in those years I was too young, I had a lot of turmoil inside me. In South Africa, you aren't given all these chances to articulate yourself. So you're hungry. You're yearning to have this and that and that at the same time.

I had one year of professional training. And I'm having piano lessons, so I'm still developing. I haven't stopped as yet.

I have two children with a South African. There we come to this fact – that when South Africans come out of South Africa, they change. The men get so extreme, terrible, that there's nothing you can do with them. I said to myself: oh well, he's going through a period of getting at forbidden fruit – in South Africa, black men would never dream of having an affair with a white woman. It was something that maybe even if they wished to, it's impossible. It's very dangerous.

And when they come you find out that what you are striving for, it's not in their mind. They just want to have fun. And I understand it, you know. At long last they can really breathe out, take a hunk of bread and say: Now I am my own master. I can do what I want to do, how I want to do it, when I want to do it, with whom I want to do it. And you, as a black woman, you are really left on the side. So either you live with him, you accept all these things, or you say: 'Not with me.' And so I decided: Not with me. So I separated from him.

Then I got married to a man from West Africa, which is also very funny because it's a different culture altogether. But my husband and I, we really found a way of getting along with each other. I took a bit from his culture, and he took a bit from my culture. So we just made it a point to find a neutral way which is good for both of us, and for the children.

Do my children know what nationality they are? We do talk about it. I asked my daughter once: 'In which language do you dream?' She says, 'In German.' I said to her, 'So you feel German?' She says, 'Not really; I think German; I speak German; but I don't feel German.' I said, 'But you behave German.' She says, 'Well, how does an African behave then?' So it was difficult from my side to explain to the child how an African behaves.

So we went through a lot of things. I said, 'Look. We automatically respect grown-ups in South Africa; doesn't necessarily have to be your mother – can be somebody who's just a grown-up. And you don't have this respect in Germany. For you, you just talk anyhow and behave anyhow to anybody you feel like – that's a typical European way of living. We don't do this kind of things.' I had to go through a lot of things to show her the difference between our culture and the German culture. But she couldn't get along with it, because she couldn't see anything wrong in what they are doing. She saw how we go along with our behaviour in South Africa . . . she saw it as being restricted. She said, 'Then the children don't have a freedom to articulate themselves if they have always to be told, do this, don't do this. When do they have a time to say that I don't want to do it?'

To make it all worse, my husband is Muslim, he's West African. So it's two ways: you have this African chauvinistic way; you have this typical hyper-religious way of behaviour of Muslims. Say when we get visitors, he wants the children to wear scarves on the head and all that. I said, 'Look, you can't do that. You can do that if you were married to a Muslim woman – she would easily accept that. But I don't. I don't go around hanging things on my head because I have to satisfy your friends or whoever comes in the house. This is our house, this is not their house. This is not your house alone – if you are living alone you can do all that.' So it's not an easy marriage. It might be from the love side of it very easy, but from living together it's not an easy marriage. And for the kids it can be really suppressive sometimes. Most of the time it's only the boys who get the best, ja, who have the freedom, and even access to everything. But the girls always have: 'Don't do that. Do this. Don't do this.' And this is not good at all.

My girl, the fourteen-year-old, she plays classics, she plays piano. And so my nine-year-old plays piano too. They always sit down together. Ah! So you want to train all the kids to be like you! Because with the Muslim way of thinking, women don't have to be musicians or do something like that, because music is parallel to prostitution.

My eldest daughter, she grew up in South Africa. She came over here to join me at nine, so she knows South Africa very well. But the others, who've never been to South Africa, they are very sceptical about it, they're not sure whether that's the right decision to take – to go back there.

Me? I say, in a way I'm scared. Or I would say I'm not ready enough. Or maybe I push it most of the time away from my mind. Or maybe I would say that I've developed musically much too much, that I wouldn't accept all those things I used to accept before. Then there would be some kind of problems for me too. So I don't think at this stage – when things are still not as good, as quiet as all that – that I'm really ready to go home.

I just want to be able to reach a point where I can be able to help my people and do something for them. Like, when I feel that I'm ready to go

back to South Africa, I can go there to try to work with children, to teach
them what I've learned musically. Voice training, what I've learned here.
I can just turn it back and say, 'Look kids. Come. It's what I've learned –
let's do it together.' These are the things which are very important for me
– learning, learning, learning.

The other important thing is a closer communication with white
people, which I never had in South Africa. I think, in a way it has helped
me to come down a bit, because you get too rough with yourself; and you
say: Oh, I hate these people. Look what they did to us! But now I'm
learning to differentiate. I know it's not all of them who were like that.
There are some who really are trying to do good.

I think the black people who have lived outside, we've gained more
than the owners of the countries where we live. They don't know us; but
we know them. We know them much more than they think. And we
accept their wrongs – they don't accept our wrongs. We accept their
good – they don't know anything about us.

The Europeans themselves, they haven't changed at all towards each
other. They are not cosmopolitan at all. We Africans are. We live
everywhere, we live with everybody. Because we are open to the world,
and they are not as yet open. They are not open to themselves: how can
they be open to us, the Africans?

They only know that we are primitive creatures. That's all they know
about black people. Nothing more.

WELCOME MSOMI and THULI DUMAKUDE
New York 1991

WELCOME: 'When you are in exile you are not looking for sympathy,
but you can create things with people; you can inspire people, make them
aware of what is around them.'

He is a sophisticated, charming theatrical producer who has also
been an actor and a writer. 'I am part of the world,' he says.

THULI: 'It doesn't mean that because America is one of the richest
countries in the world, somebody hands you a bag of gold when you get
out of the airport. You're still just as poor.'

She is Welcome's young-looking, vivacious wife, with expressive
face and gestures. Her eldest child is twenty.

WELCOME: I produced a show called *Umabatha*, which was a Zulu
version of *Macbeth*. It went to London in 1972/73 and it was a great

success. Then after that it went to Italy, Zimbabwe and other places, then came to the United States in 1978.

THULI: I was a teacher with the Durban Adult Choir. Then I couldn't continue with my teaching profession so I decided to join a theatrical group. I was involved in stage production of *Umabatha*. That brought me to this country. I wouldn't say it was my decision to stay, it was his decision! [Laughs] He told me, before he left South Africa he had already done almost everything he could do in the country to grow as an artist. Now he needs to go somewhere else and face new challenges. And I think by the time we got here, his mind was already made up that whatever happens, I'm not going back.

But having left my family – we had a house, children at home – I didn't tell anybody that I wasn't coming back; it was really hard for me. But we've always worked together, we have always created things together; and I knew that if we stay here together and still do what we had already started in South Africa, we might accomplish a lot. And it turned out to be good decision.

I was more excited than scared. Here I was coming to the so-called richest country in the world! Very influential. But when I got here, I was very sceptical. I found that there were just problems like in any other country. I think the picture I had in my mind was of a free, rich country where nobody suffers! [Laughs] So when I went to Harlem and saw drugs and starving people, homeless people, I said, well, I was wrong.

There were quite a number of culture shocks. I visited a friend; I saw that there were about four, five locks on the door. I said, 'Is it this bad? I mean you have to lock the door five times before you feel safe?' And he said, 'Ja, it's that bad.' And not talking to your neighbours. No. You just don't know the name of your neighbour, you hardly see them, you hardly communicate with them. So for me, all these things were . . . I mean what kind of a country is this? What kind of a neighbourhood is this? Is it me? Very, very strange and very scary.

WELCOME: When *Umabatha* closed in New York, my wife and I started a theatre company here in New York. We started with dance classes; after that we developed theatrical productions, which were showcased and performed in some of the major theatres, like the Brooklyn Academy of Music here in New York. Since we didn't have much money, I had to find a job. I worked for a pharmaceutical company in public relations, so that helped me. And so I worked from nine to five, after five I would go to my theatre company.

I found a place out in Brooklyn, where we did dance classes and music. I told people that I want to establish a theatre company in Brooklyn in a place called Bedford Stuyvesant, which is one of the run-down areas, what you call the ghettos of America. And they said, 'Why should you go there? You should be in Manhattan, that is where everything is happening, where you go for success.' For success! Then I said, 'No, I want to go to Bedford Stuyvesant, I want to work with the people.'

And so we started with dance classes, and people who came were told that after six months, when they graduate, they're going to be part of this important company. Some had never danced in their lives, and we started working with them. And after six/eight months, we formed the company and I got in touch with theatres; and when they performed, people couldn't believe it. Others thought these must be South Africans.

I wanted to do stories on South Africa, stories that depict life in the townships, stories with music, with dance. Not just the terrible side of life, but how people survive . . . sure, that's right. Because at times we can get trapped to believing that yes, the system is terrible, it's bad and we are all suffering. But then we have to look on the other side; what is it that keeps us going in spite of all that? So we had to train the Americans, not only just in the music and the dancing, but also in the languages.

Now, when the parents came, they came with their children and they would leave the children outside. And then one day, I said, 'No, let's make use of the children!' So we created the children's company. We would teach these children our National Anthem, and they sang *Nkosi 'Sikelele* in Zulu and Sotho. You know, you couldn't believe that these were American children, the way they performed, the way they danced.

THULI: But to qualify to be in the children's company, you had to be disciplined and to be disciplined, in an African context, is to listen to the elders, which they didn't do. They were demanding their own time: 'This is my time to speak, you have to listen.' And I said, 'Wait a minute, I'm the adult, I'm in control here, you have to do the listening.' And the children got used to my style and my way of doing things.

I found that they couldn't do their own laundry, and I said, 'How come an eleven-year-old, your mother does your laundry? She cleans your room? No. For you to qualify to be in this dance company, you've got to get up in the morning, do your own laundry, do your own cleaning and then come to the dance class.' And I check each and every one. And in no time, the parents were calling me, 'What did you do to these children?' Well, I don't know, it just takes a little bit of working on them.

WELCOME: People wanted to know: 'What is this language you speak?' We said: 'It's Zulu', and they said, 'Can you teach us?' So we started language classes, and among the people who came there was John Soaries. He was very enthusiastic. He wanted to learn the language; and in eight months he was teaching the language. Then he suggested we should write a book together, *The Student and the Teacher*. And we did, and we have a book which is out with cassettes that teach the language.

Getting back to Bedford Stuyvesant: I said to them, 'We can create Broadway, here in this place.' And they said, 'No it's impossible, you don't have any chairs, there are no lights, there is no sound system.' I said, 'I'll show you how we're going to do it. We will create our own money. If you each put in $10, or $20, we can get these things.' They all said, 'It's never going to work – things tried in this place have all always failed; maybe ten or twenty people show up.' So I said, 'No, we will work hard, advertise, get great lights; we are going to rent the chairs, all the things that we need.'

On the day of the performance, everybody was afraid for me. They didn't think anybody would come, that all this money was going to be lost. I went to the police station and asked for barricades, because I was expecting big crowds; and they said, 'Where are you going to perform this?' I said, 'At the Armoury in this area.' They said, 'No, but nobody goes there – where're you from?' I told them that I'm from South Africa; and they said, 'Well, it's understandable, you wouldn't know.'

On the day of the performance, at 7 o'clock, I was busy setting up the lights and someone came and said, 'Go outside and see what has happened!' I said, 'Something wrong?' I went outside. There was a long line all around the block, people wanting tickets. We packed that place, and of course the people who had invested the money got it back and they started asking me, 'When are we going to do another one?' It was song, dance, poetry, it was cultural variety. And that is how we built the company, just inspiring people, just saying that it's possible. That is how we started to develop the theatre.

I write the scripts and my wife does the choreography. We have worked together all the time. She did the production *Poppie Nongeni* in London and won the Laurence Olivier award for that, so . . . she's a good choreographer.

A theatre or a musician is not just someone who keeps people entertained; you have to reach out to people, to the community. And it is not like I'm a refugee, I'm in exile, so you must feel sorry for me. No, you say to yourself, 'I am part of the world!' And it's not just South Africa. It is America. You can create things with people, you can inspire people, you can make them aware of what is around them. And then you take them from that situation and you say, 'Now you can do this for the other people – in South Africa.'

THULI: I am a choreographer, I'm a dancer, I'm an actress, I'm a singer. I do everything. My first love was singing. Everything else developed out of singing, and the more I did it, the more I got a kick out of it. Oh my goodness, I can act! And then I started really refining that, because as you well know, we never had institutions where we could be trained to be professional actors or actresses. So I had to use my way of teaching myself. And that is how I grew, ja.

I haven't had an album, I think in fifteen years, for a simple reason. I've had quite a number of offers to do an album, but the lyrics or the style were not acceptable for big recording companies. It was either too political or – as they put it – too strong. 'People don't need to be bombarded with this kind of . . . ' you know. And I said I come from South Africa. I CAN sing things like 'I love you', but there is a lot more that we have to address as artists. It does not mean that because one is an artist, one is not politically aware of what is going on. This is my platform, this is my way of communicating with ordinary people without threatening them. So if you want me to record with you, you like the voice and yet you don't want the lyrics of my songs, you cannot have one and leave out the other. I would rather not have an album. And basically that is the reason, ja.

WELCOME: This has been a learning experience for me. I can take this back and work with the children in South Africa – it is one of the major projects that I'm planning to do, besides the revival of *Umabatha*. When I went back to South Africa I decided to have auditions to see if it could be done. In Johannesburg a thousand people came; in Durban, over two thousand people. And in Newcastle a group of children between the ages of nine and eleven inspired me. They were so wonderful, dancing and singing. Excellent! They were like professionals. They told me, 'We walked about sixteen miles to come to the audition.' And I said, 'You walked?' And they said, 'We came from a farm school.' With their teacher, a marvellous woman who believes in her work.

Then I started to look to do something for the children in South Africa. People said: Are you going to do it just for the black children? Then I said: Why not with all the children? It is my belief if we really mean a new South Africa, it has to be the children. We cannot talk about all these great ideas and leave out the children. So we're going to have these children from Newcastle, and then we are going to have children from Johannesburg, Durban and Cape Town, and establish centres where children are going to be taught all disciplines in the theatre – stage managers, lighting designers, actors, singers, dancers, and create video productions. All working together.

These are the things that excite me, that we feel need to be done; and in our own area, as we have done with American kids.

THULI: I went back to South Africa last year, 1990. That was another kind of culture shock, it really was. I was happy to be home but I was very depressed, very, very depressed. I had never been as scared as that, ever. I don't know, I even started to think that if people are anticipating freedom, does it take this route? Because I found that the state of confusion is so evident.

In Johannesburg there were a lot of people in the business world excited about the new South Africa, the merging of the white companies and black companies and white and black partners. But in the midst of all of that, I said it feels like we are leaving the children behind. I mean totally. I used to drive in the townships, maybe during the day, twelve o'clock noon, find young boys between the ages of thirteen to seventeen, eighteen, hanging around on the corners on a school day! They have absolutely nothing to do. Nothing to do!

One kid said to me, 'I haven't been in school for four years; my slogan was: freedom first, education after. And I still believe in that, but I have been left out. I have paved ways for other people and I have been left out and this is why I'm angry. People don't know what I feel inside. You don't know that kind of feeling when you just have no future. And you have opened up things for millions of people and nobody addresses your problem.' And I said, 'What would you want me to do for you?' And he said, 'To be honest with you, I don't know and I don't care!'

WELCOME: I've been here about eleven years. It's like another home. I cannot divorce myself from this place and yet I know I have a lot of work to do in South Africa. So I'm going to divide the time. Yes, I'll work in both.

Exile has been a great experience for me. It taught me to find ways of creating things for myself and creating things for other people. And that is why I cannot just forget about America. I cannot just go home and say, 'Forget America.' America has become a part of my life – also Europe. I cannot just go and remain in South Africa. I feel that I will bring South Africa out to the world.

THULI: I have four children – twenty, eighteen, seventeen and nine. The nine-year-old was born in this country and when he was conceived, I was already teaching African dance classes; and now I really do believe that a baby can hear sounds and react to things in the womb. He's a drummer, and I remember that whenever I was teaching, the minute the drums started to bang, he would literally jump up and down in my tummy! [Laughs] Three weeks after he was born, I went back to teaching classes but I checked with the doctor if the drums were not too much for his eardrums; and he said: As long as he doesn't cry, he's enjoying it. So I took him there, he crawled in the dance classes, he started to play drums in the dance classes, now he's a drummer.

Exile has given us many opportunities, but the price was very high. I learned that because America is one of the richest countries in the world, it doesn't mean somebody hands you a bag of gold when you get out of the airport. You're still just as poor. There were moments when I said, 'I was better off in South Africa.' But I remembered how my mother used to make a stew out of potatoes and pap and we had a meal! So I went back to that. It was very, very hard and nobody looks out for you.

I saw that a lot of men were very much involved in drinking, maybe to remove themselves from the reality of South Africa, and the expectations that they cannot provide for their wife and children. But I found that women would take nothing and create something out of that. A meal out of nothing. And it really . . . it hurt me. I think women do that everywhere, they do, but you just wonder. Women are hard, hard, hard workers. And the pride that I have in what they do is that they don't sit next to the sidewalk with their hands out and asking for money. You've got to go out there and be just as aggressive – and the aggressiveness in this country is 100 per cent. But you learn.

What will I take back with me from America? Aggressiveness! I like that, because it makes you . . . you crack through the little crevasses that you never thought you would. We come from a society that is very scared to explore. But in this country, one thing that I like about it is that it is aggressive, though it needs to be controlled. But I think, yeh, I will take aggressiveness with me. [Laughs]

Citizens of Two Countries

Whether or not they wished it, some of the exiles became irrevocably a part of the country to which they went. Through their work, their marriages, or their own preferences, they became firmly rooted in their host countries. In a sense they had shifted from being exiles and had become emigrants, bearing the citizenship and responsibilities of their adopted country. They dreamed of returning, when that would become possible, but only for a visit. Their children, growing up in Zambia, Canada, Germany – wherever – were aware of their South African connection, but regarded themselves as Zambian or Canadian or German. But the once-exiles, regardless of their work, their loyalties, or the passports they carried, felt that they were, and would always be South African.

There were some among the exiles who were not born in South Africa and did not grow up there. But nevertheless, for reasons they themselves explain, when they had to leave, they felt they too were being exiled from South Africa.

These are a few of many such citizens of two countries . . .

MICHAEL LAPSLEY
Harare 1990

'Just one piece of paper too many . . . I was on the hit list.'

He is forty-one, well set up, black-bearded, with a receding hair-line and a ready smile.

I was born in New Zealand. My first connection with South Africa is *Naught For Your Comfort*, Trevor Huddleston's book. As an adolescent it had a profound impression on me, but I never imagined that I would end up in South Africa. I joined an Anglican religious order in Australia, and trained for the priesthood. And then, in 1973, I was transferred to the South African province of the Society, and became a student at the University of Natal. And also subsequently Chaplain to the two-black one-white University Campus in Durban.

I was twenty-four, I had just been ordained. Being chaplain to the black medical school and to the Indian University and the essentially white campus, I lived in a South Africa that few people did, and was part of all those communities. It would have been easy if I'd simply lived in the black community, to say: well all blacks are good, all whites are bad – that kind of thing. But I was exposed to the humanity of the whole of South Africa, and was able to see very quickly the way in which the system entraps and dehumanises everybody, oppressed and oppressor. And everyone's need of liberation. The Gospel said that all people were equal. But apartheid said only white people were equal; all others were 'non-whites'.

Before I went, I thought of myself as a human being. On arrival my humanness was removed, and I became a 'white man'. There was nothing I could do to escape from my whiteness. It defined every aspect of my existence: the suburb I could live in, the beach where I could swim, the entrance to the post office that I could use, the toilet I could enter, and so on. I could say that I was opposed to apartheid, that I believed that all people are equal. But it made no difference. I was white, and had all the advantages of being white. Structurally, I had become an oppressor. As a white foreigner I would be eligible for citizenship and the vote within five years – things denied all blacks born in South Africa.

I was a convinced pacifist – which is unusual for Anglicans. We Anglicans usually bless wars. We blessed most wars in history. [Laughs] I used to explain to black students why it was better for them to use non-violent tactics in opposing apartheid. I said that I rejected apartheid – and they used to ask me where I was going to sleep – in my white suburb?

I could say that I would not pull a trigger. But it was not possible to say that I was not involved in violence. Every day I enjoyed and benefited from the fruits of violence, in a system where pigmentation decided how valuable your life is, and how long you are likely to live.

I went to South Africa with an understanding of what it meant to be a Christian, and what the Gospel of Christ meant. But that understanding collapsed totally in the face of apartheid reality. I suppose what I found was that my understanding of the Gospel was a set of words – which was inadequate for that horrendous reality. I saw the way in which faith was used as an instrument of pressure by the regime. So I began to have to rethink the entire Gospel. I realised the Gospel I had received was a spiritualised Gospel, and began to see that liberation is, in fact, the content of the Gospel.

I felt that if I stayed I would have become schizophrenic; that it was tearing me apart as a human being inside. What I was being told by the dominant reality is normal, my whole being was telling me it's not normal; it's actually evil. And yet all around me, somehow, people seemed to have acquiesced to this as a normal reality.

I tried to be consistent. So I would say to young black students, 'You should not take up arms to fight apartheid.' But I would also say to young white students, 'You should not take up arms to defend apartheid.' And that was long before the End Conscription Campaign. I would say to white students, 'It's not good to go to the army!' And so raise a moral question where the state had almost totally removed the moral question. So people would say, 'I have to go to the army' – never, 'I have decided to go to the army.' So raising the question was itself a threat.

I was deeply influenced by the whole Black Consciousness tide, which was at its height; and I saw its extremely positive role in the psychological liberation of black people. Some Christians spoke as if you had the ANC on one hand, the regime on the other, and the Church as a kind of middle way – which I came to see was a failure of analysis. I came to also see that Christianity or the Church could not be the alternative to apartheid.

Christians, like everybody else, have to make political choices in terms of the values they are committed to. And I saw what the ANC represented was clearly the values I believed in as a Christian. For me the fundamental shift was seeing that armed struggle was, in fact, morally legitimate, necessary and justified.

You know, the regime has always said of immigrants, and particularly of church people, 'You come to South Africa, you cause problems for us, but you keep your passports in your back pockets, so that when things get tough you can run away.' I agree. And therefore, when the regime expelled me, I said to the ANC, 'The illegitimate regime has denied me citizenship. I am asking to join the ANC, by which I understand I am taking citizenship in the country that we are still fighting for.'

The ANC, I think, had never been approached in those terms before. But the NEC said yes, OK. And I became a member of the ANC precisely in those terms. I saw that you can go to a place, you can have a kind of commitment, you can do a job. But particularly in a kind of life and death liberation struggle – the commitment has to be for keeps, or not at all.

So for me, membership was a way of saying, 'I will live with the implications of what I am saying. And if I walk this road with these people, I will continue to walk that road as long as we need to walk. For ever.'

It's very difficult to know what was it that said to the regime, 'This man must be expelled.' I would be very interested – if they don't destroy it before we go home – to find the file and see. I think there was just one piece of paper too many in my file. I had been speaking out. There is always a place for those who speak out. But there is also a place for those who act but don't speak. Perhaps if I had it all over again, I may have spoken less and acted more. But I suspect that finally one of the significant pieces of paper had made the file heavier, until it reached the weight when they said, 'No. That's enough!' But I was never given the actual reasons.

So I went to Lesotho, completed my degree at the National University there. They said that I was the first student ever to come from a white South African campus to become a student there. After those devastating years in South Africa, it was a greatly humanising experience no longer to be a 'white man', but a person. When I look back, I think of whiteness as a kind of leprosy. If only it would disappear and I could become a person again.

I became a student leader on that campus as well as a chaplain. It was one of the most politically conscious and politically active campuses in the whole of Southern Africa at that period. I became part of the whole exiled community.

I was away from Lesotho at the time of the massacre in December 1982, when forty-two people were shot dead by the South African army – refugees and Lesotho citizens, including some schoolchildren and babies. They were part of the community where I lived. Together we had shared hopes of a new life where children would sleep peacefully and grow up without fear.

On that day in Lesotho I made a vow that my life would be dedicated to ending apartheid and building a new society – what else could I offer my friends, who had made the ultimate sacrifice, and given me a taste of a new society where it is possible to be human, black or white?

Though I had been away at the time, many people believed that I was still on the hit list. And the Church felt very insecure; and that if I remained, the troops would come back. And so I was forced to leave Lesotho. I was in Britain for nine months, and then I came to Zimbabwe where I've been for the last six years.

> During his time in Zimbabwe he completed a Master's degree in political theology and Marxist philosophy, worked as a parish priest in Nimbari, a high-density African township; and has produced an ecumenical programme for mobilising the religious community and assisting Christians to look at 'why, as an issue of faith, we should be against apartheid'.

For many years, since my days in Lesotho, I've always had what I would describe as a chaplaincy role within the ANC. It comes out in 'rites of passage' – the weddings, the funerals, sometimes the baptisms. Those major events in individual lives, where comrades look for someone who has a religious faith together with a commitment to national liberation. That has always been a role – and particularly at the point of death – to both give thanks for a comrade's life, to articulate the hopes and the commitment, and to renew the faith of all our people, be they religious or not. I have seen the importance of spiritual values in the struggle, regardless of whether or not people are religious.

Apartheid touched within me the deepest parts of what it means to be human. And I realised that, if one is white and western, we've all been infected by this disease of racism; that though I can say I'm against racism, I cannot claim not to be a racist.

Now that things are changing in South Africa, there's going to be a need for healing, spiritually, in the deepest possible sense. For all of us, black and white; those who have been oppressors, those who have been oppressed – and those many of us who are both oppressors and oppressed all at the same time. So I think that kind of priestly role will continue to be important for many, many years, to be very important.

I hope when we are free to return that I will go back. Once the transfer of power takes place, I think that's when the real work will actually begin. The fight for the Freedom Charter, I think, will turn out to have been very easy in comparison with implementing it.

Two months after this interview took place, the Revd Michael Lapsley spent an afternoon with friends at a farewell party – he was leaving to take up a new ministry in Bulawayo. He returned home. His mail waiting there for him included a package that contained two books; it was post-marked RSA – Republic of South Africa. As he opened it, the package exploded, blowing off both his hands, destroying one eye and damaging the other, and leaving his body a mass of wounds. Father Lapsley did not die. Will he ever again be able to fulfil the tasks he had set himself? 'The God of the Bible,' he once wrote, 'I discovered is not neutral, but takes sides, not with religious people, but with the poor and oppressed. Soweto taught me that to ask people to be non-violent in the face of South African apartheid is to ask people to be collaborators in their own deaths. We owe it to our enemies to stay their bloodied hands, both for their sakes and for our own.'

SIR RAYMOND HOFFENBERG
Oxford 1991

'I did break the ban every day, many times a day. It was a strange sort of limbo.'

Before he was banned, 'Bill' Hoffenberg became known to many South Africans through frequent letters to the press, protesting against the many offences of apartheid. He was knighted on being elected President of the Royal College of Surgeons in 1983, and has been President of Wolfson College, Oxford, since 1985.

I left in 1968, largely because I had been banned in 1967. I had asked for reasons and was told that it was not in the interests of the country's security to divulge the reasons. I suppose there were a number of things really. I was the last chairman of the Defence and Aid Fund which had been banned, and after its banning, I sued the Minister of Justice Vorster, for banning the organisation improperly. We lost 3 to 2 in what was obviously a political judgment – there were three Nationalist judges and two United Party. And so I think that made me a little unpopular. We were very active in a lot of other ways. I was on about sixty different committees of one sort or another which were broadly under the umbrella of anti-apartheid activities.

I was chairman of the Board of Advisers to the National Union of Students, so I had a lot to do with the student leaders. And they, of course, really did set the pace of the local opposition from predominantly white groups anyway. I suppose that upset the government as well, because NUSAS was quietly a thorn in their side.

We had a very large number of black friends, and I think we probably knew more about what was really happening than most whites. Embassies, and journalists and correspondents coming to South Africa needed contacts, so we were able to introduce them to people. And a lot of the overseas reporting of events in South Africa would have been based on either information we gave, or information we were able to get for them. So I suppose those were the main reasons for the banning that I can think of.

The banning stopped me from entering any educational institution – I worked for the university so I had to stop that. The university was very good. They continued paying my salary, but it couldn't go on indefinitely. And, of course, the usual bannings – not meeting more than one person, not being quoted, reporting to the police once a week, confined to Wynberg in the Cape, etc. They had already taken my passport away in 1965. So when we came to leave, I had to apply to leave Wynberg. And I came out on a one-way exit permit.

I don't know what would have happened if we had stayed. I suspect I would have got myself into more trouble. I did break the ban every day, many times a day. One couldn't help it. We learned how to shake off the security cars that followed us. The telephone was tapped and the mail was opened, flagrantly . . . you'd see fingerprints and things, glue on the back . . . [Laughs] There was no attempt to disguise it. And why not? I mean everyone knew it was going on. We knew and they knew we knew. There was a nasty period when we had threatening telephone calls and abusive telephone calls, threats on my life and things like that. It was a strange sort of limbo, because I was there for about ten months under the banning order before we left.

Not working is stultifying. I don't think I could have stuck it indefinitely. I suspect I would have found it very difficult not to keep involved with politics in some way. There was a stream of police informers who used to try to trap me into saying things. Up to the moment we left we had problems with a leading member of the church who was trying to trap me into leaving things to store with him – the implication was that I had illegal possession of armaments. This sort of nonsense went on. It was very crude and very easy to see through.

Ultimately, I think I would have been trapped into something or other, because there were just so many pits that they were digging all round one's life. [Laughs] And eventually I think I'd have said or done something, and they'd have been very happy. In that sort of society so many things one did were presumably illegal in the light of their rather strange laws.

Have you been back since?

No. I made myself a personal promise that I wouldn't go back until all exiles were allowed back, and until all apartheid laws had been rescinded. I think it's more or less got to that stage now, and I'm toying with the idea for the first time. I'm not convinced that things are actually very much better, but at least the legal framework has changed. And so yes, there is a temptation to go back. I don't think it would be long term. It's more likely to be for a visit.

I came to London because the Medical Research Council here offered me a job when I was still in Cape Town and trying to make up my mind whether to leave or not. There were quite a number of good reasons for not leaving. I was quite an embarrassment to the government. There certainly was a lot of outcry over my banning, from universities and medical centres throughout the world, because I had a lot of international contacts. I was doing research supported by international agencies and so on. And it was quite tempting to stay and watch the government squirm. But then the Medical Research Council offered me a job that was as good as anything I was going to get.

My children were then eight and seven, I think; so they came to school here and I worked in London for four years and then was appointed to the University of Birmingham as Professor of Medicine there. Lived there thirteen years. I left them prematurely because I had been elected President of the Royal College of Physicians in 1983, and it was impossible to do that job in London and run a very big department in Birmingham. So I gave up Birmingham. And I'd only just given it up when Wolfson College invited me to come here as President of the college, so I accepted. And I've been at Wolfson's since 1985.

How do you feel now? Are you a South African or are you British?

Oh, I'm South African, yes. Unquestionably. And yet I've lived here now for a considerable period of time – twenty-three years, yes, and in a sense, I suppose I feel British. The country's been exceedingly kind to me and couldn't have been more welcoming and more helpful. I certainly have a considerable loyalty to it. But I feel my roots are in South Africa, yes.

My wife is also South African, but I don't think she feels quite the same. The difference is that she has been back because her mother's still there and now very elderly. So Margaret goes out twice a year. I don't think she's enjoyed it, for lots of reasons. She resents the fact I'm not there with her, and so she tends to wear a hair-shirt and not enjoy herself and not meet people. So she won't go down to the Cape and enjoy the scenery or anything like that, [laughs] so her picture of South Africa, I think, is one of a rather unattractive confinement to one suburb of Johannesburg. She's conscious of the poverty of the newspapers and the radio and television, etc., and the fact that it's a very narrow and inward-looking society. Which I'm sure was the case when we were there together, but somehow it didn't matter because our thoughts were being taken up by local problems. We were all looking inwards. Perhaps I need to go back to get it out of my system. She is increasingly conscious of the fact that it is very introspective and narrow. I haven't had that experience – so perhaps I need to go back to get it out of my system.

Children? Well that's another complication because they've emigrated to Australia, both of them. One got married earlier this year – and they're both going to be there permanently. They won't come back here, and I don't think they have their roots in South Africa – they were too young. A sadness of course that they have emigrated – I don't know whether that would have happened anyway.

Since you've been here, have you remained involved in South African affairs?

No, not really. I don't particularly like émigré politics. I think if you want to play politics, you do it on site. I don't particularly like campaigning about South Africa. I've spoken about it many times, and I've written letters and I suppose had some influence in certain circles. But I've not campaigned on that issue since I've been here. That's a personal decision again. I'm not happy with the concept of émigré politics unless you are genuinely an activist.

I think we were very lucky. I came to a fairly good job straight away, so more or less the day I arrived in this country I began to work as a doctor and as a research worker. I think wives probably suffer more, the whole thing is so much harder; particularly the first year when we didn't have a proper house and we were renting furnished accommodation. And it was a particularly bad summer, the first year; there were about four days of sunshine. [Laughs] And the kids didn't adjust well in the beginning.

But we were lucky. At the end of the year, we bought a nice house with a garden; the children went to a new school and they were happy there. And Margaret, having a house and garden and being able to unpack her own things, was happy. And in fact, it's really been a very happy period.

TOINE EGGENHUIZEN
London 1990

'I could simply not shake the dust of South Africa off my feet.'

> He came to South Africa as a missionary, and remained as a human rights activist. A tall, blond man, he is working for the ANC in London.

I was born in Holland where I was studying to become a priest, a Catholic priest of the Dominican Order which had missions in South Africa, Puerto Rico and the Antilles. I've always had greater interest in South Africa than in these other two places. During my studies I was given a specific Biblical study: to debunk the Biblical justification of apartheid in the Dutch Reformed Church. So that also set me more into the line of thinking about Southern Africa.

When I was finished with my studies and it came to deployment I volunteered to go to South Africa. I grew up during the Second World War. I may remember a bit of it. But the real significance of what happened then to the Slavonic people, the Jews, the Gypsies – it's just something incomprehensible. And this strengthened my feeling that apartheid in South Africa is just not on. I was too small to do anything about it in the Second World War, so these different factors led to the fact that I went to South Africa as a missionary.

I spent a little while learning Sesotho, and then I started working in the Orange Free State, in Viljoenskroon. And after about four/five years I just felt that the church was not the right place for me. I used to say to people: The church is more like a statue of liberty than a movement for liberation. And so I resigned. But I had been long enough in South Africa to feel South African.

Up till the point that I went to South Africa I'd been either at home where parents looked after you, or at college and the Seminary, where the congregation or the Order looked after you. In South Africa I was on my own – the first steps on my own two feet. And that helped also to make me feel like a South African.

When I was expelled ten years later, I could simply not shake the dust of South Africa off my feet and get back into Dutch society.

When Ahmed Timol was murdered by the Security Police, a couple of people formed a Memorial Committee, and quickly changed that into the Human Rights Committee. I already had contact with Helen Joseph, and, through Helen, with Indres Naidoo and Ama Naidoo. The Human Rights Committee asked me to join. It was a little committee of people which published the *Human Rights Bulletin*, in which we very carefully wrote South African history, saying on such-and-such a day in such-and-such a year, so many thousand women came together in Pretoria. And on such-and-such a day, so many people came together in Kliptown and adopted what they called the Freedom Charter.

We printed the whole Freedom Charter in the middle page – which was, of course, ideal for people to paste against a wall; we were the first people in the early Seventies who actually published the whole Freedom Charter in South Africa. We kept everything factual. And we had a picture of Nelson Mandela without any editorial comment when he was found guilty and sentenced to life imprisonment.

Of course, the regime knew exactly what we were up to, and every *Bulletin* that came out was immediately banned. So every time we went to a different printer. Then in 1976, in February, they banned not only the latest *Bulletin*, but all future publications of the HRC.

Now in 1976 the Transkei was getting its so-called 'independence'. We tried to form an *ad hoc* body to resist this, but that didn't succeed too well. So we decided on our own to place a full-page advertisement in the newspaper *World*, attacking the so-called 'independence'. It appeared four days before the 'independence' event. We had a coupon on the page asking people to say, 'I agree – or do not agree – to carving up South Africa in Bantustans'. And to send it to the Editor.

Mantanzima and all his cronies must have been livid that the *World* carried a full-page article attacking him and his brothers. And the result of that was that, within days, our Secretary Sheila Weinberg was placed under house arrest. I got a visit from Security Branch asking me where I lived, where I worked, means of transport, what church did I attend if any, did I have a sickness that needed special attention – oh, you know, a whole range of questions that they always ask when they want to put you under house arrest.

I was still carrying a Dutch passport, although I felt like a South African. I never took on South African nationality, not being able to swear allegiance to Die Stem and Vierkleur. So they must have had a little problem there, and ten days or so later I got my marching orders. I had arrived in South Africa 1967 in January, and this happened in November 1976; so it's about ten years.

When I had left the church I had gone to Germiston on the East Rand and worked in a concrete pipe factory. The company took me on because I knew an African language. And then the company was taken over, and the new management provoked a strike – through their mentality and attitude. They found out that I had known the strike was coming up and I hadn't informed them. So when the strike was over, they made me redundant.

Then I worked for a year for the Welgespruit Institute, where we set up an agency dealing with problems relating to migrant workers. We organised a Conference on Migrant Labour, bringing together experts – sociologists, some senior church people, some people in management, some politicians, a multiracial thing in one of those so-called 'international' hotels near Jan Smuts airport. And while we had one or two migrant workers, these were sort of senior clerks and not ordinary migrant workers.

Another way we tried to look at the migrant labour problem was to place about twenty-three black theological students from Lesotho in the rural areas; some of them to look at what happened in areas where the husbands had gone away; some to see what happened in the recruiting area at Maseru, where people were going coming back from the mines; and then some in the black townships, looking at the interaction between the township people and the migrant workers. And eight of the students actually got themselves recruited as miners. All the students were asked to write down everything they heard, and send us letters almost every day of their first impressions, the first things that people told them.

We did a very thorough debriefing of all these students, and we published their experience as *Another Blanket* – a real insight into what migrant work is like. The title *Another Blanket* came from the song that the men sing when they leave Maseru for the mines. It starts off: Now I put on another blanket – in English you would say 'another cap' – Now I become like a rat being chased underground. At home I am like the king in the tree. Illiterate people, but with a very fundamental understanding of the real radical change of personality that has to take place to become a migrant worker.

When we did this study, one old man, a migrant worker since 1948, illiterate, told one of the theological students, 'Imagine you have gone to town to buy some food for your children because they are starving. Now you go home, you come to the river, and the river is flooded. And Satan is standing there. If you go across with Satan, your children will eat. If you refuse Satan, your children will starve.' I've never found anywhere a more moving, more exact description of the migrant labourer's dilemma, and I've used it very often in public speaking.

I was at a conference on migrant labour in Pretoria, organised by UNISA with Judge Theron in the chair. One of the cabinet ministers was the main speaker. It was all establishment controlled. It was not to be a 'political' day; just a look at the problems of migrant labourers and the community.

A representative of the Human Science Institute was saying he had recently done a survey, had interviewed 200 men on their way home after their contract, 200 on the way to start their contract, and 200 women in the rural areas. And the overwhelming majority were happy with the system – something like 95 or 96 per cent. The people actually want that system!

Now that triggered me off because by that time I was really angry at this whole thing. So I stood up and really let fly with all the different experiences that came out of *Another Blanket*; and ended off with the story about this old man, the flooded river and Satan. There were a few black ministers in the audience – they gave me a standing ovation; some of the younger Afrikaner intellectuals were really stunned. Straightaway Judge Theron decided to have a lunch break; but I didn't have a chance for lunch because all these Afrikaner lecturers wanted to know more. To make a distinction between our study and that of the Human Resource Centre, I said to them, 'If you ask someone, "Do you want to be a migrant worker or stay at home?" that is to ask, "Do you want to work to get money, or to stay at home and starve?" Of course the choice will be to be a migrant worker. But if you ask them, "Do you want a job and to earn a wage here at home, or go to Johannesburg?" then most of them will say, "Here, where my family is." ' Oh! They had never thought of that sort of thing.

But the Human Rights Committee thing, the publication of *Another Blanket* and my expulsion notice happened almost simultaneously. The warrant officer who served my expulsion notice, being a bit stupid, gave me ten days to leave the country instead of the usual twenty-four hours. I was able to speak to all the different papers, and most of them started off their reports by saying: 'Migrant Labour study man deported' – or something like that. So the migrant labour thing got a bit of a boost.

Then I came out. And like I said, I couldn't just shake the dust off my feet and forget all about South Africa. There was this friend, the chairman of the HRC, still in Modder B prison; others under house arrest. So my first year back in the Netherlands I spent speaking at whatever platform or venue I was invited to – in Germany, France, Belgium, Canada, Ireland and all over the Netherlands. I became a regular reporter on South African issues for one of the radio stations, giving background information on whatever happened. And I wrote quite a number of articles.

Then I was offered a job at the International Defence and Aid Fund in London, and worked there for two years. The ANC asked me to take over as Secretary of the International Committee on Southern Africa (ICSA), so I resigned from IDAF, stayed with ICSA for a couple of years, and since that time I've been working for the ANC Treasury in its London office.

I think I feel more like a South African than a Dutch Nederlander. Sometimes I meet people who ask, 'What's happening in the Netherlands?' I say, 'I don't know', but ask me about South Africa and I can tell you. The Netherlands is not part of my life. It's some place where I go regularly because I've got brothers and sisters there, I can hardly say I've got many friends there. So I simply feel more South African than Dutch.

Religion doesn't play any part in my life now. No. I left the church not just to leave the ministry, but to leave religion as a whole. Even when I was ordained a priest, I had sort of doubts. A Dutch Catholic philosopher actually put it in such a nice way; I can't say it better, something like, 'If God exists and I say I don't believe God exists, he's still there. And if God does not exist and I say I believe he exists, however much I believe he's still not there. Therefore the question whether God exists or not is irrelevant.' And that was something that I really felt when I was still studying, before becoming a priest.

Then somebody asks, 'Why then did you go through and become a priest?' and I say, 'Well, in the Old Testament there's a nice story. People leave the slavery and the fleshpots of Egypt, and go into the desert. And in the desert you don't know which way to go. You feel you have to go forward – something is propelling you forward. Whether there is a Promised Land or not is immaterial. You'll find some food, you'll find some water on the way. And that's sort of what life is like.'

I felt there is something in the Bible, in Christianity – and for that matter many of the other religions – that is trying to tell you something about life. Not about life hereafter, or life outside your knowledge. It's trying to tell you that the birth of a child is important, and you give it a mythological gloss by baptism; not that the baptism makes it then a child of God. All right; say God loves you. But in fact what you're saying is, you are worthwhile in your own right. I've always viewed religion in that sort of sense – demythologised.

One of the reasons that I left the ministry was, like I said, that the church was more like a statue of liberty than a movement for liberation; saying that apartheid is bad, but in fact maintaining a seminary for blacks and a seminary for whites. Don't upset the applecart! Don't upset our white Catholics, who after all provide the money to sustain other activities. That was one aspect of it.

Another aspect: I was training black lay preachers, and up to a point that was no problem. But when it came to matters of faith – does God exist or does he not – I felt I had to convey my own view, which is contrary to the generally accepted view within the church. But can I justify that? If I leave next month, next week, next year, another priest comes in with a totally different outlook. That can create only conflict, and that's also not right.

So I had this feeling that I'd reached a point where I cannot say any more, because if I go beyond this then I go beyond what they expect from a priest. And I didn't want to be a hypocrite. Then I called it a day.

I have been back to the church, but purely to accompany my aged parents – Sunday service is an important thing so I'll go with them. And on Christmas Day. I've got no objections to going to church or not going to church, but purely as respect for somebody else's belief rather than my own. In that sense I can say I'm not religious.

I have always thought that, when everything has settled down, I'll go back to South Africa. Now with the changes taking place, specifically since 2 February 1990, I've said I'm prepared to do whatever the ANC want me to do, wherever they want me to do it, and for as long as they want me to do it to help in this process of change.

And then, I think, if I'm not too old then I go back. Definitely. Because I would feel more at home back in South Africa. Because I've belonged to South Africa for so long, and become a stranger in the country where I grew up. Although I grew up there, I'd feel far more lost over there, than I would in South Africa.

PAMELA DOS SANTOS
Maputo 1990

'The most exciting and the most important thirty years in the history of Southern Africa.'

She has progressed from a refugee, living in camps in Dar es Salaam with a whole ragbag of various liberation movements, to life in a special house in a protected area of Maputo, seeing heads of government, visiting different states – a change of enormous proportions.

We are in the house of Marcelino dos Santos, President of the Peoples' Assembly of Mozambique and member of the Politburo of FRELIMO. The spacious rooms have a large collection of pictures and objects from many different countries. Some are gifts to the President and belong to the State. But many have been collected privately. There are Makondi carvings on every step of the stairs; Marcelino's collection of carved and inlaid walking sticks; Pam's collection of exotic shells picked up on the beautiful beaches of Mozambique. There are Chinese vases and pictures and carvings, a Moroccan samovar, inlaid Indian pictures, African musical instruments from various countries, plaques, and dozens of beautiful boxes of all sizes.

I was a teenager that grew up very quickly. By the age of sixteen I was already going out a lot, going around with people amongst whom were jazz musicians. I started going to jazz clubs. And at the jazz clubs I started meeting black musicians.

Social intermingling with all these different people just quite naturally proceeded from there. I became more and more aware of the difficulties involved for people in Johannesburg to mix and inter-relate. Even socially. It wasn't anything particularly political at that point of my life. I finally met Joe Lowe who was a journalist, a photographer, and a bit of a writer. Coloured.

Joe and I had a relationship for a short while. I really had terrible problems with my mother when she found out about the people that I was going around with; she started to put all kinds of terrible pressures on me. I left home – at the time I was eighteen. I just walked out the door one day, and I was bunking around with different friends. I'd stay weeks here, weeks there, weeks anywhere.

I was staying in the flat of a friend of mine. Joe had been there for the evening, and he was waiting for somebody to come and pick him up to take him back to the township. I'd already gone to bed when the police barged in. The informer, the person who had called the police, was the African nightwatchman. [Laughs] Irony. Doing his right thing.

So we were locked up. We went through a medical examination at the police station, which was all negative. At the time I didn't think of it as being particularly humiliating. I was very defiant. But then later . . . They actually kept us I think it was three or four days at Marshall Square before they brought us up before the judge. And it was only when I was waiting that I realised that this was all done particularly to humiliate us.

They didn't have any concrete evidence of any sexual relationship, so they charged us on some kind of sub-clause of the Immorality Act which was to do with 'the intent to commit immorality'. [Laughs] It was quite a spectacular case. You know, this nice Jewish girl . . . it wasn't the usual kind of immorality case that was going on. Tremendous amount of publicity. My family was absolutely devastated. And partly as a result of this, my mother – with pressure from her family – applied to the courts to have me put into a juvenile home as 'uncontrollable', until I was 'of age' (twenty-one).

I said, 'My God! What am I going to do? I'm going to be locked up in a home for two and a half years!' And then this idea came up. Why don't you just go away for a couple of years? You can go out, do something. And in five or six years' time you can be back again.

I left South Africa in January when I was out on bail. We'd already been found guilty; and they'd remanded the court for two weeks for sentence. It was in that two weeks that I left – and Joe went to jail for four to five months. Got off a month for good behaviour.

There was a warrant out for my arrest because I hadn't appeared in Court to be sentenced. By then I was very involved also with political people. I was doing odd things around the COD office for a while. During that whole 1961 period, I was one of those nice little teenagers that used to run around and paint slogans on the bridges, you remember? [Laughs] And all those placard demonstrations outside the Town Hall, and Human Rights campaigns; and when Chief Luthuli came through Johannesburg to go to Oslo, we were at the airport.

I knew exactly where I was going. I went through Botswana by train, then on foot into the then Southern Rhodesia. I had been given names of contacts all along the way. People in Bechuanaland that put me on to people in Zimbabwe, who flew me out through Malawi to Dar es Salaam. I was met at the airport by James Radebe and Frene Ginwala. I had no papers; but the ANC asked them to admit me.

Tanzania was in the phase between independence and republic. I was authorised to stay three months – that was the usual thing. And in that ninety days I got myself reasonably organised. I found a job. Thank goodness, I had basic secretarial training. I could type and take notes and stuff.

Initially they put me to stay in the hospital with the ANC nurses – until British nurses forced the South African nurses to put me out. Then I went to stay in a refugee camp that was just outside Dar es Salaam where all the refugees from everywhere were staying. There were people from Southern Rhodesia, Northern Rhodesia, Nyasaland, South West Africa, Burundi, Rwanda, Kenya, Mozambique, Congo, Leopoldville. And I land up in that situation – the only white woman! It was absolutely incredible. The ANC guys used to literally form cordons around me every time I walked into that place. It was obviously impossible for me to stay in that situation for any length of time, so first I got a job, and then I got myself a little apartment, and some of the ANC workers came to stay with me so I wasn't alone.

Then Joe came – I suppose about the end of May, beginning of June – and he moved in with me for a while. But that relationship fizzled out very fast. I think that once we weren't under pressure, there was nothing left! [Laughs] Joe got a scholarship to the United States.

Eduardo Mondlane turned up in June for the actual formation of FRELIMO, which was a union of three groups. Marcelino was living in Morocco at the time. In September FRELIMO had its first congress, and Marcelino came back for the congress. That's when I got to know him better, and things developed more.

I stayed in Tanzania for the next five years, always under the auspices of the ANC. I worked and earned my own living – but I could only remain in Tanzania under the authority of the ANC. The ANC had to request a work permit for me, which they did every two years as it came up for renewal. And I participated in the various ANC activities that were going on, women's groups and other things. And had a daughter.

When the Swedes opened up the first SIDA in Dar es Salaam I went to work for them – they paid me twice as much. I got my life together. I had this child, this baby. I never had a great amount of money, but I earned enough to survive, pay my rent, pay my lights and water, feed quite a lot of people. It wasn't just feeding my daughter Ilundi and me. Marcelino was around, in and out all the time; and by that time I collected not only ANC comrades but a lot of FRELIMO comrades as well.

The first couple of years we never really discussed marriage seriously. The racial situation in FRELIMO wasn't very healthy. By 1968 contradictions in FRELIMO came to a head, and this resulted in the expulsion of the white members. Tanzania gave them something like forty-eight hours to get out. Marcelino and I started seriously thinking about getting married; and at the end of August that year – that's 1968 – when I went to renew my two-year work permit, I was told I had thirty days to leave Tanzania. I had been caught up with a group in FRELIMO that certain Tanzanians didn't want. The logical conclusion of that particular problem – because I still had no travel documents – was marriage.

Had an interesting wedding actually. Marcelino had to write a letter to FRELIMO requesting permission to marry me. And it was felt that I should also get permission from the ANC. So we both wrote our respective letters, and we both got our respective authorisations.

I stopped working for the Swedes. FRELIMO had a very strict policy; none of them ever worked for any organisation except FRELIMO during all those years. I became a Mozambican militant, a member of FRELIMO. And I worked in the Information and Propaganda department from 1968 to 1975, when we came back here to Mozambique for Independence.

After we married, there were security problems. [Laughs] FRELIMO couldn't pay rent on another flat and guard it, so I moved into a FRELIMO house – a communal house. And I lived communally – or in FRELIMO residences – until 1975 when we came to Mozambique. Some of it was rough; some of it wasn't. The last three or four years we moved into a tiny house that had been bought by FRELIMO. That house came to us because we were the only family small enough to fit into it! [Laughs] They actually had to erect a tent in the back yard so we could have the guards; because there was no room for them to stay anywhere else.

Virtually all the time until 1977 when we had the Third Congress, Marcelino was Secretary for Foreign Relations. And between his external missions and his internal missions to the different FRELIMO camps and to the interior of the country, it was only after 1975 that we really lived together. In all those years, Marcelino and I never actually spent three months consecutively together in the same house at the same time, eating together, going to bed together. [Laughs] In all the years that we've been together, it was only after June 1975 when we finally left Tanzania. I came to Maputo – it was still then Lourenco Marques – in order to get our living situation sorted out before 25 June, Independence Day. Midnight. 24th.

Yes, it's been an enormous change from basic living as a refugee living in camps in Dar es Salaam, to life in this protected area of Maputo, meeting heads of government, visiting different states. But one of the things that always amazes me is how quickly I got used to it. This is part of the problem. All the time you're thinking, 'Fundamentally I'm not changing. I think I'm still the same.' And I hope my friends think that I'm still the same Pam, except instead of having people over to a scruffy little house for dinner, I have them over to this huge mansion. I like to think that, in essence, Marcelino and I haven't changed really, that we're still the same people fundamentally.

But even if you think that you don't change, the way people relate to you definitely changes. Ja, definitely. People don't feel as free to say, 'Come over for a cup of coffee tomorrow night; we're having some friends down.' Or, 'Let's go on a picnic to the beach', because they think that maybe you can't do that. I think this also has to do with how the people see leadership. In any under-developed society, a chief or a leader is always somebody special. And it's not different here. It's not different here.

You lived nineteen years in South Africa, thirteen in Tanzania, and now fifteen in Mozambique. So what do you consider yourself to be? South African? Or Mozambican?

At this point, really, I must say that I'm a Mozambican. I carry Mozambique nationality. I live Mozambican privileges. And I have represented Mozambique at different levels at different times – through the Women's Organisation, as the wife of my husband, etc.

But, you know, I come from South Africa. That's where I was born. That's what made me what I am – although perhaps I learned much more in terms of political development and understanding of people through participating in the struggle for the Mozambican people's liberation.

What I've contributed to Mozambique in the long run is a contribution also to South Africa, because free Mozambique obviously means a free South Africa comes nearer. I think the two things are perfectly combined. I still do. In fact, Mozambique can never really be free until South Africa is free. So the two things – there's no contradiction at all. I had an interesting life, and I really wouldn't change it if I had to do it again. I think there have been very few people of my background that have ever had the privilege and oppoprtunity to do what I've done. Definitely. I've done a lot of interesting things. I've covered a period from the early Sixties to 1990 of the most exciting and most important thirty years in the history of Southern Africa. I know almost all the people who have been involved in it, the whole area, the whole region.

That's a big privilege. Yes, it is.

NOMSA GERTZ-MKETO
Hamburg 1990

'It's always difficult for children growing up in one society to feel part of another society they've never seen, they've never experienced.'

Her home is a contemporary house on a modern estate outside Hamburg. There are small, attractive gardens, a pleasant middle-class area, quiet and orderly.

As I grew up it became clearer that we lived in two different societies. My mother was Christian, used to go to church and listen to all these sermons and protestations of brotherhood; and in our practical life this had no meaning at all. I started questioning certain things from school, especially the history lessons where you were taught that your own history was something to be ashamed of, your own people were liars, thieves, lazy; and the other side was always the holy side. It was so obvious, if you started thinking, it couldn't be like that. There's no such situation where people are all black, or all green or whatever. And so it started a process of questioning.

I was still at lower secondary school when the Bantu Education Act was passed. Many of our teachers resigned in protest, and many things were changed in such a short time, for the bad, of course. The feeding scheme at our schools, which was discontinued; the syllabus was changed, Afrikaans was upgraded.

So by the time I went to boarding-school at seventeen to do my matriculation, I was really ripe for new ideas, for someone to come and show me the way. The members of the Youth League were getting together and trying to formulate new militancy, yes. And when PAC was formed it was a political direction which spoke, which touched us, which set off certain things going in us. We could identify with this organisation which served to give us back our pride, and told us to be proud of being Africans, stop bowing down, stop being ashamed, and stand up and fight.

So by the time I left school, 1960, I was identifying myself with the Pan Africanist Congress; and my boyfriend was a member. And one of the bitterest things: we had been opposing Bantu Education, but we needed university education; so he was one of the first to go to a Bantu college – Turfloop. There the conditions were so appalling that they immediately protested, and were part of a revolt which was stamped down by force.

I was at that time at Baragwanath Hospital undergoing training as a nurse. He was underground, hiding. With parents and friends we formed a sort of information network – you know, taking messages and bringing messages. It was a period of mistrust and distrust and fear and uncertainty in every aspect. He had to leave the country.

I continued at home. I wanted to do physiotherapy, and I knew I had no chance in South Africa. So I was not personally threatened but I'd reached a point where I had to do something positive. And that's why I left, 1963.

My parents didn't know that I was going. No! [Laughs] No. It was well known that the police would harass them – and they did, in fact. But they didn't know where I was, why I had gone; it was the safest way. My mother was visited by these people from the Security Police even up to 1976. So she used to tell them, 'You people, you're reading my daughter's letters anyway; you are better informed than I am.'

I went the usual route up north, landing in Tanzania. I was travelling alone. And I got lots of help all the way. One of the things I'm thankful for is this African hospitality. People felt that they had to do something for me; I was quite young then, and people never wanted to take advantage of me in any way. It was the other way – they acted very protective towards me. It gave me confidence that there is something very important within the African societies; which I experienced for myself.

I applied for scholarships, and two possibilities offered themselves. I decided not to go to the United States because of the racist set-up there. So I chose West Germany. At that time they were doing everything to get us to come. They were recruiting students. It's only now that I've come to understand they were using us in the East/West conflict, to stop us coming under the Soviet influence or going to East Germany.

Because the West Germans didn't recognise my matriculation I had to do one year to attain the standard. And then I started at university, doing comparative education.

I got married to a South African; he's the one who was hounded out of South Africa, and we were together then. He was doing geology. And after finishing he went down to Botswana. I studied until 1970, completed, and also went to Botswana. But then because of personal problems, I came back to Germany.

It was the conditions of exile that brought about the problems. I always felt if we had been at home, living with our parents, relatives and friends, certain things wouldn't have been so dramatic. And we would always have had help and counsel from older people. In this society we were quite isolated with our problems. So we started fighting each other. I think under different circumstances, it would have worked out.

My first-born was born in South Africa, and she was with my mother. My other children were born later. That was with my second husband. We have two children.

I'm deeply involved in organising political resistance, giving information about the situation to people here who support our movements. So our children have always grown up in that situation, from their birth onwards. And, of course, meeting South Africans, meeting different people, going with us to meetings and symposiums and things like that.

It's always difficult for children living in one society to feel part of another society they've never seen, they've never experienced. But if you ask them now, they wouldn't tell you that they were German. They would say, 'We are German South Africans, or South African Germans.' [Laughs] So they're sort of part of both worlds: the one they've never really experienced or seen; and the other in which they live, but where they're always treated as . . . yes, foreigners. You know, people will ask them, 'Where did you learn your German?' Yes. Or, 'Where were you born?' So when, like my son, they say, 'I was born in Hamburg,' they can't believe it. So their existence is always questioned in a way in this country. They can never feel totally at home; accepted, not being looked at, stared at and not being commented upon.

There is racialism in this country. At first I wouldn't believe it, because you see, I was starting to live, and nobody bothered much about my living, my occupying a flat anyway. The obvious divisions of apartheid were no longer in existence. But then as time went you felt it. The most obvious form was being looked at when you went into a tram or bus. I think I was one of the first African women at the University of Hamburg – everybody would turn to look at you, the whole bus! And if somebody was not paying attention, reading, he would be nudged, 'Look!' And children would be quite open about it, 'Look, a black woman! Why is she black?' and then the explanations for my colour, in my presence. [Laughs] 'Yes, she has been in the sun too long,' and the children would say, 'Why doesn't she wash?'

They assumed that I couldn't understand what they were saying. This wasn't bad. What was bad was trying to look for a flat or room. A vacancy would be advertised and you would phone. They might not hear from your voice whether you're African or what, but you came for an interview, and they would look at you. 'The flat is already taken, sorry!' And bang the door in your face, like that.

More and more foreigners came to Germany. At first, they were welcomed as workers – I remember the papers writing, 'Now we've got a million foreign workers to help us with our economy!' The millionth worker got a present of a VW.

And then things changed. After the oil crisis, foreigners were now those who were taking their jobs. And then racism really came out to the surface in this country. And of course, being African with a black skin, we were at the bottom of it all. Nowadays racism is increasing, you can feel it. First, I think, because of the economic situation. Many young people have no sense of direction; they do not believe in the established political parties any more. They feel cheated, and turn towards such organisations as neo-Nazis or the skinheads. They are calling for the expulsion of foreigners. 'We Germans are once more united; we need the work and the land for our own people, for Germans. So out with foreigners.'

The children always found a mechanism to deal with it. My boy who is twenty-two now would say, 'Oh well, there are some stupid guys who try to call me names.' But he usually had a lot of good friends, so he was not isolated. For the girls it was easier; you see, girls are, as the Germans say, *knidlich*, they're nice . . . nice and brown and easier for a time – up till adolescence! And then they become threatening. Especially when they start looking round for boyfriends – this is when a crisis comes. My daughter, the seventeen-year-old, is going through a difficult age. 'Why do I have such skin? Why have I got this curly hair?' But I think it's normal for children. They want to be just like the others.

I started teaching in 1970. I've been teaching for about twenty years. I enjoy it, I feel accepted, because I've been at this school now for eleven years. And I'm sort of an institution, yes. The African teacher, the strict one. [Laughs] Yes, I'm feared, I'm a disciplinarian.

When I started I was young, wanted to be friendly to the pupils and to do things exactly right. And I never got started. They started laughing at me, talking to each other – the whole lesson was catastrophe. I felt so bad. I went home and thought to myself, 'You must develop a strategy, because the minute you appear in front of class, especially those at the age of twelve/thirteen upwards, they look at you – you look different, maybe you talk differently; and they start trying out their tricks on you.' So I said, 'I'm going to be top dog whatever happens, in every class I enter. They must feel I'm there to do a job.' And I've tried to work on this. I keep them at a certain distance, not to be too tolerant of things. As I grow to know them and they me, then our relationship changes.

Of course I would love to go back to my country, even if it would not be to stay. I don't know if it were possible to live there after spending about thirty years outside. But just to be able to go back and show my children my country, their country in a way; the places where I grew up, where I went to school; and maybe some relatives.

I think for someone like me, exile has been positive. It has given me chances which I would never have had at home – to learn, to go to university. I could have gone further if I'd wanted. And it has opened channels of information for me, books, theatre, music. It's a world which I would never have known in South Africa. I have been able to travel, see lots of countries, different people, meet and get to know people. And to understand democracy; I'm not only involved in fighting against such obvious systems like apartheid, but also against systems which exist in South America or in Asia. You find that your problems are not quite so unique as you thought they were, that you can always be politically active under any circumstances. And it's widened my scope. And it has placed our struggle. Of course it is of primary importance to me, but it's part of the whole system of injustice in the world.

I think women in exile have specific problems. But it's not only a problem for women in exile, but South African women at home too. You see, apartheid has destroyed the self-confidence of our men. In fact colonialism, by taking away our values, our tradition, destroying it, has reduced our men to something which is neither fish nor fowl. They're confused. They have an inferiority complex, because they're no longer able to fulfil their role of the protector, of father, family man, provider for the family. At home there are quite a lot of women who have to do without men.

Our men are no longer able to shoulder their responsibility to keep a family intact. They resort to drinking a lot. Some become violent towards their women, because they feel helpless to do anything else against the state or state violence. And there's high incidence of divorce or broken families. And these men, our young men who come out of the country, haven't had positive example of a father, of a strong male person in the family; most of them have been brought up by mothers, or mothers have been dominating out of necessity. They come out and do not find their role in these outside societies. They're still looking for help from foreign institutions, getting help from scholarship bodies, getting papers and things. It is a situation of born begging, looking for help; and die begging, looking for help. And so they become aggressive; they are torn within themselves. They become aggressive especially towards women, who are better able to adapt. Having children to look after, you've no time to feel sorry for yourself; or you place such feelings behind you and you tackle what has to be tackled first.

This conflict is always there. And I think it becomes stronger in exile, yes. I wouldn't blame them. I would say it's our whole history of colonialism which has destroyed our men. Of course, they should know this and do something against it – not let themselves go, and say, 'We can't help it! We've been made to be what we are.'

PART FOUR

Bridging the Rift

Guardians of Continuity

> One commonly held delusion is that men are the wanderers and
> women the guardians of hearth and home. This can, of course, be
> so. But women, above all, are the guardians of continuity; if the
> hearth moves, they move with it.
>
> Bruce Chatwin, *The Songlines*

More than any others, these women expose the deep loss and deprivation
of exile; and the strength and endurance of the human spirit.

For the men, the loss of family was sad, but when they left they closed
the door on their family relationships and they went out into new worlds
unencumbered. For the women, leaving meant losing the whole support
system of parents and siblings. The enlarged family was a school for
domestic crafts, for child care, for parenthood. What they left was more
than a family of three generations; it was a social community embracing
neighbours and friends, where every adult was 'auntie' or 'uncle' to every
child, where the sun shone, and there was space, even if it was in the
dusty roads outside. The men were complete in themselves and saw change
as weakness. For women, the ability to change was both a necessity and
their strength.

In Europe they found themselves in cramped apartments in big cities
where there was no space for prams, where neighbours did not greet you,
and no one was there to care for toddlers while they went shopping or to
the laundromat.

Often, through death, divorce, or political commitment, they became
single parents, shouldering total responsibility in cold and alien lands.

Somehow the women found work to support themselves and their
children, made a home, gave the children love, educated them, and at the
same time educated and transformed themselves.

PEGGY STEVENSON
London 1990

'There is a side of me that was totally undeveloped, that needed to grow.'

> She is modest, even self-effacing. Her quiet manner conceals a
> person of enormous strength and courage, driven by the need to
> care for her small children and to educate herself.

I was extremely frightened because a lot of the people I knew were being
rounded up under 90-day and 180-day detention laws, and I just felt that
they were coming for me. I learned later that after I left, they did indeed
come for me. Because of the Job Reservation Act my work was threatened. I was a garment worker, and factories were closing all over the
place; we worked short hours; some of us were unemployed. I was just
psychologically going under. I was in a very, very bad way, because I had
very little education. I did feel a great need to develop a side of me that
was totally undeveloped. I was a terribly frustrated, unhappy person
because I felt I could do better than just working in a factory.

I had been involved in Congress. I had been a member of SACPO –
South African Coloured People's Organisation. I had been active since I
was sixteen – it just became very much part of my active life, my politics.
And so I was known to the police, although at the time when I left I had
not been active for a year, because I had just had a baby.

I now had two children. I was unmarried. I felt very guilty about
having children knowing how involved I was in the anti-apartheid
struggle; I suffered terribly because of my guilt, knowing that there
would be no one to look after those two children if I did go to prison.
That very much influenced me in wanting to get away – for the children's
sake as well.

I had by then saved £250, which took me seven years to save up, you
know, just taking into account the little I was earning and the responsibilities I had. I used that £250 to come to England. I brought the children
with me. I knew of somebody who would let me have a room, and that's
all I knew. Because I couldn't get a passport, I had to take an exit permit.

I left behind my stepfather and my mother, two brothers and a sister.
One brother lived with me; I was taking care of him. I paid for his
schooling through those years. He had just started teaching at that point,
so I felt I could leave knowing that he could help the family then.

I had a charter flight which went from Maputo – then Lourenco
Marques – to Paris, so my journey began by train from Johannesburg to
Maputo. From Paris I had to take a ferry over to England. The journey
was a nightmare. My nine-month-old baby was not very well at the time.
And the discrimination by the tour operators and crew was just so
unbelievable. In Lourenco Marques, in this terrible heat, our flight was

delayed by eighteen hours. And there we were sitting, myself and the two children, in this little airport, desperate for a meal or something to drink. And suddenly we realised – myself and two Indian youngsters going to Ireland to study – that we were all alone! All the other passengers had vanished! We got very alarmed, because it was the first time we'd flown. So we asked one of the officials where these people are, and he said, 'But didn't you know? The passengers were all taken to a hotel because of the delay.' There they had showers, meals and rest. And they'd deliberately left us out!

But we got here; by the time I arrived I had £40 in my pocket; and the suitcase; and my two children. The place where we were to stay was an empty room, but somebody gave me the loan of a bed so I went out and bought blankets straightaway. One thing I was totally confident about, that was about my ability as a garment worker. I had my scissors, I had my overall, and I had my tape measure. I knew I could walk into any garment factory, especially women's tailoring. So I set about looking through the papers for a job.

I arrived on the Wednesday, and by the Thursday afternoon I had a job to go to on the Monday. All that remained then was to find somebody to look after my babies. I went to the local Town Hall and asked for a list of baby minders; and by Friday I had a childminder. So out of the £40 I could at least buy blankets and pay for the room for a couple of weeks, and have money for the first week for the childminder, and 10 shillings for my fare back and forth to work. It didn't matter about lunch. I could do without lunch. So that was it. That's how I arrived in England.

I had one or two political friends here, and I had other friends who were outside of the Movement. But I didn't get in touch with any of them – it was my pride, you see, because I just cannot go asking people for anything. I decided I will only get in touch on the day when I can invite them to a meal in my place.

So for six months I didn't get in touch with anybody – I was too proud. I was really down on my uppers, and I didn't want anybody to see me like that. It was very, very lonely.

Lionel Morrison, an old SACPO man, heard about my whereabouts – I don't know how. He came to see me and he told me where the ANC office was and the people I could get in touch with. But even that I was too proud to do, because I felt I couldn't go asking anybody for help, knowing that probably everybody was in the same position. Or very nearly. And that they really couldn't help me.

I still didn't get involved in any kind of activity. Occasionally I used to go to a big AA or ANC meeting. But only very big ones, because at that time survival was uppermost. I just had to live for the kids, look after the kids. It was work and the children; and there was no way I could get involved.

I had also got involved again with the father of my second child, and that was a brake on my activities. You see, there's the problem with women. You're keen to become active, but when the husband fights you and stops you, in the end you try to avoid conflict for the children's sake.

But in the meantime I had another baby, which complicated my life even more; it was only when he was old enough to go into a nursery school that I could really break free from this unhappy relationship. Then I really launched myself. Since then I have brought up the children by myself.

I've always worked. First of all I was still working as a garment worker. And then somebody had enough confidence in me to offer me a little clerical job; I was terrified! But I took it, and I gained sufficient confidence to go to evening classes and do my O levels. I even attempted A levels, but couldn't make it because I just didn't have the time to study – not with family, full-time job and so on. It wasn't until 1975 that I could even qualify for a full-time grant to do a degree course. And then I was taken as a mature student.

I had this drive to get educated. It was a need! I know people say it's ambition; but it was not ambition. It was just that there was a side of me that was totally undeveloped, that needed to grow.

I studied history, yes, at the North London Poly; completed that degree, and went on from there to complete a postgraduate year at London University, doing a teacher-training course. And that was really the end of my studies. I did teach for a couple of years, but since then I've been working for IDAF.

It was extremely difficult working full-time, studying, getting involved in political work, looking after the family. My eldest daughter now lives in Canada. She's married. She went to a College of Art and became a graphic designer. My second daughter worked as a shop assistant and various other jobs, and she is now back at her studies. My son – he was really the one who benefited most from the British education system. Went through his O levels, A levels and did a degree at Sussex University. He's now teaching English in Spain.

In all those years I did make quite a few British friends, who are my friends to this day. Of course most of my friends are in the Movement, because we work together and have common interests.

I have recently gone back to South Africa for the first time – with a delegation from IDAF. And I tried to analyse this – that I was closer to some of the people here in England, people I've related to over thirty years, closer to them than to my biological relatives. So that in many ways these are the people, a lot of them, who have become my relatives over the years.

So it's more than just a political movement, you know. They are my family. The Movement is the one thing I can tell you now that has stabilised me. It was the one thing that remained constant in my life. No matter from which point I approached it, or how I strayed from it, it was there; it was always there; it was part of my life. Even at times when I've gone through patches, when I've been in my mind totally involved but not active, there's been that emotional attachment.

When I went back recently, before I left I was scared, because I came out on an exit permit. Would I be detained? I didn't know. I've got a British passport now. But I was also nervous as to what my reaction to my family would be. I'd been away twenty-eight years. And then the shock of finding how Johannesburg had changed! There was nothing I could relate to, nothing. No building, no street. I became desperate, looking for something I could relate to. For about two days people kept asking me, 'How do you feel?' Nothing! I felt nothing.

And I broke down the first time when I saw the name of the street that I'd lived in – Lilian Road in Fordsburg. And the second time I broke down crying is when we passed Kholvad House, and saw the site where the ANC office had stood. And going up Diagonal Street. For the first time I felt such deep emotion, because, of course, the office isn't there. But that was my guiding star, the whole pivot of my life there. And I think it was the shock that it was no longer there. I was very emotional.

Things have changed. But the other thing that shocked me was to see the terrible overcrowding everywhere, to see the terrible squalor and effects of apartheid was so upsetting. After all these years, to think that it could actually get worse! I didn't think it could. But it has. To see people homeless on the streets; sleeping on Johannesburg streets at night; homeless children wandering around Hillbrow and places like that. For me, the effect of apartheid was a terrible, terrible shock.

I know there are homeless people in London as well. I understand that, I understand that. I think it was just not realising that people have been driven from their own areas and that the scale of the problem is so enormous; and the evidence of loss of control was so clear. The regime can't control it, but they're not doing anything about it either. It seems to me that they're just waiting for the ANC to come and clear up this terrible mess. That was my personal point of view.

The highlight of my personal experience was meeting with my family. And that was extremely emotional, but also disappointing, because I found the racism among my relatives was worse than I remembered it. Coloured people who find other coloured people unacceptable because of their skin colour; who look down on them; who will not associate with them; who look down on African people; who will not associate with African people. And it's not as though they're light-skinned like me – they're all dark, dark people. To other people they're all African when you look at them! We only had a few hours together, and after twenty-eight years I didn't want to quarrel with them. Because, at a very deep level, I did relate to them. And it was such a healing process for me to meet with them.

I have been in a terrible quandary about going back to stay, because I've put down roots here. I have become a human being here. One of the reasons I left was because I felt so negated – I didn't use that word earlier – as a human being. I felt such a nothing. And England helped me to develop myself as a person, to become a person here, an ordinary person, nothing special. Just learning how to make use of yourself, how to be a person in your workday life, in your dealings with other people, your expectations.

Also, I just lived better here. For the first time I got a flat, whereas we had lived – four of us – in a room that was just slightly bigger than this, in the most squalid conditions. My life had been one of great poverty. But as a person with a conscience who has had some political education, if the Movement says, 'Now this is where you need to be deployed,' there would be absolutely no hesitation. I would go. There would be no hesitation.

But my time in exile has been a productive one, worthwhile. Very much so.

ZATOON VANIA
Toronto 1990

'I think one has to go back and embrace even your enemy for things to work out in South Africa.'

Twenty-seven years on from the time she left South Africa, she still has the wedding-dress that she never wore. She is highly educated, good-looking. For her it has been 'a very hard, very lonely life'.

I was engaged to be married to Solly Vania. He was very deeply involved in the struggle then, and our wedding was going to be on Sunday 4 October. It was 1964.

I was working as a dress designer. I had my own school, and it was flourishing. Our wedding date had been set. We had sent out invitations, booked the hall, ordered the flowers, the catering and everything. On 6 September it was Solly's birthday, and his parents had given a huge family dinner for him. After the dinner he walked me home.

At my house a friend was waiting for us. He told us certain people had been detained. Solly was a member of that cell that had been picked up. We did not dare send him back home; we decided to try to get him out of the country. He did not have travel documents. I had a brother who was a science teacher at Lenasia and he had travel documents, so there was a bit of forgery to get a passport, because these were desperate times, and that was the only way. We had to act very quickly, and he skipped to Nairobi.

So I found myself at home with a wedding without a groom! I remember so distinctly the dress – my dress. I was doing the beadwork on it; it was a beautiful peau-de-soie with embroidered flowers, and I was sewing all these beads they call teardrops. I had been working on it, and had just thrown it aside when I had gone out.

The day he left, our house and his house were raided; they were looking for him. Our telephone was being tapped; our house was under surveillance; a plain-clothes black policeman watched our house all the time. It was a very uncomfortable experience.

That time was really the start of a new phase where the struggle wasn't passive any more. It was just after the Rivonia trial, a very tense time in South Africa. Most people were afraid even to look at you if you were politically involved, in fear that they would be arrested.

We pretended that the wedding was going on as planned. I think they left me alone because of that, waiting for the wedding day to nab him. So we didn't cancel any of the arrangements; we didn't tell the guests. And then I received a letter from the police that I must go to the Grays. But my father said to me, 'You are not going to go. You must get out!'

But my father, being very old fashioned, wouldn't let me leave the country if I were not married. He said, 'I will not send you off like this. I do not know where you're going to go, I can't send you away like that.' But he would agree to let me go if I got married by proxy. This was extremely difficult because we were so closely watched, and we wanted the police to still think the wedding is going to take place on 4 October.

It was more like a funeral than a wedding; no one was dressed; no guests were invited; the only people that came were two of Solly's brothers and his father and mother. His younger brother stood in as his proxy. I'm a Muslim, and so we just had an Imam come and perform a very simple ceremony.

Before this happened, all the women had come and given me a very big shower; I had received many wonderful gifts. And I could take nothing – just my clothes. But I left. And Solly was at Nairobi airport to meet me; and the very first thing he said to me was, 'Are we married?' [Laughs]

We had some very strange experiences. You had to show that you were a resident of the country; we didn't have that, and for the first six months we had a terrible time. We were living in a very cheap hotel, right in the district where there were lots of prostitutes – that was the corner where everyone came to pick up women. But that was all we could afford. Almost every day we went to Immigration, trying to get work permits. In the meantime I became pregnant. Solly tried to get a teaching job, but they wouldn't allow him to teach. But privately he did some kind of work. And then, after six months, our money ran out and we just had nothing.

We were desperate. We'd kept on going to Immigration saying, 'Yes, we are political refugees; when are you going to give us work permits? We need to work. We are both capable, etc. etc.' But the head of

Immigration Department was a South African Boer. Yes! That was the most alarming thing. Imagine a South African Boer being the head of Immigration in a newly-independent African country – it was such an anomaly! I think that he was determined not to get us our papers.

So we did a very bold thing. We walked to parliament; of course, we were very nervous when we got there. There was this huge man in a beautiful uniform, with white gloves. He said, 'Who would you wish to see?' We didn't know anyone – we just said, 'Tom Mboya,' because it was the only name we knew. We were amazed. After half an hour, the man came out! I couldn't believe it – he came and spoke to us. And we told him that we really are political refugees; we were actively involved in the liberation movement – well, my husband was; he was in the underground, and everyone in his cell had been arrested. Isso Chiba. the leader of that group, was sentenced to eighteen years which he served on Robben Island and another member, Mac Maharaj, fourteen years. Yes, they had all been together in one cell.

We told him this, and we told him that Kenyan Immigration wouldn't give us refugee status. Please help. We have no money, we're going to be kicked out of the hotel, there is nothing we can do. I think I cried. He said, 'I will see to everything; come and see me at my office.'

Solly went to his office and told him the whole story, and they said they would confirm it with ANC officials in Dar es Salaam. And they did. Mboya called us, he shook Solly's hand and said, 'I'll do all in my power to help you.' And then he wrote a note which was put right on the cover of the brown immigration file, saying: Give these people all consideration.

It opened doors. Within a week we had working permits. Because of what he did for us I felt deeply sorry when I heard that this man was assassinated.

I was very sick. I guess it was the anxiety in a way, and being pregnant; and I had to be in bed; I couldn't keep anything down. Solly couldn't take me to hospital because we didn't have money – there was no such thing as health services. So I had to lie at home. It was a very difficult time for us.

When I was eight months pregnant I decided there was no way I could let my child be born in Kenya – she wouldn't be Kenyan; she would be stateless. So I was willing to take a chance to go back to South Africa.

I couldn't go and see my family; I couldn't go and see friends; I moved around, almost in hiding, because I didn't know who I could trust. My daughter was born at Baragwanath Hospital. And she was eighteen days old when I got a letter from the Grays again, summoning me there. I just didn't wait. I left that day. Just left. I don't know how they knew I was back in the country.

But Solly was fortunate to obtain a job in a school where all the diplomats sent their children. We lived there for around three years, although Solly felt useless in Nairobi; he wanted to do something for the

Movement, but there wasn't any organisation he could work in. And then things became very bad again; there was the Asian exodus, and of course we were not identifiable as South Africans. We looked Asian like all the other Asians, and there were very many attacks against Asians. That was terrible, because in Nairobi the Asians never had any political organisation that really assisted black struggle. I think they helped financially but never openly, ja.

At the school Solly met quite a few of the ambassadors. And when she heard what had happened to us, the Canadian ambassador said, 'You realise it's not safe here any more, and your work permit could be taken away any time and you would have to go to the refugee camp?. So what are you going to do?' By that time I had had my second baby. And when she suggested that we could go to Canada as immigrants, it was arranged, and we came to Toronto.

It was easy to settle down here, easy to find a job, because we came at a time when they needed teachers and when most apartment buildings had vacancies. And in addition, as Asians we were still, in a way, a novelty. I'm sure racism was there. But there was no overt expression of it. Solly got a job at once as a senior lecturer in maths and science. I did supply teaching for six months. My mother, my brother and my sister came – accepted as immigrants. My mother did a very kind thing. She said, 'I'll spend my time with the three of you; and I'd like you to share the money that I have, and each take it as a down-payment on a house.' So this is how we were able to buy a little semi-detached house in the northern area. It was still very under-developed. We moved into the house, and we were so excited about it, happy and planning for our future.

I had a teaching position with the Noveo Board of Education, and had been teaching for two months – just two months it was. It was on the 2nd December. I had a parent interview until late that evening. Normally I was home by about five, but this particular evening I sat and chatted with the lady, who told me how she had just lost her husband and how hard it was being a widow. And I listened, and kept on thinking I should be going.

When I got home that evening, there was a strange smell in the house. I knew it was gas and was very worried; opened the doors, found my kids half asleep. My mother was dozing off; and I didn't know where my husband was. I called his sister and said, 'I'm worried. Where's my husband?' They didn't know where he was.

I called the gas people. And then my sister went to the bathroom and said, 'The kids have thrown some toys in the toilet, and now it won't flush.' I said, 'There's a bucket in the garage, get it.' When she went into the garage, she yelled and screamed, 'Come down quickly!' And my husband had . . . it was a very cold, cold winter then . . . it was a new garage, the garage door had slipped; and he had vacuumed . . . he had the vacuum

cleaner in his hand and he had slipped down, and the vacuum cleaner . . .
He must have turned the engine on to listen to the car radio or something.

And he was dead.

And so this was after . . . we were here for about a year and six months. And then I was alone with the two babies, but was fortunate that my mother was here.

Basically it's been a very hard, very lonely life. I had no degree and they wouldn't let me teach any more – you have to get some kind of certification. So I worked during the day, and studied at night. I did this for twenty years. I did my BA degree; and then my Master's in Education; and then a Special Certificate in Gifted Education. It was very, very hard work. I still had to do everything. I had wonderful neighbours who were very good, and I had very supportive family. And there was my mother.

I think the reason why I studied so hard was really to block out the loneliness. That's really why. Because I don't think anyone could work as hard as I did . . . my summers and my winters. I was so terrified of aloneness.

Do you know, it was very strange. Sometimes I think one has a premonition that something is going to happen. One thing he said a month before he died, was, 'If you could wish for anything, what would you wish for?' And I said something flippant: 'Oh, enough money to have everything I want – what would you wish for?' And he said, 'To be instrumental in liberating South Africa.'

I realise that racism is much alive here in Canada. I am, I think, more qualified than my Director of Education. For the last six years I have applied for a promotion here – I have outstanding evaluations each year. I have given workshops to teachers for the last fifteen years. I have an outstanding reputation with the parents, people clamour to have their kids in my class. I teach at the university; I was an Adjunct Professor in the Faculty of Education here in teacher training; I teach a summer course at McGill University. These kinds of qualifications. I'm saying all this to you so that you can understand the ridiculousness of the situation, that I could not get from the level where I am as a teacher, to the next level in my Board.

My research for the Noveo Board took me to the area of racism and the damage it does to people here in Canada, to our children. And I see this in my own pupils – the low self-esteem. They want to be white. They almost deny self, deny heritage, deny origin, deny race; and want to be white.

I think I almost have two roles. When I go to school I am part of the world there, part of the Canadian way. And when I come home it's almost as if I take off that dress and put on another; and I find I am this woman, I go into the kitchen, I cook, I do all the things that you expect of a good Muslim woman.

Canada has been very good to me. I think it is a good country, one of the best. There are a lot of good anti-racist structures, there are a lot of very good people who are working towards a multi-culture and a better country.

But I've been out of my country for almost twenty-eight years. I think rationally that this is where I should be, but emotionally I am still very much attached to South Africa. I get upset sometimes. I find myself longing . . . there's a nostalgia for people, for familiar things.

My two children are grown up now. Shera is a doctor, and the younger one is doing her final year of chemical engineering. They both studied at the Toronto University. They are very, very good children. My only regret is that my children don't feel a commitment to South Africa. I think it is because I didn't talk to them about it, I found it too painful to talk about.

I went to see a South African play recently, *Songololo*, and I just felt very emotional, and I knew I wanted to go back. I have a deep longing, I want to go back to be useful. I hope I can. I'm impatient for my retirement to come up, because I want to work in South Africa – I have so much to offer in the line of education. I want to go back.

I want to give it. I want to give it free. This is how I feel. I can't see myself staying in this country any more. I feel so unfulfilled. I feel as though I have so much and . . . I think I would very much like to be there. I would very much like to be part of the building up of the country, the putting things together.

I know that real change only took place within myself when I did a lot of internal reorganisation and realised where I'd gone wrong. And I'm wondering in South Africa: would the government ever admit to the crimes they've committed against humanity, against the blacks, against the people? Will they ever admit it?

And at the same time, you have to rid yourself of hate and bitterness for what happened to your life, for what they did. I think one almost has to go back and embrace even your enemy then, for things to work out in South Africa. Christ said 'Love thine enemy.' I think that's very hard. That's going to be so hard. But only then, do I think, one will be able to become basically useful.

NANCY MOATLHODI
Copenhagen 1990

'I now realise there's nowhere in the world you feel at home except in your own country . . . the colour of one's skin, it's worse. You are always a stranger and you are always stupid.'

Sitting in Denmark, she says 'I am just a useless somebody, sitting here, doing nothing.' Now she is no longer young, and suffers from asthma. Social welfare will never be enough for her. She needs to work, to be useful, to be independent.

Since I was a child I have been a seeker, spiritually and otherwise. And that is actually where my political outlook began – from my spiritual need. And I couldn't find what I was looking for. No, I didn't know what I was looking for, it was something that I could not explain as a child. But there was something inside that I wanted.

And this search made me realise the unfairness of our country, of our rulers. I am not educated. I left school at Form 3. Later I worked in a factory and belonged to a trade union and we used to have protests, not going to work. And that started building up in me that we have to try and find a solution. We have to fight for our rights.

During Sharpeville one of my relatives was shot and killed and I became very bitter. And during the burning of passes so many people were killed, I felt, we have to do something. Politically and individually we have to contribute towards the freedom of our country.

At this time I had joined the ANC already, because of a friend who was later arrested and sent to Robben Island. It was the opening of Orlando High School, and he stood up and protested that why should the Bantu Education Minister, being a white person, come to open a Bantu Education school? He stood up during the ceremony and said this, and on that day he was arrested. I felt bitter that it seems very clear that we have no freedom of speech; and I decided that I'm going to leave the country.

I was looking for an escape. I left with my children, six children. I was thirty-two. My husband remained because he didn't approve of me leaving the country. I had to make a decision that I'm going to Botswana, where I could have my children educated and have a different outlook of life, rather than growing up in South Africa, where they will always feel inferior to the white people.

This was in February 1963. I had heard that a school was going to be opened by Patrick van Rensburg, a multiracial school; and I was wishing for my children to go to school with the white people, the same school, taught the same lessons. So I went and settled in Serowe, in Bechuanaland. The school was started that year. I helped with the fund-raising for the school, and I worked there as dormitory matron from 1965 to 1969.

I was a garment worker and I had a sewing machine. And because also I didn't want to work for white people any more in a factory, so I thought I would establish myself as a dressmaker; I thought: I am doing the work for them, and they are getting better off, and I am not getting better.

So I started dressmaking, and fortunate for me I was the only experienced dressmaker in the country at that time. I had bought a lot of materials in South Africa before leaving the country, and I was making garments as ready-made and selling them to nurses and teachers; and they were going just like hot cakes because they were good quality, the workmanship was very good.

I was the first woman to start a small industry; and I built it up to thirty-three trainees. We had fashion shows at the Holiday Inn; people used to ask, not: 'Who made this?' but: 'Where did you buy this?' I started with one machine. I got a second. We were never given enough when we applied for a loan – they always seemed to reckon that being an African, and probably being a woman too, that you can't handle money.

Then I met up with a woman who had one of those home knitting machines. There is not much market for knitwear in Botswana because it is hot, so she was pleased to join up with me. We moved into making school uniforms, and this provides a permanent market – with knitwear to match the uniform.

Although I'm a so-called uneducated person, I have proved I can make something of myself. Sometimes I say, when you look at South Africa and at the working force, it's the black people; the buying force, it's the black people; and the garment factories, many of the black people are there. They know the skills, but they only need to be developed, how to start off, and to run it.

I was approached by the Botswana government to assist in starting small industries; they had set up a development bank for anyone who had skills to start small industries.

At that time in Botswana, there was nothing for refugees from South Africa; they were just passing through to other countries, to Zambia or Zimbabwe. There was not yet a refugee office whatsoever. Later there was the ANC office, and then I started working with the organisation.

After independence in Botswana we were told that those children whose parents are South Africans, they'll have to leave the schools to be educated somewhere else. This was a shock to us. Now what do I do? Because, well, since now I'm also involved with the ANC, I don't want to go back – I can't go back. I decided, well, I will have to take citizenship to safeguard my children in their education. So that's how I've been living in Botswana, but being fully committed to the ANC; and I was doing, you know – this kind of work [A gesture indicates underground] – ja, you know what I mean? Ja. And because I had a travel document from Botswana I could go in and out. I was doing the work in and out. The document was sort of covering me. Ja. I was also housing people.

During the 1976 uprising of students, on that particular day I happened to go to South Africa. I did my shopping, and after I'd finished I went back to Soweto. But as I was leaving the Main Reef road, there was a roadblock; all the white people who were trying to go to Soweto were prevented, but all the black people could go through. In my mind I thought maybe there has been a bank robbery or something.

I drove on and got back to Botswana. When I arrived, my children were very worried, and they said, 'Mama, how did you escape?' I said, 'What do you mean, escape from what?' And they said, 'Haven't you heard what happened in Soweto?' I said, 'Come on, nothing has happened.' And they said, 'You wait for the news.' And in no time, there was the news. I never believed it! When I heard the number of children killed I said, 'I'm going there tomorrow, I want to go and see, I want to investigate.' The following day I took the car again and I went back.

I've seen it. I watched it. I saw, I was there. Oh, it was terrible! But the children – you know, I don't know who taught those children how to drive tractors. They were driving these tractors which collects garbage, and that's how they broke these bottle stores. They were so happy. They had wires, and they would tie the wires to the tractors; one drives, the other instructs; as they pull the tractor the door comes down. They went in, they take the liquor out and pour it away. They went to a butchery also in what is now called Rockville, ja. And this guy when he saw these children coming with stones, he was reaching for a revolver. Hau! It was a big mistake he did. They went for him with all these stones, and they took him and pulled him into the deep freeze and took out all the meat and gave to everyone who was passing.

And the children could conduct even the taxis. A child stops the taxi, they will drain the petrol out saying, 'We just wanted a little bit of petrol,' and take that. And then they'll take the injured ones in the taxis. They were so angry the children, very angry, because they've been killed without doing anything, so they became wild.

The police were doing their own thing too! They were just shooting, killing, you know. But did this stop the children? No! Our children are so brave. They couldn't care less. They will try and run away, but they will come back again.

I did other things in Botswana. I was one of the first to work with family planning – the International Planned Parenthood. I used to go round villages teaching women. I would also go around speaking to women about nutrition, the need to grow vegetables, emphasising self-help projects, telling them why we should grow vegetables.

There was a Swedish man who was thrown out of South Africa. He came to Botswana and started screen printing, so I also learned from him and started teaching screen printing.

There came a time when I had to leave Botswana. It was discovered that I was doing that kind of underground work. The office in Gaberone got the message that I shouldn't attempt again, ja, I should now lie low. And so I had decided to take a job outside Gaberone, in a mine hospital, a place called Janini.

I was a sort of housekeeping matron, and my administrator was from South Africa. And, oh my God! 1985! when the regime invaded Botswana! That morning I heard the news, that in Gaberone the regime was in and had killed fourteen people. The administrator said mockingly, 'Well, the Boers have been here last night, and the next step they're coming here, and of course they know who they're looking for!'

I didn't realise how shocked and afraid I was when he said this. And suddenly I started having problems in breathing, I didn't understand what was happening. It was getting worse and worse. I rushed to the doctor's office; he just called the ward for admission. I passed out. And for the whole of that week, I just kept on getting the attacks. I couldn't even attend the funerals of those people killed, I was hospitalised.

After being discharged, some people visited me and said there is a story going around that the Boers are coming tomorrow, they want Ma'Moatl-hodi, meaning me. The next night there were some Boers seen in Janini. They went to a restaurant with their guns, they picked up a young Botswana boy to go and point out places which they want. But they were reported, and they were taken to the charge office, and said they were just hunters.

Then I received a telegram stating that my mother had passed away, that the funeral is tomorrow. One of my children decided to go. And my mother was not dead, not even ill. The telegram was not sent through the post office, somebody just threw it through my letterbox.

Then the police came to me and said, 'The Boers are trying to get you back. They say you've got important information about the ANC. So you must be careful and don't open any letter that comes from outside. You bring the letter to us and we will do that for you.' Now this was a frightening life for me. Janini is a very remote place. I have to leave Gaberone very early, 3 o'clock in the morning, when nobody's going to see me. And when I come back I never sleep in my own house. I used to sleep in different places.

Then the second telegram came after some months, stating the same death of my mother, and the date of the funeral. And I felt now, this is it. I can't stay any longer. I was on a list of the people most wanted by the regime which the government of Botswana had. So I had to leave.

I had some Danish friends, and they knew my situation, so a family from Denmark sent me the money for the ticket, just to get out, So I ended up here in Denmark. I decided to seek asylum. It was granted after five months.

My children are still in Botswana, except one son who came here after I left because he had to escape too, mainly because we were doing the same job for the ANC – me and my other two sons, going in and out of the country and doing the work.

Now I have been in Denmark for four and a half years, and I find it very difficult and very depressing, because I have been a very active person, not only politically, but I mean in my life. Then suddenly I find myself being so dependent, that I'm a useless somebody sitting here, doing nothing. And that depresses me very much. I find it difficult to be a refugee or an exile. I've realised that there is nowhere in the world one feels at home, except in your own country. It's very clear now to me. And it hurts. It hurts. Also when you are ... the colour of one's skin, it's worse. You are always a stranger and you are always stupid. You are never looked at as somebody reasonable, or somebody with under-standing. You know, people are always pitying you like a fool. And that hurts, that hurts.

I don't like idling. I've been working with rural grass-root projects among people. Whenever there are groups of Danish people who are going to Africa, I am asked to come and talk to them. These are people who are going to be working in rural villages, volunteers. And one time, I felt I must ask them if they cannot use me, because I have been connected with such projects in Botswana. The leader of the group said, 'No we can't use you.' I said, 'Why not?' And she said, 'You don't speak Danish.' And I just blew up! I said, 'Don't you think you are unfair, that you send people to Africa, who don't speak a word of my people's languages, but they go there to help. Why should I have to speak Danish to go to Africa? I don't want to go and teach Danish, I just want to go and work with the people you are talking about, I have already done that, I know exactly what is needed.'

I don't have any high qualifications but I've got the experience. I identify with the village woman, I can just as well contribute like those people with qualifications. But the problem is, if you've never been to university you are never seen as somebody sensible. And this is the same with our own people, and it makes me sick and mad. Education is not only to enter university. Education can be even ... your experience of cleaning the toilet; putting stamps on envelopes – it's all education.

But our people don't see it like that, they don't see practical experience as important. They see the papers from university as being important. And sometimes they can't do anything, it's just the papers. We still have a long way to go. Now, what I am trying to say is this; no matter what, here I cannot be useful. I want to go home, even if I have to go to Botswana if I can't go to South Africa. I can still contribute.

And that's why I want to go back. Carry what I have experienced, and make my people understand that even this Europe didn't just become like that overnight. Each and every one of us has a role to play. I believe that we are all like a jigsaw puzzle and we all fit, there's a place for all of us to fit given the chance. It is the people with the practical work who have to be recognised.

Wasn't it difficult to go into exile with so many children to care for?

I didn't really feel the weight of those children, because I knew I could make it. I'm not afraid. I'm brave.

ELEANOR KHANYILE
London 1991

'I wasn't aware that my life is part of the struggles in South Africa. I thought if you are a woman, that is what you do, this is your participation.'

> On 30 January 1981, South African commandos raided two houses in Matola, a suburb of Maputo, killing nineteen members of the ANC and SACTU who were living there. Her husband William was one who died in that raid. For most of their married life apartheid kept them apart.

My husband William was in jail for eight years, on Robben Island. I met him for the first time when he came out – we had not met before. When people were arrested and detained, we used to send them food in prison. So that is when then we sort of grew closer and closer; and we kept on writing, we wrote to each other; and our love developed when he was in prison. And when he came out, then we got married.

I had promised that I will come and fetch him when he came out of prison. It was a dramatic story, because we never had any contact, any visit, never any talk between ourselves. And all of a sudden I got a call – I was working in the operating theatre. They said, 'Come, come! There's a call for you, it's 'Maritzburg.' And I answered. It was a voice I'd never heard. It was William. He was saying, 'Well, I am here. I was expecting you to come.' And he was out!

Then he came to Durban, and we arranged to get married quickly. But by the time we got married, he was already banned, and he had to apply to come to my mother's place. We got married. He was unemployed.

He used to work at home, in the trade union sector. He used to do translations into Zulu for *Workers' Unity*, and for *Umsebenzi*; and other work which he never told me about. My task in his political work was maybe to send a parcel to Swaziland, Johannesburg, Cape Town. I was working as a nurse in a theatre in Durban, with Farouk Meer and Dr Chiwa. They were also quite involved politically, so they understood my position. Even if I get calls from all over the world that would come in there, they would not object, because they knew it was ANC work.

Sometimes there would be someone coming from Swaziland. They will phone and say, 'Someone is looking for you. Can you come?' Or sometimes I will have to go to Swaziland – they will say, 'Come immediately.' I'd just tell Dr Chiwa, 'Well, I have to go to Swaziland.' They used to let me go whenever I wanted to.

Really and truly, married life with me and William was two years only. We got married, and then he was banned, and banished with house arrest in an outer suburb of Pietermaritzburg. And I was working in Durban at Umlazi. So I used to visit him on weekends when I was off.

Then in 1975 in November, he was arrested again, under the Terrorism Act. So I never saw him; because after he was arrested, I was up and down, organising with other women the welfare for the children of all the people that were arrested and in detention.

But apart from that, I never stopped doing the courier work. But because my husband had taught me not to talk about what I was doing, I never used to tell him. I realised when he was in jail that he was the one that had been setting all this work for me – what to do and what-soever.

Eleanor had been working with a man called Mkhuthuzi Mdluli. One night he disappeared. Although nobody knew for sure that it was the police who had come to his house and taken him away, it was assumed that he had been arrested. Mdluli died in detention within twenty-four hours. Eleanor was advised that it was unsafe for her to stay.

The comrades told me that if I leave the country I will still be able to come back. I'll go and train. It will take six months and I'll come back home. And I was quite happy about that, because I thought: well, six months – it's not much.

But what was good for me at the time was that I didn't have anxiety about leaving my son and my family and the house and everything. I thought I was coming back.

When we came to Swaziland we were two women and two men. Mabida was there and he said to us, 'Right. You can just stay here underground. We will give you a pseudonym; the next two or three days you will go for training, or if you want to, go to school. The choice is yours. And you can still go back.' I . . . oh, I was so thrilled. I definitely needed to go back.

But that same night we were arrested by the Swazi police, and then we were taken to the police station and we had to give our real names. So by that time we were exposed; we couldn't go back, we had to remain in Swaziland.

My son was left in Durban. I had to tell my sister to take him to my mother in the rural area. So he stayed with my mother. And then I stayed in Swaziland for a year. It was quite good; I worked there. There were women who didn't want to know anything about ANC. They only knew that they are there with the refugee status which does not allow them to do anything – no political work. It must just be cooking, washing, or we sell cakes together and do some sewing.

I was lucky; I got a job the first day after we arrived. One of our comrades told me, 'Oh, you are a nurse! So you can start tomorrow. I'm leaving to go to South Africa for treatment.' She had a third stage cancer. So I started working immediately. At that surgery there was a back room which was unused; so we opened it up to be used as an ANC women's centre, so we could do sewing and some cooking and other things. On Sunday we used to meet there. The old women used to teach us how to cook and how to sew, but we never used to talk politics. The women said, 'No politics, or you will be chucked out!' But the men were busy doing political work just the same. They were involved in underground work, and they used to meet. It was really a frustrating thing, because even in the house where we used to stay, they used to have political classes every day; they used to have a news-reading in the mornings which we used to attend. We used to have ANC underground work there. It was also a transit area for students during the time of the uprisings. There were lots of young students who used to come in and we used to sit and discuss; and when it was news time, we used to listen to the news. We used take turns together with the young students to analyse what was happening. Sometimes Mabida will give us history of Kwazulu, or you will read about Shaka, so that people should know and read and understand the history itself.

During this time, I never heard anything about William. There was only one letter which I got by the time he had been charged and was on trial with others. William sent me a note saying that he might be acquitted, and if he is, then he will have to come and join me or I could come back home.

Now I was having mixed feelings. I had already applied for a job and obtained a post in a London hospital, which was waiting for me; and I had a ticket and I had already packed and everything was ready. So I discussed it with the comrades and they said, 'No, the best thing, you go to London; there is no way that you could go back to South Africa having stayed in the ANC house. So many people have been arrested, others have been kidnapped to South Africa and it will be a risk.' And we had been raided in that house about twice by the South African police together with the Swazi police. Oh yes, they worked closely.

In the end, William was discharged. By that time, I was already here in London. My son was at home still. William remained there, and he got in touch with our son. But he didn't stay long. He had to leave in 1978. He was based in Lusaka, working for SACTU, then later in Maputo. During this time I only saw him once. He was invited by Anti-Apartheid to come to London for a special meeting of political prisoners. He stayed here for three weeks and then he went back to Mozambique.

He was living in this SACTU house in Matola. He wrote to me, we were communicating very strongly then on the phone and he told me that it would be nice if I come and stay in Maputo, then it will be easy for us also to bring our son, Vusi, and we'll stay together as a family. So I decided that in the coming year, which was 1980, I will go to Maputo for a holiday just to see how it was in Mozambique and the possibilities of me being based there with Vusi. He was then ten.

IDAF had offered me a job. The day when I went for an interview, it was the day . . . oh, William had said he will phone me that evening. So I waited and waited, but we were very busy in the theatre and each time I was free I would rush and try and make a call but it was just an engaged signal. And I kept on trying. Then the phone was just dead, and I thought, oh well, the phone is not working.

We were busy right through the night, so I couldn't communicate with him. In the morning I was told someone had phoned for me, but I was busy. Again the calls kept on coming, people phoning me. We normally finish at seven, but we were busy until about half seven, quarter to eight. So I just rushed to the room and changed to take a bus to the interview at IDAF.

Came to IDAF. You know, everybody was sort of sad and looking at me, sad, and I thought, oh, ah well, maybe it's one of those days, they are busy. So I went to see Barry and Barry kept on taking me around, showing me the books and everything. But I was looking at the time, because I was timing to go to see someone. Thereafter he says, 'Well, Ismail is coming to see me and then you can go with him in the car.'

Then I waited. Ismail came and then they took me and then they told me on the way. They told me that William was late, he was killed in Matola. I couldn't believe this. Oh. They told me in the car while I was travelling, I just fainted then; I couldn't believe it. But when I woke up it was like a dream to me. Then I thought maybe William didn't die, you see. It might be a camouflage story. Maybe they will take him into the country in disguise. Because I had been reading William Pomeroy's book about the Philippines, and how they used to infiltrate the people and then say well, so-and-so died. And I thought maybe that's what has happened to William and others.

The ANC flew me out to Mozambique. When we arrived in Matola, we were met by comrade J.S. and comrade Masondo. We went in through this guest lounge and we sat down there and then they asked me, 'Have you heard what happened?' I says, 'No.' They said, Well they're sorry William was killed . . . I thought they were going to tell me that, no, William he has been taken into the country or William hasn't been killed or anything.

So there was it. The numbers who had been killed were fluctuating – one day nine, then eleven, thirteen. You know, I couldn't believe until we had seen them; we went to view them. First we were told that we were not going to view them because they were badly mutilated. We were not going even to touch the bodies because, they say, the Portuguese custom is that they are attended by men only at the mortuary, and they will be washed and buried and we won't see them. But we made a plea as women – because all the women by Saturday they had arrived – and we all discussed this and we said well, with us, it's our own customs. And we said, 'No we would like to see them.'

We saw them. To us it was an unbelievable scene because all the coffins were there. I went past first and I thought . . . you know, I didn't concentrate on William, I was looking at these others to see are they all really dead. Then I saw William, William I knew, these others I didn't know. So I went back again to see him and I literally kissed the body and everything. There you are, he's gone. And nothing can be done.

But one thing; I was not the only one, we were so many. And I'm sure that was the consolation. Because we all came together, the twelve of us, together with the relatives and parents, others. And it was just another funeral really.

My son didn't come and my mother-in-law didn't come and my families, because the lawyers were making an application for William in particular to be buried inside the country, just as a gesture for all others who have been killed there. While all others were applying for their passports and visas to go, my family was told to stay at home. They did ask me what would I do if William is being buried at home? I said, 'Well, if he is buried after the funeral, I don't mind, because it will be like a memorial.' So we agreed on that, in those terms, because I wouldn't be allowed to go back home for a funeral. And then . . . they refused the permission for the body to go back.

After that then, I worked for IDAF. My son came to join me. He was fifteen. I went to Maputo again in 1982 to meet Vusi, and it so happened that it was during the anniversary of William's death. It was a very big anniversary and my son was lucky to join in that, and we went to see the graves. Samora Machel was addressing the rally at the graveyard.

So during all those years, my son and I were separated, from 1976 right up till 1982 when he came to join me here in London and we stayed together. He started school here and then he did engineering and computer studies, but he hasn't drawn himself into this British community. He still speaks his own language, he's never forgotten it, and he still has memories of the family and home. But I must say exile is bad for him. I think it was so traumatic for us to leave him behind. He always asks, 'But why was I left behind?' And as a result he always says, 'I don't think I will return home.' That was the greatest mistake I think I have done in my life, not to take him with me. But, as I say, my understanding was that I'll go and then I'll soon come back. Everybody thinks the same when they leave, that they will come back.

I started my full-time work with IDAF and at the same time, I continued working in the ANC's Women's Committee. I drew my inspiration of work from the comrades I met in Swaziland in particular. They were the ones who told me to read, and also they were the ones who told me the background history of the women's struggle. When I came to London, most of the women encouraged me to work in the women's field. I saw the ANC women's work growing in the region.

Each year I was learning a new form of women's struggles. Dulcie September came to tell us, 'This is not solidarity work, this is your struggle; you will have to go and do the speaking at meetings.' And she said, 'You are not going to talk about what you have learnt in the ANC, you are going to talk about yourself, your experiences.' I didn't know what she meant about this, but she meant about what has happened to my life. I wasn't aware that my life is part of the struggles in South Africa. I thought it's nature, that is how I've been brought up, that is how I grew up. I thought, if you are a woman, that is what you do, this is your participation.

In my family, in my married life with William, the short time I stayed with him, we never had divisions in the family – that there was you cooking, you washing, you ironing. The only thing which was a division in our family was that we were never in the house at the same time!

William was doing the ANC work, I was working. I used to work either in the morning or evening so when I came home, William used to take Mvusi. When Vusi goes to school, William was at home doing his work in the house; and when I used to come in the evening, William was going out to do his ANC work outside. So he used to do the cooking, washing, ironing, marketing. My task was to work and bring the income into the family.

My adult life was to work and bring the money, but I never saw it as my role as a woman in the political sense. I never saw it in that way – that I was one of the freest women in the world! [Laughs] I mean in the history of South Africa. My neighbours used to say, 'What kind of a man is this?' They'd never seen this, a man hanging the washing; he used to wash and rinse it outside in the tap, and my neighbours used to come and look at him. And I used to tell him, 'You know, the neighbours were looking at you and saying, what type of man – ' and he used to laugh. Because his politics were far advanced from mine and he knew what they meant. But for me, it never meant anything.

But over the years, our work in the Women's Section has changed a lot. Even in the ANC as a whole, our work has been growing and changing its face from that time up till now. When I left the country, as I was telling you about Swaziland, women didn't want to know anything about politics. If they could come in and sew and cook and talk about their own family lives, that was enough. But now, when you talk of family lives, the separation of families, the divided family lives, I can see what the women in London were challenging at that time. Women were challenging the ratio of women within the organisation itself and their position in the ANC executive, in all the positions. What is their role, and the percentages. Is it because the women aren't good for these positions? They are challenging all these issues, which were never challenged before.

If I had never left home it would have been a different life. But I think I wouldn't have gone astray there. I would have developed as well and moved forward.

I'm looking forward to going home, I think that is where I belong. But I wouldn't like to return in a vacuum – just to go home. Because now I won't have a home and I don't think my family has that level of political understanding. My home life is talking about the ANC work, about political work, I've got no other conversation. But if I go home, not to go to do ANC work, I'll really feel lost and I think it will be a waste of my time. So I'm waiting to go back with the ANC, to go back and do the ANC work on the ground. Over ground, yes. On the ground, over the ground! [Laughs]

It was traumatic for us to know that we had never had a home together, a family life. I never really stayed with William for long, had a home and stayed together. Never. To be in the organisation is hard, because you have to take everything as is. But one thing in the organisation I've learnt, that you are in a home. You know that whatever happens to you, you can call on them at any time. The way they buried William, it was not something I could have done. For me, it was all done in the family way.

DIANA WILLIAMS
Lusaka 1990

'Separation just destroys relationships.'

> She is secretary to Tom Nkobi, Treasurer General of the ANC. It is a job full of frustrations and difficulties – nothing is easy, particularly making phone calls on the antiquated and malfunctioning telephone system. She is quiet and self-effacing.

My parents were never racist in that die-hard racist's way. They were sort of liberal, they voted PFP, they'd always taught us to be respectful towards people and all that sort of thing.

I came into exile mainly because my husband was involved inside the country. We were living in Jo'burg at the time, and neither of us nor any of our group at the time were in contact with any formal structures of the ANC, because at that time we didn't have those sort of contacts.

My husband was working on the newspapers, incredibly frustrated with how little could be done because of the self-censorship of the press and so on. So we formed a little study group with some other people, and we started studying radical literature and whatever readings we could get hold of. It was quite a large group in the beginning, and from there came a smaller group who felt they wanted to take more decisive action. I was pregnant, so I didn't get as involved as they did. I went away for a short holiday and it was while I was away that they did this bombing for which he's now been convicted. And after the bombing, he left the country and I followed him. I was about six months pregnant. I wanted to go with him, I felt the same way he did about what was happening inside the country.

My husband skipped over the fence, but I had a passport. We went to Botswana. Because I was pregnant I had to stay there. I couldn't fly anywhere by that stage, so I had my children there, in Gaberone, ja, the twins. And when they were about three months old we came to Lusaka and waited in a transit residence. My husband had already decided he was going to go for military training.

We were there for about three months waiting for him to go, it was a pretty rough time for me. I felt incredibly . . . well, culture-shocked I suppose. But it was a difficult time in Botswana then. People were suspicious of us, you know.

Shortly after my husband left, I was asked to go to Tanzania to help teach in the ANC primary school. I got to Tanzania, but they had no arrangement for looking after the children. The only place was not at the Mazimbu complex itself, it was at a really dreadful place in the town, in Morogoro.

In Mazimbu, the Women's Section came along and decided that because I was a mother of two children and without a husband around, that I should be with all the other mothers and children at this place in Morogoro, which was really a very bad place. My children got extremely sick when they were there. This is before they had the day-care centre at Mazimbu; they were building it at that time. There were too many women and too many babies and young children stuck into this very small and very unsanitary place, ja. But I wasn't there long – my kids got so sick they nearly died there. It was gastroenteritis; they were very sick.

Comrade Tikly, who was the Director of Mazimbu at that time, came to see us, and found us in a really bad state. I was also a bit sick myself so we were really at our lowest. And against the Women's Secretariat decision, he took me back to Mazimbu. And then I finally started teaching – after about a year! I could send the kids to the day-care centre, which was then complete.

I didn't have any training, not at all. It was very challenging that. Not just because I didn't have any training, but because at Mazimbu Primary School at that time there were absolutely no course books; they were struggling to write up a syllabus. They had very few qualified teachers, so what they tried to do was put one qualified teacher with what they called an assistant teacher – and that's what happened to me. But I was very fortunate. I was with a Swedish primary school teacher, a really wonderful woman. I learned a lot about teaching-aids; it even helped me with my own kids, seeing how they're being taught here, and knowing what's wrong, and perhaps a little about how to counteract. But it was tiring, exhausting work in fact, ja, preparing all your own lessons and even writing some of your own little books and things.

All this while my husband was away. In fact, for the first six months or so I didn't even hear from him; I didn't even get a letter. It was only after he had finished his basic training that he was allowed to write, and then it was intermittent. I'd get a group of letters; and then four months and another batch of letters would come. Ja.

The kids were growing up. They took some time to get over their illness, but after a while they were OK; they went from the day care to the nursery school. And then my husband came back; he stayed for a year or so, just wanting to be with the family and sort himself out. He helped out teaching photography for a while. And then he was recruited to go to the Forward Areas. I didn't want to stay in Mazimbu – I found the place really very suffocating, insular.

I decided to go with him. But our relationship was also having serious problems, due to the separation: partly from growing apart; partly from another relationship which I had, a very short and meaningless relationship really. But it destroyed my husband, because he'd been waiting for me in an unrealistic sort of way. I really feel that separation, unless you are incredibly strong and incredibly understanding and mature – just destroys relationships. There's so much evidence of it in the Movement.

Ja. Anyway, we came to Lusaka, and waited again for months and months before he was actually sent down south. We were waiting at the farm, Chongela. When I was at home I was a secretary; but I wanted to get away from it completely, I didn't want anything to do with it, so I never told anybody I could even type. [Laughs] I was even thinking of going to study teaching. But it didn't work out. Having two small children that you're not prepared to leave in the care of an institution makes it virtually impossible. But I kept hanging on to my secret about secretarial work. But at the farm, I was going out of my mind with nothing to do; total boredom, just looking after the kids. And they were more independent by that stage, out most of the time, so I was really, really bored.

And so I offered my services to the ANC Preparatory Committee for a fundraising workshop. From there the TG got to hear about me. He was in need of a secretary – dire need, he'd been without one for some time. And I was taken on there.

So I moved into Lusaka, and I've been working for the TG ever since March 1986. I knew nothing of what my husband was doing. I had actually seen very little of him for the previous two years. He'd been in Swaziland. He'd come back, go back to Swaziland; come back again, stay a few weeks, go to Angola, come back; that sort of thing.

And then left, saying he was going inside the country, and that I would next see him . . . ja, when he came back, or when we were free.

And now he's serving twenty-five years*.

I wasn't in touch with my own family for years. At first, when we were in Botswana, Damien's parents and my parents came out to see the kids. And then, after that, we lost contact. When I came to Lusaka, I wrote to them and gave them an address; they wrote once. And then I never received another letter, so I just sort of shut them out. I felt my life was so far away from them that I couldn't relate to them at all. But I was in a rather depressed state and couldn't see the common ground that we had. All I could see was the difference.

From the middle of last year, people had been asking if my kids could go to South Africa to see their father. And I'd been really scared of it. There were a lot of complicated things. Our relationship had been on the rocks, but I had not known about this woman, or that she would be going into the country with the group. So when I found out all about it – there was all this scandalmongering in the press and so on – I felt very hurt by it. Also he didn't write to me, and I felt afraid that if I sent the kids inside the country to see him, they might not come back. That was the one issue.

I also felt that it was dangerous for Damien while he was still on trial; that the Boers might do something to the kids, or might use them in some way. But then the trial was over, they were just awaiting sentence; and one of their lawyers told our people in Harare that it was vital for his morale – and even for the kids' development – for them to see him. So we started organising their visas within about ten days.

When I first told the kids, I took them into the bedroom and sat them down and said, 'I've got something really exciting to tell you – you're going to see daddy!' Both of them seemed a bit stunned. The younger, Kieran – he is younger by ten minutes – he was excited, thinking about all the things he could get inside the country. But Seamus, who does tend to be much more serious and sensitive just said, 'I don't want to go.' I asked why, and he said, 'Boers are there; and there's a war there.' And then he started crying. It was really quite a trauma. We watch things on TV and always talk about it. It had obviously gone deep with him. Anyway I managed to persuade them that it would be OK. A sociologist working with Damien managed to get the kids a number of visits, including a contact visit, which was really good for them.

On the way back from the airport when they returned I tried to ask them a lot of questions about the visit. But it was mostly just . . . sort of vivid impressions, the clanging of the doors. 'Were you scared?' 'Yes, yes, we were a bit scared; the doors clanged and the key turned twice – it went once around and then it turned again' – things like that. You could see that actually going in was not exactly traumatic, but it made a dramatic impact, ja. They're only eight.

* Damien Williams has since been released under an amnesty for political prisoners.

But Damien had been in good spirits as well, so the meetings with the kids was good. He made a lot of jokes, and seems to have told them that he was being well looked after, not beaten up or anything – sort of dispelled some of their fears.

The main regrets I have are that we could have done far more inside the country before we left, but we were not in touch with the ANC. I was really on the periphery of political activity. I don't regret having come into exile. I've learned and developed an enormous amount, but exile is difficult for everybody. I think whites in exile have a particular experience – not more difficult but just different. From the time I've come into the ANC I haven't really had a time when I've felt close to people – our own people. I think this is my particular personality. I'm not extrovert at all; I'm a shy person, have always been. Having two children and coming into exile at the same time set me back. I couldn't get involved in the structures because the kids took up so much of my time; in Mazimbu I felt very isolated. In Lusaka I just couldn't talk to people at all; I'd lost all confidence in myself.

I think to be of any use in the future I would have to study in some way, something. You see the problem is I'm already thirty-one, I dropped out of university, I've missed out on years of opportunities to do things, make decisions that I should have made at that time. But I think I would like to study history again, and become involved in researching the history of South Africa. But it's a bit late.

EMILY DENNIS
Dakawa 1989

'We just felt we had never been parted, although we had been parted for sixteen years.'

Her garden in Dakawa is brilliant with flowers and flowering bushes and trees. She has made this place beautiful with native plants that flourish in the dry but fertile ground. She is slightly built, with light, rather sharp features. She was reluctant to talk about her life. A quiet and reserved woman, fifty-three years old.

I grew up in a village just outside Pietermaritzburg, in a place called Ixopo. My parents were farmers; we were many kilometres from the school, so we moved into the village, which was still about a mile away from the school. I had to leave school at fifteen because we were a big family, and it was very difficult for my parents to send us all to school. I worked in a sewing department. At twenty I was married and my first child was born when I was twenty-one.

My husband worked out, mostly away from home. He was a builder and he always had to travel from one building site to another.

After our second child was born, we moved into Pietermaritzburg to be closer to his workplace. But he wasn't very happy about his work, and he decided to move on to Swaziland and there we joined him again. We were always somewhere in the back, waiting for him to set up before we joined him again. It was just about that time when a lot of the people who were leaving South Africa for political reasons were drifting into Swaziland. There we met some South African exiles. These people really influenced Ossie politically. I was not interested in politics; I was just interested in bringing up the children. And I was worried actually, when I realised what was involved. I knew that we were foreigners in Swaziland, and this guilt by association could jeopardise our stay there; and I nagged maybe quite a bit about our security, 'Wouldn't it be better then if we went back home?' But, in his own way, Ossie tried to tell me, 'You know, going back home is no security.' So I tried to keep in the background.

But still I was worried, I was worried about the security of the children. I was interested in their education. I didn't want them to suffer the way I had because of a lack of education. I realised that education is the most important thing in anybody's life. No matter how difficult things get, if you are educated then you have something to fall back on.

I got a job and I started working. That did ease the situation. And with also his way of politicising me, his gentle way, I began to understand that politics was your everyday life.

But, of course, the time came when he had to leave. It was at the time of the 90-day detention, and the Security Police were visiting his parents down at Transkei, making a lot of enquiries about him. We were not permanent residents of Swaziland, we had only temporary working permits. The Swazi police started putting pressure on his employer, and then his work permit was withdrawn. Fortunately his employer then got him another work permit; he had to fight very hard to get it. But when that one was also withdrawn, then there was no other way. Going back to South Africa would have meant 90-days detention. And so it was felt then that he should then leave the country.

I had my job, I was working, the three children were at school. When the children were finished their year at school, I went back home to South Africa, and I moved down to live with his parents in the Transkei from about 1964.

At that time there was still some communication. Ossie had reached Dar es Salaam, and he had written to tell me that he would go to Europe to study for some time; and then there might be some possibility that we could join him. So in that hope, we continued.

But after two years, it was obvious that it wasn't as easy as we thought it would be. The children were living somewhere else, going to school, and I was living with his parents at a trading station in the Transkei, so there was this total separation of the whole family. And our youngest son had had a terrible accident, and it was necessary for me to get closer to the hospital where he would have attention. I decided that I should move, together with all the children, back to my home, closer to this big hospital.

I lived there until 1972. He was in Europe, but we used to get a letter occasionally from him, so there was some contact. But from 1972 there was a complete break. And that was quite difficult. We didn't hear anything from him from that time. We lost contact.

I moved from my parents; I went to live on my own. I started a little business which was paying better than working for a boss, and I did quite a lot of dressmaking in my spare time. Later on the children were at boarding-school – it was not easy, but I'd set myself a goal. I had decided that the most important thing is that they must get the best education that I can get for them. So I sacrificed the whole of my life to achieving this, yes.

It was difficult explaining to them things which I didn't quite understand myself. I had accepted the fact that he was now dependent on an organisation, that he was not free to do as he likes. Maybe I had also matured a little bit politically, and I understood things better.

Out on this little place to which I had moved – it was a sort of a settlement – and there was no doctor, there was no clinic, there were some schools. The visiting doctor who went through this place twice a week, would just stop his vehicle at the store and he would examine the patients; if they needed injections he would just inject them there in the open. So the women of that area, we decided to get together. With the help of some of the white comrades who lived in the same area, we set up a club and mobilised the women around the issue of building a clinic – not really a clinic, but a doctors' consulting room. We collected quite a lot of funds, and we put up this little clinic. Which was really very good.

I was president of this club; but I didn't realise that it was, well, drawing the Security attention to me. They started visiting my place. Then somebody would say to me, 'But why are the Security Police visiting your place so often?' And I said, 'But I don't know.' And they said to me, 'Well, I have heard the rumour that you are getting instructions from your husband to mobilise the people.' But, of course, it didn't worry me, because I knew it wasn't true.

But even before that, the Security Police were following me around. When Ossie left I was under a sort of observation. They followed us right from the beginning, when we moved from the Transkei back to our village. They wanted to know about Ossie, always asking questions about Ossie, where he is, what he is doing, has he contacted you?

I had applied for a new passport because mine had expired; and they just withdrew it – and without reasons. They asked questions, they took all our particulars, myself, my family, the children. And when the children grew up and they moved to college in Cape Town, the Security Police were there immediately to find out: Where are the children?

Then after we had built this clinic, one day a new Security Police came under the guise of a building inspector; and he walked into our little shop and he said to me, 'Mrs Dennis, I want to examine your surroundings.' So we walk through the building with him, and we went to examine the back of the building. But it was obvious he was not interested in the building, because immediately he started talking to me about my husband – this was about late 1979. And he said to me, 'You know, I think that I have met your husband in Zambia.' So I said, 'Well that's strange, I didn't know that my husband was in Zambia. I haven't seen him for many, many years.'

I found out much later – when I came out here – that at that time he was in Zambia. So they were watching him. This went on for all the time that I was there; they kept on watching us. And there's nothing worse than the feeling that you are being watched; we had information that our telephone was tapped; we knew that our letters were censored; we knew that there were people who were particularly watching our house. There was nothing, nothing that we could do. We knew that whoever we talk to is under some kind of suspicion, so we were really very isolated from people.

That's the political side. But the other side, the social side, was even more difficult for a woman on her own, especially if you are young. I was only twenty-eight when my husband left, and I had his three children to bring up. Financially it was very difficult because I had to work, but with the help of family, we managed.

It was very difficult for the children to understand. There were days when they would ask, 'But where is Daddy?' And fortunately for myself, I did not hide anything from them. When they were young I told them, 'Daddy's gone, and he's not coming back; but maybe one day you will join him.' And as they grew up, and time went on, and we were not joining him, then they would ask other questions. And I would try to answer them to the best of my ability and according to what I thought they would understand, without making up stories.

So they did understand, eventually, that he was involved in politics. And it brought us closer together, because not once did they ever feel that he should have not done it; and not once did I make them feel that I was ever against anything of the sort. They learned a little bit, maybe, from friends. They read a lot, so they understood quite a lot. So they grew up with the feeling that they would like to see their father.

But, of course, there was no contact with him; and there was no contact with other political people who could have enlightened us or even maybe helped us to . . . what shall I say . . . to get more involved in some way. So there was this isolation. But I had set myself a goal, and that was to bring up these children. And that's what I was doing. I had in other words cut myself off from everything else.

Time went on, and time went on, and there was no communication. One son was then at the University of the Western Cape, and he wanted to know very much more at a higher level. About 1979, fortunately, his father was able to make contact with us.

He was somewhere in Africa – he invited us to join him. So my son said, 'Mum, I don't know about you; but this is what I have been waiting for. So I'm going!' Ai, it was a hard decision to make. If either of my sons had refused to come out, then I would have had to stay behind, because they were still dependent on me. Our daughter was self-supporting at the time, so she was all right. But the boys felt that they would like to come, and the bigger one said, 'Well, that's it! This is what I've been waiting for.' The younger was a bit hesitant because he said, 'I don't know my Dad, but I would like to see him.' So then I said, 'Well do you want to go?' and he said, 'If one goes, we all go. If one stays, we all stay.' Eventually we decided that the three of us would leave.

It was not easy, slipping away the way we had to. We had no passports. Well – maybe this is a part I'd rather not talk about – but anyway we managed to slip out of the country, and then we met him in another country.

It was ... we just felt that we had never been parted. Although we had been parted for sixteen years, it was just normal; because I think that we had been waiting for such a reunion, and we were confident somehow that as long as there was life there was hope. So it was ... we felt quite naturally together. So then we came to Mazimbu.

It was right at the beginning. There was nothing at Mazimbu at all. They had just started building the first dormitory – Unit 1. So we settled in Mazimbu and we've watched it grow ever since.

There was a lot of work to be done. I felt that, well, there's nothing really I can do to help the situation. But my husband said to me, 'You know, every little bit, every small contribution helps to turn this big wheel.' Then, together with another comrade, I got involved in the sewing department, which was something that I could do. And then George Ponen, who was a tailor, came along, and with machines donated by the Holland Committee we started a small tailoring department. From there we went on and worked in the garment factory. And then after six years of that kind of work, Ossie had to move to Dakawa, so then I moved with him.

Dakawa was also right at the beginning, and most of the women were not working. There was only the day-care centre as a source of work for the women. We were able to organise the women into work in the sewing department, in the day-care centre, and others in the building works. That's it.

Well, I've come a real long way from the days when I thought that politics were for other people, and not for me, ja. I realise that you can't live apart from politics. Both my sons work full-time for the Movement.

Being in exile is being in exile. You are separated from your family, from your home, from your culture even. In exile you learn to live with other people. It's really an eye-opener; because it is what we talk about in South Africa, but it's something that we can never practise there, this living together. Here in exile we say 'comrade'; and you can really live as comrades, which is really very different from what you can do in South Africa.

You know, we were only married from 1956 to 1964, before he went away. But I didn't have any doubts about us not meeting again. Maybe it is because of the kind of life we had. I had this total faith and confidence that what we had discussed and what we had promised would eventually materialise. I knew that he was not independent. If it was his own will, he would have got us out immediately. But I told myself that, well, he depends on an organisation now; and until that organisation makes it possible for us to join him, then we have to wait. But I knew that only either that or death will part us. I had always lived for that moment – that one day we might have to leave. It was always at the back of our minds that one day, when Ossie can, he will send for us. So when the opportunity came, it was just a normal thing.

THOKO MAFAJE
Guelph, Canada 1990

'There is this thing that a soldier doesn't cry . . . you don't have to cry if someone is gone. Which I feel it's the wrong thing. It is hard. I've experienced it. It is hard.'

> A light snow covers the November landscape – grey, drained of colour – and adds to the feeling of isolation, of loneliness, of being far away from the familiar. She left South Africa a year after the 1976 uprising, and went to Mazimbu to finish her education.

My grandmother knew I was leaving. My mother didn't know. From my father's side they were people who didn't want to break any law; they still are. From my mother's side, they are ANC people, my grandmother was an ANC member all these years, so she knew when I was leaving; I told her, but I didn't tell my mother. I was more close to my grandmother than my mother, because she was taking care of my sister and me. I think it was good, because we began to know more; she knew what was happening. She died in 1989.

I was five years in Mazimbu, because the scholarships by then were difficult to get. I was working at the childcare centre.

I met my husband in Mazimbu in 1982. Then he went to Zambia to go and work at the Chongela farm. I got a scholarship to Zambia but it was in Quito the Copperbelt. For two years I was there. We were seven South Africans and seven Namibians. At least it was better than being in Mazimbu! [Laughs] When I finished at Quito, I joined Aaron on the farm. I was helping with the visitors, I had to help cooking, maybe show them around; and there was a school for the workers, so usually I would teach there.

In 1987 he got a scholarship with the Commonwealth to come to Canada, to the university. And I was studying teacher training. But I stopped . . . after he passed away.

Here in Canada he was sick. He had cancer. But the most troublesome thing he had was the eyes. They gave him a wrong medication . . . the eyes were sort of getting cloudy like . . . I think that sort of killed him. He was thirty-five. He was ill three months. He started in September but he wasn't that serious. In November he was just ill, he went to London, Ontario for treatment and he was sort of getting . . . then the doctor changed him to another one. There was a problem between the doctors. They couldn't decide on the treatment, because each wanted to treat him his own way. He got serious then . . . then he was admitted and died on 12 January.

When we arrived here, it was terrible! Because well, you know, the snow, you'll put on boots and . . . oh, there were a lot of things. I wrap myself with a towel underneath when it's cold, do all those things. Find that when I get into the classroom, it's hot. I start to sweat. It is only now that I've adjusted to the weather, I got used to it. But it's cold, especially in January and February, it's terrible. It goes to my nerves . . .

The Canadians, they are good. They are good. But the organisation . . . well, maybe the organisation I was dealing with, WUSC, they were mean. They were just mean towards students. One lady told me that this is how we are told to treat you, you shouldn't come and think that you are in a better place; we should treat you the way you've been treated where you come from, from your camps, especially refugees. In fact they call us refugees, I don't like it really because I think I'm not a refugee. Anyway, that's what I feel. No, I'm not a refugee. I will be going home when things are good. When things are settled, I will . . . I would love to.

I have one friend from South Africa here, he's married to an Egyptian, very nice lady, so they are my friends. That's all. We are the only two South Africans in Guelph.

I have two children, they are at school here. My sister is married, she's in Pretoria now. She called me. I was so happy. It was the first phone call since I left home, I was so happy that she surprised me.

But I'm not used to Aaron not being here, going on. I still can't believe it because there are times when sort of I'm expecting him, I am waiting. Then I say to myself, oh, by the way, he's not here. And helping the

children to adjust – that is hard; the younger one always comes and asks
. . . they know he's no longer coming . . . And the other one. They saw
their grandmother, so I have a photo of her, that's their daddy's mum,
when she was here. But I think they're taught something at school about
Africa, because immediately we mention Africa, 'No, I don't want to go
there, I will die if I go to Africa, they don't have food.' They talk about
it at school and then they think it's the same as Ethiopia . . . the same.

In fact, even adult Canadians are like that. They think that Africa, it's
just one small place where there are all these starving people, nothing . . .
there's nothing progressing on the other side. They have a high standard
of living, but they don't know what is happening in Canada, so you can't
expect them to know what is happening outside.

But there are some things we could learn from their approach towards
children. Their children understand. Our education at home is that if a
child doesn't behave you have to hit; which doesn't work, I feel it doesn't
work. They have a better approach.

I thought I was a strong mother, but – it's difficult to express this, I had
a tough time. So . . . but I managed, I don't know how. At least I'm
living, I'm OK. I thought I will break down with . . . maybe I'll go to
their mental hospital, that's what I was expecting but . . . I didn't, which
was something great for me. Well, since there were churches here, and at
home I was in the church choir, so I thought I would rather go and join
the United Church. So that's what happened. Maybe God helped me,
if there is God . . . though I don't believe . . . No, I don't believe that
there's God because if he was there, he wouldn't let some nations have
difficulties and other nations have nice times and so on. But I just got
support from the people of the church and talking about my experiences,
which is . . . well something I've never done before. But I think Aaron's
death made me have to talk about it, maybe by then sort of relieving
myself.

I used to just come in . . . from school I'll come in the house, lock
myself in the house, because I didn't see people. When people see me, it
was sort of . . . the way they will maybe talk about me: 'Thoko, oh, that
South African woman who lost her husband.' They are to look at me as
a widow, someone who has lost a husband, not just as myself, Thoko.
But I talked about it, I told people, 'No, it's not that, I need support,' I
used to tell them. Even my counsellor, I had a counsellor at school, I'd
go to her office, ja. Well . . . she was good because that gave me . . . ja,
the only place I could go and cry. So at least when I know that, I will
just go to her; whenever she sees me, I don't know, maybe something
happened, because whenever I go to her office, immediately I see her, I
start crying, because she was my counsellor and Aaron's counsellor.

I was sort of tough before. Anything will happen: 'No, let me do it.'
And be strong. Since I came and I met this woman, she told me, ja, you
have to cry it out, you have to cry. And there was another family in

Toronto, Mr and Mrs Wayer, they supported us, and took us as part of their family. They also go to the United Church in Toronto. Maybe I'll go to her house for a weekend, she'll tell me, 'Thoko, you have the right to cry. If there's something upset you, you have the right to cry. Don't keep it in . . . within you.' Because I just became ill, I didn't know what was wrong. Doctors couldn't know what was wrong. She was a nurse for twenty, thirty years, so she retired. I used to go and stay with them, cry, get it over, and they would take care of me and the children. Which supported me. Which helped me a lot.

Before, when they say somebody is dead – especially within the organisation: 'Somebody's dead.' In Tanzania we had so many funerals, malaria . . . you bury one one day, you know that maybe if you don't bury two today, next week you're going to bury three people. No, there's no longer a point of crying. And there is this thing that a soldier doesn't cry. If a soldier's gone, you don't have to cry. So we had that thing, that no, you don't have to cry if someone is gone. Which I feel it's the wrong thing. I've experienced it. Maybe it's because it's something which came to my side, I've experienced it. It is hard. When you lose someone, it's hard.

It was hard also being not at home. When Aaron died, I was in the hospital. Hospitals here allows families, if you want to come and stay there. You spend the whole night there, they'll just leave you. So ja, when he died I was with him. And I had one lady, Elizabeth Coben, who was with me. She's Canadian, she's a nice lady, she was with me and one friend from Cameroon. I went to the nurses' room and slept. But I was dreaming . . . I had this funny dream. When there's someone going to die, I dream that my grandfather, from my father's side . . . will come – I haven't seen him since he died in 1950. But he will come to me – he came when my grandmother died – and he came and said, 'No, wake up. It's time.' But they never told me what it's time for? It was sort of a knock on the window, I was dreaming.

When I woke up, I went up . . . tired, tired, I couldn't even walk, the nurses asked me what's wrong. I said, 'No, nothing.' I didn't tell them about the dream. So the other one said, 'No, nothing's going to happen.' But I said, 'No, I know there's something going to happen.' It was just about two, we were still there. After some time, Aaron started trying to talk, he couldn't talk. Then we were sitting. I didn't . . . I was sort of sitting on the bed and talking with these other people . . . I didn't see what was happening . . . so these people just . . . the other girl just stood and ran to the nurses. So I sort of got scared. And when the nurses were coming, I saw him kicking, well, I was scared. I was very scared, so they came, they just held me, I didn't know what was happening. They just pushed me, said, 'You come this side or . . . ' The other one was saying, 'No, let her be here.' So that he just . . . he just changed his eyes, and he was . . . It was my first time to see a dead person, with him. It was sad.

Families

The children had no choice. They were left or they were taken, but either way they had no part in the decision. Expressed or repressed, they bear a burden of resentment towards their parents for leaving them behind, or equally for taking them away; and, if taken, additional resentment towards the host country for its subtle exclusions; and to friends who, unlike themselves, belong where they live; which is where they were born.

What history can they claim? Their history is that of their parents, and their parents' history is not present – it is elsewhere. The drama of their parents' lives has overshadowed the small, daily, social problems of their own. They are aware of the enormity of the malign power that has shattered the continuity of their lives. But they feel 'small and inadequate in the face of something that is world-size'.

The children cannot encompass the whole picture. If the rest of the world has taken decades to encompass it, how could they be expected to understand? The parents acted under the compulsion of a powerful morality, and the children, even when young, know that this is so. But at the same time they are rendered insignificant by the insistent priorities of their parents' lives. If their politics are so important, why did they have us?

'There were times when I felt I was competing with 30 million blacks for my parents' attention,' says Nicholas Wolpe. 'I knew he was on the side of the good,' says Christopher Kasrils, 'but I didn't really understand why he was putting his politics before us.' And Gloria Nkadmimeng thought her Dad 'didn't really like me much. He's much more in love with his cause than with us, his children.'

As the children grow up in exile they want to be able to choose an identity. They need that sense of inheritance, of belonging. But as adolescents they inherit what they want least of all – their sense of being different; the difference of their home, their parents, their accents.

They are pulled two ways. Everything in the home, the concentration on news from South Africa, the conversations of their parents' friends, gatherings of the exiled community, all assert that they belong to another country; while school, friends, social habits, the desire to be accepted, immerses them in the culture of the host country.

In turn the children bring to their parents the unwelcome reality of the here and now; forcing them to slot into routines imposed by the daily tasks of living, making a home, working, shopping, mingling with other parents at the schools – all the things that insidiously corrode the temporary nature of exile and force down reluctant roots.

Exceptionally, some children of exiles triumphantly combine the opposing influences, as in the case of Lamakhosa Kunene in America, involved as much in her school's activities as she is with the cause of South Africa.

Place, race and strength of cultural traditions influence attitudes. The black children are closely attuned to their South African background and strong cultural patterns that differ from those in the West. White children from English-speaking homes are already steeped in a culture not markedly different from that in Britain. So in the West, black children know they are different and do not strive to integrate; while white children know they are different and want to remove the invisible barriers.

The extended family and the nuclear family reveal their cultural differences. White mothers took young children with them, or sent for them very soon. Many black mothers left babies or children behind in the belief that the separation was temporary, but secure in the knowledge that grandmothers and aunts embraced the child into the family. The Soweto uprising was another factor; white children were not involved in this. Young black women, schoolgirls, fled into exile in conditions of terror and danger, and lived precarious lives in the Frontline States. They had no advice; no one told them about birth control or child rearing, and if they became pregnant the babies were safer with the family at home; or left in the care of the facilities at Mazimbu while the mothers went away to finish their education. Can any judgments be made? Communication became a dangerous hazard. For security reasons the ANC would instruct its members not to write home. A letter from the exile invariably brought reprisals on the family – police raids, interrogations, harassment.

The mothers who left their children in South Africa were riven by the separation, the guilt, the loss. If the fathers felt the same they buried it very deeply, for none spoke about it. Often they did not even mention the children they had left unless asked.

The longing to make contact, as Ruth Mompati and Ray Simons describe, never left the mothers. Lulu Mabena had her first child when she was seventeen and still at school. 'My father blamed my mother. Ja – they always blame the mothers. It's not the mothers. It's something I decided to do myself.' But when she went into exile she left behind her daughter and her second-born, a son.

'The first time I tried to contact my family after I left was in 1977. I felt, now I can't take it any more; I am going to try and write to them. I wrote; and the reply came, "It's better you don't write any more because of the harassment we received from the police immediately after your letter arrived" ... then I never wrote again. Until 1983, when I felt I would break now – I must take this chance. It was terrible, especially when I was so far away. I felt – I didn't know if my parents and children were still alive, or what. I even imagined how it is to be dead. I felt: so this is how it is when one is dead – because you don't know. They don't know anything about you.'

There was no 'right' answer. The children who went with their parents were robbed of that larger family – the grandparents, aunts, uncles, cousins, that for the majority of South Africans are such an important part of their lives. Fritz and Mala Dullay, far away in Århus in Denmark, feel so guilty because they cannot give their daughters this extended family life.

'When we first got to Denmark we used to find Simmy sitting in the corner of the room there and crying all by herself. She had been torn away from the larger extended family love and security, and now we were the only ones who could give her this love, and it was simply not enough because we were facing an enormous number of adjustment problems ourselves. Once we received a taped message from her grandfather, to whom she was very close; she was about four and a half. The grandfather is saying, "Simmy, how are you? I hope you are well." And she was replying to the tape recorder, "I am well, Aja, I am very well; how are you?" She was talking to the tape recorder, and it really broke our hearts.'

TEMBEKA NGELEZA
London 1990

'Going back home it's like rewinding back to the times before Nelson Mandela was detained. Yes, with all the sufferings, we have to go back to square one.'

Her eleven-year-old daughter, who she last saw when she was six months old, is visiting her in London, but must go back to the grandmother in South Africa who brought her up.

I had a boyfriend, and he was harassed; the police used to visit his place and look for him. When they realised that they couldn't find him at his place, they'd come to my place looking for him, or even looking for me. It was becoming too dangerous; he couldn't go to work. He had difficulties even attending his father's funeral. Then he decided that if he had to leave, I had to go with him because it couldn't be safe for me either. I would have had to answer where his whereabouts were, even if I didn't know. And, of course, I wouldn't have known, because he wouldn't tell me.

My family even did not know I was leaving. When I was already in Botswana, my mother wrote me a letter. And it made me cry, because she said it was very hard for her to take it that I took a decision to leave the country – to leave my family, go to where it will be very difficult for me to go back and bury them, even if they were dead. I'll never forget that letter.

I did not have a passport. I skipped. We were only two women in a group of men. We did not have means. We did not know which way to go, and they did not agree in the group. So they ended up splitting us into different groups.

We had to cross . . . footing from Johannesburg to Botswana. They took us; they've been helping people to cross, so they knew, and they did manage to help myself and my girlfriend to cross. But the other members of our group, they were not helped. And as a result they ended up in Swaziland with my boyfriend, and we ended up in Botswana. And we couldn't trace each other in any way.

I managed to get in touch with him only after years. We left in 1977 and I met him in 1982 in Germany, when I'd gone there to study, and he was also studying there. We got married there.

When we arrived near Botswana – I never knew the area, and I don't know where it was – we had to walk a very long distance. In Lobatsi we had to stay a week without declaring ourselves, because the feet was swollen, and we were so sick we couldn't do anything. It was after a week we took a bus to Gaberone, and then we declared ourselves as refugees. That's where we were also so scared, because the police didn't want to believe us, and they wanted to take us back to South Africa. They said we must tell them the truth or they're going to deport us.

Psychologically it was killing. But maybe they enjoyed it. They couldn't really take our story, because we said we came from Port Elizabeth; and we were only two girls – we crossed without having passports. It was, in a way, not credible. In the end they let us stay.

We had to remain with the group. We were really lost in a way. The people that helped us cross, we had to stay with them in a house with many men, more than twenty I guess. And we were only two women. And whatever we were getting, the money from the Botswana Christian Council – we had to give it to them for the communal cooking and whatever. But they never thought of – they never thought of getting pads, and whatever we needed as women. We had difficulties. We couldn't have even a penny to go and buy ourselves something to drink, because they took everything to the last penny. So for whatever we wanted, we had to go to them, and they were not happy if you wanted this and this and this. Even getting stamps to communicate with your parents, it was not easy. Actually they discouraged us from trying to contact our parents. So it was just difficult.

They were a political group. I never knew what name was it, although I stayed with them. And in the evenings they used to have political discussions on Mao Tse-tung and whatever, and brought very big volumes of books. One couldn't understand them.

We met some South Africans who were staying in a house that was sponsored by the YWCA, and they are asking us, 'How do you come to stay in such a place?' And they really could see that we were having difficulties, and they told us no, we could go and stay with them, even if we did not even have money to contribute. They said, 'Go to the YWCA and explain your positions.'

I went to the YWCA to report and they accepted me without having a cent. And I stayed there. And after a while, when I'd stayed longer in Botswana I could see who was who; and what was the ANC, what was the PAC; and I had to take my own decision. I'm glad I took my own decision to join the ANC. Nobody else told me to join the ANC.

The YWCA had some project where you could go and keep the time moving. There was really nothing special; there were no teachers, and you had to get papers and read to do some O levels. But you couldn't go any further because it was not a proper school. When I left South Africa I was doing Form 4. But to go on to A levels and without teachers, it was just not possible.

One girl that stayed in the house – the police in South Africa cheated her mother; told her mother to get the daughter and they wouldn't do anything to the daughter. Really the mother wanted her daughter back, and innocently told the daughter, 'OK, I'm visiting you and I'll be here for this period.' Everybody enjoyed each other. The day the mother was leaving she had to take her mother to the station, and she was kidnapped right into South Africa. But the mother, she had trusted the people who told her, 'No we won't do anything to your daughter.' And that was it. She was put in prison. I didn't hear anything after. It was the end of her.

The very same thing that happened to this girl, it was attempted by the police to my parents. They told my mother that I could get a Red Cross passport and go back to South Africa. Because I had done nothing to them, they wouldn't do anything to me. And my mother believed them in a way. But because of this other experience, I told her to forget about seeing me.

I had a baby, my daughter was born in Botswana in 1979, and my mother had to come and collect her. I had to write her a telegram to say somebody was dead, for her to be given a paper to allow her to come to Botswana. So she was given four days to stay, and she picked up my daughter on a Saturday and she went back on a Monday.

My daughter was six months. It was hard. I couldn't accept it. And the main reason for me to give my daughter really to my parents was, I knew I still wanted to go to school. And with her it was going to be really impossible for me to do that. So the only decision – and I thought it was the right decision then – was to ask my mother to help me with her. And she did.

I did not see her again for . . . I only saw her this year actually, because my mother never trusted that if she comes to me I will send her back to her. I had to convince my mother that I will do that. It's only when I was here and I started working, it's then at least with my first salary I bought her a return ticket. She has to go back again, because my mother wants her back there. And I appreciate the fact that my mother did help me and brought her up, and I can't just take her from my mother just like that. It's my mother's daughter. Biologically my daughter, but physically my mother's daughter.

I left Botswana after three years. I went to Mazimbu to go to school, to SOMAFCO. It was very difficult, but it was comforting because we were all having the same problems and we were all together. Whenever we had problems, we would sit down and solve our problems. Of course, we couldn't solve the starvation problem at that time, because Tanzania itself had nothing in terms of food, and we really used to starve some of the time. We would go without breakfast, and had to go to school; and sometimes had to break school and go for maize harvesting – otherwise you couldn't have anything to eat. It was end of 1980, 1981. Very bad conditions in Tanzania. It was terrible. Soap was a luxury. If you smell anybody who just came from Botswana into Mazimbu who had Lux, you really feel that it's something you never had before, it was a dream. Sometimes you could go without pads, and you had to wash whatever we'd been using and dry it and re-use it again. It was really hard.

We did some help in the construction especially on school holidays. But I was not fortunate. I wanted to help so much, but was a victim of malaria. I would go to work the first day, the second day, and the third day I'm down with malaria. I had no resistance, because I did not have food and I think maybe I was weak, I don't know, because some of the people really could go to work, maybe for a week or so without getting an attack. Or maybe it was a relapse, I don't know, because I used to get it every two, three days after that.

I decided to go and take some vocational training in agriculture in the GDR. I was there for three years. I was opposed to many things that were happening there, and now and then I had to go and face the director and told him how I felt about whatever I thought was wrong. They thought I was influencing the other students. Of course they wouldn't be influenced by me, because I was the only woman in the group, they were all men.

Some things I objected to: If we had to do some training, they will give it to boys; they won't give it to girls because they said they were women. We would go and pick up stones from the field instead of going to do something practical that was part of the study. So . . . I was against such things. There were fields where they could say, 'No, this is for men; women couldn't do.' And I'd say, 'What is the use really of the course? You shouldn't have allowed women to come and do the course if you can't allow them to do certain things.' Especially when it came to mechanics – they gave more opportunities to boys and not to us. But I did finish the course although I finished it with difficulties, as a woman.

After I finished I went back. I was deployed in Zambia. I left my husband in the GDR because he had to continue his studies. He was studying polygraphy. He followed me after a year or so.

In Zambia we had difficulties. We had problems there, because we couldn't agree with the manager of the ANC farm where I was working. He had not studied agriculture, and I felt he was not doing things the right way, and I challenged him. And he was also ill-treating some of the comrades, the older comrades who were not educated. He was sort of screwed up in a way, and I had no room to accept whatever I thought was not correct. I ended up disagreeing with him; and I left the farm at the end and I stayed in town.

Then I went to Sweden, I took a course in public administration for a year. While I was in Sweden, my son was with my husband in Zambia. There were lots of separations. And I feel so guilty that I left my son. I spoke to him. He agreed that I go to school, but I think he did not understand to what he was agreeing. He didn't know what a year was. And after that he was so bitter, saying, 'Mum, I don't know, why did you leave me?'

I tried so hard to get him joining me in Sweden, but with the structures of the ANC that made it impossible. People were ready to help me; but with the bureaucracy of the Movement it was absolutely not easy. After that year in Sweden I had to come to this side, Britain, to join my family.

Of course, men they have problems when they are left with children. I think my husband had problems in looking after him – he ended up giving him to other people. And when I saw him for the first time I almost cried, but I didn't want to cry because it would hurt him as well. He was so lean I couldn't believe it; he had sores on his head – patches and whatever; he was neglected. And when I came here I had to make up for that. And I promised I will never leave him again.

But now he is healthy again. He is OK. He is almost forgetting it, that's what is important. He's more secure now, and he knows that I don't have to leave him again. Whenever he annoys me or whatever, and I tell him, 'OK, if you make me mad like this, I will leave you again!' he cries so. I don't ever want to do that again, because it hurts him so much. It hurts him so much.

At the beginning things here were so difficult, because we didn't have enough money. I was not working. My husband is working for the ANC, and the little that he gets from the ANC had to maintain us. But now things are much better that I got a job, and now I'm working, ja, much better, although I'm going back to school at the beginning of the term. I want to do another course on agriculture. I'll have him with me. Whatever difficulties we face, we'll face them together.

But returning home, it has many real implications. As things are right now going back home it's like taking the ANC and rewinding back to the times it was before Nelson Mandela was detained. Yes, with all the sufferings, we have to go back to square one. And with all the lives we have lost. You know that finding a job, it's still going to be a problem. And at this age, to go back and hassle your parents with a place to stay, it's just not going to be easy.

And with all the freedom you have now, to go back to the locations? I have a child who goes to school in London, and to go back to the location life it's not going to be easy. And all the friends now we have – I mean, we are a community who are the ANC – we do not speak of a black and a white; we are all together, we stay together, we have parties together. But when you go back, it's not going to be the same. They'll go back to where they came from, and we'll go back to where we came from. It's how politics are.

I'm worried about my son returning to South Africa – he has never known what apartheid means. He will go to Bantu education at schools. Here he doesn't learn about black and white. One day someone asked him, 'Is your teacher black or white?' He was puzzled. He didn't know what to say. Then he said, 'I don't know.' You see, here we are a community in the ANC. We are all together, black and white; and he just saw his teacher as a person. And that's how I want him to see people – as persons, not as the colour of their skins.

And after that, this is what we really have to go back for. People are dying. So it's going to be a long road home, and yes, I'm scared. What are the parents of the deceased going to say? Here you are, you are back – what happened to my son? And the son is dead one way or the other. I mean, not even to be able to explain how. How are you going to answer such question? It's not going to be easy.

My mother is looking forward to seeing me. Yesterday I spoke to her; she asked me, am I coming back? I said, 'No, I'm waiting. We still have to be organised.' So the first possible time to go home, I will go home. And I will see them. I feel at her age, she needs me to help her now! And here Tembeka is, in London.

We are victims, we who are exiles. We are all of us victims.

ROBYN SLOVO
London 1990

'I found a world of my own where nobody else belonged.'

> She is the youngest daughter of two famous parents. Her mother, Ruth First, a writer, academic and political activist, was a victim of South Africa's Death Squad, killed in 1985 in Maputo by a letter bomb. Her father, Joe Slovo, a lawyer, was the Secretary of the South African Communist Party.

I was ten years old when I left South Africa in 1964. And I didn't return for twenty-seven years.

My memory of leaving South Africa is of being incredibly relieved and incredibly excited. It didn't feel to me that I was leaving anything behind. And I think the most important thing for me was that I'd be reunited with my mother, and that I was going somewhere with her. I didn't feel that I have left friends behind – I don't to this day remember that I had close friends there.

I went back for the first time last February. I've always thought that – of my family – I'm the English one. You know, because I didn't fit . . . I felt I didn't fit in other ways. So the one thing that surprised me when I went, was that I discovered a whole layer of people I'd completely forgotten about. I was given the most wonderful welcome by this whole generation of my parents' age and above, a lot of old women who, in fact, I had remembered all the time. But what I didn't remember is how important they were to me. And on this visit, I spent the most wonderful times.

My fantasy of going back to South Africa was that I was going to really assert my Englishness, to just sort of cut it all away – go back to this place that I'd sort of carried around on my back. And say: Look here! I'm Robyn, and I'm English. I know I was born here, but I've come to show you that my life's been completely different.

And the experience of it was actually not like that. I stayed for five weeks. I did visit our old home. [Pause] Yeah, I think I . . . No. The problem was I didn't go inside the gates; I went and looked around it, and I was too frightened. I say that today, but I don't think at the time I felt frightened. I just thought of a reason that I shouldn't go in and say to the people: Look, I used to live here. Can I look around? So I went to the outside. I regret it now, I wish that I had – I have a lot of feeling for that house.

Visiting South Africa has changed me. For whatever reason, it gave me a tremendous amount of self-confidence. I came back feeling that I'd faced one of my biggest fears. I had made my own connections there; this feeling of being South African isn't actually something that I was lumbered with by others, but was partly of my own experience. I responded so well, and felt so good with these people that I met and also contemporaries of mine. I felt I had the right to be there, that's the difference. And before I went I'd always felt incredibly ashamed that I was this South African exile, with this enormous past with a lot of media attention. And I felt that I had no place within that.

So it made an incredible difference. I went back there to declare myself English, but there was a small part of me that thought: Ooh, I'm going to find I'm completely South African. And actually I came back with this feeling that I'm not either, I'm quite comfortable with that.

I think my determination to be English was in part an attempt to identify with the people around me in Britain, but also in part a sort of rebellion against my parents. The one big thing about my South African childhood is that I never fitted in. I just didn't fit in. I felt very isolated in school; I always knew that other people's parents were very wary of me. And in England I wanted more than anything to fit in. And, as well, it was a rebellion. I'd had enough of my life being influenced by what was happening to my parents. I had had a terrible time because of it, and I thought if I could assume my own identity in this new country, that would stop happening.

I got very involved in working-class society, and I used it desperately to try and criticise my parents. I had, in fact, come from a very elite society of people. And it was kind of thrown into relief when I got here. So I not only wanted to become English, but I wanted to be part of the English people and put aside the sort of conversations that I used to hear – the political phraseology of my family . . . I wanted to be the only one who really experienced English life, to be accepted, and to be part of what I saw in the street. I didn't want to be separate any more, and that was the most accessible way to do it.

When I got to England, I was sent to a semi-private school which caused me enormous distress. Not intellectually; but I found myself in very much the same environment that I had had in South Africa. I think today I could sit down and talk about it and recognise that actually my parents weren't perfect – which I didn't recognise at the time. I just interpreted it as the ultimate betrayal. I don't know if that makes a lot of sense, betrayal of my need to never again be – like I had been in South Africa – different, in any kind of small group where I didn't belong. And every move, like sending me to a semi-private school miles from my house, I reacted to and felt extremely angry about.

That was why I was so rebellious at school. A lot of my experiences in South Africa I played out when I got to England, when I was a young teenager, thirteen, fourteen, fifteen. There was a lot of rage about what had happened to me, and a lot of rage about separation. The big thing about coming to England had been that I would be with my mother – which I was for a year which I still remember as the happiest year of my life. Subsequent to that she started to get work and to travel again. I got just totally enraged about the whole thing.

I went to two secondary schools in fact, because I got expelled from the first one, and ended up in a basically working-class school. By the time I was eighteen, nineteen, I was actually such a mess I had no idea what I wanted to do. It was expected, because I was bright, that I go to university. I think I just went to university for my mother, like I did everything for her, anything, to actually make her appreciate me. I lasted two years. Academically, as I had in school, I always held my own. But I hated it.

There always came a point when I just would refuse. I left after the end of my second year. I hadn't done anything the whole of the second year, and I knew that I wouldn't actually get through.

I went to art school for three years, which I had always thought was what I wanted to do, and I'd always been told that that's what I shouldn't be doing. What I should be doing is history at Sussex! You know, actually if I was given the same choice today at Sussex, I'd do history! [Laughs]

I don't think I liked being at art school, but by that point in my life nothing really would have made any difference. I was so unhappy and so lost at that point. What was wrong with me was not not knowing what I wanted to do with my life. It was much, much more basic. [Sighs]

My father Joe never existed for me until Ruth died. I keep thinking to myself: no, that's not true; no, that's not true. But actually I have thought about this for years. When I used to describe my family, I sometimes used to forget to mention him. I would include my grandmother, but I would forget to mention Joe when somebody said, 'Tell me about your family.' I don't remember him being around at all. Very, very little. I remember him being around years and years ago, but that's all, really. I know it's real for me. That was my experience of him.

I think it was an awful lot to do with the fact that, with Ruth, there was no room for anybody else. She was so important to me. She really was. I didn't have any room for Joe at that point. I only started to recognise Joe really after Ruth died; that's where my relationship with him really starts.

Dropping out! It's . . . you see, it's quite hard for me to talk about. I'm kind of trying not to introduce the subject of drugs; but it's very important. It punctuates the whole of my story, which makes no sense unless I do.

I started taking drugs when I was fourteen. I started at school. What I discovered from the use of drugs is that they stopped me being angry. And in a way, maybe it was . . . Oh, I don't know . . . maybe it was the only way that I had at the time to survive, because I couldn't communicate what was wrong with me. The more angry I got, the more I felt I had to say, the more I got pushed into a corner. And the more people – particularly in a girls' public school – just didn't respond.

Although my drug use was quite slow to begin with, it's almost like: as soon as I started using drugs, I discovered that I didn't have to fit in. Firstly I found a world of my own where nobody else belonged, which I think was true of the whole time that I continued. And secondly, like I say, I stopped having the need to communicate. It completely shut me off. I felt I was in this enormous cloud of cotton wool. It felt like the only solution. It involved all the things that I found difficult. Although I had this reputation of being this pretty, jolly little girl, I was incredibly shy and incredibly wary, and frightened of other people. And taking drugs coincided with the first boyfriends, first friends, all outside of the school and outside of institutions.

It was all kind of illicit and subterfuge. I started sleeping with boys very early – during this drug phase. It just kind of liberated me, because I didn't have anybody I was accountable to. No one. I found somebody to look after me, and it just carried on and on and on . . .

About the time I was eighteen going on nineteen, I had really entered a whole society that nobody else in my family could enter, and particularly not my mother. My boyfriends were her nightmare. I don't remember consciously thinking it's the biggest way I could hurt her. I do remember – this is one of my first recognitions of feeling angry and embarrassed about this great heroine in my life – that she would say things – like she couldn't understand the paper-sellers because they talked in cockney accents. And I was excruciatingly embarrassed about this, and very angry with her.

My early boyfriend came from an Irish family; they lived in the most appalling conditions in Highbury – really appalling. My mother was completely unable to deal with this man – completely. I could go to his flat – it was unbearable. There was damp streaming down the walls; his mother, his sister, him, slept in one room, and it would feel to me like absolute refuge. I would actually – once I'd been going out with him for a year and a half – I would sleep in the same room. But it felt to me like an absolute haven.

It was partly really creating my own world that I felt comfortable in; partly getting back at my mother; and partly I think just really self-destructive. It was totally out of pain. The kind of relationships I started having were not stimulating. They were a lot about drug-taking and having a good time, but the way that I did it was extremely self-destructive.

I got on to harder and harder drugs. I started with glue sniffing. And from then it was just a really classical progression, very, very quickly. By sixteen I can remember taking LSD, I was taking barbiturates and amphetamines; and by the time I was nineteen I was taking morphine and heroin.

It went on with some breaks because I never really thought: this is what I want to do. So I had a few months there, a few months here; and eighteen months at one point of being off. But basically I would say, my use is from fourteen to thirty-three. I think it's generally true that I didn't understand. That's easy for me to say today, because I feel like I've found the way which I needed to. It seems very simple and obvious to me today, but actually then I didn't . . . I don't think I had the kind of help or the information or . . . I'm not really clear about it.

But what I do know is after a drug-free period I started using drugs again as soon as Ruth was murdered. I had stopped when she went to Maputo. I had been in an institution for a year; and then I was in a kind of semi-institution for six months connected with the same place. And about five days after I left, I got the phone-call that Ruth had been blown up in Maputo.

What happened to me with Ruth's death is that I had a real total crisis, loss of identity. Because I had done so much for this important figure, my mother, I actually didn't know how to do anything for myself. And I think that a lot of my wanting to clean up, stop using drugs, was to reach the ideals that she had always taught me to believe in. I didn't have a clue how to find those ideals myself. It took me another eight years.

I'm not saying that if she had lived I would have stayed off drugs. But it was a very extreme way to discover that I had very little identity of my own, and I was still suffering from the same kinds of pressures and childhood memories and unfulfilled needs. And I hadn't learnt how to replace them.

In my twenties I did all sorts of itsy bitsy jobs. Drugs took away any facility I had to fulfil commitments. Even when I was using them I was able to get very good ideas, to get excited about things. But I was so inconsistent. People didn't realise that I was using drugs. Employers didn't realise for years. I would have these terrible black weeks when I would be late, but unbelievably late – quarter to midday or half past eleven, no explanation for it, and when I was talked to, I would totally pull myself together for two or three weeks. I was good at my job as well. But just so unreliable.

I always thought that I was the only person in the world who could get away with this, and actually I was fine because I could. Then that began to fall away. I began to get an enormous fear that I couldn't fulfil the commitments I'd been given, until really I ended up like somebody . . . You know, I couldn't walk to the corner shop, I was so frightened. I'd have to drive a hundred yards. To expect me to actually do anything out in the open was too much.

The first time after I'd stopped taking drugs, I started to work in a theatre. I started writing. I wrote a play about my experiences. It was the beginning of a new phase. I'd started slowly to get back to what I think I probably would have chosen to do without all this; and that's the point at which Ruth was murdered.

When I think back over Ruth's funeral itself, I was the first one to leave Mozambique – I couldn't actually bear to be with my family. We stayed in Maputo for the funeral itself, and then we went on a family holiday to Pemba – Gill, Shawn, Joe and I. And I don't know quite how early I went back – but I think it was after a week or ten days. I just remember feeling desperately I had to get back and be with my own people. Which is extraordinary really, considering I was with my closest family, and I couldn't bear it.

So I went back and probably within four to five weeks, I started using drugs again. In three months I was very chaotically using – I think using in a worse way than I had before Ruth had died. It lasted for seven years. Ja, seven years. I didn't go off drugs again until '89, so seven years – seven years!

And now I'm off. But will I stay off? It's a very difficult question to answer, because . . . Yes and no. I think the problem for me is that I'm thirty-six years old. My entire teenage and adult experience has been caught up with drugs. And it's not just the taking and the getting of drugs; it's all my friends, my whole society, everything I've ever done has been in some way linked with drugs, or the drug world. And now, eighteen months away from that, it feels like the most enormous break-through! And like I would never, ever choose to go back there again. But I feel extremely cautious as well.

I think that I was very damaged from my childhood; but also really did a lot of damage to myself. Part of it was the political involvement of my parents, and that they were different from the other white families we lived among. It's a factor – I'm not sure it was the biggest factor . . . I don't know. I'm really not sure. I haven't worked it out and that's my problem. Sometimes I think it's absolutely that.

I did have a very extreme experience. And what I think about South Africa is not only that I had a family that couldn't fulfil my needs, but actually the whole of society seemed unable to do that. There was not one . . . I had no close . . . I mean, I just had nobody. I feel like I'm not being very clear about it, and that's probably because I am not clear about it.

The important part of the politics is that I always felt that it was a very clear choice – that my mother and father were totally absorbed – particularly my mother . . . And I always interpreted that as being my fault, because I wasn't interesting enough, or I wasn't important enough. I grew up with such a sense of – I don't know – just feeling so insubstantial. And I think that really was the politics. And they were so wordy about everything – political people are so wordy all the time. I was taught to use words and to be articulate.

And yet with all these words flying about, and all this analysis of what people needed, there were no words in my family to express what I wanted. I just couldn't find the words. Those sort of words, very simple stuff, didn't exist. And I think that is part of coming from a political background.

And also an enormous sense of guilt that my problems were nothing. I've thought about the times that I was young in South Africa, how it was. And when I think that sort of pain that I was experiencing had no validity, that I felt that I wasn't allowed to be in that pain – it makes me extremely angry, because that kind of damage could have been undone. I think I was taught that pain is relative. That there's others always worse off than you are.

I think today my pain is my pain, regardless of the circumstances. You still hear that stuff though – I suppose not only about South Africa, but in a lot of arenas.

When my mother was murdered, one of the most striking things I remember is my grandmother's attitude, which is: we must be brave and we must be strong! And in one way I know what she was talking about. But the problem was with feeling any kind of pain, or expressing any kind of loss, or even missing my mother when she was in prison, or feeling frightened when we suddenly got woken up in the middle of the night and found ourselves in another country. Not only was it extremely weak to say, 'I'm scared.' Or, 'Please. What about me?' But it was actually injurious to Ruth and Joe, that what I was doing was weakening their struggle, and struggle was clearly the most important thing as I was clearly told. In the same way when my grandmother saw us crying she said, almost like a command or an instruction: we must be strong. Like: Don't cry in public.

When I was young in South Africa, my friends were my sisters; they were my whole world. I really idolised my elder sister. In England I think I knew deep down that they were actually coping much better than I was. My middle sister almost . . . well, she mothered me for a long period, during the period I was using drugs, and before, really. When my mother was away, Gillian would tend to look after me. I relied on her a helluva lot, but consequently I didn't see her as a young person. They have both been, in different periods of my life, hugely supportive no matter what's happening to me.

And whereas it seemed to me my mother couldn't ever really see for herself what was happening, it was much clearer to my sisters. In fact, they noticed my behaviour much earlier. My elder sister had a very early argument with my mother and tried to tell her what was happening; she refused to accept it. After that, there was a whole period when Gillian did the same thing. And basically, as it went on, I just couldn't bear to be with them.

Today we're extremely close. But although I always felt this enormous closeness, I had the same inability to communicate to them what was happening as I had with my mother – and certainly my father. At the time of Ruth's death – we couldn't share our experience. We just couldn't do it. And that's still a problem. In some ways, in terms of Shawn's film, or Gill's books . . . each of our experiences belongs to them only.

The film opened it up in the sense that we now have an arena in which to discuss it. Because of *A World Apart*, we actually discussed it. We did all get together with other people and talk about Ruth and so on. But it's still very hard – I think that Shawn and Gill would probably say the same. It's very hard for us to admit that we have experiences in common.

It took me a long time to realise that using drugs had stopped serving the purpose that I'd originally started taking them for. Towards the end, every area of my life collapsed, including my physical health. It wasn't one specific thing, it was the total realisation that it wasn't working. It had worked for a few years; it was my method of survival . . . I had good times and bad times. It's not a kind of stereotypical, constant misery. But I think towards the end, it really was.

It stopped working and . . . I don't know . . . I've had enough. I don't know any other way to put it. The pain of using drugs is worse than the pain of not using.

One of the biggest reasons I stopped using was that in the past I always felt that other people wanted me to stop, particularly Shawn, Gillian and Joe and Ruth; and I didn't. And towards the end I really do think other people had given up. They were going to try to accept that this is my choice, and this is the life that I was going to lead. And at that point, when I felt that I had been given full permission and nobody cared any more, I couldn't bear it. I could not be with myself. I just couldn't stand it. They've all accepted it!

I think that every child feels powerless to a certain extent when you go to school. There's this big institution! But my experience in South Africa was the state. It was so enormous. I was so tiny. For such a huge piece of machinery to be affected by anything – I can't imagine it being more extreme.

Some of the ideals, the values I was given about the freeing of humanity, were actually a positive advantage to me – or have become so now. But at the same time were so hard to live up to. They were so enormous. The guilt and the sense of one's own inadequacy and of how small I was as a six, seven, eight, nine, ten-year-old, in the midst of something that was literally world size, that was very hard to deal with. It's very hard to accept both that I was important, and it was important.

I had a conversation with Ruth just before she died. She came to London and we spent an afternoon together. The one thing I really wanted to know – I wanted to know if she was frightened when she was in prison. It was the most important question to me. And I kept asking her, I kept on and on and on, saying, 'How did you feel when you were in prison?' I didn't want all this 'I felt I had no choice'. I just wanted her to say that she was frightened, and that she missed me. Which she did end up by saying. It is important.

I wanted to know that she was vulnerable. I wanted to know that she got frightened and did stupid things. Because that's the other thing about being brought up in a country-size struggle in the camera's eye, public: there isn't room for imperfection within that. There's a lot of humanity that gets lost in that. You lose the little details. And the little details was what I was most concerned with.

I never read anything about South Africa in the newspapers. I never read my mother's books, I never read *117 Days* until very recently. What I did, I flipped through and looked for my name, and I saw 'jolly Robyn' and I just thought, I don't want to read this. I couldn't bear it. I never admitted that I hadn't read it. I pretended that I had. The only one of her books that I ever read was *Olive Schreiner*, because that was different. Because that was about a writer.

Going to South Africa made the most enormous amount of difference. I started to read lots and lots of South African novelists. I was avidly reading newspapers. Now when I get the newspaper I always go to the international page and see what's happening in South Africa. Channel 4 were making this documentary on street children in South Africa, and they asked me to write the commentary. I felt I'd gone on for too long saying, 'I can't do this.' I thought: I can't go to South Africa unless I agree to do this. It was like a test, the test of courage. When I sat down to do it I found it incredibly easy. I thought I had no knowledge at all, but I have an intrinsic awareness – that's absolutely vital. You know, it's about more than just going and looking up facts and statistics.

So I am thinking about going back, at least for a while. I'll go back and spend a few months and just see what happens and . . . check out. Because it was such a wonderful experience just being there for five weeks.

It's a whole different experience to go and live somewhere permanently, and earn a living. So I don't think . . . It's not suddenly the answer to my problems. But it has become an option.

GILLIAN SLOVO
London 1991

'Ruth's death made me feel I can't actually escape South Africa. The country's following me wherever I go.'

She is a writer who has already published five novels. Her daughter, Cassie Ruth, has the dark-haired good looks of her mother and grandmother.

I arrived in England on my twelfth birthday. I remember leaving very acutely but I don't really know whether I remember how I felt. I know I remember arriving in England and feeling this place was a total dump and I wasn't going to fit; feeling like I didn't belong here and I didn't belong with the people meeting us. So I suppose I was unhappy to leave. I can't remember feeling unhappy about leaving. I just remember complete confusion.

Now I obviously fit in; but there is some way that I feel I'm not English and I'm a stranger in this country. My whole life is fitted into here, and I'm not sure that I would ever go back to South Africa and live there.

I don't know how long it took me to fit in. The first year was very, very miserable. Nothing fitted properly, I couldn't even cross the roads. The first time I ventured out on my own, getting to Swiss Cottage, trying to cross the road and being unable to, and having to ask a policeman to help me; he took me to a phone box, I rang home and Ruth came and got me because I couldn't go any further.

And going to a school where I was just a freak! I was a goody-goody. I'd come from this exclusive girls' school to Hampstead Comprehensive where there were both girls and boys. They were more mature emotionally than me, and I was much better educated than they. So the teachers used me as an example . . . always reading out my stuff as an example; and the others hated me. I was just very uptight and I didn't know how to socialise, and they didn't know anything about me. It was like another culture. Basically I had no understanding of the British class system so I didn't really know why I didn't fit in. I was just all wrong. And then I was sent to a more middle-class girls' school, and fitted in better.

But I've always felt that I was different, and I think that partly has to do with all the secrecy in our lives – the fact that there was another world that nobody ever talked about. Even though it was not necessary when we came to England, it carried on. My best friends were French, one Spanish, and one German. Either there were no children of English people in Camden, or I deliberately chose the ones who would have a similar feeling – that their cultural background was different from the mainstream.

After I left school I went to Bristol University to do psychology; left after a year and got a degree in Liberal Studies and Science in Manchester. I used university to leave home, like a lot of people do. Then I worked for a few years in the Open University doing so-called research for somebody who was writing a book on Science in Society. It was a very depressing time of my life. Then I left the Open University, took my pension, and went travelling for a year, I started writing fiction and at the same time, I worked for a film group. And now I just write full-time.

Joe seemed to be very absent from our lives. I'm not sure whether he was as absent as much as he seemed to be, because some of my warmest childhood memories involve Joe. I remember being woken up in the middle of the night by him. He had just come to kiss me, it felt absolutely wonderful that he was there – I must have been very young – and me saying, Oh, you must do this every night; and he said, But I do. They both came to kiss us before they went to bed and I just happened to wake up, so I remember this as a very, very warm moment. There is a whole thing in our family about Joe being the warm one. But he wasn't that present.

Ruth was present. My comparative memory, also in the middle of the night, is of Ruth typing away, you know tippy-tappying in the middle of the night. Yes, she was definitely present. But I find these things very difficult to talk about, especially since I've done all this media stuff where they've asked me about my family and I've censored the whole thing and now I no longer know what the truth is! [Laughs] When I'm talking about it, I know that I'm censoring it. I'm not going to talk about my family in public to a journalist who knows nothing about South Africa or my family or anything, in a way that will throw anybody in a bad light. So I just throw out all that stuff and I don't know whether I can ever talk about it again.

I don't have very strong memories of all of my childhood of South Africa. What I have is very strong memories of certain periods, and one of those was 1963, because that was the year that Joe left, and when Ruth was in . . . under 90-days. I also remember the State of Emergency very strongly; I remember going to Swaziland and the difficult times. When Ruth was detained it was quite obvious to me that we were just living on another planet compared to my school friends, even though the school was wonderful and the teachers were sympathetic, and one of the teachers used to take me home. But the kids had absolutely no understanding of what was going on. I got asked if my mother was a kleptomaniac – they didn't even know that anybody could be imprisoned for political reasons. I think my way of dealing with the whole situation was to be very resentful. I protected Ruth from my resentment. I was never critical of what they did, I always thought it was wonderful. And in some ways there was something nice about being special, something exciting about going to visit Ruth at the prison in the middle of the day. But I don't think I ever put the blame on Ruth or Joe because that would have been too scary. Who else was there really?

I was very highly attuned to what was going on, as well as to things I shouldn't have known at the time; such as: I knew who it was who had helped Harold [Wolpe] to escape and I shouldn't have known. I was a very good eavesdropper. Look at me – I ended up writing detective stories! [Laughs] I got very good at finding out what was happening. I didn't discuss it with Shawn and Robyn – that was a strategy, somehow, because for us all to share it was to make it real. But maybe also to make myself special and separate myself from their distress. And I think that's a strategy that we all used. So although we all experienced the same thing, we've always found it very hard to be in the same situation together.

What effect did Ruth's assassination have on your life?

A number of things, I think. I had a child afterwards, which I probably would have done anyway, but I remember hearing about her death and thinking I had to have a child now. I think that's about continuity. Feeling like it can't end here. In some ways it made me feel less crazy. In some ways, it confirmed to me that the fears I had been living with all my life were actually not in my own head, that they were a reality, and therefore I was less crazy. I just felt this isn't right, people cannot do these things to shut other people up.

I think I spent a long time moving around the perimeters of my parents' activity, in the sense that when I was in Manchester I was politically involved, I did take an interest in it, I was a Maoist for a while. I was this, that and the other; but always avoided South Africa. And I think Ruth's death and Ruth's funeral made me feel I can't actually escape South Africa. You know, this country's following me wherever I go; and that I have to find out more about it. It feels like it's still very much part of me.

Do you identify yourself as a South African?

[Pause] I would say South African yes, not British. But I'll probably end up living in Britain, partly because I don't know South Africa, and partly because Andy doesn't know it and couldn't work there, I don't think. And partly because . . . I don't know if I could do that to Cassie, take her back to that place.

I went back at the end of July [1990] for two weeks. I was going back to do promotion for my book, *Ties of Blood*. It was a very, very confusing visit altogether and my reaction is partly about what happened after I came back. The plane was twenty-two hours late, and then it didn't land in Johannesburg because there was fog; it landed in Durban. So I felt like I can't get there . . . This is my relationship to this country: I have this strong relationship, but I never actually have any solid contact with it, and I'm never going to get there. By the time we did get to Johannesburg there was nobody to meet me at the airport, because the people who were to meet me had already come and gone. And I just . . . I burst into tears because I couldn't carry my luggage and I didn't understand how this society worked and I had to get a taxi; and it was just horrible.

Then I did a week of book promotion which is always awful, and I was in the Sandton Sun – you've ever seen the Sandton Sun? Oh God! It's one of Jo'burg's five star hotels above the huge shopping mall that was not there twenty-six years ago. And it is South African money gone as vulgar as South African money can get. Totally vulgar. Everything is fake marble.

I think I was wandering around in a kind of a dream. I met people, friends of the family; I went to the ANC office. I met a lot of relatives.

And once in a shopping mall, I was getting off an escalator and somebody came up to me and said, 'You're Gillian Slovo, aren't you?' She'd recognised me from twenty-six years ago, a friend of the family's. Then I went into the bank to change money, and I had to show my passport; and the teller looked at my name and said, 'Any relation?' and I said, 'Yes, he's my father.' And he shouted across – they were all black there – 'Hey, this is Slovo's daughter!' and half the people in the bank were clapping me on the back and saying welcome to South Africa, which I completely didn't expect; and half of them were glaring at me, but being silent about it. Joe's very famous in Johannesburg now; and people come up for his autograph. I think, in a way they forget who he is because all they notice is that he's famous. There's something weird about what celebrity status does to you.

I felt very rootless. I was staying in the wrong place, so if I wanted to be on my own, I was often in shopping malls – that's why a lot of my story is about shopping malls. I was wandering around. I was either eating meals or engaging in frantic conversation with people, so to be on my own I was walking around shopping malls and I felt very rootless. And also I didn't have Cassie, so that the day didn't end at six o'clock, I wasn't having to put her to bed. I felt I was adolescent.

Then I realised that what moving from South Africa to England had done to me was to deprive me of my adolescence, because I didn't have an adolescence in England. By that time I was twelve, and I never had an adolescent rebellion. I don't think I lived for myself until I was in my early twenties. And when I went back to South Africa, I felt the feeling of being adolescent . . . of feeling rootless, that I can behave as I want; and that I'm on my own. I'm adrift from my family and my responsibilities – which I think is partly what the experience of adolescence is about.

What felt familiar was being in South Africa, and the people felt familiar. And that's why I can't be English. I felt there is part of me which belongs in that country. Both the good and the bad. The tremendous hospitality and friendliness and expansiveness; and the anger and the exclusion.

SHAWN SLOVO
London 1990

'I feel that I am South African, but I don't feel that I have a country.'

Her film, *A World Apart*, shown internationally to great acclaim, was the fictionalised story of her own relationship with her mother, Ruth First.

Coming into exile was a very damaging experience for us individually and as a family. For our family, it was the end of the uncertainty and the fear of the years preceding exile. And it was also a reunification of our family which had been separated for the year that Joe had been out of the country. That was a positive thing about it.

But it was also a very sad experience. Even at the young age of thirteen there was a great sense of loss that I experienced. It was the loss of saying goodbye to the servants, to the house and the animals – all that terrible loss. In fact, I insisted that I didn't want to go with everybody else. For some reason it seemed to be extremely important that I be on my own to go into exile; and also I wanted to go by boat because I wanted to sail up the west coast of Africa. Most of all I wanted to be on my own ... I wanted to be separate from the family.

But I wanted the family united. Well, there was a contradiction there. I'm the oldest so I always have to be kind of special and different anyway because that's my role. And I think there was a lack of information. Ruth had had a pretty damaging time in solitary confinement for 117 days, and yet she was very stoic and didn't talk about it. But it was obvious that she was quite disturbed by it, so there was that area that was uncomfortable.

It's a great shock, even at that age, facing the differences, the topographical differences between places, the cultural differences. And also, although I don't think I was aware of it at the time, of the difference between being a middle-class exile white family in England, and a middle-class white family in South Africa. The economic difference, material difference. There's suddenly no space for a start – not the space that we're used to in South Africa. There were not those wonderful summers, holidays at the Cape, and the rhythm of that sort of life.

I think this is also a beautiful country, England. But it's not even the beauty, it's more than just a kind of 'paradise lost' aspect of it. I think there is something quite special and different about South African culture. And about growing up in Africa, in African culture, in a black majority country. It's a completely different atmosphere. The rhythm is different here.

It was also very difficult to arrive here with a South African accent. At that age the last thing you want is to be different, you want to be part of your peer group. So that you tend to over-compensate and go to extremes. It's amazing how Robyn in particular, suddenly got this incredible Cockney accent. But I think we all were trying to over-compensate. I had been at a private school in South Africa, Rhodean, and suddenly I was in North London Comprehensive in its first year.

It was supposed to unite our family and in fact, it drove us apart. It certainly drove wedges between me and my sisters, for all sorts of varied and complex reasons. It made my relationship with my mother very difficult, and Joe became an absent father. He will deny this and say that he was around; but the thing is, his concentration and focus certainly wasn't on his family at that time – and I think there were tensions between him and Ruth as a result. I'd wish we'd gone to Italy or somewhere. We should have gone to a Latin country in a way, because these early life experiences do affect your later relationships. The British are very cold.

I don't think I've ever adjusted to that question: Are you South African or are you British? I'm definitely not British and have never felt British. I'm quite grateful for the passport – it's better than going round with a South African passport. The experience of one year, travelling around Europe with a South African passport was . . . I went on a camping holiday and I had to have visas for every single country in Europe, and I always had to go in different channels to everybody else. So I'm grateful that I have a British passport.

I feel that I'm a South African but, I don't feel that I have a country – that's the awful thing. I feel more South African the older I get. I like South African music, I like the company of South Africans, I feel very nostalgic and very sentimental about South African art and beads and stuff like that, but . . . I don't feel as if I have a country. That's the problem. I don't think I've ever felt a sense of belonging in a community anyway.

At the same time there was ambivalence about being a South African. I didn't want to socialise or identify with other South African exiles. I think it was . . . too painful. I don't know. I thought I didn't want to be identified with a group of victims, which is what I suppose I felt being in exile is. I found it depressing to be in large gatherings of South Africans. I was also extremely angry with my parents, with the political choices they had made and the way that had affected us as a family and me as an individual. I am a member of the ANC but I can't operate within the ANC because of this anger that I feel.

I've never not sympathised, or felt that they had not made the right choices. But I just felt, at what an expense! at what a cost to themselves, and most particularly to me. For them it fulfilled some kind of need obviously. But I just thought that the consequence can be very damaging to emotional development. So that's why I didn't like the South African community because it reminded me of all that.

I went to university and I wanted to excel. But I wanted to do it in an area that was just as far away from Ruth's as possible; and Joe's – well, particularly Ruth's. Which I think is why I chose the film industry. I did always love films when I was growing up. Would I have felt that even if we hadn't come into exile? I don't think you can separate the experience of exile from the experience of belonging to an activist family. Exile is part of that experience. You can't separate the disruptive experience from the physical fact of going into exile.

It goes back to something Ruth said: that had they realised the way the situation in South Africa was going to develop, they would have thought twice about having a family at the time they did. Which is easy to say in hindsight, but I think to their credit. When we were conceived in the early 1950s, it was a very different time in South Africa. No one could envisage the way things were going to develop. It was fun, the political games; and you were all young, you were all in your twenties and thirties. It was subterfuge and plotting and planning and meeting in cars and having parties and turning up the music loud, to drown out the buggings; and multiracial socialising; you were one of the few South Africans that could move with ease in different societies and dance and have the benefit of the music and the foods and the curries. It was a very exciting life.

The thing is that yes, you couldn't have seen the way things were going to go. But I also think that there could have been a different way to handle the whole experience as well; in my family anyway. We were never told the truth because they wanted to protect us. They tried throughout my childhood to have us lead as normal a middle-class family life as possible ... let us have a childhood I suppose. But at the same time, we were conscious of being excluded from so much. And at the same time, what happens when you're growing up as a middle-class child is this terrible guilt. Because you face the physical actuality of apartheid in a way that most white South Africans don't. Particularly with Ruth, going into her office, looking at the walls of her office with all the photos of her potato farm labourers in sacks and that kind of stuff.

We had all that. And then we had those normal middle-class demands. We wanted horse-riding and birthday parties. So there was this incredible dichotomy with what you have and what the masses don't have. And parents as communists on top of that, where everybody should have the same! This goes right through life, this terrible ... Personally, I have it at the moment. I am now in a position to earn a lot of money and I have to battle with recognising the worth of what I do. I think I'm working in an industry which, as I explained, is as far removed from my parents as possible. My concerns are now frivolous, superficial, not addressing anything important – you know everything that Hollywood involves. And that's the battle of being part of a political family as well.

If we hadn't left I think it would have been much harder to avoid the contradictions. If one had stayed, it would have been impossible ... It would have been impossible to avoid involvement by staying, active involvement in politics. What are the alternatives? Become a kind of Houghton Madam? I don't think there's any way we could have become ... so maybe I would have left the country and come to England in any case! [Laughs]. I think I would have done that. But it would have been very different, because it would have been a kind of independence bid, rather than a forced resort.

Do you think Ruth's death brought the family closer together?

Oh, ja. Yes, it did. I became closer with Gillian and Robyn as a result of that. I think it has been a way of confronting the past; not immediately, but more lately. Personally for me it was a complete watershed event in my life, because up until then I had been wavering and not committing. The most immediate effect of *A World Apart* for me is I couldn't put off that confrontation any more. And who knows? If she'd still been alive I think we still would have . . . Though before her death she was beginning to change and I was beginning to change. I just don't think my parents were equipped really to deal with the family situation. We know such an awful lot more about parenting now, these days, and the importance of a new kind of therapy as a way of addressing problems. So things might have changed anyway. We were getting to be on the way to having a civilised relationship.

But Ruth's death made me address that. I had to come to terms with the end of what had been a very unsatisfactory relationship. There was no shortage of love – that was never in question on either side; but it's just that we could not get on. You're supposed to work through those things.

You say the secrecy was to protect us and to protect yourselves; but there's another element – I think it's also to protect yourselves from having to deal with the consequences of your political activities on your children. I think it's much easier not to have to explain than to try to explain, isn't it?

Did A World Apart *work out a lot of the anger and resentment?*

Ja, but the film's got a film-ending. There's the thirteen-year-old showing an enormous amount of maturity and stability by accepting the fact that this is the way that things are going to be – so she might as well raise her clenched fist. But real life is much more complex than that; and yes, it was very cathartic, but it was just the beginning of a kind of massive exploration. There's more to be done about fathers and daughters as well. *Granta* want me to do a piece on Joe, they want a kind of profile; a personal profile; and I just cannot do it. It's just . . . I'm so angry with him still, and I'll be angry with him all my life.

MATHABO KUNENE
Los Angeles 1991

'I sacrificed my own ambitions because I felt that I had made the choice to have the children and I wanted to make it my business to raise my children.'

Although she has made bringing up her children her first priority, she is a professional caterer and a capable organiser. Her house in Los Angeles has an open door; friends and neighbours come in for a chat, stay for a meal.

When I finished high school I always had the dream of just driving ten/eleven miles to the University of Cape Town. But unfortunately it was the very first year of the Bantu colleges, and so the University of Cape Town turned me down. My father tried to appeal, but they still turned us down. I always wanted to go to law school, or medical school.

I stayed home for a year and helped my father in his business, and then after that I decided to go to nursing school; which I resented, but it was the only alternative at the time. We had family friends, Stanley and Edna Uys. And after I had completed my training and was working as a midwife, they arranged with Professor Hoffenberg to get me to come to England in 1971.

In London I looked up a teacher I had known in high school – the only person I knew in England. And well, I finally found him and one thing led to another and we got married! [Laughs] That's where I met him, yes. At the time when I met him, he was going through all kinds of . . . ja, a crisis in terms of his work and where he was in life. So I made it my priority to nurture him to the point where I thought that he would be . . . we would continue with life. And the first thing I decided very definitely was to leave England, because I thought he had been there too long.

When I met Mazisi, he had done nothing else but work for the ANC, and I thought he had reached a point where it was interfering with his creativity. He's a very creative person, but the other one took over; and I think it was the creative part in him that was almost destroying him, because he wasn't using it, wasn't responding to it.

Then we came to America and he found a job with UCLA. And we've been living here ever since.

I went home to South Africa to have my first child, Lamakhoshi. I wanted to be with family and we also thought maybe it was good for her to have some kind of identity; so she was born in Cape Town. The second one I had the sentiment of going back to England to have him. And then the twin boys were born here in the United States.

I think that it's very important for people who are exiled or move away from their native land to try and make a home, especially when you are raising children, because if you hold on to sentiments of bitterness in exile then you cannot cope. And you simply pass that on to your children. I sacrificed my own profession or whatever other ambitions that I had because I had made the choice to have the children, and I wanted to make it my business to raise my children and help them. America is a very, very difficult place to raise children, so it became my new profession to raise them the way that I thought they should be raised, with a level of consciousness about their home country, and understanding of something other than American values; and building a nice community where they can survive. Somehow when you do that with the children, they always seem to team up with children of like values and families.

I first went home when my father passed away in 1975, and then I went again in 1981, with the children. There was this funny experience when we got to the airport. I had a British passport; my daughter was on my British passport, but born in South Africa; my eldest son was a South African but born in England, and I had two children who were South African but born in the United States. And this Afrikaner immigration man at the airport looked at this thing, and says, '*Here God*! *Wat gaan aan nou hier?*' He gave one look at me with all this mixture of passports and he just didn't know what to say. He told us to step one side and pressed the button; two stern-looking men came up, and the first question was, 'Where's MaKunene?' Just like that. I said, 'He's not here.' 'And is he coming home?' I said, 'I'm not sure'; and they became very aggressive, they wanted to make sure that we had all our return tickets, which we did; and they made us wait at the airport five hours. The twins were just barely twenty-one months, after almost a twenty-four-hour flight from England through Nairobi. It was awful. They let us in, but they gave us the minimum time to stay.

1981 in South Africa was a very, very confusing time. Everybody was afraid, everybody was hopeful, everybody was angry, everybody was anxious. It was all kinds of feelings around. In a sense, I felt more afraid then of being in South Africa than I was when I left. I felt insecure, I felt threatened at all times.

My children think of themselves as South Africans, absolutely, there's no question. Lamakhoshi went out one day with a neighbour of mine in Gugulethu when she was five. She saw this tall white sergeant and coming from America, didn't feel any fear. So she walks up to him and says, 'Is that a real gun?' [Laughs] And the sergeant said, 'Yes.' She says, 'Oh, I've always wanted to touch a sheriff.' And he says, 'Well I'm not a sheriff, I'm a sergeant; and where are you from?' And she said, 'I'm from America, but I'm South African.' [Laughs] This confused him completely. And then he asked, 'Where are your parents?' She said, 'My mum is here, but these white people won't let my father come here.'

But . . . oh, my children have always been ready to go home. We speak Zulu here, and they participate in all kinds of organisations. In fact, my daughter has been the leading spokesperson for South African children, since she was nine. She has written incredible poetry. I think most of her writing started from watching the crisis on television. I would discover these little snippets under her bed, culminating with what she wrote when the Gulf War exploded, it was absolutely incredible for a child her age. You see all those awards? [Gesturing to the wall] She is part of an organisation called the Los Angeles Student Coalition, this is young people fourteen, fifteen, sixteen years old, involved in community things; they decided to extend a hand into black-white relationships, and from then it moved into the situation of the homeless, and all the other social conditions around Los Angeles.

This student organisation expanded to involve almost fifty high schools, and my daughter was part of it. Then they brought in the issue of apartheid, because at that time, 1984, they were killing so many young children in South Africa and closing the schools. The television pictures were horrible. And this group of young children did such an incredible job on raising the level of consciousness in Los Angeles about apartheid. They planned to go inside the South African consulate, bring their knapsacks and stage a seven-day sit-in; shut it down for six days, completely. They had their little strategies, I don't know how they worked it out. People saw it on television that evening, all these children, with their knapsacks and their homework and their lunches and everything, right inside the consulate on the third floor. And it was closed. As soon as the elevators opened they would all jump in, lock hands and say, 'Sorry! this is place is closed for business.' We parents supervised them so that they didn't get into trouble. The Beverly Hills police would then come in and kind of monitor them. The first time they called it off themselves. The second time, the police called the FBI in and took them to prison, ja. But then they would mount a long protest outside the consulate. And she was a spokesperson, as a South African child who was born in South Africa.

Because she had been seen on television, she started getting invitations from organisations. There was some major conference here about the plight of the immigrant child in Los Angeles and they invited her to come and speak about her feelings as an immigrant child.

She also belongs to the Children of War organisation; that brings together children from war-torn areas of the world – Cambodia, Nicaragua, Palestine, and all the other places – and then they can talk about their own personal experiences. She always was there to portray the South African child. Then this other award; she had to write an essay and compete in a regional contest: 'What I will do in the Year 2000'; and she wrote an incredible essay and she was honoured by the State Assembly for her part.

One morning I counted the people in my house, and there were nine mouths to feed. There were three South African students living here without any contributions, and we are a family of six; and I didn't know what to do with only Mazisi's salary. I found out where to get used clothes that were in good condition around Beverly Hills; I found where to buy food and I discovered that you could actually go to the market downtown and get fresh food and vegetables in large containers. So my neighbours, six or eight of us, decided that's a good idea, that once every two weeks two women would go down there and buy these boxes and boxes of fruit, come to my yard here and divide them. Ten apples for you, ten cabbages for you. These were lawyers, doctors, women who had never even entered into any kind of co-op. I said I need it, you people don't need it, but thank you for the support.

It was also wonderful because it meant that you would see your neighbours regularly; we would have iced tea in summer; and we would have coffee and we talked about the children; and this created a very, very strong bond of ten strong families who were raising children in this neighbourhood. One of my friends said, It had to take this woman from Africa to come and teach us market economy! [Laughs] That's how we created a neighbourhood and a life for ourselves. We're very happy here, and I think that even if we go home we'll miss it because my children were happy here.

But we were always, always involved in South African politics. The first time I decided to organise a political protest, it was the most incredible thing. This is 1986, when there was really bloody stuff going on; my sister called me from South Africa at one o'clock in the morning. I said, 'Don't you ever learn what time it is in the United States?' She said, 'You've got to get up, they're killing people here. What are you people doing over there?' She was hysterical. They were clearing out the people in Crossroads in Cape Town; and she said, 'You know, we were there all night, my mother was there, everybody in Gugulethu was there, picking up kids who were destroyed; there was just so much killing.' And so she said, 'What are you going to do?' She says, 'Tell the world!' And I said, 'Yes, I'll tell the world.'

I put the phone down. I decided, yes, I'm going to tell the world, I'm going to organise a big protest in this city myself, because I was angry, I didn't know what to do; but that day I decided I was going to do it. Mazisi was on his way out to some conference in Europe the same day, so he said, 'You do it, but I have to leave.' And I asked one of the students how to make a flyer about the protests; and he showed me, and we printed . . . we went to all the printers that I knew, photocopied all these things; my children and I went distributing. I went to the churches, I called people at random out of the phone book. By the third day we had decided, yes, there would be a protest; and we had one of the biggest protests in this city in front of the Consulate here. Over 2,000 people turned up.

One of the people I called up was a friend of ours, a white South African who lives in the city. I said, 'There's going to be a protest at 5 o'clock outside the South African consulate, will you come?' He was stunned; he said, 'What do you mean? I have all my money invested in South Africa, I go there so often, how could you ask me?' And I said, 'If you're my friend, you're gonna have to come.' Five minutes later that phone rang, it was his secretary and she says, 'He wants to know what

he has to do.' I said, 'I want him to be there to be one of the monitors.'
And I saw him there, disguised in some khaki outfit, had a cap. He said,
'I don't know what you expect me to do?' I said, 'I expect you to be here
because we're talking about people dying! It's just a principle.' Well of
course my neighbours all came with me, they were there and their
families; we gathered together for twenty-seven days, almost 2,500
people in front of that consulate.

And my children were always with us. My kids come from that
tradition. Doing something and being part of something.

LAMAKHOSHI THAKANGOAHA KUNENE
Los Angeles 1991

'Children don't determine wars; adults do. And children are usually the
worst sufferers.'

> She combines the self-assured openness of an American with her
> own strong sense of identity as a South African. On the wall of her
> home are the commendations and awards she has won for essays
> and public services.

My academic education has come from the United States; my true
education has come from my South African background. So I'll be happy
to go back – yes! I'm the biggest pusher for going back home – started a
new campaign recently.

I was working with a group called the Los Angeles Student Coalition,
who decided that something had to be done about the apartheid situation. They started with this small little demonstration; a couple of
friends came, and you know invited family, more people heard about it.
We had meetings every Sunday and the organisation grew, mostly because young people really wanted to be involved. They had nowhere to
take all that energy, and this was a place where they could take it.

Our goal was to move the South African Consulate, which was in
Beverly Hills, out of LA. Through sit-ins and demonstrations and press
conferences and all that they had moved it out of Berkeley. And so we
had about three sit-ins at that office. And they moved. And we found
them a couple of blocks further down from their initial place, and we had
more sit-ins and more arrests. The sit-ins were amazing experiences
because it was about thirty young people who had dedicated themselves –
with or without the support of their family; usually with sceptical
support. Most of them Americans. Also Latino people, mixed race, from
Asia. We had a pretty mixed group. We would come in early in the
morning and fill up both the elevators, go upstairs. We'd practise civil

disobedience beforehand, and were taught by different people who had done that. Peacefully blocked the entrances and exits, and we let people out but we wouldn't let anyone in. So a lot of sit-ins, a lot of demonstrations which have been growing within the past year in front of the consulate. We speak at high schools and make other young people aware of what's going on there.

There's also Children of War, which is another organisation I'm in. It's a youth based organisation for young people who have come from war situations, and that includes young people from the United States, because we consider this situation that they're living under with gang violence and with the US sponsoring wars in other countries, is a situation of undeclared war. Youth empowerment is our ultimate objective and that's in the abstract. But for a lot of the young people in the organisation, the power that they have as young people is taken away from them through these war experiences. And for them a lot of the time it's the first time they've ever spoken about the horrors that they've seen, or the sacrifices they've made in their lives. They gain power from talking about these experiences, and in turn agitating other young people as to the reality and pain of war. Young people, children, don't determine wars; adults do, and children are usually the worst sufferers of it.

We speak at high schools and have conferences, we deal with different issues besides just the war experience – racism, sexism; and adultism, which is a new term! [Laughs] In American society, we tend to underestimate the power and the contributions that young people can make, and I think that's accurate in most societies. We talk and meet with other young people who aren't necessarily activists or involved in any particular organisation, but they really want to be able to do something. For a lot of them, it's the first time they're realising that there are wars going on in Central America that this government is supporting, and there's a lot of guilt that comes from that. And usually we work towards getting away from that guilt and redirecting that energy to stop what's going on.

I don't feel when I go back to South Africa that I will feel like a stranger. Definitely no, because there's a pretty large growing South African community in LA, so I spend a lot of time together with the community, and go to community events. I'm very connected and very much a part of my culture. Living here hasn't taken that away from me. I think it's reinforced that even more. Because I've had to deal with a lot of . . . especially in elementary school, a lot of teasing, because I had a very bizarre accent when I first came. We lived in England for five years and then moved here, so it was like a mixture of a South African and an English accent, and a kind of a 'wannabe' American accent. I talked strange and dressed differently, and my parents talked totally differently, so it was very hard to adjust with the other young people. Mostly people are turned off by what they don't know and what they're not used to. But I've been able to take that. And that in fact had strengthened me as a person and strengthened my cultural identity. So in terms of being a foreigner and feeling foreign, I think it's just going to be the readjustment to the society – a different society from the American.

I was brought up on our own South African habits and culture. My parents never compromised their own upbringing and culture and beliefs to help me to adjust to the American culture. It would be harder for me, on both sides, to adjust to my own culture and to try to find a place in this culture without quite having a strong identity of my own.

PETA WOLPE
London 1990

'I still don't like telling people where I'm from.'

> Peta, Tessa and Nicholas Wolpe came to England as children when their parents left South Africa. Their father, Harold, a lawyer and political activist, escaped from jail in 1963 in dramatic circumstances, and managed to get out of the country. In England he worked as a sociologist, and has written extensively on South African politics from a Marxist standpoint. Their mother, Anne-Marie, entered academic work as her children got older, specialising in the sociology of education; she is a member of a collective producing the magazine *Feminist Review*.

I actually remember very little about South Africa. I've got sort of odd specific memories like the tree in the garden where we lived, and the dogs. And I remember when Harold was in prison being told by the kids at school, 'Yes, your daddy's in prison.' You know, that kind of thing. I don't remember actually what they said, I just remember that feeling. I was six when we left.

For a long time, living here, I wouldn't tell anybody what happened about Harold's escape. It was a sense that I had to be quiet about it, and nobody should know because it would be like a risk. That's what I felt. And for years, and even still now, I don't like telling people where I'm from if they don't know me or they don't know the history; because I think they'll think as I'm white I must be a part of the racist society there, and I don't feel like having to explain myself to them.

Our whole lives have been influenced, or more than influenced, by what happened. The family is very close, almost in some ways too close, and I'm sure some of that's to do with what's happened. When Harold, for instance, goes off travelling, I feel slight anxiety about what will happen; and if people who are close to me are going away, and if I don't know exactly where they are, I have a sense of anxiety about it. Not terribly so that it disables me in any way, but sort of the back of my mind.

Coming over here was difficult for me, even things like my name. In fact, I changed my name; we hadn't been in this country very long and I was going to a new school and I just couldn't bear my name being so different. We were driving to this school and I was panicking, 'Give me a name!' Anne-Marie could only think of Margaret because we were staying in the house of somebody called Margaret; and it was really humiliating, because I could not spell this name, it was so long! [Laughs] I couldn't spell it. When my friends came home, everyone kept calling me Peta and I eventually got everyone trained to call me Margaret; and then when I eventually changed back to Peta they were all calling me Margaret.

Everything about me seemed wrong. My hair – years ago there was a time when curly hair wasn't fashionable like it is now, and I had curly hair. I felt different to people here, and I still don't feel English really. I don't feel English and I don't really feel South African either. I don't identify myself as being English, but I don't really know South Africa; and I've never been involved politically. Yet I feel emotionally attached. When I hear about certain things that are happening, I feel part of it – and yet I don't.

It's a subject that's never out of my home; it's always here. There's always a worry. When Harold was away in America and I was checking the post and so on, I had to be careful for letter bombs and things like that, which are not part of most people's everyday life. They don't worry about their father being killed. When Ruth [First] was killed, it was just . . . it was awful, it was just . . . so close . . . much closer, in a way, than it ever had been before, because I was that much older and I knew what was happening. I find it quite difficult to explain.

I'd like to visit South Africa and maybe I will live there. I feel we've been deprived of something by not having been brought up there – that should have been our home. I think a lot of the sort of difficulties that I have arise from not really belonging here.

I feel proud of my parents; but we should have grown up where we came from, not here where I basically feel I don't really belong. I don't feel a sense of this is my country, I don't feel patriotic or anything towards this country. I can't help thinking things may have been different for me, had we been brought up in South Africa with a sense of an understanding of what the fight was about; instead of the years of feeling I couldn't really talk about what happened.

I think I was told not to, because one day when we were living in Yorkshire, I was telling the milkman, or somebody rather inappropriate about what happened, and Anne-Marie and Harold said, 'You mustn't talk about it.' And I took that to an extreme and I wouldn't tell anybody after that. For years. Quite recently I've told people at work, but before that I wouldn't talk about it. The other day at work we had an anti-racist training and they asked us to talk about our origins; and I was listening to people and I was thinking, what am I going to say, how much do I want to tell these people? I told them very briefly what had happened. I told them I was South African, and about my father's involvement, and I still felt quite anxious about telling them and got quite upset.

But ... I don't know, it's very ... In Anne-Marie's book that she's writing, she describes how one night I came into their bed and I was screaming; Harold wasn't there because he'd been taken away in the night; I don't remember that because I was only three, but I can identify almost with what a small little girl must feel like if her daddy's there one minute and the next minute he's gone.

I've formed a relationship with a man, Yves, in France, and there's a child now. Anne-Marie and Harold feel I shouldn't go and live there with him because they think there are too many cultural differences between us; and in some respects they're right. In other respects what attracts me to this man and the life there is somebody who's committed to family life. He hasn't got interests in politics, it's a million miles from his world, which is around his interests and family. And I have a kind of battle between wanting to have a professional life and feeling I should be involved politically and wanting ... Harold says social work in South Africa would be very interesting and I'm sure it is, but then there's this other side of me which sees what happened to us; politics has always really come first. I don't want my child to have that sort of experience, I want him to have an experience that's different. He comes first.

When I look at the people who've been involved politically, my parents' friends, I sometimes think, 'Should they have had children?' I don't know. I don't know how you get that balance. But they did have children. Maybe if we had lived there I would have more of a sense of a belonging and been involved politically myself ... but, coming into exile has sort of pushed me out of the picture, as it were. I think it did and it was always a conflict really between the politics and Anne-Marie and Harold, and keeping the family together; it's always been there.

I've lived here twenty-seven years now; it's a long time. Most of my life. And I am thinking about the possibility of going back. I had an argument with Harold about the Movement; I said, 'It's a very good organisation in terms of what it's trying to do at a political level, and I think it stinks the way they treat individuals.' I just think that an organisation that's fighting for what it's fighting for should be able to treat people a bit better. I know a bit about psychology because of my work and I know what separations do; especially for Nicholas, because he was just a tiny little baby and I don't know how she left him. Now that I've got Jonathan, I just don't know how she did it. I just could not ... I couldn't envisage being separated from him. And I suppose that comes back to my wanting him to have a different sort of experience. I've chosen to have this child, it wasn't planned, but I've got him and I now feel I have a responsibility.

TESSA WOLPE
London 1990

'For the first time in my life I could talk about feelings, emotions, and hatred and despair. Or just anger at our parents.'

I remember my fifth birthday party because Anne-Marie and Harold weren't there. And I have very clear memories of getting a doll. I always wanted a wedding doll and Anne-Marie would never let me have one – and I was given one. And our nanny, Angelina, who was very loving and supportive . . . The only other memory I have of South Africa is of going to the airport when we were leaving, Peta and I, and Angelina wasn't allowed to sit down because she was black. We had a lot of people there, watching . . . seeing us off, but I have this very clear memory of her not being able to sit and I asked her, 'Why can't you sit?'

But of coming here, I don't really remember anything at all. I remember Cantley Mansions where we lived. But I had lots of nightmares. And there was one where . . . Along Cantley Mansions there's a road that leads up to the tube station, ja. In this dream I was always walking up this road; there was always a car that would stop and some men would get out and start following us – I don't know if I was with Harold, or Anne-Marie, or who I was with – and then I'd start running up the road; and you know when you're running and running but you're not getting anywhere, and they were always behind. And that's always the memory of Cantley Mansions. But other than that, I don't really remember much.

I always felt sort of different at school – I think about the age of eight – because of the way our household was, where people were always coming and going; and with a name like Wolpe, and always being conscious of being Jewish and not wanting to be Jewish, certainly later on, anyway. The older I got, the more I wanted to be like normal . . . what I saw as a normal person, and not to be singled out, and not to look different. Because a lot of people always thought that we weren't English, didn't sound English. But that was much later. A lot later.

Actually I felt very proud of my parents. But I never wanted to let anyone know that we were South African or had been born in South Africa because of people's reactions to white South Africans, and being scared that you were going to be called a racist or something. And then that: 'Gosh, you're funny people, you know; you eat differently, you do things differently and the way you run your lives is so different.' I don't think it had so much to do with politics really. I don't think so. It was more cultural. Because the politics you could shrug off in some ways, you could keep it very quiet. You didn't need to talk about it; you didn't need to say, we came to this country because of what had happened – just happened to be here. Or pretending that we always lived here. With some people it didn't matter, but then a lot of people don't actually understand, and can't communicate or understand your feelings about it. Or the depressions that you might have.

When Ruth got killed, that was an important time; I spent a bit of time with Shawn and it was . . . I just felt for the first time in my life I had somebody who was outside of the family who I could sit and talk to about feelings, emotions, and hatred and despair, or just anger at our parents. The fact that we were uprooted, that we had to leave the country, that things might have been very different. We wouldn't be so messed up.

Or rebelling. Because I was very intelligent at school, I was top of the junior school, top of the secondary school, I was the brightest pupil in the first year; and then I rebelled. I feel that had I not been living around here, had I not gone to such a big school, had we stayed in South Africa, things would have been very different for all of us. And I've always had that feeling . . . It's probably absolute nonsense, but you feel that because . . . you feel angry at what's happened. You've been torn apart from the rest of your family because . . . you know, we're all divided, aren't we? We're all over the place. And we had no choice. And that seems unfair. When you spend so much of your younger years moving from town to town, you can never really make friends or settle down. You never really had a base; and you always felt a bit like a gypsy, if that's the right word. Moving round and round. It obviously affected all of us.

I have this terrible fear about Anne-Marie and Harold dying, and things going wrong and bad things happening. Ja, I've been in and out of therapy for years now, but I've only come to realise more recently that other children also fear that that can happen. But it still doesn't make you feel any better or have more of an understanding of it, because it's been around for so many years that it's just a part of me now.

And now for them to be going back – I'm just . . . I'm very bitter in a way. I feel they're dividing the family again. They are! Harold said to me, This time you have a choice. Well, I don't have a choice really; my life has been here. I have a small desire to go to South Africa, but I don't see . . . You know, it divided the family.

They should have thought about us as children. You make a decision about what you're going to do; you have children, and you are aware that you're bringing other people into the world, so therefore you have to think of them first. It's an irrational thought but it's . . . in a sense, the same thing now. You feel that there hasn't been any thought, really. Because Harold is determined to go back, and for a long time said that we should all go back together. But how can I go back now when I've lived here for so many years, my whole life except for five years? And I'm now thirty-two. It's impossible. I think I said I don't have any love for that country because of what it has done, and a lot of anger towards it, and why go somewhere where you feel . . .

And at the same time I don't feel English because of the way that the English people are. I don't think I explained properly why I feel that, and I'm not sure I can. It's just . . . our house has always been a very open house and you never have to ring; people just wander around, come round, knock on the door and they come in. But here in England, you have to always phone and say, 'Can I come round? Is it OK to come round?' And I find that a pain in the arse – that people are so reserved. You have to be invited round. You have to be asked if you want to sit down and have a cup of tea. And I just find that it's an alien way of life for me.

But then I couldn't go and live in South Africa. Our home here has been very much South African-orientated. It has really. Or not just South African, but people from other parts of the world. So it hasn't been a very English household at all. Most of Anne-Marie and Harold's friends aren't English.

The job I'm doing now does not enable me to have any social life at all really. I feel quite lonely and I think that with Anne-Marie and Harold going, I'm going to be devastated by that. I'll be losing Peta and Jonathan at the same time, and there'll just be Nick; and it's a very scary thought. But it's also probably a good thing for me.

But I am also thinking that maybe I will have to make my life differently. I keep saying, well people do . . . that you've got to forget about South Africa and forget about the past and live your life now, not blame your parents for everything, for all the mishaps and depressions throughout your life. But we still can't help feeling those feelings.

ELLWYN OTHNEIL BECK
Oslo 1990

'The way we lived in South Africa, it was this black-white thing. There was no reconciliation, there was no understanding.'

Halfway up the coast of Jutland is the town of Århus, an unlikely home to a small colony of South Africans. The nucleus was Godfrey and Irene Beck who, with nine of their eleven children, were brought to Århus from Botswana by the Danish Refugee Council. Godfrey Beck was a trade union secretary in Johannesburg who was banned in 1966 and put under house arrest. In 1969 he left for Francistown in Botswana. Ellwyn Othneil Beck is third of the large Beck family, he now lives in Norway.

I was thirteen when I left South Africa for Botswana with my family to join my father in exile. Conditions were not of the best; South African refugees were being harassed by the local police, there were a lot of kidnappings and there were a lot of deportations.

I attended a secondary school called Swaneng built by Patrick van Rensburg. There we were taught to be self-reliant – the school was built for South African refugees to combat Bantu Education and to prepare us for a post-apartheid society.

We lived at the White House, a refugee camp in Francistown with all other refugees and we shared among ourselves. My mother was like a mother to almost everybody, she could solve social problems, girlfriend problems with other comrades; and she was largely respected. We used to cook together and share food among refugees together. My father was elected the chairman of the organisation and our social relations with other refugees was good; people took care of one another, because we were in the same situation at the time.

After this we were deported from Botswana. All of us. The Botswana government didn't like it because it was an embarrassment to them with all the animosity still continuing and the deportations of refugees and kidnappings. The next thing we knew, the whole family was deported back to South Africa. I had lived in Botswana for five years. We were escorted from Francistown to the border; the police in charge was a white Rhodesian colonel. When we got to the border, the South African Special Branch waited for my father. When we got to the gates at the border the Special Branch said, 'Welcome back, Boetie, it's nice to see you!' And I didn't see my father for nearly a year. He just disappeared. He was in prison.

We lived with my granny and we were about twenty people in one house, that is three rooms plus a kitchen and a toilet outside. After a year my father was brought to court. We finally left South Africa on exit permits in 1974, the whole family with my father included.

We came to Århus in Denmark. My father started the first Anti-Apartheid Movement in Århus with local church groups and grass-roots organisations. My family were stripped of South African citizenship, and we became stateless. We travelled on diplomatic documents, and the family was accepted immediately on the same level as any Danish citizen. We got residents' permits, work permits, everything; the Danish refugee council took care of us for two years after that. We made such remarkable progress with our assimilation with Danish people, we were regarded as being Dane after two years and were entitled to the social benefits that every Dane could have. After three years, the family became citizens.

I went to university. I studied English and History. I didn't take up my profession as a secondary school teacher. I went into the Anti-Apartheid

Movement which my father had started, because there was so much to do. I came to Norway almost eight months ago to work here for the ANC.

I think exile has contributed something good to my identity because it opened up areas which I did not know. The way we lived in South Africa, it was this black-white thing. There was no reconciliation, there was no understanding of the opposition, and I always had this belief that if it was not because of that racist regime, I should not have been here, I could have lived happily with my family and kids in South Africa. But then coming to Denmark, I discovered that we as immigrants in the country we do cause a lot of problems, because we do not have the tolerance. People who are oppressed are always more sentimental, they are temperamental.

I think mothers in South Africa are very passive. My mother's relations with my father was . . . how I can say? . . . very passive. My father was a teacher, he was very oral. He was very active, and this created that my mother was very passive – she has to take care of us while my father was just around South Africa somewhere. And when she came to Botswana, she was changing from being this passive to a person with her own mind, being active.

But when she came to Denmark, it's like a stage; she just exploded! She just exploded, she became more . . . she's so active today, you know I can't even explain it to you. She's in the ANC Women's Section in Denmark, she works with an organisation that the family has started called HOSA, which collects clothing for refugees in Southern Africa. You just name it, she's just wherever; and she's a member of the anti-apartheid movement in Denmark.

After the death of my father in 1986, my mother became very lonely. But then what has happened to her, she's more active to escape that loneliness.

I want to go back home but I do have my hestitation. I do have doubts – unemployment, housing, health – because I have all these benefits in Denmark. As far as health is concerned, it's free in Denmark. I still have a flat in Denmark, earn a lot of money and this might not be there in South Africa; and these are things I consider a lot. But I also feel that I have to contribute to a post-apartheid South Africa. I have the education for it and I feel I have to contribute; so it's a commitment somehow for me to return to South Africa.

But then the uncertainties of everything . . . that goes through every person's mind, it's there. I have known a girl for the last fifteen years, I met her just a year after I came to Denmark and I still live with her. We have no children; she's a nurse. She's here in Norway now. She's Danish, yes.

I have a lot of friends in Denmark, in the Anti-Apartheid Movement, school friends. I also worked at the town council in Århus; I made a lot of friends because there are so many people there working in the town council. I was the chairman of the immigrants in Århus and I have many friends from various countries.

The thing is that if you are known, as for example my family in Denmark, you cannot do whatever you want to do, you have to consider things twice before you just say something. And I feel that I would like to explode . . . to burst out of this balloon, you know, and somehow be myself, where my politics and my feelings somehow are connected – instead of having them separate.

ROLAND and IRENE BECK
Århus, Denmark 1990

Irene Beck is the mother, and Roland – Ronnie – is her eldest child.

'I also gained something in exile. A person has learned a lot, that's what I think.'

'I think I'm neither South African any more and I can never become a Dane, so I'm in a limbo.'

IRENE: When we joined my husband after he went to Botswana we had to leave Ronnie and Denise who were working, so they could send us money. We had to stay in a refugee camp and times were very, very difficult.

We stayed a little more than six years. We got aid from the Botswana Christian Council, but it wasn't much. There were a lot of refugees, something like close to two hundred. Caritas helped support us. They sent the money to my husband and he distributed it to the refugees. There were some that did not get anything, no money at all. They were refugees from different places: Namibia, Angola, Mozambique and Rhodesia, as well as South Africans. It was in Francistown, yes.

ROLAND: I suspect that pressure was applied on the Botswana government to get rid of my father. That's why we got deported back to South Africa. We stayed there something like two years, ja.

IRENE: When we went back, we were living in a coloured township, Noordgesig, adjacent to Soweto. It was a difficult time because the children couldn't go to school. They gave as the reason that they didn't want communists. I think it was an excuse because they were first accepted and then two days afterwards they changed their minds.

ROLAND: I got sacked from work; I couldn't get work due to the fact that most newspapers wrote about the old man's return South. Then I worked for an insurance company. One Monday morning when I got to work, the director told me that my presence doesn't happen to be welcome there. Exactly, ja.

After having stayed in South Africa for two years, we had to leave. Thanks to Amnesty International, representations were made to get the Nordic countries to grant the family asylum. The Danish Refugee Council arranged for us to come.

IRENE: We didn't know anything about Denmark. We knew that it was very cold. Ja, this was the first time we're out of our own country, being a European country, it was strange. It helped in a way being a large family because actually Danish people are very cold people. They're very cold. They keep to themselves.

At first it was difficult getting around; in the bus, you know you're in a ... well, it's just European people, and you would stand at the back, you wouldn't go and sit next to them because we're not used to sitting next to whites. So we'll just stand at the back. And then afterwards we start moving in seats. It was much better if you could speak the language and understand it, so it wasn't so bad afterwards.

ROLAND: I can remember when we came here the loneliness that we experienced, the way we'd turn on one another, the fights we had, fights I had with my old man. But to look at things in hindsight as regards my old man, I regret it, I really regret it. He played a very central role. He was rather domineering at times. Strong personality. He always said one should not be dependent too much on other people, always be self-reliant.

When we arrived I used to ask myself whether it would be possible for me to return to South Africa again. On the other hand, I said to myself too that one has got to make the most out of life here in Denmark. And then finally, one comes to the conclusion that one isn't a South African any more and neither does one happen to be a Dane. And for me that's the most difficult to cope with. But well, of course, granted the latest developments back home this gives one the opportunity to return. But then again one has got to have the financial resources.

IRENE: My husband was very active politically, but the Danish said that he should not take part in any of their politics. But he was very, very active, organising South Africans and the South African Committee – he established that. Everyone knew him; he knew a lot of Danish people.

ROLAND: When we came the only anti-apartheid work then being done was by MS – Mannenvolke Samwerke – it's an aid organisation, partially state financed. My father was contacted by MS to try and expand the local Anti-Apartheid Movement here. This he did. We embarked on a comprehensive programme . . . we started with a fruit boycott, we agitated for the boycotting of all South African farming produce. There we succeeded. Afterwards we started with a coal boycott – a total ban on all South African coal. This country imported something like 90 per cent of its energy needs from South Africa. My father started working on a comprehensive economic boycott of South Africa. Unfortunately he died a week before the Danish State wrote this into law.

IRENE: I was working at that time as a garment worker, seamstress, working for the Danish commune. Pascal was at a day-care centre, but the others they were attending school. So, well they'd come from school and each one looked after one another; then I would come in the evenings and see what there is to be done, like cooking food and so on. But the girls also see to that. And then in the evenings my husband would go to meetings and so forth and I'm home with the children.

The children were all told that they should not speak English to me, so that I would learn the language. Well for me . . . at first it was very difficult for me to speak . . . then I would just keep quiet, they'll speak and I wouldn't know what's going on around me! Sometimes when I sit at the table with them eating, then I would say a prayer to myself, 'Please don't speak to me, please don't speak to me, because I can't speak!' Then I started learning slowly but it came. So all of a sudden when they spoke, then I could also speak to them. They got a shock!

Sometimes I would sit and cry, yes. I was homesick, and I would think of my mother, because I left her behind. We were here two years, then she died. We couldn't go . . . it was impossible for us to go. We came out on an exit permit.

The younger ones, Natalie, Mark, Gavin, Glen, they fit in, because they were quick to learn also the language. We put the children into local schools, made friends. Oh, we had every night the house full with Danish boys and girls coming to visit us. So they fitted in very, very quickly. It was like a college, nê, where they could stay and come home weekends.

ROLAND: Right now I'm working with Mannenvolke Samwerke. We have established a little organisation called HOSA, an acronym that simply means Helpe Organisation fur die Sude Afrika; but it also comes from the African term 'Hosa' which means, 'Come on, come on, let's get going . . . arise!' ja.

I suppose to a large extent I am happy here. To a large extent, though I must admit that at times I do grow despondent, simply because I don't know what the future might hold. And should I return back home?

IRENE: I do think of going back home, because I still have my family, brothers and sister. Perhaps I'll stay in Denmark. But most of my

children – like my daughters – they want to go back; they want to go
back, ja. But Derrick doesn't want to.

When we first came here, there was no racialism, no. But now one can
see there is, because they just come up to us and say, 'Why don't you go
back home? We don't want you here.'

ROLAND: I think that this is due to the current economic morass that
this country happens to find itself in. Foreigners become the scapegoat.
The largest minority group in this country are Turks, and they've got it
– hell, worse than the Africans. Worse than Africans. They're not needed
any more.

I think I'm neither South African any more and I can never become a
Dane, so I'm in a limbo. I mean, I'm really in limbo. I think it's pretty
difficult for the older generations to integrate, unlike younger South
Africans. Take Pascal, for example; Pascal to a degree happens to be
Danish; he grew up here, has attended school here, knows the culture.
Unlike me. What I mean by saying I'm no more a South African is
because I have been from the country for so many years, and things have
changed so dramatically.

If I'd stayed in South Africa I think I'd be dead by now. Yes, because
staying in Soweto, you can't stop taking part in the fights, because you
see and you want to help. I think that being black in Soweto is living on
borrowed time, and this is something that every black man simply
realises – that he's living on borrowed time.

Finally, I would like to say 'Unitary, non-racial, non-sexist South
Africa!' Even though I may not be able to return to South Africa, this
happens to be my wish for my countrymen.

IRENE: Oh, well, I'll never be a Dane, that's for sure! But I wouldn't say
I'm not South African, because I am a South African, and I'll stay a South
African. I'll never be a Dane. I don't feel part of this culture, this society.

But I think I gained something in exile. We've become more stronger in
political terms and you know a lot. A person has learned a lot, that's
what I think.

DALI TAMBO
London 1990

'I feel like a cultural freak, I do feel that; and I think many people do.'

His father, Oliver Tambo, was President of the ANC throughout its
long years in exile. His mother worked, brought up three children
and ensured that they had a good education. He speaks without

trace of a South African accent. He describes himself as 'a little black Englishman' who plans to return to South Africa.

I came to England with my mother when I was just about to have my second birthday. They sent me to a convent school and so I was surrounded by nuns. I didn't really understand who I was at that stage. I knew that my father was some kind of a lawyer, and that he wasn't around a lot; and so the nuns at this convent kind of became my family if you like, because I spent so much time with them. My mother was always coming up with many presents and food, taking me out and all this. But basically I guess I looked to the nuns for guidance on everything.

I don't remember being unhappy in any way. It was a school where there were a lot of disadvantaged kids, black and white. I found it fairly easy to settle in. It was later when I became more conscious of who I was, and started asking more questions of my mother. 'What is my father doing?' 'What are we?' 'Who are we?' When I left this convent and went to a prep school, she would say to me, 'Tell the boys that your father's a lawyer.' Which of course was true; but not really the whole story! But we didn't really talk about the South African situation. But for me, it gave me at least some kind of reference for myself that I could say, well, he was a lawyer.

At prep school I became more interested in Africa and South Africa, I knew things were bad down there; I knew that we'd had to leave for various reasons; I was conscious of the ANC. But because I was always at boarding-schools, we were kept away from the South African community and became much more Anglicised. My mother told me she remembers us going to school and coming back after two years and speaking our own language (Xhosa) that we'd always spoken. And then the third year, when we came back, we were saying, 'Speak English to us!' [Laughs] We had lost it basically by the third year. I remember quite vividly, because I was very insecure not being able to speak English properly at that time and was getting special lessons, this mental transition when I said to myself, I'm going to speak this language so well. And if my mother said a word wrong, it would be me who'd correct her.

But at the same time we lost all our kind of cultural identities, and picked up those around us in the boarding-schools – first at the Cathedral school in Chichester and then at Lancing. So I'd come back for holidays and think about South Africa, go back to the college and not think about it at all. I didn't feel at that stage that I was British – definitely not, because I didn't equate black with being British. I felt you could only be British if you were white. But I had a real hard time. I remember lying in bed at night thinking maybe this is all a dream, or maybe they're protecting me from something. Maybe – this sounds incredible, this is what was going through my mind – I thought, well maybe we're stinking rich and they don't want me to know, because it would spoil me. The reason I thought that was because everybody around me was stinking rich, their parents were all millionaires at these boarding-schools. I'd go and stay with them, I'd see all this wealth and splendour, and we were living in a small flat in a London suburb. Somehow I knew my father was a big man; I knew people respected him, and I couldn't understand why he didn't show more visible wealth, why we had to struggle with things when all these people were . . . Just naturally I assumed that well, if he's so famous and all these people respect him, he must also be a wealthy man; but obviously I'm being kept protected from something. And that lived with me for quite a while. I was always suspicious that there were things they weren't telling me.

But I didn't realise that it was politics basically that they weren't telling me. They didn't. My father never spoke to me about politics, never, when I was young. My mother would tell me what he was doing; but at the same time, when it came to what do I say when the boys ask me or when the boys' parents ask me? She would say, 'Tell them he's a lawyer.' So, in a way, it stopped me thinking deeply about what he was doing in politics.

Funnily enough, my political awakening was sparked by a student at Lancing, who was extremely intelligent, top of the whole place really; a Marxist even at that age. People were always coming to argue with him. The only books about Marx and such things were on his desk; they just acted as a magnet. People would come and have their arguments and go away and then somebody else would come; or a lecturer would come. His name was Ross Cooper, and I really liked him, we got on very well. And he would just sit down and tell me about it, and it became almost . . . I don't know, I just liked the rebellion side of the thing. I liked the fact that people reacted in the way they did, and seemed scared by this book and by the fact that Ross was talking about those kind of things.

When I got back home over a period of time I started equating that with wider politics. But very little really came from my father sitting me down and saying, 'This is what I do, son.' [Laughs] It wasn't like that. It was more gradually getting to know what he did. When I came back from holidays, for example, I would go up to his office and I would read all kinds of papers when he was asleep, a bit like a spy! [Laughs] But I would read everything; and that's how I got to know him. I would read his letters, read all kinds of things about him. I read so many things about him and so much on him that later in life, when I wrote a speech for my mother or something like this, he would say to me, 'That's exactly how I would have put it.' And that's just because it was coming out verbatim almost! [Laughs]

But it was very confusing, and I didn't really know who I was for a long, long time; and not until about ten years ago did I think: Right! This is me!

Another side was the constant thought in my head, when I was older, that my father would never live to see South Africa free. I always expected him to be assassinated, and in a way mentally prepared myself, because I knew that my mother would lean heavily on me. I kept saying to myself, right, you're going to have to be strong when this happens. Every time my sister or mother would ring and leave a message for me to ring back urgently, I would panic. I would think, oh my God, it's happened, the day has come! I thought he would die in the struggle. I knew that he could never retire from it – not when there was work to be done. I had many talks with my sisters when we were young about that kind of thing, about who are we? Who were they? Is daddy going to live? Or is he going to be assassinated?

He would play games. For example, one time I was in the car with him, and he and a guy called Mfundisi would play games. If there was a car following us they would take this car on all kinds of little trips, they'd pull up round a corner, let the car go past, then follow, come next to it, and Mfundisi would look at the guy in the window, and they . . . they just had fun, you know.

But all of that, although it was done in a very sort of nice way, probably for my benefit, it still scared me. I knew there were guns around, I knew . . . I'd see big suitcases full of money. My father would be coming from Algeria, going to Lusaka, or somewhere like this and I'd see big suitcases full of money, big notes and things like that. And I remember opening a suitcase up one time, and my father coming in – I thought it was toy money – and I said, 'Can I have some?' He said, 'No, no, that's for our people.'

And so a lot of things like that made me realise, I guess. The big meetings they would have at my mother's flat, and uncles and aunts constantly coming in. I got a feeling that we were involved in something. Both my parents were always glued to the television whenever the news was on, and there was always a lot of discussion. I would always sit right up next to the TV so that I didn't have to listen to them talking through it.

There were so many things pulling me in different directions. My mother was constantly saying, 'Look I've got two men in this family, and one of them is already in politics, I don't want you to go into politics. You must earn money, be independent.' All this kind of thing; and so that was pulling me in that direction. On the other hand, I was fanatical about politics at that stage and was just about to go to university in France and do a degree in politics. I was more conscious of what was going on inside the country. I'd started to have black South African friends; I was beginning to feel like an exile. But at the same time, I felt more British even at twenty-one I guess, than I did South African. I recognised that South Africa was where I was from, but I also recognised that I didn't have the same kind of inherent culture. Culturally I was a little black Englishman! [Laughs] But at least I did know who I was. At least I'd stopped saying to people that he was a lawyer, and that we were nothing to do with any political situation and things like that. But it's been a very gradual thing. I don't think there's ever been a point – and I don't think there will be until I get back – where I really can say, 'OK, I'm fully confident that this is me.'

I feel like a cultural freak, I do feel that! And I think many people do. When you sit in a room with your parents, even at twenty or twenty-one, you just feel, why am I the only person who doesn't understand what they're talking about? Because I've lost all my knowledge of our own languages. I never really had an opportunity to get them back because I've been educated away from my parents. And so as a result, away from the community and away from even the daily contact of saying a few things in Xhosa, Zulu or whatever, with my mother or sisters or friends.

Then I went to Paris, and again another European language and another culture, which I got into very heavily. I really adore French culture, and so I was very happy to be there, and got engrossed in it. I thought that I could spend the rest of my life in France, and I very nearly didn't come back. But by the time I left Paris I felt I am an international person. I have no particular nation. I also had a dislike of nationality, as it had been interpreted in the modern world, and in history – the damage it had done. I really felt that I wouldn't fight for any particular country except South Africa. But the only reason I still kept that identity with South Africa was because of the struggle. And in a way, I felt justified because I didn't go and choose these cultures, they were given to me! [Laughs] They were kind of thrown upon me. So I felt, OK yes, one day I'll go back to South Africa, but I would be quite happy if it was necessary to spend the rest of my life in exile. It's a kind of back-up. I don't know. I'm very scared about going back to South Africa. [Laughs] I remember when people asked, 'Where are you from?' saying 'Nowhere!'

In Paris I studied international affairs and political science. Then Dulcie September arrived in Paris as the ANC rep, and I lived with her for a while. We became very good friends and she did a lot to add to my politicisation, because I was a kind of textbook radical. And Dulcie, because she was always challenging everything you said, would force you to think things through. I was at the Sorbonne and the American college, two different places with two very different attitudes. At the Sorbonne, they were fairly left-wing. At the American college, they were very right-wing. Although I didn't have a personal ideology I had a political ideology, and in a way that protected me. But the experience of doing that degree nonetheless, I think was very good.

I worked at the ANC office as Dulcie's secretary for a while, and that consolidated what I was learning. We always used to say that this ANC office is crazy. It was in this block of apartments which was off the street; it had its own courtyard, but all the other rooms and flats around the office were either deserted, or no one seemed to be there. Walking in and out and you'd just have these people sitting in the hallways, eating bread or smoking ganja, or whatever, doing all kinds of weird things. So it was a really crazy place for us to have an office. But it was very shocking the way that they killed Dulcie.* I went back for the funeral.

I started getting into film, doing research work for documentaries. Ever since I left Paris, the only projects I've worked on, apart from a spell in an advertising agency, have been projects that have something to do with South Africa. I was very politically conscious by the time I left Paris. I've always said to people, 'I don't identify myself as OR's son, I have my own identity.' So it became a very sore point for me when people would introduce me as OR's son, which ANC people always did. I hated it. I knew that there was no way I was like him. I have had different influences upon me. At the same time I felt kind of robbed because I knew that if I had grown up in South Africa, that I would have been a Movement person without any doubt. Or dead, or something! [Laughs] But since I wasn't there and since that hadn't happened, I just figured I have to try to contribute in my own way.

My mother's always saying to me, 'Look at Mbeki's son! Look at Sisulu's son! Where are you?' [Laughs] Which I think is quite a cruel thing to say, but also expects too much. They were born into a situation and I was born . . . how the hell [Laughs] . . . out in a nunnery and then a prep school and a public school, how would I be a Zweleke Sisulu or a Thabo Mbeki? I'm me and I've had to accept that.

But I know that in the West we've affected people with Artists Against Apartheid and things like that; we have pulled a lot of people into the struggle. And soon as you realise that, OK this is how I can contribute, you start to feel more secure as a person in yourself.

I think that I'm definitely going back. I love our people as people. I don't know one single place in the country, and so I have reservations about that, but I expect it to be a very beautiful place. But the beauty of it for me is the people. I'm not an exile that has been lost. We're not lost at all, we're totally there. But we go back to that country as victims like all the others are – victims of apartheid. We didn't choose to go out, we weren't on holiday. We were in exile.

* Dulcie September was assassinated by two gunmen outside her office, as she arrived with an armful of mail and was unlocking the door.

PRENAVEN NAICKER
Lusaka 1990

'I feel an alien everywhere.'

Pren's father, known as 'M.P.', had been a trade-union organiser and a leading member of the Natal Indian Congress and the Communist Party. He had been arrested many times before he left the country illegally while the police searched for him once again. He came to Britain, worked in the ANC office in London, and edited the ANC monthly: *Sechaba*. He was on a mission for *Sechaba* when he died suddenly of a massive heart attack, on a plane somewhere between London and Berlin. Heart attacks and strokes were the executioners of many political leaders in exile.

The first thing I can remember of my life back in South Africa is when they were taking my dad away to prison. I had been asleep, and I could feel somebody putting his hand on my shoulder ... And I turned and I could see my dad kneeling down next to me. And he says ... but before I could really understand what he's talking about, I could see a white hand and a gun. And that's all. Somebody was standing behind him, I don't know who. And I can remember him saying: OK son. I'll be away for at least two months. Look after mummy – and he kisses me on the forehead. And then somebody else says: OK now. Let's go.

A little more frightening for me at that age was when the police used to come to my house. They used to do it in a rather aggressive manner. They would bang on the door and say: Open up! They would keep shouting until my dad would open it. He would tell us: OK. You stay here in the kitchen, all of you! And he would go out there alone.

And they'd come, pushing their way in, push him aside and say: OK. Get your things! – or something like that. And it was moments like this I used to shy away from with fear. So that fear over white people doing this, or the police doing this – it affects me to this very day, because I dream about it sometimes. It gives me nightmares.

I get a little bit emotional no matter how often I speak about this. To try and speak about some of my problems to my closest comrades and friends – I always end up getting a little emotional. Yes. I feel it does help. What is happening with many of our comrades is that they bottle it in a lot. I've noticed that problem. People feel ashamed to talk about it. I'm not. I think ... we must see this.

In Durban when we used to go to the beach – we had to walk through the white beach first before we could get to the Indian beach. And here we were always harassed and called names, shells and rocks thrown at us, and things like that. Always harassed. We used to go in groups, and we would respond with threats and punches. I grew up with that sort of thing.

And again, walking back into our area we had to walk through a white area – Overport. Here all of us . . . there's no noise; we used to walk very orderly; we weren't free; we knew in this different area we had to keep quiet. All the chatter would slowly die down, we used to walk on the pavement, be very orderly about what we were doing, until we would get into our area which is further down, past Macaws Hospital, into the Indian area. And this is where we start kicking stones, and picking stones and trying to hit some birds.

My grandmother used to tell me a lot that England is the greatest place. England has it all! I mean, the place that's the best – it's Britain, Great Britain! And on one occasion my grandmother calls me. She says: Pren! Come and see! This is a doctor from England – you know he studied in England! And I would become extremely subdued and approach with respect. Oh God! And she would always say: And I want you to be a doctor! So Britain was a faultless country – it's great there! It has everything!

And there you are. That's how I've really lived – up to that standard. Whether it was a good thing or not, I don't know.

We travelled to England on a British liner – my mother, myself, my sister and my cousin. My mother said: Feel free son, you know; get into the swimming-pool. So I put on my costume and I approached the swimming-pool. There were all whites – I couldn't differentiate who was English white, who was South African white – but they were all whites. I got into the swimming-pool; and believe-you-me, everybody left. Except one man, and he was from London. He was an Englishman.

I was sixteen years old then – this is in 1967. All of them got out! I was a very good swimmer; in fact I swam for Natal – the non-European section. I felt very, very self-conscious. But this man he didn't move out. He stood at the rails, and I went and I stood next to him. I felt so uncomfortable, I couldn't stand on my own. And he just asked me a few questions: What's your name? and Where you're from? and I found that consoling. I looked up, and I could see people staring down at me as though I was a monkey in a cage. I couldn't take that any more. I didn't enjoy my swim.

Well, those were an uncomfortable three weeks. We managed to get to Dover, were met by my father, drove up to London. And then, not very long after, William Ellis Grammar School in London.

I became extremely withdrawn; I did try to socialise – I just met one or two who I would find responding to me as an individual, but I couldn't get involved in a group or anything like that. The only time when people responded was in a negative way. I was teased because I had an accent; I was teased all the time.

A group of students from the school invited me out to a party. I didn't know them, but they were from my class. I said OK, why not? We went to the house of one of them. His parents were away.

It was the first time I realised they were smoking hashish. They wanted me to try this. And so the whole exercise was to see how Pren behaves when he gets high! They gave me some; but I wouldn't have any more because I wouldn't be able to face my parents – especially my mother. I wasn't so frightened of my father because I knew he wouldn't beat me – he's never beaten me. My mother used to beat me up and I used to take it. And of course I deserved it! [Laughs]

The London underground was a frightening experience for me – I always felt people were hostile. I used to get harassed in the streets by youths; skinheads attacked us in the pub; I was abused many times by youths Paki-bashing and all this business. Had a tremendous negative social effect on me. Eventually I was frightened of getting out of the house, wanting to avoid contact with people.

There was another circle – that is the children of people from the Movement. And I've stuck with them ever since.

I hardly knew my father, that's true. I hardly knew him. I know that when I was at school in South Africa, the principal, Sister Teresa, used to call my sister and me during school hours and say: Children, your father is back from prison. Go my dears! And she'd make the cross on our foreheads and say a little prayer, and we'd rush off. Soon as we turn our backs away from her, my sister would burst out crying. I wouldn't understand, but she would run off – and I'd walk behind her and think: What a silly girl! Papa is home. So what?

I mean – Jesus! – I never thought that going into prison was so serious. But the emotion of my sister, really, was the thing that stirred me. She used to run screaming, crying – and she'd run home, I'd follow after her. And approaching home I could feel the emotion developing. Then I walk a bit faster, walk . . . run up the staircase. When I'd see my dad, I'd go and jump on him, OK?

But I don't think that I've really understood everything I felt emotionally. Once I went with my mother to give food. We have a Diwali celebration, and we used to pack little foodstuffs for all the prisoners in my father's prison – he was in Tongaat then. And my mother took me along to go and give the stuff into the prison.

So we walked into this place – and I remember this very vividly, you know – we gave the stuff in; and then as we were walking out I could hear somebody saying: Son! Son! And we looked up. And there he was holding on to the grilles, like this! I think he was probably trying to lift himself up by his hands, to such high windows. But then he spoke to my mother in Tamil. All I can remember was: And how are you, son? And I said: Fine. And that was it.

But still then there wasn't any feeling that this is dad, this is a warm feeling. I hardly knew him.

He left before we did, and went to Botswana. And when he used to phone home, for me there wasn't any urgency – Oh, this is dad! Let me speak to him! There wasn't really anything like that. My mother used to go into hysterics, my sister as well. But for me, it was . . . it was: Let me take my football and go and have a game. I never felt it. I never felt any warmth or anything like that.

Once I came home late. I was building a relationship with a girl, so I spent time after school with her. I should have been home by half past four, instead it was now going on to six; it was getting dark and my parents were frantic. Why hadn't I come from school yet? He was coming along the road; and he stopped the car and he said: Get in. I thought: I'm going to get a thrashing now!

So he brought me home. But he wouldn't, he couldn't . . . He just wouldn't lift a finger. He even found it difficult to shout at me. I could feel his voice was breaking – I would burst out crying. He didn't do anything to me, he didn't hurt me at all – but I would start crying. And then my mother would say: Go and tell him sorry. And that was it – that sort of a relationship.

If we wanted something he would always give it to us. Even when he was very low on money. And that was a wonderful thing. We played a lot of billiards together, snooker, and this is what built our friendship.

There were moments when he'd talk about prison and I used to enjoy and listen – like when the police warders were harassing political prisoners. He would talk about how others were behaving, and I'd listen to those. But I can't remember anything he related where he was involved – I think I'd walk away or shut myself off. I would probably tell myself: Oh no, it's lies anyway. I could never take it. Now I can't understand that behaviour.

My cousin was more mature than I, and he used to read a lot – I only read science books. When my father started talking politics to my cousin I'd start listening; and then I'd put my head down and I'd think of something else. And when I think back, I hate myself for doing that because I could have understood more. But it's a sad thing that I didn't.

Later of course, after he died, I started trying to – and my mother's collecting all the stuff for me to read and all that sort of thing. And I'm understanding more now. My experience in Africa for the last decade has been tremendous really. I feel different. But I hardly knew him, I hardly knew him.

I know he tried to be a model father. For an Indian father to stand naked in front of his son was something . . . something unimaginable. But the first time we went swimming together with relatives of ours in Scotland when we were visiting our sister; after the swimming we were drying ourselves, and he stood naked – he didn't cover himself.

And smoking – he found out that I was hiding the smoking; and now in an Indian family that's very difficult. You don't just allow people to smoke. But he tried to be a modern father, so he says: Son, if you're smoking, you smoke. Do it in front of me. I don't like you hiding behind my back – that's what I don't like. But I'd still hide – it felt uncomfortable to smoke in front of him, and I didn't.

I don't think I could understand why he was away so much. I knew he was in prison, but not the details of it. And even when we came to England, he was away; he used to travel a lot.

So I hardly knew my dad. And for some reason or the other, I was always trying to keep away from him or not being responsive to him – and I don't think he was to blame for it. I don't know who's to blame or what. I don't think I know how to analyse it, really. I think it must have been difficult for him to get into my heart and mind, as much as it was difficult for me to get into my dad's mind and heart. I don't think I could understand why he was away so much. I knew when he was in prison, but not the details of it all. And even when we came to England he used to travel a lot.

MATSOBANE SEXWALE
The Hague 1990

'I am always scared that maybe I don't belong . . . But it's exciting to go back to this mystified place. This place, I've never lived there.'

She is a younger version of her mother, Bunie Sexwale. As a child she was a participant in a battle she could scarcely comprehend.

In a way, sometimes it's as if I was born in exile. OK, it's true enough that Lesotho is very, very similar to South Africa; it's basically one thing, except that it has its own border and it's independent. We used to go from Lesotho and visit our grandparents in South Africa, and that's when you realise that, hey, you have not really experienced all these things. OK, you've read about them, but you've not really had point-blank experiences – petty things like different toilets for whites and blacks, and stuff like that.

Once we took a trip with this family who were visiting Lesotho from Norway. But it became so complicated – this is in the Eighties somewhere. When we stopped for lunch we had to use different toilets from the ones they used, because they were white. And that was something I hadn't experienced in Lesotho.

I do remember the raid, yes, I do. It's pretty vivid. I have a very vivid memory about that. I was ten at the time. I don't know how exactly to describe it . . . baffling experience. It was in December, the middle of summer. I was sleeping in my aunt's bedroom; and I don't know why but there was an ironing board that hadn't been folded. So that's the first thing that woke me up, I just heard the ironing board BOOM! on the floor. 'Oh Mama! Mama! Auntie! what's happening?' And then the next thing I remember was my father trying to get into the room. For some reason the door wouldn't open, and he opened from the bottom and he just said, 'Down!'

And I knew what it meant, we'd kind of been prepared for it, if you can say that, because in Lesotho they have this LLA, Lesotho Liberation Army, in opposition. But they were based outside Lesotho in one of the Bantustans, and they used to have bombing raids into Lesotho. We knew that they were working with the Boers; and my parents prepared us for . . . just in case, they might go to the extent that they come and bomb ANC members' houses. So my father used to play little army games, throw a pretended hand-grenade and shout 'Down!' and we'd all go down. I mean, it's only later when I grew up that I noticed that it was kind of training. We took it as a game.

So it was like I knew immediately what he meant when he said, 'Down!' My aunt leapt out on one side of the bed and I went on the other side. I don't know how long it was – it felt like a very long time to me. All the shooting was going on and I remember very well that I wanted to go to the toilet badly, but I would not dare to pee on the floor. Because it was like the only thing that was going through my mind was that when all this is over, when mama comes in . . . they find that I've peed on the floor, I would get into trouble. I would probably be beaten for it! [Laughs]

I kind of knew it was the Boers, but it was all very hazardous and confused and I was very frightened. I was. I was. I just remember trying to whisper to my aunt, I want to go to the toilet, I want to go to the toilet. I don't remember if in that room they threw any grenades or anything, but later she told me she was trying to tell me to grab something to put over me, because I was scared and shivering from fright.

My sister was in another room, with a friend of ours, also a South African, Nomagqabi, and that's where the main thing took place. We hadn't moved into that house for very long, and the person who lived there before us installed burglar proofs in that room only. So I don't know; they probably assumed it was the main bedroom. I know they were spying on us. There used to be a car that came. The first few times we thought that the person has lost his way – it was a white man. Our house was at a corner, so he'd just come around the corner. When he gets close, slow down, go round the corner and then a few minutes later he comes back, the same direction, the same speed and everything. Fast, slow. So I would have thought that they would know that it wasn't the main bedroom.

I think my sister and Nomagqabi woke up because their duvets were burning or something; the blankets were burning. Their school classes had been learning about fire; this fire drill leapt into their minds. Hey, fire! The first thing is you close all the windows. So they tried to close the windows, but all the glass was broken. So they went into my parents' room next door and they lay low. The shooting went on for a while, felt like hours to me. And then it stopped. I remember somebody saying, 'Let's go!' I was too scared to move from where I was; I didn't even dare to look up and shout to my auntie. And then after a while the shooting started again; and then . . . a short while later, ja, my father came and we went out of the room. And I remember I was about to go out and I was just caught by fire coming from the room opposite.

Anyway we went out, and into the neighbour's garden, and found that they'd shot the cow next door, I have no idea why. We went into that other house and found that a woman in there had been shot as well. Apparently her baby had woken up and was crying, I suppose from all this commotion, so she lit a candle and they shot at that. She died that night, I remember.

And it's funny; the first thing I thought about when we were outside and our house was burning, was that my mother had bought us a cake the previous day, because we'd cleaned up our rooms. That's the first thing I remembered: oh, that lovely cake we had in the fridge! It's all gone now! [Laughs] It's quite amazing that that was the first thing that struck me, instead of: the house is burning down, I don't have any more clothes, I don't have anything actually, because I was sleeping only in a vest. But I was worried about the cake! And my father had these special boots he really loved. That's the first thing he thought of: Ah, my boots! [Laughs] My aunt was supposed to go the next day back to South Africa. And that's the first thing she remembered: Oh, I was going to go home!

We tried to phone the fire brigade. Behind our house there was a policeman who lived there; so my aunt and my mother went to get him to use the phone, but he wouldn't open. But then we got through at another house and the fire brigade said all their cars were broken or something like that; which I thought was an excuse, because I don't think it's possible that throughout the whole of Maseru they wouldn't have at least one fire brigade working.

It remained with me for a long time. I had nightmares. It does affect me. I have, I hope, worked it out and I think I've learned to live with it. But I do get those things once in a while. Like my last school was next to an army training base; once I was just sitting in the study room, and from there, I could always hear shooting when they were practising; but that particular day I just started shivering and shaking and I was . . . it just came back altogether as a nightmare. It just came all over me and I was really in a bad state. And it happened another time – not very long ago – that I went with some friends to the beach, and there were fireworks. I've never been allergic to fire-crackers or anything, but that day I was just reliving the whole nightmare and it was really quite bad. I was with two friends and I don't think either one of them understood – OK they may have sympathised, but they didn't understand. I mean, it's just fire-crackers! What exactly is it?

Now that I know more I think it would have been nice to have professional help to deal with this, ja. But one thing I'm thankful about was that family help was available to me, so I was able to work it out. I talked about it with my mother as well so it's like I've kind of reconciled with it. But there's still that lacking . . . the need for professional help, psychological help or something. Ja, I think it would have been helpful.

With the current things happening in the country, it would be nice to return to South Africa, it really would. But I still think that for a long time, I will face the same thing I'm facing in most of the countries that I've lived in: that OK, I'm there, physically I'm there; but it doesn't matter how much your friends or people around you make you feel welcome, you still don't feel you belong. You go around the world, and when anybody's asking, 'What are you?' you say, 'I'm South African.' I eat pap, I eat samp, I eat all sorts of South African food. But I am always scared that maybe I won't belong there either. OK, I'll proudly say I'm South African. But I don't want to say that I'm scared to go back to that mystified place. This place I've seen; I've never lived there. So I will see.

It is exciting to think about it. But I don't know . . . I think I would love to live there, settle there. I think, ja I will. Being over eighteen, I'm in a better position than people who are younger. A lot of children are going to be in a helluva situation in that they do not have a choice. Their parents want to go back, so they have to follow because they're too young to stay. I can make a choice.

But I would like to go back educated. If I do get a scholarship to go to university, I'll grab that chance and take it; get myself educated and be hopefully more productive, have something to give to the country than just being unemployed or doing unskilled things.

But I feel it's wrong to say I'll go back after apartheid is over. Because if you say that, who is going to fight for that apartheid to be over? If you are sitting out here and are not doing anything about it?

Born in Exile

They must establish their own sense of identity; and perhaps their loyalties will always be split between the place where they were born and spent their early years, and the country to which their parents belong.

But that place is remote, unknown. The reality is where they are now. In fact their parents, like so many exiles, have often moved around to different countries and their children have become cosmopolitan. They will be fortunate if they can feel that the world is wide open to them and that they can live anywhere.

TANYA HODGSON
London 1990

'I'd say I'm largely South African, but I think a little bit will always be German and a little bit will always be British.'

Her father Spencer came into exile with his parents – Jack and Rica – when he was still young. He trained as an architect in Leipzig, then went to work as chief architect in Mazimbu for many years. Since this interview, she and her parents have all returned to South Africa.

I was born in Leipzig in the GDR, 1970. My mother's German and my father's South African. Lived there until I was four and then we came to England, stayed here until I was nine and then went to Tanzania to the ANC School. My father and my mother worked there for ten years, and I went to school there; finished my O levels, and then came back to England to do my As. And I'm about to emigrate again! [Laughs] I'm going to join my parents in Zimbabwe.

I can vaguely remember coming to England. I can remember the language barrier – it gave me a bit of a hang-up about languages forever, because we were speaking English at home all the time so that my mother could learn English quite quickly. I found it very inhibiting, because I didn't feel comfortable speaking with my parents in German when they were speaking English; and I didn't feel confident enough in English. Finally my mother got quite concerned and discussed it with the teacher and the teacher said, 'Well, I'm afraid your daughter speaks better English than you do; she has to get the courage to speak it.' Ever since then I've always been very sort of shy about starting any new language.

I went to two schools within a very short space of time. I remember finding that quite frightening because I'd just come out of a small kindergarten. All of a sudden you're in a big school of about five hundred pupils, in a class of about thirty, and you don't speak the same language they speak.

I can't remember a time when South African politics wasn't there – it's always been there in our home one way or the other. My father was a member of the ANC in the GDR; and so South Africans have always been there, we've always mixed with South Africans. I can remember vaguely lying awake one night – I must have been six – and having these images of what I would do if only I was powerful enough. Very childish, that big feeling of wanting to do something and do it instantly. Not quite realising that I couldn't change South Africa by just waving a wand, you know. I was sure that if I wished hard enough it would happen.

When I first went to Mazimbu in 1979, which was only two years after it was established, they didn't have a primary school; they only had about thirty students and one teacher for the secondary school, and a small so-called International School in Morogoro – that's where I went for about a year and a half. And then the primary school in SOMAFCO got under way and I went straight into that.

We were in a small community, and English was spoken by . . . well, almost everybody over fifteen spoke English, so the language question didn't affect me much. I can't say I found myself terribly isolated ever, although for years I was the only white student in the school. But it wasn't ever a major problem, no.

I have very happy memories of that primary school but then I was in a very small class of four, an advanced class, the only one at the time. And then when I went into the secondary school I was also again in this quite small class of about fourteen. But I knew the core of the people so well. We all went straight through together.

I was very happy there in many ways. In a lot of ways I still consider it a home, even though I know that that isn't home, and that isn't a normal way to live. Between nine and seventeen are very formative years of your life, and living in such a closed community was all I knew as a teenager. It never really bothered me much. Having my parents there helped. I have to admit that, if my parents hadn't been there, I would probably have felt very different about it. But mine were always there.

We used to spend a lot of time just sitting and chatting with each other or getting around the complex. I spent a lot of time working on a student committee – I was eventually on the Student Council. I've always been a great reader, so I spent masses of time reading; I used to eat up books. It doesn't sound like much. There wasn't anything specific there, but there was just so much space to do what you wanted. You could create huge massive games, taking vast amounts of space, all in your imagination; you'd play the whole day away and would suddenly realise that you've got to get home before it gets dark. It was great, because you just had loads of exercise and you're outside all the time, you're relatively safe. It was a lot safer than in London. And you were exhausted at the end of your day, you just went and conked out! [Laughs]

They only went up to O levels at SOMAFCO, so when I was seventeen I applied to do A levels in England, got a scholarship and spent two years there. Didn't do very well, so I decided to take a year off and work. That's what I'm doing now, but not for much longer because I want to go back to school soon. I want to study urban and rural planning.

How do I identify myself? I'd say I'm largely South African but I think a little bit of me will always be German and a little bit will always be British. I'm not sure that I could ever live permanently in either of those countries. I haven't been to Germany for too long but I've lived in England for three years. I still don't feel at home here, this isn't my place. But there are things I like about England, just small things; the way people can be friendly on the streets, the way you can go into a shop and end up in a conversation about something completely irrelevant for twenty minutes.

Although being the only white student in Mazimbu didn't create any specific problems, there were things that I only realised afterwards . . . things that you didn't do, or things that you always did do, because you were white and you stuck out. It wasn't conscious, but simply engrained. You didn't not go to a meeting and you didn't not attend a class – not that bunking's a good thing to do, but loads of my friends got away with it and I probably wouldn't. Somebody would have noticed immediately that I wasn't there.

And you don't realise it, but South Africans in Tanzania were very obviously foreigners, regardless of the fact that they were black. In Tanzania it creates an immediate barrier when you walk into a market or when you walk into a shop. Even if you speak the rudiments of Kiswahili, people don't communicate beyond a certain point with you. I've enjoyed leaving that behind and being able to just talk to anybody, and to have them happy to talk to you not treating you like a foreigner.

I hope to go to South Africa and make my home there. I do hope to go, I do, very much. Eight years of living in a South African community has given me quite a strong South African identity, and I very much want to go and at least give it a try and give it my all. That's maybe one of the reasons why I don't feel at home here – I haven't tried to feel at home because I've always felt it's temporary.

I'm very scared of going back to South Africa – you live with a dream for twenty years and all of a sudden it's going to be reality, and it is a bit frightening. But I'm sure that's not just for me, I'm sure that's for everybody. I am nervous of having to start again, starting to settle down somewhere else, find new friends again. But I'm also very excited about it. You know, I want to try and study there possibly, and see what I can give back to the society, and see if it can be a home for me. And if it can't, then I don't know where I would go, but that's a bridge I'm going to cross when I get there. I'm not going to worry about it too much, because I can't solve those problems now.

Mazimbu gave me a very strong sense of identity as a South African. I've noticed in my own peer group who were either born outside South Africa or left very young, a part of them will always be connected to South Africa. It's not something that they can just forget about, especially if their parents have been involved in the struggle. But at the same time they're not very sure that they are South African. Whereas growing up in Mazimbu always made me very sure that I was a South African, and a little less sure about everything else.

I remember once at Mazimbu talking with some friends about the possibility of going home, jokingly. I was just sort of voicing my fears and saying that, you know, I was scared because I didn't really feel that I had a right to claim my South African citizenship. And the most heartening thing was that they turned round and said, 'Of course you do. You're a South African! We'll vouch for you!' It was . . . it was such a strong sense of identity. I've never had it about somewhere else.

PAUL MOHAMED
Århus, Denmark 1990

'It was an experience for us who never had seen so many things. We'd never even seen buses.'

His father Amin left South Africa because 'he just couldn't stick house-arrest'. He worked as a fisherman on the lakes and rivers of Botswana until Godfrey Beck arranged for the family to move to Denmark so that Paul's autistic brother could receive treatment.

My parents were living in Botswana for ten years or something; and then they got me. I was born in Botswana. I was just got eleven years the time I came here to Denmark.

My parents left South Africa because those Boers, they promised that next time if they would catch my father they will take his head as a souvenir, ja! [Laughs] So, well, I mean, he was very politically involved in what was going on against apartheid. He was one of those who would speak up. He could make people, through talk, to go in action. So there was a necessity to move to Botswana. My mother came a few years after, together with my bigger brother. My father ran away from South Africa without giving any information of his going because he couldn't take any chances. Because otherwise people will talk with their mouths. After two years, when he'd settled down in Botswana, he wrote, so then she found him good and safe.

I was living at Lake Nkapi I think the name is, out in the forest. We had crocodiles and giraffes and lions and buck – all kinds of animals there. It was up north. My father was working as a fisherman. He'd done a lot of small jobs, with cars and with meat and clothes and donkeys. We were living right out in the forest, and it was also very near to the border, so we were taught that you can't trust anybody.

I was taught to be on my toes all the time. We practised being prepared to get my brothers together and to divide ourselves, because any car that came might be a car with bombs, from the Death Squads. As one of seven years old I had an experience of one of fourteen years old. I had to grow up fast.

My father had to leave Botswana – it was a matter of force – because they found out at last where we were in Botswana, so we had to do something. My big brother is autistic and handicapped, so it was the ANC who helped.

I just got eleven years when we came to Denmark, and everything was new for me because as a little boy I lived a different kind of life.

So we entered Denmark in 1980 and here it was an experience for us who never had seen so many things. We'd never even seen buses; to climb on the buses and ride down town it was kind of an experience; to switch on all the electric lights because we'd grown up in the bush, ja, in the bush me and my big brother. And there our enjoyment, our pleasure, was to go out into the lake and take a nice swim. We were aware of crocodiles – sometimes there might come a crocodile and try to swim after us, but there was always my father around to hit it over the nose with a stick or something. So well, ja! It was very strange here. But ja, it was just like an adventure.

It was not so difficult to learn Danish because my parents speak Afrikaans. It is, so to say, a mixture of all kinds of languages from Germany, Denmark, Holland, so it was not so difficult to learn Danish.

But I'm not Danish. I will always be a South African in Denmark! [Laughs] I've spent most of my life here, never actually been to South Africa. But I've spent most of my life here as a South African. I would like to go back one day but . . . yes, but first I want to have had all my education and then I'm ready to go back. That's my weapon and I'm ready. I'm prepared that one day when I go back then it's not going to be silk and stars, it's going to be rough and raw and hard. I'm prepared for that.

NANDI SILENA VILEIKA
Stockholm 1990

'I don't know if I'm South African, I don't know if I'm a Brit. But I'll never be a Swede.'

> Her mother, Madi Gray, said, 'There is an old British law which allows unmarried mothers to choose a surname for their children, so we thought that we would give Nandi her own independent name.'

My naming was a hangover from the flowerchild, hippy days of my parents. My father is Swedish, Bertil Ergero, and my mother is South African, Madi Gray. They never married, and when I was inside my mother's tummy they discussed names and asked friends in different countries to send in names. They liked Nandi and Silena, and neither are very common names.

The reason I have my own surname is because Nandi doesn't go with Ergero or Gray. I'm my own person, so I should have my own surname.

I was born in London. I think we lived there for a few months and then we moved down to Tanzania. We moved around in Southern Africa for a couple of years. When I was about two, we came to Sweden for the first time. I lived a few years with my father in Mozambique and I've gone back down there as much as I can.

Otherwise I've basically lived in Sweden. But I'll never be a Swede, I can tell you that. I'll never be able to identify with them, never. I know the Swedish system and I know the Swedes. And I know I'm not the same. I don't know if I'm South African, I don't know if I'm a Brit. I've always considered Mozambique to be my second home. Then . . . now, maybe, South Africa; I will see what happens. But here, I don't identify with the culture, different ways of communicating between people. Nobody would smile in the streets here. Nobody would help anybody here. In Mozambique, if a car broke down, everybody came out of their stores and just said, 'OK let's get the car going.' They didn't even ask. Here one can be ten years old, crying in the street, and nobody will help you. They'll just look at you as if you're a maniac, an alien or something. Things like that are very vital for me.

I've recently been to South Africa with my mother. I felt that it was different there to Swedish ways. One registers each other in a different way. There's more space for love, for humanity there than here. Here things are concentrated on getting . . . what's it called? ja, possessions and positions and trying to get high status. Down there, you know, it's more a question of surviving; which means there's more space for being together, caring for each other. Different.

My friends were mostly so-called coloured. We were in Cape Town and ja, there were occasional whites and occasional blacks but most of them were so-called Cape coloureds. I suppose, I'm not very good at this ... [Laughs] ... I actually had to ask a friend there, who was what! And, ja, we were out in townships. Friends of Madi offered to take me out into townships and so on; but I've seen them before, I don't need to see them again and I don't want to see them again, not as they are now. There's no point of my going in there, I don't want to go as a tourist just to have a look.

My friends were all very politically conscious. The whites that I met were family and old friends of friends and so on with daughters my age. They only looked straight ahead and didn't see very much. They didn't see any ... oh, what's the word? – context, they couldn't put anything into any context. I mean they'd really been fooled into the South Africa white system. They asked me things like how do you look at South Africa coming from Europe, and so on. We were just not at all on the same level. It was very difficult to understand them and for them to understand me.

Is this not going to make it difficult for you to adjust to living in South Africa?

Well, there's always those kinds of problems. In Sweden, I've chosen my friends who have the same basic ideas of life and politics and living as I have, and I'll probably have to do the same thing there. The problem there will probably be that they are about twice my age, most of them! [Laughs] I don't know why. The thing is, here in Sweden, everybody is very, very tied up on age. Very tied up on age. If you meet somebody in a pub or something, the first thing they'll ask you is your age, not your name. In South Africa, it's like, 'Hello, who are you?' And we're two people that are meeting and the age isn't as important.

I'm thinking, OK, say I don't want to live in South Africa? Do I want to live in Sweden? And I know I don't want to live the rest of my life here. Then the question comes, where do I want to live? Those kinds of things, I'm not really sure of, but I suppose they'll sort themselves out sooner or later.

Where is Home?

CLAIRE RANDEREE
Berlin 1990

'I have the hope that maybe after a short while we go to South Africa, because things are changing and we want to have a home together in a country where one of us belongs.'

> The place where she was born was known as East Germany, Soviet Occupied Zone. Then it became the German Democratic Republic. Now it is part of Germany. There she met her husband, a South African living in exile.

He was a student, he came here in 1974 and I met him in 1976. Our daughter was born 1978. Then we got married in 1983. The problems were that we had to apply for a permit; you first apply to get the permission to apply. So this first application for the application took us about seven or eight months. [Laughs] And then we had to state whether we intend to stay in the GDR or abroad, and if we say abroad, that means I must go for good.

So we said, OK, we go abroad, we don't stay in the GDR, because my husband didn't like to stay, he wanted to go back to Africa.

After getting married, we stayed in the GDR for two more years because he was still a student. And when he finished he was supposed to leave the country, but he waited for me. I didn't get the permission until September and then there was another delay because I didn't get my passport. They said we can have the passport in four weeks; and the air tickets were ready, everything was booked – a cheap flight, where you have to either take the date or lose the money, paid by my father-in-law. But it took four months.

We first applied to go to Canada for a visit because my husband's parents are staying there since 1980. But that was refused. To go to Canada for permanent stay was complicated, because Canada didn't consider us immigrants. We could go to Canada only on a tourist basis, and that the GDR wouldn't accept. So for Canada I applied to come as a tourist but for the GDR I declared to go to Canada as an immigrant.

We went to Canada, and we stayed with his parents just four months. Then my husband got a bit impatient because we wanted to start working in East Africa. We didn't have anybody to ask how it would be there; we just knew that the ANC is expecting us to come as soon as we can.

We went to Mazimbu straight from Winnipeg, for me to work as a doctor and my husband as an agriculturalist. In the end he became manager of the farm in Mazimbu. We came in April 1986 and stayed until 1989.

In the beginning, of course, it was very hard, because we didn't know what to expect. I must say I expected it worse, ja, because there was no information on life in Africa; nobody could really tell me. Some people who had been there exaggerated and say, 'You don't need to take anything from your household because they provide you with everything.' Then some others we met in Canada had been in Mazimbu and came back for health reasons; and they said, 'It's terrible, it's just terrible. You'll be hungry, you'll be crowded in your house and there is just nothing you can do because everything is limited; the administration allows nobody any freedom.' Now, I found it was something in between.

We had to share a house. You know, I have been working for fourteen years before we left, I was independent all the time even as a student. When I was eighteen I left home, I was always independent. So now to be dependent on the administration and to integrate with other people in the house was very hard. As a family you want your privacy sometimes, and you don't want anybody to interfere with the treatment of your child, and so on. That was very difficult, because when we wanted to talk harsh to her, others were interfering. When we thought something is right, others were saying, 'Well it's not right'; and so on. People trying to educate our child.

She had just started Grade 2 when we left Germany; then came to Canada and she didn't speak a word of English. So we decided just for a few months, we will send her to school in Canada. But she was there for one day only, they didn't allow her to stay in school as a child from behind the Iron Curtain, ja. This is a border town to the USA, Anderson, near Winnipeg, and some parents complained to the director. She was very unhappy when she was dismissed from school, she was bored in the house, she was all alone, she didn't know any children. Then the first day, she found the children were sociable, and she came back full of joy at lunchtime and then after half an hour, there was a call, 'Please don't send the child back in the afternoon.' And she cried for the whole afternoon, she was sitting in the corner crying. Nobody could comfort her. And we all felt so bad about that.

After some days my father-in-law complained to a parliament member of Manitoba about this, he said a child of seven years can't be a spy, and then it was decided she can go back to school.

Then we come to Mazimbu, and the language was no problem at all. She started with Zulu right at the first day. Children are integrating very fast. Some children tried to be her friends, but there were some other children who shouted at her and threw stones and beat her with sticks, saying, 'Go away, you're white!' And such things, you know? And that went throughout the whole time there in Mazimbu, that always some children said, you're white. Although she isn't, I mean according to South African rules, she's coloured.

Malaria was the main health problem, and gastro-intestinal infections, skin problems. But a very important point: psychological problems. Some of these problems at Mazimbu could have been solved very easily by changing the conditions in the place. Many students came with problems and these were not recognised as health problems. It was said, 'They are just lazy to study; they think Mazimbu's a holiday resort, but this is a liberation movement, there are hardships to be taken.' I think it was very wrong, because there are hardships enough for exiles anyway, so if there are ways to relieve this a little bit, these ways should be taken. But the administration seemed to think: the harder the better. We had it tough when we were young in the struggle, so these people have to get harder. And they didn't care for these problems.

They even tried to ignore problems of people who had been in jail, who had been tortured. We had a social worker from Ireland and she reported about the treatment in Denmark or Norway of torture victims. And it was said right in this meeting, 'We don't have this problem; we don't need to send our people there, we can deal with this.' It's so infuriating! There were many students who had psychological problems.

I mean, I'm telling my own opinion now. When we came the majority of the students were over-age, nearly all of them between twenty and thirty, most of them twenty-five, twenty-six. So at home they had been either working or they were in prison, but all of them independent, out of school for a long time. Now they came to Mazimbu and they are treated like children of twelve. The bell rings, they have to get up; they have to do an hour of labour – which is not bad, but before school it's a bit bad. All these fixed hours . . . and no time for leisure. In the afternoon, classes. After supper, evening studies, news, discussions and then bedtime.

I found it very terrible the way pregnancies were treated, the involuntarily pregnant. These young girls were punished; when the pregnancy was discovered they had to go out of school for a long time, they stay in the Charlottes until the child is two years old. That means nearly three years of interruption. So for them it was better to have abortions.

But this was such a contradiction. They were punished for that, for an abortion, sent to Dakawa and the one who was responsible for the pregnancy was sent also for punishment.

So that was one of my own psychological problems which I found too tough to deal with. The other problem was that I didn't develop in gynaecology and forgot too many things. I was there for three years. I could see that my own profession is not improving. I lose what I have done because there are not enough instruments for doing gynaecology the proper way, and no possibilities of thorough check-ups.

And then the other problem was our child who was in the primary school. Many of the teachers were not trained; sometimes you find that the teacher himself can't spell English but he's teaching English. And we found she was not improving at all. She came in Grade 2 and she left with a standard of late Grade 2 – after three years! And that was the main reason we said, 'No, it's really time we must go.'

We left to Canada. It was offered to us by my father-in-law, that we come there. We stayed there from February until July, and during the whole time we wrote letters and applications. We wanted to settle somewhere – South Africa, that's really what we wanted. We wanted to work in a country which needs us. We thought about Zimbabwe, and we didn't get a reply; then we tried Nicaragua, no reply. Botswana, Lesotho. Saudi Arabia, rejected us straight away because of the communist background.

While this was going on, I had a letter from Zimbabwe saying that they wanted me, but I should have patience. I said I don't have any patience any more because it's five months without work, five months sitting at my parents-in-law's house and only my father-in-law who was working; so it was five people living on one salary. It's too much, five months, it's just too much. And for us, no work, no friends, no nothing, no connection to the outside world. Canada is terrible in itself because of the climate and also the importance money has got, the importance . . . consumption, ja. Advertisements everywhere, everything is interrupted by this; and your eye first jumps to such a thing, and it's disturbing your whole life. I found it so . . . what can I say . . . detestable.

I didn't want to live for ever in such conditions. My husband, Hassan, was saying that he wants to stay in Canada for as long as it takes to get a Canadian passport.

Then I said, 'But I can't stay on. I don't want to be Canadian.' I have to work, and in Canada it's very difficult to find work because our degrees are not recognised. You have first to do the exams again; and I don't have much trust in my abilities after three years of just doing this narrow spectrum of things. I'm forty-two and my memory is not that well any more.

So I came to the GDR and I found work immediately. After two weeks I started working and fortunately I found a place to stay; which isn't my own and nothing belongs to me – not even a cup, not a fork but . . . [Laughs] . . . it's home. It's a home.

I have the hope that after maybe a short while we go to South Africa because things are changing and we want to have a home together in a country where one of us belongs. Hassan would never agree to come here and be the victim of all kinds of racialism. It was bad before, but nobody actually attacked us. But that is what is happening now. You cannot be safe, especially if you're a couple like we are.

But for my daughter, it's difficult for her to have a sense of identity, of what country she belongs to. Something very terrible happened the Thursday before Easter. She went to a park to meet some friends there. It was afternoon, four o'clock. Three girls approached her and said, 'Foreigner! Foreigners out! Germany belongs to Germans!' And then she shouted back, she said, 'First of all I'm not a foreigner, I have been born here, and secondly what do you have against foreigners?' And then they said, 'They've taken our jobs away' – they were children, maybe fourteen, fifteen, not really adults, but bigger than she is – 'they are taking our jobs and they don't belong here and they are raping our women!' You know – children! Girls! So she said, 'You stupid fools,' or something, and they started already chasing her and slapping her and she ran away out of the park, to the home of a girlfriend.

There she said, she must go back to the park . . . she explained to me that she wanted to go back to the park to play, but I think now she had somebody else for support, she wanted to deal with them again. She went there and they were still there and started afresh. And then two boys joined these three big girls and all five of them started to beat my daughter, threw her down, kick her with feet. And some adults have been observing this and they didn't interfere. Only one old man, he said, 'You are Nazis!' And they threw stones at him, so that he had to run away, the old man.

She came home; she was full with sand and tears and everything. And then she said she wants to go home. And she wants to know: 'Where is this?'

EPILOGUE

The Return

'Before' does not exist for 'them', the 'others', those who stayed behind. For 'them' it was all continuity, for you it was a fugue of disruptions. The thread is lost. The telling has shaped the story. You made your own history at the cost of not sharing theirs. The eyes, having seen so many different things, now see differently.

Breyten Breytenbach

While I was wandering around Africa and Europe and North America interviewing exiles, the talks that prefigured apartheid's admission of failure had already begun in Pollsmoor Prison, and the era of going into exile was coming to an end. By the time the stories had been collected and edited and put in the hands of the publishers, many of the people in this book – probably the majority – had returned to South Africa. SOMAFCO had been disassembled and the sites at Mazimbu and Daka-wa with all the buildings, the school with its laboratories and equipment, the dormitories and administration blocks, the many houses, the farms and small industries, together with all the plans for future projects, had been given to the Tanzanians.

The communities of exiles in Dar es Salaam, Lusaka, Harare, London, were being dismembered, the continuity of companionship shredded, individual families once again divided. Those who stay are lonely, bereft, they feel deserted. Those who have gone enter a different country to the one they left, physically different in the thirty-year growth and change of towns and populations, subjectively different in unshared experiences and burgeoning new generations, where the familiar has become unfamiliar, and 'one must learn, all over again, each time from the beginning, the trick of going on.'*

Nobody had envisaged that freedom to return would come this way. The dream had been of a return one day when apartheid was finished,

---

* Eva Hoffman, *Lost in Translation*, Mandarin, London, 1991.

when it was overthrown. Now the road had opened up while apartheid was still in operation; white government, racial laws, Bantu education, Bantustans, political, economic and social discrimination and oppression – the whole ghastly structure. It was the exiles' opposition to apartheid that had driven them away and kept them out. Now this was no longer an insurmountable barrier to returning home, but there was no sense of triumph or fulfilment.

The traditional extended family that had been left behind had been reshaped in exile in a different form. Its members were no longer blood relatives, but relatives of heart and mind, bound together both by the immorality that had driven them out and by the loss and bereavement of what they had left. Memories of events, place, shared experience, under-standing without explanations – these brought South Africans together wherever they were.

Now this family in exile was itself to be broken, its members dispersed, its generations separated. The declaration of 2 February 1990 imposed on them a future for which there had been no prior preparation, and one filled with palpable uncertainties.

The excitement and joy of return, of reunification, is soon tempered by the practical problems of settlement and readjustment. And the deeper problems of reconciliation, to heal the wounds of pain and resentment arising from all those separated years; from those who left, a sense of loss from having been absent from and becoming marginal to an essential period of their own history, and guilt for having gone; from those who stayed, the hurt at the feeling of betrayal, of having been abandoned. Each holds their own pain of separation, of all the fears, the terrors, they have experienced, of the lost years. But they are different fears, not shared experiences; the time was too long, so neither can understand fully the pain of the other.

After an agreement for the repatriation of 40,000 exiles was negotiated between Nelson Mandela and F. W. de Klerk, the UN High Commis-sioner for Refugees in August 1991 described this as 'the beginning of the end of a thirty-year-old human tragedy'.

To believe that the exile story is coming to an end is like believing – as evidently many people do – that apartheid is now finished. The scaffold-ing – the laws and edicts – on which apartheid was constructed has been removed; but the edifice that apartheid built remains: the divided popu-lations in Soweto, Lenasia, in Mitchell's Plain, in the Bantustans; the generations deformed by an educational system that has now reached complete breakdown; an economy built on grossest inequalities so that today 7 million people live in shack settlements. Apartheid was an economic tool, and as yet the transformation has hardly begun.

And so it is with the exile experience. 'The inescapable fact is that no return is solely a return; it is a new migration. Those who return are not the same people they were when they left, and the place they return to is not the same place.'*

The dead are buried, but on the living the scars remain. The rift can never be healed.

* L. and R. Grinberg, *Migration and Exile*, Yale University Press.

Appendix

I interviewed more than 330 South African exiles, who gave freely of their experiences and their feelings. All the stories were worthy of inclusion and I was loath to relinquish each one, but I had obviously interviewed far more than could be incorporated in one book. The objective was to include as wide and representative a selection as possible, and the decision as to which stories to select was made – with some disagreement – by myself and my editor.

It was only through listening to so many that the themes and structure of the book emerged, and all the interviews contributed significantly to the final formation. I am therefore deeply grateful to these exiles whose generosity made the book possible, but whose interviews could not be included.

All the interviews have been deposited in the history archives of the University of the Western Cape in South Africa.

In addition to those who appear in this book, I interviewed also: Alan Abelsohn. Anthony Akerman. Zubeida Barmania. Steve Batji. Pascal Beck. Terry Bell. Hamid and Zabie Bhyat. Naeema Bhyat. Dr and Joan Bismillah. Maggie and John Bizzell. Kagiso Boipelo. Thami Bonga. Vuyiswa Bonga. Kami Brodie. Angela Brown. Cheryl and Ian Bruce. May Brutus. Margie Bruun-Meyer. Ann Burroughs. Hajoo Carim. Mac Carim. Joel Carlson. Grace Cloete. Marcus Cloete. Neville Colman. Stelios Comninos. Joe Cotton. Archie Criel. Gemma and Jeremy Cronin. Rosemary da Silva. Lungi Daweti. Janice Dembo. Prakash Diar. Ramnie Dinath. Esau du Plessis. Fritz and Mala Dullay. Enoch Duma. Joan Fairweather. Barry Feinberg. Basil Freeman. Doodles Gaboo. Hotep Galeta. Tandi Gcabashe. Denis Goldberg. Phyllis Goldblatt. Enoch Gqomo. Madi Gray. Joe Gumede. Eve and Tony Hall. Andrew Hall. Trish and Derek Hanekom. John Hansen. David Hartman. Rica Hodgson. Jonathan Holman. Gerry and Sally Israelstam. Anton Johnston. Stanley Jonathan. Catherine and Richard Jurgens. Kavan Kajee. Kamoo Kajee. Andrew and Christopher Kasrils. Mpho Keagile. Helaine Kentridge. Ian Kerkhof. Kgaugelo Kgosana. Thami Khaya. Norma Kitson. Graham Koch. Sam Kotane. Theo and Helen Kotze. Barto, Blanche and Eugene la

Guma. Heather Lang. Mandla Langa. Sonny Leshika. Norman Levinrad. Hugh Lewin. Lulu Mabena. Ilva Mackay. Ace Magashule. Mac Maharaj. Vincent Mahaw. Mailie. Abbe Maine. Nontutuzela Majija. Ephraim Make. Malatje. Christina Mamogale. Lindsey Manicom. Duncan Manzini. Barbara Masekela. Gandhi Maseko. Tim Maseko. Boikie Masha. Tieho Masinga. Leo Masoetsa. Andrew Masondo. Wilson Matidze. Aubrey Matlole. Elizabeth Matsemba. John Matshikiza. Gilbert Matthews. Gertrude Matuti. Cedric Mayson. William Mbalosi. David and Judy Mbatha. Blyth Mbityana. Patrick McGluwa. Michael Meli. Gordon Metz. William Mlangeni. Mpho Mmutle. Billy and Yolise Modise. Silver Mogale. Amin Mohammed. Jimmy Mokgosi. Tshepo Molape. Ben Molewa. Mehroonisha Moola. Kesval Moonsamy. Jackie Moroke. Ribbon Mosholi. Peter Motaung. Jackie Motsepe. Motsumi. Fezile Mpehle. Livingstone Mqotsi. Mendi Msimang. Welcom Msomi (Berlin). Jeff Mtembu. George Naicker. Saru Naicker. Indres Naidoo. Shanti Naidoo. Sylvia Neame. Mary and Mike Ngozi. Buras Nhlabathi. Makhunga Njobe. Fanny Nkabinde. Mo Nkadimeng. Solly Nkadimeng. Zinjiva Nkondo. Pitika Ntuli. Sifiso Ntuli. Doctor Nxumalo. Regina Nzo. John Osmers. John and Karin Pampallis. Zandisile Pase. Rashid Patel. Simon Paul. Leshy Paynter. Rose-Innes Phahle. Maud Phillips. Livy Rabalao. Peter Radisi. Freddie Ramaphosa. Thandi Rankoe. Mike Revow. Micky Rosen. Albie Sachs. Michael Sachs. Dunja Sagov. Bobby Sanjay. Mongezi Saul. Michelle Schubert. Aubrey Sedibe. Arnold Selby. Tshepo Selebi. Bert Seraje. Pearl Serote. Evalina Setlogo. Moses Shabangu. Sikhule Shange. The Shikisa Troupe. Larry Shore. Gifford Silayelo. Zoni Silwana. Ray Simons. Eric Singh. Siphiwe. Earl Smith. Brigid and Garth Strachan. Clifford Subayeko. Adelaide Tabela. Adelaide Tambo. Ernie and Liese Tamsen. Matthew Temple. Noma Themba. Steve Thorne. Saeeda Vally-Naidoo. Patrick van Rensburg. Thabisile Vikalala. Mfundi Vundla. Shepherd Williams. Willie Williams. Terence Winburg. Anne-Marie and Harold Wolpe. Nicholas Wolpe. Edith Yengwa. Yelledth Zungu.

Chronology

1948: Election of the first National Party government, led by Dr. D. F. Malan to 1954, succeeded by J. G. Strijdom to 1958; Dr. H. F. Verwoerd to 1966; B. J. Vorster to 1978; P. W. Botha to 1989; F. W. de Klerk.

1950: Suppression of Communism Act, outlawing the Communist Party, and giving Ministerial powers to ban or proscribe other organisations at his discretion. 'Communism' defined *inter alia* as aiming to 'bring about any political, industrial, social or economic change' by unlawful acts or omissions.

26 June. One-day national protest strike called jointly by the Congresses and Communist Party – the first 'Freedom Day'.

Group Areas Act introduced, enabling the government to define which racial group could live, trade or work in any area. 'The paramountcy of the white man and of Western civilisation in South Africa must be ensured . . . '

1951: Joint Planning Council established by ANC and SA Indian Congress to organise Campaign for the Repeal of Discriminatory Legislation – the 'Defiance Campaign'.

1952: 26 June. Freedom Day, the Defiance Campaign starts; over 7,500 volunteers court imprisonment by breaking racially discriminatory laws, and are arrested.

1953: Public Safety Act gives the executive the power to declare a State of Emergency.

Bantu Education Act introduced to limit black education to the degree that it serves the white economy; control of black education transferred from Department of Education to Department of Native Affairs. Minister empowered to decide what schools may exist, terms of teachers' service and content of education; all independent education services for Blacks outlawed, except with Ministerial permission.

1955: Forcible evacuation of people of Sophiatown, Johannesburg, and surrounding black suburbs comprising the Western Areas, all houses bulldozed. Sophiatown subsequently declared to be for 'Whites only' and renamed Triomf (Triumph).

1956: 26 June. Approx. 3,000 delegates from all parts of the country assemble at Kliptown, Johannesburg, for the Congress of the People (COF). The Freedom Charter is adopted in the midst of a police raid.

9 August. In protest against the extension of passes to African women 20,000 women march to Union Buildings, Pretoria.

December. 156 Congress activists from all around the country arrested and charged in Johannesburg with Treason, for campaigning in support of the Freedom Charter – the first modern Treason Trial.

Treason Trial Defence Fund established in South Africa and in London as forerunner to the Defence and Aid Fund.

1959: Extension of Universities Act closes existing universities to Blacks; 'ethnic colleges' established on a tribal basis in black rural areas.

26 June. Anti-Apartheid Movement established at public meeting in London on South African Freedom Day.

1960: 21 March. Shootings at Sharpeville by South African Police leave 69 dead, 180 wounded. Nation-wide protests, strikes, demonstrations and pass-burnings follow.

28 March. National Day of Mourning called by ANC, with nation-wide stay-at-home.

30 March. State of Emergency declared, legal processes suspended, approximately 12,000 people detained and held without trial. Unlawful Organisations Act outlaws ANC and PAC.

1961: March. The Treason Trial finally ends after more than four years, with all accused acquitted.

31 May. South Africa becomes a Republic outside the Commonwealth – without any consultation with the black majority.

October. Whites-only general election called to ratify the Republican constitution. National All-in Conference to oppose the racially exclusive election meets in Pietermaritzburg; Mandela, as keynote speaker, calls for a national General Strike on election day in protest at black exclusion, and then disappears underground. All public meetings prohibited, thousands arrested and detained without trial.

ANC and PAC establish offices 'in exile', and in Dar es Salaam form a SA United Front together with the SA Indian Congress.

16 December: Umkhonto we Sizwe issues its first proclamation explaining its aims and purposes. The first acts of organised sabotage take place in main urban centres.

1962: Arrest of Nelson Mandela on the road between Durban and Johannesburg. Subsequently charged with leaving the country illegally and sentenced to three years' imprisonment.

Sabotage Act introduced, providing a minimum sentence of five years and a maximum of death for sabotage; and house arrest without legal hearing at Minister's discretion; bans on publishing any writings or quotes from banned persons.

1963: General Law Amendment Act allows for prosecution of members of any organisation in existence since 1960 that has subsequently been declared illegal; provides for further bannings of periodicals, individuals and organisations; 90-day detention incommunicado at Minister's discretion; and continued detention of prisoners after the completion of their sentences – the 'Sobukwe clause'.

July. Arrest of Sisulu and other ANC leaders at Rivonia, Johannesburg, all later charged together with Mandela with attempting to overthrow the government by force and violence – the so-called 'Rivonia' Trial.

November. First Urban Bantu Councils set up to 'represent' urban Blacks.

Publications and Entertainments Act gives final absolute control over media.

1964: July. Eight of the Rivonia accused found guilty and sentenced to life imprisonment; one discharged.

General Laws Amendment Act: 'recalcitrant' witnesses can be jailed until prepared to give evidence.

1965: January. 90-day detention replaced by 180-day limit, and extended to permit detention of those required only as witnesses against others.

Criminal Procedure Amendment Act legalises arrest and detention of state witnesses for up to six months; safeguards under Children's Act no longer applicable to 'political' juveniles.

Suppression of Communism Amendment Act extends prohibitions on publication of writings or speeches by banned people, including those in exile.

1966: September. Dr Verwoerd assassinated in Parliament. Minister of Justice B. J. Vorster takes over as Prime Minister.

Defence and Aid Campaign declared an unlawful organisation; receipt of funds from abroad for political purposes prohibited.

1967: July. Combined Umkhonto (MK) and ZAPU force stage incursion into Rhodesia in Wankie (now Hwange) game reserve area, MK intending to carry on into South Africa. First armed clashes between MK and SADF forces leave casualties on both sides.

Defence Act amended to extend period of compulsory military service of white youths, and make all ex-servicemen liable to recall to active service over a twenty-year period.

Terrorism Act extended to cover actions retrospective to 1962, providing also for summary trials with no jury, no bail, unlimited period of detention, and for maintenance of secrecy about detainees even from Parliament.

1968: Prohibition of Political Interference Act prohibits racially mixed membership of any political party.

December. South African Students Organisation (SASO) formed.

1969: Bureau of State Security (BOSS) set up, with extension of Official Secrets Act to cover all information relating to munitions, police or military matters. Prohibition of evidence in any court on matters of state or public security.

1970: July. 2nd SASO Conference; formally adopts designation 'black' to replace 'non-white'.

1971: International Olympic Committee withdraws recognition of South Africa for Munich Olympics in 1972.

Ahmed Timol dies; police say he 'fell from the 10th-floor window at police headquarters, Johannesburg while being interrogated'.

1974: Decree that all black – 'Bantu' – schools must use Afrikaans equally with English as medium of instruction.

1975: August. Unita declares war on MPLA in Angola; SADF armoured column enters Angola, attacks MPLA town of Ngiva; secret build-up of SADF air and land forces in Angola begins.

1976: 16 June. Students massacred in Soweto as police fire on demonstrations against apartheid education and use of Afrikaans as medium of instruction. The protests develop into a general youth uprising.

1977: 12 September. Steve Biko, leader of the Black Consciousness movement, killed by police while in detention.

October: Banning of 18 organisations, including most of Black Consciousness organisations and two newspapers with black readership.

UNHCR estimates that a total of 3,000 South African refugees are now living in Southern African states.

November: UN imposes arms sanctions on South Africa.

1978: B. J. Vorster becomes President, and P. W. Botha Prime Minister.

'Muldergate' scandal reveals use of secret state funds to suborn the SA press.

Swaziland establishes police links with South Africa to 'control the refugee situation', estimated to number 8,000.

May. SADF launches massive air strike against Namibian (SWAPO) refugee camp at Kassinga, killing over 300 unarmed men and women, almost 300 children, and 12 soldiers. Over 600 refugees wounded.

First 150 students arrive at Mazimbu, Tanzania, where an ANC school for South African students in exile is being built. Studies start at SOMAFCO.

1979: Vorster resigns as President in aftermath of Muldergate scandal. P. W. Botha becomes President.

February. SADF joins Rhodesian Air Force units to attack ZAPU training centre in Boma, killing 198 and wounding 600.

June. ANC guerrillas sabotage Sasol oil-from-coal complex.

1981: SADF military raid on houses in Matola, Mozambique; 13 South Africans and 1 Mozambican killed.

ANC Representative Joe Gqabi assassinated in Zimbabwe.

1982: National Party splits; *'verkramptes'* hive off to form a separate Conservative Party.

June. ANC Representative Petrus Nzima and wife Jabu assassinated by car bomb in Mbabane, Swaziland.

October. SA agents arrested after break-in at ANC offices in London; released and flee to South Africa while awaiting trial.

December. SADF launch armed raid on ANC houses in Maseru; 3 South African refugees and 12 Lesotho nationals killed.

ANC activist Ruth First assassinated by parcel bomb in Maputo, Mozambique.

1983: New Constitution proposed, with tri-cameral Parliament to include Indian and Coloured Houses, but exclude representation of Africans.

UDF (United Democratic Front) formed as alliance of organisations to oppose the new Constitution.

19 May. MK plant sabotage bomb at SA Air Force offices in Pretoria; 19 killed.

SA Air Force makes 'revenge' air strike on Maputo, allegedly aimed at ANC bases; kills five Mozambicans, 1 SA refugee, and hits Maputo oil refinery.

End Conscription Campaign (ECC) launched by white conscripts to SADF.

1984: Confederation of SA Trade Unions (COSATU) formed.

16 March. Nkomati Accord: Mozambique to prevent ANC using its territory for military action against South Africa and reduce ANC presence to skeleton; SA to end military support for Renamo rebels and their campaign of destabilisation.

June. ANC member Jeanette Schoon and daughter killed by parcel bomb in Lubango, Angola.

September. New Tri-Cameral Parliament established after massive boycott of elections by Coloured and Indian voters for 'own House' representatives.

Spread of violent attacks on members of Black Urban Councils, and resignation of many Councils and Councillors.

1985: Widespread strikes, school boycotts, violent confrontation with armed forces in the black townships, attacks on government 'collaborators'.

February. Nelson Mandela refuses Botha's offers of release if he renounces use of violence.

Vernon Nkadimeng, son of ANC Executive member John, assassinated by car bomb, in Botswana.

June. SADF attack on ANC refugee houses in Gaberone, Botswana; 12 killed, and houses destroyed – 'a blood-curdling act of murder' (President Quett Masire).

12 June. National State of Emergency declared. SADF troops occupy urban black schools, and start military occupation and patrolling of urban black townships.

August. Botha retreats from talk of reform with defiant 'Crossing the Rubicon' speech in Durban.

1986: March. State of Emergency is lifted, coinciding with visit to South Africa of Commonwealth 'Eminent Persons' Group to explore possibilities of negotiation between government and black majority.

June. National State of Emergency re-imposed.

The squatters' camp, Crossroads in Cape Town, is razed by vigilantes while police look on; 70,000 people driven from their homes, hundreds killed.

1987: After one year of the State of Emergency, with 97 townships under military occupation, intensive repression and mass resistance nationwide.

Strikes on mines, industry and public-sector undertakings.

June. One and a half million stay away from work to commemorate the Soweto uprising of 1976.

1988: Eighteen anti-apartheid organisations including UDF prohibited from engaging in any political activity.

March. Defeat of South African forces at Cuito Canavale, Angola; heavy casualties including white conscripts, at hands of a combined Angolan-Cuban force.

Negotiated agreement reached on independence for Namibia; South African forces to withdraw in exchange for withdrawal of Cuban forces from Angola and closure of Umkhonto's Angolan bases.

Dulcie September, ANC representative in France, is shot and killed outside her Paris office.

1989: Mass defiance campaigns, including Detainees' hunger strikes in prisons.

August. OAU adopts ANC proposals as basis for negotiations between Government and opposition – 'the Harare Declaration'.

September. F. W. De Klerk replaces P. W. Botha as State President.

October. Release of 8 political prisoners convicted in the Rivonia Trial – but not including Mandela.

1990: 2 February. De Klerk announces that the ANC and PAC are to be unbanned, Mandela released, and other political prisoners and detainees progressively released.